Building Cocoa Applications
A Step-by-Step Guide

Building Cocoa Applications
A Step-by-Step Guide

Simson Garfinkel and Michael K. Mahoney

O'REILLY®

Beijing · Cambridge · Farnham · Köln · Paris · Sebastopol · Taipei · Tokyo

Building Cocoa Applications: A Step-by-Step Guide
by Simson Garfinkel and Michael K. Mahoney

Copyright © 2002 O'Reilly & Associates, Inc. All rights reserved.
Printed in the United States of America.

Published by O'Reilly & Associates, Inc., 1005 Gravenstein Highway North, Sebastopol, CA 95472.

O'Reilly & Associates books may be purchased for educational, business, or sales promotional use. Online editions are also available for most titles (*safari.oreilly.com*). For more information, contact our corporate/institutional sales department: (800) 998-9938 or *corporate@oreilly.com*.

Editor:	Deborah Russell
Production Editor:	Rachel Wheeler
Cover Designer:	Emma Colby
Interior Designer:	David Futato

Printing History:

May 2002:	First Edition.

Library of Congress Cataloging-in-Publication Data

Garfinkel, Simson.
   Building Cocoa applications / Simson Garfinkel & Michael K. Mahoney.
      p. cm.
   ISBN 0-596-00235-1
   1. Mac OS. 2. Operating systems (computers). 3. Macintosh (Computer)--Programming. I. Mahoney,
      Michael K. II. Title

QA76.76.O63 G37 2002
005.4'469--dc21
                                                       2002023320

[M]

For the kids:
Nina, Timmy, Sonia, Jared, and Draken

Table of Contents

Part I.   Cocoa Overview

Preface

Welcome!

Building Cocoa Applications describes how to write Objective-C programs for computers running the Mac OS X operating system, using the object-oriented Cocoa application framework. The book covers a wide range of technologies:

- The Aqua graphical user interface, Cocoa developer tools, object-oriented concepts, and the Objective-C language
- Cocoa programming and graphics concepts: nibs, icons, delegation, resizing, events, responders, tasks, pipes, color, Rich Text, the mouse, zoom buttons, pasteboards, modal sessions, and drag-and-drop
- The Cocoa environment: Darwin and the Window Server, the document-based architecture, the Quartz drawing system, Cocoa's preferences and defaults systems, and facilities for saving, loading, and printing

Building Cocoa Applications is a no-nonsense, hands-on book that's intended for serious developers. It's filled with extended examples illustrating complete applications written in Objective-C. As you proceed through the book, you'll take a step-by-step approach to building a series of applications of increasing complexity, adding features as you go.

Although we do not assume prior knowledge of the Macintosh or any other window-based operating environment, we do assume some familiarity with programming in general and the ANSI C language in particular.

Our primary goal is to get you up and running as quickly as possible. If you carefully read this book from cover to cover and diligently build the sample applications along with us, we're confident that you'll soon be writing your own sophisticated Cocoa graphics applications.

While this book is fast moving, we start by laying a solid foundation. Part I of the book explains how to use Aqua, the Mac OS X graphical user interface (GUI), and describes the Cocoa developer tools you'll use to build applications. It also introduces two simple but complete Cocoa applications—one built with Cocoa's Interface Builder tool and one built without it. Parts II, III, and IV are organized by application: we'll build three major, highly useful graphics applications and, in doing so, teach you how to build your own applications with Cocoa. The applications we will build are:

Calculator (Part II)
> A simple, four-function calculation application that's similar to the calculator that comes with Mac OS X

MathPaper (Part III)
> An application that is similar to a word processor but that solves equations you supply

GraphPaper (Part IV)
> A more complex, multithreading application that graphs a formula in two dimensions

The first chapter in each of these three parts introduces the application and builds its most basic functionality. Each subsequent chapter adds a new layer of functionality. For example, Chapter 6 shows how to add an icon to the Calculator application so it will display nicely in the Finder, Chapter 12 enhances MathPaper so it displays Rich Text, and Chapter 19 adds zoom buttons to GraphPaper.

We'll also build numerous additional simple applications throughout the book to demonstrate specific features of Cocoa and Mac OS X. You can build all of these applications right along with us—we provide simple but complete instructions on how to do whatever is necessary. Code for all of the applications we'll build is provided on the O'Reilly web site (see "Comments and Questions," later in this Preface).

Cocoa and Mac OS X

Cocoa is an object-oriented development environment that runs in the Mac OS X environment. Cocoa software has previously been bundled with the Mac OS X user system on a separate developer CD-ROM, but newer systems come with a package that users can install—the package name is Developer.mpkg, and it's found in /Applications/Installers/Developer Tools. Although there are many ways to write programs for Mac OS X, we think you'll find Cocoa is both the easiest and the most powerful.

Mac OS X and Cocoa Components

From the user's point of view, Mac OS X is a unified operating system and graphical operating environment that makes computers easy to use. It includes:

Aqua

Apple's revolutionary GUI, which is both visually pleasing and very easy to use.

Quartz

A comprehensive two-dimensional drawing system that can be used to display text and graphics on a computer screen or on a printer and to create Adobe Portable Document Format (PDF) files.

The Finder

A graphical interface to the computer's filesystem and to running applications.

Mail, TextEdit, Terminal, Console

Some of the Apple-supplied applications included in Mac OS X.

Foundation

An underlying set of operating-system services that are provided to Carbon, Cocoa, and Java programs.

System Preferences and the defaults system

Enable users to store their preferences for individual programs without having to directly modify special files stored in their home directories.

The HFS+ filesystem and UFS filesystem

Organize the way that files and folders are stored on the computer's disks.

TCP/IP networking

Allows Macintosh computers to communicate with each other and with the Internet.

Darwin

The underlying Unix operating system on which Mac OS X is based.

Figure P-1 shows the relationship between these technologies in the Mac OS X operating system.

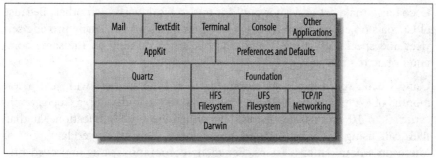

Figure P-1. The Mac OS X architecture

The Mac OS X operating system can run programs with many different kinds of user interfaces, including:

- Programs written with the Cocoa development environment. These programs display natively with the Aqua user interface.

- Programs that use a restricted part of the Mac OS 9 interface called Carbon. These programs also display with the Aqua user interface.

- Programs written in the Java programming language. Java programs can use either the Cocoa or Swing application frameworks.

- Programs written for the Mac OS 7, 8, and 9 operating systems. These programs are run in the Mac OS X "Classic" environment and appear as they would on a Macintosh computer running Mac OS 9.

- Programs written for the underlying Unix operating system. These programs either do not display a user interface at all, or implement a character-based interface from the Unix command line.

This book focuses on the Cocoa development environment, but we will mention the other user interfaces as necessary. From the programmer's point of view, Cocoa includes two distinct frameworks:

Foundation
> A collection of Objective-C classes for managing memory, interfacing with the computer's operating system, and performing other functions that are independent of the GUI.

Application Kit (AppKit)
> A collection of Objective-C classes that give Cocoa its distinctive look and feel.

By using Cocoa, your programs automatically get the Aqua look and feel. Although every application is different, Cocoa makes it easier for all applications to work in similar ways, which in turn makes it easier for people to learn new applications.

Cocoa also makes it easier for applications to work with each other. Because of Cocoa's object-oriented nature, Cocoa applications can easily provide services and special functions to other applications running on the same computer or across the network.

Using Cocoa speeds your development time. Programmers with just a few months of experience with Cocoa report that they can develop a Cocoa application 3 to 10 times faster using the Foundation and Application Kit than they can using other application frameworks such as PowerPlant, Qt, or Microsoft's Foundation Classes. For many corporations, this improved productivity justifies the decision to deploy Macintosh computer systems.

Object-Oriented Programming

Writing programs for Cocoa is similar to, and yet significantly different from, writing programs for other environments. As with other modern application development environments, you write Cocoa programs by building systems of related but distinct parts, or *objects*, and connecting them together to form an integrated whole. Confining different aspects of a program to different pieces makes those pieces easier to design, implement, debug, and reuse. This is what is known as *object-oriented programming* (OOP).

Unlike development systems based on the C++ programming language (such as Microsoft's Foundation Classes and Code Warrior's PowerPlant), however, Cocoa is built on top of the Objective-C programming language. As we shall see, Objective-C is a simpler and more powerful object-oriented extension of the C programming language than C++.

Cocoa embodies the principles of object-oriented programming from its user interface down to its very core. This greatly simplifies the task of building applications for Mac OS X. The down side is that it makes the Cocoa environment very different from the environments to which most programmers are accustomed, and consequently, although it is an easy-to-program environment, the initial learning curve is quite steep.

The Roots of Cocoa

Cocoa is a relatively new offering from Apple, but the underlying operating system on which Cocoa is based is more than a decade old. Although today Cocoa is an integral part of Mac OS X, much of the Cocoa application framework dates back to the NeXTSTEP operating system (and subsequently the Open-Step system) developed by NeXT Computer, Inc., during the late 1980s–mid 1990s. When Apple bought NeXT in 1996, it also bought the right to use the software created by NeXT. The fact that Mac OS X is based on such a solid and long-lived operating system is very important: Cocoa is not some new fad technology that Apple is trying out today but might soon discard; it is a mature, time-tested development environment that has been used and improved by many thousands of programmers over the course of more than a decade.

Cocoa Versions

All the examples in this book were developed and tested under Mac OS X Version 10.1. Although future versions of Cocoa are sure to add new features and visually change some of the user interfaces, Objective-C's dynamic binding all but assures that any Cocoa program developed under Version 10.1 will continue to run on future versions of the Macintosh operating system. Furthermore, we've tried to focus the subject matter of this book mainly on the underlying concepts and features of the operating system—and many of these haven't changed much since the initial release of NeXTSTEP 1.0 in 1989. For these reasons, this book is likely to stay in print, and be very useful, for quite some time after it is published.

Cocoa, Objective-C, and Java

Although the Cocoa Foundation and the Application Kit are written in Objective-C, Cocoa programs can be written in either Objective-C or Java. This freedom comes from the fact that Java and Objective-C have very similar models of object-oriented programming, which has allowed Apple to create a "Java bridge" that allows Java objects to invoke Objective-C methods and vice versa. Java can even be used to subclass Objective-C classes!

Despite the ability to intermix Objective-C and Java within a single program, this book focuses solely on the Objective-C programming language. Objective-C is the native environment of the Foundation and the Application Kit, and it is generally easier to debug Cocoa programs written in Objective-C than to debug the same programs written in Java. Furthermore, there are performance considerations: Cocoa-based programs run faster if they are written in Objective-C than if they are written in Java.

One significant advantage of Java over Objective-C is the large number of third-party class libraries that are now available for Java. If you need to use one of these libraries, you can benefit from using Java for some or all of your Cocoa applications. In particular, Apple's Enterprise Objects Framework now supports only the Java-based application programming interface (API).

One of the primary differences between Java and Objective-C is memory management: Java has automatic garbage collection, whereas Objective-C has a reference-count-based memory-management system. The Objective-C system is cruder, but it gives programmers greater control and generally produces applications that run faster.

For detailed information on programming Cocoa applications in Java, see the upcoming O'Reilly book *Cocoa and Java*. (And for those interested in writing Perl applications for this new platform, watch for *Programming Cocoa Applications with Perl*, also coming soon from O'Reilly.)

The Foundation Classes

Many of the Cocoa class libraries are actually implemented with the Apple Foundation library. The Foundation provides a series of highly efficient, low-level services for building advanced applications. Built into the Foundation is support for Unicode strings, XML property lists, URL resources, preferences, and other key Mac OS X technologies.

The Foundation library is used by both Cocoa and Carbon, and it provides for improved compatibility between applications written with these two application frameworks.

You can find out more about Foundation by reading the documentation that comes with the developer tools (it is installed in /Developer/Documentation/CoreFoundation). For the latest updates, check out the version at:

```
http://developer.apple.com/techpubs/macosx/Cocoa/Reference/Foundation/
ObjC_classic/FoundationTOC.html
```

Drawing with Quartz

One of the most important differences between Mac OS 9 and Mac OS X is the way these systems draw on the computer's screen. Mac OS 9 does all of its drawing with Apple's QuickDraw APIs. Mac OS X, in contrast, does its drawing with Quartz.

Quartz integrates into the Macintosh operating system many advanced features that were previously available only in Apple's QuickDraw GX and NeXT's Display PostScript drawing environments. Quartz also brings native support for Adobe's PDF. Programs written for Quartz can display PDF files as a native file type. They can also capture their drawing commands and generate PDF files directly, without having to use a PDF Writer or Distiller program.

Besides looking great, Quartz makes it much easier to move completed documents from Mac OS X systems to computers running the Windows or Unix operating systems, because both of these systems have freely available readers that will display PDF-encoded files.

You can find out more about Quartz by reading the documentation that comes with the developer tools (it is installed in /Developer/Documentation/CoreTechnologies/graphics/Quartz2D). For the latest updates, check out the version at:

```
http://developer.apple.com/quartz/
```

Mac OS X and Classic Mode

Of course, Apple couldn't release a new operating system for the Macintosh and not allow existing Macintosh programs to run on it, so Mac OS X also supports the "Classic" Macintosh environment. If you double-click on the icon for an application that runs on older Mac OS computers, a Mac OS X system will launch a copy of Mac OS 9 within Mac OS X. When you activate this application, the desktop will take on the look and feel of the Mac OS 9 environment. It's weird, but you can run those old applications quite well in Classic mode, and it works better than an emulation because it's actually a full version of Mac OS 9.x running in protected memory space under Mac OS X.

However, while Mac OS X systems will run Classic and Carbon-based applications, the future is Cocoa. Apple says that all new applications for the Mac should be written with the new Cocoa APIs, rather than with the old ones. And because it is so easy to use Cocoa, why would you want to do anything else?

Organization of This Book

This book is divided into the following four parts.

Part I, Cocoa Overview

The first part of this book introduces the Mac OS X interface (Aqua), Cocoa developer tools, the Objective-C language in which Cocoa is written, and Cocoa programming itself.

Chapter 1, *Understanding the Aqua Interface*, contains an overview of Aqua features and behaviors that programmers should understand so that they can build applications that look and feel like Mac OS X applications. In particular, programmers writing new Mac OS X applications should follow Aqua's stringent interface guidelines so as not to confuse users. Chapter 1 also contains a tutorial on how to become a power user of Mac OS X and the Aqua GUI. Although people familiar with Mac OS X and Aqua might want to skip this chapter, it contains many hints and shortcuts with which even experienced Cocoa programmers may not be familiar.

Chapter 2, *Tools for Developing Cocoa Applications*, contains an overview of Project Builder, Interface Builder, and the gdb debugger, the three most important Cocoa developer tools. It also contains an introduction to the (Unix) Terminal and several other useful developer tools.

Chapter 3, *Creating a Simple Application with Interface Builder*, uses Interface Builder, a revolutionary program for drawing and wiring together objects in application interfaces, to build a very simple application without any coding whatsoever. We'll use it to create a little program that plays a sound and updates a text field when the user moves a slider.

Chapter 4, *An Objective-C Application Without Interface Builder*, builds an application from the ground up, using only Objective-C and the Cocoa Application Kit. This will give you a hands-on feel for what Interface Builder is actually doing. We also use this chapter to introduce the syntax and framework of the Objective-C language.

Part II, Calculator: Building a Simple Application

The second part of this book is focused on building a simple application—a calculator—which we extend piece by piece through four chapters.

Chapter 5, *Building a Project: A Four-Function Calculator*, introduces the Calculator application project. We create the calculator's window and build a simple Objective-C object that handles the math features of the calculator. At the end of the chapter, you'll have a working four-function calculator.

Chapter 6, *Nibs and Icons*, adds an About box to the Calculator application. This gives us an opportunity to use some additional features of Interface Builder. We also clarify Cocoa's system of outlets, connections, and actions. At the end of this chapter, we show you how to add an application icon that identifies the application in the Finder and the Dock.

Chapter 7, *Delegation and Resizing*, introduces the concept of *delegation*— designating objects to perform functions for other objects. In this chapter, we make the four-function calculator work with other bases (binary, octal, and hexadecimal) and use delegation to set the initial base. In the second half of the chapter, we use an example of programmatically resizing a window to introduce Cocoa's NSWindow and NSView classes.

Chapter 8, *Events and Responders*, introduces the *responder chain*, the chain of objects that Cocoa uses to process events such as keypresses and mouse-clicks. At the end of the chapter, we use our newfound knowledge to modify the calculator so that users can enter numbers by typing on the keyboard, in addition to simply clicking with the mouse. This chapter completes our work on the Calculator application.

Chapter 9, *Darwin and the Window Server*, provides background on the Mach operating system upon which Mac OS X is based and on the Quartz Window Server that Mac OS X uses to draw on the screen and manage events. This chapter provides useful, general information that will help us build more complicated applications in subsequent chapters.

Part III, MathPaper: A Multiple-Document, Multiprocess Application

The third part of this book focuses on building a new application called Math-Paper. MathPaper is similar to a word processor in that it supports multiple windows, but it behaves very differently. Users can enter mathematical expressions in a MathPaper window, and the application will solve the expressions that were typed. The application uses a back-end mathematical processor called Evaluator to do the mathematical calculations. Chapter 15 leaves Math-Paper but includes several small examples that demonstrate drawing in NSView objects.

Chapter 10, *MathPaper and Cocoa's Document-Based Architecture*, introduces the MathPaper application and shows you how to write applications that control multiple windows. We also build MathPaper's back end (Evaluator) in this chapter, but we don't connect it to the application until the next chapter.

Chapter 11, *Tasks, Pipes, and NSTextView*, ties MathPaper's front and back ends together with a Cocoa object that can spawn subprocesses. By the end of this chapter, MathPaper will be able to calculate mathematical expressions typed in by users.

Chapter 12, *Rich Text Format and NSText*, discusses Microsoft's Rich Text Format (RTF), which Cocoa uses to encode information such as font, point size, and alignment into a text stream. We use RTF to make MathPaper's output look more professional.

Chapter 13, *Saving, Loading, and Printing*, introduces Cocoa's facilities for dealing with document files. Using MathPaper, we show how to register a filename extension with the Finder, how to archive information into streams, and how to save and load files with the Save and Open dialogs.

Chapter 14, *Drawing with Quartz*, shows the basics of how to draw in a window. We demonstrate this by making an animated About box for the Math-Paper application.

Chapter 15, *Drawing in a Rectangle: More Fun with Cocoa Views*, leaves MathPaper. The chapter explores the NSView class in general and the **drawRect:** method in particular. We build several small programs in this chapter to show how NSViews work.

Part IV, GraphPaper: A Multithreaded, Mouse-Tracking Application

The fourth part of this book focuses on building one last major application, called GraphPaper. Given range and step, GraphPaper will graph a mathematical function in color and use mouseovers to identify graph points. We also embed in GraphPaper many of the standard features of commercial Mac OS X applications, such as services, copy and paste, and the use of the Mac OS X preferences database.

Chapter 16, *GraphPaper: A Multithreaded Application with a Display List*, introduces GraphPaper, a complex application that graphs a function in two dimensions. This application is *multithreaded*, meaning that it has several execution threads and does several different things at the same time. It uses the same Evaluator back end that MathPaper used.

Chapter 17, *Color*, continues our discussion about drawing in color with Quartz. We show how to enable users to change the color of the graph, axes, and label via a Preferences dialog.

Chapter 18, *Tracking the Mouse*, shows how to catch mouse moves and handle more kinds of mouse events. We do this by modifying the GraphPaper application so that it displays the (x,y) coordinates of the graph for wherever the user places the mouse.

Chapter 19, *Zooming and Saving Graphics Files*, shows how to put a zoom button on a view to change its magnification. We also show how to save a graphic image as a PDF file or as a TIFF image.

Chapter 20, *Pasteboards, Services, Modal Sessions, and Drag-and-Drop*, shows how to put data on and remove data from the pasteboard (clipboard). We also show how to make GraphPaper a Mac OS X service that shows up in the Services menu, so you can graph functions that are selected in other applications.

Chapter 21, *Preferences and Defaults*, shows how to build a multi-view Preference panel and how to save its contents into the defaults database.

This book also contains an appendix, *Cocoa Resources*, which lists other books and online resources that you might find helpful in programming Cocoa.

What You Will Need

To use the examples in this book, you will need a computer running Mac OS X Version 10.1 or later. You will also need a copy of the Mac OS X developer tools, which Apple currently distributes for free along with the Mac OS X operating system. The Developer Tools distribution contains everything you need to develop a Cocoa application, including the GNU Objective-C compiler (developed by both Apple and the Free Software Foundation), the assembler, the linker, all of the libraries, and all of the Cocoa header files. The Developer Tools distribution also contains Apple's online developer documentation, although this information can also be accessed for free from Apple's developer web site at:

```
http://developer.apple.com
```

Conventions Used in This Book

The following conventions are used in this book:

Italic
> Used to emphasize new terms and concepts when they are introduced.

Bold
> Used for method names in the text.

`Constant width`
> Used for code examples and any system output. It is also used for file, directory, function, and variable names, and for commands and URLs.

Constant width italic
> Used in examples for variable input or output.

Constant width bold
> Used in examples for user input and to highlight new code that is being inserted into existing code.

→
> Used as shorthand to represent menu command choices. For example, choosing the Copy command from the Edit menu will be written Edit → Copy.

Comments and Questions

Please address comments and questions concerning this book to the publisher:

> O'Reilly & Associates, Inc.
> 1005 Gravenstein Highway North
> Sebastopol, CA 95472
> (800) 998-9938 (in the United States or Canada)
> (707) 829-0515 (international/local)
> (707) 829-0104 (fax)

There is a web page for this book, which provides code and lists errata and any additional information. You can access this page at:

> http://www.oreilly.com/catalog/buildcocoa/

From that page, you can download all of the code that we developed throughout this book. However, we recommend that you use the online code as a last resort. We believe that you'll learn more about programming Cocoa if you take the time to type in the demonstration programs, thinking carefully about the code as you type it, rather than simply downloading and running the finished programs. We've provided the full code, however, so you'll have something to fall back on in the event that the programs you type in don't work.

To comment or ask technical questions about this book, send email to:

> bookquestions@oreilly.com

For more information about books, conferences, Resource Centers, and the O'Reilly Network, see the O'Reilly web site at:

> http://www.oreilly.com

Acknowledgments

This book is an outgrowth of a book we wrote back in the early 1990s called *NeXTSTEP Programming, Step One: Object-Oriented Applications* (Springer-Verlag). Many NeXT people helped us with that original project (and quite a few of them are now at Apple Computer, Inc.); others helped when we made an attempt to update the book for Apple's Rhapsody system back in 1997 (that system was never released). Many more Apple employees contributed time and energy reviewing this book, helping us obtain software and other resources, and answering our many technical questions. A very big and sincere thank you to all of these Apple employees.

We are also very grateful to the following people who provided technical reviews and other support while we were working on this book:

- Bill Bumgarner at CodeFab
- Andrew Stone at Stone Design
- Carlos Weber, Kristofer Younger, Kurt Revis, Lance Bland, Simon Stapleton, Tom Waters, and Eric Peyton, via the cocoa-dev mailing list
- Gary Longsine at illumineX, inc.
- Ondra Cada at OCSoftware
- Mike Beam at the University of Texas
- Scott Anguish at Stepwise
- Don Rainwater at the University of Cincinnati
- Michael "wave" Johnson at Pixar
- Louise Mahoney

Thanks as well to both Apple and James Duncan Davidson for providing some of the source material that we used in writing the appendix.

Our editor Debby Russell did a fabulous job of championing this book with O'Reilly, working with Apple, and editing this book. Jessamyn Read created illustrations that helped convey some of the more difficult ideas. Many thanks to Rachel Wheeler, the production editor and copyeditor for this book; Emma Colby, who designed the front and back covers; David Futato, who designed the interior format and wrestled the many icons into submission; Leanne Soylemez, the proofreader; and John Bickelhaupt, who indexed the book.

Cocoa Overview

Part I, Chapters 1 through 4, introduces the Mac OS X interface (Aqua), Cocoa developer tools, the Objective-C language in which Cocoa is written, and Cocoa programming itself.

- Chapter 1, *Understanding the Aqua Interface*
- Chapter 2, *Tools for Developing Cocoa Applications*
- Chapter 3, *Creating a Simple Application with Interface Builder*
- Chapter 4, *An Objective-C Application Without Interface Builder*

Understanding the Aqua Interface

The Mac OS X graphical user interface (GUI) is called *Aqua*. Aqua's advanced use of color, animation, and transparency and its plethora of powerful user-oriented features make it a true delight to use for both novices and power users. To write applications that function well in this environment, a developer should first become proficient at using Aqua as a power user. This means knowing Aqua's GUI guidelines and how applications are structured well enough to accomplish tasks quickly and efficiently. You can then use this knowledge to write applications that provide better interfaces for others.

This chapter contains an introduction to the Aqua GUI and its guidelines. The references at the end of this chapter contain the web addresses for Apple's guidelines. No previous experience with Mac OS X is assumed. All screen shots were taken from Mac OS X Version 10.1.

What Makes Mac OS X So Special?

Mac OS X is special for two important reasons. First, it brings the popular Macintosh operating system interface into the 21st century with a new, object-oriented environment that is almost as easy to program as it is to use. Second, Mac OS X brings the world's easiest-to-use interface (Aqua) to the venerable Unix operating system, which is the underlying basis of Mac OS X. This has allowed Apple almost overnight to claim the largest installation of Unix operating systems on the planet: tens of millions! There are now more installed copies of Mac OS X than of all other desktop Unix variants *combined*, including Sun, Linux, HP, IBM, and more. Unix lovers, take note!

Aqua is the interface to all of the next-generation Mac OS X applications, including the Finder, the Dock, Mail, TextEdit, and many other applications that are bundled with Mac OS X. The most important of these applications is the Finder, which is an improved reimplementation of the traditional Finder for the Macintosh.

The Mac OS X Finder lets you start up programs and manage the filesystem primarily through point-and-click activities that are natural to the user. With the Finder, you can copy 10 MB of files from one disk to another, launch (run) several programs, open and print an 80-page document, recursively change the permissions on files, and view a graphics file in a panel all at the same time! That would not be possible with previous versions of Mac OS.

Mac OS X is also special because of its embedded imaging model, *Quartz*. (An *imaging model* does the actual drawing on the screen or on a printer.) Based on Adobe's Portable Document Format (PDF), the next-generation version of Adobe's PostScript page-description language, Quartz provides a true WYSIWYG ("wizzy-wig," or *what-you-see-is-what-you-get*) capability because the imaging model for printing is the same as that for the screen. This is a marvelous asset for any application that uses text or graphics (and what application doesn't?).

Where Mac OS X shines brightest, however, is in its development environment, *Cocoa*. As you'll discover by working through this book, the object-oriented Cocoa environment makes it surprisingly easy to design new applications and then turn them into working applications. Our main design tool is *Interface Builder* (IB), perhaps the world's most powerful tool for building application interfaces. With IB, you can create menus, windows, controls, etc. and make connections between them graphically. IB allows easy access to Cocoa's *Application Kit*, a set of more than 120 powerful classes that define and create objects for use by your applications. We'll discuss these powerful tools in the next chapter.

A Quick Look at the Mac OS X User Interface

Let's take a look at the main components of the Mac OS X user interface. Figure 1-1 contains a screen shot of a typical Mac OS X user's screen. The screen background, called the *desktop*, is light gray (you can change the color). The always-available Apple system menu at the top left opened when the Apple icon above it was clicked. The Mac OS X Finder is the *active application*, and thus its menu populates the rest of the menu bar at the top of the screen. The Finder window at the top of the screen is the *active window*, and its Info dialog is at the bottom left. (A *dialog* is a special type of window that gives information about or instructions to an application.) The *Info dialog* contains a number of labels that show information about the selected folder and a checkbox to set a folder attribute. It also contains a pop-up menu that can be used to change the view (information) that the Info dialog currently displays. We'll discuss these screen objects in more detail later in this chapter.

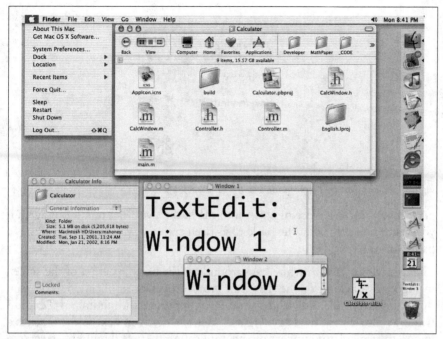

Figure 1-1. Mac OS X user's desktop

The Dock at the right of Figure 1-1 contains 14 icons, the first 12 representing applications (programs). (The Dock can also be positioned at the bottom or left of the screen; it's the user's preference.) The two icons at the bottom of the Dock represent a minimized document window and the Trash. The Finder ("Happy Mac") icon, which represents the Finder, is always at the beginning (left or top) of the Dock. If you move your mouse over an application icon in the Dock (i.e., move the mouse pointer over an icon without pressing or click- ing), the application's name will be displayed next to the icon. If you press and hold the mouse button down on an application icon (e.g., the Finder icon) in the Dock, a menu will pop up and display (as menu items) the names of the windows that are currently open for that application (see Figure 1-2). If you continue to hold down the mouse button and then drag it and release it over one of those menu items, the corresponding window will come to the fore- ground. This is especially handy if an application has many open windows or has windows buried under the windows belonging to other applications.

The Trash icon at the end of the Dock represents a *folder* (directory) where files are temporarily stored for later deletion or restoration. Files are deleted *only* when the Empty Trash command is chosen from the Finder menu. Files are restored by clicking the Trash icon and then dragging the files out of the resulting Finder window and dropping them into another Finder window or onto the desktop. The real-life analogy of a trash basket in your office works

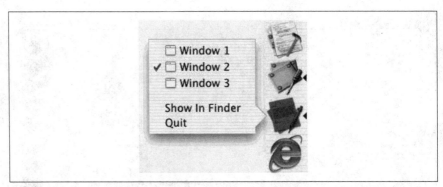

Figure 1-2. The TextEdit icon in the Dock with associated menu

here: if you throw a piece of paper into the basket, you can pull it out again if you want; however, after the basket has been emptied, you've lost the piece of paper forever.

TextEdit

Calculator alias

The text windows with white backgrounds at the bottom center of the screen in Figure 1-1 belong to the TextEdit word-processor application. The icon directly above the Trash icon in the Dock represents a minimized TextEdit window. The icon at the lower-right corner of the screen next to the Dock is a link to the Calculator application, an application that we'll build from scratch starting in Chapter 5. Double-clicking this icon (or any application icon in the Dock) will launch the application.

There are many other application icons in the Dock. If a small black triangle is shown next to an application icon, then the associated application is running (although its windows and menu might be hidden from view). The applications without triangles next to their icons are not running. Single-clicking any icon representing an application (running or not) in the Dock causes the associated application to become the active application, with its menu displayed in the menu bar at the top of the screen.

Basic Principles of the Aqua Interface

Before the release of the original Macintosh, different applications running on the same computer in environments such as MS-DOS had wildly different interfaces. Some applications used the mouse; others used only the keyboard. Some applications were character-oriented; others created their own primitive window systems. This was a heavy burden on users and severely limited their overall productivity.

One of the primary goals of the original Macintosh was that different applications running on the same computer would have a consistent user interface.

Consistency helps users because they don't have to learn a new set of rules to perform the same basic operations as they move from application to application. (Think of how easy it is to drive different brands of automobiles—no additional training is required because they all have steering wheels, brakes, and accelerators that work the same way.)

The Toolbox, Carbon, and Cocoa

The original Macintosh delivered this consistent user interface through a set of procedures stored in a read-only memory (ROM) called the *Toolbox*. Developers who wrote applications for the Mac, regardless of whether they were writing a word processor or a spreadsheet, were encouraged to use the Macintosh Toolbox to display the application's user interface. This made things easier for users, because all applications behaved in the same way. It also made things easier for developers, because they did not have to reimplement things like scrollbars or menus for every application that they wrote.

Over the years, another advantage of the Toolbox became evident; as the operating system was improved and new features were added to the Toolbox, existing programs could get new functionality "for free." When Apple moved from Macintosh System 6 to System 7, well-behaved applications could suddenly operate in a multiapplication environment. Likewise, when System 7 gave way to Mac OS 8, applications that used the Toolbox and followed its conventions were able to take advantage of Mac OS 8's visual enhancements to the Macintosh interface. Indeed, the Toolbox was so integral to the Macintosh platform that many applications built without the Toolbox proved to be buggy and crashed a lot, and as a result, they were not successful in the marketplace.

Unfortunately, the reliance on the Toolbox came with a price: once a function call was placed in the Toolbox, Apple could not remove it, for fear of breaking existing applications. Over the years, the Toolbox became cluttered with many slightly different versions of the same function, some of which had been developed long ago and had inherent problems. The Toolbox was, in a word, bloated.

With the move from Mac OS 9 to Mac OS X, Apple revised the Toolbox and removed many of the early application programming interfaces (APIs). Apple gave the name *Carbon* to the remaining Macintosh APIs, which are natively supported by the Mac OS X operating system. Applications that use the original "Inside Macintosh" Toolbox APIs can be run on Mac OS X only inside the Macintosh "Classic" environment, which is essentially a copy of the Mac OS 9 operating system that runs within the Mac OS X environment.

With Mac OS X, Apple also introduced a new set of APIs known as *Cocoa*—a set of APIs for the 21st century. Because these APIs were developed independently of Apple,[*] they are fundamentally different from the original Macintosh APIs. Whereas the Toolbox and Carbon APIs are in the C programming language, the Cocoa APIs are written in Objective-C, an easy-to-use, object-oriented programming language that is well suited to writing GUIs.[†] The Cocoa environment provides consistency and ease of programming that are unparalleled among the other programming environments available today.

Consistent Aqua

Aqua's consistency means that windows in different applications have the same appearance and functionality; for example, mouseclicks and drags perform the same kinds of actions, and common menu commands are in the same place and have the same names, the same keyboard equivalents, and so on. The overall look and feel of all Mac OS X applications is the same. Contrast this with the haphazard way that interfaces to some Microsoft Windows applications have been developed over the years, and you'll begin to see why we like Mac OS X so much.

Mac OS X and Aqua put you in charge of your desktop and its windows. Through preference settings, info panels, resize controls, icon dragging, and other means, you can change the size, visibility, and location of almost every object on your desktop, decide when your Dock is visible and what it looks like, change the size of most text, and even determine which icons represent your folders.

With Aqua, the primary instrument that you use to interact with the computer is the mouse. Compared with the computer's keyboard, the mouse seems more natural for most users, because using the mouse is a better analogy for how we interact with objects in the real world. For example, if a window on the desktop represents a piece of paper on a desk, it's more natural for a user to move that window by dragging the window to a new place on the screen than by typing a sequence of keyboard commands.

Unlike previous versions of the Macintosh operating system, however, much of Mac OS X can also be controlled from the keyboard. Many common commands have keyboard equivalents, such as Command-X for Cut and Command-V for Paste, that will help you use applications more efficiently. Thus, people who lack the dexterity or the vision required to accurately use a mouse

---

[*] The Cocoa APIs are based on the NeXTSTEP operating system and APIs that Apple acquired when they bought NeXT Computer, Inc. in 1996.

[†] The Cocoa APIs can also be called directly from the Java programming language.

can still benefit from the Mac OS X environment by using the keyboard (in particular, the tab and arrow keys). Universal access and speech features are also available in Mac OS X.

The Mouse and Cursor

You can do two basic things with a mouse: move it and click its button.[*] Four different mouse *events* (actions) can be derived from these basic actions:

Clicking (single-clicking)
> Pressing and releasing a mouse button (mouse down and mouse up) without changing the position of the mouse.
>
> Clicking (or single-clicking) is used to select an object or location on the screen. For example, you can click a button or menu command to select some action, click an icon or filename in a list to select it for further action, click in a window to bring it in front of other windows, or click on a piece of text to select an insertion point.

Multiple-clicking
> Pressing and releasing a mouse button two or three times in rapid succession without changing the position of the mouse.
>
> Multiple-clicking extends the action of clicking. For example, you can click on a piece of text to select an insertion point, double-click to extend the action to select the nearest word, and triple-click to select the entire line or paragraph. Likewise, you can click a file icon in the Finder to select a file and double-click the icon to open the file in its associated application.

Dragging
> Pressing and holding down a mouse button and then moving the mouse (and thus the cursor); release the mouse button to end.
>
> Dragging is used primarily to move an object or define a range. For example, you can drag a window's title bar to move the window, drag a file icon to reposition it in a Finder window, or drag the knob on a slider or scroller to select a value or scroll through a window. You can also use dragging to define a range of characters in a text area, or to select a group of graphics in a drawing area or icons in a file area. The last two operations use a technique known as *rubberbanding*, where a lightly drawn rectangle indicates the selection range.

---

[*] Mac OS X also supports a two-button mouse with a scroll wheel. Under normal circumstances, the left button is used for selection and the right button brings up a context menu. If you have a mouse with a scroll wheel, moving the wheel will cause the view underneath the mouse to scroll. In the interest of brevity, this section considers only the standard Apple one-button mouse. Chapter 8 discusses mouse events in more detail.

Pressing

Pressing and holding down a mouse button in place; release the mouse button to end.

Pressing is used mainly as a substitute for repeated single-clicks. For example, you can repeatedly click a scroll button to move through the contents of a document window, or you can simply press the scroll button and let the window scroll.

The terminology we'll use in this book is that one *chooses* menu commands, *clicks* or *presses on* buttons or icons, *selects* items in a list, *drags* icons across the desktop, and *drags* across items in a list (e.g., files in a Finder window).

Mouse Action Paradigms

It's not crucial for users to know Aqua's mouse action paradigm terminology, because most Aqua actions are fairly intuitive. However, Cocoa developers should understand these mouse action paradigms (patterns, archetypes) and the associated terminology. You need to be aware of the paradigms so that you don't disrupt their naturalness for users of your applications. You also need to understand the terminology in order to properly use the procedures that come with Cocoa and to understand Apple's documentation. Following are the four Aqua mouse action paradigms, and some examples of each:

Direct manipulation

A user drags a window's title or resize bar to move or resize the window, clicks in a partially obscured window to move the window to the front, or drags a file's icon to the Trash icon to delete it. The user directly manipulates these objects.

Target selection

A user drags across a sequence of characters to select them for a change in font, or drags a rectangle around several graphics objects to select them for copying. These objects have been selected for some targeted action.

Targeted action through controls

A user clicks a button to change a text font, drags a slider knob to change the size of an object, or clicks a menu command to make a panel appear. We'll discuss control objects in depth later in this chapter.

Modal tool selection

A user clicks a pencil or rectangle icon in a palette of tools in a graphics editor to select a drawing tool, and the cursor changes to indicate the mode of drawing. The word "modal" implies that the application has distinct modes. When an application is in a modal state, some (or most) of its commands may be unavailable, or subsequent mouse actions may be specific to that mode.

Fortunately for developers, most responses to direct manipulation and target selection by the mouse are handled automatically by Cocoa objects and by Quartz. For example, a developer doesn't have to do anything to make a button highlight or a window move in response to user actions; Cocoa button objects automatically highlight when clicked and Quartz handles all window movements directed by users. On the other hand, an action in response to a change in a control object (e.g., a button click, slider drag, or menu command) or a cursor change in response to a modal tool selection is usually handled explicitly by the developer.

Cursors

The Cocoa *cursor* is a graphics image 16 pixels square that moves with the mouse. (A *pixel* is the smallest addressable point on the computer's bit-mapped display.) Moving the mouse quickly moves the cursor farther than moving it slowly—even if the distance moved is the same. Picking up the mouse and placing it elsewhere does not change the position of the cursor.

The cursor can take many different shapes, depending on the context. Its shape can change in response to entering or exiting a window or graphics area and in response to tool or target selection. The most common cursors are shown in the following list. The *hot spot*, or the exact location (point) of the screen referred to by the cursor, depends on the type of cursor currently displayed.

Arrow
For selecting, clicking, etc.; the hot spot is at the tip of the arrow. This is the most common cursor.

Arrow with plus sign
Indicates that a copying operation is about to take place in the Finder or another application. The hot spot doesn't matter, because this cursor appears only when the user is dragging another object.

Arrow with link
Indicates that a link (reference) operation is about to take place in the Finder or another application. As with the arrow-with-plus-sign cursor, the hot spot doesn't matter.

I-beam
For text input positioning, editing, etc.; the hot spot is at the center.

Spinning disk
This "wait" cursor indicates that an application is performing an operation that must be completed before you can continue your work in that application; however, you may activate another application by clicking in one of its open windows or its icon in the Dock, and you won't have to wait to use the new application. This is a huge user benefit provided by Unix. The hot spot is at the center.

✐ *Pencil*
For drawing lines in a graphics editor or other such program; the hot spot is at the tip. Other, similar drawing cursors include the paintbrush, paint pot, etc.

+ *Crosshair*
For drawing shapes such as rectangles or circles in a graphics editor; the hot spot is at the center.

Window Types and Behavior

On-screen windows fall into four principal categories, which vary in appearance and function:

- Document windows
- Utility windows
- Dialogs (includes sheets)
- Alerts

TextEdit

We'll describe each of these window types in the following sections. After that we'll discuss how and when these four types of windows become the *main* or *key* window in an application. For many of our examples we'll use the TextEdit application, the basic word-processor application bundled with Mac OS X and located in the /Applications folder.

Document Windows

A *document window* is file-based and is the main working area of an application. A window containing a text document being edited in a word processor is a document window, as is a window containing a spreadsheet in a spreadsheet application or an image being manipulated in a graphics editor application. Most document windows, like some of the windows in Figure 1-1 and the window in Figure 1-3, have resize controls and close, minimize, and zoom buttons. The resize control is at the lower-right corner of a document window, while the three window-control buttons are on the left side of the window's title bar.

The small *proxy* (file) *icon* to the left of the title in a document window can be manipulated with drag-and-drop, as can a file icon in the Finder. Command-pressing the proxy icon causes the complete folder path of the document file to appear, and when a user drags to one of those folders and releases the mouse button, the corresponding folder opens in the Finder (even if the proxy icon is in a document window from another application, such as TextEdit.)

A document window's close button displays an X inside it when the document is saved to disk and a dot when the document has not been saved. Document windows usually contain vertical and/or horizontal scrollers when the

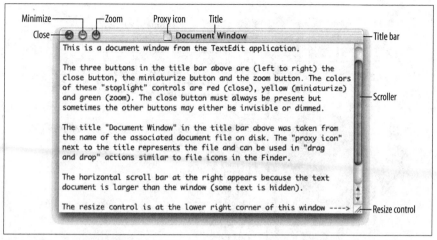

Figure 1-3. A document window in TextEdit editing a file called "Document Window"

window contents are too large to fit in the window. An application can have many document windows open at the same time.

Utility Windows

Utility windows provide tools or controls that support document windows. The Font and Colors windows that are available in many applications are utility windows (see Figure 1-4). Utility windows float over document windows and are distinguished by their shorter (in height) title bars and lack of a (working) minimize button. Utility windows sometimes have no title and have only the close button visible (unlike those in Figure 1-4). Cocoa programmers and former NeXTSTEP users refer to utility windows as *panels*. The Mac OS X terminology guidelines reject use of the term "panel," but we will use it in this book anyway because the Cocoa API uses it extensively.

Dialogs

A *dialog* is a window that seeks input from a user in response to a specific request. Examples include the familiar Open, Save, and Print dialogs. The Show Info dialog in the Finder is another example. Dialogs come in three types—modeless, document modal, and application modal:

Modeless dialog

Does not prevent the user from working in any other window of the application. Users can change settings in a dialog while still interacting with document windows. The Find/Replace tool in a word processor (see Figure 1-5) is an example of a modeless dialog; Preferences is another. In a modeless dialog, the close button is usually the only window-control button that is enabled.

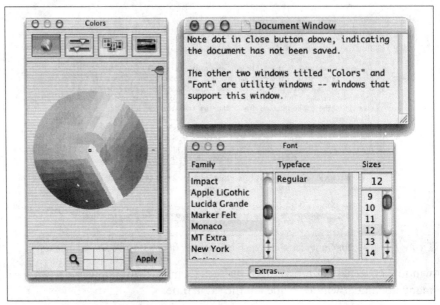

Figure 1-4. The Colors and Font utility windows in TextEdit

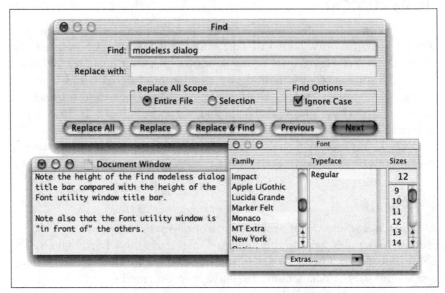

Figure 1-5. The Find modeless dialog in TextEdit; compare with document and utility windows

Document modal dialog

Prevents the user from working with a particular document, but not with other documents in the same or in other applications. Document modal dialogs are always rectangular *sheets* that animate downward from a document window's title bar; see Figure 1-6 for an example. Each sheet is attached to a document window, so there is no way that a user can be confused about which document will be saved, printed, etc.

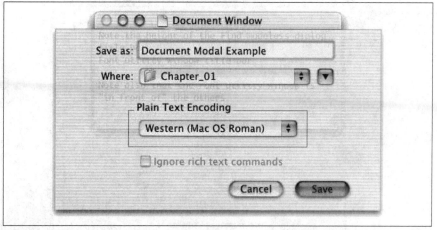

Figure 1-6. The "Save as" document modal sheet (window)—the document temporarily can't be edited

Application modal dialog

Prevents the user from working anywhere else within the application. The user can still switch to and work in other applications. An Open dialog is a common example of an application modal dialog. In TextEdit, for example, no document window can be edited while the Open dialog is displayed (see Figure 1-7). However, you can switch to the Finder or any other application and use it as you would normally. Application modal dialogs typically display their functions in the title bar (e.g., Open) and do not have any window-control buttons (e.g., no close button) because they are dismissed with an OK, Cancel, or other push button at the bottom of the dialog. Application modal dialogs float above document and utility windows, which makes sense because of the user's need to dismiss them before working elsewhere in the application.

Alerts

Alerts are displayed in windows or sheets. *Alert windows* pop up in the center of the screen and display important messages to notify users that a potentially negative event is about to occur. If a user tries to quit the TextEdit application when two or more documents are unsaved, for example, an *application* modal alert will be displayed, as shown in Figure 1-8. Another common example is the Finder alert that pops up when you try to empty your Trash.

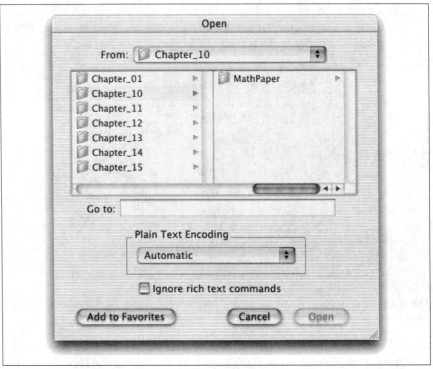

Figure 1-7. The Open application modal dialog in TextEdit

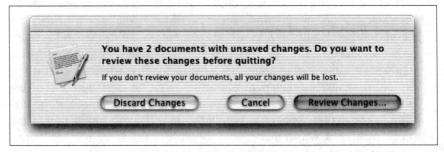

Figure 1-8. Alert displayed after a user tried to quit TextEdit without saving documents

An alert can also be *document* modal (i.e., the alert applies to only a single document), in which case it is displayed as a sheet. For an example, see Figure 1-9. Note also that the "Save as" sheet in Figure 1-6 is *not* an alert; it's a dialog.

Application modal alerts have no title in the title bar and are displayed front and center so the user takes notice. Document modal alerts are sheets attached to document windows. Both types of alerts display the application icon, a large, bold-font message, and some smaller-font informational text. A Cancel button (if possible) and default action button also appear near the bottom of the alert.

Figure 1-9. Alert for a single document displayed as a sheet in TextEdit

Info Dialogs

Info dialogs are common in Mac OS X. They provide details about selected files, objects, and so on in the active application. For example, the Finder and Interface Builder rely heavily on modeless Info dialogs. Two examples of the Finder Info dialog for two different selections are shown in Figure 1-10.

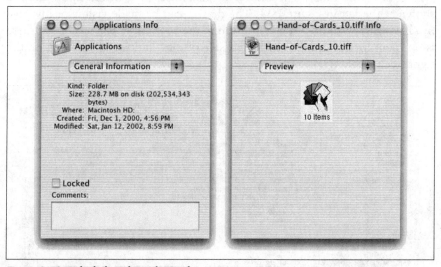

Figure 1-10. Info dialogs from the Finder

Some people refer to an Info dialog as an *inspector*, because the Info dialog allows you to inspect attributes of the selected item.

Under normal circumstances, an Info dialog is on the screen only while its associated application is active. By pressing the Info dialog's close button, you can close the dialog without adversely affecting any of the application's documents.

Multi-View Windows

Some applications support multiple views within the same window. For example, every Finder main window supports three different views: the icon view, the list view, and the column view. The System Preferences application also displays many different views in the same window. These views can be selected by clicking an icon-button in the toolbar. In some multi-view windows, different views can be selected by clicking a tab. The System Preferences Displays and Sound windows are examples of multi-view windows with tabs. Each view in a multi-view window is called a *pane*.

Windows with Drawers

Mailbox

A few Mac OS X windows have "child" windows called *drawers*. A drawer slides out from its parent window and typically contains controls that are used regularly but don't need to be visible all of the time (contrast drawers with utility windows, which typically contain controls that often need to be visible *all* of the time). The drawer of mailboxes in the Mail application is shown at the left in Figure 1-11. The drawer can be made visible or invisible by clicking the Mailbox (toggle) button in the Mail window's toolbar. If there is no room for the drawer on the left side of the window, it will open on the right side.

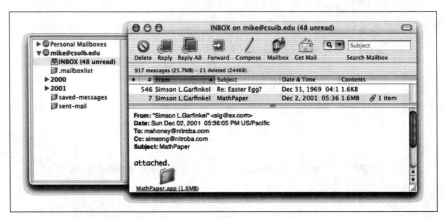

Figure 1-11. Drawer (left) of mailboxes in Mail application

Main and Key Windows

The *key window* is the window or dialog that will respond to the Mac keyboard. The *main window* is the document window that corresponds to the active document (e.g., a document window in a word processor or image window in a graphics editor). The main window is usually also the key window, because users work in the main window most of the time. A main window relinquishes its key-window status temporarily while a user gives instructions to an application, usually in a dialog or utility window that has become the key window. The key window's title bar is always highlighted, and its title is displayed in black. The main window remains highlighted even when it's not the key window.

We'll give you two examples of main and key windows in TextEdit. The first example, which has two document windows, is shown in Figure 1-12. The document window being edited (Doc 2) is the main window, while the Find dialog is the key window. The other document window is neither main nor key.

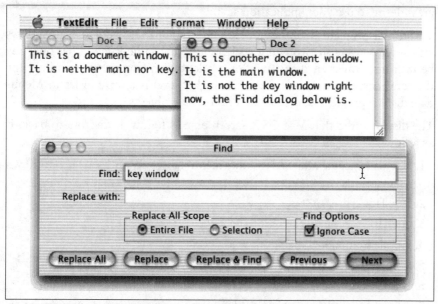

Figure 1-12. Main window (Doc 2) and key window (Find dialog) in TextEdit

For a second example, suppose that you are using TextEdit to edit a file in the main document window, and you type Command-T to display the Font utility window. The main document window will remain the key window. If you then click the mouse in the Sizes text field that is used to control point sizes in the Font window, the Font window will become the key window, but the document window will remain the main window. When you close the Font window, the main window will go back to being the key window.

Window Order

When you are using Mac OS X on a large display, you may often see 20 or more windows and other objects on the screen. Without a clear ordering scheme, a user's screen would often be in chaos, and the GUI would lose much of its ease of use. For example, suppose that a new user had spent hours editing a document within an application without saving her work. Suppose also that an alert window for that application popped up and demanded her action before she could save the document. If the alert window were completely hidden by other windows, the user might think she had a hung application, resign herself to losing hours of work, and kill the application (or worse, restart). If the alert window were front and center, this probably wouldn't happen. As another example, suppose that user couldn't find a window for an application you wrote because it was hidden under several other windows. She wouldn't be very productive if she regularly had trouble finding the window when she needed it, and she probably wouldn't have a great desire to use your application again!

To prevent problems like these, Mac OS X organizes the on-screen windows into several layers. If two windows belong to the same layer, either one may be in front. However, if two windows belong to different layers and occupy the same screen space, the one in the higher level is always in front. Menus take display precedence over all other on-screen objects.

The display order that Mac OS X screen objects follow, from front to back, is as follows:

1. Regular menus attached to the menu bar, pop-up menus, pop-down menus
2. The Dock
3. Alerts
4. Application modal dialogs
5. Utility windows
6. Modeless dialogs
7. All other windows, including document windows and document modal dialogs attached to document windows

The frontmost window is called the *active window*. It is distinguished by a title with black text and colored view-control buttons at its upper-left corner.

Menus and the Menu Bar

Menus contain a list of commands, states, and submenus that can be chosen with the mouse. The Mac OS X *menu bar* stretches across the top of the screen and is always visible, except when a slide show, full-screen video, or some other display application takes over the entire screen. The *Apple menu*, which drops down when the Apple icon () at the top left of the screen is clicked, is always available, even during application and document modal periods. The Apple menu, shown in Figure 1-13, is controlled by the operating system, not by any one application or by the user.

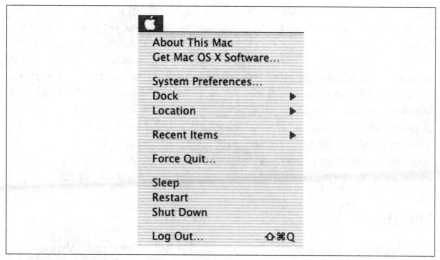

Figure 1-13. The Apple menu is always available and is controlled by the operating system

To the immediate right of the Apple menu is the *application menu*. The application menu changes depending on the active application, and it displays the active (or current) application's name in bold text. By convention, the application menu contains commands that affect the entire application, such as Preferences, Hide Others, and Quit. The application menu for the TextEdit application is shown at the left in Figure 1-14.

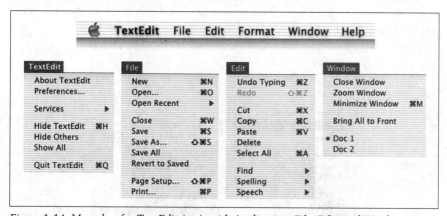

Figure 1-14. Menu bar for TextEdit (top), with Application, File, Edit, and Window menus

Each application has its own set of menus, and we've exploded four of Text-Edit's six menus in Figure 1-14. In addition to the application menu, the File and Window menus should be present for all applications. Edit, Format, and Help menus are common but are not required by the Apple interface guidelines. Other application-specific menus (e.g., the Go menu in the Finder) may also be present.

A dark gray *disclosure triangle* (▸) at the right side of a menu cell is a *submenu indicator*. A key combination containing the cloverleaf symbol (⌘)—also known as the *Command key*—in combination with a character key and possibly modifier keys (e.g., Shift, Option) is called a *keyboard equivalent*, or *key equivalent*, to the mouse. Key equivalents are used in combination with the Command (Apple, cloverleaf) key (or keys) at the bottom of the keyboard. Menu commands that bring up dialogs are usually followed by three dots (an *ellipsis*), indicating that additional information must be provided to complete the command. Grayed-out (or *dimmed*) menu commands are disabled in the application's current context. Menus and submenus float on top of all other windows and are visible only when the associated application is active.

The Dock

The Mac OS X Dock replaces the Mac OS 9 Application menu. Always available (though it may be temporarily hidden), the Dock is designed to reduce on-screen disorder and help users organize their work. The Dock always contains the Finder icon and the Trash icon in the first and last positions, respectively, as shown in Figure 1-15. The Dock can also contain any number of additional icons that fall into four groups: running applications, minimized documents, file/folder icons, and application icons for commonly used applications (running or not) such as Mail, iTunes, and Internet Explorer. Every *open* application's icon and every minimized document icon (for non-hidden applications) is in the Dock. The commonly used applications that populate the Dock are the choice of the user.

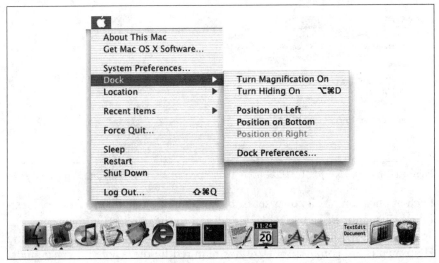

Figure 1-15. The Dock (bottom) location and appearance can be controlled via the Dock submenu

By choosing a menu command from the Dock submenu located in the Apple menu (see the top of Figure 1-15), a user can turn magnification and hiding on or off. When turned on, the magnification feature causes each icon in the Dock to enlarge when the mouse is positioned over it. When turned on, the hidden feature causes the Dock to "hide" off-screen unless the mouse is positioned over it. Users can also position the Dock as a whole at the left, right, or bottom of the screen. We prefer the Dock on the left or right side of the screen because most documents are portrait-shaped, and a Dock at the bottom of the screen gets in the way.

Users can access additional Dock preferences through the System Preferences application. We'll experiment with those preferences in the step-by-step exercises later in this chapter.

The example Dock in Figure 1-15 contains 15 icons, 6 of which represent running applications (indicated by a black triangle below each icon). The first icon on the left is the Finder, which is always running. The second icon from the left is the running Mac OS X Mail application, which sports a "live" badge with the number of unread mail messages. The last three icons on the right are separated from the others by a slight gap with a barely visible line. This part of the Dock contains minimized document windows and is where the user can place file and folder icons from the Finder for quick access. The user's Library folder icon is second from the right, and a minimized TextEdit document is third from the right. Minimized document icons are actually miniature versions of the windows they represent—great feedback for the user.

All the icons in the Dock provide a name when the mouse is positioned over them, as with the iTunes application at the left in Figure 1-16. When the mouse is pressed and held down on a Dock icon, a menu appears, as shown in the screen shot in the center of Figure 1-16.

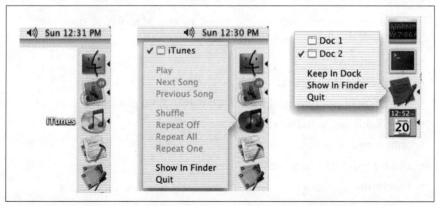

Figure 1-16. Mouse positioned over (left) and pressed on (center) the iTunes icon; mouse pressed on the TextEdit icon (right)

If the Dock icon over which the mouse is pressed and held down represents an inactive application, the Show In Finder command is the only menu item available. If chosen, this menu command activates the Finder and selects the application, folder, etc. in the filesystem. If the application is active (i.e., running) when the mouse is pressed, the application icon in the Dock will display a special Dock menu containing Show In Finder and several other useful commands for quick access, as follows:

- At the top of the Dock menu associated with an active application is a list of each of the application's document windows; selecting one of these menu items brings the corresponding window to the front of the desktop. For example, the Dock menu for the running TextEdit application at the right in Figure 1-16 shows Doc 1 and Doc 2.

- At the bottom of the Dock menu is a menu option labeled Quit. Selecting this option terminates the application.

- If the application was not in the Dock prior to its being run, the menu option Keep In Dock will appear as well. Choosing this menu option causes the application's icon to remain in the Dock after it is terminated.

Controls

Mac OS X *controls* are on-screen graphical objects that perform like physical control devices we use every day. Consider a car stereo system that has an on-off switch with an indicator light, a row of buttons to select a radio station, a sliding knob to set volume, and a push button for ejecting an audio CD. Each of these devices is a control device with a different function. The on-off switch is a toggle, the radio buttons allow a choice of one out of many options, the slider sets a level or value, and the push button causes an action. All of these physical control devices have analogous on-screen controls that can be manipulated by the mouse in Mac OS X.

There are several common control types in the Mac OS X user interface, which we will discuss in the following sections:

- Push buttons
- Radio buttons and checkboxes
- Pop-up menus, command pop-down menus, and combination boxes
- Text fields and scrolling lists
- Sliders and scrollers
- Color wells and image wells
- Disclosure triangles

Buttons

There are several types of on-screen buttons. They fall into two main groups: action buttons and two-state buttons. An *action button* performs a single task, such as opening a dialog, saving a file, copying text, or closing a window. A *two-state button* sets a single feature or attribute on or off, such as whether text should be in bold font or a drawer should be displayed. In the car stereo analogy, the eject button is an action button, while the on-off switch is a two-state button. The set of car radio buttons is analogous to a matrix (group) of two-state buttons, each indicating whether the associated radio station is selected. There is more structure to this matrix of radio buttons, however, because only one of the two-state buttons may be selected at any one time. A checkbox is another example of a two-state button.

Push buttons

A *push button* looks like a rounded rectangle with a text label on it. Clicking a push button performs an immediate action, such as printing a document, canceling a dialog, or responding to an alert message. Push button names should be verbs (such as Open, Print, Save, or Cancel) that describe the action to be performed.

Push buttons should not be used to indicate a state such as on or off (use checkboxes instead). When a push button represents the default action that can be initiated by hitting the Return key, the button is shown in a darkened form (see the button at the edge of the page). Push buttons are sometimes completely round, like the Back button shown at the edge of the page, which was grabbed from a Finder window.

Radio buttons and checkboxes

We discuss these two types of buttons together because they are often confused with one another. *Radio buttons* should be used for a group of mutually exclusive, but related, choices. As a group, they have functionality similar to the radio buttons on your car stereo. A group of radio buttons should contain at least two choices. If you need more than five choices, consider using a pop-up menu (discussed in the next section).

Checkboxes should be used to indicate options that must be either on or off (toggles). A checkbox can stand alone if appropriate to the application. Checkboxes in a group, like those at the edge of the page, are almost always independent of one another (unlike radio buttons). Checkboxes should be labeled so that it is clear what actions the checked and unchecked choices will perform. In contrast to radio buttons, checkboxes usually initiate actions.

Pop-up Menus, Command Pop-down Menus, and Combination Boxes

A *pop-up menu* is a menu-like list that appears on top of a button when the button is pressed. Like a set of radio buttons, a pop-up menu displays a list of mutually exclusive choices—only one can be chosen at a time. Pop-up menus are preferred over radio buttons when the number of choices is more than five, when the user doesn't need to see the choices all the time, or when window or dialog real estate is at a premium. Unlike menu commands, a pop-up menu item should set a state rather than initiate an action.

As shown at the edge of the page, a pop-up menu has a *double-triangle indicator* and a label that displays the currently selected choice, and it "pops up" when the double-indicator triangle is clicked. To select an item from a pop-up menu, a user must press the pop-up menu button, drag the mouse pointer to the desired item, and release the mouse button. The chosen item will be displayed on the pop-up menu button. Pop-up menus are sometimes given numeric keyboard equivalents (e.g., Command-1). See Figure 1-17 for an example of how a pop-up menu functions.

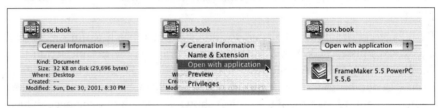

Figure 1-17. A pop-up menu before, during, and after a selection

Command pop-down menus are like regular drop-down menus, but they appear in windows rather than in the menu bar. The Extras pop-down menu from the Font window is shown at the edge of the page. Command pop-down menus aren't used very often and are sanctioned for use only in windows that are shared among multiple applications (e.g., the Font or Color utility window). The label of a command pop-down menu is similar to that of a regular menu (and unlike that of a pop-up menu) in that it doesn't change.

A *combination box* is a combination of a text entry field and a pop-up menu or a drop-down scrolling list, as shown at the edge of the page. A combination box is useful for displaying a list of common choices while still allowing the user to type in an item not in the list, sometimes with text completion, as in the "First" example at the edge of the page. *Text completion* means that a user can quickly select an item by typing only the first few (unique) characters (this is similar to filename completion in a Unix shell and web-address completion in a web browser).

Text Fields and Scrolling Lists

There are two types of text fields, input and static. A *text input field* is a rectangular area of text that is editable by the user, although it can be disabled in
some contexts. The text is selectable, so the user can drag across it or multi-
ple-click it for subsequent cut, copy, and paste operations. Some input text
fields allow only one short line of text and can restrict input to certain characters and formats (e.g., uppercase letters only). Text input fields are often
arranged in groups, where the Tab key can move the selection from one text
field to the next. When the user types some text and then hits the Return key,
the text field usually makes something happen; typically, the text is read and
some action is performed with it (e.g., a file is saved under a name typed into
a text field in a Save panel). This functionality makes the text field a control.

A *static input field* is a rectangular area of text that is *not* editable by the user
but that may be selectable and may be dimmed in some contexts.

A *scrolling list* contains as many list items as needed and typically resides
inside a scrolling area in a window or in a pop-down menu (see the next section). Both the list view and the column view in Finder windows use scrolling
lists; another example is the list of running applications in the Finder's Force
Quit Applications utility window.

Sliders and Scrollers

Scrollers let you scroll through a text or graphics area that is larger than the
displayed view. *Sliders* let you set a value (e.g., floating point, integer) and are
often accompanied by a text field displaying the value. You can grab a scroller or slider knob anywhere to drag it. You can also click anywhere in a scroller or slider well for larger movements. The center of the knob will move to
the position clicked (this scroller behavior is called "scroll to here" and can be
changed to "jump to the next page" in the General preferences pane in the
System Preferences application).

The *size* of a scroll knob within the scroller well indicates the relative size of
what you see compared with the total area. For example, in Figure 1-18 the
scroll knob fills about 60% of the scroller well, so we would expect that about
60% of the choices in the scrolling list are visible (in fact, 8 of 13 choices are
visible in Figure 1-18). The *position* of the scroll knob indicates the relative
location of what's visible within the entire list or document. Thus, in
Figure 1-18, the 8 visible choices are at the top of the list of 13 total choices.
Scrollers usually contain *scroll arrows* for slow, consistent scrolling through a
document. In some applications you can make the scroller move more quickly
by holding down the Option key when pressing the scroll arrows.

Text Field

Text Field

Sliders can be horizontal or vertical and can be discrete or continuous. When they are discrete, they accept only grid values and should thus have tick marks. There are two continuous sliders in the window in Figure 1-18.

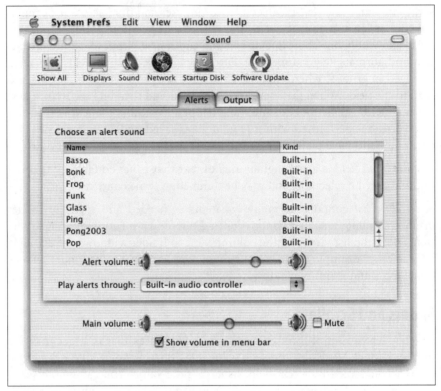

Figure 1-18. Sliders and a scroller in the System Preferences application

Color Wells and Image Wells

A *color well* is used to select and manipulate colors. If you press the mouse down inside the color area of a color well (the dark area in the center of the color well at the edge of the page) and drag outward, you will drag out a little chip of "color" that can then be dropped on certain other on-screen objects, such as an image well. Alternatively, you can click the mouse on the edge of a color well to bring up a Colors utility window, which can also be used to change the color well's color. The Colors utility window itself has a color well in its lower-left corner, as shown in Figure 1-19.

An *image well* serves as a drag-and-drop target for an icon, picture, or color chip (as shown at the bottom of the Colors window in Figure 1-19). Another example of an image well can be found in the Desktop pane of the System Preferences window. A set of image wells would serve well as a set of thumbnails for a photo album.

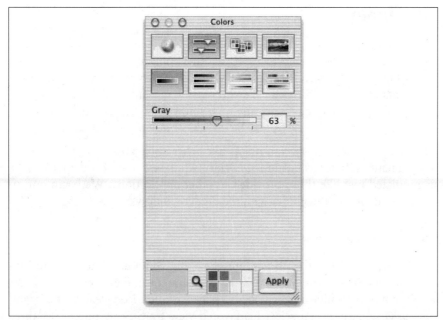

Figure 1-19. Colors utility window with a color well (lower left) and eight image wells (lower center)

Disclosure Triangles

Disclosure triangles (▸) are common in menus, the Finder, and many other applications that display hierarchical information. Clicking a disclosure triangle next to a folder in list view in a Finder window, for example, will "disclose" the files in the folder.

Other Controls

There are several other types of controls in Mac OS X:

Bevel buttons
    These display text, an icon, or a picture and usually replicate the behavior of a push button.

View-control buttons
    The button in the Finder's toolbar (shown at the edge of the page) is an example of three bevel buttons in a matrix.

Tab controls
    These change the view pane of a window (for example, the Alerts and Output tabs in Figure 1-18).

Placards, progress indicators, and relevance controls
    These are less-often-used controls; information about them can be found in the online reference materials.

The Finder

 The Finder is a special application in Mac OS X, because it oversees the Aqua environment and allows easy access to all other applications. It never stops running while you're logged in. The Mac OS icon shown at the edge of the page represents the Finder, just as the TextEdit icon represents the TextEdit application. You can activate the Finder any time you want by clicking this icon in the Dock—it's always available (it may be invisible, but it's easy to find).

Although the Finder is special, it acts like other applications in most ways. It has a menu, submenus, windows, utility windows, and so on that can be manipulated just like those provided in other applications. We begin our in-depth discussion of the Finder with the Finder window.

The Finder Window

The Finder window is the primary interface that you will use for viewing and manipulating files in the Mac OS X (Unix) hierarchical filesystem. The Finder window supports three different views (panes) of files: *icon view*, *list view*, and *column view*. A user can select his favored view by clicking one of the three mutually exclusive *view-control buttons* at the left of the Finder's toolbar. We present the same Finder window showing three different views of the commonly used /Applications folder in Figure 1-20, Figure 1-21, and Figure 1-22.

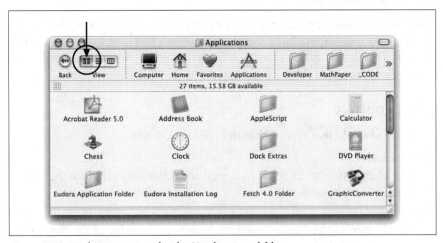

Figure 1-20. Finder's icon view for the /Applications folder

No matter which view you choose, the Finder window's content area consists of three main parts: the toolbar, the status bar, and the view pane. The toolbar and status bar can be hidden via the Finder's View menu, but the view pane is always visible. The Finder status bar displays the number of items

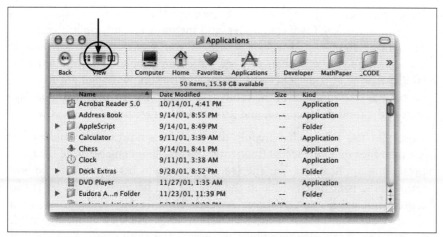

Figure 1-21. Finder's list view for the /Applications folder

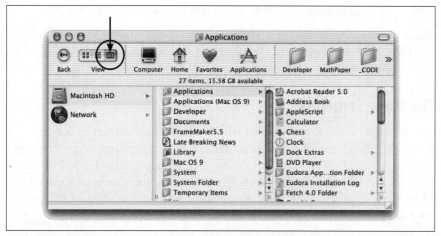

Figure 1-22. Finder's column view for the /Applications folder

(files and folders) in the selected folder and the space available on disk. The Finder toolbar contains several types of buttons for viewing and manipulating files and folders, including the three view-control buttons discussed previously. Like the Back button on a web browser, the Back button in the Finder toolbar returns you to the previous view.

The Toolbar

For quick access, file and folder icons can be placed in the toolbar to the right of the view-control buttons. After being dropped in the toolbar, these icons work like shortcuts (although that term isn't used). The first icon (Computer) in this area of the toolbar represents your computer, the second icon

(Home) represents your Home folder (~), the third icon (Favorites) represents your ~/Library/Favorites folder, and the fourth icon (Applications) represents the system /Applications folder. If you single-click on any one of these icons, the view will change to the represented folder. You can add a file or folder icon (e.g., Developer in Figure 1-22) by simply dragging it from the view pane and dropping it in the toolbar. To remove a file or folder icon-button from the toolbar, drag it off and drop it on the desktop.

You should use the toolbar mainly to store icons representing folders and document files that you access frequently. The toolbar can also store file icons representing applications, but the Dock is usually a better place to do that because there isn't much space in the toolbar and because the Finder is file-oriented, not application-oriented. A single-click on any folder icon in the toolbar opens that folder in the browser. A single-click on a document file icon in the toolbar opens that file in the associated application. A single-click on an application icon launches that application, as in the Dock. Thus, files, folders, and applications that you access regularly are only a click away.

You can radically change the contents of the toolbar via the View → Customize Toolbar menu command. We'll revisit this in the step-by-step exercises later in this chapter.

The Menu Structure

As with all Mac OS X applications, the Finder menu structure is hierarchical. When the Finder is active, the menu bar at the top of the screen displays eight menus: Apple, Finder, File, Edit, View, Go, Window, and Help. The menu bar and the contents of the seven Finder menus are shown in Figure 1-23. Most of these menu commands are obvious; we'll utilize some of the not-so-obvious ones in the step-by-step exercises later in this chapter.

To see the contents of a menu, single-click on the menu name in the title bar. The menu will stay open, or stick (no pressing is required). The submenu displayed will be attached to the title bar, and you can then choose a menu command by clicking it. Alternatively, you can press down on a menu title in the menu bar, drag the mouse down to the desired menu option, and then release the mouse button to select it.

Support Windows and Dialogs

There are several useful Finder utility windows and dialogs that can be displayed via menu commands. Perhaps the most useful is the modeless Info dialog, which shows up when the user chooses File → Show Info and provides detailed information about individual files and folders. The Edit → Show Clipboard menu command brings up the Clipboard, which displays the cut or

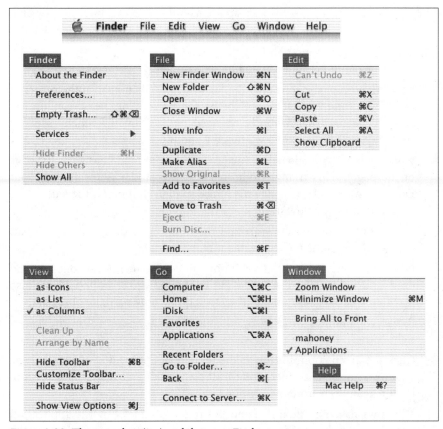

Figure 1-23. The menu bar (top) and the seven Finder menus

copied contents currently available for pasting. The Finder's Clipboard, Preferences, and About windows are all modeless and will stick around while you work elsewhere in the Finder. The Go → Go to Folder menu command brings up the Go to Folder dialog, a document modal sheet attached to the main Finder window (a Finder's view is considered a document in a window). These windows will be discussed later in this chapter.

Configuring Your Desktop, Step by Step

This section takes you on a guided tour of the Mac OS X Finder and System Preferences applications. We assume that you have the Mac OS X Developer Tools installed. All of the steps work under Mac OS X Version 10.1.

To get the most out of these exercises, we recommend that you follow them precisely. For example, start by logging in and do not close any windows or dialogs unless instructed to do so. If you do not follow a step precisely or if you skip a step, subsequent steps may not make sense.

The steps in configuring your desktop are as follows. As with all step-by-step exercises in this book, we recommend that you follow these steps precisely.

1. Start up your computer and log in.

   The Finder will be running, and the Finder menu will appear in the menu bar at the top of the screen. A Finder window will appear in the center of the screen, and the Dock will be at the bottom of the screen (unless you've closed it or previously changed its position, in which case you should choose Finder → New Finder Window).

   Note the black triangle below the Mac OS Finder icon (shown at the edge of the page). This triangle indicates that the Finder is running. If your Dock is on the side of your screen, the triangle will be on the side of the icon, rather than below it.

2. Move your Finder window around the desktop by dragging its title bar. Any window can be moved in this way.

   Note that you cannot drag a window above the menu bar, but you can drag it partially off-screen to the left or right or at the bottom. Note also that the window goes "under" the Dock but is only partially obscured.

3. Resize your Finder window by dragging the resize control in the lower-right corner.

4. Click the green zoom button at the top left of the window. Note that the window changes size (perhaps to fill the working area). Click the zoom button again to restore the previous size.

   Windows have an initial size and position that are set by the application and are called the *standard state*. If a user resizes or moves a window, the window is in the *user state*. The zoom button simply toggles between the standard and user states. Each of the three views in the Finder has its own standard state.

5. Make sure you are viewing files in your Finder window in column-view mode by clicking the column-view button (the one on the right) in the Finder's toolbar.

Working with the Dock

6. Remove all of the icons from your Dock (except for the Mac OS and Trash icons, which cannot be removed) by dragging them from the Dock and dropping them onto the desktop (background). Each icon will disappear in a cloud of dust.

   If any applications are running, you must quit them before you can drag them out of your Dock. Running applications are those that have a small triangle below the icon in the Dock. To quit a running application, press and hold down the mouse on its icon in the Dock, and choose Quit from the menu that pops up.

7. Select (i.e., single-click) the hard disk icon labeled Macintosh HD in the Finder window. This represents the top (root) of the filesystem hierarchy for the Mac OS X filesystem.

Macintosh HD

8. Now select the /Applications folder (directory) in the Finder by clicking its icon. The /Applications folder should have an A-like picture (made up of a pencil, pen, and ruler) on it, as shown at the edge of the page.

Applications

9. Add the Mail application to your Dock by selecting it in the Finder, dragging its icon from your icon path, and dropping it just below the Mac OS icon in your Dock.

Mail

10. Use the same procedure to add the TextEdit application to your Dock.

11. Open the Utilities folder by selecting the folder icon at the bottom of the column that holds the list of applications. This folder contains applications that are useful for power users but that are not normally needed by beginners. (If you aren't already a power user, you need to become one!)

TextEdit

12. Add the Terminal and Console applications to your Dock, as you did with Mail and TextEdit. Only one application can be dropped into the Dock at a time.

Utilities

13. Open the /Developer/Examples/AppKit folder in your Finder by selecting Developer (from the second Finder column), then Examples, and finally AppKit.

Terminal

14. Drag the AppKit folder icon to the "end" of the Dock, near the Trash icon. Folders and file icons can be placed only in the part of the Dock between the Trash icon and the faint line.

Console

15. Now remove the AppKit folder icon from the Dock by dragging it out to the desktop and releasing it. The Finder toolbar is a better location for folders.

The AppKit folder contains good examples of Cocoa applications that show off different aspects of the Foundation and Application Kits, the two fundamental frameworks of the Cocoa development environment. (When you are finished with this book, you should go through the examples in this folder, build each with Project Builder, run them, and then look at the code to see how they work.)

The Finder's Viewing Options

16. Open your Home folder again by clicking the little house icon in the Finder window's toolbar.

Home

17. Choose View → Show View Options to bring up the View Options utility window. If necessary, drag this utility window so that it doesn't

share screen space with the Finder window. If you are still in column-view mode, no options will currently be shown in the View Options window.

18. Experiment with the three different ways of displaying files (icon view, list view, and column view) by clicking the three different view-control buttons (shown at the edge of the page) in your Finder's toolbar. (These views were covered earlier, in the section "The Finder.") Note that the View Options window changes to show the options for the selected Finder view, as shown in Figure 1-24.

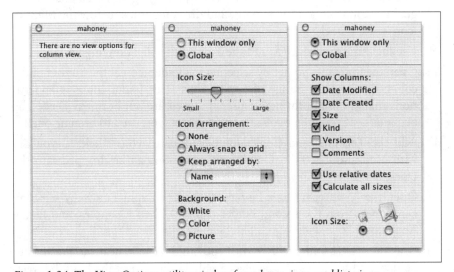

Figure 1-24. The View Options utility window for column, icon, and list views

19. Choose the Finder's View → as List menu command. Note that you are provided with more information about the files in the list view than in the other views.

20. Click the Name column header, and note that the files are ordered alphabetically by name. Click the Name column header again, and note that the order is reversed.

21. Click the Date Modified, Size, and Kind column headers, and note that while in list view you have many ordering options for the files in a folder. You can also add more columns with similar functionality, as indicated in Figure 1-24.

22. Choose the Finder's View → as Columns menu command, an alternative way of selecting the column view (the view-control buttons are quicker).

23. Open another Finder window by choosing the File → New Finder Window menu command. The new window will probably open with the root Computer folder displayed in the view pane, but it might open with your

Home folder displayed. This is a user preference that can be selected in the Finder Preferences window.

24. Click in one Finder window and then in the other (this is known as *click-to-focus*).

Note how each window is displayed "on top of" the other after it is clicked (using the desktop analogy, where windows are pieces of paper). Note also that the title of the window in front is displayed in black instead of gray and that the window-control buttons are colored red, yellow, and green instead of gray.

25. Minimize (iconify) one of the Finder windows by clicking the yellow minimize button in the window's title bar.

The window will animate into a minimized Finder icon (shown at the edge of the page) in the Dock with either the Genie effect or the Scale effect. The animation effect is a user preference and can be changed in the System Preferences application. The mini-window icon in the Dock should resemble the full-sized window.

26. Open your Home folder by selecting (with a single-click) the little house icon in the still-open Finder window's toolbar.

Home

Finder Preferences

Many Mac OS X applications allow the user to set *preferences* that change the way the application behaves. Your preferences are stored in your ~/Library/Preferences folder. If different people use the same computer with different login accounts, each person will have her own set of system- and application-specific preferences. In the following steps, we will look at the Finder's preferences.

27. Choose the Finder → Preferences menu command. The Finder Preferences dialog should appear, as shown in Figure 1-25 (your preferences may differ).

28. Click the "Hard disks" checkbox, and the icon(s) representing your computer's hard disk(s) will appear on the desktop (the icon(s) might be hidden behind a window). Uncheck the checkbox (i.e., click it again), and the hard disk icon(s) will disappear.

Macintosh HD

---

* The Unix-based X Windows windowing system supports *point-to-focus* (or *mouse-to-focus*) in addition to click-to-focus. With point-to-focus, windows become active when you move the cursor on top of them; no click is required. Point-to-focus can result in commands being accidentally sent to the wrong window if your mouse is bumped. This is one of the reasons that the Macintosh and Windows operating systems don't use point-to-focus. On the other hand, some people prefer point-to-focus because it requires less clicking.

Figure 1-25. Finder Preferences dialog

29. Click the "Always show file extensions" checkbox and look in a Finder window. File extensions will appear after the names of the files that have them.

30. Click the red close button to close the Finder Preferences dialog.

31. Now click the button (⊖) in the upper-right corner of the Finder window. Note that the toolbar disappears.

32. Click the button in the upper-right corner of the Finder window again. The button is a toggle, so the toolbar will return.

    Use this button to hide the toolbar quickly when you need more space in the view pane. Note that you can also hide the status bar that lies between the toolbar and the view pane by choosing View → Hide Status Bar.

33. Choose the Finder's View → Customize Toolbar menu command to change the Finder view pane into a cornucopia of useful icons and tools that can be dragged to your toolbar for quick access, as shown in Figure 1-26. Note that the window in Figure 1-26 has the default set of icons in its toolbar.

34. Click the Done button. (You can customize your toolbar later, when you have a feel for Aqua. We prefer the default set as a starting point.)

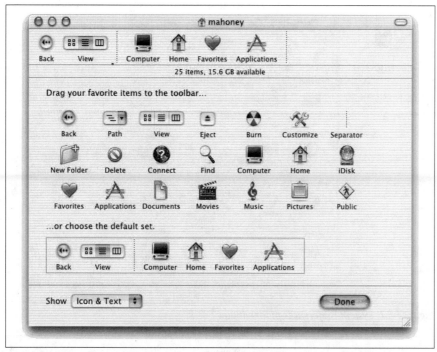

Figure 1-26. For quick access, drag icons from the View pane into the toolbar

System Preferences

The Finder preferences affect only the Finder. Many Mac OS X preferences affect your entire operating-system environment. These preferences can be modified using the System Preferences application. This application replaces the Control Panels system used in previous versions of Mac OS (and it's similar to the Microsoft Windows Control Panel).

35. Choose System Preferences from the Apple menu to launch the System Preferences application, as shown in Figure 1-27.

36. If your System Preferences window doesn't look like the one in Figure 1-27, click the Show All icon-button in the toolbar (the row of icons just below the title bar).

37. Click the General icon-button in the Personal row in the System Preferences window. Note that the new preferences pane (view) that shows up (see Figure 1-28) is slightly smaller than the previous one, and the window shrinks accordingly.

38. Press the Highlight color pop-up menu button, drag to Graphite, then release the mouse button. (Change it back if you prefer.)

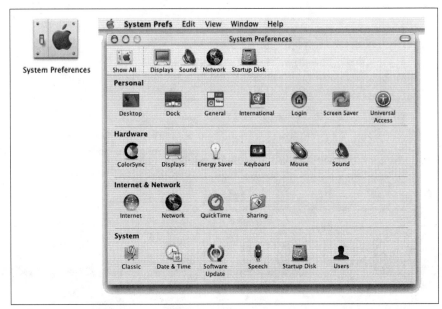

Figure 1-27. System Preferences main window

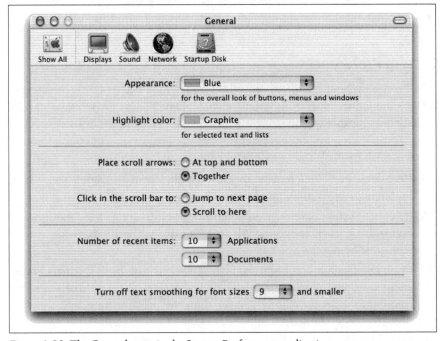

Figure 1-28. The General pane in the System Preferences application

39. Click the radio button labeled "At top and bottom" in the "Place scroll arrows" section of the General System Preferences pane.

40. Now click the Finder icon in your Dock to make the Finder active. Note that the highlight color is Graphite (or whatever you chose for a highlight color) and the "up" scroll arrow is at the top of the scroller instead of the bottom.

41. Choose Finder → Hide Finder (or type Command-H) to hide the Finder. The System Preferences application should become active, because it was the active application before the Finder was made active.

42. Click the radio button labeled "Together" in the "Place scroll arrows" section of the General System Preferences pane.

    We recommend keeping both scroll arrows together because this makes it easier to switch from scrolling up to scrolling down. In fact, you can switch the scrolling direction while pressing the mouse button by simply sliding from one scroll arrow to the other.

43. Now single-click the Apple icon () in the menu bar, then position the mouse over the Recent Items.

    Note that there is a list of recently launched applications and another list of recently opened documents in the menu. This is a very useful menu that defaults to lists of length 5. We'll change the lengths to 10 in the next step.

44. Back in the System Preferences application, press the "Number of recent items: Applications" pop-up menu button, drag to 10, then release the mouse button. Do the same for the number of recent documents.

45. Click the Show All icon-button in the System Preferences toolbar.

Show All

Dock

46. Click the Dock icon-button in the Personal row in the System Preferences window to get the pane shown in Figure 1-29.

47. Click the "Right" radio button to position your Dock at the right of your screen. Note that you can also have your Dock hide automatically and change the animation effects applied to applications as they open. When turned on, the Magnification feature will cause icons in your Dock to enlarge when the mouse is positioned over them, a wonderful feature if you have lots of icons in your Dock or if your vision is poor. Some of these preferences are available via the Apple menu.

48. Click the Show All icon-button again and then click the Screen Saver icon-button in the System Preferences toolbar. Note that you can choose from a variety of screen savers, specify the number of inactivity minutes before your chosen screen saver takes effect, and also choose corners where you want to position the mouse to force the screen saver to take effect.

Screen Saver

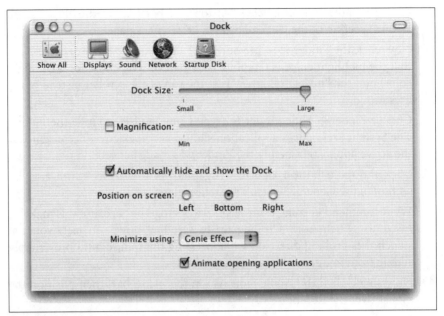

Figure 1-29. The Dock pane in the System Preferences application

49. Click the Show All icon-button once again, then click the Sound icon-button in the System Preferences toolbar (see Figure 1-18 for a screen shot of the Sound pane). Note that you can choose from a variety of sounds for system alerts and specify the volume.

50. Click the Show All icon-button one last time, then click the Software Update icon-button in the System Preferences toolbar. We recommend that you visit this pane regularly and click the Update Now button to download updates from Apple's web site. Or, you can click the "Update Software Automatically" radio button and select "Check for updates Daily" (or Weekly), so you won't have to remember to update your software.

51. Choose System Prefs → Quit System Prefs to quit the System Preferences application.

Menu Guidelines and Keyboard Equivalents

Developers should follow Aqua's menu guidelines carefully so users of their applications can learn and work faster. Common menu structure and commands are crucial to better user productivity within a GUI. In this section, we discuss most of the standard Mac OS X menus and associated keyboard equivalent guidelines. For further details, see the "Introduction to the Aqua Human

Interface Guidelines" at Apple's developer web site or in the /Developer folder (references are provided at the end of this chapter).

A *keyboard equivalent* is a way of manipulating a graphical object (usually a menu) using the keyboard rather than the mouse. To use a keyboard equivalent, type a single key (perhaps modified by the Shift key) while pressing one of the Command keys near the bottom of the Apple keyboard (depending on your Mac, you may have only one Command key on your keyboard). Experienced users use keyboard equivalents because they are faster than manipulating the mouse. Using the mouse is a more natural way to manipulate graphical objects, but it's often slower and less convenient, either because the user's hands are already on the keyboard or because mouse (cursor) movements across a screen are time-consuming and clumsy.

A keyboard equivalent usually substitutes for a click on a menu command from the menu bar, but it may also substitute for a pop-up menu command. Pop-up menu key equivalents should be digits (e.g., Command-2 activates the second item down from the top of a pop-up menu, as shown in Figure 1-30).

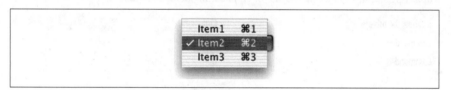

Figure 1-30. Command-2 activates the second item of this fictional pop-up menu

Because most keyboard equivalents are common across applications, a user will need to learn only a few of them to work considerably faster. The most common and useful keyboard equivalents are listed in the tables in the following sections. Others can be seen in the screen shots of the menus themselves. Note that the keyboard equivalent labels on Mac OS X menus are displayed in capital letters, but you must actually use lowercase letters to make the commands work (unless the label contains the shift icon—for example, File → Save As).

Application Menu

Every application has an *application menu*, the menu to the immediate right of the Apple menu. Figure 1-31 contains a screen shot of the application menu for a generic application template. Application menus contain commands that affect the entire application, including the following: display the About window, display the Preferences dialog (if any), Hide the application, Hide Others (i.e., all other applications), Show All (applications), and Quit. We'll discuss the Services submenu later.

Figure 1-31. Generic Application menu and menu bar for a Mac OS X application

The standard key equivalents for Application menu commands are listed in Table 1-1.

Table 1-1. Standard key equivalents for Application menu commands

Keyboard equivalent	Command
Command-H	Hide
Command-Q	Quit

The menus (File, Edit, etc.) to the right of the application menu in the menu bar are application-dependent, but if included they should be placed in the order shown in Figure 1-31. If additional menus such as View, Format, and Tools are included, they should be inserted between the Edit and Window menus. Mac OS X users are accustomed to finding the File, Edit, Window, Help, and other menus in the same place for every application, so don't frustrate them by moving the menus around when designing your application.

A command from a submenu is sometimes promoted up a level to the main menu if it's essential to the application. For example, the Font command might be promoted from the Format submenu to the main menu in a word processor or other font-dependent application. If this decision is made, the promoted command should immediately follow the submenu where it would normally be found. Thus, a promoted Font command, for example, would follow Format in the main menu.

File Menu

The File menu contains commands that affect a document (or file) as a whole. These commands are used to open, create, or save the type of document(s) associated with the application. As with the application menu, not all of the commands in the File menu are required, but if included they should be ordered as shown in Figure 1-32.

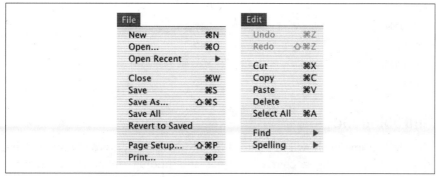

Figure 1-32. Generic File and Edit menus

The Save and Save As commands will both save the contents of the main document window to a file, but Save As allows you to save the file to a name that is different from the current name. The standard key equivalents for the File menu are listed in Table 1-2. Note that the Save As and Page Setup key equivalents are three-key combinations requiring the Shift key.

Table 1-2. Standard key equivalents for File menu commands

Keyboard equivalent	Command
Command-N	New
Command-O	Open
Command-W	Close
Command-S	Save
Shift-Command-S	Save As
Shift-Command-P	Page Setup
Command-P	Print

Edit Menu

The Edit menu commands can be used to manipulate text, graphics, and other objects in the key window (i.e., the one with keyboard focus). Edit menu keyboard equivalents—listed in Table 1-3—are perhaps the most worthwhile to learn, because they are used very often and in a variety of places. The Cut, Copy, Paste, and Select All commands can be used in most text and graphics areas in any main window or dialog that is key. Edit menu key equivalents are very convenient for right-handed people, because they can be performed easily with the left hand while one's right hand is on the mouse.

Table 1-3. Standard key equivalents for Edit menu commands

Keyboard equivalent	Command
Command-X	Cut
Command-C	Copy
Command-V	Paste
Command-A	Select All
Command-Z	Undo

Find Submenu

The Find submenu shown in Figure 1-33 allows easy access to common activities such as finding a character string and finding the next or previous appearance of the same string. The common key equivalent Command-F brings up the Find dialog (window) for specific searches.

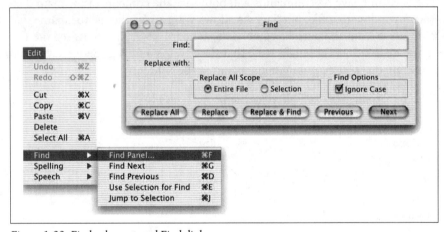

Figure 1-33. Find submenu and Find dialog

The Use Selection for Find command finds the next string that matches the current selection. The standard key equivalents for the Find menu are listed in Table 1-4.

Table 1-4. Standard key equivalents for Find submenu commands

Keyboard equivalent	Command
Command-F	Find, Find Panel
Command-G	Find Next
Command-D	Find Previous
Command-E	Use Selection for Find
Command-J	Jump to Selection

Format and Font Menus

Format menu commands affect the layout of text and graphics documents. The Format menu is not available in every application, but it is usually found in applications that deal with text, such as TextEdit. The Font submenu is usually a choice in the Format menu (as in the TextEdit menu shown in Figure 1-34), but it can be promoted to the main menu, as described previously. There are no standard keyboard equivalents for the Format menu, but there are many for the Font submenu (the Format key equivalents in Figure 1-34 are specific to TextEdit).

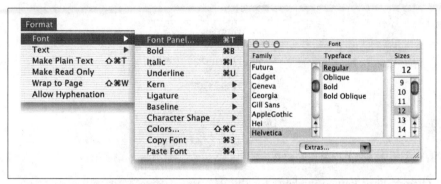

Figure 1-34. The Font submenu and Font utility window in TextEdit

Font submenu commands such as Bold and Italic affect one aspect of the text font. There are several other common Font submenu commands that affect font size and style, some of which are shown in Figure 1-34. The Font Panel command brings up a standard Font utility window with font family, typeface, and size choices, as shown in Figure 1-34. The standard key equivalents for the Font menu are shown in Table 1-5.

Table 1-5. Standard key equivalents for Font submenu commands

Keyboard equivalent	Command
Command-T	Font Panel
Command-B	Bold
Command-I	Italic
Command-U	Underline

Window Menu

Window menu commands such as those in Figure 1-35 apply to windows within the active application. The Close, Zoom, and Minimize Window commands apply only to the key window. (Close Window is usually in the File menu, with the Command-W key equivalent, but it can also be placed in the Window menu.) The Bring All to Front command brings all the windows in the active application to the front of the desktop. The Doc 1 command brings the Doc 1 document window to the front and makes it the key window (the Doc 2 menu command works similarly). The dot next to Doc 1 in Figure 1-35 indicates that it has not been saved to disk (same meaning as the dot in a document window's red close button). These two menu commands that affect document windows were added to the Window menu dynamically, as the corresponding documents (files) were opened.

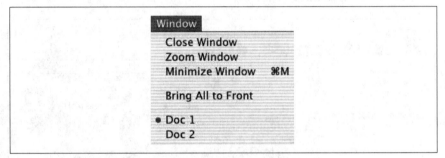

Figure 1-35. The Window menu in TextEdit

The standard key equivalents for the Window menu commands are shown in Table 1-6.

Table 1-6. Standard key equivalents for Window menu commands

Keyboard equivalent	Command
Command-M	Minimize Window
Command-W	Close Window

Services Submenu

The Services submenu commands like those in Figure 1-36 allow for communication between different applications. Most services take the selected text or object in the key window and perform some sort of function with it. For example, if you select some text in TextEdit and then choose Services → Mail → Mail Text, the text will be sent to the Mac OS X Mail application, which will place it in a Compose window that opens automatically. Likewise, you can choose Services → Mail → Make Sticky to turn the selected text into a "sticky note" on your screen (launch the Stickies application in the /Applications folder to find out about stickies).

Services such as these enable applications to interoperate with each other without any prior arrangement on the part of the programmer or the user. Unique

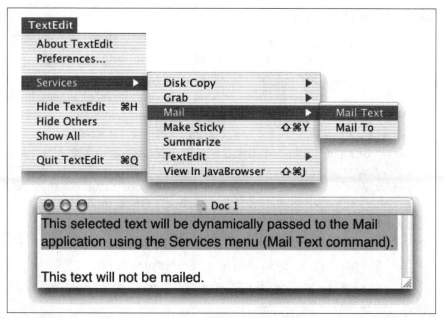

Figure 1-36. *Using the Mail Text command under the Services submenu to email the selected text*

to Mac OS X, services are an extremely powerful aspect of the operating environment that result from the dynamic binding of the Objective-C language. We'll learn how to create an application that provides services functionality in Chapter 20.

Working with the Filesystem, Step by Step

The Mac OS X Finder is primarily used for managing files stored on your computer's hard and floppy disks, and over the network. This section discusses many of the Finder's operations and menu commands for managing files and folders.

1. Log into your account on a computer running Mac OS X. Make sure that the Finder is the active application and that only one of its windows is open.

2. Open your Home folder (directory) by selecting (with a single-click) the Home icon toward the center of the toolbar in the Finder window.

3. Switch to icon view in the Finder.

Working with Folders

untitled folder

stuff

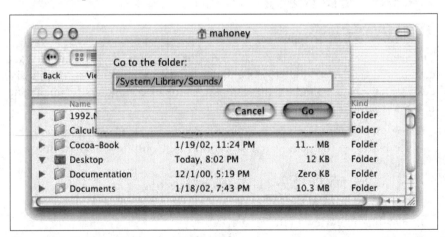

Macintosh HD

4. Create a new folder in your Home folder by choosing File → New Folder from the menu bar. The new folder will be named "untitled folder".

5. Make sure the text "untitled folder" is selected (in your highlight color), as shown at the edge of the page. If it isn't, double-click the text "untitled folder" to select it.

6. Rename the new folder stuff by entering "stuff" on the keyboard.

7. Make your stuff folder easily accessible by dragging its icon from your Finder view pane and dropping it on your Finder toolbar (widen the Finder window if necessary). Whenever you need to access the stuff folder, all you need to do is click its icon in the Finder toolbar.

8. Switch to column view in the Finder.

9. Open the /System/Library/Sounds folder in the Finder window by:

   a. Clicking the Computer icon in the Finder's toolbar

   b. Clicking the Macintosh HD icon (or wherever your Mac OS X operating system is located)

   c. Clicking the System folder, then the Library folder, and finally the Sounds folder (you'll probably have to scroll down to see it)

   Traversing through the filesystem this way is easiest in column-view mode. Icon-view mode requires double-clicks, and the folders are more difficult to find. However, there's an even easier way to get to the Sounds folder, as we'll see next.

10. Choose Finder's Go → Go to Folder menu command, and note that a sheet drops down from the active Finder window (see Figure 1-37).

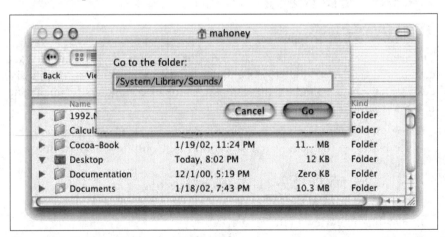

Figure 1-37. The Go to Folder sheet in the Finder

11. Type in "/Sys" in the Go to Folder sheet, and the Finder will complete the folder name to "System" for you. Hit the Tab key to accept the completion.

12. Finish typing the path /System/Library/Sounds (with tabs), as shown in Figure 1-37, then click the Go button. This is a quick way to access a folder for which you know the path but that you don't have in your toolbar.

The case-sensitivity of filenames depends on the kind of disk volume on which your file resides. Most Mac OS X computer disks are formatted with Apple's HFS+ filesystem. With HFS+, the case of filenames is preserved but ignored. This means that you cannot have files named "apple" and "Apple" in the same folder. On the other hand, if your disks are formatted with the Unix filesystem, filenames are case-sensitive—an uppercase "A" is a different character from a lowercase "a"—so files named "apple" and "Apple" can appear in the same folder. This can be confusing!

Working with Files

13. Select the Glass.aiff file by clicking the filename Glass.aiff in the Sounds folder in the Finder.

14. Click the arrow in the right column to play the "glass" sound (see Figure 1-38).

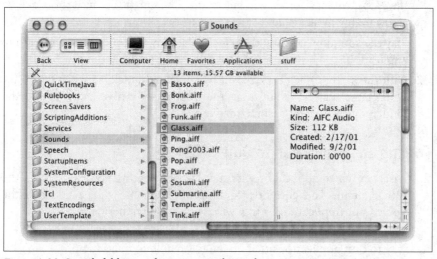

Figure 1-38. Sounds folder in column view in the Finder

15. Switch to icon view in the Finder.

16. Press down on the Glass.aiff icon and drag it so it's on top of the stuff folder icon in your Finder toolbar. Don't release the mouse button yet.

Note that the cursor changes to the standard arrow-with-plus-sign cursor, indicating that a copy operation is about to take place.

17. Now drop the Glass.aiff icon on top of the stuff folder icon (i.e., release the mouse button). The file will be copied into the stuff folder.

18. Again drag the Glass.aiff icon from the icon path and drop it on top of the stuff folder icon in the Finder toolbar. A Finder alert labeled "Copy" pops up to warn you that the file Glass.aiff already exists in your stuff folder, as shown in Figure 1-39.

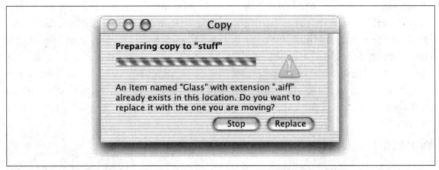

Figure 1-39. Finder alert warning that a copy command may replace an existing file

19. Stop the copy operation by clicking the Stop button on the Copy alert.

QuickTime Player

20. Double-click the Glass.aiff icon. The QuickTime Player application in the /Applications folder will automatically launch (because the player is associated with .aiff files).

21. Play the sound by clicking the big circular Play button in the center of the application.

22. Quit the active QuickTime Player by choosing QuickTime Player → Quit QuickTime Player. Note that the previously active application, the Finder, automatically becomes active.

Forcing an Application to Quit

23. Discover which applications are running by selecting Force Quit from the Apple menu. The currently running applications will be listed in the Force Quit Applications utility window, as shown in Figure 1-40.

The Force Quit button shown at the edge of the page provides a simple way to quit applications that are *hung* (unable to continue processing). If an application is hung, select it from the list of running applications in the Force Quit Applications window and then click the Force Quit button. Do not use this method to quit an application unless it is hung.

This feature of Mac OS X is made possible by the protected memory architecture provided by Darwin/Unix that allocates a unique memory space for each application. We recommend that you remember the key

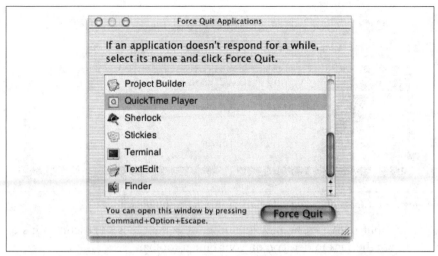

Figure 1-40. The Force Quit Applications utility window

equivalent, Command-Option-Escape, that brings up the Force Quit Applications window without using the mouse (which might be temporarily out of service).

24. Click the red close button at the top left of the Force Quit Applications window.

25. Still in icon view, open your Home folder again by clicking the Home icon in the Finder's toolbar.

26. Create another new folder called junk in your Home folder by typing Shift-Command-N (the key equivalent of choosing the File → New Folder menu command) and renaming the untitled folder. (To type Shift-Command-N, hold down one Shift and one Command key simultaneously while typing the N key.)

junk

27. Make your junk folder easily accessible by dragging its icon from your icon view pane and dropping it in your Finder toolbar.

28. Open the stuff folder by clicking its icon on your Finder toolbar.

Moving and Copying Files

29. Select the file Glass.aiff in your browser (use a single-click).

30. Make a copy of the Glass.aiff file in the stuff folder by choosing File → Duplicate from the Finder's menu (or typing Command-D).

Glass copy.aiff

A new file named Glass copy.aiff, which is a copy of the Glass.aiff file, will appear in your stuff folder. Your Finder window should look like the one in Figure 1-41.

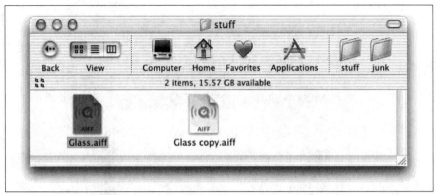

Figure 1-41. Glass.aiff and a duplicate copy of it in the stuff folder

31. Without releasing the mouse button, drag the Glass.aiff icon so it's on top of the junk folder icon on your Finder toolbar.

    The plus-sign cursor does not appear this time; instead, the cursor remains an arrow. The arrow indicates that the file Glass.aiff will be moved to the junk folder, not copied.

32. Release the mouse button and check the contents of the stuff and junk folders. Note that the Glass.aiff file appears only in the junk folder.

    If you are the owner of both folders and they reside on the same physical disk, the default behavior for drag-and-drop operations is to move files, not copy them. This behavior also applies when you drag and drop multiple files or folders.

33. Open the junk folder by clicking its icon in the Finder toolbar.

34. Select the Glass.aiff file in your browser.

35. Without releasing the mouse button, drag the Glass.aiff icon and let it hover over each of the icons (Computer, Home, etc.) in your Finder toolbar.

    Note that some of the icons in the toolbar highlight, indicating that they will accept the Glass.aiff file. The Computer icon will not accept it (unless you are logged in as superuser). Note that the cursor changes to the arrow-plus-link cursor over the Favorites icon (because Favorites stores only aliases to files, not the files themselves).

36. Keeping the mouse button pressed, drag the Glass.aiff icon on top of the stuff folder icon on your Finder toolbar and press the Option key. Note that the plus-sign cursor appears. Release the mouse button while pressing the Option key, and note that the Glass.aiff file is copied into the stuff folder.

    You have forced a copy by using the Option key.

Moving Without Activating

37. Type Command-N twice to make two more Finder windows appear.

38. Holding down a Command key, press on the title bar of one of the windows that is in the background and drag the window to a new location. Release the mouse and Command key.

    Notice that you can move this window around the desktop without bringing it to the front. If the window belonged to another application, the Command key would allow you to move the window without activating that application. This technique can be useful for clearing your work area or finding windows.

39. Close the two new Finder windows.

Getting Information About Files

40. Select the stuff folder icon in your Finder toolbar to open that folder.

41. Select the Glass.aiff file.

42. Choose File → Show Info (or type Command-I) to display the Glass.aiff Info dialog, as shown on the left side of Figure 1-42).

The General Information pane displays general information about the file or folder that is currently selected in the Finder. For a file, this includes the kind of file that is selected and its size. For folders, the Info dialog displays the total size of all of the items in that folder. If you click the Locked switch for a file, no changes to the file will be permitted (although the file may still be moved to another location). If you click the "Stationery Pad" checkbox, when the file is opened, a new, untitled copy of the original is opened. This is useful for storing file templates.

43. Choose Name & Extension from the pop-up menu in the Info dialog (see the right side of Figure 1-42). This pane shows the true name of the file as it is stored in the filesystem (later try looking at an application file, and you'll see the .app extension). You can also control whether the extension for this file will be displayed (e.g., Glass.aiff will become simply Glass).

44. Choose "Open with application" from the pop-up menu in the Glass.aiff Info dialog (see the left side of Figure 1-43). This Info dialog pane shows which applications may be associated with the Glass.aiff sound file.

45. Press the bevel button with the QuickTime icon on it to see a pop-up menu (see the screen shot on the right of Figure 1-43).

46. Drag to iTunes and release the mouse button.

47. Double-click Glass.aiff in the Finder, and iTunes will open and play the "glass" sound.

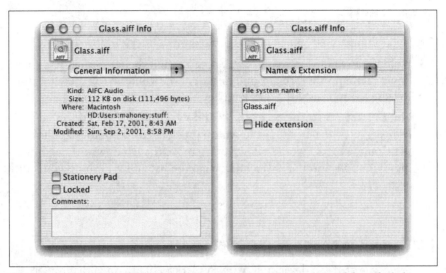

Figure 1-42. The General Information and Name & Extension panes of the Info dialog

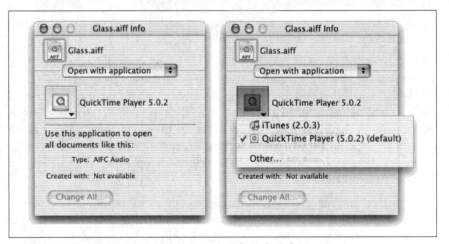

Figure 1-43. The Open with application pane of the Info dialog

iTunes

48. Choose iTunes → Quit iTunes.

Note that AIFF files can be opened with either QuickTime Player or iTunes. Mac OS X applications contain information about what kinds of files they can open; the Finder reads this information and displays the results in the Info dialog's "Open with application" pane.

49. Press the bevel button in the Finder's Info dialog again and drag to QuickTime Player. iTunes is not the best application to associate with simple sounds.

---

50. Choose Preview from the pop-up menu in the `Glass.aiff` Info dialog (see the left side of Figure 1-44). The Preview pane allows you to see the contents of some files without actually launching an application program. The Finder knows how to preview sound, graphics, and some plain-text files, but not many others. In this case, you can preview an AIFF sound.

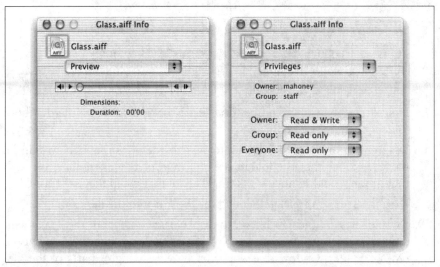

Figure 1-44. The Preview and Privileges panes of the Info dialog

51. Finally, choose Privileges from the pop-up menu in the `Glass.aiff` Info dialog (see the right side of Figure 1-44).

    The Privileges pane allows you to control the security of the file. Each file has a specific owner and a group to which it belongs (these are Unix concepts). If you are the owner of the file, you can change its privileges.

52. Change the Owner privilege from "Read & Write" to "Read only" via the Owner pop-up menu. The file `Glass.aiff` will then be read-only for you, the owner. Consequently, you won't be able to delete it, but let's try anyway.

53. Drag the `Glass.aiff` file icon from your `stuff` folder and drop it on the Trash icon in the Dock. You'll get the alert shown in Figure 1-45. Click OK.

Filling and Emptying the Trash

54. Change the Owner privilege of `Glass.aiff` from "Read only" back to "Read & Write" via the Owner pop-up menu (i.e., reverse Step 52).

55. Still in icon view in the Finder, click the Home icon and then select the `stuff` folder.

Figure 1-45. Alert indicating that a read-only file cannot be deleted

56. Hold down the Command key and select the junk folder. Note that both folders are now selected.

57. Drag either of the two selected folders to the Trash, and both will be moved. Notice that the folders are still in your Finder toolbar (we wish that Apple would remove icons from the toolbar when they are trashed).

58. Drag the stuff and junk folders off the toolbar into the desktop.

59. Double-click on the Trash icon to display the contents of the Trash window, as shown in Figure 1-46. Note that the Trash window is a special type of Finder window that does not allow viewing of parts of the file-system other than the Trash folder.

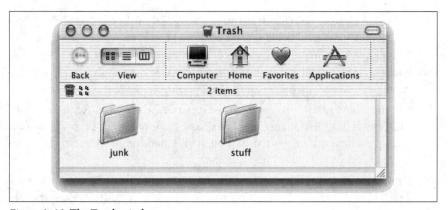

Figure 1-46. The Trash window

60. Choose the Finder → Empty Trash menu command. You will be prompted to see if you are sure that you wish to remove the folders, as shown in Figure 1-47.

61. Click OK.

Congratulations for making it all the way through!

Figure 1-47. The Finder wants to know if you really want to dump your trash

Summary

Although there is more to learn about using Mac OS X, this introduction is probably enough to get you started and feeling comfortable with the interface. Keep the user guidelines you learned in this chapter in mind when designing application interfaces—your users will thank you for it. You might also want to bookmark the references shown at the end of this chapter.

In the next chapter, we'll learn how to work with some of the most important Cocoa developer tools. Then, in Chapter 3, we'll create our first program.

Exercises

1. Go through "Configuring Your Desktop, Step by Step." Make a list of the things you discovered while working through the steps.

2. Open document windows, utility windows, and dialogs in the TextEdit application to convince yourself that the window order we discussed in this chapter is accurate.

3. Open two viewer windows, utility windows, and dialogs in the Mail application to convince yourself that the window order we discussed in this chapter is accurate. Note how the Colors and Font utility windows are the same from application to application.

4. Look at the Services menu for several Mac OS X applications, including the Finder, Mail, TextEdit, and your web browser. Determine why services are included for some applications but not others. Also determine the context in which services items are dimmed and unavailable for these same applications.

5. See how many violations of Aqua user interface guidelines you can find in the bundled applications in the /Applications folder. Look for naming,

menu placement, key equivalents, and window-order violations. Use the references in the next section.

6. Go through "Working with the Filesystem, Step by Step." Make a list of the things you discovered while working through the steps.

References

Many of these references are installed on your computer when you install the developer tools; they're also on Apple's web site (`http://developer.apple.com`). The advantage of using the pages on your computer is that they should match whatever version of Cocoa you are using, whereas the version on the Apple web site will match Apple's most recent version of Cocoa. However, we prefer the version on Apple's web site, as those pages seem easier to use and frequently have more complete descriptions of Cocoa concepts.

1. Cocoa developer documentation:

   `http://developer.apple.com/techpubs/macosx/Cocoa/CocoaTopics.html`

2. Mac OS X terminology guidelines:

   `http://developer.apple.com/techpubs/macosx/Essentials/AquaHIGuidelines/`
   `AppBTerms/index.html`

3. Introduction to the Aqua Human Interface Guidelines:

   `http://developer.apple.com/techpubs/macosx/Essentials/AquaHIGuidelines/`
   `AHGIntro/index.html`

   This document is also available at:

   `/Developer/Documentation/Essentials/AquaHIGuidelines/AquaHIGuidelines.pdf`

4. User interface elements:

   `http://developer.apple.com/techpubs/macosx/Cocoa/TasksAndConcepts/`
   `ProgrammingTopics/Misc/UIElementsPage.html`

CHAPTER 2

Tools for Developing Cocoa Applications

There are several applications bundled with Mac OS X that are very useful for writing Cocoa programs. Most of these tools reside in the /Developer/ Applications folder, but some reside in the more user-oriented /Applications/ Utilities folder. We'll discuss the most helpful of these tools in this chapter.

Developer Tools

The two most important Mac OS X developer tools by far are Project Builder (PB) and Interface Builder (IB). These tools reside in the /Developer/ Applications folder, shown in Figure 2-1.

The third application you'll need to learn as a Cocoa developer is the gdb debugger. We'll discuss gdb and how it's used at the Unix command line and with PB toward the end of this chapter. We'll also take a quick look at the ObjectAlloc, PropertyListEditor, IconComposer, icns Browser, Console, ProcessViewer, and Terminal applications.

Project Builder

Project Builder is Cocoa's integrated development environment (IDE), used to manage application development projects. For each application, developers will use PB to create a skeletal application framework, organize the application's resources, edit the Objective-C source code files, run the compiler and the rest of the build process, control the debugger, add application and document icons, and set up other application features. PB does a lot for developers—it's a wonderful tool!

Project Builder

The PB menu bar and main window for an under-construction application called Calculator are shown in Figure 2-2. The buttons on the left of the toolbar are for building (compiling), cleaning, running, and debugging applications. The pop-up menu that currently displays "Calculator" is for switching

Figure 2-1. The developer applications bundled with the Mac OS X developer system

build targets, whereas the buttons on the right of the toolbar are for stepping through an application being debugged. The Groups & Files pane at the left of the window in Figure 2-2 shows the files that make up the project, including the Classes files where you add your application-specific code. The top-right pane shows the output from a compilation process, and the bottom-right pane shows a file (`Controller.h`) being edited. We'll discuss all of these PB features in great detail as we build applications throughout this book. We'll show you how to open a project in PB and also how to use the `gdb` debugger in PB later in this chapter.

Interface Builder

Interface Builder

Interface Builder is used to create application interfaces (e.g., menus, windows, buttons) and make connections between interface objects. It is also used to connect interface objects to Objective-C data structures called *objects*.

The IB menu bar and the interface for an under-construction application called Calculator in IB are shown in Figure 2-3. Both the small MainMenu menu bar

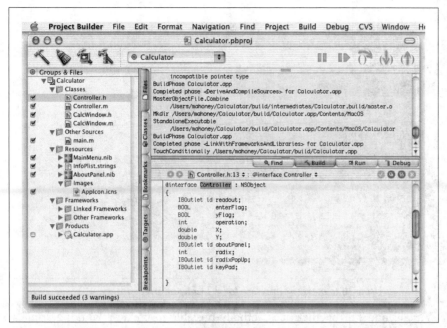

Figure 2-2. Using PB to build and manage the Calculator application

below IB's menu bar and the window titled "Calculator" on the left are part of the interface for the Calculator application being built. The window on the right (Cocoa-Views) shows a palette of user-interface objects (e.g., Button, Switch) that can be dragged and dropped into an interface window. The button and text field objects inside the Calculator window were taken from this palette and then modified. The buttons in the toolbar at the top of the Cocoa-Views palette allow developers to access a great variety of user-interface objects for building application interfaces.

In Figure 2-4, our second IB screen shot, the window at the lower left displays icons representing some of the (instance) objects that are part of the Calculator project. For example, the icon labeled "Window" represents the Calculator window, and the icon labeled "MainMenu" represents the Calculator's menu. The icon labeled "Controller" represents an Objective-C object that has no associated on-screen object such as a button or window. The "connection" line from this Controller icon to the "readout" display in the Calculator window represents a path so that messages can be sent by the Controller object to the readout display to update the output. It's really just a pointer called "readout" from one piece of code (the Controller object) to another (the text field object). The Info window on the right in Figure 2-4 provides information about existing connections and enables developers to set up new connections. The Info window also displays information about objects' (e.g., button, Controller) attributes and allows them to be modified.

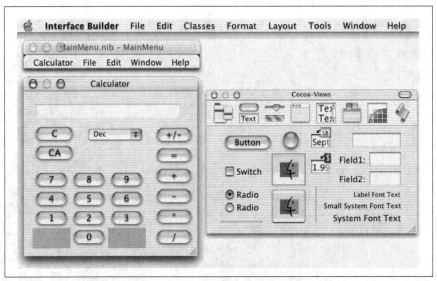

Figure 2-3. Using IB to build the interface for the Calculator application

With IB and PB together, it is actually possible to create a working application without any programming whatsoever! Of course, the application won't do much until you add application-specific code, but it will look good and it will run. We'll learn more about how to use IB beginning with Chapter 3 and PB beginning with Chapter 4. In the meantime, let's look at some other important developer tools.

ObjectAlloc

Memory management is one of the most complicated issues that you will encounter as a Cocoa programmer. That's because unlike in the C programming language, where memory management is completely up to the programmer, or the Java programming language, where memory management is completely automatic, in the Cocoa environment, memory management is *semiautomatic*. The programming environment does most of the work, but you need to do some of it too. And because memory management is semiautomatic, it's possible to make mistakes.

ObjectAlloc

You can use the developer application ObjectAlloc to watch a Mac OS X application as it allocates and frees objects. This is not only a useful tool for finding memory leaks and other problems in your programs—it is also a fun way to learn about Cocoa.

To run the ObjectAlloc application, double-click on the ObjectAlloc icon in the /Developer/Applications folder. When the application launches, you'll be

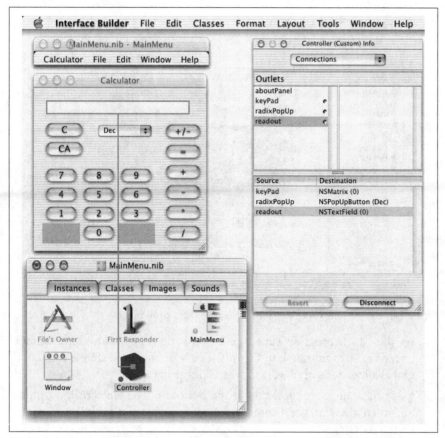

Figure 2-4. Connection between on-screen and "code" objects in IB

prompted with an Open-like dialog titled "Run". Within this dialog you need to navigate to the actual executable file in the `.app` folder (directory) of the application you wish to run. Here's how:

1. Launch the ObjectAlloc application, and you'll get a dialog titled "Run".

2. Resize the Run dialog so that at least four columns are visible, as shown in Figure 2-5.

3. Navigate through the filesystem to the `Clock` file in the `/Applications/Clock.app/Contents/MacOS/` directory. Select this file.

Clock

4. Click Open in the Run dialog, and you'll see the ObjectAlloc main window.

5. Click the bevel button with the green "play" arrow on it to start the Clock running under ObjectAlloc.

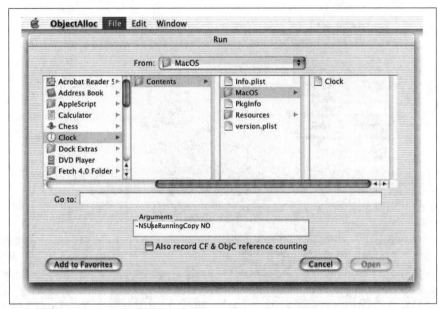

Figure 2-5. Opening the Clock executable file with ObjectAlloc

6. As the Clock program runs, the bars on the right side of the window change in size, as shown in Figure 2-6. These bars indicate the number of global allocations of objects for the Clock program.

7. Click the Auto-sort checkbox at the bottom of the ObjectAlloc window and then the Category column header, so that the table rows remain sorted by category.

8. Scroll down to where the categories begin with the letters "NS". Objects with names that begin with "NS" are objects from Cocoa's Application Kit that are being allocated and destroyed by the Clock program.

9. Click the Instance Browser tab to look at specific instances of each object.

10. Click the Call Stacks tab to see what the call stack was at the time that each object was created.

11. Quit the ObjectAlloc application.

Programs run much more slowly when they are run from within the ObjectAlloc application, so you generally won't use it to observe programs that you are not debugging. However, when you need to use it, ObjectAlloc can be handy.

PropertyListEditor

PropertyListEditor

The PropertyListEditor application is used to view and edit property lists stored in .plist files. A *property list* is a list of information that is read by applications while they are launching. The list often contains information

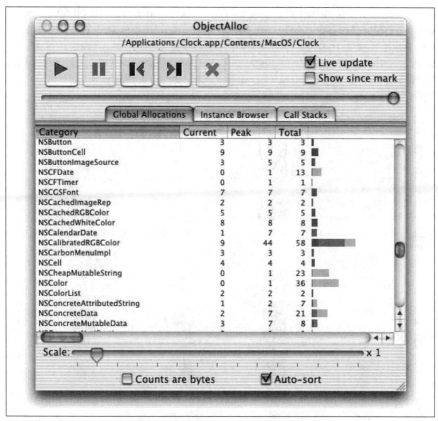

Category	Current	Peak	Total	
NSButton	3	3	3	
NSButtonCell	9	9	9	
NSButtonImageSource	3	5	5	
NSCFDate	0	1	13	
NSCFTimer	0	1	1	
NSCGSFont	7	7	7	
NSCachedImageRep	2	2	2	
NSCachedRGBColor	5	5	5	
NSCachedWhiteColor	8	8	8	
NSCalendarDate	1	7	7	
NSCalibratedRGBColor	9	44	58	
NSCarbonMenuImpl	3	3	3	
NSCell	4	4	4	
NSCheapMutableString	0	1	23	
NSColor	0	1	36	
NSColorList	2	2	2	
NSConcreteAttributedString	1	2	7	
NSConcreteData	2	7	21	
NSConcreteMutableData	3	7	8	

Figure 2-6. Watching the Clock's ObjectAlloc application

such as user preferences, window position and size when the application was last terminated, and so on. We'll use the PropertyListEditor application later in this chapter.

IconComposer and the icns Browser

The IconComposer application is used to create .icns files that contain application and document icons of various sizes. It's not a graphics editor like PhotoShop; rather, IconComposer accepts icons that you create in applications such as PhotoShop and bundles them together in one file for use in a Mac OS X application. The icns Browser application simply displays the contents of .icns files. We'll use IconComposer in our applications later in the book.

IconComposer

icns Browser

Utilities

In addition to the applications found in /Developer/Applications, there are several useful developer tools in the /Applications/Utilities folder. These applications are bundled with the user system, but they can still help developers. The /Application/Utilities folder is shown in Figure 2-7. The icons in this folder are rather plain (look at your screen, not the screen shot in the book), indicating their utility status (compare them with the more colorful icons for the "fancy" applications in the /Developer/Applications folder).

Figure 2-7. The /Application/Utilities folder contains useful tools for developers

The Console displays information that other applications print on the system console. This should be familiar to the Unix-savvy. Many Mac OS X programs display error messages on the system console rather than writing them to a file. The Console application can also show you a stack-trace of a program that crashes. We suggest you keep this application handy when programming and testing.

The ProcessViewer graphically shows you all of the processes that are currently running on your computer. Its output is similar to that of the common Unix programs top and ps, which can be run in a Terminal window in Mac OS X. A screen shot of the user processes for the logged-in user (as opposed to the administrator processes) is shown in Figure 2-8.

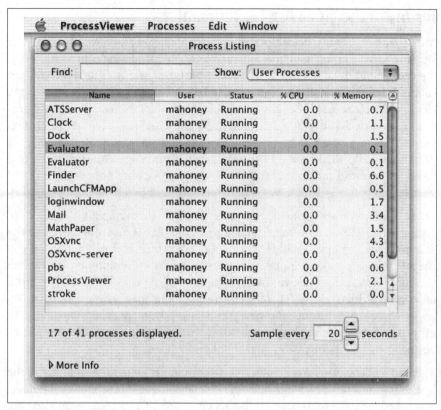

Figure 2-8. ProcessViewer displaying user processes

The Terminal enables you to work at the Unix command line. There is no counterpart for Terminal in previous versions of Mac OS, and it's much more powerful than the DOS command line familiar to Microsoft Windows users. Within Terminal, you can fully explore the file and operating systems, directly run compilers, run programs, and do much more. If you are familiar with other Unix operating systems such as Solaris or Linux, Terminal will make you feel right at home. In the next section, we'll set the scene by explaining some of the history behind Unix and computing in general. Then we'll show you a little about Terminal itself.

Working with the Terminal

In this section, we'll cover the details of the Mac OS X Terminal application. Before getting into those details, though, we'll take a step back to look briefly at the history of the video display terminal itself. That should give you some insight into why the Terminal application developed in the way it did.

History of the Video Display Terminal

Many years ago, long before personal computers were developed, computer systems were too big and too expensive to put on a single person's desk. Instead, computers were put in special-purpose rooms (called "computer rooms"), where a staff of highly-trained professionals worked around the clock to keep the machines running. Many computer systems read their programs from decks of 80-column computer punch cards, each of which was punched with a series of holes that represented a single line of text. When a program was finished running the results were printed on a line printer. These systems were said to implement "batch mode processing" because programs were run in batches—there was no interactivity at all!

One of the first revolutions in computing was the development of interactive systems. In addition to being attached to a card reader and a line printer, the computer was equipped with a modified teletype printer. Every time a key on the teletype was pressed, a distinct code was sent to the computer. Every time the computer sent a code to the teletype, the teletype would literally print a letter onto a roll of paper. These interactive systems made the computer much easier to use. Over time, the teletype printers were replaced with special-purpose printing terminals that were designed specifically for interactive computing, rather than for sending telegrams and telexes.

The first video screens were connected to computers by the U.S. military in the late 1950s, and by universities and research labs in the 1960s. These computer-controlled video systems were incredibly expensive. The screens were also very specialized: usually, each video system was designed to run a specific application. Over time, however, the video systems became more general-purpose.

In the mid 1970s, there was a breakthrough: instead of having the computer directly control the video screen, a number of companies started to build special-purpose desktop boxes called *glass teletypes* or *video display terminals* (VDTs). To the computer, a VDT looked like a traditional printing terminal. But instead of having paper, it had a video display, a character generator, and a small amount of memory. By the late 1970s most of these systems had standardized on a display that was 80 columns wide and 24 lines high, but that's about the only thing that was standardized: different VDTs from different manufacturers had different capabilities and used different codes to do things such as clear the screen or move around the cursor.

The Unix operating system (Darwin) that underlies the Mac OS X operating system still shows much of this evolutionary history. Every copy of Mac OS X comes with a program called ed, a line-oriented editor designed to be used with printing terminals. Likewise, there is a file called termcap in /usr/share/misc/ that contains the actual control codes used by thousands of different kinds of printing and video terminals. (You'll even find Simson's name and email address in this file, with the terminal definition of an emulator that used to run on the Atari ST!) The termcap file allowed a single program, such as vi or GNU Emacs, to run on many different kinds of displays. Over the past 25 years, these programs have become highly tuned by generations of programmers. They are now ideal environments for writing and debugging programs.

Most of the terminals whose names appear in the termcap file are long gone. If you wanted to, you could hook your Mac OS X laptop up to a model 33 teletype and start typing in all of the example programs in this book! But you wouldn't do that, of course. Aside from the fact that you probably couldn't *find* a working ASR 33, most computers in use today are built around bitmap displays, rather than character terminals.

Bitmap displays were invented along with VDTs in the 1970s, but they didn't become popular until the 1980s. The reason was cost: because each pixel of a bitmap display is individually accessible, the displays required more memory and thus were more expensive to produce. Of course, today memory is cheap, so practically every computer (from simple handhelds to ten-thousand-dollar workstations) has a bitmap display. But in the early 1980s, some people were using computers that had bitmap displays while other people had character-oriented terminals. In some cases, single computers had both bitmap displays *and* terminals. Because of this ambiguity, the most popular application for the early bitmap displays was the "virtual terminal" program—a program that let a single bitmap display multiple rectangular "terminal" windows, each one simulating a VDT.

This, in a nutshell, is the history behind the Mac OS X Terminal application. Now let's move on to see how today's Terminal application operates.

The Mac OS X Terminal Application

Like other terminal emulators, Terminal displays rectangular windows on the Macintosh bitmap display. This virtual terminal responds to the escape sequences contained in the /usr/share/misc/termcap file. (If you want to look at this file, you can view it in the Terminal or by using the Finder's Go → Go to Folder command. The termcap file doesn't show up automatically because the Finder hides system details such as the /usr directory from users.)

Terminal

The Mac OS X Terminal actually emulates the escape sequences of the Digital Equipment Corporation VT100 terminal. As such, it provides a conventional interface for running standard Unix editors, debuggers, and other programs that do not have Mac OS X interfaces. Figure 2-9 shows a screen shot of a Terminal window running GNU Emacs, the popular editor available for every version of Unix.

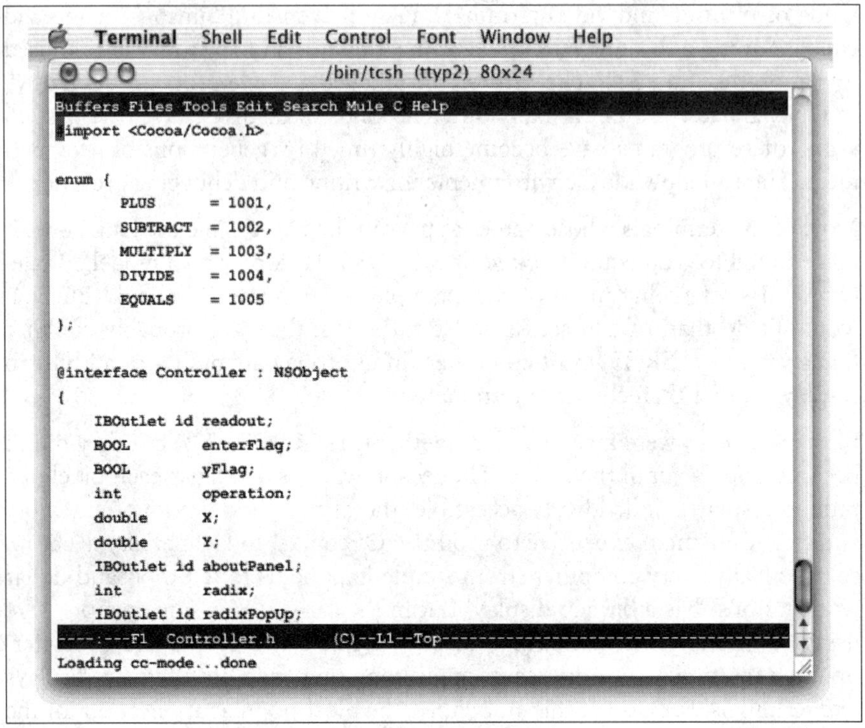

Figure 2-9. Terminal with the GNU Emacs editor running inside

The Terminal's application menu contains the standard Mac OS X application menu commands. As required, there are About, Preferences, Services, Hide, Hide Others, Show All, and Quit commands (in the correct positions).

Next to the application menu in the Terminal's menu bar is the Shell menu, which is located where the File menu usually sits. The Shell menu makes sense in this position because the Shell → New command creates a new (Unix) shell window in Terminal, just as File → New in a text editor creates a new file or document in the editor application. (A Unix shell is a command language interpreter that provides an interface to the underlying Unix operating system—Darwin, in Mac OS X. Users can change their shells from the default tcsh to others, such as csh, sh, or zsh, via the shell pane in the Preferences dialog.)

The Terminal's menu bar also contains the standard Edit, Window, and Help menus, together with a Control menu and a (promoted) Font menu (there is no need for a Format menu). The uncommon Control menu contains commands to move around in a Terminal shell window.

By choosing Terminal → Preferences you can bring up the Terminal Preferences dialog. The Preferences dialog, shown in Figure 2-10, displays the Window pane, which allows you to change the size and title-bar contents of your

Terminal windows. There are many other preferences available to the user (click the icons in the toolbar to see them), and Unix aficionados will find that they can set preferences to emulate the type of Unix environment to which they are accustomed. We recommend that you take a few minutes to explore the various preferences available.

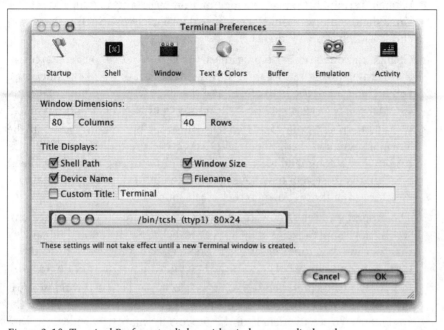

Figure 2-10. Terminal Preferences dialog with window pane displayed

Terminal also has a related Terminal Inspector dialog (which you can open with the key equivalent Command-I) that allows items specific to a particular Terminal window to be modified. The panes in this dialog are similar to the panes in the Terminal Preferences dialog. These panes are not redundant—the panes in the Terminal Preferences dialog change preferences throughout the application, while the panes in the Terminal Inspector dialog change settings only for the specific Terminal window that is active (these settings will not be "remembered" as preferences).

If you try to print the contents of a Terminal window, you will be given the choice of printing all the text output (which is stored in a buffer) to the window, just the selected text, or just what's visible in the window. You can also copy information from the Terminal window into other applications or paste information from other applications into a Terminal window, and you can drag a folder or an icon from the Finder into the Terminal window (which will result in the path for that folder being entered into the Terminal as if you had typed it on the keyboard).

Working in a Unix Shell, Step by Step

Next we'll run you through a few steps so you can become familiar with Unix and Terminal. Since we're working with Unix, we will use the term "directory" instead of "folder" in this and the gdb sections below.

Terminal

1. Launch Terminal (from your Dock or from /Applications/Utilities). A Unix shell window should open (if it doesn't, choose Shell → New and check your Startup preferences).

2. Change the directory by typing the Unix command cd /Applications in this Terminal window and then hitting the Return (Enter) key. Make sure you include the space between cd and the slash, and remember that Unix commands are case-sensitive, so the letters cd need to be lowercase.*

3. List all the files in the /Applications directory by entering ls -l in the Terminal window, as in Figure 2-11. (We use the term "enter" to indicate that the command should be followed by hitting the Return key.) Note that your system may have some different files in the /Applications directory from those shown in the screen shot.

   The programs in the /Applications directory are actually directories themselves, not simple files as they appear to be in the Finder. (You can tell that they are directories because the first character on the left in the directory listing output for Mail.app is the letter d, which stands for directory.)

4. List all running processes by entering ps aux in the Terminal window (ps is the Unix command that lists all of the processes currently running on the computer). To see the details of the process listing better, widen the window and enter ps auxww; the ww will force the output to be in wide format.

5. List your user processes by entering ps auxww | grep *username* (where *username* is your account username) in the Terminal window. The output should be similar to that of the ProcessViewer application's listing of user processes. (The vertical bar character, |, is the pipe symbol that takes the output from ps auxww and pipes it to input for the grep, or search, utility. For more on grep, enter man grep in a Terminal window.)

6. Enter top in a Terminal window to run the top program, which will display a real-time view of system-usage statistics and the running processes, as shown in Figure 2-12. Your top output will definitely be different from that in Figure 2-12.

The top process list automatically updates every second. The first line of the top display shows the number of processes that are running. The second line

---

* On most Unix systems, filenames are case-sensitive. However, Mac OS X uses the Hierarchical File System (HFS), which preserves the case of filenames that are entered but ignores case when files are opened, moved, copied, or deleted.

```
   ○ ○ ○                    /bin/tcsh  (ttyp2)  80x28
[mmosx:~] mahoney% cd /Applications
[mmosx:/Applications] mahoney% ls -l
total 0
drwxrwxr-x   4 root     admin   264 Oct 14 16:41 Acrobat Reader 5.0
drwxrwxr-x   3 root     admin   264 Sep 14 20:55 Address Book.app
drwxrwxr-x   5 root     admin   264 Sep 14 20:49 AppleScript
drwxrwxr-x   3 root     admin   264 Sep 11 03:39 Calculator.app
drwxrwxr-x   3 root     admin   264 Sep 14 20:41 Chess.app
drwxrwxr-x   3 root     admin   264 Sep 11 03:38 Clock.app
drwxrwxr-x   3 root     admin   264 Nov 27 01:35 DVD Player.app
drwxrwxr-x   3 root     admin   264 Sep 28 20:52 Dock Extras
drwxrwxr-x   7 mahoney  admin   264 Jul 12  2001 Fetch 4.0 Folder
drwxrwxr-x   3 root     admin   264 Dec  8 11:33 Image Capture.app
drwxrwxr-x   3 root     admin   264 Sep 14 20:55 Internet Connect.app
drwxrwxr-x   3 root     admin   264 Oct 28 10:49 Internet Explorer.app
drwxrwxr-x   3 root     admin   264 Dec 14 14:30 Mail.app
drwxrwxrwx   3 root     admin   264 Nov 25 17:34 OSXvnc.app
drwxrwxr-x   3 root     admin    58 Sep 14 21:01 Preview.app
drwxrwxr-x   3 root     admin   264 Sep 14 20:57 QuickTime Player.app
drwxrwxr-x   3 root     admin   264 Sep 14 21:02 Sherlock.app
drwxrwxr-x   3 root     admin   264 Sep 11 03:36 Stickies.app
drwxr-xr-x   3 root     wheel   264 Feb 18  2001 System Preferences.app
drwxrwxr-x   3 root     admin   264 Sep 11 03:39 TextEdit.app
drwxrwxr-x  26 root     admin   840 Jan 26 22:04 Utilities
drwxrwxr-x   3 root     admin   264 Aug 26 12:06 iMovie.app
drwxrwxr-x   3 root     admin   264 Jan  2 10:26 iPhoto.app
drwxrwxr-x   3 root     admin   264 Dec 10 14:25 iTunes.app
[mmosx:/Applications] mahoney% ▮
```

Figure 2-11. Terminal window listing of /Applications folder

displays the load averages, or the number of processes that are currently in
the run queue—that is, the number of processes that are ready to run at any
given time. The three numbers that follow Load Avg represent the load aver-
aged over the last 5 seconds, the last 30 seconds, and the last 60 seconds. The
next four lines contain information about the shared libraries and virtual
memory system. Finally, there is a tabular display for each of the currently
running processes. For each process, the percentage of the CPU resources that
the process is using is displayed, along with the time that the process has been
running, the number of threads that the process has, and other information.

7. With the top program still running, activate the Finder and launch the
   ProcessViewer application in /Applications/Utilities. As we saw earlier
   in this chapter, ProcessViewer will display a list of user processes.

ProcessViewer

8. Select a process (e.g., Clock) in ProcessViewer's window, then click the
   small arrow next to the phrase "More Info" at the bottom left of the window to see more information about that process. Select the Process ID
   and Statistics tabs and compare the information with that in the top output in the Terminal window.

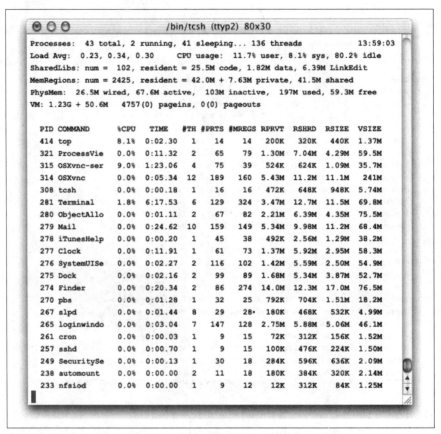

Figure 2-12. Output from the top program in a Terminal window

9. Now reactivate the Terminal window and type q to terminate the top program.

To see the text that scrolled outside the Terminal window, drag the scroll knob upward. Try selecting some of the text in the window with your mouse. The standard Edit submenu commands Copy, Paste, and Select All work as you would expect (although Paste forces a scroll to the bottom, a user preference).

The Defaults System

Next we will investigate the *defaults (database) system*, which records user preferences and other information that must be stored when applications aren't running. The stored information includes default fonts, window positions and sizes, toggle settings, etc., most of which is accessible via an application's Preferences dialog but some of which is not. For example, the size and position of the main Mail window is stored in the defaults system when the application is terminated. This stored size and position will be read by the Mail application when it next launches. Mail will then use this information to place its new main window in the same position with the same size as when Mail was last terminated. Note, however, that the stored size and position are not preferences that can be set in a Preferences dialog; rather, they are values that the user implicitly set by moving or resizing a window using direct manipulation. (For more information on the defaults system, enter `man defaults` in a Terminal window.)

10. Enter `defaults read com.apple.Terminal` in a Terminal window, and you'll see the current defaults for Terminal.

If you have not made any changes to the Terminal's preferences, you will see very few lines of detailed output from this command. On the other hand, if you have been working with Terminal for a while and have changed your preferences, you may see as many as 50 lines of detailed information. Let's look at part of the output ("localhost" is the name of the host computer—yours will be different):

```
localhost> defaults read com.apple.Terminal
{
    AlwaysPromptOnQuit = 1;
    Bell = 1;
    BlinkCursor = 0;
    Columns = 80;
    DockLaunchHide = 0;
    ...
    NSPreferencesContentSize = "{594, 399}";
    Rows = 30;
    SaveLines = 10000;
}
localhost>
```

These defaults mean that Terminal will prompt before quitting, "ring" the system bell (beep) when appropriate to alert the user, use the block (and not the blink) cursor, open new windows with 80 columns and 30 rows, open the Preferences dialog with a specified size, save up to 10,000 lines in the output buffer, and so on.

11. Back in the Finder, type Command-~ (tilde) or choose Go → Go to Folder to open the Go to Folder sheet.

12. Type "~/Library/Preferences" (use the Tab key for folder-name completion) in the sheet and hit Return to open the folder.

Terminal's defaults information is stored in the file `com.apple.Terminal.plist` in your `~/Library/Preferences` folder. This folder contains a variety of property lists that control the way that the Mac OS X environment is customized for your account. Because this information is stored under your Home folder, different users of the same computer can have different environments.

PropertyListEditor

13. Double-click the `com.apple.Terminal.plist` file, and the PropertyList-Editor application will launch. Remember that PropertyListEditor is another developer-only application that allows you to view and edit the defaults stored in a property list (`.plist`) file for any application.

14. Click the triangle next to Root in the PropertyListEditor window. You should see the same defaults that you saw in the Terminal window.

In later chapters, you'll create your own property list, which will be stored in your `~/Library/Preferences` folder (the same place as the property lists for Mac OS X bundled applications). We'll discuss the defaults database in more detail in Chapter 21.

 Do not edit the property lists for applications while they are running! If you do, the application may overwrite your changes. Exit the application first.

15. Open another application, such as `com.microsoft.explorer.plist`, in PropertyListEditor.

16. Quit the PropertyListEditor application.

17. Hide Terminal by choosing Terminal → Hide from its main menu or by typing Command-H. We'll use Terminal again in the next section. (Clicking the red close button in the Terminal window closes only that window, not the actual application.)

Debugging Programs with gdb

The GNU debugger is gdb. It was written and is maintained by the Free Software Foundation. gdb is a powerful tool for looking inside a running program and trying to figure out why that program is not behaving as expected. Apple has modified gdb to be aware of Objective-C syntax and objects, and to work together with the PB and Terminal applications.

The gdb tool is located in the directory /usr/bin. If you click the Computer icon in the Finder's toolbar and then select Macintosh HD, you will not see /usr listed. Mac OS X and the Finder hide many system details from the user, including Unix system directories such as /usr/bin, /bin, and /etc. You can view these directories in the Finder using the Go to Folder sheet, but you cannot see all directories in the Finder (e.g., the .app directories are hidden). You can, however, see all the filesystem directories in a Terminal shell—your vehicle for exploring the guts of Mac OS X.

Using gdb in Project Builder, Step by Step

The easiest way to use the gdb debugger is in PB. We'll show you how to get started with that in this section. First, we must have an application to work with, so we'll use a copy of the CircleView example application that is bundled with the Mac OS X developer system.

When you debug a running program within PB, you can access some of the most useful gdb commands graphically. You can set breakpoints by clicking the mouse next to a line of code (a *breakpoint* is a place where a running program stops executing and control is returned to the debugger). When a breakpoint is reached in a running program, the stack frame and the variables on the stack will be displayed in the debugger window. You can also use the buttons on the upper-right side of the PB window to control execution. The up and down arrows will step you up and down the call stack. The arrow over the parenthesis will execute a gdb step command. The pause button will pause execution, and the button with the triangle will continue program execution.

Let's try a few of these commands on a real example:

1. Open the Go to Folder sheet in the Finder and enter "/Developer/Examples/AppKit".

2. Copy the CircleView folder into your Home folder by Option-dragging the folder and dropping it on your Home icon. (If CircleView is not available, choose another example application in the same folder.)

3. Click your Home icon and then click the CircleView folder. You'll see the files in the folder in column view, as shown in Figure 2-13.

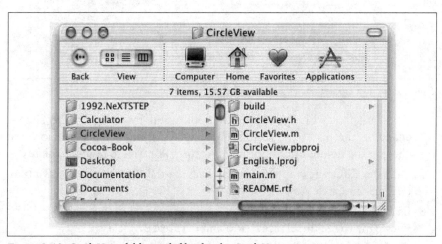

Figure 2-13. CircleView folder with files for the CircleView project

4. Open the CircleView project in PB by double-clicking on the Circle-View.pbproj project file in the CircleView folder.

5. Click the build and run button ( ) above the Groups & Files pane in PB.

    After a few seconds, the application will be built (compiled) and will run. The build and run button will turn into a stop button ( ). The running CircleView application is shown in Figure 2-14.

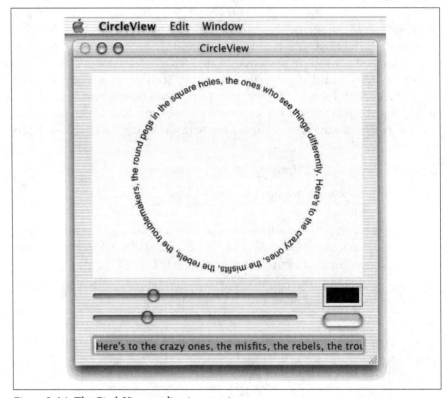

Figure 2-14. The CircleView application running

6. You can play with this fun little application by dragging the sliders, changing the text (try entering "Mac OS X"), changing the color, and clicking the nondescript button below the color well to animate the text.

7. Quit the CircleView application by clicking the stop button in PB's toolbar (or quit CircleView directly).

8. Back in PB, click the disclosure triangle next to Classes in the Groups & Files pane to see the CircleView.h and CircleView.m class files.

9. Single-click the CircleView.m file to open it in the lower-right pane in PB's main window, as shown in Figure 2-15.

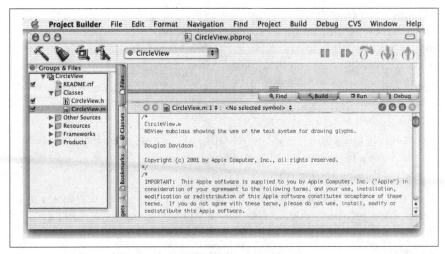

Figure 2-15. The CircleView project in PB

10. Press the up-down ("stepper") arrows (⇕) to the right of "<No selected symbol>" in the middle of the PB window, drag to "-setColor:", and release the mouse button. This action takes you to the "-setColor:" method (like a function) in the CircleView.m file.

11. Set a breakpoint by clicking the mouse in the white column to the left of "-(void)setColor:". An arrow (➡) should appear, as in Figure 2-16.

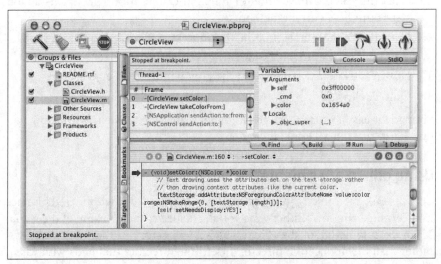

Figure 2-16. Stopped at a CircleView breakpoint in PB

In a moment we'll run the CircleView program in debug mode within PB. PB will run gdb in the background and provide us with a nice graphical interface to many of its commands. (If you want to see that gdb is running in the background, look at your running processes in ProcessViewer). We'll test some of the graphical commands available in PB, but first we'll clean out (remove) all of the derived build files in the project to ensure that we start from scratch:

12. Clean the CircleView build files by clicking the clean active target (whisk-broom) button (🖌) in PB's toolbar. Click the clean active target (blue) button in the resulting sheet.

13. Now click the build and debug button (🔨) in PB's toolbar. The button displays a hammer and a bug spray can icon that turns into a stop button when the application runs.

The CircleView application should now be running in the foreground. Because we set the breakpoint at the **setColor:** method, we won't reach it until we try to change the color.

14. Click the border of the color well (shown at the edge of the page) in the CircleView window.

You might expect the Font window to appear, but it doesn't because of the breakpoint. Your PB window should now look like the one in Figure 2-16. You can see the "Step into method or function call" button (🔽) at the right of PB's toolbar. This action executes one step (line of code). You can use it repeatedly to step through your program and debug it line by line.

15. Click the "Step over method or function call" button (🔽). This action steps out of the current method.

16. Click the "Continue execution" button (▶). This action continues execution of the CircleView program.

17. Now reactivate CircleView, and the Font window will appear.

18. Quit CircleView.

PB made it easy for us to use gdb to debug CircleView. Next, we'll show you the "hard" way, in a Terminal window.

Using gdb in a Terminal Window

You can run gdb directly in a Terminal window, or from within GNU Emacs in a Terminal window. Either way, you must specify the filename of the actual Mach executable file in the /Contents/MacOS directory in the "app wrapper," rather than the application directory itself (the directory that ends with .app). Thus, to debug the program CircleView.app with gdb at the Terminal shell command line, type the text shown in bold below.

```
localhost> cd ~/CircleView/build
localhost> gdb CircleView.app/Contents/MacOS/CircleView
...
```

gdb now starts up with about 10 lines of output. Next, we'll set the same breakpoint that we set earlier, in PB (line 160 is where the **setColor:** method begins in CircleView.m):

```
(gdb) b CircleView.m:160
(gdb) help
(gdb) quit
```

That's enough to get you started. Now, to run gdb from GNU Emacs, use the Emacs command:*

```
M-X gdb <return>
```

After this, Emacs will prompt you for:

```
Run gdb on file: /Users/me
```

where /me is the user's home directory.

At this prompt, type the name of the file that you want to debug:

```
Run gdb on file: ~/CircleView/build/CircleView.app/Contents/MacOS/CircleView
```

The advantage of using gdb from Emacs is that Emacs will automatically split the screen into two windows, giving you a gdb buffer in one and following the program that you are debugging in the other. Many programmers find this an effective way to work.

gdb Commands

gdb is a complicated program with dozens of commands. Fortunately, to get started you need to know only a few basic commands.

Typically, when you are using gdb, you will set a breakpoint and then run your program until you reach that breakpoint. Your program will then automatically stop running, and you will be free to inspect the contents of the variables. Table 2-1 lists the commands you would use to set breakpoints at a few sample locations.

Table 2-1. gdb commands for setting breakpoints

Use this gdb command	To set a breakpoint at
b myFile.m:53	Line 53 in the file myFile.m
b printer	The function printer( )
b [MyView drawrect:]	The Objective-C method **drawRect:** in the class MyView

To run your program, enter run in the Terminal window. After your program reaches a breakpoint (or if your program crashes), you will return to the gdb

---

* To type M-X gdb <return> into the Emacs editor, press the Esc key, press the X key, type gdb, and press the Return or Enter key.

command line. You can also interrupt your program's execution by typing Control-C. From the command line, you may find the commands in Table 2-2 useful in debugging.

Table 2-2. Useful gdb commands

Command	Purpose
run	Starts your program
where	Shows a stack-trace of your program
list	Lists part of your code
print *expr*	Displays the value of a local variable (*expr*); p is a shortcut

You can control program execution using the n command in gdb to execute the next statement and the s command to execute another step of your program. The difference between these two commands has to do with how they handle function calls. If the next statement to be executed is a function call, the s command will step into the function, whereas the n command will cause the entire function to be executed and then stop the program. When you are stopped within a program, the up command will jump you up the call stack, while the down command will take you down the call stack.

That's enough of gdb for now. Use gdb's help command to learn more.

User Interface Design

Although not strictly a development *tool*, user interface design is certainly something that developers need to be concerned about. Some developers spend far too little time designing the user interface of an application, yet that is the part that makes the first impression on most users. An application's user interface may well determine its success or failure.

To properly address all user interface design issues would take another book. However, user interface design is so important that we've listed a few tips for novice designers here:

- When developing a new application, create the user interface *first*. Then the user interface will more likely be written for the user, not the programmer. There's nothing worse than making an interface conform to code. Remember, you are writing your application for users, not for yourself.

- Don't put too many windows on the screen when your application is launched. If you do, the user may be confused and may not even know where the focus of your application lies. Also, don't start up your application with windows overlapping one another.

- Don't violate users' expectations. In part, this means that you should follow the Aqua user interface guidelines for menus, windows, panels, and so on. If you don't have the time to read the interface guidelines (they are long, but are discussed throughout Chapter 1), try to make your application look and work like other Aqua applications, such as the Finder, Mail, and TextEdit.

- Don't confuse the grouping of functionality. Some applications are riddled with menus and dialogs that confuse functionality. For example, viewing and font options should not be in the same menu.

- Balance your menus so that there are no more than 10 items per menu. Also, avoid creating short menus (i.e., one or two items) between the standard Edit and Window menus.

- Don't use too many different fonts and styles for your application. Keep the interface as simple as possible, and show your tricks in the About box.

- Provide sufficient WYSIWYG before a choice is set so that the user knows what the result of an action will be. For example, in the General pane of the System Preferences application, the Appearance and Highlight colors are displayed in the pop-up menu before they are selected.

Summary

In this chapter, we started out by taking a brief look at many of the Cocoa development tools. In /Developer/Applications, where most of the tools are located, we looked at PB, IB, ObjectAlloc, PropertyListEditor, IconComposer, and the icns Browser. There are other useful tools in that folder that we did not cover—launch them and find out what they do. In /Applications/Utilities, we looked at Terminal, Console, and ProcessViewer. We spent the most time with the gdb debugger, because it's an essential developer tool. We also worked with the filesystem and took a quick look at user interface design.

In the next chapter we'll take a closer look at IB, Apple's powerful tool for building application interfaces, and create our first program.

Exercises

1. Work through the steps in the "ObjectAlloc" section.
2. Work through the section "Working in a Unix Shell, Step by Step." Make a list of the things you discovered while working through the steps.
3. Work through the section "Using gdb in Project Builder, Step by Step."
4. Copy the /Developer/Examples/AppKit/TextEdit folder into your Home folder and build and run it—it's the same TextEdit application that we used in the last chapter. Explore the files associated with the TextEdit project in PB and IconComposer.

CHAPTER 3

Creating a Simple Application with Interface Builder

Interface Builder is Cocoa's main development tool for creating user interfaces for your applications. It lets you graphically design the windows that your application will use, together with all of their associated menus, buttons, sliders, and other objects. After you've put together the basic interface for your application, IB lets you "wire" (connect) together the parts (objects) and save all these specifications so that your application can use them when it runs.

This chapter introduces you to IB. We'll build a very simple interface for an application and test it with IB's Test Interface command. We won't use this interface beyond this chapter; we won't even save it. Our only goal here is to give you a sense of the ease and power of IB.

Let's start by taking a look at a typical Cocoa developer's screen, shown in Figure 3-1. The application being built is a simple calculator, and the IB development tool is the active application. The window at the top left that looks like a calculator is the interface for the calculator application under development. Similarly, the small window below the calculator window is the menu interface for the calculator application. The window at the bottom left and the two windows near the Dock are IB development support windows (and therefore aren't part of the calculator application itself). In the center of the screen is a Project Builder window containing source code for the calculator application. We'll use both PB and IB in Chapters 5 through 8 to create this very calculator application. An important icon in the Dock is the icon for IB; a copy of it is shown at the edge of this page. Note the screwdriver in the icon.

Interface Builder

At first glance you might think of IB as only an application prototyping tool. While IB can be used for prototypes, its primary use is to build the actual graphical user interfaces for Cocoa applications. IB is much more than a prototyper; it is an integral part of the Cocoa programming environment.

Project Builder

IB works together with PB (see the icon at the edge of the page) to provide a skeleton of source code to which a developer can add application-specific code. Note the hammer in PB's icon.

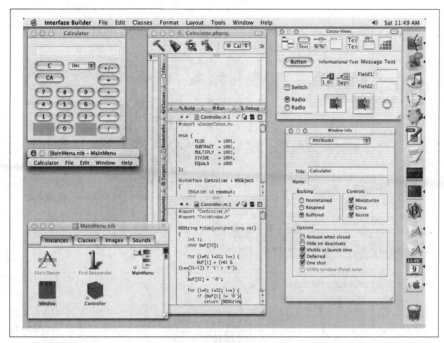

Figure 3-1. A Cocoa developer's screen

To keep things simple, we won't even use PB or build a complete project until the next chapter. However, in this chapter we do hope to delight you by demonstrating the powerful object-oriented development environment of Cocoa.

Getting Started with Interface Builder

1. Launch IB by clicking its icon in your Dock (or Finder).
2. Choose Interface Builder → Hide Others to simplify your screen.

Interface Builder

Your screen should look similar to the screen shot in Figure 3-2. IB's main menu is at the top of the screen, its Starting Point window is on the left, and its Palettes window is on the right of the screen. The windows on your screen may be in different locations, and the Palettes window may show a different palette from the Cocoa-Menus palette shown in Figure 3-2 (click the buttons in the Palettes window toolbar to change the palette). You can specify which windows show up at launch time in IB's Preferences dialog. Also, as with many Mac OS X applications, IB will remember its state from when it was last terminated.

Now that we've launched IB, we can start building our own application.

3. Make sure that Cocoa → Application is selected in IB's Starting Point window (as in Figure 3-2), then click the New button.

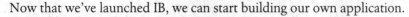

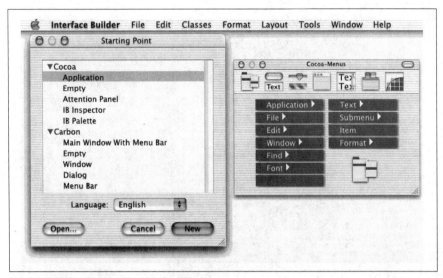

Figure 3-2. IB immediately after launch

The screen has now become more interesting, with the addition of three new items (see Figure 3-3). Near the top of the screen in Figure 3-3 is an empty window titled "Window" (again, note that the locations of these windows on your screen may differ slightly). On the left in the middle of the screen is a menu bar titled "Untitled - MainMenu". Don't try choosing commands from this menu right now—it's the main menu for the application that you are building. In subsequent chapters we'll show how you can tailor this menu with commands and submenus to suit a particular application.

In the lower-left corner of the screen in Figure 3-3 is the Nib File window for the new application. The Nib File window and menu are titled "Untitled", because you have yet to give the application a name. A *nib* is a file that contains information about an application's interface; we'll discuss nib files in great detail later. (Note that the Palettes window at the right in Figure 3-3 shows a new palette, the Cocoa-Other palette. We clicked the third item from the left in the Palettes window toolbar so you could see this palette in the figure).

> Instances

The icons in the Nib File window under the Instances tab in Figure 3-3 (e.g., File's Owner) represent predefined objects available to your new application. If you add more windows or panels to your application, icons representing these objects will also appear under the Instances tab in the Nib File window. When clicked, the other tabs (Classes, Images, Sounds) in this window show other resources available for your application. If there are too many objects to be displayed in the Nib File window, you can drag the window's vertical scroll knob to see them all. You can also resize this window if you want. Most windows that have a scroller should be resizable; this is important to remember when you start designing your own applications.

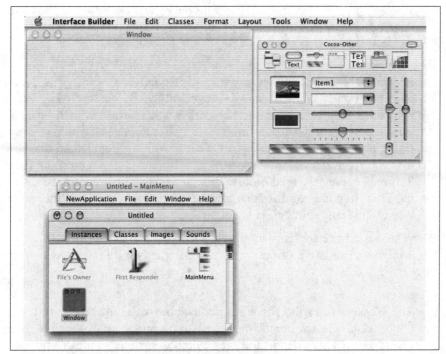

Figure 3-3. IB after creating a new Cocoa application

Let's look at the individual objects under the Instances tab for a *new* application, like the one shown in Figure 3-3:

File's Owner

In this example, the File's Owner icon represents the main object in charge of running your application. This object is called "NSApp" and is of the NSApplication class type. We'll go into more detail about what this object is and what it does later in this book. For now, just think of this icon as the object that controls the nib.

MainMenu

The MainMenu icon represents the new application's menu structure. At this point it consists of the five submenus (NewApplication, File, Edit, Windows, and Help) shown in the associated menu in the middle of Figure 3-3. These menu commands don't do anything significant until you test or run the application.

Window

The Window icon in the Nib File window represents the application's main window—the bland window titled "Window" that IB automatically created when you chose Cocoa → Application. The Nib File window will contain an icon for every standard window and panel in your application. If a window or panel in the application you're building isn't visible (e.g., if it's behind another window or was closed to simplify the screen), you can make it visible by double-clicking its icon in the Nib File window.

First Responder

A *responder* is an object that receives and responds to Cocoa events. Most of these events come from the keyboard or the mouse. The First Responder icon represents the object that will receive keyboard events. This is usually the active control of your application's key window—that is, the object inside the window (or dialog) with the highlighted title bar that will receive keyboard events. As your application executes, the First Responder changes based on user events. Being able to send messages to the First Responder, rather than to a specific object, is one of the many very useful features in Cocoa!

We've discussed the contents displayed under the Instances tab in IB's Nib File window. Next, we'll discuss what's under the Nib File window's other three tabs:

Classes

The Classes tab in the Nib File window shows the hierarchy of all the Objective-C classes that your new application knows about (see Figure 3-4). Classes define and create objects such as windows and buttons, as we'll see in subsequent chapters. IB's Classes menu commands work together with the classes in this hierarchy. You can add, modify, and perform other operations on classes within IB. In Figure 3-4, you can see the hierarchy of classes for the NSWindow class. We'll discuss this hierarchy in more detail in later chapters.

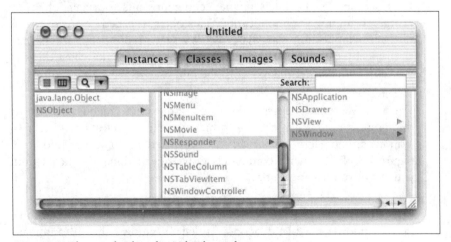

Figure 3-4. Classes tab selected in Nib File window

Images

The Images tab in the Nib File window displays representations of the icons and other images that are available to the application. When you click the Images tab, IB will display the available images in the Nib File window, as shown in Figure 3-5.

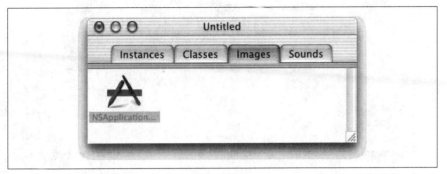

Figure 3-5. Images tab selected in Nib File window

Every Cocoa application is provided with a system icon called NSApplicationIcon—the generic application icon that shows up in the Dock and elsewhere for a running application that has no custom application icon. You can add your own image by dragging its file icon from your Finder and dropping it in the Nib File window. Alternatively, you can add an image by pasting it into this window.

All of the icons in the Instances, Images, and Sounds views in the Nib File window have their names displayed below them. Some of the names are in black, while others are in dark gray. The names in gray cannot be changed, but you can change a name in black by double-clicking it and typing a new name. Changing an icon's name in the Nib File window has no effect on the rest of the application you're building. For instance, if you change the name of the icon "Window" to "Steve's Window", the window itself will still be titled "Window". These icon names in the Nib File window are generally only for the convenience of the developer.

Sounds

The Sounds tab in the Nib File window displays representations of the sounds that are available to the application. When you click the Sounds tab, IB will display icons for the available sounds in the Nib File window, as shown in Figure 3-6 (we've resized the window so you can see all of the icons).

Sounds are an integral part of many Cocoa applications. Used appropriately, sounds can make an application easier and more fun to use. One very appropriate use of a sound is to alert the user to an unexpected

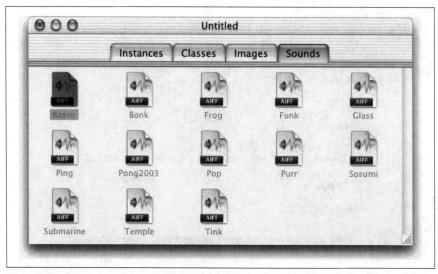

Figure 3-6. Sounds tab selected in Nib File window

event. For example, when you try to copy a file to a folder that contains a file with the same name, the Finder alerts you by playing your chosen system beep.

Every Cocoa application is provided with numerous system sounds, such as Basso, Bonk, and Frog. These sounds are located in the /System/ Library/Sounds folder. As with the Images tab view, you can add your own sounds to the application by dropping their file icons in the Nib File window.

Adding Objects to Your Application

In this section, we'll customize our new application's main window, "Window". It's wonderful that IB automatically provides every new application with this window, but it's rarely the right size. Sometimes it's too small; usually it's too big. Fortunately, we can easily resize the window as we would any Mac OS X window.

4. Resize the window titled "Window" to a height of about one inch and a width of about three inches.

Notice that you don't need to know the exact height and width of this window to set its size; you simply resize it visually and you're done (remember, you're building an application here). This is a good example of the basic philosophy of IB—graphical things are best done graphically. This philosophy is at the heart of Cocoa's ease of programming. (On the other hand, you can resize the window to precise dimensions using the NSWindow Info dialog, if necessary.)

Adding a Button Object to Your Window

The IB Palettes window near the upper-right corner of the screen contains seven (or more) palettes of objects that can be dragged into your application. By clicking one of the selector buttons in the toolbar near the top of the Palettes window, you can choose which palette is visible. The Palettes window is a *multi-view window*, in which one of several different views (panes) can be displayed depending on your selection of a tab, pop-up menu item, or other item. The Nib File window is also a multi-view window, but its different views are selected via tabs rather than via toolbar icons.

One of the most useful palettes in the Palettes window is the Cocoa-Views palette. The 14 objects in this palette are mainly Control objects (see Chapter 1) and are labeled in Figure 3-7. (Note that some objects are of the same type but have different attributes; also note that palettes may be different in future Mac OS releases.)

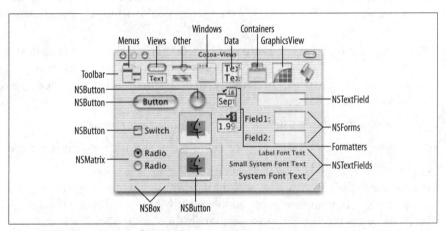

Figure 3-7. Cocoa-Views palette in IB

You can drag an object from the Cocoa-Views palette and drop it into any window or panel of the application you're building. Let's see how this works:

5. Make sure the Palettes window displays the Cocoa-Views palette by clicking the second icon from the left (shown at the edge of the page) in the Palettes window toolbar. The window's title bar should read "Cocoa-Views", as shown in Figure 3-7.

6. Add a button to your application by dragging the Button icon from the Cocoa-Views palette and dropping it into the window titled "Window". The window should look something like the one in Figure 3-8.

You can resize this new button by dragging some of the little gray circles, or *handles*, around the button's perimeter (the handles on your screen may be a different color, depending on your highlight color preference). You can move

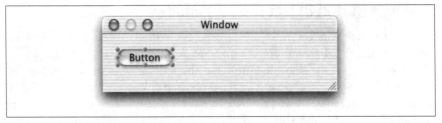

Figure 3-8. Window with selected button in IB

the button by pressing in the center of the button and dragging the button to the desired location within the window.

7. Resize the button so it's a little wider by dragging the right-middle handle on the button.

8. Move the button so it's in the same location as in the earlier screen shot. (Note that blue guidelines pop up as you move the button near a border of the window. These can be useful when you're arranging the contents of a window.)

9. Change the name of the button to "Noise". To do this, double-click the button's title ("Button")—the button's text will highlight (as shown at the edge of the page) to indicate that it's been selected. Then type "Noise" and hit Return.

Now you've got a simple window with a button. Let's try it out!

10. Choose the File → Test Interface menu command (or type the keyboard equivalent, Command-R).

All of the standard IB windows will disappear (as shown in Figure 3-9), and you'll be left with your new application's main window and menu (except for the IB name on the left). It looks as though the new application is running, but in fact we're only testing its interface within IB; there is no executable file.

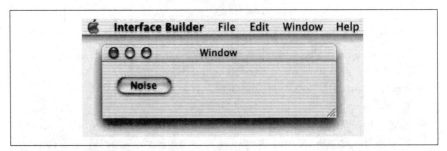

Figure 3-9. Testing the interface of a new application

Notice that the IB icon in your Dock has changed from its original Build mode to the "Frankenstein switch" icon shown at the edge of the page. This new icon indicates that your program is now in Test Interface mode. You can move, resize, miniaturize, and even close the window titled "Window". Several of the menu commands work, too! Try the File → Close menu command, for example (of course, the application doesn't do much at this point). Press the Noise button and note that it turns blue, as if it had been pushed (clicked).

11. Quit the Test Interface mode by choosing Quit NewApplication from the IB menu (or by typing Command-Q).

Giving Your Button a Funky Sound

Next, we'll show how easy it is to add sound to a button:

12. Click the Sounds tab in the Nib File window to see the sounds available to the new application.

13. Drag one of the sound icons (e.g., Funk) and drop it on top of the Noise button in the window, as shown in Figure 3-10.

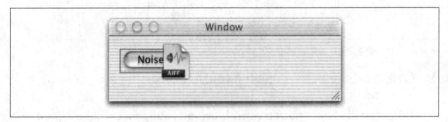

Figure 3-10. Dropping a sound on the Noise button

The button will highlight, indicating that it will accept the noise as an attribute. Also note that IB's inspector (or Info) window opens at the lower right of the screen and shows the attributes of your Noise button.

Inspecting and Changing Your Button's Attributes

Next, we'll show how easy it is to change a button to act as if it has been clicked when the user hits the Return key:

14. Make sure the Noise button is selected (handles appear around its border) by clicking it once.

15. Choose Tools → Show Info to display the Info dialog (window), shown in Figure 3-11 (the Info dialog was probably already open). Select Attributes in the pop-up menu if it isn't already selected.

    The Info dialog contains information (attributes, etc.) about the selected button. Note that the title (Noise) and sound (Funk) associated with the button show up in this window.

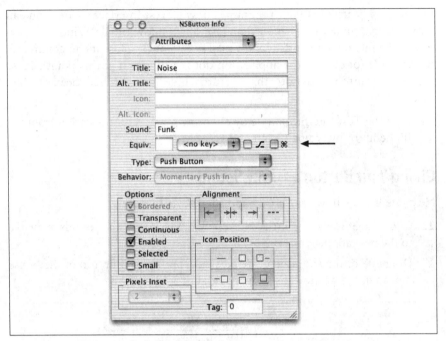

Figure 3-11. NSButton Info dialog for Noise button

16. Click the "<no key>" pop-up menu and choose the Return menu item from the list.

Note that the Noise button turns blue, indicating that it's the *default* button. When a user hits the Return key, the default button acts as if it has been clicked.

17. Choose File → Test Interface again.

18. Click the Noise button, and you'll hear the sound that you dropped on top of the button.

19. Hit the Return key, and you'll hear the sound again (because you made the button the default).

20. Choose Quit NewApplication from IB's main menu to return to IB's Build mode.

Objects, Messages, and Targets

The Cocoa Application Kit is written in Objective-C, a hybrid language based on ANSI C and SmallTalk that was developed by Brad Cox. The principal building block of object-oriented programs is the *object*. Objects can be thought of as bundles of related ANSI C variables and functions with lots of extra functionality.

Objective-C objects are self-contained code entities that communicate by sending *messages* to one another. A message is like a function call in a traditional programming language in that it causes a procedure to be executed. However, a message is unlike a function call in that it is sent to a specific object; it is not simply "called." The procedures that are executed—called *methods* in Objective-C—are "encapsulated" inside objects, and thus different objects can respond to the same message in different ways.

Unlike some object-oriented languages, Objective-C doesn't require that you know the type (class) of an object before you send it a message. This is known as *dynamic* or *runtime binding*; the message is bound to the object at runtime instead of compile-time. It allows for much greater flexibility, because certain decisions can be made following a user's action. For example, when a user chooses Cut from an application's Edit submenu, a **cut:** message is sent to a target object (the colon is part of the message). If an application lets a user cut text, graphics, and other types of data, the **cut:** message will have varying targets that won't be known until runtime. With runtime binding, the application doesn't need to know the class of the target object before the **cut:** message is sent.

Objects and Classes

Under Cocoa, every on-screen object is represented by an Objective-C object inside the computer's memory. In our little Noise button application, there's an NSWindow object that displays and controls the application's on-screen "Window" window, and there's an NSButton object that displays and controls the Noise button. There's yet another object for the application's "Untitled - MainMenu" window, and one additional object for each of the individual menu items inside the menu.

Every Cocoa object belongs to a *class*, which both defines and creates the object. Many of the Cocoa class names are fairly self-explanatory. For example, the classes of the on-screen objects in the application we just described are listed in Table 3-1.

Table 3-1. On-screen objects in the application

Object in the application	Class
The window ("Window")	NSWindow
The button ("Noise")	NSButton
The main menu ("Untitled")	NSMenu
The menu items (Info, Edit, Hide, Quit)	NSMenuItem

The "NS" in the prefix to each class name is a holdover from NeXTSTEP (NS), the application framework that spawned Mac OS X.

There are many other objects present in this application that aren't immediately apparent because they have no obvious corresponding objects on the screen. Some of these objects are listed in Table 3-2.*

Table 3-2. Additional objects in the application that aren't immediately apparent on-screen

Object name	Class	Purpose
NSApp	NSApplication	The application's main controlling object
[myWindow contentView]	NSView	Defines the content area of the window where the application can draw
n/a	NSButtonCell	The Button's supporting Cell object, which actually displays the button

Notice that the second object in Table 3-2 has a funny name with square brackets. The square brackets are the Objective-C *messaging operator*. The phrase "[myWindow contentView]" means "send the **contentView** message to the object pointed to by the variable called myWindow and return the result." The result is a pointer to the contentView object (or simply "content view") inside myWindow. A pointer to an Objective-C object is called an *id*. When the application starts up, we don't have the id for myWindow's content view object. We can get it only by sending a message to the myWindow object (myWindow here is the Objective-C variable name for the pointer that points to the Window object titled "Window").

Messaging is one of three major elements of the Objective-C language that you need to learn about in order to write Cocoa programs. The second is how to construct your own classes. The third is how to use a few of the important classes that are part of the Cocoa environment—in particular, the classes NSWindow, NSView, and NSApplication. Once you understand these three things, the very heart and soul of Cocoa, you will understand most of what you need to know to write Cocoa programs.

Targets, Actions, and Connections

Many of the objects in Cocoa's Application Kit are set up so that when you manipulate an on-screen object in a running application, a message is automatically sent to a second object. These objects are called *control objects*. (The Noise button object we discussed earlier is a control object.) The object that receives the message is called the *target* of the sending object. The procedure (method) that the target is instructed to perform is called the *action*. We'll refer to this as the *target/action paradigm*.

---

* It's not imperative that you understand everything in the remainder of this section right now, but we're going to give it to you anyway. We'll return to these subjects in later chapters.

For example, when you choose the Quit menu command from an application's menu, the associated NSMenuItem object sends a **terminate:** message to the control object, NSApp (also known as the File's Owner).

The **terminate:** message has the form [**NSApp terminate:self**]. The action is **terminate:**, and **self** is an argument specifying the object that sent the message. This message causes the NSApp object to execute its **terminate:** method, which terminates the program. Likewise, the NSMenuItem object associated with the Hide menu command sends the **hide:** message to NSApp, which causes NSApp to remove all of the application's windows from the screen. Note that the colons (:) shown above are actually part of the Objective-C method names.

To see how this works in practice, let's add two more control objects—a text field and a slider—to the new application's window. First we'll put them in the window, and then we'll wire (connect) them together so that a message can be sent from the slider to the text field.

1. Return to the application you built previously within IB's Build mode.

2. Drag the icon for the simple NSTextField object (shown at the edge of the page) from the Cocoa-Views Palettes window into the window titled "Window".

3. Click the Cocoa-Other button at the top of the Palettes window to display the sliders available to applications under construction.

4. Drag the icon for the horizontal grid slider object from the Cocoa-Other Palettes window into the window titled "Window".

5. When you're done, you should have a window that looks like the one in Figure 3-12.

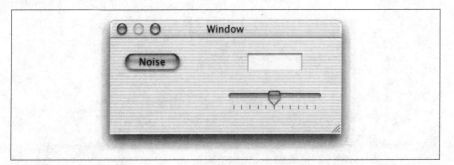

Figure 3-12. Window with new text field and slider in IB

Next, we'll make a connection so that the slider (NSSlider) object can send a message to the text field (NSTextField) object whenever the slider's knob is moved.

6. Hold down the Control key on the keyboard and drag from the slider object to the text field object (note the direction). You will see a "connection wire" linking the slider to the text field, as shown in Figure 3-13.

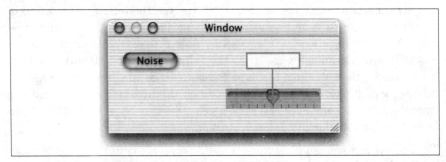

Figure 3-13. Connection wire from slider to text field in IB

7. Release the mouse button, and IB's Connections Info dialog (NSSlider Info) will appear near the lower-right corner of the screen (see Figure 3-14). The Connections Info dialog lets you make or break connections between objects.

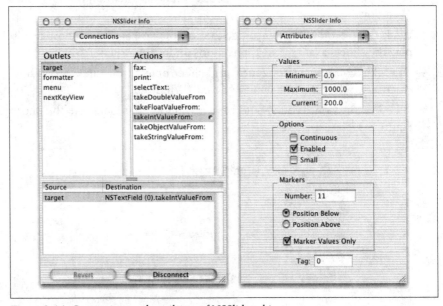

Figure 3-14. Connections and attributes of NSSlider object

Connections from a control object (i.e., the slider) to another object have two parts: a target and an action. You already specified the NSTextField object as the target (or receiver or destination) of a message when you connected the NSSlider object to the NSTextField object (in that direction). You specify which action (method) the target should perform in response to an event in the NSSlider Info dialog. Your choices for the action are listed under "Actions" in the Info dialog on the left of Figure 3-14. (If you had connected the NSSlider object to a different target, such as the NSButton object, you would see a different list of actions, because an NSButton object can perform a different set of actions from those performed by an NSTextField object.)

The action we'll use here is **takeIntValueFrom:**, which causes the NSText-Field object to ask the sender (the NSSlider object) of the original message for its integer value (only the grid marks have values on this particular slider). This integer corresponds to the position of the NSSlider object's knob.

8. Select the **takeIntValueFrom:** action in the Connections Info dialog and then click the Connect button. (Alternatively, you can double-click the **takeIntValueFrom:** action.)

After you make the connection, the Connect button becomes a Disconnect button, as in the inspector window on the left of Figure 3-14, and the connection dimple (⌐) appears next to the action name in the Info dialog.

9. Make sure the slider is selected (handles appear), then choose Attributes from the pop-up menu in the NSSlider Info dialog.

10. Change the Maximum value of the slider from 100.0 to 1000.0 and change the Current value to 200.0. Note the other attributes, such as Marker Values Only, in the Info dialog on the right of Figure 3-14.

11. Test the interface again by choosing IB's File → Test Interface menu command or typing Command-R.

12. Drag the NSSlider object's knob. As you move it, the NSTextField object will update the integer it displays according to the knob's position (see Figure 3-15).

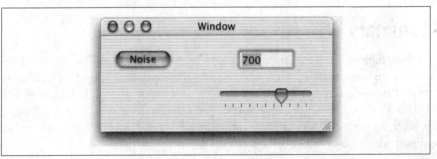

Figure 3-15. Testing the slider connection to the text field in Test Interface mode

13. Choose Quit NewApplication from IB's main menu.

Figure 3-16 shows the communication between the NSSlider and NSText-Field objects. A mouse-drag event on the slider knob causes the NSSlider object to send the **takeIntValueFrom:** message to the target NSTextField object, which executes its **takeIntValueFrom:** method (this results from the connection we set up). The **takeIntValueFrom:** method then sends the **intValue** message back to the NSSlider object, which returns the slider's current value of 700 to the NSTextField object, and then the NSTextField object displays the result. (We didn't have to tell the NSTextField object's **takeIntValueFrom:** action procedure to send the **intValue** message back to the NSSlider object; the NSTextField object is smart enough to know how to get an integer value from the sending object.)

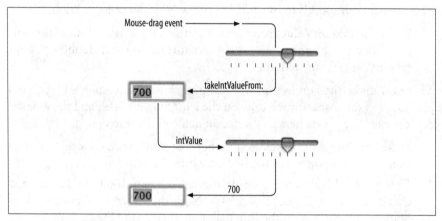

Figure 3-16. Communication between NSSlider and NSTextField objects

This may seem like a lot of overhead, but messaging is actually quite fast—only slightly slower than a standard function call. And the benefits are wonderful, as we'll see.

14. Quit IB. There's no need to save any of the files or interface specifications.

Summary

In this chapter, you've learned a little about the workings of IB and Objective-C. You've seen that on-screen objects have corresponding Objective-C objects stored in the computer's memory. You've also seen a special class of object called a *control* in action, and you've seen that a control can have a target, which is another object that is automatically sent a message to perform an action when the control object is manipulated by the user.

In the next chapter, we'll cover the basics of Objective-C, Cocoa's native programming language. We'll also take a look at the basic Objective-C classes that Cocoa provides to make writing complicated programs much easier.

Exercise

Work through all of the steps in this chapter, but use different on-screen objects. For example, use a rounded bevel button from the Cocoa-Views palette (instead of a push button) and a continuous vertical slider (instead of a horizontal one with markers). Find a icon in the filesystem and figure out how to place it on the bevel button. Also, use the **takeFloatValueFrom:** method to connect the slider to the text field. Use Test Interface mode to test your work.

CHAPTER 4

An Objective-C Application Without Interface Builder

As we saw in Chapter 3, Interface Builder is a tremendously powerful program. But IB also hides a lot of the nuts and bolts of how Cocoa applications work, and a knowledge of those nuts and bolts will serve you well as you learn Cocoa programming. In this chapter, we will create a simple Cocoa application in Objective-C without using IB. In the process, we'll learn the fundamentals of the Objective-C programming language, the Cocoa class hierarchy, and memory management under Cocoa.

The Tiny.m Program

In this chapter, we'll discuss a small application called Tiny.m (the .m extension means that the file contains Objective-C code). This program will bring up a window and will draw a dodecagon (12-sided polygon) with a fancy pattern in it (see Figure 4-1).

Before discussing the application in detail, we'll show you the complete Objective-C source code for Tiny.m—Example 4-1. We're showing you this now because the best way to learn a new language is to read a program that's written in that language. As you'll see, much of the code in Tiny.m that relates to on-screen objects will not be necessary when we combine Objective-C with IB.

Throughout this book, we've elected to include comments in the programming examples, even though we are also explaining the code within the book's text. We do this because it is good programming style to include comments in the code. We hope you'll get used to using comments in the code that you write.

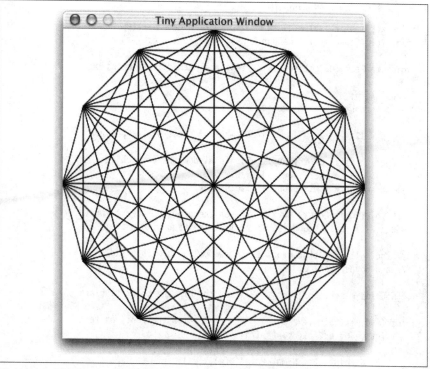

Figure 4-1. The Tiny.m application window

Example 4-1. Tiny.m

Tiny.m

```
/* Tiny.m
 * A tiny Cocoa application that creates a window
 * and then displays graphics in it.
 * IB is not used to create this application.
 */

#import <Cocoa/Cocoa.h>          // include the Cocoa Frameworks

/***********************************************************
** A DemoView instance object of this class draws the image.
***********************************************************/

@interface DemoView : NSView     // interface of DemoView class
{                                // (subclass of NSView class)
}
- (void)drawRect:(NSRect)rect;   // instance method interface
@end

@implementation DemoView         // implementation of DemoView class
```

Example 4-1. Tiny.m (continued)

```objectivec
#define X(t) (sin(t)+1) * width * 0.5      // macro for X(t)
#define Y(t) (cos(t)+1) * height * 0.5     // macro for Y(t)

- (void)drawRect:(NSRect)rect    // instance method implementation
{
    double f,g;
    double const pi = 2 * acos(0.0);

    int n = 12;                    // number of sides of the polygon

    // get the size of the application's window and view objects
    float width  = [self bounds].size.width;
    float height = [self bounds].size.height;

    [[NSColor whiteColor] set];    // set the drawing color to white
    NSRectFill([self bounds]);     // fill the view with white

    // the following statements trace two polygons with n sides
    // and connect all of the vertices with lines

    [[NSColor blackColor] set];    // set the drawing color to black

    for (f=0; f<2*pi; f+=2*pi/n) {          // draw the fancy pattern
        for (g=0; g<2*pi; g+=2*pi/n) {
            NSPoint p1 = NSMakePoint(X(f),Y(f));
            NSPoint p2 = NSMakePoint(X(g),Y(g));
            [NSBezierPath strokeLineFromPoint:p1 toPoint:p2];
        }
    }

} // end of drawRect: override method

/* windowWillClose: is a delegate method that gets invoked when
 * the on-screen window is about to close (user clicked close box).
 * In this case, we force the entire application to terminate.
 */

-(void)windowWillClose:(NSNotification *)notification
{
    [NSApp terminate:self];
}
@end   // end of DemoView implementation

/*
 * setup() performs the functions that would normally be performed by
 * loading a nib file.
 */

void setup()
{
    NSWindow *myWindow;       // typed pointer to NSWindow object
    NSView   *myView;         // typed pointer to NSView object
    NSRect    graphicsRect;   // contains an origin, width, height
```

Example 4-1. Tiny.m (continued)

```objc
    // initialize the rectangle variable
    graphicsRect = NSMakeRect(100.0, 350.0, 400.0, 400.0);

    myWindow = [ [NSWindow alloc]               // create the window
               initWithContentRect: graphicsRect
                       styleMask:NSTitledWindowMask
                                 |NSClosableWindowMask
                                 |NSMiniaturizableWindowMask
                           backing:NSBackingStoreBuffered
                             defer:NO ];

    [myWindow setTitle:@"Tiny Application Window"];

    // create amd initialize the DemoView instance
    myView = [[[DemoView alloc] initWithFrame:graphicsRect] autorelease];

    [myWindow setContentView:myView ];     // set window's view

    [myWindow setDelegate:myView ];        // set window's delegate
    [myWindow makeKeyAndOrderFront: nil]; // display window
}

int main( )
{
    // create the autorelease pool
    NSAutoreleasePool *pool = [[NSAutoreleasePool alloc] init];

    // create the application object
    NSApp = [NSApplication sharedApplication];

    // set up the window and drawing mechanism
    setup( );

    // run the main event loop
    [NSApp run];

    // we get here when the window is closed

    [NSApp release];        // release the app
    [pool release];         // release the pool
    return(EXIT_SUCCESS);
}
```

Before we analyze the program, we suggest that you type it in and save it in a
file called Tiny.m.

Tiny.m

We strongly recommend that you type the examples within
this book by hand, rather than downloading them from the
Web. You will learn more about Cocoa programming by actually typing in the examples—and then finding your typos—
than you will by merely reading them.

You can use any of the text editors that come with Mac OS X: Project Builder, TextEdit, GNU Emacs, vi, or ed. If you're just starting out with Unix, you'll probably want to use PB or TextEdit, because they work like most other Cocoa programs and have several nice features for writing code. TextEdit is the basis of the editor that's built into PB. It is extended in PB with some powerful features for browsing a program's source code and interfacing directly with gdb, the GNU debugger we discussed in Chapter 2.

Using Character-Based Editors with Mac OS X

Mac OS X comes with a variety of "programmer's editors" that you can use for editing text files. These editors include TextEdit, GNU Emacs, vi, and ed. With the exception of TextEdit, all of these editors were developed for character-based terminals and must be run from the Terminal application, which we described in Chapter 2.

Don't be scared off from these other editors just because they may seem antiquated. Many programmers and system administrators use GNU Emacs. It's a powerful editor that can handle dozens of files at the same time. It's programmable, and it has a built-in mail reader, a development environment, and many other tools. Unlike TextEdit and PB, GNU Emacs can, for example, automatically reindent a block of text that's been copied from one place in your program to another. GNU Emacs has a "tags" system that allows you to place your cursor on a function call and automatically jump to where that function is defined. All in all, it is a considerably more powerful tool for editing code than PB. What's more, GNU Emacs is available for Unix, Windows, and Mac OS 7 and above, allowing you to use a consistent editor on all platforms.

The vi editor is the descendant of the Unix "visual" editor that Bill Joy (of Sun Microsystems, Inc.) wrote in 1976. The vi editor is included with Mac OS X because some people have hardcoded it in their brains and really love it.

After you've typed the source code in the file Tiny.m, open a Terminal window and change to the directory where the file resides. Compile Tiny.m and then (if there are no errors inadvertently introduced by typing mistakes) run the executable Tiny with the commands shown here in bold type:

```
% cc -Wall -o Tiny Tiny.m -framework Cocoa
% ./Tiny
```

Tiny is now running—look for its window.

The components of this compiler call command are described in Table 4-1.

Table 4-1. Compiler call command components

What you typed	What it means
cc	Invokes the C compiler. (In Cocoa, the C, Objective-C, and C++ compilers are all invoked with this same command, although the C++ compiler is usually invoked with the /usr/bin/c++ command.)
-Wall	Makes the compiler list *all* warnings.
-o Tiny	Places the result of the compilation in the Tiny file.
Tiny.m	Compiles the program in the Tiny.m file (which resides in the working directory).
-framework Cocoa	Instructs the linker to use the Cocoa "framework."

If the program compiles without errors (and there should be no errors, not even any warnings), you can run it as specified above, by typing "./Tiny" and hitting Return.

You should see the window displayed earlier, in Figure 4-1.

 This demo program lacks many fundamental elements of a standard Cocoa program, and therefore it does not interact properly with the Mac OS X environment. In particular, this program does not display a menu, it does not bring its window to the front of the window stack when it starts up, and it does not appear in the Dock. A side effect of these characteristics is that you may find it difficult to find the Tiny window. If this happens to you, try hiding your running applications until the Tiny window appears.

You can close the Tiny application by clicking the red close button at the top-left corner of its window or by typing Control-C in the Terminal window.

Before we explain how Tiny works, let's take a detour and look at some basics of the Objective-C programming language. This discussion is not meant to be exhaustive, but rather a foundation on which we can build throughout the rest of the book.

An Introduction to Objective-C

We discussed Objective-C briefly in the last chapter. In this chapter, we'll go into a lot more depth.

The Objective-C language was invented by Brad Cox in the early 1980s and was based on the object-oriented principles of SmallTalk. Cox wanted to create a computer environment that could be used to build *software-ICs*— software components that could be used to create large programs in much the same way that discrete integrated circuits are used to create computers. Cox wrote a book, *Object-Oriented Programming: An Evolutionary Approach,* in which he outlined his strategy of grafting object-oriented technology onto existing programming languages (e.g., C), rather than creating fundamentally new languages (e.g., Simula and SmallTalk). And he founded the Stepstone Corporation to bring his brainchild to the market.

Objective-C is based on two important principles. First, Cox wanted to create a language that offered much of the object-oriented programming power that existed in SmallTalk. Specifically, he wanted a language in which both classes and instances of classes were objects, a language that allowed introspection, and a language that performed the runtime evaluation of messages. Second, he wanted a language that was easy to learn and as similar to C as possible. He came up with Objective-C.

Objective-C is quite similar to the ANSI C language, but it introduces a single new type, one new operator, and a few compiler directives. These additions are summarized in Table 4-2.

Table 4-2. New features in Objective-C

New feature	Example	Purpose
#import	#import <Cocoa/Cocoa.h>	Includes a file if it has not been included before. Similar to #include.
id	id anObject;	Pointer to an object.
[ ]	[anObject aMethod];	Messaging operator; sends a message to an object.
self	[self display];	Pointer to the current object.
super	[super display];	Pointer to the current object's parent class. Allows a method implementation in a class to call another method implementation in the superclass. This is most commonly used when overriding method implementations.
@interface	@interface MyClass: NSObject	Marks the beginning of a class declaration. Usually appears in a .h file.
@implementation	@implementation MyClass	Marks the beginning of a class implementation. Usually appears in a .m file.
@protocol	@protocol DrawProtocol	Marks the beginning of a protocol declaration. Usually appears in a .h file.
@class	@class NSString, NSDictionary;	Tells the compiler that a class will be referenced before it is defined. Similar to declaring a struct name * in ANSI C.
@end	@end	Notes the end of an @interface, @implementation, or @protocol section.

Table 4-2. New features in Objective-C (continued)

New feature	Example	Purpose
+	+(id)alloc;	Introduces a class method in an @interface or @implementation.
-	-(id)init;	Introduces an instance method in an @interface or @implementation.
@""	@"a string"	Used to create an unnamed NSString object. Equivalent to [NSString stringWithCString:"a string"].

Objects and Classes

An Objective-C *object* is a self-contained bundle of code containing data and procedures that operate on that data. The data is stored in *instance variables*, and the procedures are called *instance methods*. For example, an NSWindow object, which controls an on-screen window, contains a frame instance variable that stores the window's location on the computer's screen. The NSWindow object is self-contained, or encapsulated, in the sense that instance variables such as frame are not directly accessible from outside the object; you can modify them only by invoking the object's methods. These methods assure that all access to instance variables is carefully controlled, which helps ensure the integrity of the instance data. This whole process is sometimes called *data encapsulation*.

An Objective-C *class* is a template that defines characteristics that are common to all objects that are members, or *instances*, of that class. For example, the NSWindow class defines the instance variables and methods that comprise NSWindow objects. The NSWindow class also defines special *class* or *factory* methods for creating new objects.

Objective-C is different from other object-oriented languages, such as C++, in that Objective-C classes are objects themselves—you can send them messages and pass references to classes as arguments.

When a class creates an object using a class method, it sets up memory for a new data structure containing the instance variables defined by the class. It does *not* make a copy of the instance methods that the object can perform. There is only one copy of the instance methods, and they are stored as part of the class's definition in the computer's memory. These instance methods are shared by all instances of the class, which makes memory usage more efficient. This also means that every member of a class responds to a message in the same way. (This is not the case in some other object-oriented languages, where individual objects are allowed to "specialize" a class.)

For example, suppose that an application requires two on-screen windows. The application will send two separate requests (messages) to the NSWindow class to create two distinct NSWindow objects. Each NSWindow object will contain its own class-defined data structure with its own copies of the instance variables (e.g., frame). If one of the NSWindow objects is asked to perform the **setFrame:** action (which changes the window's origin and size), the window object will go to the NSWindow class definition in memory for the actual **setFrame:** code, but it will change only the frame instance variables in its own data structure, not those in the other window on the screen.

Figure 4-2 shows an application with two windows on the screen; each window has a corresponding NSWindow object inside the computer's memory, and each NSWindow object has its own set of instance variables but shares the same methods.

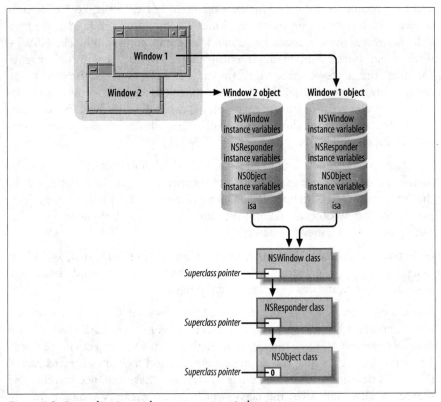

Figure 4-2. An application with two on-screen windows

Inside the computer's memory, objects are implemented as data structures that contain the instance variables as well as pointers to the objects' classes. It's the Objective-C runtime system that brings all this to life.

Methods and Messaging

An Objective-C *method* is invoked by sending the object a *message*.* Objective-C messages are enclosed in square brackets, as follows:

```
[receiver message]
```

The **receiver** can be a class or an instance object, while **message** is a method name together with arguments. We will refer to the entire bracketed expression **[receiver message]** as a *message* as well, although some prefer to call it a *message expression*.

For example, suppose that you have an NSWindow object variable called aWindow. You can send aWindow the message **orderOut** with this statement:

```
[aWindow orderOut];
```

The terms *method* and *message* may appear to be used interchangeably and to mean the same thing, but they actually have slightly different meanings. A method is a procedure inside a class that's executed when you send that class or an instance of that class a message. The method is executed when the object is sent the corresponding message. Indeed, the same message sent to objects of different classes will usually cause methods with different implementations to be invoked.

 Although the phrase "sending a message" suggests concurrency, message invocations are similar to traditional C-language function calls. If your program sends a message to an object, that object's corresponding method has to finish executing before your program can continue with other tasks.

One nice thing about Objective-C is that the same syntax is used for sending messages to both classes and instances. For example, this code sends the message **alloc** to the NSWindow class:

```
[NSWindow alloc]
```

while this code sends the **display** message to the object pointed to by the object variable aWindow:

```
[aWindow display]
```

Messages can have *arguments*. For example, this code sends a message that has a single argument:

```
[aCell setIntValue:52];
```

---

* The Mach operating system, upon which Mac OS X is based, offers another kind of messaging called *Mach messages*. Mach messages should not be confused with Objective-C messages.

This next line of code sends a message that has two arguments:

```
[myMatrix selectCellAtRow:5 column:10];
```

It tells the myMatrix object variable to select the cell of the matrix at position (5,10). The full name of the message is **selectCellAtRow:column:**, which is what you get when you remove the arguments and the spaces from the message invocation. The message name contains all of those letters and both colons.

By convention, class names usually begin with uppercase letters, while methods and instances begin with lowercase letters. This convention is occasionally violated, however, when using nonstandard case improves the readability of a program's source code.

The id Data Type

Objective-C adds one new data type, id, to the C programming language. An *id variable* is a pointer to an object in the computer's memory. (The variable myMatrix in the previous section could have been defined as an id variable.) You can think of an id as somewhat analogous to the ANSI C void * pointer, but whereas a void * pointer can point to any kind of *structure*, an id variable can point to any kind of *object*.

There is an important difference between a void * pointer and an id—a function that receives a void * pointer has no way of knowing what the pointer really points to. On the other hand, Objective-C objects contain type information, so it is possible for an Objective-C function to examine an id and determine the kind of object that it points to, or *references*.

Looking at an id pointer and figuring out what kind of object it points to is called *introspection*, and it happens often when an Objective-C program runs. The Objective-C language uses introspection to implement *dynamic binding*. When you send a message to an Objective-C object, the Objective-C runtime system literally hands that message to the object and asks the object "Which function call do you want to run in response?" Dynamic binding allows different objects to respond to the same message in different ways, which gives Objective-C programmers a tremendous amount of power and flexibility.

Similarities and differences between void * pointers and the id data type are summarized in Table 4-3.

Table 4-3. Pointers to structures versus pointers to Objective-C objects

Characteristic	Pointers to structures	Pointers to Objective-C objects
Pointer type	void *	id
Sample declaration	void *ptr;	id obj;

Table 4-3. Pointers to structures versus pointers to Objective-C objects (continued)

Characteristic	Pointers to structures	Pointers to Objective-C objects
Size of pointer on 32-bit PowerPC microprocessor	4 bytes	4 bytes
Points to	Any kind of structure	Any kind of object
To determine the kind of object pointed to	Impossible unless the type is encoded inside the structure itself	Send the object a message—for example, **[obj class]**

In the next section, we'll continue our exploration of Objective-C by creating an actual class.

> The Objective-C runtime is extremely fast. Although it is true that Objective-C messages take somewhat longer to execute than do traditional C function calls or C++ member function dispatches, the actual amount of clock time is measured in microseconds—under normal circumstances, you should not be concerned with the overhead of an Objective-C method invocation. Remember that the Objective-C runtime that you are using can directly trace its lineage to a version that ran on a Motorola 68030 computer running at 25 MHz! It was plenty fast then; today's computers are at least 20 times faster.
>
> Don't spend your time trying to "get around" the Objective-C runtime by looking for ways to replace Objective-C messages with traditional function calls. Instead, use the Objective-C runtime to your fullest advantage. It will save you time developing your application, allowing you to concentrate on issues of design. If your application seems to run slowly, this is almost certainly the result of poor design, not of the minor overhead caused by Objective-C method dispatches.

A Simple Class Example

Suppose that a friend asks you to help debug a program that is supposed to help ninth-grade students in a chemistry course by drawing pictures of molecules. To draw the atoms on the computer's screen, your friend has created a class called Circle. Instances of this class will be used to draw the atoms on the computer's screen. The class is called Circle, rather than Atom, because your friend hopes to reuse this class for a graphics package that he is creating.

To perform the necessary functions, your friend has implemented in his program a variety of methods that respond to messages. Instances of the Circle class respond to an Objective-C **drawSelf** message that causes them to display themselves in the currently selected window. A second method, **set-Radius:**, sets the circle's size.

Let's look at these methods in practice. At part of the program your friend is debugging, there is a variable called aCircle that points to a particular circle that is being acted upon. At this point in the code, the program can force the circle to display itself with this excerpt of code:

```
[aCircle drawSelf];
```

Likewise, the radius of the circle can be set to 5.0 with this statement:

```
[aCircle setRadius:5.0];
```

There is no limit to the number of methods to which a class can respond. For example, your friend has implemented a method that can be used to set the center of the circle to a particular (x,y) coordinate:

```
[aCircle setX:32.0 andY:64.0];
```

Methods can also return values. In this example, your friend has implemented a method that allows the program to determine the x and y coordinates of the circle's center. For example:

```
printf("aCircle centered at %f,%f\n", [aCircle x],[aCircle y] );
```

The methods **setX:andY:**, **x**, and **y** are called *accessor methods* because they give you access to a variable encapsulated inside the aCircle object. In this case, the methods **x** and **y** return floating-point numbers (the values in the instance variables), and the output would be:

```
aCircle centered at 32.0,64.0
```

Accessor methods free the programmer using a class from having to know the details of how the class is implemented. For instance, the Circle class might store the location of the circle as a center (x,y) and a radius (r). Alternatively, the Circle class might store the location of the circle as the bounding box (x1,y1) to (x2,y2), or as a bounding box with an origin at (x,y) and an extent (width,height). Each of these representations has certain advantages and disadvantages to the programmer implementing the Circle class. But as programmers using the Circle class, we don't really want to know how it is implemented—we just want to be sure that it works properly.

 When you create your own classes, you should first consider what kinds of accessor functions the programmers using the classes will require. The initial design of the class will often be dictated by the accessor methods, but if you use well-defined accessor methods, you will be able to change the implementation of your class without needing to make many other changes in your software.

Creating and Initializing Objects

Every computer language provides a facility for allocating and initializing new regions of memory. In ANSI C, memory allocation is done with the functions malloc( ), calloc( ), and memset( ). C++ allocates new objects with **new**. The Objective-C methods for allocating and initializing memory are **alloc** and **init**.

The **alloc** method is a class method: you send the message **alloc** to a class, and the class allocates the memory for that object and returns a pointer to the object that it just allocated. In our example, we will send the **alloc** method directly to the Circle class.* Because the **alloc** method creates a new object, it is often called a *factory method*.

The **init** method is an *instance* method; you send the message **init** to an object that was just allocated and the object initializes itself. So your friend's program might have a bit of code in it that looks like this:

```
id aCircle;                     // declare object pointer

aCircle = [[Circle alloc] init];   // create aCircle instance

[aCircle setX:32.0 andY:64.0];  // set center of circle
[aCircle setRadius:10.0];       // set radius of circle
[aCircle drawSelf];             // display circle on screen
```

The aCircle = [[Circle alloc] init] statement sends the **alloc** message to the Circle class, asking it to allocate memory (create) a new Circle object. The **alloc** method returns the id of an uninitialized Circle object. This object is then sent an **init** method, causing it to be initialized. The **init** method returns the id of the object that we are supposed to use. This id is usually the same as the id that the **alloc** method returned—but it is not always the same, which is why it is important to nest the **alloc** and **init** methods.

Another feature of Objective-C is that it allows you to tell the compiler that a pointer will point only to an object of a particular type of class (or one of its subclasses). For example, we could rewrite the previous code in this way:

```
Circle *aCircle= [[Circle alloc] init];

[aCircle setX:32.0 andY:64.0];  // set center of circle
[aCircle setRadius:10.0];       // set radius of circle
[aCircle drawSelf];             // display circle on screen
```

This notation is called *static (strong) typing*. The advantage of static typing is that the compiler can perform a limited amount of checking and can issue warnings if you seem to be sending a message to a class or an instance of the class that is not implemented.

Because initializing an object and setting its instance variables is a common operation, most Objective-C classes provide special-purpose initializers that perform both of these functions. Let's say the Circle class has such an initializer,

---

* One of the interesting aspects of Objective-C is that the Circle class is itself an object. In C++, classes are not themselves objects.

called **initX:Y:radius:**. Using this initializer, we might simplify the previous code fragment to look like this:

```
Circle *aCircle = [[Circle alloc] initX:32.0 Y:64 radius:10];
[aCircle drawSelf];
```

There are many kinds of messages that you can send to an object. These messages are defined in the class interface definitions.

The @interface Directive

To use a new class in your program, you need some way to tell the Objective-C compiler the names of the class, its instance variables, its methods, and the superclass from which it is derived. This is done with a *class interface*—a fancy name for an included file that is brought to the compiler's attention with the #import directive.

The Connector class example we'll use here has a relatively simple class interface, shown in Example 4-2.

Example 4-2. The Connector.h class implementation file

```
/* Connector.h:
 * The Connector class interface file
 */

#import <Foundation/NSObject.h>

@interface Connector : NSObject
{
    id start;
    id end;
}
+ (id) connector;
+ (id) connectorFrom:(id)anObject to:(anObject);
- (id) init;
- (void) setStart:(id)aStart;
- (void) setEnd:(id)anEnd;
- (id) start;
- (id) end;
- (float) length;
- (void) drawSelf;
@end
```

The following line in Example 4-2 begins the class interface:

```
@interface Connector : NSObject
```

This line tells the compiler that we're about to define the Connector class and that the Connector class *inherits* from the NSObject class. This means that each instance of the Connector class has a copy of the same variables that the NSObject objects have, and that they respond to the same messages as other

NSObject instances. Connector objects also have additional variables and methods, as defined by the programmer who created the class. We'll discuss inheritance in greater detail a bit later.

The next two lines in the example define the instance variables (start and end) that every Connector object contains.

The block of lines that begins with plus signs (+) and minus signs (-) defines the class and instance methods of the class. Those lines beginning with plus signs are class methods; you send the corresponding message to the Connector class itself. Those beginning with minus signs are *instance methods*; they are invoked by messages sent to class instances. Following the plus or minus sign is a C-style cast that shows the type that will be returned when the method runs. If no type is declared, (id) is assumed (it's the default).

 You can have class and instance methods with the same name; the Objective-C runtime system automatically figures out if you are sending a message to a class or to an instance of that class.

Let's skip over the class methods for now and focus on the instance methods. The **init** method should be familiar by now: that's the method that initializes an instance of the Connector class that's been allocated with the **alloc** method. The methods **setStart:**, **setEnd:**, **start**, and **end** are all accessor methods: they allow you to set and inspect the values of the Connector's instance variables. The **length** method returns a floating-point value that corresponds to the distance between the centers of two objects. Finally, the **drawSelf** method can be sent to the Connector to ask it to draw itself.

The #import Directive

Did you notice that Example 4-2 started with an #import preprocessor directive, instead of the more traditional ANSI C #include? This was not a misprint.

The Objective-C #import statement is similar to C's #include statement, but with an improvement: if the file specified in the #import statement has already been #import-ed, that file doesn't get #import-ed a second time. This is an incredibly useful feature, because it avoids all sorts of "kludges" for which C #include files are notorious. Here is an example of the type of kludge we mean:

```
/* kludge.h:
 * A kludgy C #include file
 */
#ifndef __KLUDGE__
#define __KLUDGE__
...
/* code that we wanted to include, but just once */
...
#endif
```

ANSI C #include files typically check to see whether some symbol (in this case, __KLUDGE__) is defined and, if it is not, define the symbol and process the rest of the #include file. This methodology is both inefficient and dangerous. It is inefficient because every #include file is typically processed numerous times. It is dangerous because different files can inadvertently have the same __KLUDGE__ symbol defined, which causes one of the files to prevent the contents of the other file from being processed.

Objective-C's #import statement actually does what programmers want done—it reads in the contents of the file if the file has not previously been read. With Objective-C, the previous example could be rewritten as simply:

```
#import <kludge.h>
```

Destroying Objects

When you are done using a piece of memory, it is polite to return the memory to the computer so that it can use that memory for other purposes. Well, it's more than polite—if you don't free memory when you're done using it, your program will require more and more memory over time, and eventually it will run out of memory and crash. Let's look at how that problem is handled in several programming environments:

C/C++

In ANSI C, memory that is alloc-ed with malloc( ) or calloc( ) is freed with the free( ) function. C++ uses new to create new objects and delete to free them. If you are a programmer who is using these languages, you need to manually keep track of all of your memory; when you no longer need a piece of memory, it's your responsibility to free it. That's not much of a problem for simple programs, but it can be a problem when objects are created in one part of your application and used in another part; frequently, objects end up never being freed, or being freed multiple times. If either of these things happens in a C or C++ program, the program will eventually crash.

Java

In contrast, the Java programming language does not have an explicit way to free memory. Instead, it has a garbage-collection system that automatically frees objects when they are no longer referenced anywhere in the running program. This eliminates the memory-management problems inherent in C and C++, but it creates a new class of problems. Garbage collection is almost impossible to implement efficiently, and it's easy for a programmer to make a relatively minor mistake that prevents memory from *ever* being freed. Just ask any Java programmer!

Objective-C

Cocoa has a third approach to memory management that is a hybrid of these two approaches. When you write a Cocoa program with Objective-C, each part of the application needs to notify the underlying system when it is using an object and when it is finished with an object. The underlying system maintains a reference count for each object, which keeps track of whether any other part of your program is using the same object. When the final part of your program releases the object, the object is automatically freed. From here on, we'll concentrate on this approach.

When Objective-C objects are initialized, they are given a reference count of 1. When you're done using an Objective-C object, you send it a **release** message. This message causes the object to decrement its reference count. If the reference count is decremented to 0, it's time to free the object. In this case, the Cocoa runtime system sends the object a **dealloc** message.

The **dealloc** method is similar to C's free( ) function: send an object the **dealloc** message and the memory associated with the object is freed—the object literally frees itself. But as a Cocoa programmer, you will never send the **dealloc** message to an object. You just send **release** messages.

The reverse of the **release** message is the **retain** message. This is the message that you send to an object to increment its reference count. If you create an Objective-C object that is going to be working with another object, that first object should **retain** the id of the second object. This will prevent the second object from being inadvertently **dealloc**-ed somewhere else in the program.

Let's see this process in action. Remember the Connector class from Example 4-2? The Connector class draws a line from one object to a second object. What's particularly clever about the Connector class is that it doesn't know where it's located—it simply knows the objects to which it is connected. It then asks each of these objects their position to determine where it should draw its line.

To set up a connector between the objects circle1 and circle2, we might create a snippet of code that looks something like this:

```
Connector *aConnector = [[Connector alloc] init];

[aConnector setStart:circle1];
[aConnector setEnd:circle2];
```

The implementation of the **setStart:** method might have a code fragment that looks like this:

```
start = [anObject retain];
```

When the **retain** message is sent, the reference count on the object pointed to by the variable anObject will be incremented. The id of this object will then be assigned to the variable start, which is an instance variable within an instance of the Connector class.

When the instance of the Connector class finishes working with this object, it will release it with a line of code that looks like this:

```
[start release];
```

When the **release** method is called, the reference count is decremented. If it is 0, the object will automatically be sent a **dealloc** message, which will cause the object to be freed. Remember, you should never send the **dealloc** message yourself.

The @implementation Directive

Objective-C uses the @implementation directive to tell the compiler that the following methods are method implementations. Implementations are stored in files that have the extension .m. The syntax of these files is somewhat similar to the syntax of the class interface files. Example 4-3 contains an excerpt of a sample Connector.m implementation file.

Example 4-3. The Connector.m file, our first try

```
/* Connector.m:
 * The implementation of the Connector class
 */

#import "Connector.h"

@implementation Connector

-(void)setStart:(id)anObject
{
    start = [anObject retain];
}

-(void)setEnd:(id)anObject
{
    end = [anObject retain];
}

@end
```

Following the @implementation directive are the actual class methods that are being defined. The two methods in Example 4-3 each begin with a minus sign (-), indicating that they are instance methods. In fact, these methods are accessor methods, designed to set the values of the start and end instance variables.

At the end of the class methods, there is a line containing the @end directive. This tells the compiler that you are done defining methods.

When your program is running, the Objective-C system knows to run these snippets of code if the **setStart:** or **setEnd:** message is sent to a Connector object (that is, an instance of the Connector class).

These methods are pretty good, but they both contain a significant bug: they can leak memory if they are ever called a second time. This is because both the **setStart:** method and the **setEnd:** method discard the old values for the start and end variables without first releasing them. So a better implementation for these methods might look like this:

```
@implementation Connector

-(void)setStart:(id)anObject
{
    [start release];
    start = [anObject retain];
}

-(void)setEnd:(id)anObject
{
    [end release];
    end = [anObject retain];
}

@end
```

(Notice that the newly added code is highlighted in bold; this is a convention that we will use throughout this book when we mix "old" code with "new" code to be inserted.)

Because the **setStart:** and **setEnd:** methods retain the object that is passed in as an argument, it is important that this object be released when it is no longer needed. We can force the Connector to do this by overriding the **dealloc** method in the Connector class:

```
-(void)dealloc
{
    [start release];
    [end   release];
    [super release];
}
```

This method will release the variables start and end, then call [**super release**]. This expression passes the **release** message to the superclass of the Connector class—that is, the class from which the Connector class is derived. We don't yet know what that class is—that information is contained in the Connector class interface definition.

What about the **length** method? This is a method that returns the length of the connector, or the distance between the two objects. It's not an accessor method, because there is no length instance variable. In fact, the Connector class has no idea where the connector object is actually located; this information is stored in the objects pointed to by the start and end instance variables.

One way to implement the **length** method is like this:

```
- (float) length
{
    float dx = [start x]-[end x];
    float dy = [start y]-[end y];
    return sqrt(dx*dx+dy*dy);
}
```

As you learn to program in Objective-C, you'll discover that it is common to implement one method by having the method send other messages.

The +alloc Method and the NSObject Root Class

In the previous example, there is an important method that the Connector class responds to that you do not see in the interface file. That method is the **+alloc** method—the method that creates new objects (or instances) of the Connector class. The plus sign (+) means that it's a *class* method—a method that is invoked by a message you send to the Circle class itself, rather than to an instance of the class.

The Connector and Circle classes do not have their own **+alloc** methods. Instead, they inherit this method from their common superclass, the NSObject class. We won't show the entire interface NSObject root class because it's pretty big, but here is a small portion of it:

```
@interface NSObject
{
    Class       isa;
}

+ (void)initialize;
- (id)init;

+ (id)new;
+ (id)allocWithZone:(NSZone *)zone;
+ (id)alloc;
- (void)dealloc;

- (id)copy;
- (id)mutableCopy;

...
@end
```

As you can see, an NSObject has a single instance variable called isa. This variable is of type Class, which is a typedef for an ANSI C structure that contains the class information for this object.

Every* class in Cocoa inherits from type NSObject, and therefore every object contains this isa pointer to its class type. Likewise, every class includes the class methods that are present in the NSObject class. The most important of these class methods is +**alloc**, which allocates new objects of the class.

The NSObject class is part of Cocoa's Foundation class library. As this book progresses, we will explain more aspects of the NSObject class and the class methods that it contains. (If you are curious, you can put down this book now and read the documentation for the NSObject class.)

NSString, NSMutableString, and NSLog

Two other important Objective-C classes that you will use often are the NSString and NSMutableString classes. These two classes allow you to construct and manipulate strings that are coded in standard 7-bit ASCII, 8-bit Unicode, 16-bit Unicode, or the traditional Macintosh coding system. These classes provide for practically everything you could ever want to do with a string, including copying it, performing string searches, creating a substring, formatting printing, and more. The vast majority of Cocoa methods that expect a string as an argument use an NSString, rather than a traditional ANSI C char *.

Because the NSString class is so widely used, Apple modified the Objective-C compiler to make it easy to create these strings. Once again, it's done with the at sign (@). Whereas ANSI C uses a pair of double quotes to create a byte array, Objective-C uses the at sign (@) followed by a pair of double quotes to create an NSString. For example:

```
char     *str = "this is an ANSI C string.";
NSString *str2 = @"this is a Cocoa string.";
```

Strings created with the NSString class are *immutable*, meaning that they cannot be changed. If you want to be able to make changes to the string after you have created it, you need to use the NSMutableString class instead. In this example, we will create a string and then append a message to it:

```
NSMutableString *str3 = [[NSString alloc] init];

[str3 appendString:"This is how you build "];
[str3 appendString:"a Cocoa String."];
```

---

* Actually, virtually every Objective-C class inherits from NSObject. There are a few special-purpose classes that do not, but these classes are not important for the purpose of this discussion.

The Cocoa NSString class has nearly a dozen different initializers that allow you to create an initial string from another string, from traditional ANSI C strings, and even from printf-style formats. Consider these examples:

```
NSString *str4 = [[NSString alloc] initWithString:@"a String"];

NSString *str5 = [[NSString alloc] initWithCString:"a C String"];

NSString *str5 = [[NSString alloc] initWithFormat:@"3+3=%d",3+3];
```

If you want to print the value of an NSString, you should use the NSLog( ) function. This function is similar to the ANSI C printf function, but with three important differences:

- Instead of taking a char * as its first argument, it takes an NSString *.
- In addition to the standard printf formats, it understands %@ to print the object's description.[*]
- In addition to printing the requested format, it also prints the date and time.

Example 4-4 shows a small program that illustrates both string processing and the NSLog( ) function:

Example 4-4. A small example of NSString

```
#import <Cocoa/Cocoa.h>

int main(int argc,char **argv)
{
    int i;

    for (i=1;i<5;i++) {
        NSString *str1 = [[NSString alloc]
                        initWithFormat:@"%d + %d = %d",  i, i, i+i];

        NSLog(@"str1 is '%@'",str1);
        [str1 release];
    }
    return(0);
}
```

Type in this program and save it in a file called adder.m. You can then compile the program as follows:

```
localhost> cc -o adder adder.m -framework Cocoa
localhost>
```

---

[*] In the case of the NSString class, the description of an object is simply the contents of the string. For other classes, the description of an object might be a human-readable form of its class name, the object's location in memory, and some instance variables. You can control how instances of a class will display in an NSLog( ) format by overriding the class's description method. This method returns an NSString object.

Then you can run it:

```
localhost> ./adder
2002-02-13 08:27:10.752 adder[3004] str1 is '1 + 1 = 2'
2002-02-13 08:27:10.753 adder[3004] str1 is '2 + 2 = 4'
2002-02-13 08:27:10.753 adder[3004] str1 is '3 + 3 = 6'
2002-02-13 08:27:10.753 adder[3004] str1 is '4 + 4 = 8'
localhost>
```

autorelease and the NSAutoreleasePool Class

As a Cocoa programmer, you will frequently write methods that need to return an object. You'll also often want to create and use objects without having to worry about destroying the objects when you're done. Cocoa makes both of these tasks easy with its memory-management system.

Function calls that return objects or allocated blocks of memory are the bane of programming languages such as C and C++. This is because it isn't always clear where the objects or memory should be deallocated. Cocoa gets around this problem by having two different methods for releasing objects that have been retained—the **release** method and the **autorelease** method.

When you send an object a **release** message, the object's reference count is immediately decremented. If the reference count reaches 0, the object is sent a **dealloc** message. The **autorelease** message does not cause the object's reference count to be decremented immediately. Instead, it causes the object to be added to a list of objects in the current *autorelease pool*. Objects in the autorelease pool are sent a **release** message when the current autorelease pool is deallocated.

Rules for alloc, release, and autorelease

Memory management under Cocoa may seem complicated at first. In time, however, you will find that it is quite easy to use. Here are some rules that you will find helpful in deciding when to use the messages **retain**, **release**, and **autorelease**:

- If part of your program (e.g., a class that you write) creates an object with an **alloc** message, you must ensure that your program sends the object either a **release** or an **autorelease** message.
- The accessor methods of your classes should **release** the old instance variables and then **retain** the ids of any objects that are passed in as arguments.
- The **dealloc** method of your class should **release** all previously retained objects.

Typically, the Cocoa system creates an autorelease pool at the beginning of each pass through the event loop; this autorelease pool is released when the event is done being processed. If you're writing a function or a method that returns an object, you can autorelease and then return the object. The caller to the function then has the option of either retaining that object itself, in which case the object will not be freed, or doing nothing, in which case the object will be freed when event processing is over.

Let's see how this works in practice. Example 4-5 shows our NSString example rewritten to use the autorelease pool (NSAutoreleasePool). The pool is created before the loop starts and is released when the loop finishes executing.

Example 4-5. The NSString example rewritten to use the autorelease pool

```
#import <Cocoa/Cocoa.h>

int main(int argc,char **argv)
{
    int i;

    NSAutoreleasePool *pool = [[NSAutoreleasePool alloc] init];
    for (i=1;i<5;i++) {

    NSString *str2 = [NSString stringWithFormat:@"%d + %d = %d",i,i,i+i];

        NSLog(@"The value of str1 is '%@'",str2);
    }
    [pool release];
    return(0);
}
```

Notice that this line of code from Example 4-4:

```
NSString *str1 = [[NSString alloc]
                initWithFormat:@"%d + %d = %d", i, i, i+i];
```

was replaced with this line:

```
NSString *str2 = [NSString stringWithFormat:@"%d + %d = %d", i, i, i+i];
```

These lines are not equivalent. In the first case, the object pointed to by str1 is an allocated, initialized object that has a string and a reference count of 1. In the second case, the object pointed to by str2 is an allocated, initialized object with a reference count of 1, but the object's id has further been added to the NSAutoreleasePool. This code is actually equivalent to the following:

```
NSString *str2 = [[[NSString alloc]
                initWithFormat:@"%d + %d = %d",i,i,i+i]
                autorelease];
```

That is, the single method **stringWithFormat:** replaces the methods **alloc**, **initWithFormat:**, and **autorelease**. Many Foundation and Application Kit classes have class methods that return objects that have been autoreleased.

Don't worry if this seems confusing. In subsequent chapters, we'll use the autorelease system so much that it will be second nature to you by the time you're finished with this book.

Tiny.m Revisited

Now let's take another look at Tiny.m. Here is the start of the Tiny.m program:

```
/* Tiny.m
 * A tiny Cocoa application that creates a window
 * and then displays graphics in it.
 */
```

Like any well-written program, Tiny.m begins with a set of comments describing what the program does. Objective-C supports the standard ANSI C style of comments. That means that anything enclosed between a /* and a */ is a comment. Anything on a line following a double forward slash (//) is a comment as well. Thus:

```
/* This is a comment */
// This is a comment as well
```

The next line of Tiny.m imports the Cocoa header files for the Foundation and Application Kit frameworks:

```
#import <Cocoa/Cocoa.h>
```

This statement brings in the Objective-C class definitions for the entire Cocoa framework, including the Foundation and the Application Kit. Recall from earlier chapters that the *Foundation* is a collection of tremendously useful classes for managing strings, arrays, queues, and other traditional data structures. The *Application Kit* is the collection of classes that are used to display the graphical user interface; often called the *AppKit*, this framework includes the fundamental NSApplication, NSWindow, and NSView classes.

 You might think that importing such a large number of files would slow down the compilation process. In fact, it does not, because all of the Cocoa headers are precompiled. As long as you #import <Cocoa/Cocoa.h> before you do anything else in your program, the required time is practically nil.

Every Cocoa program has one, and only one, instance of the NSApplication class. It's usually created inside a function called NSApplicationMain( ) by sending **sharedApplication** messages to the NSApplication class. In our example, we will create it in the function called main( ).

The NSApplication object is the most crucial object in the program because it provides the framework for program execution. The NSApplication class connects the program to the Window Server, initializes the Quartz display environment for this application, and maintains a list of all of the application's windows. The NSApplication object receives events such as keypresses and mouseclicks from the Window Server and distributes them to the proper NSWindow objects, which in turn distribute the events to the proper objects inside the on-screen windows.

The NSWindow class is where the master control of your program's on-screen windows is defined. For every window that your program displays, there is an associated instance (object) of the NSWindow class inside the computer's memory. You can send messages to NSWindow objects that make the associated on-screen windows move, resize, reorder to the top of the window display list (placing themselves on top of the other windows), and perform many other operations.

The NSView class is the class that plays the most central visual role in Cocoa applications. Many of the classes in the AppKit inherit from the NSView class. NSView objects are responsible for drawing in windows and receiving events. Each NSView object can contain any number of NSView objects, called *subviews*. When a window receives a mouse event, it automatically finds the correct NSView object to receive that event.

You can look at the interface (#include) file NSView.h in the /System/Library/Frameworks/AppKit.framework/Headers folder if you are interested in seeing the names and arguments of the methods that the NSView class implements. In fact, all of Cocoa's Application Kit framework classes have interface (.h) files in the same folder. Because you will frequently refer to its contents, you may want to create a shortcut to this folder from your computer's root folder. For convenience, we'll use such a shortcut—from now on we'll use the notation /AppKit/ filename.h to stand for the file /System/Library/Frameworks/ AppKit.framework/Headers/filename.h.

You can also view the documentation for the Foundation and AppKit frameworks on your hard disk using PB and on Apple's web site.

The Objective-C program Tiny.m consists of a function called main( ), which is called by the operating system to start the program. The main( ) function in Tiny.m isn't very complicated. Here it is:

```
int main( )
{
    // create the autorelease pool
    NSAutoreleasePool *pool = [[NSAutoreleasePool alloc] init];

    // create the application object
    NSApp = [NSApplication sharedApplication];
```

```
    // set up the window and drawing mechanism
    setup( );

    // run the main event loop
    [NSApp run];

    // we get here when the window is closed

    [pool release];                    // release the pool
    return(EXIT_SUCCESS);
}
```

The first statement in the main( ) function creates an NSAutoreleasePool, which is used by Cocoa's garbage-collection system.

After the autorelease pool is created, the program allocates an NSApplication object by sending the **alloc** message to the NSApplication class (every Cocoa program must have exactly one NSApplication object). This object is created with the **sharedInstance** method, which automatically allocates an NSApplication object, initializes it, and adds the object to the autorelease pool. The id of this object is then assigned to the global id variable NSApp. Global variables are a rarity in Cocoa for style and software-engineering reasons, but it makes sense to be able to send messages to the NSApplication object from any part of the program because of its crucial role.

 The name "NSApp" violates the convention that class names start with capital letters while variables that point to objects start with lowercase letters; alas, NSApp is a very special object!

The second statement in main( ) calls the function setup( ), which contains the code that makes the Tiny program unique. We'll discuss this function in detail in the next section.

The third statement, [**NSApp run**], is a message to the NSApplication object to run the program's main event loop. The *event loop* is a system that usually sits idle, waiting to respond to the user's pressing a key on the keyboard or moving or clicking the mouse. It can also respond to timed and internal events. The event loop is part of the NSApplication class—you never see it or have to do much with it. Unlike event loops in some other window systems, Cocoa's are mostly automatic. The event loop terminates when the NSApp object is sent an **NSApp** or **stop:** message; this usually happens when the user chooses the Quit menu command. The **NSApp** message causes NSApp to call exit( ), terminating the program. The **stop:** message causes [**NSApp run**] to exit. This distinction can be useful for advanced Cocoa programming, as we'll see later in this book.

The next line in Tiny.m frees the autorelease pool. Although you don't strictly need to do this—the underlying operating system will automatically free those resources when the application exits—it's good programming style to free memory that you no longer need.

Windows, Views, Delegates, and the setup( ) Function

Now it's time to look at the workhorse of Tiny.m, the setup( ) function. We'll try to digest it in pieces. Here is the first part of the function:

```
NSWindow *myWindow = nil;
NSView   *myView  = nil;
NSRect    graphicsRect;

// now create the window

graphicsRect = NSMakeRect(100.0, 350.0, 400.0, 400.0);
```

The first two lines set up local variables that will be used to hold the ids of the NSWindow and NSView objects that will be created. They are initialized to nil, which is a pointer to the empty object. (That is, it is a pointer to 0; messages sent to nil are ignored.) The third line creates a local variable that will hold the location on the screen where Tiny.m will draw its window.

The Cocoa Foundation provides three C typedefs for doing graphics (NSPoint, NSSize, and NSRect), which are defined in the following code. If you're interested, you can find their declarations in the file NSGeometry.h in the /System/Library/Frameworks/Foundation.framework/Headers directory (we'll refer to this file as /Foundation/NSGeometry.h).

```
typedef struct _NSPoint {
    float x;
    float y;
} NSPoint;

typedef struct _NSSize {
    float width;        /* should never be negative */
    float height;       /* should never be negative */
} NSSize;

typedef struct _NSRect {
    NSPoint origin;
    NSSize size;
} NSRect;
```

The function NSMakeRect( ) is simply a convenient shorthand for creating a rectangle that has a particular origin and size. Instead of using this:

```
graphicsRect = NSMakeRect(100.0, 350.0, 400.0, 400.0);
```

we could have used:

```
graphicsRect.origin.x =      100.0;
graphicsRect.origin.y =      350.0;
graphicsRect.size.width =    400.0;
graphicsRect.size.height =   400.0;
```

The graphicsRect contains the details of where the new window will be located and how big it will be. The window itself gets created in the next Tiny.m program line, when the **alloc** message is sent to the NSWindow class (recall that **alloc** is a class method). The new instance object is then initialized within the nested **initWithContentRect:styleMask:backing:defer:** message. The id of the new NSWindow object that is created is assigned to the variable myWindow:

```
myWindow = [ [NSWindow alloc]
            initWithContentRect: graphicsRect
                      styleMask: NSTitledWindowMask
                                 |NSClosableWindowMask
                                 |NSMiniaturizableWindowMask
                        backing: NSBackingStoreBuffered
                          defer: NO ];
```

One of the many nice features of Cocoa's Objective-C interface is that arguments are labeled, which makes Objective-C programs easy to read. In the example above, the four arguments are **initWithContentRect:**, **styleMask:**, **backing:**, and **defer:**. After each colon are the arguments themselves.

Let's look at each of the arguments:

initWithContentRect: *graphicsRect*

Specifies where the window will be created and how large it will be. In this case, the location of the lower-left corner is at (100.0,350.0) and the size is 400 pixels square. (The screen origin—the point (0.0,0.0)—is the pixel at the lower-left corner of the Mac OS X screen.)

style: *NSTitledWindowMask|NSClosableWindowMask| NSMiniaturizableWindowMask*

Tells the Window Server to display the window with a title bar, a close button, and a miniaturize button. (The vertical bar is the Objective-C bitwise OR operator, which causes the bits within the numerical constants to be OR-ed together.) Most Mac OS X windows have title bars that contain titles. To set up a window without a title bar, omit the NSTitledWindowMask argument. These and other window attributes are defined in the file /Appkit/NSWindow.h.

backing: *NSBackingStoreBuffered*

Specifies which kind of backing to use. Windows can have three kinds of backing: retained, buffered, or none. Retained backing means that visible portions of the window that a program draws are written directly to screen memory, but that an off-screen buffer is set up to retain nonvisible portions that are obscured by other windows. Thus, if the window is covered by another window and then exposed, the Window Server can redraw it without any work on the part of your program. Buffered windows use the off-screen buffer as an input buffer, and the buffer's contents are transferred to the screen when the window is flushed. Windows with no backing have no off-screen memory; if they are covered and then exposed, they must be redrawn, and might momentarily flash white while that redrawing takes place. Buffered windows are most common in Cocoa.

defer: *NO*

Tells the Window Server that we want our window created right away, rather than later.

Pass Small Structures, Not Pointers to Structures

Cocoa frequently passes entire structures on the stack as arguments to functions and methods, whereas other frameworks more often will pass pointers to structures. In the previous example, for instance, the entire graphicsRect structure, rather than a pointer, is passed.

Even though it's faster to push a pointer on to the stack than to push the entire structure, once the structure is on the stack, the called subroutine can access the structure's element very quickly. By contrast, if a pointer is pushed onto the stack, referencing each element requires a pointer de-reference.

If the called function is going to access every element of the structure, it is considerably faster to push the entire structure onto the stack. And as added benefits, passing complete structures on to the stack results in cleaner code, eases memory management, and improves threading.

Remember, all of these arguments make up a single Objective-C method, whose proper name is **initWithContentRect:styleMask:backing:defer:**.

Unlike in C++, you cannot leave off an argument and get a default value!

After the long myWindow statement executes, the myWindow variable contains the id of the window created with the attributes provided. We can then send messages to the window by sending messages to that id, as we do in the next statement. The following message sets the window's title to the string "Tiny Application Window". The at-sign directive, @"", tells the compiler to create an NSString object with the text "Tiny Application Window", rather than creating a char * string:

```
[myWindow setTitle: @"Tiny Application Window"];
```

The next four statements in `Tiny.m` create an object of the NSView class and set up the window for drawing. We need to describe the NSView class before we can discuss these statements thoroughly.

Views

The NSView class and its subclasses are the primary mechanism by which Cocoa users and applications interact. To draw on the screen, an application invokes NSView instance methods to establish communication with the Window Server and then sends the NSView instance Quartz drawing commands. Going the other way, the AppKit will send a message to an object of the NSView class when the user does something which creates an event, like clicking the mouse or pressing a key on the keyboard.

NSView objects represent rectangular chunks of screen real estate inside a window. Many of the interesting Cocoa objects—sliders, buttons, matrices, and so on—are instances of NSView subclasses. Programmers use the NSView class by subclassing it. NSView is an *abstract superclass*; it contains the functionality that many other classes need and therefore inherit, but instances of the NSView class itself are rarely used.

One of the most important methods in the NSView class is **drawRect:**, which is invoked when its containing view (or window) wants your view to draw itself. (Cocoa invokes the **drawRect:** method automatically for you.)

For this example, we created a subclass of the NSView class called Demo-View. This subclass adds no instance variables to what it inherits but it does override NSView's **drawRect:** method with a new one that draws the fancy design shown in Figure 4-1. Here is the interface for the DemoView class:

```
@interface DemoView : NSView
{
}
- (void)drawRect:(NSRect)rect;
@end
```

This class is referenced by the last four lines of the setup( ) function, as follows:

```
// create the DemoView for the window
myView =[[[DemoView alloc] initWithFrame:graphicsRect]
                        autorelease];
[myWindow setContentView:myView ];
[myWindow setDelegate:myView ];
[myWindow makeKeyAndOrderFront: nil];
```

The first of these four statements contains nested messages that create and initialize the DemoView object called myView. The second statement sets up the myView that we've just created as the *content view* of the NSWindow object that we created earlier. Every window contains precisely one content view, which represents the area of the window that is accessible to the application. That is, the content view contains the entire window except the title bar, border, and scroller (if present). The **setContentView:** method also changes the offset and the size of the myView object that we created, so that it is precisely aligned with the window.

The third statement, [**myWindow setDelegate:myView**], delegates to the myView object the responsibility of responding to certain messages sent to the myWindow object. One such message is **windowWillClose:**; we'll see how it works shortly.

The final statement sends the **makeKeyAndOrderFront:** message to myWindow. This message forces myWindow to be displayed in front of (on top of) all the other on-screen windows and makes it the *key* window, or the window that accepts keyboard events. The argument nil doesn't do anything here; it's just a placeholder. The reason that the **makeKeyAndOrderFront:** method contains the argument is so that it can be used with IB.

 As we noted earlier, the **makeKeyAndOrderFront:** message in this example does not result in the window's being brought to the front of the view screen. We think that this is because the message is sent before the application's main event loop is running. One day we hope to have a solution to this problem. If you find the answer, please send it to us and we'll post it on the O'Reilly web site.

Drawing with Quartz Inside a View Object

The actual drawing of the fancy pattern shown in Figure 4-1 happens in the DemoView **drawRect:** method. The drawing code in this example is not optimized in any way, but for now it will do.

The [**myView drawRect:**] message is invoked (called) automatically when the DemoView is first displayed on the screen. This method executes the following code:

```
#define X(t) (sin(t)+1) * width * 0.5
#define Y(t) (cos(t)+1) * height * 0.5

- (void)drawRect:(NSRect)rect
{
    double f,g;
    double const pi = 2 * acos(0.0);
    int n = 31;

    float width  = [self bounds].size.width;
    float height = [self bounds].size.height;
```

```
    // clear the background

    [[NSColor whiteColor] set];
    NSRectFill([self bounds]);

    // these lines trace two polygons with n sides
    // and connect all of the vertices with lines

    [[NSColor blackColor] set];

    for (f=0; f<2*pi; f+=2*pi/n) {
      for (g=0; g<2*pi; g+=2*pi/n) {
        NSPoint p1 = NSMakePoint(X(f),Y(f));
        NSPoint p2 = NSMakePoint(X(g),Y(g));

        [NSBezierPath strokeLineFromPoint:p1 toPoint:p2];
      }
    }
}
```

The variables width and height are set up to be the width and height of the myView object. We get these values by invoking the **bounds** method on the current object ([**self bounds**]). This returns the exact size of the area in which the myView object is allowed to draw.

Because the coordinate systems of NSViews can be scaled and translated, Cocoa provides two methods for determining the current size of each NSView. The message [**self bounds**] returns the size of the NSView in its own coordinate system, whereas the message [**self frame**] returns the size of the NSView in the coordinate system of its containing view. If this sounds confusing, don't worry: we'll explain coordinate systems in considerably more detail in Chapters 14 and 15.

The next statement sets the current drawing color to whiteColor. Then a built-in Mac OS X function, NSRectFill( ), is called that fills the rectangle returned in [**self bounds**] with a white background. This has the effect of making the entire myView area white. We then change the current drawing color to blackColor before drawing the lines of the pattern.

The #define statements create two macros that will be used for translating from polar to rectangular coordinates. Once these two functions are defined, we create an inner loop and an outer loop that connect all of the lines. To draw the lines we use the NSBezierPath class, which has a collection of class methods for drawing lines, circles, and Bezier paths.

This completes our discussion of the Tiny application. Don't worry if you don't understand all these statements (especially those starting with the macros) at this point.

Summary

In this chapter, we wrote a program that used Objective-C but not IB. In Chapter 3, we were limited by the tools that IB provided us: there was no way to let the programmer create loops, do math, or perform most other tasks that we associate with "programming" a computational engine. We did lots of programming in this chapter, but we had to think a lot about the mechanics of the program that IB supplied for us in Chapter 3.

The real power of the Cocoa programming environment is that it lets you *combine* IB (and PB) with Objective-C, taking advantage of what each one does best: IB for creating the interface and making connections that lead to message passing, and Objective-C for creating new classes and for the actual writing of the computational engine. Throughout the rest of this book, we'll learn how to create powerful applications while writing a relatively small amount of code.

Exercises

1. Rework the DemoView class in Tiny.m so that the program draws a series of concentric squares or circles.
2. Read the header files for /AppKit/NSColor.h and modify DemoView so that the drawing appears in many different colors.
3. Read the header files for /AppKit/NSStringDrawing.h and add text to the DemoView display.

References

1. Objective-C:

   http://developer.apple.com/techpubs/macosx/Cocoa/ObjectiveC/AppendixA/
2. *Object-Oriented Programming: An Evolutionary Approach,* by Brad J. Cox and Andrew J. Novobilski (Addison Wesley)
3. *Objective-C: Object-Oriented Programming Techniques,* by Lewis J. Pinson and Richard S. Wiener (Addison Wesley)

Calculator: Building a Simple Application

Part II, Chapters 5 through 9, is focused on building a simple application—a calculator—which we extend piece by piece through these chapters.

- Chapter 5, *Building a Project: A Four-Function Calculator*
- Chapter 6, *Nibs and Icons*
- Chapter 7, *Delegation and Resizing*
- Chapter 8, *Events and Responders*
- Chapter 9, *Darwin and the Window Server*

Building a Project:
A Four-Function Calculator

In this chapter, we'll build a simple Calculator application with four functions: add, subtract, multiply, and divide. When we're done, our Calculator will contain the menu and window shown in Figure 5-1. In the process of building the Calculator, we'll learn about Interface Builder, connections, and some of the commonly used Cocoa Application Kit (AppKit) classes.

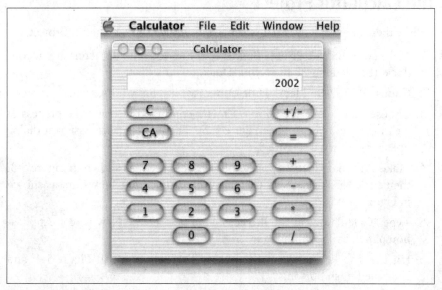

Figure 5-1. Calculator application window and menu bar

We've chosen to build a calculator as the first "real" application in this text for several reasons. First, calculators are familiar; we've all used one, and we sort of know how they work. (When creating an application, the first thing to understand is the problem you need to solve.) Second, calculators are useful. As programmers, we're constantly having to do silly little things like add two numbers together or convert a number from decimal to hexadecimal (the hex part will be built in Chapter 7). It's a tool that you can put to work after you build it.

More importantly, a calculator is a good starting point for budding Cocoa developers. In subsequent chapters, we'll use the Calculator as an infrastructure for learning about Cocoa graphics, printing, multiple windows, file handling, and many other features.

Creating your own calculator puts you in charge of its design. After all, there are many kinds of calculators: some are scientific, some are financial, and some are just simple four-function calculators. Our Calculator will let you key in the sequence "3+4=" by clicking four buttons in a window. The Calculator will display (in order) 3, 3, 4, and 7 in a text output area. If you don't like the decisions we've made and want to change or add functions and features, go right ahead! Our aim is to give you the know-how to create your own applications.

Getting Started: Building the Calculator Project

Follow these steps carefully to get started building your Calculator project:

Project Builder

Interface Builder

1. Make sure that the Project Builder and Interface Builder icons are in your dock, then launch PB from your Dock.

2. Choose Project Builder → Hide Others to simplify your screen.

3. Choose PB's File → New Project menu command to begin the process of creating a new project (see Figure 5-2). The New Project Assistant dialog opens, as shown in Figure 5-3.

4. Make sure that Cocoa Application is highlighted, as shown in Figure 5-3, then click Next. The New Cocoa Application dialog shows up, as shown in Figure 5-4.

5. Type "Calculator" in the Project Name field of the New Cocoa Application panel, as shown in Figure 5-4.

6. Hit the Tab key to fill in the second line, as shown in Figure 5-4, and click the Finish button.

PB's main window for the Calculator project opens; it should look similar to the window in Figure 5-5.

The main window in PB contains several buttons. The four buttons that look like tools (hammer, whiskbroom, etc.) at the left of the window just below its title bar are "action" buttons that can build, clean, run, and debug your project. The five disabled (dimmed) buttons near the top-right corner of the window are used with the debugger (as discussed in the section "Using gdb in

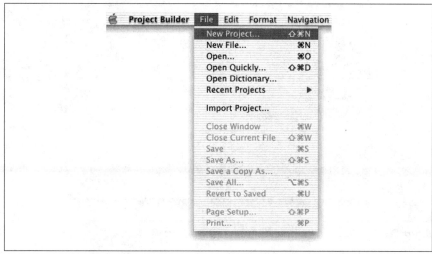

Figure 5-2. Choose PB's File → New Project command to create a new project

Figure 5-3. New Project Assistant in PB

Project Builder, Step by Step" in Chapter 2). Going from left to right, these debug buttons allow you to pause execution, continue execution, step *over* the method or function call, step *into* the method or function call, and step *out of* the current method or function call. Descriptions of the buttons pop up as you move the mouse over them.

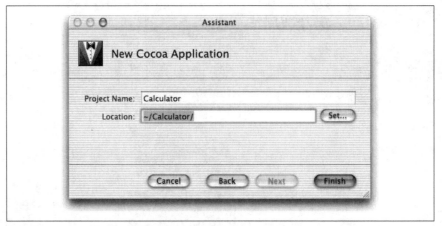

Figure 5-4. Providing the name and location for a project

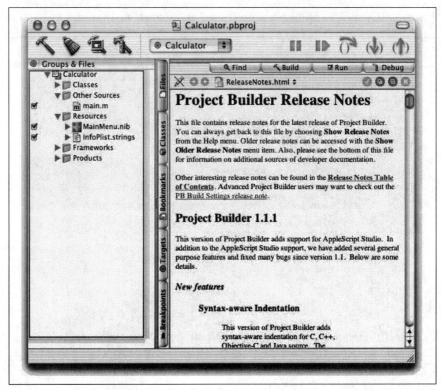

Figure 5-5. Main window in PB

The rest of the PB main window is divided into two sets of tabbed views. The vertical set of tabs controls what is seen in the lefthand pane of the window.

This pane (or view) can display one of five different types of information:

- The files in your project
- The classes in your project
- The bookmarks that you have set in your project
- The build targets
- Any debugging breakpoints that you may have set

The horizontal tabs near the righthand side of PB's main window display either the Find feature, the Build output, the Run (logged) output, or the Debugger output in the pane that opens above the tabs. Finally, the lower-right corner of PB's main window is where you can browse or edit a file. The first file that is displayed when you create a new project is the Project Builder Release Notes. Normally, you would edit your source code or display Help or AppKit headers in this (text) pane.

When you first see PB's main window, the Files tab is highlighted and groups for five types of files (Classes, Other Sources, etc.) associated with your project are shown. You can click the little gray disclosure triangles next to the labels in this Groups & Files pane to show the names of the files in your project. We'll discuss these different file types later, in "The Files in a Project."

7. Click the disclosure triangle to the left of the Resources label in the Groups & Files pane to reveal the `MainMenu.nib` and `InfoPlist.strings` files, as shown in Figure 5-5.

   The checks (☑) next to these files in the target column (◉) at the left of PB's main window mean that the files are part of the Calculator target.

8. Double-click the `MainMenu.nib` file icon in PB's main window.

IB will launch and display the `MainMenu.nib` interface that was automatically created by PB when we created a new Cocoa application. This interface includes a main menu titled "MainMenu" and a main window titled "Window". An associated Nib File window is also displayed in the lower-left corner of the screen, below the new menu.

Interface Builder

9. To simplify the screen, choose Interface Builder → Hide Others.

   Your screen should contain the same objects as the one shown in Figure 5-6 (although probably not in the exact same location, and the Palettes window may show a different palette).

Building the Calculator's User Interface

The `MainMenu.nib` file created by PB and opened in IB above is called, aptly enough, a *nib file* (nib stands for *NeXT Interface Builder*—a holdover from the

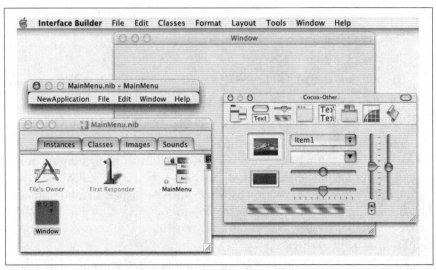

Figure 5-6. IB with the MainMenu.nib file for the Calculator project opened

pre-Apple life of this development environment). A nib file stores information about all of the user interface objects in your program, including the windows, controls, and menus; the connections between those objects; and some other objects that IB knows about. When you compile and link the application you are building, the application's nib file (or files, if the program uses more than one) gets bundled together with the program's executable code and stored in a package, or *app wrapper*, folder. This folder has a .app extension and looks like an executable application in the Finder.

The nib files are stored in an undocumented Cocoa proprietary binary format. Fortunately, it doesn't need to be documented—all of the nib-file management is done by IB. IB is basically a nib editor: when it opens a nib file, it reads the specifications and displays the associated objects. After you make your modifications to the program, IB writes out a new nib file, replacing the old one.

Now that we've created the project, we'll add and customize the windows, panels, and menus needed for our Calculator's user interface.

Customizing the Main Window

The main window in the Calculator's interface, currently titled "Window", doesn't look anything like a calculator: it's the wrong shape, it shouldn't have a resize handle, and it doesn't even have the right name! Fortunately, these are all properties that we can easily change by using IB's NSWindow Info dialog.

To see this Info dialog for a particular window, you must first select the window by either clicking in its background or clicking on its icon in the Nib File window's Instances pane. If you click on an object (e.g., a button) inside a window object in IB, the button, not the window, will be selected.

In general, the title and contents of IB's Info dialog change in response to which object in the interface is selected. When the Info dialog changes in response to a selection, you may still have to choose which aspect of the object you want to inspect: its attributes, its connections, or something else. You can make this choice by dragging to it in the Info dialog's pop-up menu or by typing Command-1 for Attributes, Command-2 for Connections, and so on.

Next, we'll go through the steps to customize our Calculator's window in IB.

1. Select the newly created empty window in IB by clicking in its background.

2. Choose Tools → Show Info to display the NSWindow Info dialog. If necessary, press the pop-up list button in the NSWindow Info dialog and select Attributes. (You can accomplish both of these actions by simply typing Command-1.)

Interface Builder

The NSWindow Info dialog should now look like the one shown on the left in Figure 5-7.

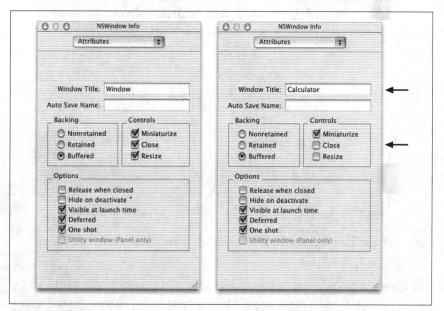

Figure 5-7. NSWindow Info dialog before (left) and after (right) changes

3. Change the title from "Window" to "Calculator" and hit Return.

4. Turn off the Close and Resize attributes in the NSWindow Info dialog's Controls box by clicking their checkboxes so the checkmarks disappear (see the resulting Info dialog on the right side of Figure 5-7—the arrows indicate where the changes were made).

Although the red close button and resize handle do not disappear from the Calculator window in IB, they will no longer be present when the application is running.

5. Resize the Calculator window so that it is about three inches square.

Adding Controls in a Window

Next, we'll drag the buttons and text display area that the Calculator application will need from IB's Palettes window into the main Calculator window:

6. Make sure the Cocoa-Views palette is visible by clicking the Views button at the top of IB's Palettes window.

7. Drag an NSTextField object from the Palettes window and drop it near the top-right corner of the Calculator window. Use the blue guidelines to position the object. (If you release the dragged object when it is near a guideline, the guide will actually grab and align the object, helping make your layout visually attractive.)

When you are finished, your window should look like the one shown on the left in Figure 5-8. A border in the current selection color surrounds the NSView object that is ready to accept the new NSTextField.

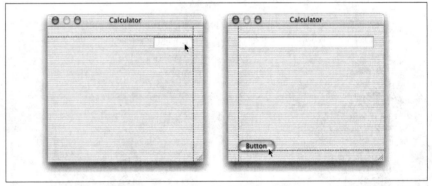

Figure 5-8. Calculator window with new text field (left) and button positioned using guidelines

8. Drag the NSTextField's left-middle selection handle to the left to widen the NSTextField object so that it is almost the width of the Calculator window, as shown in the window on the right in Figure 5-8.

9. Drag an NSButton object from the Palettes window and drop it in the lower-left corner of the Calculator window, as shown in the window on the right in Figure 5-8. Use the blue guidelines.

10. Double-click the center of the NSButton object, change the text "Button" to the digit "0", and hit Return.

11. Make the width of this button smaller by clicking the button once and then dragging the button's right-middle handle to the left until the button stops getting smaller. (When necessary, you can make buttons even smaller using the NSButton Info dialog.)

12. Make sure the cursor is positioned in the window, and press the Option key on the keyboard to see the layout information, as shown in the window on the left in Figure 5-9. Note that the guidelines gave us a 20-pixel buffer between the button and each edge near it. Release the Option key.

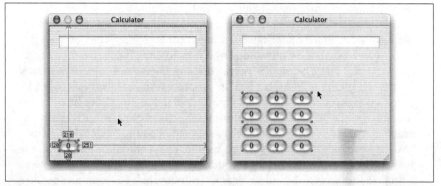

Figure 5-9. Layout information (left) and creating an NSMatrix of NSButtons (right)

Next, we'll create the Calculator's keypad, using the great power of IB!

13. While pressing the Option key on the keyboard, drag the upper-right handle of the NSButton up and to the right. Release the mouse button when there are four rows and three columns of buttons, as shown in the window on the right in Figure 5-9.

Congratulations—you've just created a matrix (NSMatrix) of buttons (NSButtons)! The NSMatrix is one of the classes provided by the Cocoa Application Kit. An NSMatrix object is a two-dimensional array containing other objects that are subclasses of the NSCell class.

Every Cocoa NSControl subclass, including NSButton, NSSlider, and NSText-Field, has an associated NSCell subclass (e.g., NSButtonCell, NSSliderCell, and NSTextFieldCell). These cell objects do the actual drawing of the controls that we put into the window. When you drag a button, slider, or text field off the IB palette and into your window, you are actually dragging out two objects—an NSControl and a corresponding NSCell.

You can also display NSCell objects in a rectangular NSMatrix. As before, the NSCell objects handle the drawing. When you drag one of the resizing handles with the Option key pressed, IB automatically converts the NSControl and its associated NSCell into an NSMatrix and a whole set of NSCell objects.

The NSControl object is used for handling events from the keyboard or mouse. IB hides this split between the NSControl and NSCell from us and makes the control and its associated cell look like a single object. This is often a source of confusion for programmers new to Cocoa.

Cells and Controls

You may wonder why Cocoa uses this combination of objects—an NSCell and an NSControl—rather than a single object. You may also wonder why the NSCell inherits directly from NSObject and is not a subclass of NSView. Certainly, it can be more complicated to implement an NSCell class because it is not a view: NSCells are commanded by a view to draw themselves at a particular location. The NSCell/NSControl division dates back to Cocoa's early days, when it ran on 25-MHz 68030 microprocessors, and was developed by Cocoa's designers because NSViews require a floating-point coordinate transformation, while NSCells do not. Drawing a matrix of buttons, such as a calculator pad, could have required literally a thousand floating-point calculations if NSCells were full-fledged views, each with its own coordinate system. So the division is largely a performance optimization. Once the optimization was developed, however, other advantages were discovered. For example, because the handling of events is separated from the drawing on the screen, with a clear partition between the two, it is easy to change one of these behaviors without affecting the other. This is not the case with other application frameworks.

Now we'll resize the NSMatrix as a whole to fit the area we want:

14. Drag the right-middle handle of the NSMatrix to the right so that the NSMatrix is almost the same width as the NSTextField. This time, all 12 of the buttons titled "0" will get wider simultaneously. (Don't worry about being exact at this point in the interface.)

NSMatrix Dragging Options in IB

When you drag a handle on a matrix object, one of three things can happen, depending on which modifier key is pressed (we saw the first two of these in the previous example):

None
> Changes the size of all cells in the matrix

Option (Alt)
> Changes the number of cells in the matrix

Command (Apple)
> Changes the spacing between cells

These values can also be changed using the NSMatrix Info dialog.

The buttons in the NSMatrix we created will be used to represent digit keys on our Calculator, and thus we'll change their names from "0" to the 10 decimal digits (and disable the remaining 2 buttons). We also need to set some less obvious attributes of the buttons, called *tags*, to make the buttons work properly. In order to explain how tags work and help you better understand why we make certain choices while creating an interface, we'll postpone finishing the interface for now to discuss the Objective-C class that we'll create to handle the button clicks.

Building the Calculator's Controller Class

It's time to start thinking about the Objective-C object that will control our Calculator—that is, respond to button clicks, calculate the values that the user wants, and display the results. By convention, this kind of object, which performs behind-the-scenes work and communicates with the user interface, is called a *Controller*.

Controllers generally don't have main event loops; instead, they perform actions in response to events that are received and interpreted by other objects. A good rule of thumb is to place as little code in your Controller as is necessary for it to do its job. If it is possible to create a second Controller that is used only for a clear, particular purpose, do so—the less complicated you make your application's objects, the easier they are to debug. In addition to controlling the overall flow of the application, Calculator's Controller will contain the code to perform the basic arithmetic and thus can be thought of as the *computational engine* or *back end* (albeit a very simple one) of the application.

Designing the Controller Class

Cocoa doesn't provide you with a Controller class—it's up to you to write one for your application. (IB and the AppKit are fabulous, but they can't do everything for you—at least not yet!)

Before you start coding, it's a good idea to sit down and think about your problem. What does the Controller have to do? What kind of messages will it need to respond to? What kind of internal state does it have to keep in order to perform those functions? Recall that we want our Calculator to allow a user to type in the sequence "2*5=" by clicking four buttons in a window and to display (in order) 2, 2, 5, and 10 in a text output area. Thus, for our Calculator, the answers are fairly straightforward.

Here's what our Calculator must do:

- Clear the display and all internal registers (value holders) when a "clear" button is clicked.
- Allow the user to click a digit button on the numeric keypad and display the corresponding digit immediately after it is typed.
- Allow the user to click a function button (e.g., "add", "subtract").
- Clear the display when the user starts entering a second number.
- Perform the appropriate arithmetic operation when the user presses the "equals" button or another function button.

Our Calculator must also maintain the following state to perform these functions:

- The first number entered
- The function button clicked
- The second number entered

It turns out that to work properly, our Controller object needs two more pieces of information:

- A flag that indicates when a function button has been clicked—if the flag is set, the text display area (which we'll call *readout*) should be cleared the next time that a digit button is clicked, because the user is entering a second number
- The location in the readout text display area where the numbers should be displayed

These bullets indicate that we are using Objective-C to create a simulation of a real, physical calculator. That's what object-oriented programming is often about: constructing progressively better simulations of physical objects inside the computer's memory, and then running them to get real work done. When the simulation is functionally indistinguishable from the real-life object being simulated, the job is finished.

Creating the Controller Class

Every Objective-C class, except NSObject, is based on (and inherits from) another class. The NSObject class itself is the most fundamental Objective-C class, because it defines the basic behavior of all objects and is at the root of all inheritance hierarchies. Because we don't need any special behavior in our Calculator other than what is already defined in the AppKit, our Controller class will be a subclass of NSObject.

We'll start building our Controller class by subclassing it from the NSObject class in IB.

1. Click the Classes tab in IB's Nib File window to view the AppKit's object hierarchy. Classes

2. Scroll to the far left in the Classes pane using the horizontal scroller at the bottom of the Nib File window, and then select the NSObject class by clicking it. (See Figure 5-10.) You can also rapidly jump to the NSObject class by typing the word "NSObject" into the Classes pane's Search field.

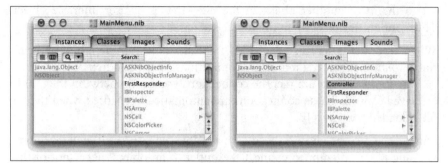

Figure 5-10. NSObject (root) class (left) and new Controller classes (right)

The NSObject class name is displayed in gray, which means that you can't change any of its properties or built-in behaviors without subclassing it. So that's what we'll have to do.

3. Click IB's Classes menu item at the top of the screen, then choose Subclass NSObject, as shown in Figure 5-11 (or simply hit the Return key when NSObject is highlighted).

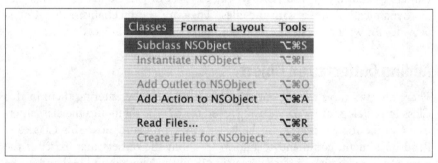

Figure 5-11. Classes menu in IB

4. A new class called MyObject will appear under NSObject in the class hierarchy.

5. Change the name from "MyObject" to "Controller", and hit Return. (See Figure 5-10.)

You've just created a new Objective-C class called Controller. Right now it doesn't do anything different from the NSObject class. Next, we'll give the Controller class some custom behavior by adding some outlets and actions.

Outlets and Connections

Cocoa uses a powerful system known as "outlets and connections" to give you an easy way to send messages between user interface objects such as windows, buttons, other controls, and your own custom objects. An *outlet* is simply an instance variable in an Objective-C class that has the type id and thus can store a pointer to an object. The value of this instance variable is usually set to the id of another object in the nib—that is, a user interface object. Thus, outlets normally point to interface objects.

When an outlet is set to store the id of another object in the nib file, IB calls this a *connection*. Cocoa maintains connections for you. When object specifications are saved in a nib file, the connections you set up between them in IB are saved as well. These connections are automatically restored when the nib file is loaded back into IB.

Outlets can also be given a specific type. When you do so, IB will give you a warning if you attempt to connect the outlet to an object that is not of that type (or a class of that type).

For example, suppose that you have two object specifications in a nib file: objects A and B. Suppose also that object A contains an outlet, or id variable, that points to object B. When Cocoa loads this nib file, it will first create new instances of object A and object B, then will automatically set the outlet in object A to point to object B; that is, it sets the outlet A to be the id of object B.

Outlets therefore give you an easy way to track down the ids of objects that are dynamically loaded with nib files. They are the mechanism that Cocoa provides for wiring up an interface in IB without writing any code.

Adding Outlets to an Object

There are two ways to add outlets to a class: either by entering them in IB's Class Info dialog, or by hand, using an editor to type them into the class interface (.h) file for your class. In the latter case, you can choose IB's Classes → Read Files menu command to inform IB about the outlets that exist for the class. We'll see how to add outlets using IB in this chapter and by hand in the next chapter.

After adding an outlet, you use IB to *initialize* where it points. You do this by setting up a connection from the object containing the outlet to the object to which you want it to point, and then choosing the outlet from the list of outlets in IB's Connections Info dialog. When you make a connection between an outlet in an object and another object in IB, IB sets the instance variable in the first object to the id of the object to which it is connected. That's all!

In the following steps, we'll add and initialize an outlet called readout in IB.

6. If necessary, select Controller in the Classes pane of IB's Nib File window.

7. Now type Command-1 to display IB's Attributes Info dialog for the Controller class. The Info dialog window should be titled "Controller Class Info".

8. Make sure that the Objective C radio button is selected in the Attributes Info dialog, as shown in Figure 5-12.

9. Click the Add button at the bottom of the Controller Class Info dialog, and the outlet called myOutlet will appear.

10. Change the name of this outlet to "readout" by typing the new name followed by Return.

If you make a mistake, you can double-click the outlet to change the name again. You can also click the Remove button to remove an outlet. When you're done, the Class Info dialog should look like the one on the right in Figure 5-12.

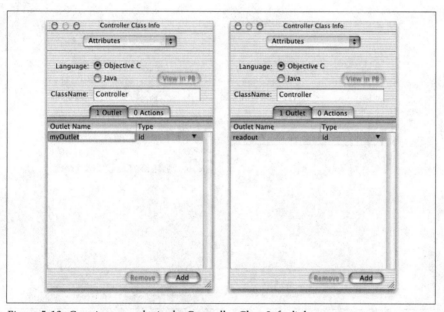

Figure 5-12. Creating an outlet in the Controller Class Info dialog

We'll eventually set the readout Controller outlet to point to the Calculator's text display area (NSTextField) object in the Calculator window. Then the Controller will be able to send messages to the NSTextField via the outlet.

Next, we'll add action methods to the Controller class.

Adding Actions to the Controller

An *action* is a special type of Objective-C method. Action methods are special because they take a single argument called *sender*, the id of the object that sent the message invoking the action method. Using IB, we can arrange for an object's action method to be invoked automatically in response to a user event, such as a button click, menu choice, or slider drag. Thus, an action method is an *event handler*.

In Chapter 3, we used the **takeIntValueFrom:** action method to make an NSTextField automatically take its value from the NSSlider object when the slider knob was moved (see Figure 3-16). Here, we'll create our own action methods in the Controller class and arrange to have them invoked when the user clicks our Calculator's buttons.

11. Click the 0 Actions tab in the Controller Class Info dialog.

12. Click the Add button at the bottom of the Controller Class Info dialog; the **myAction:** action will appear, as shown in Figure 5-13.

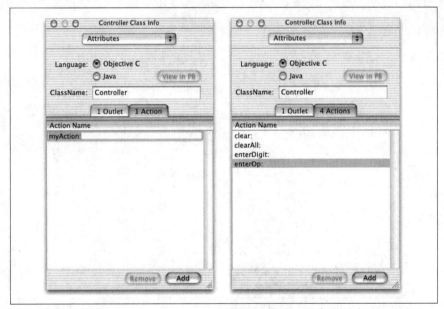

Figure 5-13. Creating an action (left) in the Controller Class Info dialog; four actions in Calculator (right)

13. Rename **myAction:** as **clear:** and hit Return.

14. Add the **clearall:**, **enterdigit:**, and **enterOp:** actions to your Controller class in a similar fashion. You don't have to type the colons (:) when renaming actions, because IB will automatically append them.

Notice that IB alphabetizes the actions as you add them. Your Controller Class Info dialog should now look like the one on the right in Figure 5-13.

In light of our discussion of the design of the Controller class, the function of these four actions should seem fairly self-evident. We'll go over the details later.

Notice that there's only one action to handle all of the digit button clicks (**enterDigit:**) and only one action to handle all of the function buttons (**enterOp:**). We'll determine which digit or function button is clicked by using the single argument of these actions, the id of the message's sender. By querying the sender of the action message, the **enterDigit:** and **enterOp:** methods can determine which digit or function button was clicked. The method will then perform the appropriate action. This is a much more economical means of method dispatch than creating a separate method for each button on our Calculator—it takes less code and it runs virtually as fast.

Creating the Controller Class Files

Now that we've set up an outlet and several actions for our Controller class, we need to tell IB to create the `Controller.h` class interface file and the `Controller.m` class implementation file. Then we'll add the appropriate functionality (code) to these class files and eventually compile them with the Objective-C compiler. IB's Create Files for Controller command in the Classes menu generates these files from the class specifications we made in the Nib File window and the Class Info dialog.

15. Make sure the Controller class is selected in the Classes pane of the Nib File window.

16. Choose Classes → Create Files for Controller.

A sheet will unfold from the Nib File window enabling you to specify the filenames for the class files to be created, as shown in Figure 5-14. Because the name of the class is Controller, the default names for the class files are `Controller.h` and `Controller.m`. After creating these class files, IB will insert them into the Calculator project.

17. Click Choose on the sheet to use the default filenames (`Controller.h`, `Controller.m`) and insert them into the Calculator project.

18. Now click the PB icon in your Dock to see how these class files fit into your project.

Project Builder

The two new files should be located in the Classes group but may be located in the Other Sources group. If you like, you can move these files from one file group to another in PB's Groups & Files pane; the organization is for your benefit only and is ignored by PB. When you have a large project, you may even want to create your own groups and subgroups of files.

Figure 5-14. Saving the Controller class files created by IB

These new Controller class files contain only a skeleton of what we want in the Controller class. To make our Controller work, we have to add some logic and write some Objective-C code.

19. Click the Finder icon in your Dock and investigate which files have been created as part of your Calculator project—there are several!

These project files reside in your ~/Calculator folder. We recommend that you compare the files in the ~/Calculator folder in the Finder with those listed in the Groups & Files pane in PB.

Adding Code to Make the Controller Class Work

To make the Controller work, we need to understand a little bit about a four-function calculator. The basic four-function calculator has three registers: an X and a Y register, both of which hold numbers, and an operations register, which holds the current operation. The readout always displays the contents of the X register. Clicking a function button stores that function in the operations register and sets a flag. If the flag is set, the next time a digit button is clicked, the number in the X register is moved to the Y register and the X register is set to 0.

We'll get the Controller class working in stages, testing them one at a time. Generally, this is a good approach to writing any program, large or small. Object-oriented programming makes it easy to test the individual parts, because they are all fairly self-contained.

First, we'll get numeric entry and the clear keys working. Later, we'll handle the arithmetic functions.

20. Back in PB, click `Controller.h` in PB's Groups & Files pane to open the file in PB's main window, as shown in Figure 5-15. (If you double-click instead of single-click `Controller.h`, a separate editor-type window will open.)

Project Builder

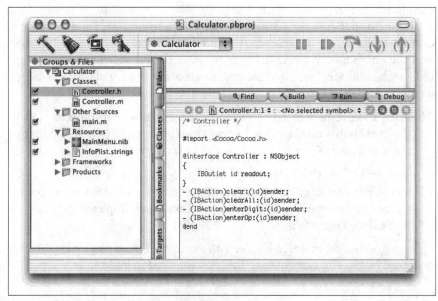

Figure 5-15. Controller.h interface file in PB

Looking at the code in PB's window (in Figure 5-15), note that the Controller class is a subclass of NSObject, as we specified in IB. Note also that Objective-C declarations have been generated for the outlet (`readout`) and the four action methods in the Controller class that you set up in IB.

Following is the `Controller.h` file. The lines generated by IB are shown in regular type, and the lines that you need to insert are shown in bold type.

Controller.h

```
/* Controller.h */

#import <Cocoa/Cocoa.h>

@interface Controller : NSObject
```

```
{
    IBOutlet id readout;
    BOOL        enterFlag;
    BOOL        yFlag;
    int         operation;
    double      X;
    double      Y;
}
- (IBAction)clear:(id)sender;
- (IBAction)clearAll:(id)sender;
- (IBAction)enterDigit:(id)sender;
- (IBAction)enterOp:(id)sender;
- (void)displayX;
@end
```

IB generated the first two (non-bold) lines because we subclassed NSObject to create the Controller class (importing <Cocoa/Cocoa.h> includes the NSObject class interface file, as well as the rest of the Cocoa classes). Because we added readout as an outlet in the Class Info dialog, IB also generated the IBOutlet id declaration for it (see the sidebar "IBOutlet and IBAction"). Finally, IB generated the four action method declarations because we added the four actions in IB's Class Info dialog. Note that the single argument for all of these action methods, sender, was generated automatically.

21. Insert the five new instance variables and one new method indicated by the lines shown earlier in bold type in the Controller.h file. We'll discuss the new **displayX** "non-action" method a bit later.

22. Save the Controller.h class file (Command-S).

23. Still in PB, double-click Controller.m in the Groups & Files pane to open a new editor-type window with the Controller implementation code inside. (See Figure 5-16.)

Following is the Controller.m file. As with the Controller.h file, we list the lines generated by IB in regular type and the lines you need to insert in bold type.

Controller.m

```
/* Controller.m */

#import "Controller.h"

@implementation Controller

- (IBAction)clear:(id)sender
{
    X = 0.0;
    [self displayX];
}

- (IBAction)clearAll:(id)sender
{
    X = 0.0;
    Y = 0.0;
```

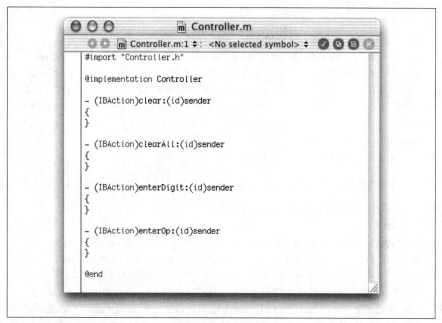

Figure 5-16. Controller.m interface file in a PB editor window

```
    yFlag = NO;
    enterFlag = NO;
    [self displayX];
}

- (IBAction)enterDigit:(id)sender
{
    if (enterFlag) {
        Y = X;
        X = 0.0;
        enterFlag = NO;
    }

    X = (X*10.0) + [ [sender selectedCell] tag];
    [self displayX];
}

- (IBAction)enterOp:(id)sender
{
}

- (void)displayX
{
    id s = [NSString stringWithFormat:@"%15.10g", X ];
    [readout setStringValue: s];
}

@end
```

IBOutlet and IBAction

IB uses the keywords IBOutlet and IBAction when it reads an Objective-C interface file to determine the outlets and actions in your Objective-C classes. The word IBOutlet tells IB that the following instance variable is an outlet. Likewise, the keyword IBAction tells IB that the following method name is an action.

Consider this example:

```
@interface ATestObject : NSObject
{
    IBOutlet id anOutlet;
}
- (IBAction)anAction:(id)sender;
@end
```

IBOutlet and IBAction are not reserved keywords in the Objective-C language. Instead, they are #define-d to have special meaning by the Cocoa #import files. The letters "IBOutlet" are actually #define-d to be nothing. Likewise, the keyword IBAction is #define-d to be the void type.

The outlet in our example can be used to point to any kind of object within an IB nib file. IB also allows the use of typed outlets. To declare a statically typed outlet, replace the "id" with the class type. For example, to tell IB that the outlet in the above example should point only to an NSWindow or subclass of an NSWindow, you could change the example to read as follows:

```
@interface ATestObject : NSObject
{
    IBOutlet NSWindow *anOutlet;
}
- (IBAction)anAction:(id)sender;
@end
```

By default, IB creates untyped outlets. You can make them typed by editing your class interface file and reading the file back into IB. An easier way is to click the down arrow (shown in Figure 5-12, to the right of id) in the Outlet pane of IB's Info dialog and choose the type from a drop-down list.

In this book, we use a combination of typed and untyped outlets.

IB generated the line that imports `Controller.h` because every class implementation file must import its own interface file. Most of the other lines generated by IB are simply stubs for the action methods that we set up in the IB's Class Info dialog. IB generates code in class files more for convenience than for any other reason.

24. Insert the code shown above in bold type into the `Controller.m` file.

25. Save the `Controller.m` class file (Command-S).

The Controller class sends messages to instances of the NSTextFieldCell and NSMatrix classes. In particular, the newly added **displayX** method displays the contents of the X register by sending the **setStringValue:** message to readout, the outlet that we created in IB. Later we'll use IB to initialize readout to point to the NSTextFieldCell object (near the top of the Calculator window).

When a message is sent to an object of a class, the class interface file definition for that class should be #import-ed in the class definition. But #import statements for the NSTextFieldCell and NSMatrix class interface file definitions are not listed in the code we've shown. What's going on? Fortunately, the `#import Controller.h` line in `Controller.m`, together with the `#import <Cocoa/Cocoa.h>` line in `Controller.h`, takes care of importing the NSTextFieldCell and NSMatrix class interface file definitions for us. In fact, they import all the Application Kit class definitions.

In Cocoa, the AppKit class headers are all precompiled, so it's quite fast to import them all, provided that `<cocoa/cocoa.h>` is imported before any symbols are #define-d. (A *precompiled* header file has been preprocessed and parsed, thereby improving compile time and reducing symbol table size.) This is why IB inserts the `#import <Cocoa/Cocoa.h>` line in all class interface files it generates.

The **clearAll:** method in the `Controller.m` file sets the X and Y registers to 0.0 and the two flags to false, and then sends the **displayX** message to self (the Controller object itself) to display 0.0 in the text display area. The **clear:** method is similar but only needs to set the X register to 0.0 and then redisplay. We'll discuss the **enterDigit:** and **enterOp:** methods after we finish setting up the user interface and making all the connections.

Customizing Buttons and Making Connections

In this section we'll use IB to add more interface specifications to the `Calculator.nib` file, including customizing buttons further and making several different types of connections between objects. In order to make connections which involve an object of the Controller class, we need a representation of it in IB.

Instantiating (Creating an Instance of) the Controller Class

Creating the Controller class isn't enough: we also need to create an object that is a member of this class, called an instance. Then we have to arrange for the numeric keypad of buttons in the Calculator window to send action messages to the instance whenever these buttons are clicked.

1. Make sure the Classes tab is displayed in IB's Nib File window (titled "MainMenu.nib"), then select the Controller class (recall that it's a subclass of NSObject). If you have trouble finding it, use the Search feature in the window.

2. Choose IB's Classes → Instantiate Controller menu command.

This will create an icon called "Controller" under the Instances tab in the Calculator's Nib File window, as shown in Figure 5-17 (IB automatically displays the Instances tab view). This icon represents an instance object of the Controller class—it can be used as the target object of action messages and also to initialize outlets. You can change the name from "Controller" to something else if you like—the name isn't used for anything except your convenience in IB. Note the little circles with exclamation marks in them next to the instances in Figure 5-17. They represent tiny alerts that can be discovered by mousing over the instances. For example, if you mouse over the Controller instance, you will discover that its readout outlet is unconnected (see Figure 5-17).

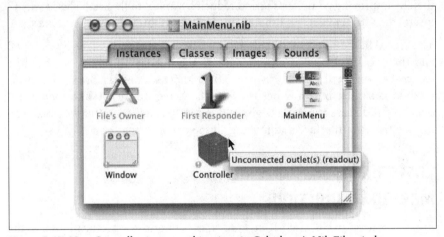

Figure 5-17. New Controller instance object icon in Calculator's Nib File window

Setting Up Tags and Titles for the Keypad Buttons

Next, we'll set the buttons on the Calculator's numeric keypad to the digits 0 through 9 and arrange for each one of them to send a message to the Controller object.

A *tag* is a reference integer for a Control object that can be set and read in IB's Info dialog. The purpose of tags is to allow your program to distinguish cells in a user interface from one another, which lets you use the same Objective-C method to handle several different but closely related functions.

To differentiate between the buttons, the Controller object will read the tag of each button.

3. Double-click the button at the upper-left corner of the matrix in the Calculator window.

   The button highlights with a darker version of your current selection color to indicate that it is selected, and the NSButtonCell Info dialog displays information about the button (see Figure 5-18).

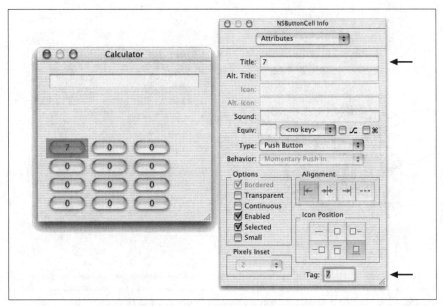

Figure 5-18. Setting the title and tag of a Calculator button in IB

4. If necessary, select Attributes in the pop-up menu in the Info dialog. Note how the window changes to show information about the selected object.

5. Change the title of the NSButton from "0" to "7" in the Info dialog and hit Return.

6. Change the tag of the NSButton to "7" at the bottom of the Info dialog and hit Return.

When the Calculator is running and one of the buttons in the matrix of digit buttons is clicked, we'll arrange for the NSMatrix object to send the **enter-Digit:** message to our Controller object. The Controller object needs to know which button (i.e., which digit) was clicked, so it will send a message back to the sender (the NSMatrix object) to determine which of the button cells in the NSMatrix object was selected. The Controller can then get the tag for that cell and use it in the **enterDigit:** method as if it were a digit (which is why we set the tags equal to the value of the NSButton).

7. Change the titles and the tags of the other keypad buttons to reflect the digits that they represent, as shown in Figure 5-19. You can use the Tab key to move between buttons in the NSMatrix, but setting the tags is a bit of a nuisance. (Make sure you set the tags properly—we've found that this is an easy place to make a mistake.)

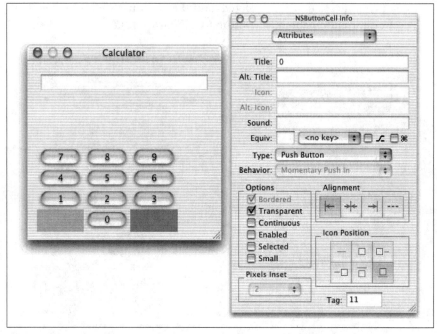

Figure 5-19. Making two buttons transparent and unenabled in IB

8. Select the lower-left button in the NSMatrix (it's invisible in Figure 5-19).

9. In the NSButtonCell Info dialog, deselect the Enabled switch to make the on-screen button in our running Calculator unclickable.

10. Now click the Transparent checkbox in the same NSButtonCell Info dialog to make the button disappear, as in Figure 5-19.

11. Repeat the previous two steps for the lower-right button, so that only 10 of the original 12 buttons in the NSMatrix are used. (See Figure 5-19.)

12. Click in the Calculator window background (where there are no buttons or text) to select the window, then click the button matrix once to select the NSMatrix as a whole.

13. Type Command-T to bring up the Font panel.

As with most Cocoa applications, IB lets you change the font family, typeface, and size of most text it displays. Here we want to change the way our application looks.

14. Choose the Lucida Grande 14-point font. (You may have noticed that if you make the text inside a standalone button too large for the button to display the information, IB automatically resizes the button. However, IB does not automatically resize the cells inside an NSMatrix if the text is too large to display. This behavior is somewhat inconsistent and may be changed in the future.)

Making the Connections

15. Connect the NSMatrix button object to the Controller instance object by pressing the Control key on the keyboard and dragging the mouse cursor from the middle of the NSMatrix to the Controller instance object icon in the Nib File window, as shown in Figure 5-20.

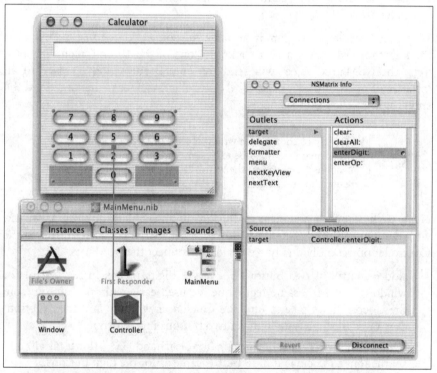

Figure 5-20. Target/action connection from NSMatrix to Controller instance

When you make the connection between the NSMatrix and the Controller instance, it is very important that you press the mouse button when the mouse cursor is over the NSMatrix and release the button when the cursor is over the Controller icon. The order matters, because the NSMatrix will be sending a message to the Controller, not the other way around. (Later in this chapter, we'll drag the connection in the other direction to accomplish something else.)

Figure 5-20 shows the resulting "connection wire" between the NSMatrix and the Controller instance icon. The small square in the middle of the NSMatrix indicates the source of the connection, while the square around the Controller instance icon indicates the target. Make sure you have connected the whole NSMatrix and not one of the individual buttons in the NSMatrix.

After you release the mouse button, IB will display the NSMatrix Info dialog (see Figure 5-20). You can determine the source object of the connection by the name in the title bar of the Info dialog—in this case, it should be "NSMatrix Info". The column in the window should include the four action methods we set up earlier in the destination object, namely the Controller instance.

16. Click the **enterDigit:** action method and then click the Connect button in the NSMatrix Info dialog. The dimple (☞) next to the method indicates that the connection was made. See the NSMatrix Info dialog at the right in Figure 5-20.

When the Calculator program is running, the connection we just made means the following: whenever a user clicks any one of the 10 on-screen digit buttons, the NSMatrix object will send the **enterDigit:** action message to an instance of our Controller class. The Controller instance is the target and the **enterDigit:** method is the action.

 It's easy to connect the wrong objects or to disconnect a connection you want, so be extremely careful when making connections and check them in IB if your application isn't responding properly.

Next, we'll add clear and clear all buttons in an NSMatrix object, as we did with the digit buttons. This time, however, we'll connect each button to the Controller object individually—we will not connect the NSMatrix.

17. Add a matrix of two buttons above the digits matrix in the Calculator window, using the same technique we used earlier (drop a button from the Cocoa-Views palette into the Calculator window and then Option-drag on a selection handle to get two buttons in a matrix).

18. Rename the two new buttons "C" (for clear) and "CA" (for clear all) and set the font to Lucida Grande 14, the same as for the digit buttons.

Your window should now look similar to the one in Figure 5-21. If you don't remember how to add a matrix to your window, refer back to "Adding Controls in a Window." If you can't find the Palettes window, choose IB's Tools → Palettes → Show Palettes menu command.

19. Double-click the CA on-screen button to select it. The NSButtonCell Info dialog (not the NSMatrix one) should appear.

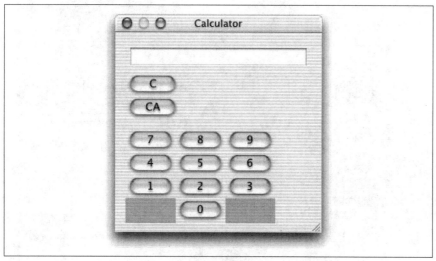

Figure 5-21. Adding another NSMatrix of NSButtons to the Calculator window

20. Connect the CA button to the Controller instance object icon by Control-dragging from the button to the icon and then double-clicking the **clear-All:** action in the NSButtonCell Info dialog (double-clicking has the same effect as clicking the action name and then clicking the Connect button). See Figure 5-22.

21. Similarly, double-click the C on-screen button to select it and then connect it to the Controller instance icon. This time, double-click on the **clear:** action to complete the connection.

You can make IB show you an existing connection from a source object by first selecting the source object and then clicking either the target or the action method with a dimple (•) in the Connections Info dialog. You might try this by selecting the CA button again and single-clicking the **clearAll:** action method. Don't double-click **clearAll:**, because that will break the connection.

Next, we'll set attributes of the Calculator's text (actually numeric) display area:

22. Select the NSTextField object that is the white display area in the Calculator window.

23. If necessary, select Attributes in the NSTextField Info dialog (or type Command-1).

24. Deselect the Editable option in the NSTextField Info dialog (near the bottom) so that the text in the NSTextField object is not editable by the end user of the Calculator.

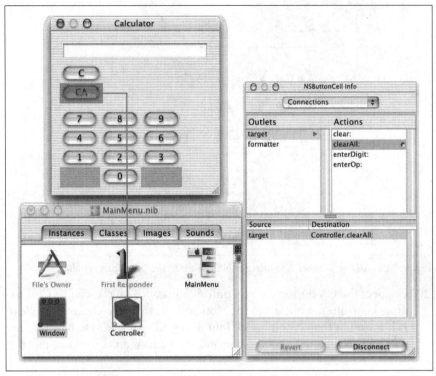

Figure 5-22. Target/action connection from NSButtonCell to Controller instance

Be sure that you leave the Selectable option enabled, as this makes it possible for your user to copy the answer into another application. Many programmers inadvertently make their text not selectable or editable, which can produce significant frustration on the part of users!

25. Set the alignment to be right-justified by clicking the icon that looks like this: ⟶ .

26. If necessary, resize the window. Also, resize the text field so that it goes across the top of the window but stays within the blue guidelines.

The NSTextField Info dialog should now look like the one in Figure 5-23.

The source of all three Calculator connections we've made so far has been a user interface object, while the destination has always been the Controller object. In the next connection we make, the direction will be reversed—the source will be the Controller and the destination will be an interface object. This second type of connection requires an outlet, and we will refer to it as an *outlet connection*. Fortunately, we've already declared the outlet that we need (readout).

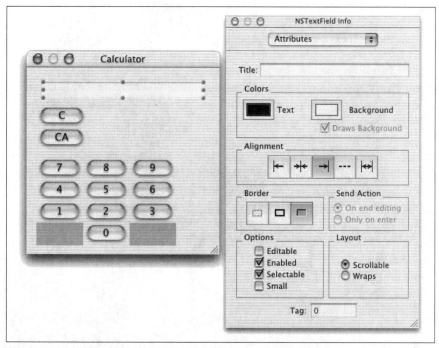

Figure 5-23. Setting the attributes for the NSTextField in the Calculator

27. Control-drag from the Controller instance object icon to the NSText-Field object. The connection wire (in your current selection color) should look like the one in Figure 5-24.

28. In the Connections Info dialog, double-click the readout outlet to complete the connection, as shown in Figure 5-24.

Connecting the readout outlet to the NSTextField object causes the readout instance variable in the Controller object to be initialized to the id of the NSTextField when the nib section is loaded at runtime. Initializing an outlet in an instance object is the only way to determine the id of an object created with IB, so outlets must be used when sending messages to user interface objects.

29. Type Command-S in IB to save the MainMenu.nib file.

Compiling and Running a Program

At this point, we're ready to test the keypad of digit buttons. To do this, we must compile the Controller.m and main.m source code and link them together with the MainMenu.nib file. (We'll discuss the main source file later, in the section "The Files in a Project.")

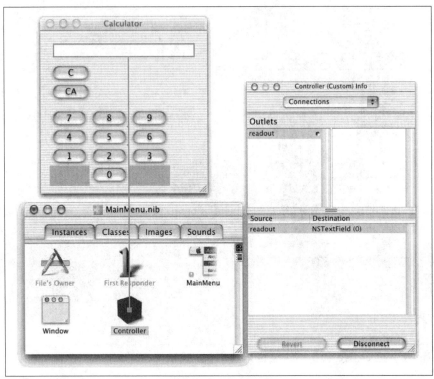

Figure 5-24. Outlet connection from Controller to NSTextField

There are three ways to compile a Cocoa program:

- From Project Builder
- From a command-line prompt
- From GNU Emacs

We'll describe each of these approaches in the following sections.

Compiling and Running a Program from PB

The following steps will compile (make, build) and run your Calculator program directly from PB:

Project Builder

1. Activate PB and click the horizontal Build tab (Build) near the right side of PB's main window to see the Build pane (above the tabs).

2. To have PB include debugging information in the executable, you must select the vertical Targets tab and make sure that the Development build target is selected, as shown in Figure 5-25.

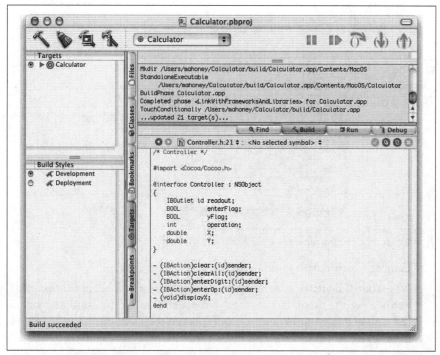

Figure 5-25. Compiling the Calculator application in PB's main window

3. Start the compilation process by clicking the Build button (![build icon]) near the upper-left corner in PB's main window. If you haven't saved all of your files, PB will prompt you to save them before building. In this case, click the Save All button.

If there are no compile-time errors, you should see "Build succeeded" in the lower-left corner of PB's main window and the compile log. If an error occurred, first check the code in your Controller class files and then refer to the next section in this chapter.

4. Run your program directly from PB by clicking the build and run button (![run icon]) near the top-left corner of PB's main window.

This will run the Calculator.app executable file, which was created in your ~/Calculator/build folder when the Calculator program successfully compiled. (The .app extension doesn't appear in the Finder.) We didn't actually have to compile and run in a two-step process; we only needed to click the build and run button.

The main Calculator window and menu appear on the screen, as shown in Figure 5-26.

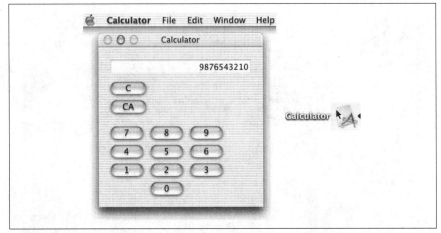

Figure 5-26. Calculator running on the Mac OS X desktop

5. Choose Calculator → Hide Others to simplify your screen.

   Note that Calculator is running as any other Mac OS X application runs, and we get the menu bar for free! Note also that the position and size of the Calculator window and its contents are the same as the way you left them in IB.

6. Try the keypad buttons to make sure every digit works. Clicking the buttons 1, then 2, then 3 in order should make the number "123" appear in the white text area. The C and CA keys should zero-out the values on the display.

Note that the new default application icon is in your Dock, shown on the right in Figure 5-26.

7. Choose Calculator → Quit NewApplication to exit the Calculator application (we'll change the menu label from "NewApplication" to "Calculator" later).

Compiler Error Messages

Sometimes (many times!) code does not compile properly, as you can see in the PB window in Figure 5-27.

If instead of a clean compile you get compiler warning or error messages, you have probably made a typographical error at some point in the code. For example, the error message in Figure 5-27 was generated by removing the first semicolon from the **displayX** method in the Controller.m file (the semicolon is missing from the statement above the highlighted statement at the bottom in Figure 5-27).

Compiling and Running a Program
in the Terminal Shell Window

You can use the pbxbuild utility to compile your Calculator program from the Terminal shell window or from within the GNU Emacs text editor. This can be handy if you want to use an editor other than PB to create your source code.

Terminal

For example, to compile the Calculator program, you might type:

```
localhost> cd ~/Calculator
localhost> pbxbuild
```

To compile your Calculator program within GNU Emacs in a Terminal shell window, type:

```
M-x compile <Return>
```

Emacs will print:

```
make
```

Press the Backspace button four times to delete the word "make," and then type:

```
pbxbuild <Return>
```

The compile log should look similar to that in PB.

If everything compiled correctly, you now have a Cocoa application called Calculator.app in your ~/Calculator/build directory. To run your program, either double-click the Calculator icon in the Finder or type the following in a shell window:

```
localhost> open build/Calculator.app
```

The open command sends a message to the Finder that it should open a file. This has the same effect as double-clicking an application icon in the Finder. See the earlier Figure 5-26—the application should run similarly. Any errors or output to the standard error or standard output devices will be visible in the Console application.

Make sure that you type the .app, or the executable won't be found! The .app extension doesn't appear in the Finder, but it is part of the Calculator application's name. It will also appear in file listings made in the Terminal window using the Unix ls command.

If you click on an error message in the top-right panel of PB's window (e.g., "syntax error, found 'setStringValue'"), the offending line of code will be highlighted in the source code file, Controller.m. If you double-click the error message, a new window will open with the line containing the error highlighted (actually, the error is in the previous line, but it doesn't cause a problem until the highlighted line). This is a great help in finding and fixing compiler errors!

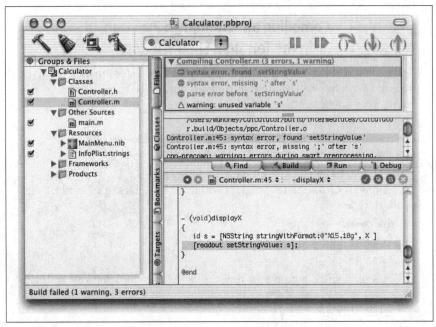

Figure 5-27. Compiler errors in PB's main window

If you get compiler errors for source code that you type in from this book, we suggest that you first reexamine your code line by line, rather than downloading our code from the Web. Examining code for errors is an important skill to develop.

As an alternative to double-clicking an error message, you can open the Controller.m file in a PB editor window, type Command-L to bring up the Goto panel, enter "45" (the line where the error was reported), and inspect the code on line 45 and previous lines.

(If you compiled your program from within GNU Emacs, you can use the Emacs command "goto-next-error" to automatically jump to the file and line containing the error.)

The enterDigit: Action Method

The **enterDigit:** method we added to the Controller class is invoked whenever a digit button is clicked. Let's look at it closely to see how it works.

```
- enterDigit:sender
{
    if (enterFlag) {
        Y = X;
        X = 0.0;
        enterFlag = NO;
    }
```

```
    X = (X*10.0) + [ [sender selectedCell] tag];
    [self displayX];
    return self;
}
```

The first part of the function is self-explanatory: if the enterFlag instance variable is set, the value of the X register is copied into the Y register and both the X register and enterFlag are cleared. Note that the *scope* of instance variables such as enterFlag is the entire class definition. All methods within a class have access to all instance variables defined in that class.

The next line contains the magic: the value in the X register is multiplied by 10 and added to the returned value, [[**sender selectedCell**] **tag**]. This performs a base-10 left-shift operation on X and then adds the last digit pressed. Let's look at this nested method expression in pieces.

[**sender selectedCell**] sends the **selectedCell** message to the variable sender. When the **enterDigit:** method is invoked (called), sender is set to the id of the object that sent the message—in this case, the NSMatrix object. Clicking a button in an NSMatrix selects that button. Thus, the expression [**sender selectedCell**] returns the id of the NSButtonCell object for the button that was clicked. [[**sender selectedCell**] **tag**] then sends the **tag** message to the NSButtonCell object; this method asks the button for the tag of the cell. Thus, the nested message expression [[**sender selectedCell**] **tag**] returns the tag of the pressed button. (Recall that the tag on the digit button is equal to the digit label on the button.)

Adding the Four Calculator Functions

We still need to add the functions that perform the calculations to our Calculator application. We'll add six new buttons in yet another NSMatrix. The Controller object will need to differentiate between the buttons somehow, so we'll assign them different integer tags.

Our first step in handling the four functions is to equip our Controller class with definitions for the mathematical operations that we want our Calculator to be able to handle. Then we'll add these functions to our Calculator's user interface.

1. Using PB's (or another) editor, insert the following enumerated data type after the #import directive in the Controller.h file (remember that bold code should be typed into class files):

Controller.h

```
enum {
    PLUS      = 1001,
    SUBTRACT  = 1002,
    MULTIPLY  = 1003,
    DIVIDE    = 1004,
    EQUALS    = 1005
};
```

These codes will correspond to the tags that we will give the arithmetic buttons in the NSMatrix (we don't want to confuse these tags with tags that we set previously). The Controller object will determine the tag of the button that sends it the action message and use that tag to figure out which function button the user has clicked. This is similar to what we did with the NSMatrix of digit buttons.

Controller.m

2. Using an editor, insert the lines shown here in bold into the **enterOp:** method in the `Controller.m` file.

You may be able to use the same PB code pane (or separate window) that you used for `Controller.h` by pressing the up-down "stepper" arrows (⇕) next to the filename and dragging to `Controller.m`. You can also type the three-key combination Command-Option-up-arrow to rapidly switch between a class's `.h` and `.m` files.

```
- (IBAction)enterOp:(id)sender
{
    if (yFlag) {              // Something is stored in Y
        switch (operation) {
            case PLUS:
                X = Y + X;
                break;

            case SUBTRACT:
                X = Y - X;
                break;

            case MULTIPLY:
                X = Y * X;
                break;

            case DIVIDE:
                X = Y / X;
                break;
        }
    }

    Y    = X;
    yFlag = YES;

    operation = [ [sender selectedCell] tag];
    enterFlag = YES;

    [self displayX];
}
```

The **enterOp:** method is the computational engine of our Calculator application. It performs the arithmetic operation that was stored in the `operation` instance variable, sets up the registers and flags for another operation or another button click, and then displays the contents of the X register in the window display area.

3. Activate IB and create an NSMatrix with six buttons, as shown in Figure 5-28. (If you don't remember how to do this, go back and review how the digit buttons were set up.)

Interface Builder

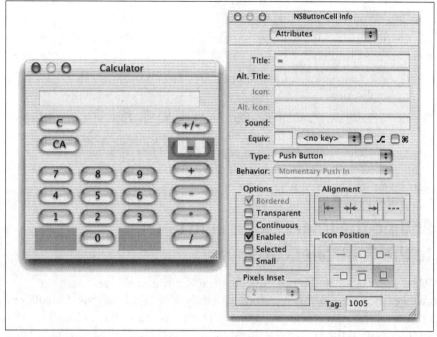

Figure 5-28. Calculator window with operations in IB

As you try to place these buttons, you may want to resize or rearrange the existing buttons on the current Calculator interface. Feel free—one of the most powerful things about IB is that you move around an interface after you have created it.

4. Set the title of each button to correspond with one of the six basic functions, as shown in Figure 5-28. You may want to use a larger font for some of the titles to make them more readable.

5. Set the tag of each button (except "+/-") to correspond with the enum defined in the `Controller.h` file above.

   To set the tag of a button, select the button, type Command-1 to display the NSButtonCell Info dialog, change the value of the tag, and press Return. Don't worry about the unary minus "+/-" button for now. Again, double-check your tags to make sure they are correct.

6. Connect the new NSMatrix to the Controller by Control-dragging from the NSMatrix to the Controller instance icon and double-clicking the **enterOp:** action in the NSMatrix Info dialog. This connection is similar to the one we made for the numeric keypad.

7. Choose IB's File → Save (or Save All) command to save the nib and Controller class files.

8. Compile your program and run it. If you use PB, all you have to do is click the build and run button (), and PB will do all the rest (including prompting for file saving).

All of the Calculator's buttons should now work properly, except for the unary minus button.

9. Choose Calculator → Quit or click PB's Stop button to exit the Calculator application.

For easy access, we recommend that you keep the PB, IB, and Terminal application icons in your Dock while developing applications. Also, when you want to switch applications, use Mac OS X's Hide command rather than Quit. This keeps your screen clear and avoids the wait of having applications start up again when you need them.

Adding the Unary Minus Function to the Controller Class

We want the unary minus function (the button with the "+/-" on it) to change the sign of the number currently displayed in our Calculator's numeric display area. One way to implement this function is to handle it with another case in the switch statement in the **enterOp:** method—we could give the "+/-" key its own tag and have the **enterOp:** method intercept it and perform the appropriate function. The problem with this approach is that the unary minus function has little in common with the other arithmetic functions: it takes one argument instead of two, and it operates immediately on the displayed value. A far better way to implement this function is to implement a new action method in the Controller class.

Using IB's Read Files Command with a New Action Method

Adding new action methods to existing classes is slightly more difficult than creating the initial class definition. Early versions of IB simply replaced the existing class files (Controller.h and Controller.m, here) with new versions, wiping out any source code that you might have added. Current versions of IB detect that you have made changes in the class files and allow you to merge the changes using the Merge Files application. Unfortunately, this can be a painful and error-prone process. The safest way to add new outlets and actions to files after they have been created and edited is to add these items directly to the Objective-C interface files in a text editor, and then use IB's

Classes → Read Files menu command to inform IB about any new actions and outlets.

Project Builder

1. Back in PB, insert the **doUnaryMinus:** action method definition, shown here in bold, into `Controller.h`. (You can tell that it's an action method because of its IBAction typing and because sender is the only argument.)

Controller.h

```
...
- (IBAction)clear:(id)sender;
- (IBAction)clearAll:(id)sender;
- (IBAction)enterDigit:(id)sender;
- (IBAction)enterOp:(id)sender;
- (void)displayX;
- (IBAction)doUnaryMinus:(id)sender;
@end
```

2. Now insert the **doUnaryMinus:** method shown here into `Controller.m`:

```
- (IBAction)doUnaryMinus:(id)sender
{
    X = -X;
    [self displayX];
}
```

Controller.m

3. Choose PB's File → Save All menu command to save the Controller class files.

It doesn't matter where you put this method in `Controller.m`, as long as it's between the directives @implementation and @end. However, for consistency, we suggest that you order the method implementations in the same way that the method declarations are ordered in the `Controller.h` class interface file.

Finally, we have to tell IB about the new **doUnaryMinus:** method and set up a connection between the on-screen unary minus button and the Controller:

4. Activate IB by double-clicking `MainMenu.nib` in PB's main window (`MainMenu.nib` is one of the Resources in your project).

Interface Builder

5. Click on the Classes tab in IB's Nib File window to open the Classes pane.

6. Select Controller in the class hierarchy in the Classes pane. Because it's a subclass of NSObject, you may have to scroll to the left (or use the Search field).

7. Choose IB's Classes → Read Files menu command.*

IB will display the Read Files dialog, as shown in Figure 5-29.

This dialog tells us that the definition for `Controller.h` will be parsed from the edited file on disk.

---

* If you have the Controller class in IB's Classes tab selected, you will have an additional menu item labeled "Read Controller.h". As you might imagine, choosing this menu option causes the `Controller.h` file to be read directly, without forcing you to choose the file in the Read Files pane. This is a faster method of reading a class description.

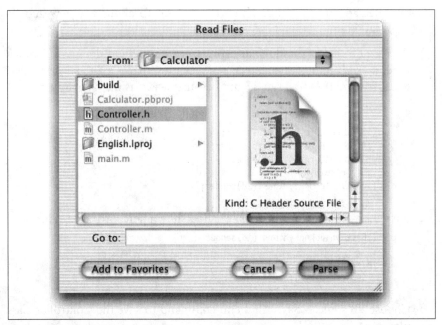

Figure 5-29. Read Files dialog in IB

8. Make sure that Controller.h is selected, as shown in Figure 5-29, and click Parse in IB's Read Files dialog to parse the saved Controller.h file on disk.

9. Make sure that the Controller class is selected in the Nib File window and then type Command-1 to see the Controller's attributes in the Info dialog.

The new **doUnaryMinus:** action method should appear in the Controller Info dialog, as in Figure 5-30, indicating that the Read Files command worked.

10. Double-click the unary minus ("+/-") button in the Calculator window. Make sure that the NSButton, not the NSMatrix as a whole, is selected.

11. Connect the selected unary minus button to the Controller instance. Do this by Control-dragging from the button to the Controller instance in the Nib File window (note that the Instances tab view displays automatically) and then double-clicking the **doUnaryMinus:** action in the NSButtonCell Info dialog.

When a button in an NSMatrix object has its own target, as in the previous example, the button's target overrides the target of the NSMatrix. Thus, when the user clicks on the unary minus button, the button will send the **doUnaryMinus:** message to its own target, rather than sending the **enterOp:** message to the target of the NSMatrix.

12. Back in PB, build and run the program (note how PB nicely prompts to save files).

Project Builder

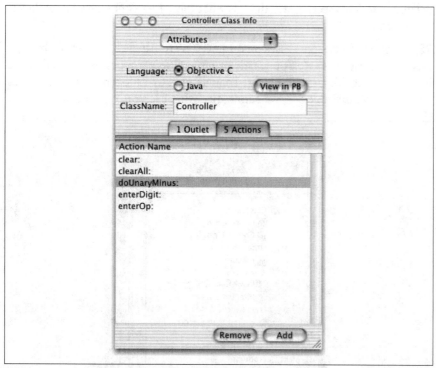

Figure 5-30. New doUnaryMinus: action method in IB after Read Files command

The unary minus function should now behave as expected (although the application isn't perfect yet—it has some bugs).

You might be wondering why IB's Read Files command didn't bring in the definition of the **displayX** method in addition to the **doUnaryMinus:** method. The reason is that IB only looks for action methods when parsing a class interface (.h) file. An action method should always be declared in the form:

```
- (IBAction)methodname:(id)sender;
```

with a single argument called sender. As we'll see later, IB will also bring in outlet declarations when parsing a class interface file. These outlet declarations must be instance variables of the form:

```
IBOutlet id outletname;
```

Action methods and outlets are the *only* types of information that IB learns about a class when it parses a class interface file.

The Files in a Project

If you've been checking your ~/Calculator directory while stepping through this chapter, you'll probably have noticed that several files were automatically created in it. This section will discuss what these files contain and how they fit into a project.

PB's Groups & Files pane uses an outline view to list each project file by type, as shown in Figure 5-31. You can display the different types of files in this outline view by clicking the disclosure triangle next to a file type (e.g., Resources, Frameworks). In Table 5-1, we summarize what each file type means.

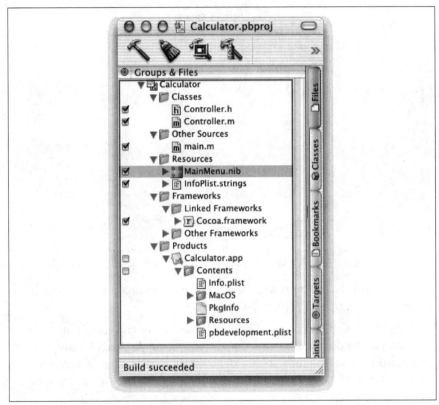

Figure 5-31. Groups & Files pane in Calculator's main window in PB

Table 5-1. Cocoa file types

File type	Typical extensions	Meaning
Classes	.h, .m, .mm	Objective-C class interface (.h) and implementation (.m) files. The .mm extension is used for Objective-C++ source code files.
Other Sources	.c, .m, .mm	ANSI C (.c) and Objective-C (.m) source code files (e.g., main.m).
Resources	.nib, .strings	Resources used by the application, including the IB (.nib) files and strings tables.
Frameworks	.framework	Library files that are linked into your program (e.g., Cocoa and Foundation).
Products	.app	Applications that have been built with PB.

The main.m Program File Generated by PB

When you create a project, PB generates an Objective-C file called main.m containing the program's main( ) function. The main( ) function is where every Objective-C (and C) program begins. The following code in the main.m file is generated in the Calculator project:

```
#import <Cocoa/Cocoa.h>

int main(int argc, const char *argv[])
{
    return NSApplicationMain(argc, argv);
}
```

As you can see, this is a very simple function! All it does is run the NSApplicationMain( ) function that is built into the Cocoa Application Kit framework.

The Cocoa documentation for the NSApplication class (not function) defines the NSApplicationMain( ) function as the following:

```
void NSApplicationMain(int argc, char *argv[]) {
    [NSApplication sharedApplication];
    [NSBundle loadNibNamed:@"myMain" owner:app];
    [NSApp run];
}
```

This function creates the NSApplication object, which creates the autorelease memory pool that we discussed in Chapter 4, then loads the application's main nib file (MainMenu.nib in Calculator) and starts the NSApplication object's main event loop. The main event loop handles menu clicks, keystrokes, and all of the other events to which an application can respond.

Control doesn't return to main( ) until the NSApplication object receives a **stop:** or **terminate:** message, which usually happens in response to a user's choosing the application's Quit menu item. At that point, the main( ) function receives the return code from the NSApplicationMain( ) function.

Other PB-Generated Files

In addition to creating the Objective-C .h, .m, .nib, and main.m program files for a project, PB created the following files for us:

Calculator.pbproj
    The directory containing the project files, which keep track of the individual parts of the project. You might investigate this directory in a Terminal window because, like Calculator.app, it appears to be a simple file (not a folder) in the Finder.

Calculator.pbproj/project.pbxproj
    The project file that keeps track of the parts of the project.

`Calculator.pbproj/`*`username`*`.pbxuser`
> The project file that keeps track of the preferences for the user *username*.

`English.lproj`
> A directory that contains the information for an English-language version of our project, including the `MainMenu.nib` file (discussed earlier) in our example.

`English.lproj/InfoPlist.strings`
> A string table that references all of the strings inside the English-language project.

Summary

We got a great start programming in this chapter! We started by building a real project with PB. Then we used IB and Objective-C to build user interface objects, create and customize our own class, and connect these user interface objects with an object of our new class. We also learned a little more about Objective-C and some AppKit classes, and a lot about the files that PB generates. In the process, we used four important operations that IB can perform on classes: Subclass, Instantiate, Read Files, and Create Files. These operations were all found in the Classes menu in IB (some of these operations can be performed in ways other than using the menu commands).

These operations are the basic building blocks that you will use to create your own applications, although the order in which you use them will vary from project to project. Typically, the steps for creating an application are the following:

1. Create a project using PB.
2. Build the application's user interface using IB.
3. Customize the buttons and other user interface items in IB.
4. Design the application's Controller class.
5. Connect the controls to the Controller, and vice versa.
6. Add code to make the Controller class work.
7. Compile, test, and fix the code that you have created.
8. Tweak the user interface as necessary.

In the next chapter, we'll add an About box (dialog) and some icons to our Calculator application, and we'll find out how to increase the efficiency of a Cocoa application by using separate nib files.

Exercises

1. Instead of creating a **doUnaryMinus:** method to handle the "+/-" function key in Calculator, add the unary minus function to the **enterOp:** method.

2. Instead of creating a single **enterOp:** method to handle the four arithmetic operations, create four separate methods to handle the four operations.

CHAPTER 6

Nibs and Icons

In the previous chapter, we created our simple four-function Calculator application. Although our Calculator works, it lacks the nifty presentation and many of the basic features of most Mac OS X applications. Some aspects were simply not implemented. In this and the following two chapters, we'll use our simple Calculator as a starting point and slowly expand it, adding new features one by one.

In the first section of this chapter, we'll configure the Interface Builder–supplied menus for the Calculator application and make some minor changes to the default About box (window) that is provided. Typically, the About box informs users about the version, author, and copyright of the application.

After seeing how the Cocoa-bundled About box works, we'll create a new About box from scratch for our Calculator. We will use this new About box to demonstrate how to manage multiple nibs (interfaces) within a single application. In the last section of this chapter, we'll see how Cocoa allows you to specify an icon for an application.

Customizing MainMenu.nib

As we saw in Chapter 5, Project Builder creates your application (i.e., new project) from a stored template. It's up to you to customize this template to fit your own needs. We've done a lot of that already, but there are a lot more possibilities, as we'll soon see.

Changing the Application Menu

MainMenu.nib

Perhaps the most obvious part of PB's application template interface (provided in MainMenu.nib) that needs customization is the menu bar. In Figure 6-1, on the left, we show the main application menu as it is delivered to us in the PB template. The first thing we'll do is to change the application name and the appropriate menu items.

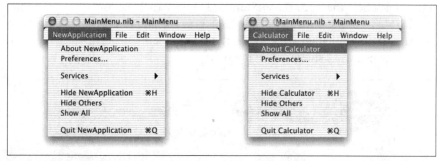

Figure 6-1. Application Menu before (left) and after (right) customization

1. Launch PB by double-clicking the file `Calculator.pbproj`. (We recommend that you keep this file's icon in the Finder's toolbar or in the Dock.)

Project Builder

2. Double-click `MainMenu.nib` in the Resources section of PB's Groups & Files browser to launch IB.

3. Choose Interface Builder → Hide Others to simplify the screen.

Interface Builder

4. If you don't see a small menu titled "MainMenu.nib - MainMenu" on the screen, then double-click the MainMenu icon in the `MainMenu.nib` Nib File window.

5. Double-click NewApplication in the menu bar titled "MainMenu.nib - MainMenu". The word will highlight in your highlight color. Type Calculator and hit Return to change the application's name in the main menu.

6. Single-click Calculator in the menu bar to open up the Calculator menu.

7. Double-click on the first menu item and change the title from "About NewApplication" to "About Calculator".

8. Similarly, change the menu items "Hide NewApplication" to read "Hide Calculator" and "Quit NewApplication" to read "Quit Calculator".

Your application menu should now look like the screen shot on the right in Figure 6-1.

9. Single-click the About Calculator menu item and then choose Tools → Show Info (or type Shift-Command-I) to see the NSMenuItem Info dialog.

10. If necessary, choose Connections in the pop-up menu to see the NSMenuItem Connections Info dialog (or type Command-2).

Note that there is a target/action connection indicated by the dimple (▾) next to the **orderFrontStandardAboutPanel:** action method. This method causes the NSApplication object to display a standard About box. (Note how the programming environment uses the term *panel*, whereas the Aqua interface guidelines reject that term. In our discussion, we'll use whatever term is appropriate in the given context.)

11. Single-click the **orderFrontStandardAboutPanel:** action method in the NSMenuItem Connections Info dialog to see a connection wire between the About Calculator menu item and the File's Owner icon in the Nib File window, as shown in Figure 6-2.

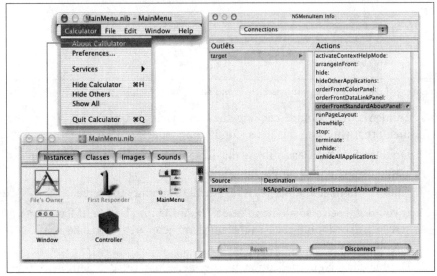

Figure 6-2. Connection between About Calculator menu item and File's Owner

Recall that the File's Owner icon represents the object of type NSApplication in charge of running your application and interfacing with the Mac's hardware. Thus, when the Calculator application is running and the About Calculator menu item is clicked, this target/action connection means that the **orderFrontStandardAboutPanel:** action message will be sent to the NSApplication object. The **orderFrontStandardAboutPanel:** method does exactly as its name indicates—it displays the standard About box (panel) in front of all other on-screen windows.

12. Repeat Step 11 for the last four menu items in the Calculator menu, beginning with Hide Calculator, to find out about their preset connections and action methods.

Some of the menu items in other menus have additional preset connections. For example, the File → Close menu item sends a **performClose:** message to the FirstResponder object (probably the key window). You might take a few minutes to investigate these connections, but be sure not to disconnect any of them.

Note that there has been no change to the Calculator application in the last four steps—we've just been poking around. If you want, you can now build and run your application and see the new Calculator menu. We'll do that in a later step, after we modify the About box to fit our application.

Changing the Strings in the About Box

Every Mac OS X application should have an About box. The About box displays basic information about the application, such as who created it and what version is currently running. About boxes are so important that they are built into the Cocoa AppKit. An About box is occasionally referred to as an *About panel*, especially in the programming world.

The left side of Figure 6-3 shows the Calculator application's default About box (except the application's name, which was changed to "Calculator" when we first named the project in PB). You can display this About box by running the Calculator application and choosing the Calculator → About Calculator menu item. As you can see in Figure 6-3, the About box displays the same application icon (currently the default one) that PB uses to identify the Calculator program in the Finder. It displays the name of the program and a version number. But what's this "MyCompanyName" company? And where are these strings coming from in the first place?

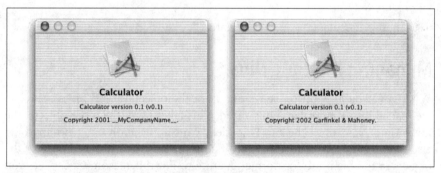

Figure 6-3. Default (left) and modified (right) About boxes

Just as the Cocoa development environment allows you to store the interface of your application in a resource called a nib, you can also store string resources in special files called *plists* (short for *property lists*), or string tables. When you create a new project, PB creates a file called `InfoPlist.strings` that holds a series of name/value pairs for textual information about your application. The built-in AppKit About box uses this string table to determine what information should be displayed inside the About box for your application.

13. Back in PB, select the `InfoPlist.strings` file in the Resources section of the Groups & Files pane. The contents of the file should be displayed in the lower-right pane of PB's window.

Project Builder

14. Change the copyright year from "2001" to "2002" and the company name from "MyCompanyName" to "Garfinkel & Mahoney" (or anything else you want!) in the NSHumanReadableCopyright string. See Figure 6-4.

15. Click PB's build and run button (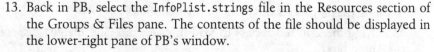).

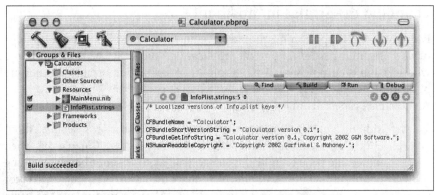

Figure 6-4. Editing the InfoPlist.string property list table

16. Save the `InfoPlist.strings` file (and any other file) when prompted.

17. With the Calculator application running, choose Calculator → About Calculator. You should see the new About box shown on the right in Figure 6-3.

18. Choose Calculator → Quit Calculator.

Managing Multiple Nibs

When a Cocoa application starts up, all of the objects stored in its main nib are loaded into memory and initialized. This takes time (the more objects, the more time), and until the nib is loaded, your application can't do anything else. This can be real drag, especially if your program doesn't need most of the objects in the main nib for normal operation. For this reason, Cocoa lets you take objects that you don't use often and place them in separate nibs. You can arrange for these auxiliary nibs to be loaded only when they are needed.

Auxiliary nibs should be used for most panels that do not need to be displayed when your program first starts up. Instead, the files are loaded the first time that the panel is needed. Once the panel is loaded, it is resident in your computer's memory—additional attempts to make the panel display go much faster.

Now we'll arrange for our Calculator application to use a separate nib for its About box. This will consist of three steps:

i. Creating the new nib that contains the About box

ii. Modifying the Controller class to load this new nib (and thereby display the About box)

iii. Modifying the Calculator's `MainMenu.nib` accordingly

For pedagogical reasons, we'll perform these steps in the order (ii), then (iii), and finally (i).

Modifying the Controller Class

To start, we'll modify the Controller object to add two things:

aboutPanel

> A new outlet that holds the id of the About box

showAboutPanel:

> A new action method that displays the About box

You might think that the easiest way to create the new outlet and action method is to add them in IB's inspector window, as we did in the previous chapter. You can do this. However, because we have added code to the Controller.h and Controller.m class files, if you add the outlet and action methods in IB, you will need to use Apple's File Merge utility to merge the changes that you made in these files with the changes that IB makes. This can be somewhat complicated, and if you make a mistake, you will lose all of the specialized coding that you have added so far!

Instead, we believe that the easiest way to add new outlets and action methods to the Controller class is to use a text editor to add them directly to the Controller.h and Controller.m class files, and then use IB's Classes → Read Files command to read them into IB's internal description of the class. The new outlet and action will then appear in IB's Controller class inspector, and we'll be able to use them to make connections with user interface objects. (Recall that we parsed an outlet from the Controller.h file into IB in the previous chapter; here we'll parse a method in a similar fashion.)

1. Back in PB, insert the two lines shown here in bold into Controller.h, and save the file:

Project Builder

Controller.h

```
@interface Controller : NSObject
{
    IBOutlet id readout;
    BOOL       enterFlag;
    BOOL       yFlag;
    int        operation;
    double     X;
    double     Y;
    IBOutlet id aboutPanel;
}
- (IBAction)clear:(id)sender;
- (IBAction)clearAll:(id)sender;
- (IBAction)enterDigit:(id)sender;
- (IBAction)enterOp:(id)sender;
- (void)displayX;
- (IBAction)doUnaryMinus:(id)sender;
- (IBAction)showAboutPanel:(id)sender;
@end
```

The aboutPanel outlet will eventually be set to the id of our new About box object. The **showAboutPanel:** action method will be coded to display the

About box in response to the user's choosing the Calculator → About Calculator menu command.

2. Make sure you save the edited `Controller.h` file at this point, because IB will read the class interface file from disk, not from your edited but unsaved copy.

Interface Builder

3. Now double-click the `MainMenu.nib` resource in PB to open the interface in IB. (Following that, you again might want to choose IB's Hide Others menu item to simplify your screen).

4. Select the Controller class (under NSObject) under the Classes tab in IB's `MainMenu.nib` window and choose IB's Classes → Read Files menu item.

5. Double-click `Controller.h` in the Read Files panel that opens to parse the new definition of the Controller class from the updated `Controller.h` file on disk.

6. Type Command-1 to display IB's Attributes Info dialog; you should see the new `aboutPanel` outlet and the new **showAboutPanel:** action method, as shown in Figure 6-5. (If you don't see them, you probably didn't save the `Controller.h` file after editing).

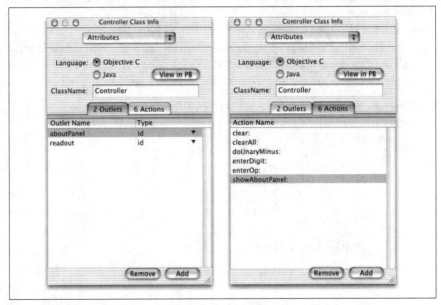

Figure 6-5. New outlet (left) and action method (right) in Controller class

Controller.m

7. Back in PB, insert the entire new **showAboutPanel:** method, shown here in bold, into `Controller.m`. We suggest that you place it just before the `@end` directive.

```
- (IBAction)showAboutPanel:(id)sender
{
  if (aboutPanel == nil) {
    if (![NSBundle loadNibNamed:@"AboutPanel.nib" owner:self] ) {
      NSLog(@"Load of AboutPanel.nib failed");
      return;
    }
  }
  [aboutPanel makeKeyAndOrderFront: nil];
}
```

Every Objective-C instance variable is initialized to nil (0) when an object is created.* When the Calculator application starts up, the aboutPanel outlet in the Controller instance will not be explicitly set, so its value will be nil. Thus, when the **showAboutPanel:** method is invoked the first time, the conditional if statement will cause the **loadNibNamed:owner:** message to be sent to the NSBundle class.

A *bundle* in Cocoa is a collection of files in a folder that is used to store dynamically loaded code, icons, sounds, objects, and/or other kinds of information. A nib is a special kind of bundle that is used by IB to store user interfaces. Applications are another special kind of bundle that are created by PB and used by the Finder to put together all of the files that go into an application. Frameworks and IB palettes are additional examples of bundles.

The call to the **loadNibNamed:owner:** method loads the nib bundle containing the About box (which we'll create later in this chapter) from the nib AboutPanel.nib. When the nib is loaded, it automatically initializes the aboutPanel outlet of its owner to the id of the About box. (We'll show you how to create the About box and set up this initialization a bit later.) Finally, the **showAboutPanel:** method will send the About box object the **makeKeyAndOrderFront:** message, which makes the About box the key window and brings it to the front of the window display list (making it visible). If something goes wrong with the loading, the NSLog( )† function will display an error message in the system console and in PB's Run pane if the application is run from PB. This can be very useful in debugging.

The second time the **showAboutPanel:** method is called, the aboutPanel outlet will already be initialized. Thus, the statement sending the **loadNibNamed:owner:** message will be skipped, preventing a second copy of the nib from being loaded. Because the nib that we loaded the first time through is still in memory, the About box will be displayed without the loading delay.

---

* Note that Objective-C initializes only instance variables. Variables that are static or local to a method are still uninitialized, just as in standard ANSI C.

† NSLog( ) works a lot like printf, except that the first argument is an NSString and the result is sent to the system console.

Apple's "Aqua Interface Guidelines" say that bringing up a panel should be a safe and reversible option. A user should be able to make the panel disappear by clicking a cancel or close button without any ill effects for the application. Our About box will meet this requirement.

Modifying the Main Calculator Nib

Next we'll modify the About Calculator menu item command in the Calculator's main menu so that it invokes our **showAboutPanel:** method.

As we saw earlier in this chapter, the Cocoa development environment gives every new Cocoa application a built-in About box. This panel is displayed by the NSApplication object when it receives the **orderFrontStandardAbout-Panel:** message. To have our application display our custom About box (which we haven't created yet), we'll need to change the About Calculator menu item so that it invokes our method, instead of the default method.

To do this, follow these steps:

Interface Builder

8. Back in IB, click Calculator in the Calculator main menu to open the submenu.

9. Select the About Calculator menu item.

10. Type Command-2 to display the Connections Info dialog for the NSMenuItem, as shown earlier in Figure 6-2.

11. Make sure that the **orderFrontStandardAboutPanel:** action method is highlighted in the Connections inspector and then click the Disconnect button to remove the default connection. The dimple next to the method should disappear.

12. Control-drag from the About Calculator menu item to the Controller object in the MainMenu.nib window to create a new connection, as shown in Figure 6-6.

13. Select the **showAboutPanel:** action in the NSMenuItem Info dialog (see Figure 6-6), and then click the Connect button at the bottom of the dialog. The Connect button will become a Disconnect button, as shown in Figure 6-6. (You can also double-click the action method.)

We have now arranged for the About Calculator menu command to invoke the Controller's **showAboutPanel:** action method.

There is one other modification that we should make to the Calculator menu, concerning the menu command that brings up a Preferences panel. Because our Calculator application doesn't have a Preferences panel, we should remove this menu item.

14. Still in IB, select the Calculators → Preferences menu item by clicking it once.

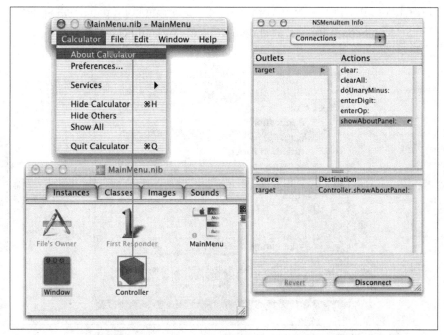

Figure 6-6. New connection between About Calculator menu item and Controller instance

15. Type Command-X to cut the menu item from the menu. Your menu should now look like the one in Figure 6-7.

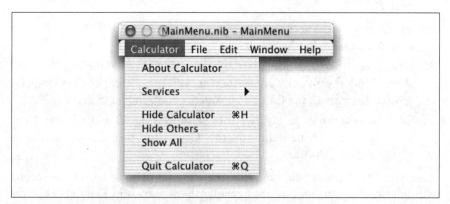

Figure 6-7. Newly configured Calculator application menu in IB (no Preferences item)

16. Type Command-S to save the MainMenu.nib file.

Creating the About Box Nib

To complete our About box addition, we will create a separate nib for the About box. This nib will be loaded by the **loadNibNamed:owner:** message that the Controller's **showAboutPanel:** method sends to the NSApplication object.

17. Choose IB's File → New command. IB's Starting Point panel will appear.

18. Select Cocoa → Empty, as shown in Figure 6-8, and click New.

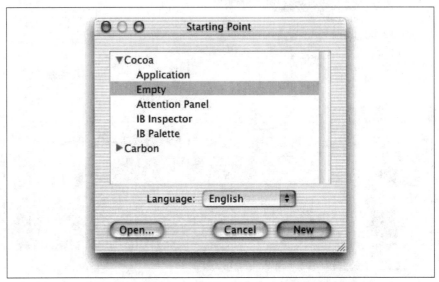

Figure 6-8. Creating a new empty nib in IB

Note that there are now two Nib File windows at the lower left of the screen, one for `MainMenu.nib` and the other ("Untitled") for the new nib that we created.

19. Type Command-S to save this new nib, and you'll see a "Save as" sheet slide out from under the title bar.

20. If necessary, click the down arrow button (▼) to reveal the full "Save as" sheet. Find the folder `Calculator/English.lproj` (the English-language project directory of the Calculator source code), shown in Figure 6-9.

21. Save the new nib as `AboutPanel.nib`. Before saving, IB will ask you if you want to add the new nib to the Calculator project, as shown in Figure 6-10. Click Add.

AboutPanel.nib

After you add the new nib, note that the name in the title bar of the second Nib File window changes to `AboutPanel.nib`, as shown in Figure 6-11. Note also that there are only two instance objects, File's Owner and First Responder, in the new nib (compare with `MainMenu.nib` in Figure 6-11). Because IB knows this is an empty auxiliary nib, it doesn't automatically provide you with MainMenu and Window instances, as it did for the main nib. Clearly, another MainMenu object is not needed. Also, if you activate PB, you'll notice that `AboutPanel.nib` has been added to the Calculator project as

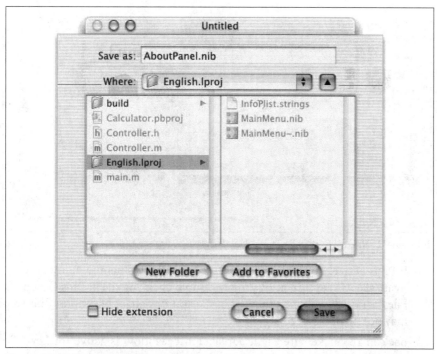

Figure 6-9. Saving a new nib for the About box in IB

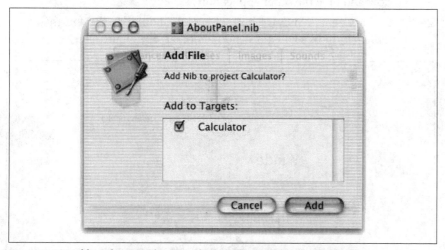

Figure 6-10. Adding the new AboutPanel.nib to the Calculator project

a resource, alongside MainMenu.nib and InfoPlist.strings. Thus, when the Calculator application is built, AboutPanel.nib will automatically be copied into the Calculator.app application bundle.

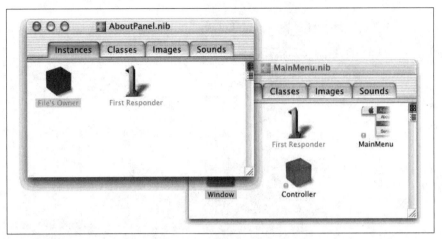

Figure 6-11. New AboutPanel.nib window (left)

22. If PB is active, double-click AboutPanel.nib in PB's main window to reactivate AboutPanel.nib in IB. (If you double-click any file in PB's Groups & Files pane, PB will open that file in the appropriate application.) This step may not be necessary.

23. Back in IB, make sure the AboutPanel.nib window is active (or *key*). To simplify the screen, we recommend that you minimize the MainMenu.nib window and hide the other applications.

24. Click the Cocoa-Windows button (which should be the fourth button from the left) in IB's Palettes window toolbar. See Figure 6-12.

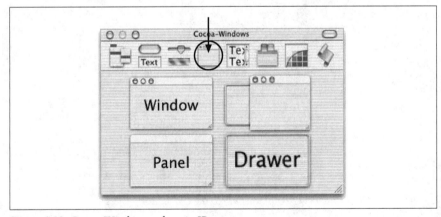

Figure 6-12. Cocoa-Windows palette in IB

25. Drag the icon with the Panel label from the Cocoa-Windows palette and drop it in the AboutPanel.nib window (you can also drop it on the desktop). This will create an empty panel with the title "Panel" and will add the panel to the AboutPanel.nib nib. See Figure 6-13.

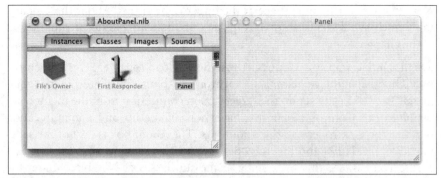

Figure 6-13. New panel (right) and updated AboutPanel.nib with panel icon

26. Click anywhere inside the new panel to select it, then type Command-1 to bring up the NSWindow Attributes Info dialog (NSPanel is a subclass of NSWindow).

27. Change the title of the panel to "About the Calculator" in the Info dialog.

28. Click the Cocoa-Views button (which should be the second one from the left) at the top of IB's Palettes window.

29. Customize the panel's text by dragging and dropping text icons (e.g., System Font Text) from the Cocoa-Views palette into the panel.* Type Command-T to bring up the Font panel to change the size, etc. of the type. See what we did in Figure 6-14. (Your About box won't look exactly the same as our screen shot yet, but it doesn't matter.)

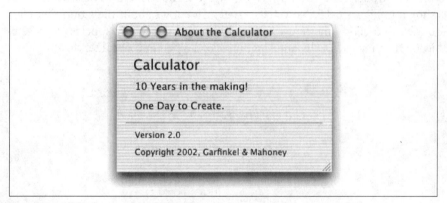

Figure 6-14. Newly customized About box

30. Now drag the horizontal-line icon from below the radio buttons in the Cocoa-Views palette and drop it in the new panel. Resize it and change its location to be a separator, as shown in Figure 6-14. Also, resize the panel itself as appropriate.

* It's possible that the names of the text icons will change in later releases. Palettes may change too.

Note that we've left some space at the upper right of the "About the Calculator" panel. We'll use that space to place our application icon before the end of the chapter.

Recall that we want the Controller instance to load AboutPanel.nib when the user chooses our Calculator's Calculator → About Calculator menu command. We've already set up the target/action connection from the menu command to the Controller, but we have not yet set up any communication between the Controller and the About box. The About box is part of the separate AboutPanel.nib, and this nib doesn't even "know" that a Controller class exists. You can see this by looking at the subclasses of NSObject under the AboutPanel.nib Classes tab—there's no Controller class. We'll set up the required linkage between the new nib and the Controller in the next few steps.

31. Select the NSObject class in the Classes pane in the AboutPanel.nib window.

Note that the Controller class does not appear (recall that it did show up in the MainMenu.nib window). To change this, we'll make IB read the Controller.h information into AboutPanel.nib.

32. Choose the Classes → Read Files menu command, and the Read Files dialog will open.

33. Browse the filesystem to select the Controller.h file (under ~/Calculator) in the Read Files panel, then click the Parse button.

The Controller class should now show up in the AboutPanel.nib window, as shown in Figure 6-15. Now AboutPanel.nib knows about the Controller class outlets and action methods, and it also knows that it is a subclass of NSObject. Of course, all of this information is contained in Controller.h.

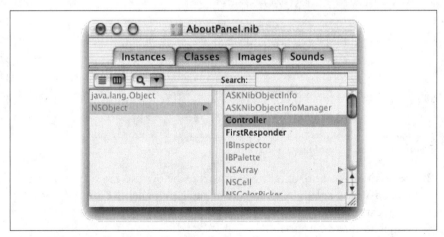

Figure 6-15. Controller class in AboutPanel.nib window

Alternatively, you could have informed AboutPanel.nib about the Controller class by simply dragging the Controller.h file icon from the Finder or PB and dropping it into the AboutPanel.nib window. When you do this, IB will automatically parse the Controller class definition on disk and insert the Controller class into the AboutPanel.nib class hierarchy. We'll use this quicker technique in subsequent chapters.

We still need to make a connection from the Controller instance (created by MainMenu.nib) to the About box object (created by AboutPanel.nib) in order to initialize the Controller's aboutPanel outlet. We cannot do this using a different Controller instance instantiated by AboutPanel.nib—we must use the instance instantiated by MainMenu.nib, because that's the one that controls the running Calculator application! To do this, we will use the File's Owner icon in AboutPanel.nib. The File's Owner is an object that "owns" a nib.* It's the argument that is passed to the NSBundle class when the nib file is loaded. We've already arranged for this argument to be the id of the Controller object that is running the Calculator application, so all we need to do is to make sure that AboutPanel.nib sets the outlet when it is loaded.

34. Click the Instances tab in the AboutPanel.nib (not MainMenu.nib) window to see the three objects for this nib.

Instances

35. Inform IB that the File's Owner in AboutPanel.nib will be of the Controller class. Do this by clicking the File's Owner icon in the AboutPanel.nib window and then selecting Controller in the File's Owner Info dialog, as shown in Figure 6-16. (If the Info dialog isn't visible, type Command-1).

36. Make the aboutPanel outlet in the File's Owner point to the About box. Do this by first Control-dragging from the File's Owner icon in the AboutPanel.nib (not MainMenu.nib) window to the (About) Panel icon in the same window. Finish the job by double-clicking the aboutPanel outlet in the File's Owner Info dialog. See Figure 6-17.

When AboutPanel.nib is loaded, it will create the About box. The last step we completed arranged for the aboutPanel outlet in the File's Owner object (i.e., the Controller object that loads AboutPanel.nib) to be set to the id of this newly created About box (represented by the Panel icon in AboutPanel.nib).

You might still be wondering about the File's Owner. Recall the following Objective-C statement in the Controller's **showAboutPanel:** method; when the program runs, this statement loads AboutPanel.nib:

```
[NSBundle loadNibNamed:@"AboutPanel.nib" owner:self]
```

---

* The File's Owner icon is actually a proxy for the object id that is passed to the method that loads the nib into memory.

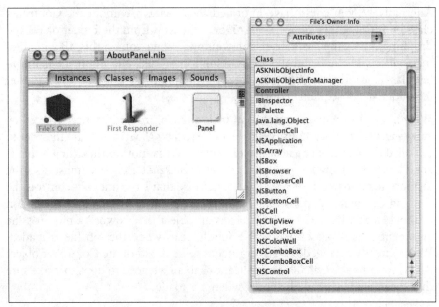

Figure 6-16. Changing the class type of the File's Owner in AboutPanel.nib

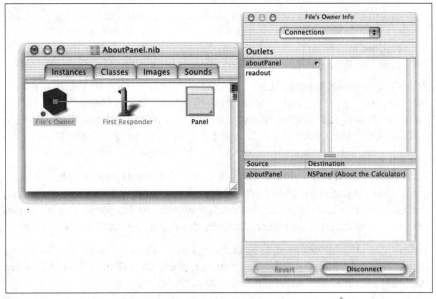

Figure 6-17. Setting the aboutPanel outlet to point to the About box

The File's Owner is the object that is specified by the **self** in the clause **owner: self**. In this case, the owner is the Controller instance (**self**) that sends the above message to NSBundle. Thus, the aboutPanel outlet in the Controller instance is set to the id of the About box that is loaded.

The File's Owner icon is called a *proxy object* because it is not a real object; instead, it is a proxy for a real object that was instantiated when another nib was loaded (in this case, that nib is MainMenu.nib). Setting File's Owner outlets and sending messages to a File's Owner object are the easiest ways to communicate between nibs.

Now, let's run the Calculator application and see how it works:

37. Activate PB and click the build and run button for the Calculator target. Save all files before building.

38. With Calculator running, choose Calculator → About Calculator.

The first time you choose the Calculator's Calculator → About Calculator menu command, you may notice a slight delay before the About box appears (and you may hear your hard drive reading the nib file). This delay is the time that it takes to load the nib file AboutPanel.nib into memory. However, if you close the About box and then choose Calculator → About Calculator again, the About box should appear immediately because it's being read from memory, not from disk.

39. Choose Calculator → Quit Calculator.

Adding Icons to Applications

Mac OS X uses icons—little descriptive pictures—in many places to represent programs and their documents. Mac OS X also allows applications to change their icons while the applications are running. For example, the Mail program uses the icon containing an envelope (shown at the edge of the page) to represent the application in the Dock and Finder. When Mail is active and you have unread mail messages, the Mail program adds an *icon badge* to its icon in the Dock to display how many messages are unread. As we've seen already, folders and documents also have icons.

Viewing Icons with the icns Browser Application

Application icons are typically stored in a file with a .icns extension. Each such file contains several images, of various sizes and bit depths, that are used by the Finder and other applications. A .icns file can also contain an icon mask that is used for transparency. Because bitmap images do not scale well, the .icns file format stores only icons that are 12×16, 16×16, 32×32, 48×48, or 128×128 pixels. You can simultaneously view all of the images for a given file with the icns Browser application, located in the /Developer/Applications folder.

icns Browser

The Mac OS X Mail application icons are stored in the file /Applications/ Mail.app/Contents/Resources/app.icns. This file doesn't normally appear in the Finder because the Finder hides system details from users. However, you can see the contents of the `app.icns` file by first choosing Finder's Go → Go to Folder command and then entering `/Applications/Mail.app/Contents/Resources/` inside it. Following that, select the `app.icns` file and drag and drop it on the icns Browser application icon in your Dock to see the window shown in Figure 6-18.

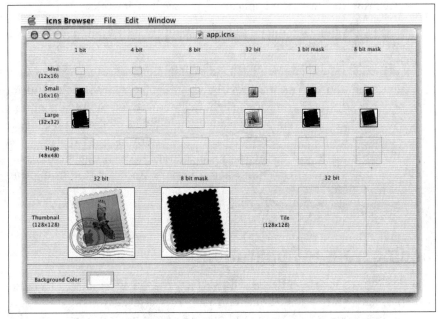

Figure 6-18. Viewing Mail's icons and masks in the icns Browser application

Creating Application Icon Files with IconComposer

IconComposer

To create a `.icns` file, use the developer's tool called IconComposer, which we described briefly in Chapter 2. This tool's icon is shown at the edge of the page, and it resides in the `/Developer/Applications` folder. Note the screwdriver on IconComposer's icon, and contrast it with the icon for icns Browser, which is a viewer, not a tool. IconComposer does not actually let you edit the icons. Instead, it allows you to create a `.icns` file that is built by importing image files created by other applications. For example, you might use Stone Design's Create program to create a large image, then import this image at several resolutions into the `.icns` file.*

---

* For icon design guidelines, we suggest that you consult a book or web site on user interface design. Search the Web for design experts such as Jakob Nielsen and Ben Shneiderman. O'Reilly's OnLamp online service also has an excellent article on designing icons for Aqua applications (see `http://www.onlamp.com/pub/a/muc/2001/05/24/aqua_design.html`).

We're not very good artists, but we did manage to create the 128×128 pixel TIFF image at the edge of the page. The TIFF (Tagged Image File Format) format is a common bitmap graphics format in Mac OS X. Our image was saved in a file called calc.tiff. We then launched IconComposer and dragged the calc.tiff file icon from the Finder into each of the four icon areas in Icon-Composer's window. (You can also drag in GIF files, or files of any other image format that Mac OS X recognizes.) For each image where the resolution didn't match, IconComposer warned us of this fact and asked us if we wished to use a scaled version, as shown in Figure 6-19.

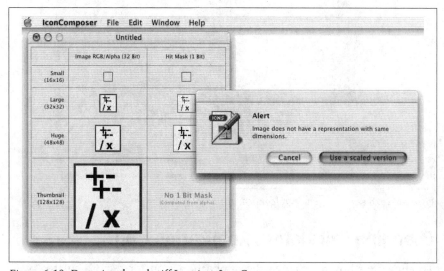

Figure 6-19. Dropping the calc.tiff Icon into IconComposer

1. Create an icon for your Calculator application using a graphics application. Store the icon in a file called calc.tiff. If you don't have time to create an icon, "borrow" one from an existing application or download one from the Web (be aware of copyright).

2. Launch the IconComposer program from the /Developer/Applications folder (or your Dock).

IconComposer

3. Drag the calc.tiff icon for your application into each of the icon wells in the IconComposer's "Untitled" window, as shown in Figure 6-19.

4. Choose IconComposer's File → Save menu command (or type Command-S) and save the file in your Calculator project folder with the name AppIcon.icns, as shown in Figure 6-20.

In this example, we use the name AppIcon.icns for our application icon. However, you can use any filename, provided that you tell PB which filename you are using. We shall see this in Step 10 in the next section.

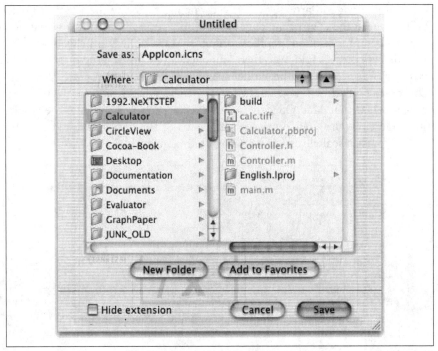

Figure 6-20. Saving our new AppIcon.icns file in IconComposer

Changing Calculator's Application Icon

To show you how to change the application icon for our Calculator, we'll assume that you've saved a copy of the file `AppIcon.icns` in your `~/Calculator` folder as we described in the previous section. (If you haven't done this, copy the file with this name from `/Developer/Examples/AppKit/DotView` or some other AppKit example). Then we'll tell PB to use an image from `AppIcon.icns` for our Calculator's application icon. When the Calculator program is compiled, the icon's image will automatically be included in the Calculator's NSBundle folder.

Project Builder

1. Back in PB with `Calculator.pbproj`, choose Project → Add Files.

2. Select the `AppIcon.icns` file, as shown in Figure 6-21, and click the Open button.

As shown in Figure 6-22, PB will prompt you as to whether or not you wish to copy the items that you have just selected (e.g., the `AppIcon.icns` file) into the destination group's folder. The setting of this checkbox does not matter, because you already copied the `AppIcon.icns` file into your project directory.

3. Do not change any settings in the newly dropped sheet; simply click the Add button.

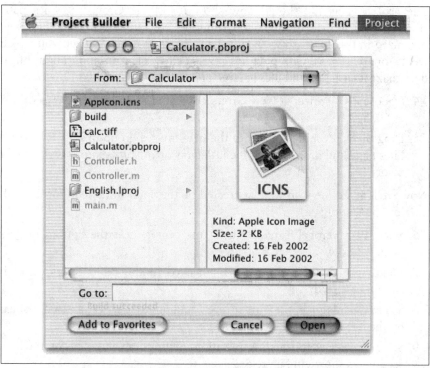

Figure 6-21. Adding the AppIcon.icns file to the Calculator project

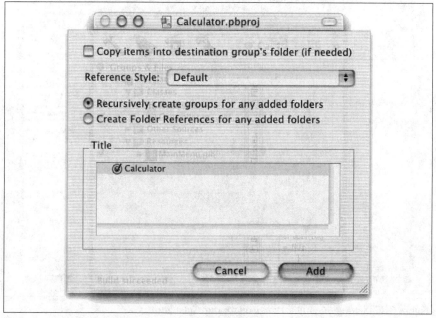

Figure 6-22. Option to copy AppIcon.icns into project directory

The `AppIcon.icns` file should now show up in the Groups & Files pane (Resources group) in the main PB window. We like keeping our files well organized in this pane, so we'll create a new group called "Images" in which we'll store our icons. Grouping has no real effect on your application, but it does make it easier to find files in large projects.

4. Choose PB's Project → New Group command and rename "New Group" as "Images".

5. Drag the `AppIcon.icns` file into the new Images group in PB's Groups & Files pane and drop it when the little gray arrow turns into your highlight color.

Now we'll make the icon we just created be the application icon for the Calculator application:

6. Select PB's vertical Targets tab (at the center, near the bottom of PB's main window).

7. Make sure that Development is checked in the Build Styles pane (it should be already).

8. Select Calculator in the Targets area, and another set of tabs will appear on the right.

9. Select the newly appeared Applications Settings tab and focus on the Icon section, as shown in Figure 6-23.

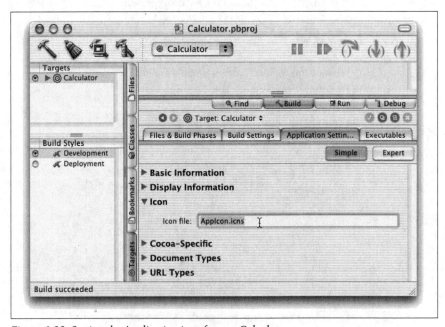

Figure 6-23. Setting the Application icon for our Calculator

10. Enter the filename `AppIcon.icns` in the "Icon file:" white text field area, as shown in Figure 6-23, and hit Return.

11. Build and run your Calculator application in PB. As usual, save all files before building.

12. With the application running, choose Calculator → About Calculator. You should see something similar to the screen shot in Figure 6-24 . Note that there is no icon in the About box, but we'll change that in the next section.

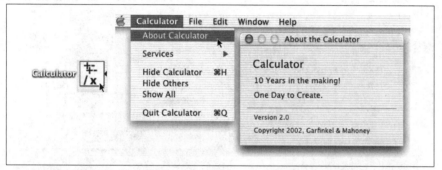

Figure 6-24. The running Calculator application with customized About box (no icon yet)

Although it doesn't always work right away, you should eventually see the application icon in your Dock to represent the running Calculator application (see Figure 6-24). You should also see it in the Finder (as shown at the edge of the page) when the Calculator application is selected in the `~/Calculator/build/` folder. If your application icon doesn't show up right away, try logging out and then logging back in—that worked for us.

13. Choose Calculator → Quit Calculator.

Making the New Icon Appear in the About Box

When we created our new About box in `AboutPanel.nib`, we left a space for the new application icon in the upper-right corner. In the following steps, we will add an NSImageView object in our About box to help display our new application icon:

14. Back in IB, be sure that `AboutPanel.nib` is the active nib by clicking in its Nib File window.

15. Click the Cocoa-Other button, which should be the third one from the left in IB's Palettes window toolbar.

16. Add an NSImageView object (seen at the edge of the page) to the About box by dragging its icon from the Cocoa-Other palette and dropping it into the top-right area of the About box.

17. Click the Images tab in the AboutPanel.nib window. Note that there are two copies of the icon we created, one labeled "AppIcon" and the other "NSApplicationIcon".

18. Add our new application icon (seen at the edge of the page) to the new NSImageView by dragging the AppIcon-labeled icon from the Images pane in the AboutPanel.nib window and dropping it on the NSImage-View in the About box. See Figure 6-25 for the result (your icon won't look exactly like this screen shot yet).

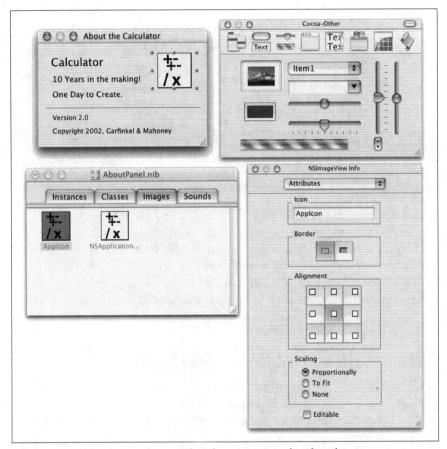

Figure 6-25. Adding our newly created application icon to the About box

19. Remove the border around the NSImageView object in the About box by clicking the icon (▢) on the left in the Border area of the NSImageView Info dialog.)

20. Make sure that the image alignment is centered and scaling is set to "Proportionally" in the NSImageView inspector. The result is shown in Figure 6-25.

21. Back in PB, build and run your project. Save all files when prompted.

22. Choose the Calculator → About Calculator menu command; you should see your custom application icon, as shown in Figure 6-26.

Project Builder

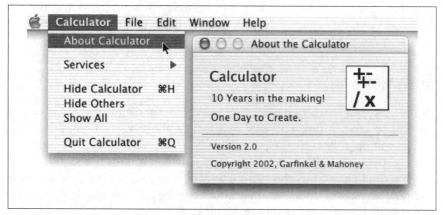

Figure 6-26. The running Calculator application with the application icon displayed in the About box

23. Choose Calculator → Quit Calculator.

There is no limit to the number of images that you can add to your application. To add an image to your project, simply drag the GIF, JPEG, or TIFF icon for that image file from your Finder window and drop it into your application's nib window in IB or in the main window in PB. Images that are stored in one nib cannot easily be used by objects in other nibs. For this reason, it is usually better to store images in the project directory rather than in a nib.

Cocoa's NSImage Class

In the previous example, we used an NSImageView object to display an image in our About box. The NSImageView class actually calls on another class, NSImage, to do its work. NSImage is the workhorse class for all images within the Cocoa development environment.

Cocoa uses objects of the NSImage class to display practically any kind of image on the screen. In Cocoa Version 10.1, the NSImage class could handle all the following types of images, and more:

- Portable Document Format (PDF)
- Tagged Image File Format (TIFF)
- Windows Bitmap Format (BMP)
- Graphics Interchange Format (GIF)
- Joint Photographic Experts Group format (JPEG)

- Macintosh Picture format (PICT)
- Untagged (raw) bitmap data

The NSImage class can also be extended on the fly by other programs that "register" themselves as *filter services*.* Because your programs will use the NSImage class, they too will be able to read images in any of these formats—without any additional work on your part.

Summary

In the first part of this chapter, we added a second nib to our Calculator application, and in doing so provided that application with an About box. Using multiple nibs is a good way to enhance the performance of your program; with multiple nibs, objects are created only when they need to be used. In the second part of this chapter, we learned how to create a Cocoa icons file and how to make this file the application icon for our Calculator. Finally, we saw how to display this icon in our About box.

In the next chapter, we'll learn about delegation, a powerful tool for controlling the functionality and extending the behavior of the Cocoa AppKit objects.

Exercises

1. Change the name of the nib name in the **showAboutPanel:** method from "AboutPanel.nib" to "No-such-nib.nib", but do not change the name of the actual nib file. Recompile and run your program. What happens when you attempt to display the About box? Why?

2. Revisit IconComposer and determine the meaning of the different icon resolutions and bit masks.

3. Investigate the .icns files in the /Applications and /Developer/Examples/ AppKit folders. Use the Terminal or Finder's Go → Go to Folder command to open folders such as /Application/iTunes.app/Contents.

References

1. General PB reference:

   http://developer.apple.com/techpubs/macosx/DeveloperTools/ProjectBuilder/ProjectBuilder.pdf

2. Creating photorealistic icons for Mac OS X:

   http://www.onlamp.com/pub/a/mac/2001/05/24/aqua_design.html

---

* We'll discuss Cocoa services in Chapter 20, but we won't implement a filter service. For more information on filter services, please consult the NSImage documentation.

CHAPTER 7

Delegation and Resizing

In this chapter, we will modify our Calculator application so that a user can choose to work with any of the following bases: base 2, 8, 10, or 16. To do this, we'll modify the Controller class to keep track of the current base and update the display accordingly. We'll also have to modify the keyboard-input routines to work with the proper base, called the *radix*, and ignore keypresses (digit-button clicks) that are invalid for a particular base. Most importantly, we will introduce the concept of *delegation*, a technique for specifying objects that perform functions for other objects. As for the user interface, we'll set up a pop-up menu (for the user to change the base) and show how to resize a window programmatically.

Handling Different Bases

The first step toward making our Calculator work with more than one base is to put a control for changing the base in the Calculator window. We'd like to use a radio button control, for several reasons. First, the radio button allows only one selection at a time, which is how our calculator will work. Second, it's both an input and an output at the same time—it shows a state and lets you change it. In addition to letting the user change the base, the radio button matrix indicates which base is currently selected and shows at a glance all of the choices. Unfortunately, the radio button idea has one major problem—it will take up too much room in our small calculator window. Instead, we'll use a pop-up menu. It has all of the qualities we need, including using only a small amount of space (although it doesn't show all choices without a click).

1. Open your Calculator project in Project Builder by double-clicking the `Calculator.pbproj` file (which you should have put in your Dock or Finder toolbar).

2. Open your project's main nib in Interface Builder by double-clicking `MainMenu.nib` in PB's Groups & Files pane.

Project Builder

Interface Builder

3. Choose Interface Builder → Hide Others to simplify the screen.

4. Select IB's Cocoa-Other palette (the one with the pop-up menu shown at the edge of the page).

5. Drag the pop-up menu icon from the Cocoa-Other palette and drop it in the middle of the Calculator window, just below the white text area, as shown in Figure 7-1.

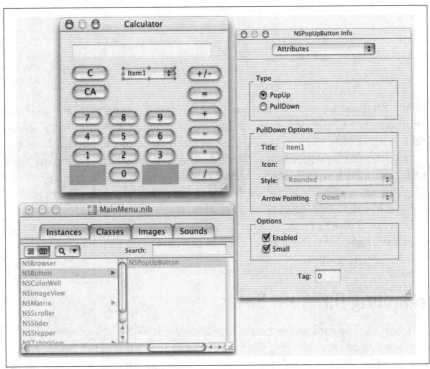

Figure 7-1. New pop-up menu in Calculator window with pertinent inspector

6. If necessary, type Command-1 to bring up the NSPopUpButton Attributes Info dialog.

Note that NSPopUpButton, the AppKit class we're using to install our pop-up menu, is not a menu; rather, it's a button that is a subclass of NSButton (see the class hierarchy in the Nib File window in Figure 7-1). When you double-click the pop-up menu button in IB, you'll see the three menu cells that the associated pop-up menu initially contains, as shown at the edge of the page.

An on-screen pop-up menu is controlled by an instance object of the NSPop-UpButton class. An NSPopUpButton object creates an NSMenu object to handle its menu-like functionality.

7. Click the Small checkbox near the bottom of the NSPopUpButton Info dialog to make the pop-up menu smaller, as shown in Figure 7-1 (we don't have much room left in our Calculator window).

8. Triple-click on the pop-up menu to expose the menu choices and simultaneously select the first choice (Item1) for editing, as shown on the left in Figure 7-2.

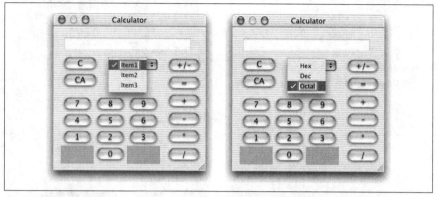

Figure 7-2. Editing the pop-up menu items

9. Change "Item1" to read "Hex", then hit the Tab key.

10. Change "Item2" to read "Dec", hit the Tab key, and change "Item3" to read "Octal". Your pop-up menu should now look like the one on the right in Figure 7-2.

We need one more menu item to allow a fourth option, "Binary" (base 2), as a choice for Calculator end users. We'll do that next.

11. Select IB's Cocoa-Menus palette by clicking the icon at the left of the Palettes window toolbar (shown at the edge of the page).

12. Drag the menu item labeled Item (Item) from the Cocoa-Menus palette and drop it below the third menu item (Octal) in the pop-up menu, as shown in Figure 7-3.

13. Double-click "Item" and change the text to "Binary" (see Figure 7-4).

14. Select the second item in the pop-up menu (Dec). We'll leave this item selected so that the application will start up as a decimal calculator (remember that the way you leave interface objects in IB is the way they'll appear when your application launches, unless you write code to change the interface).

15. Close the pop-up menu by clicking in the Calculator window's background, but not in the text area or on a button (that is, click above the text area but below the title bar).

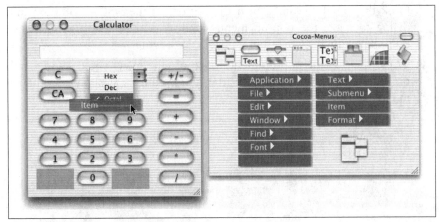

Figure 7-3. Adding a new menu item to the pop-up menu

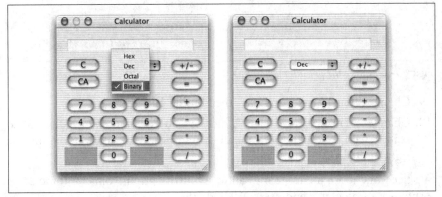

Figure 7-4. Renaming the new menu item (left) and leaving "Dec" showing on the pop-up menu (right)

16. Resize the pop-up menu so that it takes up no more room than is needed (click it once and drag a handle to make it smaller).

Your calculator window should look like the one on the right in Figure 7-4.

Pop-up menus work like a combination of the menus and buttons that we've used already. Like menus and buttons, they send messages, but unlike either menus or buttons, the last menu item selected remains visible on the top.

In a way that's similar to what we did with tags on the NSMatrix of digits in the previous chapter, we'll now set tags for the new pop-up menu.

17. Double-click on the pop-up menu labeled "Dec" to expose all four menu items.

18. One by one, select each menu item (e.g., Hex) and make sure that its tag matches the base that is displayed. That is, the Hex menu item should

have a tag of 16, and the Dec, Octal, and Binary menu items should have tags of 10, 8, and 2, respectively. (See Figure 7-5.)

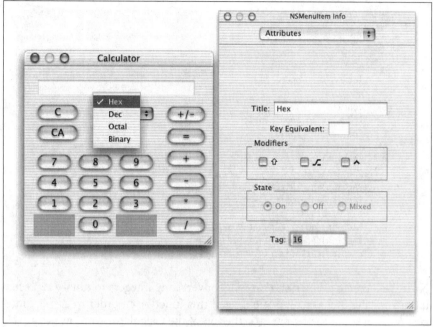

Figure 7-5. Setting the tag of a pop-up menu item

19. As before, select the Dec item and close the pop-up menu by clicking in the Calculator window's background, but not in the text area or on a button.

Your calculator window should still look similar to the one shown on the right in Figure 7-4.

 Tags have no effect on the outward appearance of any object.

Modifying the Controller Class

To make the Controller work with this new NSMatrix that contains a pop-up menu, we'll create a new action method called **setRadix:** that will be invoked whenever the user selects one of the radix choices from the pop-up menu. This **setRadix:** method will find out which base was selected in essentially the same way that the **enterDigit:** method in Chapter 5 found out which digit button was clicked—it will examine the tag of the sender of the message. To keep track of the radix that the user selected, we'll also add a new instance variable called radix to the Controller class.

Project Builder

Controller.h

20. Back in PB, insert the `radix` instance variable and the **setRadix:** action method declarations shown here in bold into `Controller.h`:

```
. . .
@interface Controller : NSObject
{
    IBOutlet id readout;
    BOOL       enterFlag;
    BOOL       yFlag;
    int        operation;
    double     X;
    double     Y;
    IBOutlet id aboutPanel;
    int        radix;
}
- (IBAction)clear:(id)sender;
- (IBAction)clearAll:(id)sender;
- (IBAction)enterDigit:(id)sender;
- (IBAction)enterOp:(id)sender;
- (void)displayX;
- (IBAction)doUnaryMinus:(id)sender;
- (IBAction)showAboutPanel:(id)sender;
- (IBAction)setRadix:(id)sender;
@end
```

Next we'll create a function that will convert long integers to binary representations in ASCII characters. We'll need this function in order to display integers of all bases in the text area at the top of the Calculator window.

Controller.m

21. Insert the following `ltob()` function into `Controller.m` before the `@implementation` directive:

```
NSString *ltob(unsigned long val)
{
    int i;
    char buf[33];

    for (i=0; i<32; i++) {
        buf[i] = (val & (1<<(31-i)) ? '1' : '0');
    }
    buf[32] = '\0';

    for (i=0; i<32; i++) {
        if (buf[i] != '0') {
            return [NSString stringWithCString:buf+i];
        }
    }
    return [NSString stringWithCString:buf+31];
}
```

A function in your class implementation file can be used by any other part of your program—it works like (and is) a regular C-language function. (Note that the function does *not* have access to the class instance variables (e.g., radix) because it is outside the class implementation.) The `ltob()` function

---

just listed changes a long integer into an ASCII binary representation. It places that ASCII representation in a buffer, then uses this buffer to create an NSString object, which is the return value of the function. We need this function because Cocoa lacks a general-purpose function for converting integers to ASCII-encoded strings of arbitrary bases.

22. Insert the following **setRadix:** method into `Controller.m` immediately before the @end directive:

Controller.m

```
- (IBAction)setRadix:(id)sender
{
    radix = [ [sender selectedCell] tag];
    [self displayX];
}
```

This method sets the radix instance variable to be the tag (2, 8, 10, or 16) of the pop-up menu item that was selected and updates the X register.

23. Replace the original **displayX** method in `Controller.m` with the new one that follows:

```
- (void)displayX
{
    NSString *s=nil;

    switch(radix) {
    case 16:
        s = [NSString stringWithFormat:@"%x",(int)X];
        break;
    case 10:
        s = [NSString stringWithFormat:@"%15.10g",X];
        break;
    case 8:
        s = [NSString stringWithFormat:@"%o",(int)X];
        break;
    case 2:
        s = ltob((int)X);
        break;
    }

    [readout setStringValue: s];
}
```

(Remember to *replace* the entire **displayX** method; do not leave the old **displayX** in place.)

This new **displayX** method converts the contents of the X register to the base (radix) that the user previously selected and displays the result in the Calculator window's text display area. (Recall that the readout outlet points to the NSTextField object near the top of the Calculator window.) Note that the base is "known" to **displayX** through the radix instance variable. Because radix is an instance variable, it is accessible to any Controller method.

In order for the radix instance variable to be set to the user-selected base, we need to arrange for the pop-up menu to send the **setRadix:** message to the Controller. As always, when we need an on-screen object to pass information to a custom object, we must set up a target/action connection in IB. But IB doesn't know about the **setRadix:** action method yet, so we must first read the new Controller class definition into IB:

24. Make sure that you save the two Controller class files in PB before proceeding (File → Save All).

Interface Builder

25. Back in IB, select the Classes tab in MainMenu.nib, then select the Controller class (under NSObject) in the class hierarchy. (The easiest way to find the Controller class is simply to type C in the Search field—try it!).

26. Choose IB's Classes → Read Controller.h menu command (note that you don't have to search for the class interface file in the filesystem, but you do have to with Classes → Read Files).

The new **setRadix:** action method we declared in Controller.h should now show up in the Controller Class Info dialog, as shown in Figure 7-6.

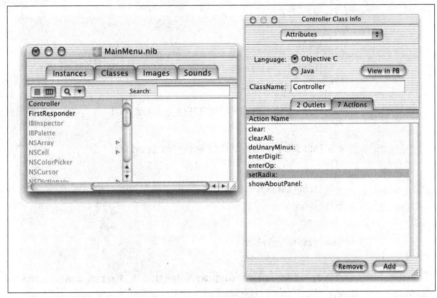

Figure 7-6. Reading the new setRadix: action method into IB

Next, we'll set up a target/action connection involving this method.

27. Select the Instances tab in the MainMenu.nib window.

28. Control-drag from the pop-up menu to the Controller object, as shown in Figure 7-7. (The previous step is actually unnecessary, because IB will automatically switch to the Instances pane when you Control-drag a connection to the Nib File window.)

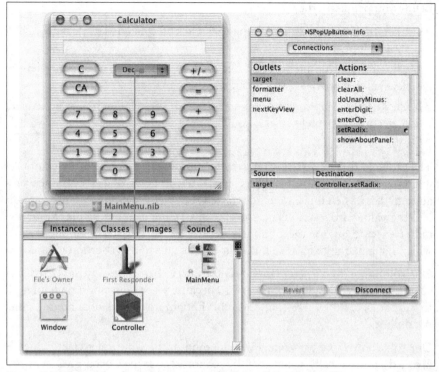

Figure 7-7. Connecting the pop-up menu to the Controller with setRadix:

29. Arrange for the pop-up menu to send the **setRadix:** action message to the Controller by double-clicking **setRadix:** in the NSPopUpButton Info dialog, as shown in Figure 7-7.

30. Back in PB, click the build and run button. Save all files when prompted.

31. With Calculator running, click the digit button labeled "9".

Nothing happens! What's worse, there are ominous messages colored in red in PB's Run pane, as shown in Figure 7-8. What's wrong?

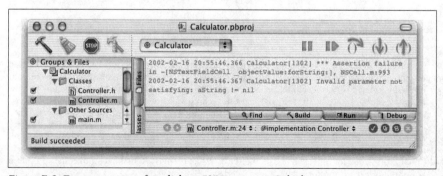

Figure 7-8. Error messages after clicking "9" in running Calculator

Before you panic, try the following:

32. Click the Dec pop-up menu and then click Dec again. The decimal digit 9 should appear.

33. Click the pop-up menu again and drag to Octal. The octal equivalent of decimal 9, namely 11, should appear.

34. Click the pop-up menu again and drag to Binary. The binary equivalent of decimal 9, namely 1001, should appear.

35. Quit Calculator.

The problem that occurred when we first clicked the 9 button is a lack of programmer initialization. Objective C initializes all of an object's instance variables to 0, so when our Calculator started running, the radix instance variable had the value of 0. As a result, the switch statement in the **displayX** method didn't execute any of the options—and no value was set to the variable s, which remained initialized to nil. That's what caused the assertion failure.

One solution is to hardcode the initialization of the instance variable radix in Controller.m. We could set radix to 10 because we set our pop-up menu in IB to start at Dec. But where can we do this initialization, and what are the other possibilities?

Our solution will be to create a new method in the Controller class, which is invoked automatically when the application starts up. Cocoa gives us three clean ways to specify initialization code for objects in a user interface:*

The **awakeFromNib** *method*

We can specify an initialization with Cocoa's **awakeFromNib** method. Cocoa automatically invokes the **awakeFromNib** method, if such a method exists, for *every* object it unarchives from a nib file. It does this after all of the objects have been unarchived and connected.

The notification system

We can use Cocoa's notification system, which allows objects to broadcast messages without designating connections in advance.

---

* Cocoa actually gives us a fourth way to initialize our objects as well. Because objects in nib files are instantiated using the NSCoder system (which we will describe in Chapter 13), we could create an **initWithCoder:** method and initialize variables in that method. The fact that we are telling you this in a footnote should be a strong signal that this technique is not to be used except under the most arcane circumstances. For starters, different **init** methods are called depending on how the object is initialized. A second problem with this method is that the **initWithCoder:** method is called after each object is created, whereas the **awakeFromNib** method is called after *all* of the objects in a nib are instantiated and wired up. That's why we wrote that Cocoa gives you three *clean* ways to specify initialization code for objects in a user interface. While there is a fourth technique, in our opinion you shouldn't use it for initializing a user interface.

Delegation

We can use a technique called *delegation*, where another object is delegated the responsibility of responding to certain types of messages sent to the delegating object.

We'll use the delegation technique to solve our current initialization problem because it fits nicely in the Calculator application. Later in the book, we'll use both of the other techniques.

Delegation

Cocoa uses a technique called delegation to allow objects to specify other objects, called *delegates*, to handle certain messages for them. Thus, one object can delegate to another object the responsibility for handling messages of a certain type. Delegation gives the programmer a system for modifying or controlling the behavior of Cocoa's more complicated objects, such as those of type NSApplication and NSWindow, without having to subclass them. Typically, delegation is used to control the behavior of an object or to invoke a method automatically in response to an action performed by a user.

An object sends its delegate specific messages under specific circumstances. Before the object sends the message, it checks to see if the delegate can respond to the message by interrogating the delegate with the **respondsTo-Selector:** message. If the delegate doesn't implement a method for a specific message, the message simply isn't sent! (The sender must interrogate the delegate, because if a delegate receives a message for which it doesn't have a corresponding method, the program will generate an error.)

For more information about **respondsToSelector:** and similar messages, see the documentation for the NSObject class. The **respondsToSelector:** method is defined in the root NSObject class and thus is inherited by *all* other objects.

Should, Will, and Did Delegates

Cocoa has three principal types of messages that are sent to delegate objects: *Should*, *Will*, and *Did* messages. Both *Should* and *Will* messages are sent *before* something happens (e.g., before a window closes). When the delegate is sent a *Should* message, the delegate can change the sender's behavior by responding in a certain way. On the other hand, a *Did* message gets sent *after* a particular event takes place (e.g., after a window closes). A *Did* message notifies the delegate object that something has occurred. At that point, it's too late to change the behavior, but you might want to do something in response to an action that another object has taken.

There are dozens of different delegate messages implemented by various Cocoa classes. In Tables 7-1 and 7-2, we list a few typical *Will*, *Should*, and *Did* delegate methods that are implemented by the NSApplication object. In these tables, as in earlier ones, we'll use the same type conventions used in Apple's Cocoa documentation: methods are in **bold** type, arguments are in *italic* type, and data types are in normal type.

Table 7-1. Typical Will and Should messages

Will message	When message is sent to delegate
(void)**applicationWillFinishLaunching:** (NSNotification *)*aNotification*	Before the application is finished launching. The argument to this delegate method (and many others) is an NSNotification object from the Foundation.
(void)**applicationWillUnhide:** (NSNotification *)*aNotification*	Before the application is unhidden.
(void)**applicationWillUpdate:** (NSNotification *)*aNotification*	Before the Application object updates the application's windows.
(NSApplicationTerminateReply) **applicationShouldTerminate:** (NSApplication *)*sender*	When the NSApplication object receives a **terminate:** message. This method lets you clean up the application—for example, shutting down databases and saving or closing any open files before it terminates. Return **NSTerminateNow** to allow the application to terminate now, **NSTerminateCancel** to cancel termination, or **NSTerminateLater** to ask for more time. (If the delegate responds with **NSTerminateLater**, it will be sent another **applicationShouldTerminate:** message.)

Table 7-2. Typical Did messages

Did message	When message is sent to delegate
(void)**applicationDidBecomeActive:** (NSNotification *)*aNotification*	After the application is activated
(void)**applicationDidHide:** (NSNotification *)*aNotification*	After the application is hidden
(void)**applicationDidFinishLaunching:** (NSNotification *)*aNotification*	After the application has been launched and initialized, but before it receives its first event
(void)**applicationDidResignActive:** (NSNotification *)*aNotification*	After the application is deactivated
(void)**appDidUnhide:** (NSNotification *)*aNotification*	After the application is unhidden
(void)**appDidUpdate:** (NSNotification *)*aNotification*	After the Application object updates the application's windows

Delegate methods let you do fairly complicated things with ease. For example, suppose that you set up a delegate object for your application's NSApplication object, and that the delegate implements the **applicationShouldTerminate:** method. When the user chooses the Quit menu command from your application, the NSApplication object receives the **terminate:** message and in turn sends the **applicationShouldTerminate:** message to its delegate. The delegate's **applicationShouldTerminate:** method could then display a panel asking the user "Do you really want to quit?" If the user answers "No," the delegate returns **NSTerminateCancel** to the NSApplication object, and the application doesn't terminate. If the user answers "Yes," the delegate returns **NSTerminateNow**, and the application terminates.

Not every class in the AppKit makes use of delegation, but many do. Frequently, you can accomplish the same thing with either delegation or subclassing. If you have a choice, use delegation! Delegation is simpler and generally easier to debug than subclassing, and it makes your code more easily reusable. Delegation frees you from having to subclass a lot of the AppKit classes. For most applications, you'll need to subclass only the NSObject and NSView classes.

One of the most frequently used of the NSApplication delegate methods is **applicationDidFinishLaunching:**, which is automatically sent after an application is initialized but before it receives any events. Later in this chapter, we'll set up a delegate for our Calculator's NSApplication object and use **applicationDidFinishLaunching:** to set the initial radix and perform other initialization tasks.

Specifying an Object's Delegate

An object's delegate is specified by an *outlet* instance variable appropriately called delegate. Table 7-3 lists the main AppKit classes that support delegates.

Table 7-3. Main delegate-supporting AppKit classes

Class	Reason for delegate object
NSApplication	To receive information about the application's state
NSBrowser	To fill the information stored in the browser
NSDrawer	To control the display and hiding of drawers
NSFontManager	To receive alerts when fonts are changed
NSImage	To notify the application if an image isn't drawn
NSLayoutManager	To alert when the text in a container has been laid out, or when a layout has been invalidated
NSMatrix	To edit information stored inside a matrix
NSSavePanel	To validate filenames
NSSound	To alert when sounds are finished playing
NSSplitView	To control resizing
NSTableView	To control when table rows and columns are selected, displayed, and moved
NSTabView	To alert when tabs are displayed and hidden
NSText	To control editing and interception of keystrokes

Table 7-3. *Main delegate-supporting AppKit classes (continued)*

Class	Reason for delegate object
NSTextField	To control editing and interception of keystrokes
NSTextStorage	To control the processing of edits
NSTextView	To control the editing of text
NSToolbar	To control the display of toolbars and the addition and removal of toolbar items
NSWindow	To receive window events and control resizing

There are two ways to provide an object with a delegate:

- Connect the object to its delegate in IB.
- Use the object's **setDelegate:** method.

Which object should be the delegate? The answer to this question depends on your application. Sometimes you will create a special object whose sole purpose is to be the delegate of one or more other objects. By using one object as the delegate for several other objects, you can centralize control for handling events for common objects. However, an object can also serve double duty, both being the delegate for another object and having a life of its own.

In our example, we'll make our Calculator's Controller object be the delegate of the NSApplication object. We'll do this for two reasons. First, the Controller class is still fairly simple. By making it the NSApplication's delegate, we eliminate the complexity of creating a second class.*

The second reason to make our Controller object the NSApplication's delegate is that the initialization we want to perform—namely, setting the Calculator's radix—needs to be done inside the Controller object itself. Thus, the Controller is the logical object to be the NSApplication's delegate object.

Setting Up a Delegate Outlet in the Nib

We'll use IB to make our application's Controller instance the delegate of the NSApplication object. Recall that the File's Owner object under the Instances tab in the `MainMenu.nib` window represents the Calculator's NSApplication object; it's the owner of `MainMenu.nib`.

Interface Builder

1. In IB, select the Instances tab in the `MainMenu.nib` (Nib File) window.
2. Control-drag from the File's Owner icon to the Controller instance icon inside the `MainMenu.nib` window.

---

* Creating too many classes to solve a particular problem is a common mistake made by some people new to object-oriented languages. It leads to lasagna code—code with too many layers stacked together. Too many classes may lead to the object-oriented equivalent of spaghetti-code. Creating too few classes is also a common mistake of newcomers.

3. Double-click the delegate outlet to complete the connection, as shown in Figure 7-9.

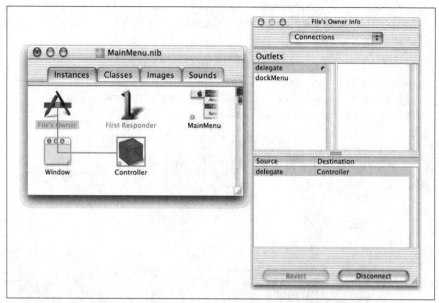

Figure 7-9. Delegate connection from File's Owner to Controller

Our Controller instance is now the delegate of the NSApplication object referred to as the File's Owner in IB. Next we'll add a new outlet to the Controller class so that the delegate method can determine the initial menu item (radix) that is selected in the pop-up menu.* This outlet, which we'll call radixPopUp, will be set to the id of the NSPopUpButton that causes the pop-up menu of radixes to be displayed.†

4. Back in PB, insert the radixPopUp outlet into Controller.h:

```
...
@interface Controller:Object
...
    int        radix;
    IBOutlet id radixPopUp;
}
...
```

Controller.h

---

* In this example, we have the Controller class determine the initialization value from the pop-up menu in the nib, rather than setting the pop-up to reflect a value that might be stored in the Controller.m file. Cocoa is a visual application development environment; when possible, the default values of instance variables should reflect what is stored in the visual interface, rather than the other way around.

† When you drag out a pop-up menu from IB's palette, you actually drag out two objects: an NSPopUpButton and an attached NSMenu.

5. Save the edited `Controller.h` file.

6. Back in IB, make sure the Controller class is selected in the Classes pane in the `MainMenu.nib` window and then choose Classes → Read Controller.h to parse the Controller class definition again (so IB knows about the new `radixPopUp` outlet).

7. Select the Instances tab in the `MainMenu.nib` window.

8. Connect (Control-drag from) the Controller instance icon to the pop-up menu and double-click the `radixPopUp` outlet in the NSPopUpButton Connections Info dialog, as shown in Figure 7-10.

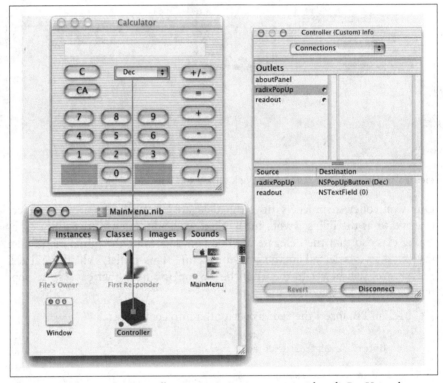

Figure 7-10. Connecting Controller instance to pop-up menu with radixPopUp outlet

Note that this connection is in the opposite direction of a previous connection between these same two objects.

Two connections are listed in the bottom pane of the Connections Info dialog in Figure 7-10 (we set up both of them). This is useful information for Cocoa programmers, because it lets you immediately see the destinations of all of the outlets that have been set for a given class (Controller, in this case). If you click on one of the connections listed, IB will redisplay the connection line for you.

Next, we'll set up the delegate method in the Controller class.

Adding the Delegate Method to the Controller

To receive the application delegate's **applicationDidFinishLaunching:** message in the Controller, all we need to do is create a method with the name **applicationDidFinishLaunching:**. You can place this method between the @implementation Controller and @end statements. Alternatively, you can create a second set of @implementation and @end statements containing the delegate methods (that's what we've done below). This separate definition helps isolate those methods specifically for delegation from the methods used for other purposes.

9. Add all of the following code after the original @end directive in Controller.m:

Controller.m

```
@implementation Controller(ApplicationNotifications)

-(void)applicationDidFinishLaunching:(NSNotification*)notification
{
    radix = [ [radixPopUp selectedItem] tag];
    [self clearAll:self];
}
@end
```

You can add as many Controller delegate methods as you want between the @implementation Controller(ApplicationNotifications) and @end directives. ApplicationNotifications is called a *category*. You can also use this syntax construct for adding methods to AppKit classes, but you will need to set up separate interface and implementation files. You cannot use a category to add new instance variables to a class, but methods in a category have full access to all of the instance variables defined in the object class itself. Next we show the matching class interface for the Controller(NSApplicationNotifications) category:

10. Insert all of the following declaration code after the original @end directive in Controller.h.

Controller.h

```
@interface Controller(NSApplicationNotifications)
-(void)applicationDidFinishLaunching:(NSNotification*)notification;
@end
```

When the application starts up, the Controller's **applicationDidFinish-Launching:** method is automatically executed. The method will set the radix* and then invoke the Controller's **clearAll:** method to display the initialized X value in the Calculator's text area.

11. Build and run your application. In contrast to the last time, your Calculator should display the numbers as soon as you start clicking the digit

---

* If we used a matrix of radio buttons instead of a pop-up menu, we could simply call the **setRadix:** method and supply the id of the matrix as the sender. Unfortunately, the NSPopUpButton uses the **selectedItem** method to find which cell is currently selected, rather than the **selectedCell** method.

buttons. However, there are other problems that we need to fix. We'll address them in the next section.

12. Quit Calculator when you're done playing around with it.

Disabling Buttons for Better Multiradix Input

You may have noticed that there is still a big problem with our Calculator—the keypad doesn't work correctly in any base except for decimal. The reason for this failure lies with the following statement in the **enterDigit:** method:

```
X = (X*10.0) + [ [sender selectedCell] tag];
```

This statement multiplies whatever is in the X register by 10 and adds the tag of a digit button each time one is clicked. Unfortunately, we don't want to multiply the X register by 10 if a radix other than base 10 is in effect; instead, we want to multiply by the current radix. So, for a first pass, the 10.0 in this statement should be replaced with radix.

Controller.m

1. Replace the 10.0 in the **enterDigit:** method in Controller.m with radix to get:

```
X = (X*radix) + [ [sender selectedCell] tag];
```

But that's not the only change we need to make; we also have to change the keypad of buttons so that particular buttons are deactivated when certain bases are selected. For example, a user shouldn't be able to press the 8 button when the Octal base is chosen. Also, it would be nice to make buttons for the numbers A, B, C, D, E, and F appear when the user selects Hex. We'll address all of these problems and add the new features in the remainder of this chapter.

Accessing NSMatrix Cells with an NSArray Object

Every Cocoa button is either *enabled* or *disabled*. If a button is disabled, the black labeling on it turns gray, and the button won't respond to the mouse. In the following steps, we'll modify the **setRadix:** method so that each time the radix is changed, the method will scan all of the buttons in the digit-button matrix and disable the ones whose tags are equal to or greater than the newly selected radix.

To scan all of the digit buttons in the NSMatrix, we'll need its id. We'll also need the id of each individual button that the matrix contains. As we will see, the id of each cell inside an NSMatrix object is stored in yet another Foundation object, called an NSArray. As its name implies, an NSArray contains an array (or list) of other objects.

2. Insert the `keyPad` outlet declaration shown here in bold into `Controller.h`:

Controller.h

```
...
@interface Controller:Object
{
...
    IBOutlet id radixPopUp;
    IBOutlet id keyPad;
}
```

3. Save `Controller.h`.

Our program will use the `keyPad` outlet to learn the id of the NSMatrix object when the application starts up. As usual, we'll arrange for this initialization in IB.

4. Now drag the `Controller.h` icon from PB's Groups & Files pane and drop it in the `MainMenu.nib` window in IB.

Interface Builder

This operation has the same effect as choosing IB's Classes → Read Controller.h menu command. You can also drag the `Controller.h` icon from the Finder and drop it in the same place. Now `MainMenu.nib` "knows about" the new `keyPad` outlet in the Controller class.

5. Connect the newly created `keyPad` outlet in the Controller instance to the NSMatrix object that contains the digit buttons for your Calculator. Make sure you connect to the matrix and not to a single digit button within the matrix (move the mouse near the edge of the matrix until you see that it's surrounded by a connection wire box, as shown in Figure 7-11).

NSArray is an important class for Cocoa programmers; it's a generic class (actually called a Foundation class) for maintaining a collection, or list, of other objects. The NSArray class has methods for:

- Creating an array from a single object, or from a collection of objects
- Sending a message to every object in the list
- Counting the number of elements in the list
- Accessing a specific element in the list by number
- Creating a new NSArray from the existing array

After an NSArray is created and initialized, the collection of objects that make up the array never changes. If you need to create an array to which objects can be added or removed, use an NSMutableArray instead. This mutable (changeable) class has additional methods for:

- Adding an object to the list
- Adding an object to the list if it isn't already there
- Removing an object from the list

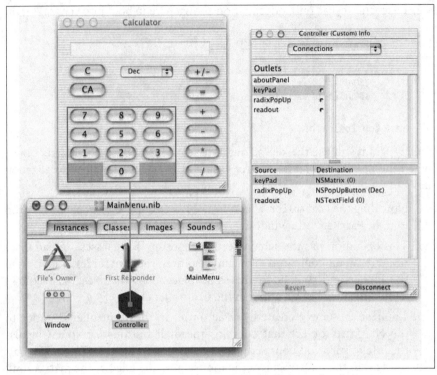

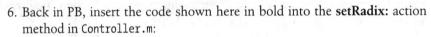

Figure 7-11. Connecting Controller instance to matrix with keyPad outlet

Refer to the Cocoa Foundation documentation for a detailed explanation of the NSArray and NSMutableArray classes.

Project Builder

Controller.m

6. Back in PB, insert the code shown here in bold into the **setRadix:** action method in Controller.m:

```
- (IBAction)setRadix:(id)sender
{
    NSArray *cells;
    int i;

    radix = [[sender selectedCell] tag];

    // Disable the buttons that are higher than selected radix
    cells = [keyPad cells];

    for (i=0; i<[cells count]; i++) {
        id cell = [cells objectAtIndex: i];
        [cell setEnabled: ([cell tag] < radix) ];
    }

    [self displayX];
}
```

We'll explain the new code in **setRadix:** line by line. The following line sends the **cells** message to the keyPad (NSMatrix) object, which causes the object to return the id of the NSArray object that holds all of the NSMatrix's (button) cells:

```
cells = [keyPad cells];
```

Once we have the id (stored in the cells instance variable) of this NSArray object, we can easily access the objects stored inside it. This line sets up a loop that will execute for each of the objects stored in the NSArray object:

```
for (i=0; i<[cells count]; i++)
```

This line sets the cell local variable to be the id of the *i*th element in the NSArray object:

```
id cell = [cellList objectAtIndex: i];
```

The expression [cell tag] < radix in the following line returns YES if cell should be enabled and NO if it shouldn't (YES and NO are specified by #define operators in the Foundation class NSObjCRuntime.h file):

```
[cell setEnabled: ([cell tag] < radix)];
```

The outermost message then sets the cell to be enabled or disabled as appropriate for the current radix. For example, if the radix is 8 (octal), all cells with tags less than 8 should be enabled (YES), while cells with tags 8 or greater should be disabled (NO).

There are a variety of ways to loop over the objects stored with an NSArray. You can create an integer variable and step through all of the variables, as we did earlier. Alternately, you can ask the array for an objectEnumerator and step that enumerator through the contents of the array. For example, the **setRadix:** method could be rewritten to look like the following (not necessary to implement):

```
- (IBAction)setRadix:(id)sender
{
    NSEnumerator *enumerator;
    NSCell *cell;

    radix = [[sender selectedCell] tag];

    // Disable the buttons that are higher than selected radix
    enumerator = [[keyPad cells] objectEnumerator];

    while (cell = [enumerator nextObject]) {
        [cell setEnabled: ([cell tag] < radix) ];
    }
    [self displayX];
}
```

This revised version of the **setRadix:** method is smaller and more object-oriented, but some people may find it harder to understand. It may also take a few thousandths of a second longer to run; on the other hand, it may not. Ultimately, both versions of the method work equally well, but the object-oriented version is easier to debug and easier to maintain. In general, you should use the NSEnumerator class for iterating through NSArrays, rather than a for loop with the **objectAtIndex:** method.

7. Save all pertinent files and build and run the Calculator application.

8. With Calculator running, click the digit buttons to display the number 258.

9. Now click the Dec pop-up menu button and drag to Binary. Note that the number 258 changes to its binary representation and all the digit buttons except 0 and 1 are disabled, as shown in the window on the left in Figure 7-12. The buttons turn gray because Cocoa buttons automatically display their titles in gray when they are disabled.

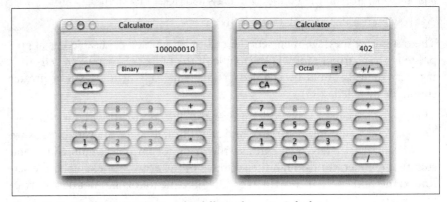

Figure 7-12. Disabling digit buttons for different bases in Calculator

10. Next, click the Binary pop-up menu button and drag to Octal. Note that the number changes to its octal representation and that the digit buttons 8 and 9 are disabled, as shown in the window on the right in Figure 7-12.

11. Quit Calculator.

Coherence in Object-Oriented Programming

The changes to the **setRadix:** method bear mentioning, because they contain the essence of another important object-oriented concept: *coherence*. Being *coherent* means being logically or aesthetically ordered or integrated. In object-oriented programming, coherence means writing as little code as necessary by writing code that figures out what it needs to know when it runs, rather than having things preprogrammed. This way, if something changes, the code automatically reconfigures itself at runtime.

In this example, the **setRadix:** method disables those buttons in the matrix that have a tag that is equal to or greater than the current radix—so, for example, the buttons labeled 2–9 don't work when the Calculator is in binary mode. But rather than hardcoding the keys, the **setRadix:** method needs to disable the keys for each radix; we have **setRadix:** find these keys by scanning through the associated NSArray object that contains the matrix cells. Likewise, rather than hardcoding into **setRadix:** the number of buttons in the matrix, we have **setRadix:** determine the number by asking the NSArray how many objects it contains. This way, we can change the number of cells in the matrix while in IB and not have to make any changes to the **setRadix:** method.

Resizing Windows Programmatically

We're not done with our Calculator—we still haven't built a system for entering the hexadecimal "numbers" A, B, C, D, E, and F. Probably the easiest way to enter these hex numbers is to add another six buttons to the keypad and put the letters on them. (Naturally, these buttons will have the tags 10–15.) Because we don't need these buttons to be displayed all the time, our Cocoa Calculator will do something that no physical calculator can do: it will make itself bigger when it is in hex mode (to make room for the extra buttons), and then make itself smaller when they are no longer needed (i.e., in other bases).

To accomplish this magic, we need to learn more about how the NSMatrix, NSCell, and NSWindow classes work:

- When we want to make our Calculator window bigger, the first question to ask is "How much bigger?" We'll need to insert space for two more rows of buttons (six new hex-only buttons in total). Each NSMatrix knows the size of its cells as well as the spacing between cells. We'll need to query our NSMatrix to find out how much larger the NSWindow needs to be in order to hold two more rows of buttons.

- After we know how much space to add, we'll need to resize the window and make sure that every object in the window moves to the appropriate place during the resize operation.

- After the window is resized, we'll need to create the six additional buttons that we want and set their tags appropriately.

- Finally, when we make the Calculator window smaller, we'll need to arrange to remove the two rows of buttons that we just added.

Modifying the Calculator's Interface

The first thing that we'll do is modify the Calculator's interface so that the resize operation happens seamlessly for the interface objects in the Calculator window.

The Cocoa *autosizing* system determines how objects shrink, expand, or move on a window when that window is resized. A nice example of autosizing can be seen in the Mac OS X Mail application, which stretches the messages list and message preview areas when you resize the main window, but does not stretch the buttons or other controls. In our Calculator application, resizing is relatively simple, because there are only two cases we need to be concerned with:

- When the user switches *to* base 16 (the Calculator window must get bigger to accommodate the two extra rows of buttons)
- When the user switches *from* base 16 (the Calculator window must get smaller as the extra rows of buttons are removed)

When either of these things happens, we want the text area display and some of the buttons to stay near the top of the Calculator's window, but we want the keypad of digit buttons to stick to the bottom. We will insert the new hex-only buttons A–F above the digit buttons 7, 8, and 9.

Interface Builder

1. Back in IB, select the NSTextField that is the Calculator's text display readout.

2. Type Command-3 to bring up the NSTextField Size Info dialog.

The Size Info dialog, which is available for all subclasses of the NSView class, enables you to control an object's position and resizing within a window. We'll start by focusing on the autosizing box at the bottom of the Size Info dialog:

3. Click the bottom-most part of the cross in the Autosizing box of the Size inspector so that the vertical line at the very bottom turns into a spring-like wire, as shown in Figure 7-13.

The autosizing we've set in Figure 7-13 means that the NSTextField display area will "give" at the bottom of the window and "stick" to the top of the window when the window is resized. Thus, during autosizing, we are allowing the NSTextField to change its position relative to the bottom boundary of the window, but not relative to the top boundary.

4. Set the autosizing for the NSMatrix containing the C and CA buttons to match the autosizing for the NSTextField display readout.

5. Set the autosizing for the radix pop-up menu and the function keys (e.g., +, /) matrix to match the autosizing of the display readout as well.

At this point, all of the interface objects in the Calculator window have the same autosizing setting, except for the keypad, or digit-button matrix. The keypad needs a different autosizing setting because we want it to stick to the bottom of the window, not to the top of it. The reason is that we will insert the six new hex-only buttons above the digit buttons 7, 8, and 9.

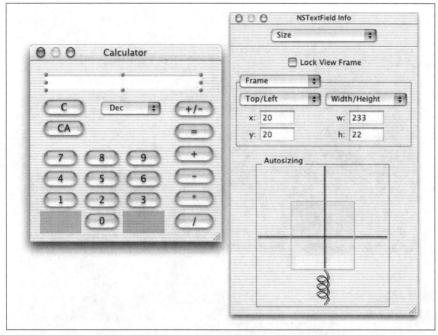

Figure 7-13. Setting the autosizing for the NSTextField display readout

6. Select the keyPad NSMatrix and set its autosizing to look like that in Figure 7-14.

We'll make only a general statement about autosizing now, and then we'll move on. You can control the selected object's *position* within a window by clicking the lines *outside* the inner box in the Size Info dialog's Autosizing area, and you can control the object's *size* by clicking the lines *inside* the inner box.

Notice that we haven't entered any sizes such as how big the matrix is, how big the Calculator window is, or how big the window has to grow. We don't need to find out this information ahead of time and hardcode it into our program. Instead, we'll arrange for the Controller object to send messages to the NSMatrix and NSWindow objects to find out this information. The Controller will then calculate how much larger the window needs to grow in order to make the additional hex buttons visible and will send a message to the NSWindow object to change its size accordingly.

Modifying the Controller Class

Next, we need to modify the `Controller.h` and `Controller.m` files to make the window bigger when we switch to base 16 and smaller when we switch from base 16 to a different base.

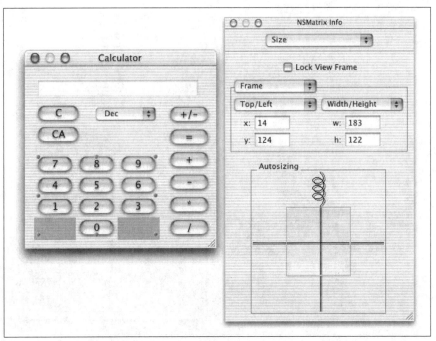

Figure 7-14. Setting the autosizing for the NSMatrix of digit buttons

Controller.m

7. Back in PB, replace `Controller.m`'s **setRadix:** method with the much longer version that follows. In contrast to the way we implemented the previous version of this method, we'll code the method the object-oriented way this time.

```
- (IBAction)setRadix:(id)sender
{
    NSEnumerator *enumerator;
    NSCell *cell;
    int oldRadix = radix;

    radix = [ [sender selectedCell] tag];

    if (radix!=oldRadix && (radix==16 || oldRadix==16) ) {

        double ysize = [keyPad cellSize].height * 2
                        + [keyPad intercellSpacing].height * 2;
        int row,col;
        NSWindow *win = [keyPad window];
        NSRect frame = [win frame];

        // If switching to radix 16, grow the window,
        // and keep the title bar in the same place
        if (radix==16) {
            frame.size.height += ysize;
            frame.origin.y    -= ysize;
            [win setFrame:frame display:YES animate:YES];
```

```
            for (row=0;row<2;row++) {
                [keyPad insertRow:0];

                for (col=0;col<3;col++) {
                    int val = 10 + row*3 + col;
                    cell = [keyPad cellAtRow:0 column:col];
                    [cell setTag:val];
                    [cell setTitle:[NSString
                                  stringWithFormat:@"%X",val]];
                }
            }

            [keyPad sizeToCells];
            [keyPad setNeedsDisplay];
        }

        // If switching away from base 16, shrink the window
        // (keeping the title bar in the same place)
        else {
            frame.size.height -= ysize;
            frame.origin.y     += ysize;
            [keyPad removeRow:0];
            [keyPad removeRow:0];
            [keyPad sizeToCells];
            [keyPad setNeedsDisplay];
            [win setFrame:frame display:YES animate:YES];
        }
    }

    // Disable the buttons that are higher than selected radix
    enumerator = [ [keyPad cells] objectEnumerator];

    while (cell = [enumerator nextObject]) {
        [cell setEnabled: ([cell tag] < radix) ];
    }
    [self displayX];
}
```

Don't worry if this code seems a bit complicated—it is a jump beyond what we've seen before! It uses a few methods from the NSWindow and NSMatrix classes that have yet to be described, but we'll get to them before the end of the chapter.

The first new line sets up the oldRadix variable to contain the old radix. We use this to see if the user has changed the radix. If the user is changing the radix, and either the old or the new radix is base 16 (hex), the window needs to be resized.

The first part of the resizing code fills in ysize, a variable that stores the amount of vertical space that the window needs to grow or shrink. Because we are adding two new rows, ysize is exactly equal to twice the height of the keyPad cells and twice the intercell spacing. We also ask the keyPad for the id of its NSWindow object, so that we can eventually send a "resize" message to the window. We also get the frame of the window, which is its current location and size on the screen.

If we are switching to radix 16, the window needs to get bigger. We add ysize to the window frame's height, then use the **setFrame:display:animate:** method to make the NSWindow bigger. This method's **animate:** argument, which we set to YES, is responsible for animating the stretching, which makes our Calculator look like other Cocoa applications that animate their resizing.

Next, we insert the two rows of new buttons, using nested for loops. Each row is inserted at position 0, which is at the top of the matrix. Each row will have three buttons: A, B, and C for the row immediately above the row with 7, 8, and 9, and D, E, and F for the new top row in the matrix. The inner loop sets the tag and title of each of the new buttons as appropriate for its position.

We follow by sending the matrix the **sizeToCells** message, which causes the NSMatrix to recalculate its size given the fact that it now has two additional rows of cells. Finally, we send the matrix the **setNeedsDisplay** message, so that the matrix automatically redisplays itself when the window is updated.

The second case—making the window smaller—is much simpler. We calculate the new smaller size of the window, remove the top two rows, resize the matrix, note that the matrix needs to be redisplayed, and finally resize the window.

8. Back in PB, build and run your upgraded Calculator, saving all files first.

9. Click the 2, 6, and 7 digit buttons, then switch to Hex via the pop-up menu. The window should resize downward, and six new buttons should appear, as in the window on the right in Figure 7-15.

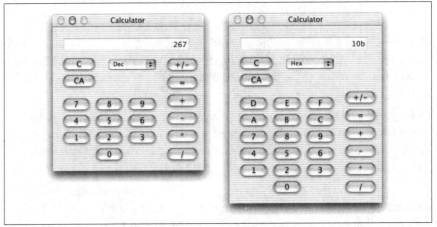

Figure 7-15. Calculator without (left) and with (right) hex buttons

10. Now switch to Binary, Octal, or Dec. The window should return to its original size.

11. Quit Calculator when you're done playing with your nifty new creation.

Strong Typing with Objective-C

There are two ways that you can specify a variable that holds a pointer to an object in Objective-C. You can use the id type to declare a pointer to any kind of object. Alternatively, if you know in advance what kind of object you are going to have, you can construct a pointer to the specific object type by using the object's class name as a type. Thus, a pointer to an NSArray object can be declared like this:

```
id anArray;
```

or like this:

```
NSArray *anArray;
```

The second way of declaring an NSArray is called *strong (static) typing*. Strong typing provides better compiler type checking and the ability to directly access public variables stored inside the NSArray object.

You can use strong typing with IB. For example, if you have an outlet that should be connected only to an object that is of type NSWindow (or a subclass), you could declare that outlet like this:

```
IBOutlet NSWindow *anOutlet;
```

You can also do this in IB's Class Info dialog, in the Outlets pane. Click the little black down arrow next to an outlet to choose its (strong) type.

Two Very Important Classes: NSWindow and NSView

In this section we'll describe the very important NSWindow and NSView classes in more detail and list many of their most useful instance methods.

The NSWindow Class

NSWindow is one of the most important classes in the Application Kit. If you want to be an effective Cocoa programmer, it is essential that you be familiar with the variety and scope of NSWindow's many methods.

Every on-screen window displayed by a program is controlled by an instance object of the NSWindow class. Each NSWindow object receives events from a program's NSApplication object. Most mouse events are sent to the object within the window where the mouse event took place (e.g., if an on-screen button is clicked, a **mouseDown:** message is sent to the corresponding NSButton object). Keyboard events are sent to the object that is the window's first responder, which we'll describe in detail in the next chapter.

Each window contains at least one instance of the NSView class (described shortly), called the window's *content view*. Although you can work directly with a window's content view, normally you will create subviews of the content view in which you do your actual drawing and event processing. We'll discuss these ideas in great depth in the following chapters.

Some of the most common instance methods for NSWindow objects are listed in Table 7-4. Recall that if an argument's data type isn't specified (e.g., *sender*), it's an id by default.

Table 7-4. Common instance methods for NSWindow objects

NSWindow instance method	Purpose
- (id)**contentView**	Returns the id of the window's content view.
- (void)**makeKeyAndOrderFront:**(id)*sender*	Makes the window the key window and places it in front of all other windows on the screen.
- (void)**center**	Moves the window to the center of the screen.
- (void)**orderOut:**(id)*sender*	Takes the window out of the screen list, which makes it invisible. The window is still in the Window Server's memory; you just can't see it!
- (void)**performClose:**(id)*sender*	Simulates a user's clicking the window's close button.
- (void)**performMiniaturize:**(id)*sender*	Simulates a user's clicking the window's miniaturize button.
- (void)**setFrame:**(NSRect)*aFrame* **display:**(BOOL)*flag* **animate:**(BOOL)*aFlag*	Moves and optionally resizes a window with or without smooth animation.
-(BOOL)**setFrameUsingName:**(NSString *)*aName*	Sets the window's frame using a name stored in the system defaults. This is handy if you want a program to reappear in the same location on the screen as the location where it was last run.
- (void)**setFrameFromString:**(NSString *)*aString*	Sets the window's frame using a representation stored in *aString*. This is handy if you want to remember a window's position and size in a file and then restore it later.
- (void)**setTitle:**(NSString *)*aString*	Sets the window's title in its title bar to *aString*.
- (void)**setTitleWithRepresentedFilename:** (NSString *)*aString*	Sets the window's title in its title bar to a filename.
- (NSRect)**frame**	Returns the window's frame; tells you where the window is on the screen and how big it is.

All of the methods available to the NSWindow class are described in the NSWindow documentation. One of the easiest ways to read this documentation is by referring to Apple's Developer web site: http://developer.apple.com. You can also use the class browser that is built into PB. To do this, click the

Classes vertical tab in PB's main window, click the disclosure triangle next to NSObject, and then click the little book icon next to a class such as NSArray. (See Figure 7-16.)

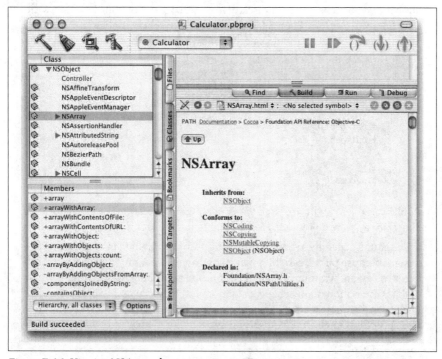

Figure 7-16. Viewing NSArray documentation in PB

The NSView Class

NSView is the basic class for creating objects that draw in windows and respond to user events. Just as everything drawn on a Cocoa screen is drawn in a window, practically everything drawn inside a window is drawn with the help of NSView objects. For example, the NSMatrix, NSTextField, and NSButton classes we've used in our Calculator application are all subclasses of NSView.

Every window contains at least one view—the content view. This view covers the window except for the title bar, resize handle, and border. The window's content view automatically stretches and shrinks with the window when the window is resized.

Every view can have zero or more subviews. After a view draws itself, it redraws any of the objects in its subview hierarchy (we'll say more about view hierarchies later) whose appearance has been changed or altered. In this way, what we see on the Mac OS X screen properly corresponds to what is stored in the computer's memory.

Objective-C Public Variables

Objective-C classes can declare specific instance variables as *public variables*, allowing them to be accessed directly from other parts of your program without the need to go through accessor methods. Public variables are specified after the @public declaration, as in the following example:

```
@implement MyClass : NSObject
{
    float val1;
    float val2;
@public
    float public_val1;
    float public_val2;
}
- init;
- (void)compute;
@end
```

Public variables can be accessed via C's arrow (->) notation, just as if the variable anArray were a pointer to a structure (which in fact it is!).

You should generally refrain from using public variables in the classes you design, because public variables make your objects less modular and more difficult to update without causing future problems. Using public variables also violates the notion of object encapsulation. Public variables are part of the language specification for those few cases when you need the utmost efficiency and speed, but in general, you should avoid using them.

The NSView class is one of the most powerful abstractions in Cocoa's Application Kit. Some of its most useful methods are listed in Table 7-5.

Table 7-5. Common instance methods for NSView objects

NSView instance method	Purpose
- (void)**addSubview:**(NSView *)*aView*	Adds *aView* as a subview to the NSView.
- (void)**display**	Causes the NSView to redisplay itself and all of its subviews by invoking the **drawRect:** method for all of these views. Do not invoke this method; call **setNeedsDisplay:** instead.
- (void)**drawRect:**(NSRect)*rect*	Implemented by subclasses of the NSView class to draw themselves. This single method handles displaying on the screen, printing, and scrolling. You normally do not call this method, but instead allow it to be called by the NSView class.
- (void)**lockFocus** - (void)**unlockFocus**	Locks/unlocks the drawing focus on an NSView, so that all future Quartz drawing commands are executed in this NSView. If you are drawing inside a **drawRect:** method, focus is automatically locked and unlocked for your program (by the **display** method).

Table 7-5. Common instance methods for NSView objects (continued)

NSView instance method	Purpose
- (void)**setNeedsDisplay:**(BOOL)*aFlag*	Causes this view (and all of its subviews) to be redisplayed after the current event is finished being processed. Call this method with the argument YES rather than calling the **display** method.
- (NSArray *)**subviews**	Returns the NSArray object that contains all of an NSView's subviews.
- (NSView *)**superview**	Returns the id of an NSView's superview.
- (int)**tag**	Returns the NSView's tag. By default, NSViews have a tag of -1, but some NSViews (such as NSControls) allow you to change their tags to distinguish them from one another.
- (id)**viewWithTag:**(int)*aTag*	Searches an NSView and all of its subviews for a view with a given tag.
- (NSWindow *)**window**	Returns the id of the NSView's window.

The rest of the NSView methods are described at Apple's Developer web site: http://developer.apple.com.

Summary

In this chapter we learned about delegation, a system that lets a programmer specify objects that should automatically be sent messages when certain events happen. We used delegation to catch the NSApplication object's **application-DidFinishLaunching:** message, which is the standard technique for specifying code that should be run when an application is initialized.

Having done this, we modified our Calculator so that it could change its size using the **setFrame:display:animate:** method. We also learned a little bit more about NSWindow and NSView objects.

In the next chapter, we'll revisit our ongoing discussion of events—the basic data type used by Cocoa to keep track of actions initiated by the user. We'll then see how events are handled by the NSResponder class, the abstract superclass of NSApplication, NSView, and NSWindow, which contains much of the Mac OS X event-handling mechanism.

Exercises

1. The **setRadix:** method has gotten unwieldy. Split the functionality into two or more methods. Justify your decisions about how you decided to break up the logic. Is it possible to split up this method in such a way that you use fewer lines of code with two methods than with one?

2. Add another base to the Calculator.

3. Add a second display to the Calculator so that it will display both hexa-decimal and decimal numbers at the same time.

CHAPTER 8

Events and Responders

Our Calculator already handles events such as mouseclicks on buttons and menu items, but all this was automatic; we haven't had to write any specific code to handle these mouse events. In this chapter we'll learn more about events and the chain of objects that Cocoa uses to respond to events. At the end of the chapter, we'll see how to "catch" events from the keyboard in our Calculator application. This is the final chapter of the Calculator application.

Events and the NSResponder Chain

There are seven basic kinds of events that Cocoa developers need to be concerned about:

Mouse events
> Generated by pressing, clicking, or moving the mouse

Keyboard events
> Generated by a keypress or release

Tracking rectangle and cursor-update events
> Generated when the cursor crosses the boundary of a predefined rectangular area (*tracking rectangle*) in a window

Periodic events
> Generated to notify an application that a certain time interval has elapsed

AppKit-defined events
> Generated by the Application Kit when a window is moved, resized, or exposed, or when the application is activated or deactivated

System-defined events
> Generated by the system—for example, when the power is turned off

NSApplication-defined events
> Custom events defined and generated by your application to be inserted into the event queue

Of these, the mouse and keyboard events are usually the most important for developers.

What Is an Event?

A Cocoa *event* is a message and a corresponding object that the Window Server sends to an application in response to some action taken by the user. Pressing a key on the keyboard generates an event, as does releasing that same key. Pressing the mouse button in a window generates an event, as does releasing the mouse button (and moving the mouse, too).

The Mac OS X Window Server, which was introduced in Chapter 1, is a low-level process running in the background that is responsible for sending events to applications and displaying images on the screen. It isolates you from the details of the Mac's hardware. We'll discuss the Window Server in detail in the next chapter.

Events drive applications. Every action that a user takes is turned into an event by the Window Server, which in turn sends the event information to the appropriate Mac OS X application. Each window has an event mask that it uses to tell the Window Server which events it wants to receive. We'll describe event masks in more detail later in this chapter.

What is actually sent to the application is an *event record*, in the form of an NSEvent object. The NSApplication object stores events in an *event queue*.

The NSEvent Object

When your program receives an event, it is packaged in an NSEvent object. The types of information that the object contains, along with the data types, is in the file NSEvent.h. Search for this file via the Find or Classes (vertical) tab in Project Builder if you're curious about the class interface.

Cocoa supports many different kinds of events. The following 21 events are listed in the file NSEvent.h:

```
typedef enum _NSEventType {
        NSLeftMouseDown         = 1,
        NSLeftMouseUp           = 2,
        NSRightMouseDown        = 3,
        NSRightMouseUp          = 4,
        NSMouseMoved            = 5,
        NSLeftMouseDragged      = 6,
        NSRightMouseDragged     = 7,
        NSMouseEntered          = 8,
        NSMouseExited           = 9,
        NSKeyDown               = 10,
        NSKeyUp                 = 11,
        NSFlagsChanged          = 12,
```

```
         NSAppKitDefined          = 13,
         NSSystemDefined          = 14,
         NSApplicationDefined     = 15,
         NSPeriodic               = 16,
         NSCursorUpdate           = 17,
         NSScrollWheel            = 22,
         NSOtherMouseDown         = 25,
         NSOtherMouseUp           = 26,
         NSOtherMouseDragged      = 27
     } NSEventType;
```

It's unlikely that you'll ever work with these event numbers, because whenever the NSApplication object receives event numbers from the Window Server, it automatically translates them into Objective-C messages. The corresponding methods are defined in the NSResponder class.

NSResponder is the abstract superclass that contains Cocoa's event-responding mechanism. Most of the classes that we have discussed so far in this book, including NSApplication, NSWindow, and NSView, are subclasses of NSResponder. The NSResponder methods are defined in the file NSResponder.h. The methods that are important for event handling include the following.

```
- (void)mouseDown:(NSEvent *)theEvent;
- (void)mouseUp:(NSEvent *)theEvent;
- (void)mouseMoved:(NSEvent *)theEvent;
- (void)mouseDragged:(NSEvent *)theEvent;
- (void)scrollWheel:(NSEvent *)theEvent;
- (void)rightMouseDown:(NSEvent *)theEvent;
- (void)rightMouseUp:(NSEvent *)theEvent;
- (void)rightMouseDragged:(NSEvent *)theEvent;
- (void)mouseEntered:(NSEvent *)theEvent;
- (void)mouseExited:(NSEvent *)theEvent;
- (void)keyDown:(NSEvent *)theEvent;
- (void)keyUp:(NSEvent *)theEvent;
- (BOOL)performKeyEquivalent:(NSEvent *)theEvent;
```

This list contains about half of the event-handling methods available in NSResponder. Each of the methods in the list has a pointer to an NSEvent object as its first and only argument. By sending messages via this pointer to an NSEvent object, you can learn about the NSEvent itself. Table 8-1 describes the messages that you would typically send to an NSEvent object from your event-handler code.

Table 8-1. Important NSEvent methods

Data element	Purpose
- (NSString *)**characters**	Returns the characters associated with a key-up or key-down event.
- (NSString *)**charactersIgnoringModifiers**	Returns the characters as they would have been received if no modifier key (other than Shift) were pressed.

Table 8-1. Important NSEvent methods (continued)

Data element	Purpose
- (int)**clickCount**	Returns the number of mouseclicks associated with a mouse-down or mouse-up event.
- (float)**deltaX** - (float)**deltaY** - (float)**deltaZ**	Returns the change in x, y, and z for scroll-wheel, mouse-moved, and drag events.
- (BOOL)**isARepeat**	Returns YES if the key event was caused by a key autorepeating when the user held the key down.
- (unsigned short)**keyCode**	Returns the hardware-dependent value of the key that was pressed for key-down and key-up events.
- (NSPoint)**locationInWindow**	Returns the location of the event in the associated window's coordinate system.
- (unsigned int)**modifierFlags**	Returns the settings of the Shift, Control, Option, and Command keys.
- (NSTimeInterval)**timestamp**	Returns the time of the event since system startup. You may find it difficult to translate this **timestamp** to an actual time, but usually it's not necessary.
- (int)**trackingNumber**	Returns the number of the tracking rectangle that was entered or exited, for tracking-rectangle events.
- (NSEventType)**type**	Returns the type of the event.
- (NSWindow *)**window**	Returns the window associated with the event.

Events and the NSApplication Object

After an event is translated into an NSResponder method, your program's NSApplication object sends the corresponding message to the appropriate NSWindow (or other) object within your application. The particular object in your application that receives the message is determined by the type of message, as shown in Table 8-2.

Table 8-2. Important NSResponder methods

NSResponder method	Sent to
mouseDown:, rightMouseDown:	The window where the mouse-down event occurred
mouseUp:, rightMouseUp:	The window where the original mouse-down event occurred
mouseDragged:, rightMouseDragged:	The window where the mouse-dragged event occurred
mouseEntered:, mouseExited:	The object that was specified when the tracking rectangle was created (see Chapter 18)
keyDown:	The key window
keyUp:	The same window that received the key-down event
performKeyEquivalent:	The key window

As we saw earlier, each one of these NSResponder methods has an NSEvent object as its only argument. This NSEvent object contains essentially the same information that the Mac OS X Window Server passes to the NSApplication object, but it's in a form that Cocoa programmers can handle.

Responders and the NSResponder Chain

As we mentioned earlier, the NSView, NSWindow, and NSApplication classes are all subclasses of the NSResponder class. NSResponder is the main class for handling events. It's called an *abstract superclass* because its functionality is used via instances of subclasses of NSResponder rather than by instances of NSResponder itself.

The NSResponder class declares a single instance variable called nextResponder, an id that points to another object and is, of course, inherited by all NSResponder descendants (i.e., by any class that inherits from NSResponder). When an NSResponder subclass (usually NSView or one of its descendants) object receives an event, such as a **mouseDown:** event, in its physical screen space, it tries to process the event. If it cannot do anything with the event, it sends the event to the object pointed to by its nextResponder instance variable—typically another NSView (called the *superview*) that "contains" the first NSView. This forwarding of the event from NSResponder to NSResponder happens over and over again until an object is found that will respond to the event, or until the event gets passed all the way up this chain to the window itself. This sequence of nextResponders forms a *responder chain*. The event-forwarding happens automatically if an NSResponder subclass doesn't implement (override) a particular NSResponder method.

Look at Figure 8-1 for a simple example of a responder chain. The button is partially obscured to indicate that it's a subview of the box. If a user clicks the on-screen NSButton labeled "Button" and it doesn't respond to this **mouseDown:** event (let's say it's disabled), the event is passed up the responder chain to the containing NSBox object labeled "Box", the NSButton's superview. If the NSBox can't respond (and it usually doesn't—NSBoxes are typically used only for appearance), the **mouseDown:** event is passed to the (invisible) content view. The content view is an NSView object that covers the NSWindow object labeled "Window", except for the title bar and border. If the content view can't respond, the **mouseDown:** event is sent to the NSWindow titled "Window". Thus, the responder chain of objects for this simple example is Button → Box → content view → Window.

NSApplication and NSWindow objects contain their own instance variables (in addition to the nextResponder instance variable inherited from NSResponder) for the processing of keyboard events. An NSApplication object

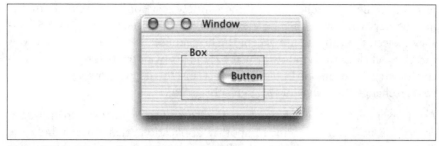

Figure 8-1. Responder chain: NSButton with superview NSBox in an NSWindow

contains an id pointer called keyWindow, which points to the window in an application that is designated to accept keyboard events (the key window changes in response to user events). Each NSWindow object contains an id pointer called firstResponder, which points to the NSView object inside the window that should be sent keyboard events when they are received from the NSApplication object.

Mouse Event Handling

Here's what happens (automatically) when you press down a mouse button in a window:

1. The Window Server sends the NSEvent data structure for the mouse-down event to your program's NSApplication object.
2. The NSApplication object sends a **mouseDown:** message (with the same NSEvent structure as the argument) to the NSWindow object that controls the on-screen window in which the cursor was located when the mouse-down event occurred.
3. The NSWindow object sends the **hitTest:** method to its content view (i.e., an NSView object inside the window) to determine the lowest descendant that contained the cursor when the mouseclick occurred. The returned view will be the NSView that is "in front of" other views on the screen.

At this point, what follows depends on whether the window is the key window:

4. If the window is already the key window, the event is sent to the subview where the mouseclick occurred.

   If the window is *not* the key window, it first makes itself the key window, then sends the **acceptsFirstMouse:** message to the subview where the mouseclick occurred. If the subview returns YES, the NSEvent is sent to it. If the view returns NO, no further processing takes place on the event.

Some NSViews, such as NSButton and NSSlider objects, accept the first mouseclick. Thus, you can click a button in a window, and have the button respond to the mouseclick, even if the window that contains the NSButton is not the key window. Other NSView-subclassed objects, such as an NSText-View object, typically do not accept the first mouseclick. This means that you must first click in the window to make it the key window before you can successfully click in an NSTextView object inside the window. You can, of course, change this behavior through subclassing.

As an example, try the following in the TextEdit application: open a non-empty file in TextEdit, activate another application (that doesn't hide the TextEdit window), and then single-click in the TextEdit window. The cursor does not move to where you clicked, because the NSTextView object inside the TextEdit window returns NO when sent the **acceptsFirstMouse:** message from the window.

If the NSWindow object is already key when the event occurs (and thus sends the event to the subview determined by **hitTest:**), the following additional processing takes place:

5. If the subview cannot process the event, it sends the event to its nextResponder. The nextResponder of an NSView object is by default its superview—that is, the NSView that contains the NSView receiving the event.

6. If none of the subviews can process the mouseclick, it gets sent to the NSWindow's content view. If the content view cannot process the event, the event gets sent to the content view's nextResponder—the NSWindow itself.

For the most part, all of this handling of responders and first responders is automatic—you don't have to worry about it unless you are trying to do something nonstandard.

Mouse events other than **mouseDown:** are handled a little differently. The **mouseUp:** event is sent to the NSView object that was sent the corresponding **mouseDown:** event, regardless of the position of the mouse when the button is released. This means that buttons that have been pressed know when they are released, even if you drag the mouse and release it in some other window.

The **mouseEntered:** and **mouseExited:** events are sent to the "owner" object specified by the **addTrackingRect:owner:userData:assumeInside:** message (you'll find more on these methods in Chapter 18). The **mouseMoved:** and **mouseDragged:** events are different from other events because they are sent continuously, and therefore tend to "drag" down the system performance. Use them only when necessary. (You can frequently get around the need to catch **mouseMoved:** or **mouseDragged:** events by overriding other methods inherited from the NSCell or NSControl classes, or by creating your own modal loops.)

Keyboard Event Handling

Keyboard events are handled differently from mouse events because a keypress doesn't correspond to a particular point on the screen. Here's what happens when you press a key.

1. The Window Server sends the NSEvent data structure for the keyboard event to the active application's NSApplication object.

At this point, what happens depends on whether a Command key is pressed (down). We'll first continue our discussion assuming that a Command key is *not* down, then discuss the case when a Command key is down.

2. Assuming that the Command key (or both of them, if your keyboard has two) is up, the NSApplication object sends the **keyDown:** message to the NSWindow object controlling the key window (via the NSApplication object's keyWindow instance variable).

3. The NSWindow object that receives the **keyDown:** message sends the message to the object pointed to by the window's firstResponder instance variable, which is usually an NSView that can handle keyboard events.

4. If the firstResponder object cannot handle the keyboard event, it sends the event to its nextResponder object. This may occur several times.

5. The nextResponder of an NSWindow's content view is the NSWindow itself. If the keyboard event is returned all the way up the responder chain to the NSWindow, the computer's system beep is played.

On the other hand, if the Command key is down, the NSApplication object sends the **performKeyEquivalent:** message to every NSWindow object that contains a menu in its window list, until one of the objects responds YES. In this way, windows other than the key window can intercept Command-key events and act accordingly. If no menu intercepts the event, Command-key events are handled just as any other event would be: they are passed to the key window, which passes the event to the content view, which passes it, in turn, down the responder chain. All of this event handling is done automatically for you by the AppKit; all you need to do is assign a key equivalent in Interface Builder, and the AppKit takes care of the rest.

An Event-Handling Example Using TextEdit

Suppose we drag the icon for a file—let's use Controller.h in this example—from the Finder and drop it on top of the TextEdit application icon in your Dock. The Finder will automatically launch the TextEdit application (if necessary) and send it a message to open the Controller.h file for editing. Inside the TextEdit application, this message is received by the NSApplication object, which translates it into an **application:openFile:** message. TextEdit's NSApplication delegate receives this message and opens the file, as shown in Figure 8-2.

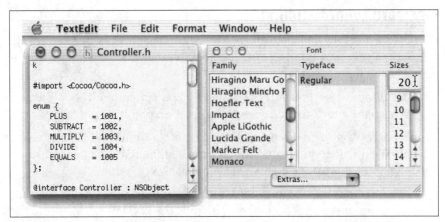

Figure 8-2. TextEdit demonstration of first responder

There are several objects in the window titled "Controller.h". The title bar alone contains three buttons, an icon, and a text field. Then there is an NSScrollView object, which contains the NSTextView that actually displays the text.

When TextEdit starts up, the NSTextView is made the NSWindow's first responder, as indicated by the blinking cursor that appears at the very beginning of the file. If you then press a key, say "k", a keyboard event will be sent to the Controller.h window because it is the key window. The letter "k" will appear at the beginning of the file, as shown in Figure 8-2.

Now suppose you type Command-T to bring up the Font panel (dialog), then click on the Font panel's title bar. If you watch carefully, you'll see that the blinking cursor in TextEdit's Controller.h window disappeared. How did that happen?

When you type Command-T, the nib* for the Font panel is loaded into the memory of the running application. When you click on the Font panel's title bar, you are telling the NSApplication object that you want the Font panel to become the key window (panels are special types of windows that are usually created as instances of NSPanel or its subclasses, and NSPanel is a subclass of NSWindow).

Before making the Font panel the key window, the NSApplication object needs to find out if the NSFontPanel object can in fact become a key window. To do this, the NSApplication object sends the NSFontPanel object the **can-BecomeKeyWindow** message. The NSFontPanel responds in the affirmative.

---

* In Mac OS X Version 10.1.2, the full pathname of this file is /System/Library/Frameworks/AppKit. framework/Versions/C/Resources/English.lproj/NSFontPanel.nib.

Although we don't have the source code for the NSFontPanel class, it's a sure bet that it has a method for this class that looks something like this:

```
- (BOOL)canBecomeKeyWindow
{
    return YES;
}
```

Once it knows that the NSFontPanel can become the key window, the NSApplication object needs to see whether the text object in the main TextEdit window is prepared to give up being the first responder. The **resignFirst-Responder** message is sent to the TextEdit's main NSWindow, which forwards the message to its NSTextView object. The NSTextView object responds YES, indicating that it is willing to give up being first responder. This also tells the NSTextView object to make its cursor disappear.

Now the NSApplication object can act to change the key window. It first sends the **resignKeyWindow** message to TextEdit's main NSWindow, then sends a **becomeKeyWindow** message to the NSFontPanel object. Finally, it sends the NSFontPanel window the **becomeFirstResponder** message, to tell it that it has become the first responder. All of this happens automatically, inside the Application Kit framework.

Suppose that after clicking the Font panel's title bar in TextEdit, you press the "2" key. You'll hear the system beep, because although NSWindow is the first responder and key window, it does not respond to the key "2". Now focus on (i.e., click in) the text area immediately below the Sizes label in the Font panel. You'll see the blinking cursor in the Font panel, and keypresses will be accepted. Try changing the font size to 20 with the keyboard. The (Sizes) NSTextField object in the Font panel has become the first responder. Before that change occurred, the NSWindow sent the **acceptsFirstResponder** message to the NSTextField and received the answer YES. See Figure 8-2 for the result of our TextEdit demonstration.

To recap, whenever you click in either an NSTextField or an NSTextView object (or on any other NSView, for that matter), the containing NSWindow sends the **acceptsFirstResponder** message to ask the object if it wants to become the first responder. If the text displayed by an NSTextView or NSTextField object is editable or selectable, as it was in our TextEdit example, the object answers YES. The **acceptsFirstResponder** method for these objects presumably looks something like this:

```
- (BOOL)acceptsFirstResponder
{
    return YES;
}
```

After the NSTextField object in the Font panel answers YES to this message, the containing NSWindow tries to make it the first responder by sending the

makeFirstResponder: message to itself (`self`), with a pointer to the NSText-Field object as the argument. The **makeFirstResponder:** method begins by sending the **resignFirstResponder** message to the current first responder. If the current first responder refuses to relinquish its role, it returns NO, and the NSWindow's first responder doesn't change. If the current first responder returns YES, thereby agreeing to relinquish its role as first responder, the **makeFirstResponder:** method sends the **becomeFirstResponder** message to the potentially new first responder (the NSTextField object). If that object refuses to become the first responder, it returns NO and the first responder doesn't change. If that object agrees to become the first responder, the NSWindow's **makeFirstResponder:** method sets the `firstResponder` instance variable to point to the NSTextField object.

The NSTextField object uses its **becomeFirstResponder** and **resignFirst-Responder** methods to control the display of the text cursor that is displayed at the point of entry. When it receives a **becomeFirstResponder** message, it displays the cursor; when it receives the **resignFirstResponder** message, it removes it.

Action Messages and the NSResponder Chain

When we described how the target and actions work in IB, we weren't entirely truthful. We said that if you specify a target and an action for a slider, the slider sends that action message to that target. For example, in Chapter 3 we connected the slider to the text field, as shown in Figure 8-3 (ignore the Noise button). We then said that the slider sent the **takeIntValueFrom:** message to the NSTextField.

This isn't exactly true, even though it appears that way in Figure 8-3. Instead of having the NSSlider object send the message directly to the NSTextField object, Cocoa uses NSControl's **sendAction:to:** method to send the action message via NSApp, the single NSApplication object that's a part of every Cocoa application. (Recall that NSSlider is a subclass of NSControl and therefore inherits the **sendAction:to:** method). This allows some actions to be context-sensitive—i.e., to change their behavior depending on which NSView and NSWindow are currently selected.

For example, suppose you had a simple window with three text fields, as shown in Figure 8-4. Suppose also that you chose the Edit → Cut menu command. Cocoa needs some way of sending the **cut:** action message to the object containing the piece of text that you've selected (we've selected Field #1 in Figure 8-4). If the Cut menu cell had a specific fixed target object—say, the middle field—the **cut:** message would often be sent to the wrong place. Clearly, the target of the **cut:** message needs to change based on which text the user has selected.

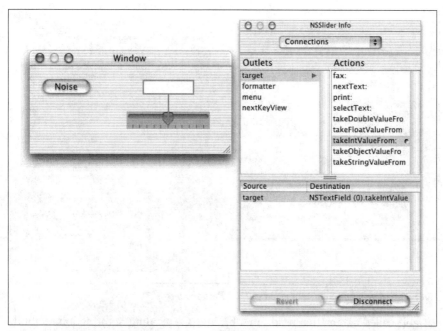

Figure 8-3. Target/action connection from NSSlider to NSTextField

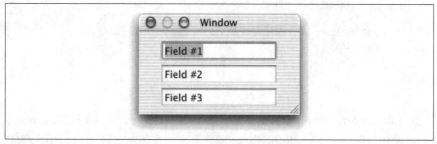

Figure 8-4. Window with three fields, only one of which can respond to the cut: message at any instant

Look at the target of the Cut menu item in IB in Figure 8-5—you'll see that it has been set to the First Responder icon, not to any specific object. Furthermore, if you look at the Connections Info dialog in Figure 8-5, you'll see a wide choice of actions to which a First Responder object can respond (scroll down in the inspector to reveal more than 50!). This is all especially confusing because there is *no* NSFirstResponder class. We describe what is happening in the following paragraphs.

IB's target/action connections are implemented by Cocoa's NSActionCell class. The NSActionCell class has an instance variable called target (actually _target) that holds the id of the object being sent the action message, and an instance

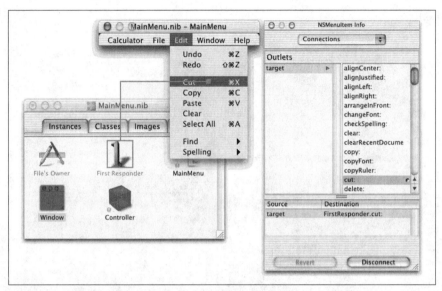

Figure 8-5. Cut menu item connected to First Responder

variable called action that holds an Objective-C encoding of the action method. Part of the Objective-C interface of the NSActionCell class is shown here:

```
@interface NSActionCell : NSCell
{
    // All instance variables are private
    int     _tag;
    id      _target;
    SEL     _action;
    id      _controlView;
}
```

If the target of an action message is nil, the Control object's **sendAction:to:** method determines an appropriate receiver for the action by checking a variety of objects. The Control object does the following, in order:

i. Begins with the first responder (typically an NSView) of the key window and follows the responder chain (via nextResponder pointers) up the responder chain through the NSWindow's content view to the NSWindow object itself, searching for an object that can respond to the specific action.

ii. If none of those NSViews (or the NSWindow) can respond, the NSWindow's delegate object is checked to see if it can respond.

iii. If the main window is different from the key window (as it was in our TextEdit example when we typed in the font size), the NSApplication object next checks the main window's responder chain and the main window's delegate.

iv. If none of those views or delegates can respond to the action, the NSApplication object tries to send the message to the NSApplication object itself (NSApp) and, finally, to the NSApplication's delegate.

The search continues until an object is found that implements the action method, and the action method returns a value other than nil. If no object handles the message, the message is ignored.

IB's list of first responder methods in the Connections Info dialog aren't defined in any single class—IB simply starts you off with all of the methods from possible target classes that Apple thinks you'll need. You're free to add your own whenever you want.

Other Kinds of Events

Other kinds of events are processed in slightly different ways. NSWindow-moved, window-resized, and window-exposed events are sent directly to the NSWindow object associated with the event. The remaining Cocoa events (application-defined events, system-defined events, timer events, cursor-update events, application-activate events, and application-deactivate events) are handled by the NSApplication object.

The Event Loop

Other than the Tiny.m program in Chapter 4, we have not written a main( ) function for any of our applications. That's because the PB template that was used to create our Calculator application already contained a main( ) function.

Let's again look at the main.m file, which contains the main( ) function used by our Calculator application:

```
#import <Cocoa/Cocoa.h>

int main(int argc, const char *argv[])
{
    return NSApplicationMain(argc, argv);
}
```

Well, that's not terribly useful. All it does is run the NSApplicationMain( ) function! What's going on here?

When NSApplicationMain( ) runs, it performs the following steps:

i. Processes any command-line options

ii. Sends the [**NSApplication sharedApplication**] class (or factory) message, which creates the NSApplicaton object, initializes the display environment, connects the application to the Window Server, and creates an autorelease pool

iii. Determines the main nib of the application (from the application plist) and then loads this nib with the owner of NSApp, the newly created NSApplication object

iv. Sends the [**NSApp run**] message to start up the application's main event loop

The last step is the most important for our current discussion; it starts off the main event loop, where much of the power of Cocoa is found.

The Main Event Loop

When the NSApplication object called NSApp receives the **run** message, it starts the object's main event loop. The *event loop* is a section of code that reads events and performs appropriate functions for those events. This is the primary place where the NSApplication object receives events from the Window Server. The event loop runs until the NSApplication object gets sent a **stop:** or a **terminate:** message. A **stop:** message causes the **run** method to stop and returns control to the caller. A **terminate:** message causes the application to quit gracefully, without returning control to the caller.

The NSApplication main event loop program does the following:

* If there is an event waiting, gets it and processes it.
* If there is a timer pending, executes it.
* If data is received at a watched Mach port, reads it and calls the appropriate function. (See the discussion of Mach in Chapter 9.)
* If data is pending at a watched file descriptor, reads it and calls the appropriate function.
* Repeats until a **stop:** message is received.

The most common way of breaking out of the NSApplication's main event loop is by sending a **terminate:** message to NSApp. Here's what happens when the **terminate:** message is received:

* If the NSApp object has a delegate that implements the **appShouldTerminate:** method, the corresponding message is sent to the delegate.
* If the delegate's **appShouldTerminate:** message returns NSTerminateCancel or NSTerminateLater, the **terminate:** method is aborted, and the main event loop continues to run. (In the case of NSTerminateLater, a timer is set that will schedule another **terminate:** message to be sent later.)
* Otherwise, the application is terminated with a call to exit( ).

The fact that Cocoa handles the main event loop for the programmer is one of the primary differences between programming in Cocoa and programming in many other window-based environments. Because Cocoa handles most events automatically, individual programmers are freed from this tedious task, which in turn makes programs behave in a more reliable and unified fashion.

Nevertheless, Cocoa does allow you to write your own event loop or take over the event loop while something out of the ordinary is happening. Typically, you would do this for a special purpose that isn't handled well by the Application Kit. For example, IB uses its own event loop when you Control-drag a connection from one object to another; this special event loop exits when the mouse button is released.

You can use the NSApplication method **nextEventMatchingMask:untilDate: inMode:dequeue:** to construct your own event loop. This method returns the next event that matches a mask that you provide. The mask allows you, for example, to read a mouse-up event but ignore a periodic event or flags-changed event. These other events will be saved until the main application event loop is running again.

Catching Keyboard Events for Our Calculator

In the remainder of this chapter, we'll make our Calculator easier to use by taking advantage of our new knowledge of events and responder chains. The goal will be to let the user type digit keys (e.g., "5") on the keyboard instead of clicking buttons in the Calculator's window.

 Some of the functionality that we will implement in the following sections could be implemented from within IB by assigning a key equivalent for each NSButton in the NSButton Info dialog. We've chosen to show you this approach instead for several reasons. First, we feel that this example shows many interesting details about Cocoa, including how the NSArray and NSDictionary classes operate. This example also shows how Objective-C allows you to "reach inside" the Cocoa classes, even though you don't have their source code, and to change or augment the way that they operate. Finally, some of the functionality that we describe—the automatic enabling and disabling of keys depending on the current radix—cannot easily be implemented from within IB.

Subclassing the NSWindow Class

We'll accomplish our goal by first subclassing the NSWindow class to form a new class called CalcWindow, then changing the class of our Calculator window to CalcWindow. Subclassing NSWindow is a common technique for intercepting all of the events that are destined for a window, rather than for a particular view in that window. (This example is slightly contrived, because Cocoa also allows you to assign keyboard equivalents to each key in IB. However, we wanted to show you how to subclass the NSWindow class, and this is as good a time as any to do it.)

In addition to catching the keyboard events, our CalcWindow object needs to know what to do with them. To accomplish this, we'll arrange for our Calc-Window object to scan its window for all buttons and make a table of each button that has a title consisting of a single character. Each time the CalcWindow object receives a keyboard event, it will consult this table to determine whether there is a corresponding button that should act as if it has been clicked.

The first step is to subclass the NSWindow class in IB:

Project Builder

Interface Builder

1. Open your Calculator project in PB by double-clicking the `Calculator.pbproj` file in your `~/Calculator` project directory.

2. Open your project's main nib in IB by double-clicking `MainMenu.nib` (under Resources in PB's Groups & Files pane).

3. Choose Interface Builder → Hide Others to simplify the screen.

4. Select the NSWindow class (under NSResponder) under the Classes tab in the `MainMenu.nib` window.

5. Choose IB's Classes → Subclass NSWindow command to create a subclass of the NSWindow class. (Another way to do this is to Control-click inside the `MainMenu.nib` window and select Subclass NSWindow from the resulting menu).

6. Change the name of this new subclass from "MyWindow" to "CalcWindow", as shown in Figure 8-6.

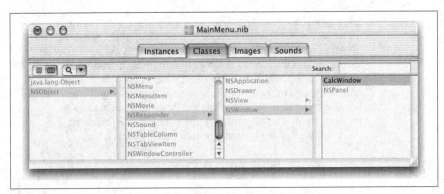

Figure 8-6. Creating a subclass of the NSWindow class

7. Choose IB's Classes → Create Files for CalcWindow menu command to create the class interface and class implementation files for the new class. The resulting new sheet is shown in Figure 8-7. (Again, this step can be done by Control-clicking in the MainMenu.nib window.)

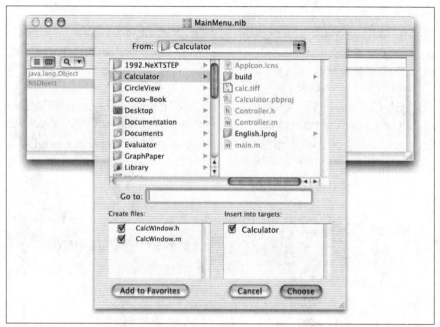

Figure 8-7. Creating class files for the CalcWindow subclass

Near the bottom of Figure 8-7, note that the files CalcWindow.h and CalcWindow.m have been created and inserted into the Calculator (target) project. Make sure that the sheet that dropped down from your MainMenu.nib title bar looks the same as the one in Figure 8-7.

8. Click the Choose button to finish the process of creating the two Calc-Window class files.

The previous two steps save us a bit of effort by creating the skeleton CalcWindow.h and CalcWindow.m class files in the project directory and adding them to our project. You might take a minute to check your ~/Calculator folder in the Finder to see that these two files were actually created in this folder. You might also activate PB to see that the files have been added to the project under the Classes group in the Groups & Files pane. By clicking these class filenames in PB, you can also see how little code has been generated for CalcWindow. There are no instance variables or action methods in the files, because we didn't specify any in IB. Currently, CalcWindow simply inherits all of its data and functionality from NSWindow and is essentially the same class as NSWindow. We'll change that soon.

Next, we'll change the class of the Calculator window from NSWindow to CalcWindow.

9. Still in IB, click the Instances tab in the MainMenu.nib window.

10. Select the Calculator window by clicking the icon labeled "Window" (you can also select the window by clicking in the background of the Calculator window itself).

11. Type Command-5 to display the Custom Class inspector for the Calculator window. The class of the Calculator window is currently NSWindow.

12. Click CalcWindow in the inspector to change the Calculator window's class to CalcWindow, as shown in Figure 8-8.

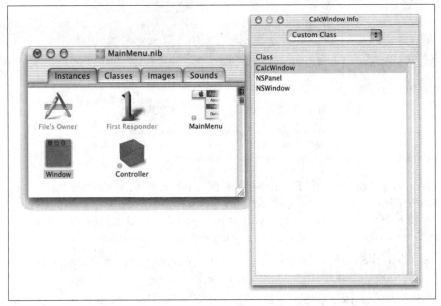

Figure 8-8. Changing the class of the Calculator window to CalcWindow

Before proceeding with our quest to capture keyboard events for our Calculator application, we need to learn about Cocoa dictionaries.

Dictionaries

We will use an NSMutableDictionary object to determine whether incoming keyboard events match button clicks in the window. The NSDictionary and NSMutableDictionary classes are provided by Apple as part of the Cocoa

Foundation framework of "basic" classes. "Mutable" means "changeable," and that describes the difference between the two classes: NSDictionary objects cannot be changed after they are initialized, whereas NSMutableDictionary objects can be changed. Dictionaries are data-storage objects; you can think of them as arrays, except that the index is an object rather than an integer. Dictionaries are basically hash tables with a nice interface.*

The following example should help you understand Cocoa dictionaries. The example creates an NSMutableDictionary that contains only two NSString objects. The first object contains the string "Garfinkel", and the second object contains the string "Mahoney". The key for the first object is an NSString object that contains the string "Simson", and the key for the second object is a fourth NSString object, this one containing the string "Michael". As the example shows, you can make a retrieval from an NSDictionary object using either the original object that was used as the key when the first object was inserted, or a second object that is logically equal to the original key. The comments mixed in with the code describe the program.

```
// Demonstrate the NSDictionary class

#import <Cocoa/Cocoa.h>

int main( )
{
    // Every program must have an NSAutoreleasePool
    NSAutoreleasePool *pool = [[NSAutoreleasePool alloc] init];

    // Create the dictionary
    NSMutableDictionary *dict =
                [NSMutableDictionary dictionaryWithCapacity:5];

    // Create the two key (index) objects
    NSString *key1 = [NSString stringWithCString:"Simson"];
    NSString *key2 = [NSString stringWithCString:"Michael"];

    // Create the first data object
    // Note that this uses a different NSString syntax than above
    NSString *dat1 = @"Garfinkel";

    // Insert data into the dictionary. Note the second insertion
    // does not assign the NSString object to a local variable.
    [dict setObject:dat1 forKey:key1];
    [dict setObject:@"Mahoney" forKey:key2];
```

---

* The term "hash table" is used because dictionaries are typically implemented as arrays in which the index is a mathematical function, called a *hash*. Indeed, Cocoa dictionaries are implemented with NSObject's **hash** method to compute a hash code and the **isEqual:** method to determine if the two objects used for keys are equal.

```
// Now show retrieval two different ways
NSLog(@"The object for key1 is %@\n",
      [dict objectForKey:key1]);
NSLog(@"Michael's last name is: %@\n",
      [dict objectForKey:@"Michael"]);

[pool release];

}
```

Terminal

If you save this program in the file dict.m, you can compile and run it in a (Unix) Terminal window as follows:

```
% cc dict.m -o dict -framework Foundation
% ./dict
2002-02-02 00:02:13.998 x[369] The object for key1 is Garfinkel
2002-02-02 00:02:13.999 x[369] Michael's last name is: Mahoney
%
```

Implementing the CalcWindow Class

To implement the CalcWindow class, we'll use keyboard characters (in the form of NSStrings) for the (hash) keys of an NSMutableDictionary and the ids of the associated NSButtons as the values. To build the dictionary (or hash table), the CalcWindow object will search for all of the NSButtons contained in the Calculator window that have single-character titles.

Methods for searching for button titles

In this section, we'll implement methods in the CalcWindow class that will search for NSButton object single-character titles such as "2" and "+" and will build a corresponding NSMutableDictionary object, as described earlier.

CalcWindow.h

13. Edit the CalcWindow.h class interface file (in PB or elsewhere) and insert the five lines shown here in bold (do not insert this code in the Controller.h file):

```
#import <Cocoa/Cocoa.h>

@interface CalcWindow : NSWindow
{
    NSMutableDictionary *keyTable;
}

- (void)findButtons;
- (void)checkView:(NSView *)aView;
- (void)checkButton:(NSButton *)aButton;
- (void)checkMatrix:(NSMatrix *)aMatrix;
@end
```

The new keyTable instance variable will point to the NSMutableDictionary object we'll create later. We'll use the four new methods (**findButtons**, etc.) to search the Calculator window for all of the buttons, as described in Table 8-3.

Table 8-3. Methods to search for buttons in the Calculator window

Method	Purpose
findButtons	Start searching the Calculator window's content view.
checkView:aView	Search the aView object. If aView is an NSButton object, check it with **checkButton:**. If aView is an NSMatrix object, check all of its buttons with **checkMatrix:**. If a subview is found, check it recursively with **checkView:**.
checkButton:aButton	Check aButton to see if it has a single-character title. If so, add the button to the NSDictionary object with the title as its key.
checkMatrix:aMatrix	Check each of the buttons inside aMatrix by repeatedly invoking the **checkButton:** method.

Now we'll describe the implementations of each of these CalcWindow methods in detail. CalcWindow's new **findButtons** method simply removes all of the objects from the NSMutableDictionary object (keyTable) and then invokes the **checkView:** method for the Calculator window's content view to set up the NSMutableDictionary.

```
- (void)findButtons
{
    // Check all the views recursively
    [keyTable removeAllObjects];
    [self checkView:[self contentView] ];
}
```

CalcWindow.m

The **checkView:** method is more interesting than **findButtons**. It can be invoked with any NSView object in the window as its argument, and it checks to see whether the NSView is of the NSMatrix class, the NSButton class, or neither. (An NSView object is any object that belongs to a subclass or descendant class of NSView.) If the NSView is of the NSMatrix or NSButton class, **checkView:** invokes the **checkMatrix:** method or the **checkButton:** method (respectively). Otherwise, **checkView:** gets the list of subviews for the NSView passed and invokes itself recursively for each one (yes, methods can invoke themselves recursively). In this manner, all of the NSViews in the window are processed. We need separate methods to check the NSMatrix and NSButton objects because the cells (i.e., NSCell objects) stored inside these objects are not subviews (cells are not views).

The following code shows CalcWindow's new **checkView:** method:

```
- (void)checkView:(NSView *)aView
{
    id view;
    NSEnumerator *enumerator;

    // Log which aView is being processed; see PB for output
    NSLog(@"checkView(%@)\n",aView);

    // Process the aView if it's an NSMatrix
    if ([aView isKindOfClass: [NSMatrix class] ]) {
```

CalcWindow.m

```
        [self checkMatrix: aView];
        return;
    }

    // Process the aView if it's an NSButton
    if ([aView isKindOfClass: [NSButton class] ]) {
        [self checkButton: aView];
        return;
    }

    // Recursively check all the subviews in the window
    enumerator = [ [aView subviews] objectEnumerator];
    while (view = [enumerator nextObject]) {
        [self checkView:view];
    }
}
```

This **checkView:** method sends the **isKindOfClass:** message to the aView argument object to determine its class (NSMatrix, NSButton, or other). If the aView object is of the NSMatrix class, the **checkMatrix:** method is invoked. If the aView object is of the NSButton class, the **checkButton:** method is invoked. If aView is neither an NSMatrix nor an NSButton object, the **checkView:** method recursively invokes itself for all of the subviews contained within the NSView. Actually, the objects that are passed to **checkView:** are instances of subclasses of the NSView class, not instances of NSView itself. However, because they inherit from the NSView class, we still refer to them as "views."

CalcWindow's **checkButton:** method, shown in the following example, checks a button to see if its title is a single character. If it is, the button is stored in the keyTable object (an NSMutableDictionary object that we'll create when the CalcWindow object is initialized, as we'll see a bit later).

CalcWindow.m

```
- (void)checkButton:(NSButton *)aButton
{
    NSString *title = [aButton title];

    // Check for a cell with a title exactly one character long.
    // Put both uppercase and lowercase strings into the dictionary.
    // The "c" key on the keyboard will clear, not display a hex "c".

    if ([title length]==1 && [aButton tag] != 0x0c ) {
        [keyTable setObject:aButton forKey:[title uppercaseString]];
        [keyTable setObject:aButton forKey:[title lowercaseString]];
    }
}
```

This method uses the NSMutableDictionary instance method **setObject:forKey:** to insert the button's id, namely aButton, into the dictionary object. The key is an NSString with the single-character title of the button.

CalcWindow's **checkMatrix:** method now checks all of the NSButton objects in an NSMatrix. NSMatrix objects must be checked separately, because the

NSButtons that they contain are not subviews of the NSMatrix. This was originally done for performance reasons.* The fact that NSCell objects are not views complicates our task, but not significantly.

```
- (void)checkMatrix:(NSMatrix *)aMatrix
{
    id button;
    NSEnumerator *enumerator;

    enumerator = [[aMatrix cells] objectEnumerator];
    while (button = [enumerator nextObject]) {
        [self checkButton: button];
    }
}
```

CalcWindow.m

This method first gets the list of cells (NSButtonCells, in our example) that are contained in the NSMatrix, then invokes the **checkButton:** method for each of them.

Now we have the four methods that we need to set up the NSMutableDictionary object with key-value pairs.

Finishing off the CalcWindow class implementation

The CalcWindow class requires two additional methods in order to work properly. The first (**keyDown:**) is the method that actually handles the keydown events. The other is the method that initializes the NSMutableDictionary object.

```
- (void)keyDown:(NSEvent *)theEvent
{
    id button;

    button = [keyTable objectForKey: [theEvent characters] ];

    if (button) {
        [button performClick:self];
    }
    else {
        [super keyDown:theEvent];
    }
}
```

CalcWindow.m

This **keyDown:** method will be invoked only when a keyboard event is not otherwise handled by an object in the NSResponder chain. It sends the **objectForKey:** message to the NSMutableDictionary object (keyTable) to obtain the

---

* When NeXTSTEP was developed in the late 1980s on 25-MHz 68030 microprocessors, it was considerably faster to instantiate a few thousand cells than a few thousand views. On today's computers, the performance speedup of using cells is no longer significant, but NSCells remain for historical reasons.

id for the NSButton whose title is the same as the keyboard character ([**theEvent characters**]) that was typed.

If no such NSMutableDictionary key exists, **objectForKey:** returns nil and **keyDown:** passes the original message to its superclass to handle the event. If the key does exist, the **keyDown:** method sends the **performClick:** message to the NSButton whose id is stored for the key. The **performClick:** message causes the NSButton target object to perform as if it had been clicked. The message is not sent if the on-screen button is disabled.

Finally, we need to set up an initialization method—the method that is automatically invoked when the CalcWindow object is created and sets up the NSMutableDictionary object.

We typically create initialization methods in our subclasses by overriding one of the parent's initialization methods. There are two NSWindow initialization methods to choose from for CalcWindow. If you look in the NSWindow.h header file in PB, you'll find the declarations of these two initialization methods:

```
- (id)initWithContentRect:(NSRect)contentRect
             styleMask:(unsigned int)aStyle
               backing:(NSBackingStoreType)bufferingType
                 defer:(BOOL)flag;

- (id)initWithContentRect:(NSRect)contentRect
             styleMask:(unsigned int)aStyle
               backing:(NSBackingStoreType)bufferingType
                 defer:(BOOL)flag
                screen:(NSScreen *)screen;
```

One of these methods is the *designated initializer* of the NSWindow class. The designated initializer is the one and only initialization method for a class that is guaranteed to be invoked by all of the other initialization methods of that same class. Thus, if you subclass a class, you need only write a method for the designated initializer method to catch all initialization events.

But which method is the designated initializer? The only way to find out is to read the documentation. The designated initializer is typically the method that has the most arguments, but the NSWindow class is different. Its designated initializer is the first (shorter) method listed. That's because the **initWithContentRect:styleMask:backing:defer:** method was designated as the designated initializer before NeXTSTEP supported multiple screens (note the one additional **screen:** argument in the last initialization method). It has thus been left as the designated initializer for historical reasons.

We discussed the **initWithContentRect:styleMask:backing:defer:** method in detail in the section "Windows, Views, Delegates, and the setup() Function" in Chapter 4. Next, we override this method to create and initialize the

CalcWindow, which is like a normal window except that it has an NSMutableDictionary that must be allocated. We also override the **dealloc** method to release the keyTable that we created to prevent a memory leak:[*]

CalcWindow.m

```
- (id)initWithContentRect:(NSRect)contentRect
    styleMask:(unsigned int)aStyle
    backing:(NSBackingStoreType)bufferingType
    defer:(BOOL)flag
{
    keyTable = [ [NSMutableDictionary alloc] init];
    [self setInitialFirstResponder:self];

    return [super initWithContentRect:contentRect
        styleMask:aStyle
        backing:bufferingType
        defer:flag];
}


- (void)dealloc
{
    [keyTable release];
    [super dealloc];
}
```

Our designated initializer method creates and initializes an NSMutable-Dictionary object (keyTable). The method then specifies that the CalcWindow object itself will be its own initialFirstResponder (this is necessary so that the CalcWindow object will receive the keypresses). Finally, it forwards the initialization message to its superclass (NSWindow) to actually do the rest of the work of initializing the CalcWindow object. This **initWithContentRect: styleMask:backing:defer:** method is invoked automatically whenever an instance of the CalcWindow class is created.[†]

---

[*] After this example was created, the definition of the **setInitialFirstResponder:** method in the file /AppKit/NSWindow.h was changed so that the method now expects an NSView * as an argument, rather than an NSResponder *. As a result, this line of code generates a warning message when it is compiled (although it still works properly). We believe that this error will soon be addressed by Apple. In the meantime, you can suppress the compiler warning by adding an explicit cast:

```
[self setInitialFirstResponder:(id)self];
```

[†] The keyTable could have been created on-demand in the **findButtons** method with a piece of code like this:

```
if (!keyTable) {
    keyTable = [[NSMutableDictionary alloc] init];
}
```

This style of on-demand resource allocation is called *lazy allocation*. Lazy allocation generally improves performance, because it defers creating objects until they are needed (recall our discussion of separate nib files in Chapter 6). If they are never needed, they are never created. "It is always a good thing and something that developers should be encouraged to do," says Ali Ozer of Apple Computer, Inc. We didn't use lazy allocation in our example because we wanted to show how to create a designated initializer for the NSWindow subclass CalcWindow.

The **dealloc** method is called when the window is destroyed. It releases the keyTable. In practice, the CalcWindow's **dealloc** method may never be called, because the window is destroyed when the application exits. We have included the **dealloc** method because it is good programming practice to write the code that releases the memory that you have allocated. Otherwise, you are likely to get sloppy, and other programs that you write will inadvertently have memory leaks in them.

Now it's time to put all this code into the CalcWindow.m file.

CalcWindow.m

14. Insert the code we discussed earlier into CalcWindow.m, including the implementations of the six new methods listed below. Note that the **key-Down:** and **initWithContentRect:styleMask:backing:defer:** methods are overrides of NSWindow methods and so do not require declarations in CalcWindow.h.

```
- initWithContentRect:styleMask:backing:defer:
- findButtons
- checkView:
- checkButton:
- checkMatrix:
- keyDown:
```

Changes in the Controller Class

The last thing we need to do to get the keyboard to work with our Calculator is to make a few changes to our Calculator's Controller class. We need to arrange for our Controller object to invoke CalcWindow's **findButtons** method when the Controller starts up and also when the radix changes.

Controller.m

15. Insert the lines shown here in bold into Controller.m:

```
#import "Controller.h"
#import "CalcWindow.h"
...

- (void)applicationDidFinishLaunching:(NSNotification*)notification
{
    radix = [ [radixPopUp selectedItem] tag];
    [self clearAll:self];
    // Set up the button NSMutableDictionary
    [ (CalcWindow *)[keyPad window] findButtons];
}
@end
```

16. Insert the lines shown here in bold at the end of the **setRadix:** method in Controller.m:

```
    // Disable the buttons that are higher than selected radix
    enumerator = [ [keyPad cells] objectEnumerator];
```

```
        while (cell = [enumerator nextObject]) {
            [cell setEnabled: ([cell tag] < radix) ];
        }
        [self displayX];

        // Radix changed, set up the NSMutableDictionary for a new base
        [ (CalcWindow *)[keyPad window] findButtons];
    }
```

The CalcWindow.h file needs to be imported into Controller.m, because the Controller invokes the **findButtons** method. We get the id of the Calculator's window (a CalcWindow) object by sending the **window** message to the keyPad that the window contains. The cast to the CalcWindow * type prevents the compiler from issuing a warning that NSWindow does not respond to the **findButtons** message.

17. Save all pertinent files and build and run your Calculator application.

18. With Calculator running, enter "12345678" by typing the eight corresponding digit keys on the keyboard. Follow that by typing the "+" key, then the "9" key, and then the "=" key. All of this should work as expected, and you should get the result 12345687 (which is the result of 12345678 + 9).

Note that as you press a digit key on the keyboard, the corresponding on-screen button will highlight (due to the **performClick:** method), and the digit will appear in the Calculator's readout text display area.

19. Now type the "c" key to clear the display.

20. Next, choose Hex mode and type "ab", followed by "-", then "d", then "=". The result should be 9e.

21. Try some more examples. What about the "0" key—does that work? How about typing uppercase letters (e.g., "A", "B") for the hex values—do they work? How about hex "c"? This program needs some tweaking—check out the "Exercises" section.

22. Quit Calculator after you have played with the keyboard a bit.

If your Calculator doesn't work correctly, make sure that you've subclassed the NSWindow and set up the CalcWindow class definition properly.

Summary

In this chapter, we took a close look at events and the responder chain and saw how they interact with the NSWindow object. We'll periodically revisit these topics throughout the rest of the book, looking more closely at how events interact with the NSView class.

This chapter also marks the end of the evolution of our Calculator application. We've certainly covered a lot of ground while developing it, and it sure was fun!

In the next chapter, we'll learn more about the system software that underlies Mac OS X and Cocoa. Then, in Chapter 10, we'll start on a new application—MathPaper—which we'll use to learn about interprocess communication and controlling multiple main windows.

Exercises

1. Modify our Calculator application by relabeling the on-screen hex buttons A–F with the lowercase letters a–f. Also, make the "c" key on the keyboard work as the hex c button, and the capital letter "C" work as the Clear button. Finally, fix the keyboard input for the "0" button.

2. Try using key equivalents for all of the buttons in the Calculator instead of the more complicated way we caught key events in this chapter. How can this be done for hex characters?

3. Add more sophisticated mathematical functions, such as sin, cos, and log, to our Calculator application. Use IB as a prototyping tool to redesign the Calculator window to accommodate these new functions.

4. From scratch, develop your own new calculator program that looks and works exactly like the bundled Calculator program in the /Applications folder.

References

1. Events and other input:

   http://developer.apple.com/techpubs/macosx/Cocoa/TasksAndConcepts/ProgrammingTopics/Misc/EventsPage.html

2. Foundation classes (NSMutableDictionary in particular):

   http://developer.apple.com/techpubs/macosx/Cocoa/Reference/Foundation/ObjC_classic/FoundationTOC.html

CHAPTER 9

Darwin and the Window Server

If your only previous exposure to computing is to previous versions of the Macintosh operating system (Mac OS) or Microsoft Windows, you've probably noticed that Mac OS X is very different indeed. If you're familiar with the "classic" Mac OS, you've probably noticed that with Mac OS X you don't need to preallocate how much memory a program uses, and that programs in the background run without any noticeable degradation in performance. If you have used either Mac OS or Windows, you've surely noticed that Mac OS X does not crash as much as these other operating systems—in fact, for most users it doesn't crash at all! In this chapter, we'll see why Mac OS X is so different.

Unix, Mach, and the Mac OS X Environment

The Mac OS X environment is built on top of the Unix operating system and the Mach kernel. Together, they form a powerful computing infrastructure that is part of what Apple calls *Darwin*. In addition to the Mach and Unix services, Darwin includes the Mac OS X networking and (multiple integrated) filesystems.

Operating Systems

An *operating system* is the master control program that loads and runs other programs and controls a computer's input and output systems, such as the keyboard, display, and disk drives. Multitasking operating systems such as Mach allow more than one program to run at the same time on the same computer; the operating system automatically arbitrates between the various programs that are waiting to run, letting one program run for a few milliseconds, then another, then another. Each program gets its own *time slice* of system resources.

In addition to dividing the CPU resources between different programs that want to run, the operating system divides up the computer's memory and controls access to the computer's input and output devices. For example, the operating system makes sure that mouse events are sent to the correct programs, even if more than one program is prepared to receive mouse events at a given instant.

Another important function of the operating system is to prevent running programs from interfering with each other. This is called *memory protection*. Without such protection, a wayward program could affect other programs or other users, delete important files, or even crash the entire computer system (users of Apple's Mac OS 9 and Microsoft Windows 98 are used to frequent crashes).

Unix

The Unix operating system was developed in the early 1970s at AT&T Bell Labs. The creators of Unix sought to create a flexible computing environment in which they could get useful work done by putting together a complex system from simple building blocks. They also wanted to create a portable operating system—that is, an operating system that could run just as easily on computers made by a variety of different vendors. (At the time, practically every computer ran an operating system that had been written specifically for that computer. It was extremely rare for computers from different companies—and sometimes from the same company—to run compatible systems.)

Unix was hugely successful. In the 1970s and 1980s, it spread throughout academia and to many research labs. But it was also a bit of an outlaw system, because no computer companies actually sanctioned Unix to be run on their hardware. Digital Equipment Corporation, for example, had been known to tell customers that running Unix voided the warranty on Digital's PDP and VAX minicomputers. Instead of Unix, Digital wanted its customers to run their proprietary RSTS, RT11, and VMS operating systems.

Things changed for Unix in the 1980s, when engineers at Sun Microsystems, Inc. and a number of other companies took Motorola's new 68000 series of microprocessors and used them to create a new kind of computer—the *engineering workstation*. Because these companies didn't have the millions of dollars to create their own operating systems, they decided instead to license Unix.

With the success of the workstation vendors, Unix went mainstream. Today it is the basis of systems sold by Sun, Compaq, Hewlett-Packard, IBM, and many other firms. Unix is also the basis for a variety of free operating systems, including Linux, FreeBSD, and NetBSD.

Mach

In the 1980s, Digital funded a project at Carnegie Mellon University to develop a new operating system for a supercomputer that Digital was creating. The group at CMU decided to build an operating system that was designed for extraordinarily high performance: most operations would be memory-mapped, the system was optimized for high-speed communication between processes, and the operating system would be multithreaded so that it could run on computers with multiple processors. When Digital canceled its supercomputer, the CMU group decided to rename the operating system "Mach" and to continue development. Avie Tevanian, now Apple's Senior Vice President of Software Engineering, was one of the lead developers of the system.

The Microprocessor

Mac OS X uses a Motorola/IBM PowerPC microprocessor, or *central processing unit* (CPU), to read and execute instructions and read and process data from the computer's memory. As of this writing, Mac OS X runs exclusively on PowerPC-based systems (G3, G4). This is actually a marketing decision, rather than a technical decision. Very little of Mach and Mac OS X are written in the PowerPC's native assembly language. As a result, Mac OS X can easily be ported to other microprocessors simply by recompiling the system and rewriting a small number of device drivers.

The original NeXTSTEP and OpenStep operating systems from which Mac OS X and Cocoa were derived ran on several different hardware platforms. NeXTSTEP was developed on Motorola 68030- and 68040-based microprocessors, but NeXT ported the entire operating system to the Intel 486 and Pentium computers in the early 1990s. After that, NeXTSTEP was ported to the Sun Microsystems SPARC and Hewlett-Packard PA-RISC architectures (and renamed "OpenStep"). Because Mach supports a "fat binary" system, it was possible for a NeXTSTEP developer to create an application on a 68040-based computer and have that application run on all three other architectures (although it was a good idea to test the application before selling it!).

In the future, it is possible that Mac OS X will once again run on other processors.

The Mach operating system consists of a kernel and a system support environment. One layer up from the hardware, the Mach kernel manages the computer's memory and schedules computing time for the various programs that are ready to run.

The kernel implements *virtual memory*, a system that uses the computer's hard disk to simulate a much larger block of *random-access memory* (RAM). Virtual memory is transparent to running programs (although it can slow them down considerably, because hard-disk access is thousands of times slower than RAM access). A program that needs a 10-MB block of memory simply allocates a 10-MB block of memory; the kernel automatically shuffles data from the computer's internal memory to the hard disk and back, as necessary. This is called *swapping* or *paging*.

The Mach kernel oversees the creation of *processes*, or running programs. Mach further allows each process to create additional "lightweight" processes, called *threads,* which run independently of each other but within the same program. Threads simplify writing programs that do more than one thing at the same time.

Mach also provides a highly efficient system of interprocess communication using *Mach messages*. These messages can be sent from one thread to another, between processes, or even from one computer to another across the network.

The Mach system support environment

Sitting on top of the Mach kernel is the operating system support environment, which runs a version of the 4.4BSD (Berkeley Software Distribution) Unix system. The Berkeley Unix system provides Cocoa with access to hard disks and floppy disks through the Unix and HFS filesystems, networking using either TCP/IP or AppleTalk, support for the network filesystems, and a variety of other important features.

Mac OS X's Unix environment also contains all of the device drivers for managing the computer's hardware devices, including the keyboard, the screen, the serial ports, and the USB and FireWire buses. Unix is an intimate part of Cocoa, and it is therefore important to understand how it manages users and processes. We'll discuss these in the following sections.

Usernames and UIDs

Everyone who uses a computer running Mac OS X has a username. When you log in, your username gets translated into a unique number called your *user identifier*, or UID. (If you don't have to log into your Mac OS X computer in order to use it, your computer has been set to "auto-login" to a particular user account. For details, look at the Login Window pane of the System Preferences application, shown in Figure 9-1.)

Unix also uses some special *system users* for a variety of special purposes:

root
> This user, also called the *superuser*, is an administrative user that performs accounting and low-level system functions.

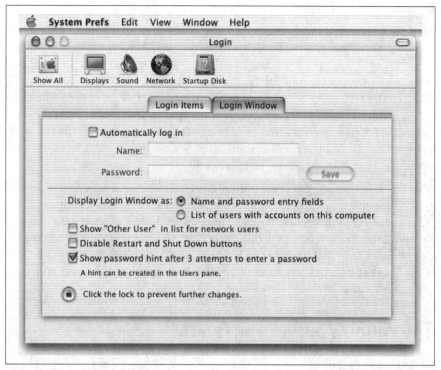

Figure 9-1. Login Window pane of System Preferences—note the "lock" icon at the bottom

daemon

    This user operates the computer's email system.

www

    This user runs Mac OS X's built-in web server.

These users are not actually people who log in, but merely different UIDs used to run background processes with different kinds of privileges.

Mac OS X largely insulates you from needing to know about the superuser and other user accounts. Some control panes that allow you to make significant system changes have a small "lock" icon at the bottom that you need to click in order to confirm that you really wish to modify the setting. Other control panes allow you to click the lock to prevent settings from being further modified (see Figure 9-1). Sometimes a superuser or other password is required to "open" the lock and enable settings to be modified.

When you create multiple users on the same Cocoa computer, the Cocoa administration utilities make sure that each user has his or her own UID. Having different UIDs prevents users from seeing each other's private files. Normally, this administrative task is taken care of by the Mac OS X's *NetInfo* (network administrative information) system.

Processes, PIDs, and UIDs

Mach is a multitasking operating system. Every task that the computer performs at any given moment (such as the Window Server, the Finder, or the TextEdit application) has an associated process. The process is the operating system's fundamental tool for controlling the computer. You can generally think of the terms *process* and *running program* as synonymous, but be careful: some applications create more than one process (as we'll see in the next chapter). You can also run more than one copy of a single program at a time, in which case you'll have only one program but two (or more) processes (we'll demonstrate that in the next chapter as well).

The Mach kernel assigns every running process a unique number called the *process identifier*, or PID. The first process that runs when the computer starts up is called *init*; this process is given the number 1. Any process can *fork*, and by doing so, create a new process. All of the processes on your computer are descendants of process number 1. Mach process numbers can range from 1 to 32767, and the kernel guarantees that no two active processes will ever have the same number.

The Window Server and Quartz

The Mac OS X Window Server manages the screen (or screens), the keyboard, and the mouse. Unlike the X Window Server and the NeXTSTEP Display Post-Script Window Server, the Mac OS X Window Server is lightweight—it doesn't actually do the drawing itself. Instead, its primary role is to manage which regions of the screen each application is allowed to use, and to allow the applications to do their own drawing. The main job of the Window Server, then, is to assure that programs draw in their own rectangular piece of real estate on the screen, and to see to it that events destined for one program aren't accidentally sent to another.

The Window Server frees you from having to worry about interactions between your program and other programs that are running simultaneously. For all intents and purposes, you can design your program as if it is the only one running.

The actual drawing on the Mac OS X screen is done with Quartz. Most Cocoa applications use Quartz to draw to an off-screen buffer that is flushed to the screen when the drawing is finished. This buffer is shared between the application and the Window Server using the Mach virtual memory system, making it very fast.

The Quartz system has native support for Adobe's Portable Document Format (although Apple's implementation of PDF doesn't actually use any of Adobe's code, for licensing reasons). As a result, Quartz can both display and generate PDF files. Quartz can display text in any font size and at any angle. And because it is easy to translate PDF into the commands used by most modern printers, Quartz assures that what you see on the screen looks pretty much like what gets printed on paper (except that the printer output looks better because of its higher resolution).

Quartz is a device-independent graphics system that handles all aspects of line drawing, typesetting, and image presentation on the computer's screen. *Device-independent* means that Quartz hides all differences in resolution from your program: to draw a line; you simply tell Quartz to draw a line. Quartz automatically figures out which pixels on the screen (or dots on the printed page) should be turned on or turned off.

Quartz also handles output attributes such as line width and fill color. If you want to draw a dark gray line, you simply set the color to dark gray and draw the line. If the output device is black-and-white only, Quartz or the PDF driver for your printer will automatically dither or halftone the line as necessary (*dithering* and *halftoning* are techniques for showing continuous-tone images on devices that can display only a few shades of color, or black and white only). If your output device can handle gray tones, Quartz or the PDF driver will automatically choose values of gray according to what you've selected.

When you're programming with color, Quartz allows you to specify color using a variety of color models—for example, RGB, CMYK, and HSB—and then, as with black and white, converts the color that you requested to what is appropriate to your display. This makes the color output from Cocoa programs look as good as it possibly can on whatever display you use.

Finally, Quartz can automatically take advantage of any graphics acceleration hardware that is present on your computer.

The Application Kit and the Window Server

Recall that Cocoa's Application Kit (AppKit) is a collection of Objective-C classes that define and create objects for use by applications. Many of these AppKit objects, such as NSWindow, NSMenu, and NSButton, have on-screen representations. In this section, we'll describe how these objects communicate with the Window Server.

An application's NSApplication object (recall that every Cocoa application must have precisely one of these) is responsible for communication between the AppKit objects in the application and the Window Server. One of the main functions of the NSApplication object is to receive events from the Window Server and distribute them to the appropriate window (or windows).

NSWindow objects manage an application's representation of windows on the screen. NSWindow objects work together with the Window Server to handle window-moved, window-exposed, and other window events so that on-screen windows are kept up-to-date.

The AppKit class implementations are stored in a special file called a *shared library* that is contained within the AppKit bundle. The shared library is automatically linked with your program when your program is run. This means that Apple can make improvements in the Application Kit from release to release, and that those improvements are automatically reflected in your program when it runs on the newer release of the operating system. No recompiling is necessary! Shared libraries also make program images smaller, because the library isn't loaded into the program until the program is loaded for execution.

Terminal

You can find out which shared libraries an application depends on by using the otool command in the Terminal. Enter the following commands, shown here in bold, to find out which shared libraries Mac OS X's Clock.app application uses:

```
% cd /Applications/Clock.app/
% otool -L Contents/MacOS/Clock
Contents/MacOS/Clock:
    /System/Library/Frameworks/AppKit.framework/Versions/C/AppKit
        (compatibility version 45.0.0, current version 617.0.0)
    /System/Library/Frameworks/Foundation.framework/Versions/C/
        Foundation (compatibility version 300.0.0, current
        version 423.0.0)
    /System/Library/PrivateFrameworks/HIServices.framework/Versions
        /A/HIServices (compatibility version 1.0.0, current
        version 64.0.0)
    /System/Library/Frameworks/ApplicationServices.framework/
        Versions/A/ApplicationServices (compatibility version
        1.0.0, current version 16.0.0)
    /usr/lib/libSystem.B.dylib (compatibility version 1.0.0,
        current version 55.0.0)
%
```

Note that Clock.app uses the AppKit and Foundation class libraries, together with three others.

Seeing All the Processes

ProcessViewer

To see all of the processes running on your Mac OS X computer, we can use the ProcessViewer application we introduced in Chapter 2. Figure 9-2 contains a screen shot of ProcessViewer displaying the *user* processes at a given time, whereas Figure 9-3 shows the *administrator* (or *root*) processes. Figure 9-2 contains additional *process ID* information at the bottom of the window.

We can also use the ps command in a Terminal (Unix) window to see all of the running processes. The ps command has many options, but using the options a, u, and x gives us a user-readable listing of all the currently running

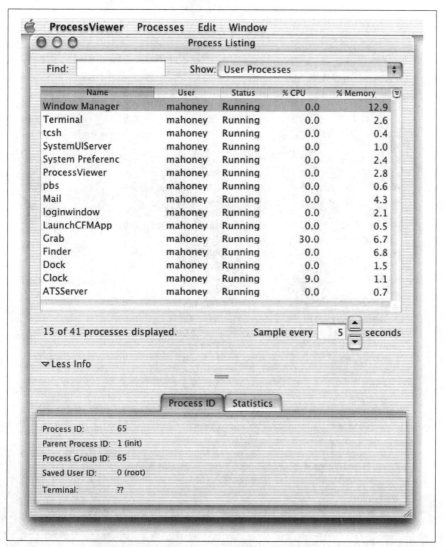

Name	User	Status	% CPU	% Memory
Window Manager	mahoney	Running	0.0	12.9
Terminal	mahoney	Running	0.0	2.6
tcsh	mahoney	Running	0.0	0.4
SystemUIServer	mahoney	Running	0.0	1.0
System Preferenc	mahoney	Running	0.0	2.4
ProcessViewer	mahoney	Running	0.0	2.8
pbs	mahoney	Running	0.0	0.6
Mail	mahoney	Running	0.0	4.3
loginwindow	mahoney	Running	0.0	2.1
LaunchCFMApp	mahoney	Running	0.0	0.5
Grab	mahoney	Running	30.0	6.7
Finder	mahoney	Running	0.0	6.8
Dock	mahoney	Running	0.0	1.5
Clock	mahoney	Running	9.0	1.1
ATSServer	mahoney	Running	0.0	0.7

Figure 9-2. User processes with process ID information

processes. (ProcessViewer's output is nicer, but it contains less information than the ps command's output.)

Terminal

Enter ps auxww in a Terminal window (the suffix ww is for wide format). Your listing should contain many of the same programs as the following listing (the processes in our ps listing differ from those in our ProcessViewer listing). Some of the processes running on your computer are bound to differ; it depends on which programs you are running and how your system is configured. wsurfer is the username of the user who logged in, and we've formatted the shell output a bit to make it easier to read.

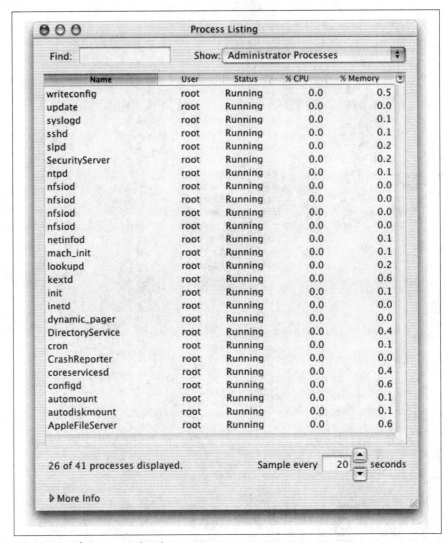

Figure 9-3. Administrator (root) processes

```
% ps auxww
USER      PID  %CPU %MEM    VSZ    RSS   TT  STAT    TIME COMMAND
wsurfer   615  4.2  5.1    38040  13248  ??  Ss     0:01.24
    /System/Library/CoreServices/WindowServer console
wsurfer    63  0.4  0.6     9400   1664  ??  Ss     0:03.35
    /System/Library/Frameworks/ApplicationServices.framework/Versions/A/
    Frameworks/ATS.framework/Versions/A/Support/ATSServer
root       41  0.0  0.6     3372   1480  ??  Ss     0:00.00 kextd
root       67  0.0  0.0     1276     96  ??  Ss     0:01.85 update
root       70  0.0  0.0     1296    108  ??  Ss     0:00.00 dynamic_pager
    -H 40000000 -L 160000000 -S 80000000 -F /private/var/vm/swapfile
```

```
root        93   0.0  0.1     2332     372  ??  Ss       0:00.38
   /sbin/autodiskmount -va
root       116   0.0  0.6     3820    1496  ??  Ss       0:00.93 configd
root       151   0.0  0.1     1288     156  ??  Ss       0:00.11 syslogd
root       157   0.0  0.0     1604     120  ??  Ss       0:00.00
   /usr/libexec/CrashReporter
root       179   0.0  0.1     1580     368  ??  Ss       0:00.23 netinfod -s local
root       186   0.0  0.2     2448     488  ??  Ss       0:01.32 lookupd
root       196   0.0  0.1     1528     300  ??  S<s      0:01.99 ntpd -f
   /var/run/ntp.drift -p /var/run/ntpd.pid
root       205   0.0  0.6     8968    1476  ??  S        0:03.54 AppleFileServer
root       209   0.0  0.4     2872    1060  ??  Ss       0:00.85
   /System/Library/CoreServices/coreservicesd
root       216   0.0  0.0     1288     116  ??  Ss       0:00.00 inetd
root       226   0.0  0.0     1276      84  ??  S        0:00.00 nfsiod -n 4
root       227   0.0  0.0     1276      84  ??  S        0:00.00 nfsiod -n 4
root       228   0.0  0.0     1276      84  ??  S        0:00.00 nfsiod -n 4
root       229   0.0  0.0     1276      84  ??  S        0:00.00 nfsiod -n 4
root       236   0.0  0.1     2192     320  ??  Ss       0:00.00 automount
   -m /Network/Servers -fstab -m /automount -static
root       239   0.0  0.4     3684    1068  ??  S        0:00.20 DirectoryService
root       249   0.0  0.3     2136     656  ??  Ss       0:00.23
   /System/Library/CoreServices/SecurityServer
root       255   0.0  0.1     1536     224  ??  Ss       0:00.42 /usr/sbin/sshd
root       260   0.0  0.1     1560     152  ??  Ss       0:00.07 cron
root       267   0.0  0.2     5108     528  ??  Ss       0:03.20 slpd -f
   /etc/slpsa.conf
wsurfer    616   0.0  1.7    46392    4464  ??  Ss       0:01.65
   /System/Library/CoreServices/loginwindow.app/loginwindow console
wsurfer    623   0.0  0.6    18624    1612  ??  Ss       0:00.93
   /System/Library/CoreServices/pbs
wsurfer    624   0.0  5.7    75876   14816  ??  S        0:02.45
   /System/Library/CoreServices/Finder.app/Contents/MacOS/Finder -psn_0_262145
wsurfer    628   0.0  1.3    53288    3292  ??  S        0:00.54
   /System/Library/CoreServices/Dock.app/Contents/MacOS/Dock -psn_0_393217
wsurfer    629   0.0  1.0    56400    2748  ??  S        0:00.46
   /System/Library/CoreServices/SystemUIServer.app/Contents/MacOS/
   SystemUIServer -psn_0_524289
wsurfer    630   0.0  1.1    59632    2960  ??  S        0:00.60
   /Applications/Clock.app/Contents/MacOS/Clock -psn_0_655361
wsurfer    631   0.0  0.5    39072    1324  ??  S        0:00.13
   /Applications/iTunes.app/Contents/Resources/iTunesHelper.app/Contents/
   MacOS/iTunesHelper -psn_0_786433
wsurfer    632   0.0  2.0    62820    5168  ??  S        0:01.37
   /Applications/Utilities/Terminal.app/Contents/MacOS/Terminal -psn_0_917505
wsurfer    633   0.0  0.4     5876     940 std  Ss       0:00.15 -tcsh (tcsh)
root       572   0.0  0.0        0       0 con- Z        0:00.00 (AEServer)
root       638   0.0  0.1     1324     288 std  R+       0:00.01 ps auxww
root         1   0.0  0.1     1292     248  ??  SLs      0:00.01 /sbin/init
root         2   0.0  0.1     1300     144  ??  SL       0:01.31 /sbin/mach_init
%
```

Table 9-1 contains descriptions of the meanings of the different fields in the ps listing.

Table 9-1. Fields in the ps command output

Field	Meaning
USER	Username of the user who owns the process; usually root, for processes run by the system, or your username.
PID	Process identifier of each process.
%CPU	Percentage of CPU time the process is using.
%MEM	Percentage of physical memory the process is using.
VSZ	Amount of virtual memory the process is using.
RSS	Amount of process resident in physical memory.
TT	Terminal being used by the process; a "??" means that the process is not associated with any terminal. Programs that are run from the Mac OS X Terminal application are usually associated with a terminal, whereas GUI programs are not.
STAT	Status of the process: R is running, S is stopped, W is waiting, N is "niced" (running with reduced priority).
TIME	Length of time the process has been running.
COMMAND	Command that ran the program that started the process.

You can look up the ps command by typing man ps in a Terminal window to learn further details concerning this command's output.

Most of the processes displayed in the ps auxww listing above have an important function. Table 9-2 lists what each one does.

Table 9-2. Description of the processes in our ps listing

Process	Function
slpd -f /etc/slpsa.conf	This command is not documented.
/sbin/mach_init	mach_init is the master Unix process that starts all other processes.
kextd	This command is not documented.
ATSServer	Although this command is not documented, we believe that it is the Adobe Type Server.
update	Flushes internal filesystem caches to the disk every 30 seconds.
dynamic_pager	System memory paging daemon.
autodiskmount	Disk automounter.
configd	System Configuration Server.
syslogd	System logging daemon.
CrashReporter	Reports crashes.

Table 9-2. Description of the processes in our ps listing (continued)

Process	Function
netinfod	NetInfo Daemon.
lookupd	Lookup daemon, which makes NetInfo run faster.
ntpd	Network Time Protocol daemon, which keeps the computer's clock synchronized with the time servers.
AppleFileServer	File server for AppleShare.
coreservicesd	Core services daemon.
inetd	Internet daemon, which starts a variety of Internet daemons.
nfsiod	NFS IO daemon, which provides a write-back cache for the Network File Service.
DirectoryService	Provides directory services.
automount	Auto NFS mounter, which automatically mounts NFS filesystems when requested.
pbs	Pasteboard Server.
SecurityServer	Core Services Security Server.
sshd	SSH server.
cron	Program that automatically runs programs listed in the file /usr/lib/crontab at predetermined times.
WindowServer	Mac OS X Window Server.
loginwindow	Process that runs the login window.
pbs	Mac OS X Pasteboard server, which coordinates sharing of data on the various pasteboards.
Finder	Mac OS X Finder.
Dock	Mac OS X Dock.
SystemUIServer	Provides command bar icon menus.
Terminal	Terminal application.
CPU Monitor	CPU monitor.
ps auxww	ps program, which generated this listing.

Summary

This chapter may not have been as much fun as the previous ones, because we didn't show you any cool Interface Builder techniques, any nicely integrated features of Project Builder, or even any powerful AppKit classes. However, we did learn a bit about the Darwin working internals of Mac OS X, things that every serious Cocoa programmer should know. There's a lot more to learn about Darwin, but we've learned enough to go on to our next (more sophisticated) example, MathPaper, in the next chapter.

Exercises

1. Run the `ps aux` command in a Terminal window. Attempt to explain every process that you see listed.

2. Is it possible for your computer to run out of processes? If you think the answer is no, explain why. If you think the answer is yes, devise an experiment to make your computer run out of processes, try it out, and explain what happens. Is there any way to recover from this situation other than rebooting your computer?

3. Explain the difference between a process and a thread.

4. Run the Quartz Debug program in the /Developer/Applications folder. Select "flash screen updates." Explain how different kinds of programs (Carbon, Cocoa, Swing) use threads differently. Can you explain the different threads running in each of your applications?

5. Type `man vmstat` in a Terminal window to review the documentation for the `vmstat` command. Explain what this program does, in your own words. Explain the output of the commands `vmstat -i`, `vmstat -m`, `vmstat -s`, and `vmstat -z`.

References

1. Darwin:

   http://developer.apple.com/darwin/

2. `ps` command:

   Type `man ps` in a Terminal window to see the full command documentation.

MathPaper:
A Multiple-Document,
Multiprocess Application

Part III, Chapters 10 through 15, focuses on building a new application called Math-Paper. MathPaper is similar to a word processor in that it supports multiple windows, but it behaves very differently. Users can enter mathematical expressions in a MathPaper window, and the application will solve the expressions that were typed. The application uses a back-end mathematical processor called Evaluator to do the mathematical calculations. Chapter 15 leaves MathPaper, but it includes several small examples that demonstrate drawing in NSView objects.

- Chapter 10, *MathPaper and Cocoa's Document-Based Architecture*
- Chapter 11, *Tasks, Pipes, and NSTextView*
- Chapter 12, *Rich Text Format and NSText*
- Chapter 13, *Saving, Loading, and Printing*
- Chapter 14, *Drawing with Quartz*
- Chapter 15, *Drawing in a Rectangle: More Fun with Cocoa Views*

MathPaper and Cocoa's Document-Based Architecture

In this chapter and in Chapters 11 through 14, we are going to start over and build a new, more sophisticated calculator-like application called *MathPaper*. MathPaper will manage multiple windows, use fonts to convey information, and use interprocess communication to make a request to another (back end) program to do the actual calculation. In writing MathPaper, we will learn a lot more about Cocoa's architecture for creating applications that handle documents in multiple windows.

The MathPaper Application

When we're done, MathPaper will be a scratchpad mathematics application that looks like a text editor: it will display a little text window into which you can type mathematical expressions. The neat thing about MathPaper is that when you hit the Return key, the application will automatically calculate the value of the mathematical expression that you've typed and display the result. Figure 10-1 contains an example of MathPaper running with three windows open.

MathPaper can handle multiple windows: typing Command-N will give you another "piece" of "math paper." In later chapters of this book, we'll use part of MathPaper to graph equations as well. MathPaper has four main parts:

Document-based architecture
  Cocoa's powerful document-based architecture manages the application's windows and some of the menus, and it handles files that need to be opened, saved, printed, and so on. The principal AppKit classes in this architecture are NSDocumentController, NSDocument, and NSWindow-Controller.

MathDocument
  MathDocument is a subclass of the NSDocument class that manages the actual opening and saving of MathPaper document files. There is a

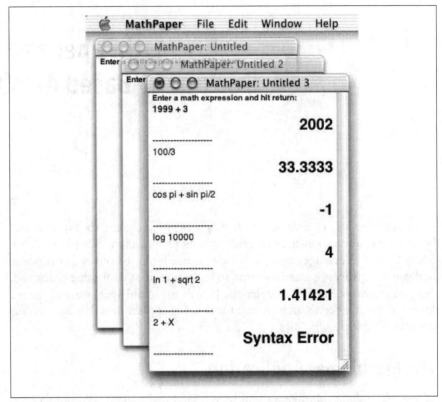

Figure 10-1. MathPaper window with mathematical expressions and results

separate MathDocument object for each piece of math paper (i.e., one for each window like the ones shown in Figure 10-1).

PaperController

PaperController is a subclass of the NSWindowController class that asks for the mathematical calculations to be performed and displays the results. As with MathDocument, there is a separate PaperController object for each piece of math paper.

Evaluator

Evaluator is a separate program that can evaluate arbitrary algebraic expressions. It communicates with a PaperController object using an NSTask object and two NSPipe objects. Evaluator is the back end (computational) part of our MathPaper application.

The Cocoa document-based architecture is part of the Application Kit framework. The document architecture manages many aspects of an application that can open multiple documents at a time, including the File → Open, Save, Save As, Save To, and Close menu options. To use this architecture, you create subclasses of the NSDocument class (and optionally the NSWindow-Controller class). The classes contain the common functionality for managing windows; your subclasses contain the application-specific routines.

In addition to handling multiple windows, MathPaper handles multiple processes: each piece of math paper is attached to its own copy of the Evaluator program, which performs calculations solely for that window. Together, the MathDocument and PaperController classes comprise the MathPaper application's front end, while the Evaluator makes up the application's back end. This technique of having separate front and back ends is a common approach used by many applications. It is also a common technique for structuring web sites. One of the advantages of this technique is that it lets you subdivide your programming efforts, concentrating on the math-solving or database part of the program in the back end and the user-interface part of the program in the front end. Another advantage is that the equation-solving back end can be used by more than one application, as long as its interface is well documented. If you are careful with your design, you can also create a portable back end that will be easy to move from one operating system to another.

In this chapter, we'll build two of the three major modules of MathPaper: the Evaluator back end, which we'll test in a Terminal (Unix) window, and the front-end interface, which we'll test on the desktop. In Chapter 11, we'll hook these two modules together with the third major module in our application, a controller. The controller will use an object of type NSTask to manage the Evaluator (Unix) subprocesses. In Chapter 12, we'll improve our MathPaper output using our own Rich Text Format (RTF) class. Then, in Chapter 13, we'll arrange for each piece of math paper to save its data into a file and then read the data back from the file when the data-file icon is opened.

The big picture of the MathPaper application, with three open math paper windows (as in Figure 10-1), is shown in Figure 10-2. It indicates that the MathPaper application creates three MathDocument objects and three Paper-Controller objects, one for each window. Each PaperController object creates its own NSTask object to manage a copy of the Evaluator back end.

The Evaluator Back End

The MathPaper back end, which we'll call Evaluator, is a program that reads a stream of mathematical expressions and displays the result of evaluating them. If you give the back end the following input, line by line:

```
1+2*3+4
2+5*sin(3)
9/4
3+
(8-76+32) / 3.2
```

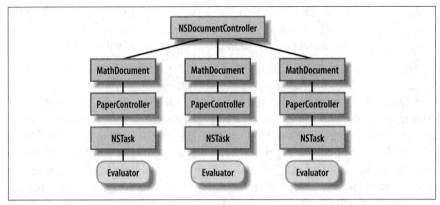

Figure 10-2. The big picture of the MathPaper application

it will return this output:

```
11
2.7056
2.25
Syntax Error
-11.25
```

The Evaluator will write its output directly to standard output, and we'll demonstrate it in a Terminal window. Later, when we run the Evaluator as a subprocess from MathPaper, the Evaluator's standard output will be returned to the MathPaper application, which will, in turn, display the contents in an on-screen window.

In the rest of this section and the next section, we'll discuss how to build the Evaluator back end. These sections use hardcore Unix development tools that are not essential to understanding Cocoa programming, and you can skip them if you want to download the source code from our web site (`http://www.oreilly.com/catalog/buildcocoa/`). You can also download a working copy of the Evaluator program from our web site. However, we recommend that you follow the steps in the next section, even if you don't fully understand what's going on. All you really have to know to continue with Math-Paper is that the Evaluator will perform the actual calculations for MathPaper and that it will run as a separate Unix process. So, if you plan to just download the source files, you can skip ahead to the section "Building MathPaper's Front End."

The task of the Evaluator back end breaks down into two parts: lexical analysis and parsing. *Lexical analysis* involves reading the input stream and determining which characters correspond to numbers and which correspond to operations. The character stream is then turned into a stream of *tokens*, or symbols. For example, the input to Evaluator shown earlier would generate the following token stream:

```
<1> <+> <2> <*> <3> <+> <4> <newline>
<2> <+> <5> <*> <sin> <(> <3> <)> <newline>
<9> </> <4> <newline>
<3> <+> <newline>
<(> <8> <-> <76> <+> <32> <)> </> <3.2> <newline>
```

The second part of the back end is the *parser*, which reads the token stream generated by the lexical analyzer, performs the requested calculations, and prints the correct result.

Parsers and lexical analyzers are not trivial programs to write. Fortunately, Mac OS X comes with two programs for constructing lexical analyzers and parsers from (relatively) simple input files. These program-generating programs are called lex and yacc. You don't need to understand how lex and yacc work in order to understand the MathPaper program. The only thing that really matters is that, using lex and yacc, we are able to build a relatively powerful and reliable back end with only a small amount of work.

The Evaluator application is compiled from three input files:

Makefile
> Input for make, the Unix utility that maintains, updates, and regenerates programs; tells make how to compile and link the Evaluator program*

grammar.y
> Input to the yacc program

rules.l
> Input to the lex program

lex and yacc

lex and yacc are programs that generate other programs. A full description of their use is beyond the scope of this book. For further information in Mac OS X, type man lex in a Terminal window. Also see the book *lex & yacc*, by John Levine, Tony Mason, and Doug Brown (O'Reilly).

yacc reads an input grammar file (in our case, the file grammar.y) that describes a particular grammar and generates two C source code files: y.tab.h and y.tab.c. lex reads the include file y.tab.h and a second file (in our case, the file rules.l) that describes a set of lexical rules and generates a C source file called lex.yy.c. The source code in y.tab.c and lex.yy.c is then compiled with the cc compiler and linked to form the Evaluator program.

We get a lot of power by using lex and yacc. Not only do we get a full-featured mathematical evaluator that properly interprets parentheses and

---

* Although we use make to build the Evaluator in this chapter, in the next chapter we'll see how to build Evaluator with Project Builder.

order of evaluation (for example, evaluating multiplication before addition), but we also get a system to which it is easy to add new formulas and rules. For example, adding a new function to the Evaluator simply requires adding two new lines, one to the set of rules and one to the grammar. We'll be doing much of our work from the Terminal command line, so make sure your Dock contains Mac OS X's Terminal application (its application icon is shown at the edge of the page).

Terminal

Building the Back End

1. Create a new folder called `Evaluator` in your Home folder.

2. Using an editor (TextEdit, GNU Emacs, or vi), create a file called `Makefile` in your `Evaluator` directory containing the following:

```
CFLAGS = -O
SRCS = y.tab.c lex.yy.c
LFLAGS =  -ly -ll -lm
Evaluator: $(SRCS)
        cc $(CFLAGS) -o Evaluator $(SRCS) $(LFLAGS)

clean:
        /bin/rm -f Evaluator $(SRCS) *.h

lex.yy.c: rules.l y.tab.h
        lex rules.l

y.tab.h: grammar.y
        yacc -d grammar.y

y.tab.c: grammar.y
        yacc grammar.y
```

It is very important that you begin the indented lines with a tab character, and not with spaces! The Unix make system distinguishes between these two types of whitespace.

This `Makefile` contains the targets install, clean, etc.

grammar.y

3. Using an editor, create a file called `grammar.y` in your `Evaluator` directory containing the following:

```
%{
#include <libc.h>
#include <math.h>

int printingError = 0;
%}

%start list

%union
```

```
{
    int    ival;
    double dval;
}

%token <dval> NUMBER
%token <dval> SIN COS TAN ASIN ACOS ATAN
%token <dval> SINH COSH TANH ASINH ACOSH ATANH
%token <dval> SQRT MOD LN LOG PI
%type  <dval> expr number

%left '+' '-'
%left '*' '/'
%left SIN COS TAN ASIN ACOS ATAN SINH COSH TANH ASINH
%left ACOSH ATANH
%left '^' SQRT MOD LN LOG
%left UMINUS    /* supplies precedence for unary minus */

%%              /* beginning of rules section */

list : stat
     | list stat
     ;

stat : expr '\n'
{
  printf("%10g\n",$1);
  printingError = 0;
  fflush(stdout);
}
;

expr   : '(' expr ')'
{
  $$ = $2;
}
     | expr '+' expr   { $$ = $1 + $3;}
     | expr '-' expr   { $$ = $1 - $3;}
     | expr '*' expr   { $$ = $1 * $3;}
     | expr '/' expr   { $$ = $1 / $3;}
     | SIN expr                        { $$ = sin($2);}
     | COS expr                        { $$ = cos($2);}
     | TAN expr                        { $$ = tan($2);}
     | ASIN expr                       { $$ = asin($2);}
     | ACOS expr                       { $$ = acos($2);}
     | ATAN expr                       { $$ = atan($2);}
     | SINH expr                       { $$ = sinh($2);}
     | COSH expr                       { $$ = cosh($2);}
     | TANH expr                       { $$ = tanh($2);}
     | ASINH expr                      { $$ = asinh($2);}
     | ACOSH expr                      { $$ = acosh($2);}
     | ATANH expr                      { $$ = atanh($2);}
     | expr '^' expr                   { $$ = pow($1,$3);}
     | expr MOD expr                   { $$ = fmod($1,$3);}
```

```
            | LN expr                      { $$ = log($2);}
            | LOG expr                     { $$ = log10($2);}
            | SQRT expr                    { $$ = sqrt($2);}
            | '-' expr %prec UMINUS
            {
                $$ = -$2;
            }
            | number
              ;

number      : NUMBER    /* lex number */
            | PI        { $$ = M_PI;          }
            ;

%% /* beginning of functions section */
void yyerror(char *s)
{
    if (printingError == 0) {
        printf("Syntax Error\n");
        fflush(stdout);
        printingError = 1;
    }
}

int main(int argc,char **argv)
{
    while (!feof(stdin)) {
        yyparse();
    }
    exit(0);
}
```

4. Using an editor, create a file called rules.l* in your Evaluator directory containing the following:

rules.l

```
%{
#include "y.tab.h"
#include <stdlib.h>

#define YY_INPUT(buf,result,max_size) (buf[0])=getchar();result=1;

int yywrap(void);
int yywrap(){return 0;}

%}

%%

"\n" return('\n');
```

---

* Make sure your rules.l file extension is a lowercase letter "l" and not the digit 1! Make sure you use the letter and not the digit in rules.l in the Makefile as well.

```
[0-9]*("."[0-9]*("e"[-+][0-9]+)?)?  {yylval.dval = atof(yytext);
    return(NUMBER);}

sin      return(SIN);      // NOTE: In this section, be sure to use
cos      return(COS);      // a tab after the 'sin' and each of
tan      return(TAN);      // the other function names. If you use
asin     return(ASIN);     // spaces, this code will not compile
acos     return(ACOS);     // properly.
atan     return(ATAN);
sinh     return(SINH);
cosh     return(COSH);
tanh     return(TANH);
asinh    return(ASINH);
acosh    return(ACOSH);
atanh    return(ATANH);
mod      return(MOD);
ln       return(LN);
log      return(LOG);
sqrt     return(SQRT);
pi       return(PI);

[ \t]    ;

.        {return(yytext[0]);}

%%
```

Unlike most lex and yacc programs, Evaluator contains all of the auxiliary C code that it needs to run in the grammar.y file. yacc automatically passes this code along to the C compiler with the parser that it generates.

5. Open up a Unix shell window in the Terminal application.

6. Compile the Evaluator program with the make utility by typing make in the Terminal window. What you should type is shown here in bold:

Terminal

```
% cd ~/Evaluator
% make
yacc grammar.y
yacc -d grammar.y
lex rules.l
cc -O -o Evaluator y.tab.c lex.yy.c -ly -ll -lm
%
```

If you get any errors, you probably made a typo.

7. After compiling the program, test it with a few mathematical expressions, as follows:

```
% cd ~/Evaluator
% ./Evaluator
10+20
        30
2002/2001
    1.0005
```

```
sin(2*pi) + cos(4*pi)
           1
^C%>
```

(Type Control-C to exit the program. The "^C", which indicates where you should type Control-C, will show up in the Terminal window where indicated.)

Congratulations—you're finished with the back end! If you don't understand it all, don't worry. All you have to know to continue with MathPaper is that Evaluator will perform the actual calculations for MathPaper and will run as a separate process.

Cocoa's Document-Based Architecture

MathPaper uses Cocoa's document-based architecture, which relies on three classes—NSDocument, NSDocumentController, and NSWindowController— for managing its windows. Part of the Application Kit, the document-based architecture includes much of the functionality needed to create an application that can manage multiple windows, each containing its own document.

Working with the rest of the AppKit, the document-based architecture system provides for the following functionality, most of which is available via an application's File (or Document) menu:

- Creating new documents (File → New)
- Opening existing documents from files (File → Open)
- Saving files, either to the names from which they were opened or to new names (File → Save, File → Save As, File → Save Copy As)
- Reverting documents to the way that they are stored on the disk (File → Revert to Saved)
- Closing currently open files, first prompting to save the files if necessary (File → Close)
- Printing documents and modifying the current page layouts (File → Print and File → Page Setup)
- Automatically handling the window's modified status and title bar, and the application's Window menu

All of these tasks are handled for us automatically by Cocoa's document-based architecture system.

Building MathPaper's Front End

The next step is to create MathPaper's front end—the user interface and the program module that starts up the Evaluator subprocesses and sends them mathematical expressions to evaluate.

The MathPaper program will consist of two nibs:

MainMenu.nib
> The main nib that will control the menu, application initialization, and launching of new windows.

PaperWindow.nib
> The nib that will control a single MathPaper window. If we have several MathPaper windows, one copy of `PaperWindow.nib` will be loaded for each window.

> Because every MathPaper window has a separate nib, we can create new instances of a window simply by loading the same nib multiple times. We'll see how this works later in this chapter.

Setting Up the MathPaper Project

1. Launch Project Builder and choose its File → New Project menu command.
2. Select "Cocoa Document-based Application" in the New Project Assistant, as shown in Figure 10-3, and then click the Next button.

Project Builder

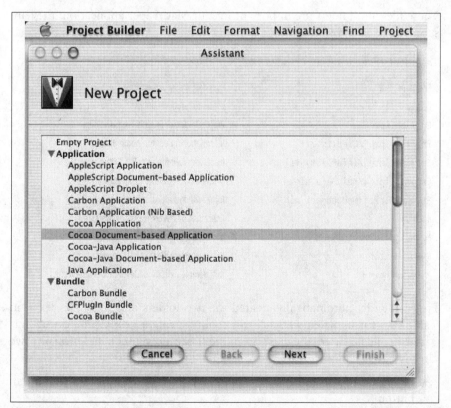

Figure 10-3. Creating a new Cocoa document-based application in PB

3. Give your new project the name "MathPaper" and click the Finish button.

Project Builder will create a folder called MathPaper in your Home folder and will populate it with files and folders, as shown in Figure 10-4.

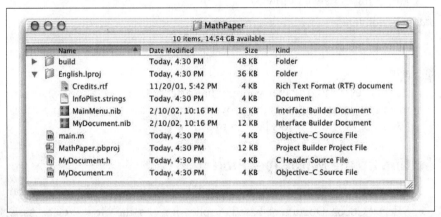

Figure 10-4. Files and folders created by PB for a new document-based application

These files and folders are important for our MathPaper application; they are summarized in Table 10-1.

Table 10-1. Files and folders created by PB for MathPaper

Filename	Purpose
build	Folder for program builds
English.lproj	Project folder for English-language nibs
English.lproj/Credits.rtf	Information for default About panel
English.lproj/InfoPlist.strings	Initial localized property list for the project
English.lproj/MainMenu.nib	Main menu nib for the application
English.lproj/MyDocument.nib	Initial window/document nib
main.m	Contains Objective-C main( ) function
MathPaper.pbproj	MathPaper PB project file
MyDocument.h	Initial interface file for MyDocument class
MyDocument.m	Initial implementation file for MyDocument class

Project Builder automatically created the two folders and eight files listed in Table 10-1 for us when we used this tool to create a new Cocoa document-based application. In the next step, we'll see how much functionality we already have.

4. In PB, run your MathPaper application by clicking the build and run button.

A "generic" MathPaper should now be running, with one document window that displays the text "Your document contents here".

5. Choose MathPaper's File → New menu command twice, and you should see two additional document windows, as shown in Figure 10-5.

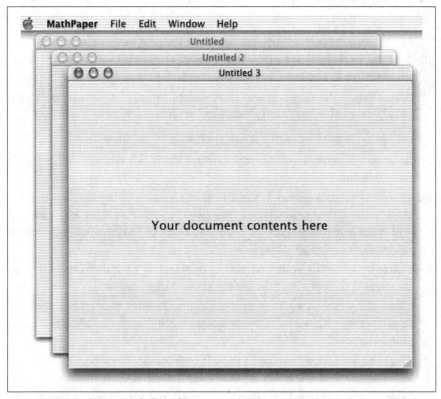

Figure 10-5. MathPaper with three documents

6. Try some of the other menu commands, such as File → Close and Window → Minimize.

Note that several of these menu items already work and were therefore pre-connected for us as soon as we chose to create a new Cocoa document-based application. This built-in functionality saves Cocoa programmers a lot of work!

7. Choose MathPaper → Quit.

Changing the Names of MathPaper Project Files

Rather than accepting the default names provided by PB, we will change the name of the nib from "MyDocument.nib" to "PaperWindow.nib". We'll also change the name of the class from "MyDocument" to "MathDocument". If we don't do this, we'll be stuck with the same (MyDocument) generic names that you see for most Cocoa document-based applications. The name-changing will take a bit of effort, but not too much.

8. Open the Finder and browse to your ~/MathPaper/English.lproj folder, as shown in Figure 10-4.

9. Change the name "MyDocument.nib" to "PaperWindow.nib" in the Finder (single-click the filename and type the new name).

10. Next, change the name of the interface file in ~/MathPaper from "MyDocument.h" to "MathDocument.h" in the Finder.

11. Also change the name of the implementation file in ~/MathPaper from "MyDocument.m" to "MathDocument.m" in the Finder.

Now we need to tell PB not to use the old nib and class filenames:

Project Builder

12. Back in PB, make sure that the Groups & Files pane is visible in PB's main window.

13. Open the Classes group in the Groups & Files pane by clicking the disclosure triangle next to Classes. The two (former) class files, MyDocument.h and MyDocument.m, should both be displayed in red because the files no longer exist in the ~/MathPaper folder.

14. Delete both MyDocument references by selecting each filename with your mouse and then pressing the Delete key on your keyboard.

15. Open the Resources group in the Groups & Files pane. The filenames Credits.rtf, MainMenu.nib, MyDocument.nib, and InfoPList.strings should appear.

16. Click the disclosure triangle to the left of MyDocument.nib to see "English", which is also colored red because the nib name has been changed.

17. Select the red-colored "English" and press the Delete key on your keyboard. PB may prompt you with a drop-down sheet that contains "Remove: Some items are represented on disk. Also delete from disk?" If you see this sheet, click the Don't Delete button.

Next, we need to inform PB about the new names we gave to the files in the Finder:

18. Choose PB's Project → Add Files menu command to add the renamed files to the MathPaper project.

19. In the resulting sheet, click the MathDocument.h file and then Shift-click the MathDocument.m file.

20. Click the Open button in the drop-down sheet, and you'll see another drop-down sheet with a checkbox item asking if you want to "Copy items into destination group's folder".

21. Because the MathDocument class files are already in the ~/MathPaper folder, simply click Add.

22. If the MathDocument files are not inserted into the Classes group in PB, drag them into it (drop the files after the disclusure triangle changes to whatever your highlight color is).

23. Again choose the Project → Add Files menu command. This time, add the `PaperWindow.nib` file that is inside the `English.lproj` folder and make sure it's in the Resources group in the Groups & Files pane.

When you are finished, the Groups & Files pane in your MathPaper project window should look like the one in Figure 10-6.

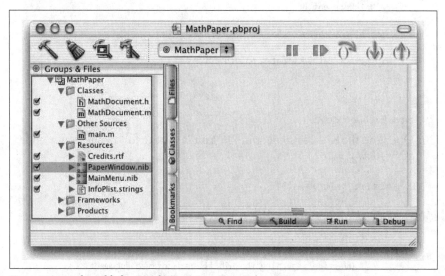

Figure 10-6. Files added in MathPaper Groups & Files pane

Finally, let's change the name representing the MathDocument class in Interface Builder:

24. Double-click the `PaperWindow.nib` filename in PB's Groups & Files pane to open the file in IB.

25. Select "MyDocument" under the Classes tab in the `PaperWindow.nib` window (use the Search field in this window to find the class quickly; it's a subclass of NSDocument).

26. Change the name of this class from "MyDocument" to "MathDocument".

The MathDocument Class

In this section, we will set up the MathDocument class as a subclass of the NSDocument class.

MathDocument.h

27. Open the file `MathDocument.h` in PB by double-clicking its name in the Groups & Files pane. You will see the following source code:

```
// MyDocument.h

#import <Cocoa/Cocoa.h>

@interface MyDocument : NSDocument
{
}
@end
```

MathDocument.h

28. Replace the comment and `@interface` statements in `MathDocument.h` with the statements shown here in bold:

```
// MathDocument.h

#import <Cocoa/Cocoa.h>

@interface MathDocument : NSDocument
{
}
@end
```

29. Save `MathDocument.h`.

30. Open the file `MathDocument.m` in PB. You'll see the following source code:*

```
// MyDocument.m

#import "MyDocument.h"

@implementation MyDocument

- (NSString *)windowNibName
{
    // Override returning the nib filename of the document.
    // If you need to use a subclass of NSWindowController or if
    // your document supports multiple NSWindowControllers,
    // you should remove this method and override
    // -makeWindowControllers instead.
    return @"MyDocument";
}

- (void)windowControllerDidLoadNib:(NSWindowController *) aController
{
    [super windowControllerDidLoadNib:aController];

    // Add any code here that needs to be executed once the
    // WindowController has loaded the document's window
}

- (NSData *)dataRepresentationOfType:(NSString *)aType
```

---

* We have taken the liberty of reformatting some of this source code so that it will fit better on these pages.

```
{
    // Insert code here to write your document from the given data.
    // You can also choose to override
    // -fileWrapperRepresentationOfType: or
    // -writeToFile:ofType: instead.
    return nil;
}

- (BOOL)loadDataRepresentation:(NSData *)data ofType:(NSString *)aType
{
    // Insert code here to read your document from the given data.
    // You can also choose to override
    // -loadFileWrapperRepresentation:ofType: or
    // -readFromFile:ofType: instead.
    return YES;
}

@end
```

31. Replace the first three lines of `MathDocument.m` with the statements shown here in bold:

MathDocument.m

```
// MathDocument.m

#import "MathDocument.h"

@implementation MathDocument
```

32. Replace the return value in the **windowNibName** method as follows:

```
- (NSString *)windowNibName
{
    return @"PaperWindow";
    // The comments have been removed
}
```

All of the changes we made in the last several pages are necessary because we want our own names (not the default ones), to better describe our nib and class files (perhaps there's an easier way to do this, but we don't know it). In making these changes, we've also gotten a look at some of the code that is automatically generated for a Cocoa document-based architecture application.

The MainMenu.nib File

In this section, we will customize the MathPaper menus that are stored in the `MainMenu.nib` file:

33. Back in PB, double-click the `MainMenu.nib` filename (under Resources) in PB's Groups & Files pane. IB will automatically launch and display the `MainMenu.nib` interface created by PB.

Interface Builder

34. Choose Interface Builder → Hide Others to simplify the screen.

35. Select IB's Cocoa-Menus palette by clicking the icon (shown at the edge of the page) at the left of the Palettes window toolbar.

The Cocoa-Menus palette is shown in Figure 10-7. Many of the menu cells in IB's Cocoa-Menus palette are preconnected (we saw such a preconnection previously with Calculator's Edit → Cut menu item, which was connected to the First Responder object's **cut:** method). We'll soon see how the File menu commands are preconnected. Also, be careful to include the desired functionality when changing names of menus and items. For example, if you drag the Window submenu into your application and then run it, the NSApplication object will automatically update the Window submenu as you create and delete main windows within your application. (Isn't object-oriented programming wonderful?!) You won't get this behavior, though, if you simply drag out the submenu called Submenu and change its name to Window.

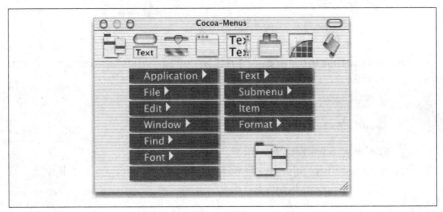

Figure 10-7. Cocoa-Menus palette in IB

In Mac OS X Version 10.1, some of the menus in the Cocoa-Menus palette differ slightly from the menus that are included in the default `MainMenu.nib` menu. For example, the Edit menu in the palette contains a Speech menu item, while `MainMenu.nib`'s Edit menu does not. This and other minor variations appear to be oversights and may be changed in a future release.

You can cut and paste menus and submenus with IB's Edit → Cut and Edit → Paste commands (what a concept!). If you want a particular submenu (like the extended Edit submenu) but you don't want a particular submenu command (e.g., Edit → Paste As), simply select the menu command and cut it out of the submenu. (You can also delete entire menus by hitting the Delete key when a menu cell is highlighted, so be careful!)

Of course, each application program that you create is likely to have its own specific collection of menus. Typically, you will initially customize the menus in `MainMenu.nib` when you first create your application. Then, as your application grows, you will modify the menus.

36. Back in IB, double-click "NewApplication" in the main `MainMenu.nib` menu and change its name to "MathPaper".

Interface Builder

37. Change the other three occurrences of "NewApplication" in the Math-Paper menu to "MathPaper", as shown in Figure 10-8.

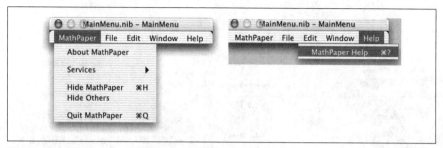

Figure 10-8. Configuring MathPaper's main menu

38. One by one, select and cut both the Preferences menu item and the space below it (we will not be creating a Preferences panel for this application). Your MathPaper application menu should now look exactly like the one in Figure 10-8.

Note that the Services submenu in Figure 10-8 is empty—it will be filled in automatically when your program runs (another free and tremendously powerful feature of Cocoa). Cocoa applications use the Services submenu to send messages to other applications.

39. Rename the Help submenu item so that "MyApp Help" becomes "Math-Paper Help", as shown in Figure 10-8.

40. In the `MainMenu.nib` window, choose File → New.

41. Type Command-2 to bring up the NSMenuItem Connections Info dialog.

42. Single-click the **newDocument:** method with the dimple next to it to display a premade connection to the First Responder (make sure you don't double-click the method and break the connection!).

Your screen should now contain something like the screen shot in Figure 10-9. (The only reason we included the previous three steps was to show you a MathPaper preconnection—these steps do not change anything in the Math-Paper program.)

The File menu (see Figure 10-9) has commands for dealing with documents as a whole—creating new documents, saving them, and so on. The Cocoa document-based architecture provides methods for each of the menu items in the File menu, as indicated in Table 10-2.

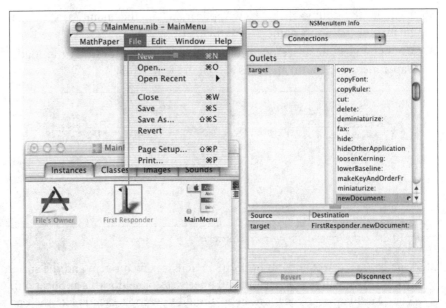

Figure 10-9. Premade connection from File → New to First Responder

Table 10-2. File menu items and their premade action messages

File menu item	Action message
File → New	[FirstResponder newDocument:]
File → Open...	[FirstResponder openDocument:]
File → Open Recent → Clear Menu	[FirstResponder clearRecentDocuments:]
File → Close	[FirstResponder performClose:]
File → Save	[FirstResponder saveDocument:]
File → Save As...	[FirstResponder saveDocumentAs:]
File → Revert	[FirstResponder revertDocumentToSaved:]
File → Page Setup...	[FirstResponder runPageLayout:]
File → Print...	[FirstResponder print:]

The First Responder will typically be the object that controls the document in the key window and thus will change as the end user changes the key window. Messages that are not handled by the key window will be passed up the responder chain; for example, the File → New command will be handled by the NSDocumentController object. The Window submenu will automatically be modified when your program is running to include additional menu cells for each document window (but not panel) that your program creates: this is done for you by the NSApplication object.

MainMenu.nib is now set up, so let's move on to customizing details about our project.

Customizing the Document-Based Project Information in PB

We must tell PB about the kinds of documents that Cocoa's document-based architecture will support. We will enter the information in the Application Settings pane under PB's Targets tab, as you'll see shortly.

For each document type, PB needs to know:

- The name of the document type
- Whether your application can edit files of this type, or merely display them
- The extension used for files of this type
- The Macintosh type and creator codes that are used when files of this type are saved
- The icon that is used to display this file type
- The subclass of the NSDocument class that should be used to read in this file type

The type and creator codes are 32-bit numbers that are stored in the file on any Macintosh HFS filesystem. These codes allow the Finder to automatically launch the appropriate application when you double-click the name of a file that stores a document associated with the application. For this reason, file extensions and creator types must be unique. To assure that they are unique across all applications, Apple maintains a registry of creator codes.

 The future of type and creator codes is currently uncertain. All versions of Mac OS until Version 10 relied on them extensively. With Mac OS X, Apple has placed more emphasis on file extensions. In part, this appears to stem from a desire to be more compatible with the rest of the computer industry. Mac OS X Version 10.0 used extensions and creator codes interchangably. With Version 10.1, Apple has tried to deemphasize type and creator codes. Because it is not clear what the future holds, this chapter shows how to use extensions as well as type and creator codes.

In writing this book, we requested from Apple a creator code for the Math-Paper application. We were assigned the code MATP. You should use this code for your copy of the MathPaper application. To get creator codes for your own applications, you must fill out Apple's Creator Code Registration form at http://developer.apple.com/dev/cftype/.

In the following steps, we will tell PB about the creator code and the Math-Document class.

43. In PB's main window, click on the Targets vertical tab.

44. Select the MathPaper target in the Targets pane at the upper-left corner of PB's main window.

45. Select the horizontal tab labeled "Application Settings".

46. Enter "MATP" in the Signature field of the Basic Information section.

47. Scroll down to the Document Types setting at the bottom of the pane and select it.

48. Enter "MathPaper" in the Name field to change the document type.

49. Enter "com.oreilly.MathPaper" in the Identifier field. The application identifier is a globally unique name that you use to identify your application. It controls, among other things, the name of the file that will be used to store the application defaults. (We'll talk more about this in Chapter 21.) You create the application identifier by reversing your Internet domain name and appending the application name.

50. Click the pop-up menu labeled "None" next to the Name field and change the Role from None to Editor.

51. Enter "matp" in the Extensions field.

52. Enter "MATP" in the OS types field.

53. Enter "MathDocument" in the Document Class field.

54. Click the Change button at the bottom of the Application Settings pane.

We'll leave the icon file blank for now. When you are finished, the MathPaper application Document Types in PB's main window should look like the window in Figure 10-10.

Setting Up PaperWindow.nib

In addition to the nib for the main menu, we will use the second (auxiliary) nib called `PaperWindow.nib` to define the window that will be used by each piece of math paper. The NSDocumentController class will load this nib each time it needs to create a new document window.

55. Still in PB, click the Files vertical tab (shown at the edge of the page) to display the files in the MathPaper project.

56. Double-click `PaperWindow.nib` under Resources in the Groups & Files pane. As we've seen before, this will open `PaperWindow.nib` in IB.

57. Choose Interface Builder → Hide Others to simplify the screen.

58. In IB, double-click the icon labeled "Window" (shown at the edge of the page) under the Instances tab in the `PaperWindow.nib` window. If it's not already displayed, this will display the generic-looking window with the text "Your document contents here" and bring it to the front of the screen.

Window

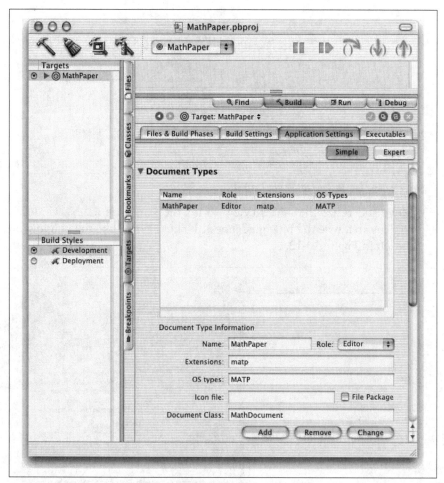

Figure 10-10. The MathPaper project with the application settings properly set

59. Select the text "Your documents contents here" by clicking it once, then hit the Delete key to remove this text.

60. Resize the new window so it's about three inches wide by four inches tall.

61. Click the Cocoa-Data button (shown at the edge of the page) at the top of IB's Palettes window to see the Cocoa-Data palette, shown in Figure 10-11.

62. Drag an NSTextView object (see Figure 10-11) from IB's Cocoa-Data palette and drop it in the window titled "Window".

If you type Command-1 with the NSTextView selected, the object will appear to be of the NSTextView class. However, if you type Command-5, the true class (NSScrollView) of this object appears. The NSScrollView actually "contains" an NSTextView "inside" it. (It also has an NSClipView.) We'll discuss NSTextView extensively in the next chapter.

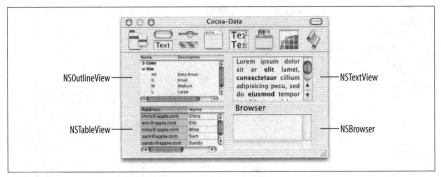

Figure 10-11. The Cocoa-Data palette in IB

63. Move and resize the NSTextView so it's the same size as the window's content area (use the blue guidelines). It should look like the window on the left in Figure 10-12.

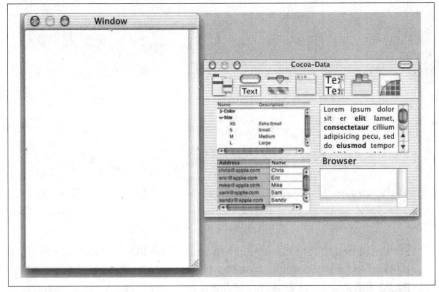

Figure 10-12. NSScrollView covering the content area of a MathPaper window

64. Select the NSTextView by clicking it once, then drag to Size in the Inspector pop-up menu (or type Command-3) to bring up the NSTextView Size inspector.

As we saw with the Calculator application, the Size inspector lets you specify how an NSView object will change in size and location when its containing view, or *superview*, is resized. In our MathPaper interface, we will specify the resizing characteristics of the NSTextView when the window's content view is resized (which occurs whenever the window is resized). In Figure 10-13, the large square labeled "Autosizing" represents the selected NSView's superview (content view, in our case), while the *inner* square represents the selected NSView (NSTextView, in our case). The origin and size of the NSTextView are set in the box above the Autosizing box.

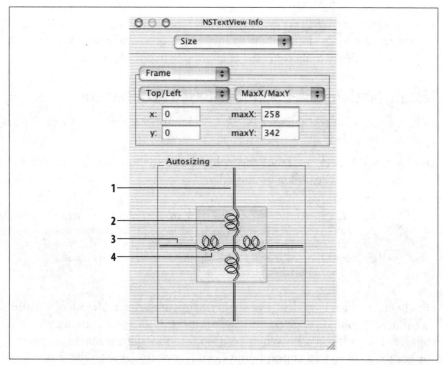

Figure 10-13. Size inspector for NSTextView object

The outer and inner Autosizing boxes each contain a set of two vertical and two horizontal lines. You can click on any of these lines to change it from a straight line to a spring, and vice versa. The straight line labeled (1) in Figure 10-13 indicates that the NSTextView will remain the same distance from the top of the window, no matter how the containing window is resized. If we change this line to a spring, the NSTextView will move up or down inside the containing window when the window is stretched or shrunk vertically. Likewise, the straight line labeled (3) indicates that the NSTextView will remain the same distance from the lefthand side of the window, regardless of how the containing window is resized. If we change this line to a spring, the NSTextView will move left or right inside the containing window when the window is stretched or shrunk horizontally. The spring labeled (2) indicates that the NSTextView will stretch or shrink when the containing view is resized vertically; a straight line here would indicate that the NSText-View does not vertically resize. The spring labeled (4) indicates that the

NSTextView will stretch or shrink when the containing view is resized horizontally; a straight line here would indicate that the NSTextView does not horizonally resize.

65. Click the lines inside the inner square in the Autosizing area of the Size inspector so that they become springs, as shown in Figure 10-13. This will cause the NSTextView to resize whenever its superview is horizontally or vertically stretched or shrunk, which is precisely what we want for an NSTextView that covers the content area (view) of a window.

Testing MathPaper's Document-Based Architecture

At last, it's time to test the skeletal MathPaper application, with some of our own features added:

66. Back in PB, click the build and debug button (shown at the edge of the page). Save all files when prompted.

> MathPaper may run but give you an alert panel that states "Can't create new document." If this happens, try cleaning out your ~/MathPaper/build folder by clicking PB's Clean Active Target button, shown at the edge of the page, and then build and debug MathPaper again.

PB will create a build folder (if necessary), copy into this folder all of the files that it needs, compile your classes, and start the application running within a copy of the gdb debugger. When your application starts running, a generic application icon should appear in the Cocoa Dock (we've seen that before). A single blank MathPaper window will be created automatically, because the application was launched without asking it to open a file.

67. Type Command-N twice. Two more windows will be created, as shown in Figure 10-14.

68. Try resizing one or more of the windows to test your Autosizing settings. Note that you can type mathematical expressions in the windows, but they are not evaluated because we haven't yet tied the Evaluator to MathPaper.

69. Quit MathPaper.

Summary

Well, that's all we've got right now—nothing else works! But marvel at how much functionality we get automatically from the document-based architecture. We've done very little to the interface, but already MathPaper has the basic architecture it needs to handle numerous documents simultaneously.

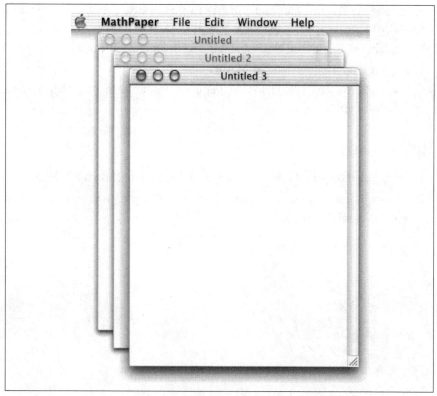

Figure 10-14. MathPaper running with an NSTextView in each window

We did, however, do a lot of work on our back end, Evaluator, in the first part of this chapter. In fact, Evaluator is now prepared to perform our requested calculations (as we saw when we ran it in a Terminal window), but it needs to be connected with the interface to work within the document-based architecture. In the next chapter, we'll tie the front-end interface and the back end together. To do that, we'll have to make some modifications to the MathDocument class and create the PaperController class. We'll also need to learn about some new Cocoa classes specifically designed to handle interprocess communications.

Exercises

1. Write short but detailed documentation on how to use Evaluator in a Terminal window. In particular, specify what types of mathematical expressions Evaluator will properly calculate.

2. What happens when you enter two consecutive "illegal" mathematical expressions in Evaluator? Fix the problem.

3. Investigate lex and yacc and enhance Evaluator by expanding the types of mathematical expressions that it implements.

4. Explain the role of the NSDocumentController class in this application.

5. Implement an About box for MathPaper.

6. Investigate Cocoa's NSHelpManager class and implement a Help system for MathPaper.

References

1. *lex & yacc*, by John Levine, Tony Mason, and Doug Brown (O'Reilly)

2. Manpages for lex, yacc, and make (type man lex, man yacc, and man make in a Terminal window)

CHAPTER 11

Tasks, Pipes, and NSTextView

In the last chapter, we built the MathPaper front and back ends. The back end (computational part) was created as a separate program called Evaluator. The front end was created using Cocoa's powerful multiple-document architecture. In this chapter, we'll tie the two ends together, learn more about processes, and modify the MathDocument class to display the results of calculations performed by Evaluator.

Processes, Pipes, and Resources

Here's the big picture of the MathPaper application: one process is responsible for all interaction with the user, while other processes are responsible for performing the actual mathematical calculations. The first process is the MathPaper process itself. The other processes are Evaluator processes that will be created by the MathPaper process using the NSTask class. Communication between the MathPaper and Evaluator processes depends on the NSPipe and NSFileHandle classes. NSTask, NSPipe, and NSFileHandle are Foundation classes that we haven't used yet; we'll describe them before using them.

The Unix operating system has always had a rich set of functions dedicated to interprocess communication. Unix uses the fork( ) system function to "spawn" (create) child subprocesses. After a subprocess is spawned, it can change what program it is running by calling the execv( ) system function. One way of communicating with subprocesses is via a *pipe*, a special kind of file object used by Unix to transmit information between processes. Unix is powerful, but the Unix functions fork( ) and execv( ) can be quite complicated to use. You can learn more about these system calls by typing man fork, man pipe, and man execv at the Terminal command line.

Rather than forcing us to use these functions directly, Cocoa gives us easy-to-use Foundation classes that provide a clean, object-oriented interface.

Objects of the NSTask, NSPipe, and NSFileHandle class type will have specific tasks in MathPaper. Each NSTask object will spawn a child Evaluator process, while NSPipe objects will be used to enable the MathPaper and Evaluator processes to communicate with one another via the Unix pipe structure. (As with pipes in the physical world, anything pushed in one end of a Unix pipe comes out the other end.) To provide for two-way communication between two processes, our MathPaper application will use a pair of pipes: one for sending information from the PaperController to Evaluator, and one for getting the results back from Evaluator.

While creating and using pipes can be complicated, the NSTask and NSPipe classes do all of the hard work for you. As with any class, you need to understand the NSTask and NSPipe class interfaces in order to use them, but you need not be concerned with the details of how these classes actually work.

Each Unix pipe has two ends, represented by a pair of NSFileHandle objects. The NSFileHandle class provides an object-oriented interface for files and communications channels. You can create an NSFileHandle that is associated with a file, with a network connection, or with a pipe.

In summary, each PaperController object in MathPaper will create:

- One NSTask object that will create and manage an Evaluator process
- Two NSPipe objects, one for sending information from the PaperController object to an NSTask object, and a second for sending information in the opposite direction between the same two objects
- Four NSFileHandle objects, two each for the two pipes described in the previous bullet

Making Evaluator a MathPaper Auxiliary Executable

In the previous chapter, we created and tested Evaluator in a Unix shell. Now we want to add the Evaluator source files (grammar.y and rules.l) to the MathPaper project and create a second target, so that the MathPaper project can create both the front end and the back end of the MathPaper application. We'll name this second target "Evaluator", and we'll make the MathPaper target dependent on the Evaluator target, which will result in the Evaluator target's being built before the MathPaper target is built. We'll also set up the MathPaper target so that the Evaluator executable is automatically copied into the MathPaper application wrapper as an auxiliary executable.

What a lot of work! Until now, the MathPaper application itself has been the only target. Let's get started on the modifications that we need.

1. Open `MathPaper.pbproj` in Project Builder.

2. Choose Project → New Target, and a new sheet will drop down in PB's main window.

Project Builder

3. Scroll to the bottom of the new sheet and select Tool, as shown in Figure 11-1.

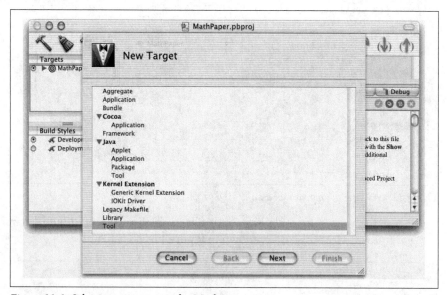

Figure 11-1. Selecting a new target for MathPaper

4. Click the Next button and a second new sheet will drop down, prompting for the name of the new target.

5. Enter "Evaluator" in the Target Name field in this second drop-down sheet, as shown in Figure 11-2. Select MathPaper as the project to which to add the new target.

6. Click the Finish button to add the new Evaluator target to the Math-Paper project.

After you complete these steps, the Evaluator target should appear next to a target icon (⊚) in the Targets pane of the `MathPaper.pbproj` project window. The MathPaper project was already in this pane because it was our first build target.

At this point, the Evaluator target has no source files with which it can build its target. Thus, our next task is to add the Evaluator source files `rules.l` and `grammar.y` to the project.

7. Choose Project → Add Files to begin the process of adding Evaluator's source files to the project. A new drop-down sheet appears with a filesystem browser.

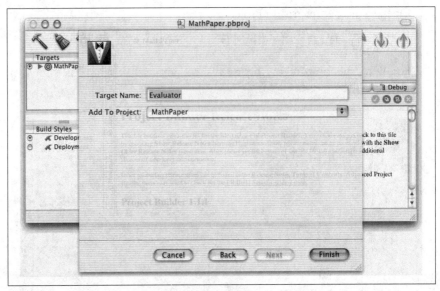

Figure 11-2. Giving the new target a name and project

grammar.y

8. Select the yacc source file grammar.y file in the browser (it should be in your ~/Evaluator folder), as shown in Figure 11-3.

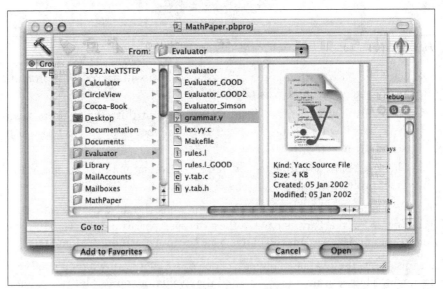

Figure 11-3. Finding the grammar.y yacc source file in the filesystem

9. Click the Open button to get a new sheet, as shown in Figure 11-4.

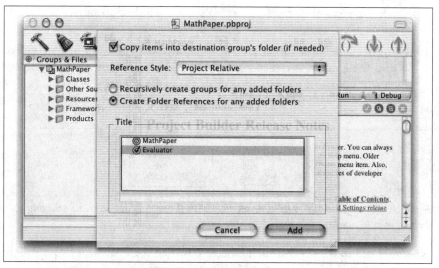

Figure 11-4. Adding grammar.y to the Evaluator target

10. Click the checkbox next to "Copy items into destination group's folder",* choose the Project Relative Reference Style, click the "Create Folder References for any added folders" radio button, click the Evaluator target, and finally click the Add button. Make sure that your settings are the same as those in Figure 11-4 before clicking Add.

11. Choose Project → Add Files again and add the lex rules file, rules.l, as you did with grammar.y. Make sure you choose the same settings as in Figure 11-4 for rules.l.

rules.l

 It is important that you add grammar.y before you load rules.l, because compiling the rules.l file requires an intermediate file produced when the grammar.y file is compiled. If you get the order wrong, you can manually change it by rearranging the order of the icons for these files within the Sources section of the Files & Build Phases tab of the Evaluator's Targets pane. The icon for the grammary.y file should be above the icon for the rules.l file.

If you check your ~/MathPaper folder in the Finder, you'll find that the grammar.y and rules.l files have been added to the folder. Next, we need to inform PB that the MathPaper target depends upon the Evaluator target.

---

* By copying the files from the ~/Evaluator folder into the ~/MathPaper folder, we make sure that the MathPaper application has its own copy of these files. All of the source code on which the Math-Paper application depends should be contained within the ~/MathPaper folder.

12. Click the vertical Targets tab in PB's main window to open the Targets pane.

13. Drag the Evaluator target and drop it on top of the MathPaper target. (Drop the Evaluator target when the disclosure triangle changes to your highlight color—it took us several tries to make it work.)

Your Targets pane should now look like the one on the left in Figure 11-5.

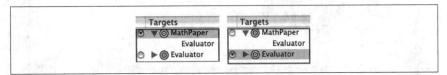

Figure 11-5. Targets pane—adding Evaluator to MathPaper target (left) and selecting Evaluator as active target (right)

Now we need to tell PB that the tool created when the Evaluator target is built is an auxiliary executable for the MathPaper target:

14. Make Evaluator the active (build) target by clicking the area to the left of the disclosure triangle next to its name. Your Targets pane should now look like the one on the right in Figure 11-5.

15. Build and run Evaluator by clicking the build and run button, shown at the edge of the page.

16. With Evaluator running in the Run pane in PB's main window, verify that it works by typing some mathematical expressions. Recall our type conventions: what you type is in bold and the results are in regular type.

```
10+20
          30
2002/2001
      1.0005
sin(2*pi) + cos(4*pi)
          1
```

The output is shown in Figure 11-6.

17. Click the stop button ((stop)) in PB's main window to terminate the Evaluator programs running within the PB environment.

As a result of our building the Evaluator target, you should now have an Evaluator executable in your ~/MathPaper/build folder. It has a little Terminal-like icon next to it. The Evaluator executable will also be listed in the Products section of PB's Groups & Files pane. We now need to tell PB that Math-Paper needs this executable in order to run:

18. Make MathPaper the active (build) target by clicking the area to the *left* of the MathPaper disclosure triangle. Your Targets pane should now look like the one on the left in Figure 11-5 again.

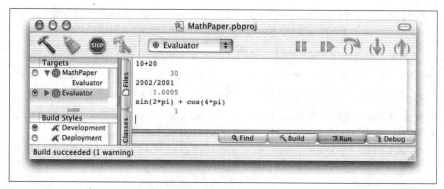

Figure 11-6. Evaluator running in PB's main window

19. Select the Files & Build Phases tab.

20. Select the Frameworks & Libraries section.

21. Choose the Project → New Build Phase → New Copy Files Build Phase command. A new section labeled "Copy Files" will appear.

22. Select the Files tab to display the Groups & Files tree view.

23. Scroll to the bottom to reveal the Products folder.

24. Open the Products folder to reveal the icon labeled "Evaluator".

25. Drag the Evaluator icon from the Products folder to the Files field of the Copy Files section.

26. Change the pop-up menu to read "Executables". The window should now appear as ours does in Figure 11-7.

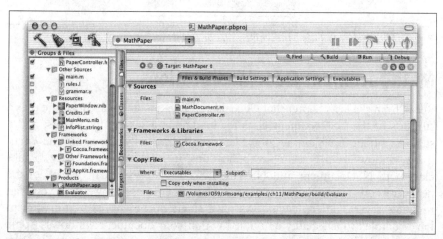

Figure 11-7. The Evaluator product is added to a newly created Copy Files section of the Files & Build Phases tab of the Targets pane

27. Type Command-S to save the project file.

Before moving on, we'll clean up our Groups & Files browser by putting all of the filenames in their correct groups.

28. Drag the recently added Evaluator executable into the Resources group.

29. Similarly, drag the grammar.y and rules.l source files into the Other Sources group. It's easier to do this when the groups are open.

If you open the groups, your Groups & Files pane should look like the one in Figure 11-8. Evaluator should be listed both as a resource for the MathPaper project and as a product itself. (The order of files within a group doesn't matter; in fact, the distribution of files into these groups is mostly a convenience for programmers.)

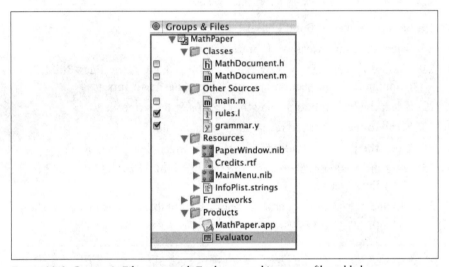

Figure 11-8. Groups & Files pane with Evaluator and its source files added

MathDocument Class Modifications

Recall from the last chapter that Cocoa's multiple-document architecture uses a subclass of the NSDocument class for loading and saving documents, and a subclass of the NSWindowController class for actually managing the document window itself. For simple applications, it may not be necessary to subclass both NSDocument and NSWindowController—you can put all of the necessary code in your subclass of the NSDocument class. However, if you plan to create several different windows for a single document, or if you want to have complex functionality embodied within your document windows, Apple recommends that you subclass NSWindowController. (For a more detailed discussion, we recommend that you read the Cocoa documentation pages for the NSDocument, NSWindowController, and NSDocumentController classes.)

In the next section, we will create a class called PaperController as our subclass of the NSWindowController class. To teach MathDocument about PaperController, we need to make two modifications to the MathDocument.m class file:

1. Back in PB, open the MathDocument.m class file (this is the file that was originally called MyDocument.m).

2. Add the line shown here in bold near the beginning of the MathDocument.m file:

MathDocument.m

```
// MathDocument.m

#import "MathDocument.h"
#import "PaperController.h"
```

Recall that the MathDocument class is a subclass of NSDocument. If we look at the code for MathDocument.m that we listed in the last chapter (or view it in PB), there is a comment in the **windowNibName** method that tells us to override NSDocument's **makeWindowControllers** method whenever we subclass NSWindowController. We'll do just that in the next step:

3. Override NSDocument's default **makeWindowControllers** method by adding the method shown here in bold just before the @end of the Math-Document.m file:

```
// Override the NSDocument makeWindowControllers
// method to specify our own controller

- (void)makeWindowControllers
{
    PaperController *ctl =
        [ [PaperController alloc]
            initWithWindowNibName:[self windowNibName] ];

    [ctl autorelease];
    [self addWindowController:ctl];
}
@end
```

This new method overrides NSWindowController's **makeWindowControllers** method. It creates an instance of PaperController, autoreleases the instance, and finally adds the instance to the list of managed window controllers using **addWindowController:**.

There is another automatically generated comment that says we should remove the implementation of **windowNibName** when overriding the **makeWindowControllers** method. We have not found this necessary using Mac OS X Version 10.1, but it may be necessary in the future.

You may be confused about why we autorelease the PaperController instance—after all, don't we want to use this object later? Well, recall from Chapter 4 that the **autorelease** message doesn't immediately release an object. Instead, it decrements the object's reference count. If no other part of our program increments the object's reference count by the time that the next event is requested from the user, the object will automatically be freed. In this case, however, the PaperController object will automatically be retained by the **addWindowController:** method call.

We need to autorelease the PaperController object because we **alloc**-ed it. But we don't want to send the object a full-blown **release** message, because we don't want it to be freed. It is for this purpose that the **autorelease** method was invented.

It's finally time to create the PaperController class that we've been discussing. Most of our "controlling" code will be placed in this class.

Creating PaperController, a Subclass of NSWindowController

In this section, we will create our initial PaperController class with the method that starts up Evaluator:

Interface Builder

1. Double-click the `PaperWindow.nib` file in PB's main window to open it up in IB.

2. Select the Classes tab in the `PaperWindow.nib` window.

3. Select the NSWindowController class (under NSObject—use the Search field if necessary).

4. Choose the Classes → Subclass NSWindowController menu command, as shown in Figure 11-9.

5. Type Command-1 to display the myWindowController Class Info panel.

6. Change the name of your new subclass from "MyWindowController" to "PaperController".

7. Add a new outlet named "theText" (note that there is already an outlet called "window").

8. Select the File's Owner under the Instances tab in the `PaperWindow.nib` window.

9. Type Command-5 and change the Custom Class of the File's Owner to PaperController (because the PaperController will load the `PaperWindow. nib` file).

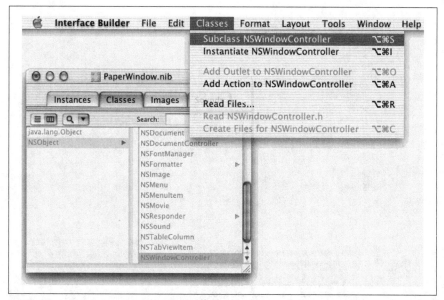

Figure 11-9. Subclassing NSWindowController

10. Control-drag from the File's Owner icon to the text area inside the window and double-click theText to make a connection, as shown in Figure 11-10.

11. Now select the PaperController class under the Classes tab in the PaperWindow.nib window.

12. Choose the Classes → Create Files for the PaperController menu command to create new PaperController.h and PaperController.m class files in the MathPaper target.

13. Click Choose at the bottom of the resulting sheet to create the class files in your ~/MathPaper folder.

14. Back in PB, check to see if the PaperController.m and PaperController.h files were inserted in the Classes group in the Groups & Files pane. If not, drag them from the group in which they were inserted into the Classes group (after all, PaperController is a class!).

Project Builder

Next, we need to add five more instance variables to the PaperController class. They will eventually be set to point to objects that we described earlier in this chapter. We will also change the declared type of the theText instance variable so that it exactly matches the NSTextView class type (theText was the name of the PaperController outlet we set up in IB before we created the class files). This second step is not strictly necessary, but it enables the

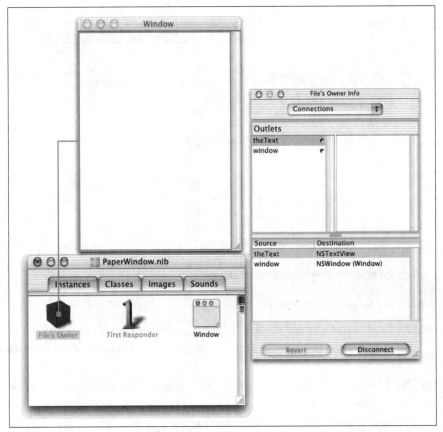

Figure 11-10. Connecting File's Owner to NSTextField inside NSScrollView

Objective-C compiler to do some additional compile-time checking for us (and it's good style!). Note that this strong typing of an outlet can also be set in IB's Info dialog.

PaperController.h

15. Still in PB, edit the `PaperController.h` file by adding or replacing the lines shown here in bold:

```
#import <Cocoa/Cocoa.h>

@interface PaperController : NSWindowController
{
    NSTask          *evaluator;
    NSPipe          *toPipe;
    NSPipe          *fromPipe;
    NSFileHandle    *toEvaluator;
    NSFileHandle    *fromEvaluator;
    IBOutlet NSTextView     *theText;
}

@end
```

Next, we'll work on the PaperController class implementation. The first method that we will add is **windowDidLoad**. This method is declared in PaperController's superclass, NSWindowController, so we are actually overriding the method. The **windowDidLoad** method will automatically be invoked after the PaperWindow.nib file is loaded and the PaperController class is instantiated.

16. Insert the entire **windowDidLoad** method shown here into the PaperController.m file (which has only three statements in it so far). Make sure you put this method between the two @ directives.

PaperController.m

```
- (void)windowDidLoad
{
    NSString *path=0;

    [super windowDidLoad];
    [ [self window] makeFirstResponder:theText];

    path = [ [NSBundle mainBundle]
                pathForAuxiliaryExecutable:@"Evaluator"];

    toPipe   = [NSPipe pipe];    // NSTask below will retain
    fromPipe = [NSPipe pipe];    // NSTask below will retain

    toEvaluator   = [toPipe fileHandleForWriting];
    fromEvaluator = [fromPipe fileHandleForReading];

    evaluator = [ [NSTask alloc] init];
    [evaluator setLaunchPath:path];

    [evaluator setStandardOutput:fromPipe];
    [evaluator setStandardInput:toPipe];
    [evaluator launch];

    [ [NSNotificationCenter defaultCenter]
       addObserver:self
          selector:@selector(gotData:)
             name:NSFileHandleReadCompletionNotification
           object:fromEvaluator];

    [fromEvaluator readInBackgroundAndNotify];

}
```

This method may look complicated, but it really isn't. Let's look at it piece by piece.

The first and third lines of the method create and initialize an NSString object called path, which will contain the file path of the Evaluator program. The next two lines invoke the superclass (NSWindowController) method and make the window's text area the first responder.

The next four lines of the method create two pipes: one that will send data to the Evaluator process, and one that will receive data from the process. For each of these pipes, we obtain the particular file handle that the PaperController will need to use.

After the pipes are created, the method creates the NSTask object that will actually spawn and communicate with the Evaluator process. We tell the task the path of the Evaluator program and give it the two pipes that we will use for our bidirectional communications. We then send [**evaluator launch**], which starts the process.

After the task is launched, we need some way of finding out when it has data available for the PaperController. We could poll the fromEvaluator NSFile-Handle class 10 or 20 times a second, but that would be incredibly wasteful. Instead, we ask the Cocoa notification system to watch the fromEvaluator object for us. When this object has data, it will emit a special message called **NSFileHandleReadCompletionNotification** to any object that happens to be observing. Our [**NSNotificationCenter defaultCenter**] message asks the default notification center to send our PaperController object a **gotData:** message whenever data is available. This notification request will remain until it is removed or our program exits.

The last line asks the fromEvaluator object to start watching for data from Evaluator. The NSFileHandle is checked for data as part of the application's event loop.

Finally, we need to write the PaperController class cleanup code. Because the PaperController registered to receive notifications, it needs to unregister when it no longer wishes to receive them. Because we have **alloc**-ed Evaluator, we should be sure to release it when the PaperController object is no longer needed. The logical place for this cleanup code is in the **dealloc** method, which is called when the PaperController is about to be destroyed.

PaperController.m

17. Add the following **dealloc** method to the PaperController.m file:

```
- (void)dealloc
{
    [[NSNotificationCenter defaultCenter] removeObserver:self];
    [evaluator release];
    [super dealloc];
}
```

We're getting closer! We have already arranged for the Evaluator program to be built automatically when the MathPaper application is built and for Evaluator to be placed automatically into the MathPaper bundle. We have created our NSWindowController subclass, PaperController, and arranged for Math-Document to instantiate PaperController automatically. The only things left to do are to write the code that will read each line of text entered when the user hits the Return key and send it to Evaluator, and then to write the code that will read the results from Evaluator and display them in the NSText-View. Before we can do that, however, we need to explain a lot more about how the NSTextView works.

The NSScrollView and NSTextView Classes

In Chapter 10 we introduced the NSScrollView and NSTextView classes when we dragged an NSScrollView object from IB's Cocoa-Data palette into a MathPaper window. At the time, we said that the NSScrollView object "contains" an NSTextView object. Perhaps a better way of putting it is to say that an NSTextView is "embedded" inside each NSScrollView. The NSScrollView object in IB's Palettes window actually contains the following nine objects:

NSScrollView
Displays the scroller and does the actual scrolling

NSTextView
Displays the text

NSClipView
Helps arrange the communication between the NSScrollView and the NSTextView

Vertical scroller
Controls up-down scrolling and shows where you are in the document

Horizontal scroller
Controls left-right scrolling and shows where you are in the document

NSTextStorage object
Holds the data that the NSTextView displays

NSTextContainer object
Defines the region where the text will be displayed

NSLayoutManager object
Controls the layout of the NSTextStorage object's information within the NSTextView

NSSimpleHorizontalTypesetter
Does the typesetting

You can control whether each scroller is displayed by sending the **setHas-VerticalScroller:** or **setHasHorizontalScroller:** messages (with the arguments YES or NO) to the NSScrollView. By default, the NSScrollView that you drag off IB's Cocoa-Data palette displays the vertical scroller, but not the horizontal one.

NSTextView objects are most frequently used with NSScrollView objects, which is why Interface Builder provides them that way. We'll learn other ways to use NSScrollViews in the GraphPaper application later in this book.

The NSTextView object is Cocoa's general-purpose text editor. An NSTextView object is used by almost every application that allows text entry. For example, Mac OS X's TextEdit text editor uses the NSTextView class as its main editing tool. It is also used by many commercial drawing applications, such as Stone Design's Create.

An NSTextView object can do all of the following:

- Display single-font (monofont) text or multiple-font text
- Automatically word-wrap
- Work with the pasteboard
- Save its contents in a stream of ASCII, Unicode, or RTF text

The NSText class supports a general programmatic interface for objects that manage text. However, you typically use instances of its subclass, NSTextView.

Every NSWindow object has a special NSText object called the *field editor* that can be assigned minor editing tasks for the NSWindow. This NSText object is shared among NSForm, NSMatrix, NSBrowser, and NSTextField objects located within a single associated on-screen window. When you are working with text in one of these objects in a window, the field editor reads in the text and lets you edit it. When you're done, the field editor NSText object spits out its contents and puts the text back into the appropriate location. The shuttling about of the field editor is all fairly transparent and is handled automatically by these classes.

NSTextView Class Basics

Like objects of the NSApplication and NSWindow classes, an NSTextView object can have a delegate object. You can use an NSTextView's delegate to find out when the user has made changes to the text or to prevent changes from happening under certain circumstances, as described in Table 11-1.

Table 11-1. Common delegate methods of the NSText and NSTextView classes

Delegate method	Purpose
-(void)**textDidBeginEditing:** (NSNotification *)*aNotification*	Alerts the delegate that the user has started to edit the NSText(View) object.
-(void)**textDidChange:** (NSNotification *)*aNotification*	Alerts the delegate that the text or formatting of the NSText(View) object has changed.
-(void)**textDidEndEditing:** (NSNotification *)*aNotification*	Alerts the delegate that the user is finished editing the NSText(View) object. This message is usually sent when the user clicks elsewhere on the window.

Table 11-1. *Common delegate methods of the NSText and NSTextView classes (continued)*

Delegate method	Purpose
- (BOOL)**textShouldBeginEditing:** (NSText *)*aTextObject*	Requests permission from the delegate for the user to edit the text contained within the NSText(View) object. If the delegate returns YES, editing is allowed. If the delegate returns NO, editing is not allowed.
- (BOOL)**textShouldEndEditing:** (NSText *)*aTextObject*	Requests permission from the delegate to allow the user to end editing. The delegate can use this method to take the opportunity to validate the contents of the NSText(View) object, and to force the user to change an invalid value to a valid value before allowing the user to do something else inside the application.

Most often, you'll use an NSTextView object to display a chunk of text for the user (e.g., the contents of an article or a mail message). Alternatively, you might use an NSTextView object to let the user enter some free-form text (again, such as a mail message). If you're writing a full-featured text editor, the NSTextView object is a great place to start. With its architecture, you can easily create an elaborate system that supports multiple columns of text, runarounds, and many other features.

When it runs as part of an application, the NSTextView object contains a copy of all of the text that you are editing. The more text that you have, the longer it will take to load the text into the NSTextView object and to display it for the first time. However, the NSTextView object collection is still extremely fast—a lot of very smart people have been working for many years on these objects. Give them a try before you try to do better.

PaperController Class Modifications

Now it's time to finish the PaperController class. To do this, we need to make the following changes to PaperController:

- Add a method that waits for the user to hit the Return key, gets the new formula that the user has typed, and then sends it to the appropriate Evaluator process.

- Add a method that gets invoked when there is data from the Evaluator process ready to be displayed in the NSTextView.

- Terminate the Evaluator process when a MathPaper window is closed.

Creating the NSTextView Delegate

There are many ways to find out when the user hits the Return key. One way is to subclass the NSTextView class and examine each event; another is to set up a delegate object that will be alerted each time the text inside the NSTextView changes. If the change results from a carriage return, our delegate can then grab the last line of the NSTextView object and send that line to Evaluator.

An NSTextView delegate can receive all sorts of special messages when things happen to the NSText object. The one that we care about here is the **textDid-Change:** message, which is sent to the delegate object whenever the text changes. To find out if the text changed because the user hit the Return key, our delegate method asks the window for the current event; it then asks the current event for its characters and checks whether the resulting string is equal to a carriage return.

After the MathPaper user hits the Return key, our delegate method asks the NSTextView object for an NSString that contains all of the text that is currently stored inside the NSTextView. It then searches backward through this NSString object for the second-to-last carriage-return character and creates a substring containing the characters located between the last two carriage returns. This substring is then sent to the Evaluator process using NSFileHandle's **writeData:** method. We also temporarily set the NSTextView in the MathPaper window to be "not editable", because we don't want to allow the user to type a new equation while Evaluator is calculating the results.

Although we could create a separate class for our NSTextView delegate, instead we'll make our PaperController class the NSTextView's delegate and implement the **textDidChange:** delegate method in PaperController.m.

1. Back in IB, open PaperWindow.nib.

Interface Builder

2. Double-click the NSTextView that's "inside" the NSScrollView object to select it (you should see a blinking edit cursor). If you only single-click the NSScrollView/NSTextView combination, you'll get the NSScrollView and not the desired NSTextView.

3. Control-drag from the center of the NSTextView object to the File's Owner icon in the PaperWindow.nib window.

4. Double-click the delegate outlet in the NSTextView Connections inspector to set the File's Owner as the delegate of the NSTextView, as shown in Figure 11-11.

5. Back in PB, insert the **textDidChange:** delegate method into the Paper-Controller.m file, as follows:

PaperController.m

```
// NSTextView delegate method textDidChange:
// If current event is a carriage return, do special processing
- (void)textDidChange:(NSNotification *)notification
{
    NSString *key = [[[self window] currentEvent] characters];

    if ([key isEqualToString:@"\r"]) {

        // Get the last line of text from theText and process it

        NSString *str = [theText string];
```

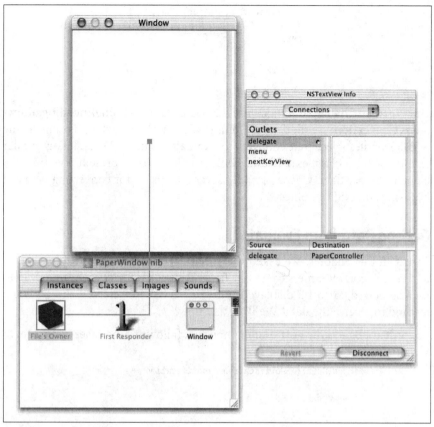

Figure 11-11. Making PaperController (File's Owner) the delegate of the NSTextView

```
int length = [str length];
int i;

// Get the last line and send it to Evaluator if it has
// anything on it

for (i=length-1;i>=0;i--) {

    if (i==0 || [str characterAtIndex:i-1] == '\n') {
        NSRange llRange = NSMakeRange(i,length-i);
        NSString *lastLine = [str substringWithRange:llRange];

        if ([lastLine length]>1) {
            NSData *sendData =
            [lastLine dataUsingEncoding:NSASCIIStringEncoding
                allowLossyConversion:YES];
            [toEvaluator writeData:sendData];

            // Do not allow any more changes to the text
```

```
                                    [theText setEditable:NO];
                        }
                        return;
                }
            }
        }
    }
```

Our **textDidChange:** method uses NSString's **dataUsingEncoding:allow-LossyConversion:** method to create an NSData object, which is sent to the NSFileHandle object that connects to Evaluator. The NSData class is similar to the NSString class, except that NSData objects can represent any arbitrary block of binary data. Cocoa provides several methods for converting between NSString and NSData objects.

Getting Data from Evaluator

Earlier in this chapter, we asked the application's default notification center to send the **gotData:** message to our PaperController object each time Evaluator has new data to be displayed, but we haven't yet created the **gotData:** method to receive the data! We'll do that now.

PaperController.m

6. Still in PB, add the **gotData:** method that follows to the PaperController.m file:

```
- (void)gotData:(NSNotification *)notification
{
    NSData *data;
    NSString *str;

    data = [ [notification userInfo]
                objectForKey:NSFileHandleNotificationDataItem];

    str = [ [NSString alloc] initWithData:data
                                encoding:NSASCIIStringEncoding];

    // Add the data to the end of the theText object
    [theText appendString:str];
    [theText appendString:@"-------------------\n"];

    // Scroll to the bottom
    [theText scrollRangeToVisible:
                NSMakeRange([ [theText textStorage] length], 0)];

    // Register to get the notification again
    [fromEvaluator readInBackgroundAndNotify];

    // Allow the user to type additional math expressions
    [theText setEditable:YES];

    // And release the string
    [str release];
}
```

This method is a little tricky because it interfaces with Cocoa's notification system. According to the NSFileHandle documentation, when the NSFile-Handle posts a notification that it has data, the data is placed inside an NSDictionary object under the key NSFileHandleNotificationDataItem.

The first executable statement in **gotData:** gets the NSData object that contains the (raw) data from the file handle, and the second statement turns the NSData object into an NSString object. The third statement sends this string an **autorelease** message, which assures that it will be released if it is not retained elsewhere in our program (and it won't be). The next two statements append the string from Evaluator to the end of theText, and then follow this with a line of hyphens and a newline that will separate mathematical expressions from one another in the window.

NSFileHandleReadCompletionNotifications are one-shot. To get the next batch of data from the NSFileHandle, the PaperController class needs to ask the NSFileHandle for the next notification. Finally, the method makes theText editable, so that the user can type in more data.

Adding a Method Using a Category

If you read the **gotData:** method and then closely read the documentation for the NSText and NSTextView classes, you'll notice something odd: the NSTextView class does not implement an **appendString:** method! This is a useful method to have, but for some reason, Apple didn't include it. Thus, we'll have to create it ourselves.

Fortunately, there's an easy way around this problem—we'll add the method to Cocoa's NSTextView class using an Objective-C *category*. Being able to add methods to existing classes without subclassing is one of the cooler things that you can do with Objective-C. We'll do just that in the following two steps, adding the NSTextView(MathPaper) category that includes the **appendString:** method we need:

7. Insert the NSTextView(MathPaper) category interface shown here into the PaperController.h file, after the existing @end directive:

PaperController.h

```
@interface NSTextView(MathPaper)
- (void)appendString:(NSString *)str;
@end
```

8. Now insert the category implementation shown here after the existing @end directive in the PaperController.m file:

PaperController.m

```
@implementation NSTextView(MathPaper)
- (void)appendString:(NSString *)str
{
    int len = [ [self textStorage] length];
    [self replaceCharactersInRange:NSMakeRange(len,0)withString:str];
}
@end
```

This category adds the **appendString:** method to the NSTextView class (not the PaperController class, even though it's located in `PaperController.m`!). The method first finds out how many characters are in the NSTextView's `textStorage` object. It then calls the `NSMakeRange()` utility function to create an NSRange object (location and length) to pass to NSTextView's **replaceCharactersInRange:withString:** method, together with the **appendString:** method's string argument. The **replaceCharactersInRange:withString:** method replaces the zero-length selection that exists at the end of the `textStorage` object with the passed-in string.

9. Now press the pop-up menu button labeled Evaluator (◉ Evaluator ⇡) near the top of PB's main window and drag to MathPaper. Note the target icon on this pop-up menu, indicating that we have just changed our (build) target from Evaluator to MathPaper.

10. Build and run the MathPaper application.

11. Type some mathematical expressions in MathPaper's window and hit Return. The expressions should be evaluated and you should get results!

12. Choose File → New (or type Command-N) three times to get a total of four MathPaper windows.

13. Type some additional mathematical expressions in the key MathPaper window, as shown in Figure 11-12.

14. Choose the Window menu and note that the four MathPaper windows are listed, as shown in Figure 11-12. These menu commands work! The multiple-document architecture provides this functionality.

15. Choose the Services menu, and note that its commands work too.

16. Do not quit MathPaper yet.

Before we move on, it's useful to see which Unix processes are running when MathPaper is running:

Terminal

17. Open a Terminal window and type `ps uxww` in it. (If you prefer, use Process-Viewer here.)

As we saw previously, the `ps` command displays processes running on your Unix box. The `u` option tells `ps` to display processes owned by the user (i.e., you), the `x` option tells `ps` to display processes without controlling terminals, and the `ww` option tells `ps` to display in the wide format (so you can see the long file paths). Type `man ps` in the Terminal window for all the gory details.

The `COMMAND` column of the `ps uxww` display contains one MathPaper process:

```
/Users/wsurfer/MathPaper/build/MathPaper.app/Contents/MacOS/MathPaper
```

The `COMMAND` column of the `ps uxww` display also contains four Evaluator processes that all look like this:

```
/Users/wsurfer/MathPaper/build/MathPaper.app/Contents/Resources/Evaluator
```

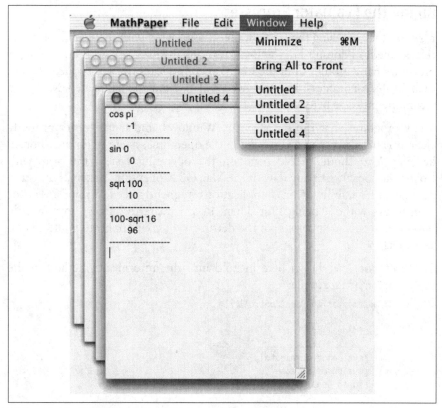

Figure 11-12. MathPaper running with several windows

Each one of the Evaluator processes is tied to one of the four MathPaper windows. If you find it's too difficult to read the output of the ps uxww command, try typing this instead:

```
ps uxww | grep Evaluator
```

This will display only the processes that include the "Evaluator" string.

18. Now close all four of the MathPaper windows by clicking their red close buttons, but leave MathPaper running.

19. Type ps uxww in the Terminal window again.

You would expect the four Evaluator processes to go away one by one as the windows are closed, but in fact they are all still running (with no useful purpose!). We will have to do something about that.

20. Quit MathPaper.

21. Type ps uxww in the Terminal window a third time, and you'll see that all five of the processes (one MathPaper and four Evaluator processes) have ceased running.

Killing the Evaluator Processes

It's clear that releasing the NSTask object associated with the Evaluator in the **release** method doesn't kill the Evaluator process itself. As a result, Evaluator processes hang around until the MathPaper application itself is killed. To kill each Evaluator process properly, we need to send the associated NSTask a **terminate** message before releasing it. We'll do that shortly.

Many programs that run on Mac OS, Windows, and Unix do not properly clean up after themselves: they rely on the operating system to do their housekeeping. You should not depend on the operating system this way with Cocoa, not because of any flaw in the Mac OS X operating system, but rather because of its stability. Cocoa applications frequently need to run for days or even weeks without being shut down. If you waste resources—even a little bit—it may become obvious (to the detriment of your application and to you as a developer!).

PaperController.m

22. Insert the line shown here in bold into the **autorelease** method in the PaperController.m file:

```
@implementation PaperController

- (void)dealloc
{
    [evaluator terminate];
    [evaluator release];
    [super dealloc];
}
```

When each MathPaper window is closed, the PaperController object will be sent a **release** message. Because this PaperController had only one reference count, this will cause the PaperController object to be sent a **dealloc** message. When this message is received, the PaperController will first terminate and then release the Evaluator's NSTask. (The NSTask will then release itself.)

23. Build and run MathPaper again. Type ps uxww in a Terminal window to test whether the Evaluator processes are killed as the MathPaper windows are closed.

24. Quit MathPaper.

Giving Proper Titles to MathPaper Windows

Do you think it's somewhat unsettling that our MathPaper application simply says the word "Untitled" in the title bar of each window, rather than stating the name of the application? If so, you can make a three-line addition to the PaperController.m class implementation file to change this. Let's do it.

25. Add the following method, **windowTitleForDocumentDisplayName:**, to the PaperController.m file:

PaperController.m

```
- (NSString *)windowTitleForDocumentDisplayName:
                (NSString *)displayName
{
    return [@"MathPaper: " stringByAppendingString:displayName];
}
```

26. Build and run MathPaper again and note the more appropriate window titles, as shown in Figure 11-13.

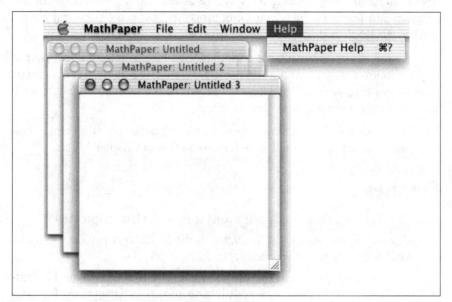

Figure 11-13. MathPaper windows with better titles

The NSWindowController class automatically invokes the **windowTitleForDocumentDisplayName:** method to determine the actual window title that is displayed. Our version of this method returns an NSString that has the title "MathPaper:" before the filename. (Recall that the NSString object is **autorelease**-d when the application returns to the main event loop.)

> This situation with the title demonstrates why it is important to read the Cocoa developer documentation. Before we wrote this chapter, we didn't know about the **windowTitleForDocumentDisplayName:** method (it wasn't present in earlier versions of the Application Kit.) But we thought that the plain "Untitled" window was too barren, so we opened up the documentation for NSWindowController and searched for the word "title". Within two minutes, we knew how to remedy the problem, and the code worked perfectly the first time.

Summary

We began this chapter by adding the Evaluator back end we created in the previous chapter to the MathPaper project. Then we created a new subclass of NSWindowController, called PaperController, where we put most of our "controlling" code—the code that ties our lex- and yacc-built back end together with the Cocoa-supplied document front end. MathPaper's parts (Evaluator, document architecture, PaperController) fit the model-view-controller paradigm nicely. Along the way, we discovered a few issues with our program and learned a bit about Unix processes and some powerful classes (such as NSTextView) in order to take care of those program issues.

We can still improve MathPaper considerably. For example, the text output in the windows is plain, and we haven't done anything about file operations such as printing, saving, opening, and so on. In the coming chapters, we'll start working on solving these shortcomings.

Another important thing missing from the MathPaper application is the ability to save and load files. We'll learn how to do that in Chapter 13.

Exercises

1. Why didn't we need to add our Makefile from the last chapter to PB?
2. Why did we choose to add Evaluator to the MathPaper project in PB as a Tool? Are there any other choices?
3. Where did we put interface and implementation code for the NSTextView category? Is there a better place to put it? What options for category placement are available?
4. Find out when and how often each of your MathPaper methods is invoked. Do this by inserting NSLog( ) function calls near the beginning of every method in the MathDocument and PaperController classes. Then run MathPaper within PB to see the logged output in the Run pane. Are you surprised at the sequence of method invocations? Does the "big picture" we described in the last chapter make sense?

CHAPTER 12

Rich Text Format and NSText

The MathPaper windows that we built in the last chapter didn't quite live up to their initial billing. We promised what you see on the left side of Figure 12-1 but gave what you see on the right. The difference between the two windows is a matter of fonts and formatting. Although the NSTextView object that we used allows a great deal of control over fonts and formatting, when we invoked the **replaceCharactersInRange:withString:** method in PaperController we were simply pasting plain ASCII text into the selection, which comes up as left-justified monofont text—not very interesting. To get the promised fonts and formatting, we'll have to learn about *Rich Text Format* (RTF). Most of today's word processors (e.g., TextEdit, Microsoft Word) support RTF, and it has been used as a cross-platform format for years, so you probably know a little bit about it already. In this chapter, we'll show you how to code RTF right into your applications.

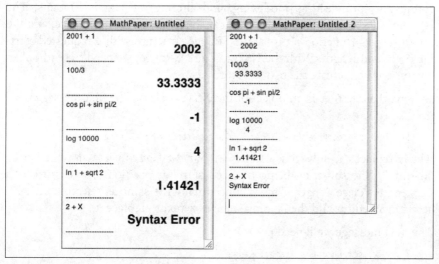

Figure 12-1. What we promised (left) and what we've delivered so far (right)

Rich Text Format

Suppose you want to amaze your friends by showing them how easy it is to create text with different font sizes in a window. You might want the final window to look something like that shown in Figure 12-2.

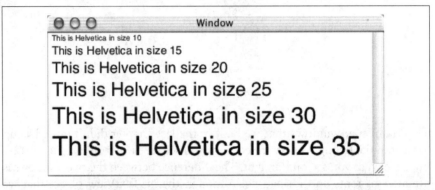

Figure 12-2. Desired text output

One way that you can do this is by using the NSText class as if it were a simple text editor, sending an instance of NSText commands to insert text, select the text, and then change the text to the desired size. Although this is an inefficient way to manipulate the NSText class, it is conceptually easy.

Formatting NSTextView Output

The NSText class (the superclass of our friend, NSTextView) provides lots of commands for selecting, modifying, and altering the text it contains. The NSFont class allows us to create a font with any name and point size, and the NSMakeRange( ) function returns an NSRange structure with a requested starting point and length. With the NSFont and NSRange, we need to send only a few messages to create the text in Figure 12-2.

Assume that theText is an object of the NSText class. The first message we'll need is:

```
[theText replaceCharactersInRange:aRange withString:aString]
```

which replaces a substring of text in our NSText object with the string "aString". The substring being replaced starts at position aRange.start and has length aRange.length. This is conceptually the same as selecting the substring in an editor and then typing some new text to replace it.

The next message we'll need is:

```
[theText setFont:aFont range:aRange]
```

which sets the text in theText (an NSText object) in the range aRange to have the font aFont.

The last message we'll need is:

```
[NSFont fontWithName:aName size:aSize]
```

which invokes an NSFont class (or factory) method to create a new font object with the name aName and point size aSize.

Following is the method we used to create the Helvetica text in the window in Figure 12-2:

```
- (IBAction)fontDemo:(id)sender
{
    float s;

    for (s = 10.0 ; s < 36.0 ; s += 5.0) {

        NSString *str = [NSString
            stringWithFormat:@"This is Helvetica in size %g\n", s];

        int length = [ [theText textStorage] length];
        NSRange range;

        [theText replaceCharactersInRange:NSMakeRange(length,0)
                            withString:str];

        range = NSMakeRange(length,[str length]);

        [theText setFont:[NSFont fontWithName:@"Helvetica" size:s]
                range:range];
    }
}
```

If you want to see the **fontDemo:** method's output, create a new project and insert the method in a new subclass of NSObject. The subclass should also contain an outlet called theText that connects to an NSScrollView in a window. To invoke the method, instantiate an object of your new subclass, make it the delegate of the File's Owner, and invoke **fontDemo:** in the **application-DidBecomeActive:** notification method. (Note that this is not the only way to do this.*)

---

* Another way to create an application to invoke **fontDemo:** is to use Project Builder and Interface Builder to create a project with an NSTextView object in a window and a menu item called Demo. Then subclass NSObject to get the MyObject class, and add an outlet called theText and an action called **fontDemo:** to it. Instantiate the subclass to get a MyObject instance, connect the theText outlet to the NSTextView outlet, and make the Demo menu cell send the action message **fontDemo:** to the MyObject instance. Finally, unparse MyObject, type in the **fontDemo:** code above, build and run the application, and choose the Demo menu command.

When we wrote our original NeXTSTEP book back in 1992, we called this method **slowFontDemo:** because it was very slow. Running on a 25-Mhz NeXTstation (CPU speed has certainly gotten better, thanks to Moore's law), you could actually watch each line of text being inserted into the text object and being reformatted to the specified size. It actually looked like somebody was sitting down at the computer's keyboard, inserting the string "This is Helvetica in size nn" into the text editor, selecting it with the mouse, and changing its size. When the method ran, it was just plain ugly. But that was 10 years ago. If you build a "quickie" application that invokes the **fontDemo:** method and run it today, the text will appear immediately. This is a testament both to the significantly faster speed of today's computers and to the improved algorithms used for rastering fonts.

Indeed, this short demonstration shows some of the significant advantages of Cocoa for handling text:

- The fonts look great, because they're automatically scaled by Quartz to whatever size you request.
- The text automatically wraps when you resize the window.
- The second time you run this demo it will run even faster, because the Window Server will have cached bitmaps for the sizes of the fonts that you have specified.

Nevertheless, it's somewhat awkward to drive the NSText object like a word processor. For our purposes, it's far better to simply load a file into the NSText object and have it display all of the fonts at the same time. To do that, we need to learn about Rich Text.

Rich Text Syntax

The other way to manipulate text is by constructing the text you want ahead of time—with all of the fonts and formatting commands already in place—and then reading it into the NSText object in a single operation. One format for this data stream, called *Rich Text*, was developed by Microsoft in the 1980s.

Rich Text looks a little like the codes used by *TeX* (pronounced "tech," as in the word "technique"), the document typesetting system developed by Donald Knuth. Here's the "raw" Rich Text code that will display the same fonts and text as the above demonstration:

```
{\rtf1\mac\ansicpg10000\cocoartf100
{\fonttbl\f0\fswiss\fcharset77 Helvetica;}
{\colortbl;\red255\green255\blue255;}
\margl1440\margr1440\vieww8320\viewh3920\viewkind0
\pard\tx1440\tx2880\tx4320\tx5760\tx7200\ql\qnatural
```

```
\f0\fs20 \cf0 This is Helvetica in size 10\

\fs30 This is Helvetica in size 15\

\fs40 This is Helvetica in size 20\

\fs50 This is Helvetica in size 25\

\fs60 This is Helvetica in size 30\

\fs70 This is Helvetica in size 35\

\fs20 \
}
```

An RTF file consists of unformatted text (e.g., "This is Helvetica"), control words (e.g., \fonttbl), control symbols (e.g., \~), and groups enclosed by curly braces ({}). Each *control word* begins with a backslash (\) and consists of a string of letters followed by an optional numeric argument. Each *control symbol* (none in our previous example) begins with a backslash and is followed by exactly one nonalphanumeric character (e.g., \~ represents a nonbreaking space). Curly braces have a special meaning: they define *groups* that support Rich Text graphics *states*. If you change the state of a font within a graphics state, the change is lost when the state is closed.

Don't be alarmed if Rich Text seems a little complicated! There are really only a few Rich Text controls that you need to be concerned about, and later in this chapter, we'll introduce an RTF object that handles them for you automatically. Many of the RTF controls that are generated by the previous examples can safely be ignored.

Using TextEdit to Explore RTF

The Mac OS X editor TextEdit is a Rich Text editor. If you open a new file with TextEdit, it will be either a plain text file or an RTF file, depending on your TextEdit preference settings. If it's plain text, choose TextEdit's Format → Make Rich Text menu command to make it RTF. Then save the "empty" file, and you'll get a file that contains the following information:

```
{\rtf1\mac\ansicpg10000\cocoartf100
{\fonttbl}
{\colortbl;\red255\green255\blue255;}
\margl1440\margr1440\vieww9260\viewh7500\viewkind0
}
```

Try this in TextEdit, save your file, and then use the Unix cat (or vi, pico, etc.) command to list the file's contents in a Terminal window. (The contents of your file may differ slightly, depending on your defaults.) If you add three lines of text in TextEdit in Helvetica (probably your default font), as shown in the window on the left in Figure 12-3, you'll end up with something like this:

```
{\rtf1\mac\ansicpg10000\cocoartf100
{\fonttbl\f0\fswiss\fcharset77 Helvetica;}
{\colortbl;\red255\green255\blue255;}
\margl1440\margr1440\vieww9000\viewh7820\viewkind0
\pard\tx1440\tx2880\tx4320\tx5760\tx7200\ql\qnatural

\f0\fs24 \cf0 This is line 1\
This is line 2\
This is line 3\
}
```

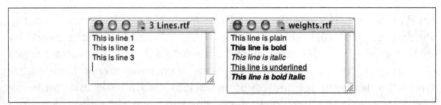

Figure 12-3. TextEdit files to examine RTF codes for text, weights, and angles

When TextEdit reads a file, it checks the first five characters to see if they are "{\rtf". If they are, TextEdit assumes that the file is in Rich Text Format.

Next, let's experiment with text *weight* and *angle* changes. The window on the right in Figure 12-3 produces the following RTF code:

```
{\rtf1\mac\ansicpg10000\cocoartf100
{\fonttbl\f0\fswiss\fcharset77 Helvetica;\f1\fswiss\fcharset77
Helvetica-Bold;\f2\fswiss\fcharset77 Helvetica-Oblique;
\f3\fswiss\fcharset77 Helvetica-BoldOblique;}
{\colortbl;\red255\green255\blue255;}
\margl1440\margr1440\vieww9620\viewh7500\viewkind0
\pard\tx1440\tx2880\tx4320\tx5760\tx7200\ql\qnatural

\f0\fs24 \cf0 This line is plain\

\f1\b This line is bold\

\f2\i\b0 This line is italic\

\f0\i0 \ul This line is underlined\

\f3\i\b \ulnone This line is bold italic\
}
```

Now let's try changing the font size. The window on the left in Figure 12-4 produces this RTF file:

```
{\rtf1\mac\ansicpg10000\cocoartf100
{\fonttbl\f0\fswiss\fcharset77 Helvetica;}
{\colortbl;\red255\green255\blue255;}
```

```
\margl1440\margr1440\vieww3560\viewh1820\viewkind0
\pard\tx1440\tx2880\tx4320\tx5760\tx7200\ql\qnatural

\f0\fs20 \cf0 This line is 10 point size\

\fs24 This line is 12 point size\

\fs28 This line is 14 point size\

\fs31 This line is 15.5 point size\
}
```

Figure 12-4. TextEdit files to examine RTF codes for sizes and fonts

Finally, let's try changing *fonts*. The window on the right in Figure 12-4 produces this RTF file:

```
{\rtf1\mac\ansicpg10000\cocoartf100
{\fonttbl\f0\fswiss\fcharset77 Helvetica;\f1\fnil\fcharset80
AppleGothic;\f2\fmodern\fcharset77 CourierNewPSMT;
\f3\froman\fcharset77 TimesNewRomanPSMT;\f4\fscript\fcharset77
BrushScriptMT;}
{\colortbl;\red255\green255\blue255;}
\margl1440\margr1440\vieww3500\viewh2020\viewkind0
\pard\tx1440\tx2880\tx4320\tx5760\tx7200\ql\qnatural

\f0\fs28 \cf0 This is Helvetica\

\f1 This is AppleGothic\

\f2 This is Courier New\

\f3 This is Time New Roman\

\f4\i This is Brush Script MT}
```

RTF Control Words and Symbols

Rich Text Format is a system for encoding various kinds of font information into a printable ASCII character stream (only 7-bit ASCII characters are used, for portability). Using Rich Text control words, you can encode font, size, and even margin changes in an application-independent fashion. There are many Rich Text control words; Apple implements only a subset of them. This brief discussion should be enough to get you going.

An RTF document begins with the character string "{\rtf0" or "{\rtf1" and ends with a closing brace, "}". Inside the RTF document, you can have control words, which begin with a backslash (\), and text. Control symbols are interpreted as commands, while text is displayed or printed.

You can have additional pairs of braces within an RTF file. Any formatting controls that you issue within a pair of braces will be used but will not be printed when the Rich Text is printed. For example, the following sequence in an RTF file:

```
This is {\b a test} of Rich Text.
```

prints like this:

This is **a test** of Rich Text.

Controls can appear anywhere in the text. For example, the strings:

```
This is \b a test \plain of Rich Text.
```

and:

```
This is \b a test \b0 of Rich Text.
```

print like this (the same as the string with braces above):

This is **a test** of Rich Text.

Normally, Rich Text ignores carriage returns. If you want a carriage return, precede it with a backslash (\). If you want a backslash, type a double backslash (\\). These are examples of control symbols.

You can define any number of fonts within an RTF document. Fonts are given numbers; you usually define them within a set of braces at the beginning of the document. In our earlier example, the following string defined a single font table, with the font \f0 being Helvetica:

```
{\fonttbl\f0\fswiss\fcharset77 Helvetica;}
```

Table 12-1 summarizes some common RTF controls.

Table 12-1. Common RTF controls

Control word	Meaning
\rtf	Declares a file to be a Rich Text file—you should use \rtf0 or \rtf1
Font control word	**Meaning**
\fonttbl	Begins definition of a font table
\f0	Selects font 0
\fswiss *fontname*	Selects a sans-serif font *fontname*
\fmodern *fontname*	Same as \fswiss
\froman *fontname*	Selects a serif font *fontname*
\fnil *fontname*	Selects another kind of font *fontname*
\fs*nn*	Selects a font size—*nn* is in half points

Table 12-1. Common RTF controls (continued)

Font control word	Meaning
\plain	Plain
\b	Bold
\b0	No bold
\i	Italic
\i0	No italic
\gray*nnn*	Gray; *nnn*= 0 for black, 1000 for white
\ul	Underline
\ul0	No underline
\up*nn*	Superscript *nn* half points
\d*nnn*	Subscript *nn* half points

Formatting word	Meaning
\xd5 l	Left-justify text (quad left)
\xd5 c	Center-justify text (quad center)
\xd5 r	Right-justify text (quad right)
\tab	Tabstop
\paperw*nnnn*	Paper width in twips[a]
\paperh*nnnn*	Paper height in twips
\margl*nnn*	Left margin
\margr*nnn*	Right margin
\fi*nnnn*	First-line indent in twips
\li*nnnn*	Left indent in twips
\ulw	Word underline
\uld	Dotted underline

[a] There are 1,440 twips in an inch.

The RTF controls in Table 12-2, while useful, are not currently implemented by Apple.

Table 12-2. Unimplemented RTF controls

RTF control	Meaning
\shad	Shadow
\scaps	Small caps
\caps	All caps
\v	Invisible text
\uldb	Double underline

If you specify a font that isn't available on the machine you're using, you are likely to get Courier.

Creating an RTF Class

Using Rich Text can be a pain: you have to remember far too many controls. There's got to be an easier way! Of course there is—create an Objective-C class for building and managing Rich Text segments. Following is the interface for such a class, a subclass of the root NSObject class, which works with the NSTextView object:

RTF.h

```
#import <Cocoa/Cocoa.h>

@interface RTF:NSObject
{
    NSMutableData *data;
}
- (void)dealloc;
- (NSData *)data;
- (void)appendChar:(unsigned char)ch;
- (void)appendRTF:(NSString *)string;
- (void)appendString:(NSString *)string;
- (void)setBold:(BOOL)flag;
- (void)setJustify:(NSTextAlignment)mode;
- (void)setSize:(float)aSize;

@end
```

This time we'll describe these methods before we show how they are coded. The interface and method descriptions are all you really need to know in order to use a class—we don't need to know the implementation details. For example, we don't know how the AppKit classes are implemented, yet we've been using them throughout the book!

Table 12-3 summarizes the instance methods declared in our new RTF class. The methods described in this table that do not appear in RTF.h are overrides of methods in NSObject.

Table 12-3. Instance methods in the RTF class

Method	Method description
(id)**init**	Initializes an RTF object, establishes a simple Rich Text header, and returns the id of the newly created RTF object.
(void)**dealloc**	Frees the RTF object and releases its internal storage.
(NSData *)**data**	Returns an NSData object for an RTF object. The RTF data is automatically terminated by a closing brace character. You can pass this object directly to an NSTextView object's **replaceCharactersInRange:withRTF:** method. This method doesn't actually return the internal NSData buffer; instead, it returns a copy.
(void)**appendChar:**(unsigned char)*ch*	Appends a character to the internal NSData object.
(void)**appendRTF:**(NSString *)*string*	Appends a Rich Text string to the RTF object stream. No translation is performed on the string.

Table 12-3. Instance methods in the RTF class (continued)

Method	Method description
appendString:(NSString *)*string*	Appends an ASCII text string to the RTF object stream. Special characters, such as newline and backslash, are automatically quoted.
setBold:(BOOL)*flag*	If *flag* is YES, the following text is appended in bold. If *flag* is NO, the following text is not appended in bold.
setJustify:(NSTextAlignment)*mode*	Sets the justification mode of the text that is appended to the RTF object. Cocoa's justification modes are defined in the header file NSText.h.

Following is the implementation for our RTF class:

```
// RTF.m:

#import "RTF.h"

@implementation RTF
- (id)init
{
    NSString *header =
    @"{\\rtf1\\mac{\\fonttbl\\f0\\fswiss Helvetica;}\\f0\\fs24 ";

    [super init];
    data = [NSMutableData dataWithData:
              [header dataUsingEncoding:NSASCIIStringEncoding] ];
    [data retain];
    return self;
}

- (void)dealloc
{
    [data release];
    return [super dealloc];
}

// Create a new NSData object that has a termination brace.
// Cocoa's NSText won't display without the brace.
- (NSData *)data
{
    NSMutableData *data2 = [[NSMutableData alloc]
                            initWithData:data];
    [data2 appendBytes:"}" length:1];
    return data2;
}

// appendChar: appends an arbitrary character to the data
- (void)appendChar:(unsigned char)ch
{
    [data appendBytes:&ch length:1];
}

// appendRTF: appends an arbitrary RTF string to the RTF object
- (void)appendRTF:(NSString *)string
```

```
{
    [data appendData: [string dataUsingEncoding:NSASCIIStringEncoding] ];
}

// appendString: appends an ASCII text string,
// all of the special characters in the text
- (void)appendString:(NSString *)string
{
    int i;

    for (i=0;i<[string length];i++) {
        unichar c = [string characterAtIndex:i];

        switch(c) {
          case '\n':    // escape special characters
          case '{':
          case '}':
          case '\\':
            [self appendChar:'\\'];
            break;
          default:
            break;
        }
        [self appendChar:c];
    }
}

- (void)setBold:(BOOL)flag
{
    [self appendRTF: flag ? @"\\b " : @"\\b0 "];
}

- (void)setSize:(float)aSize
{
    [self appendRTF:[NSString stringWithFormat:@"\\fs%d",(int)aSize*2]];
}

- (void)setJustify:(NSTextAlignment)mode
{
    switch(mode) {
      case NSNaturalTextAlignment:
      case NSLeftTextAlignment:
      case NSJustifiedTextAlignment:
        [self appendRTF:@"\\ql\n"];
        break;
      case NSCenterTextAlignment:
        [self appendRTF:@"\\qc\n"];
        break;
      case NSRightTextAlignment:
        [self appendRTF:@"\\qr\n"];
        break;
    }
}

@end
```

This class makes use of the NSMutableData and NSString classes, and of Cocoa's Unicode-based system for converting between the two. If you are not familiar with these classes, you may find it useful to review their documentation at this time.

Notice that, before the NSData is returned, a copy is made and the closing brace (}) required by the Rich Text standard is appended. The closing brace is added to the copy, which allows the RTF object itself to be used again should the caller wish to add more information. (PaperController won't, but you might in another program that you write.) The object's user doesn't have any way of knowing that this is done, and indeed, as long as the RTF class works properly for the user, the user doesn't need to know. This is another example of why it is better to use accessor methods rather than using Objective-C's @public feature and directly accessing an object's instance variables.

Integrating Our RTF Class into MathPaper

Now that we have defined the RTF class, let's integrate it into the MathPaper application to get the promised fonts and formatting:

1. Open MathPaper.pbproj in Project Builder and choose File → New File to create a new file called RTF.h.

   Project Builder

2. Select Empty File in the New File Assistant pane and then click Next.

3. Enter "RTF.h" in the File Name field, make sure the MathPaper target is checked, and then click Finish.

4. Now enter the RTF class interface code, as provided in the previous section, into RTF.h.

   RTF.h

5. Similarly, create another file called RTF.m and insert the RTF class implementation code (also provided earlier) into it.

6. If they aren't there already, drag the RTF.h and RTF.m files into the Classes group in PB's Groups & Files pane.

   RTF.m

Another way to perform the six steps presented in this section is to first create the RTF.h and RTF.m class files outside of PB, using another editor (e.g., TextEdit or GNU Emacs). Save these two files in the ~/MathPaper folder, and then drag their file icons from the Finder and drop them into the Classes group in PB's Groups & Files pane.

Now that our new RTF class has been added to the project, we proceed to make the necessary changes in the PaperController class.

NSAttributedString: An Even Better RTF Class

If you do a lot of work with Rich Text, you will quickly exceed the capabilities of the RTF class presented in this chapter. Rather than continuing to extend the RTF class, you should investigate the Cocoa attributed string classes, NSAttributedString and NSMutableAttributedString. Header files for these classes appear in both the /Foundation and /AppKit directories.

The attributed string classes allow you to effectively and easily manage text strings with associated attributes. Many classes in the Application Kit can directly handle attributed strings. If you are using an NSControl, NSCell, NSTextField, or NSTextView, you may find it easier to build an attributed string than to create an RTF string.

The "attributes" used by the NSAttributedString system are represented as name/value pairs that are stored in NSDictionary objects. Attributes can apply to all of a string or simply to a subset of the string. Some of the attributes that you may use include:

NSFontAttributeName
> The font of the attributed string (the default is Helvetica 12)

NSParagraphStyleAttributeName
> The paragraph style of the attributed string

NSForegroundColorAttributeName, NSBackgroundColorAttributeName
> The foreground and background colors of the text

NSBaselineOffsetAttributeName
> The offset from the baseline, in points

We use RTF, rather than NSAttributedStrings, in this chapter because RTF is a standard that works across platforms. If you wish to create multiple-font documents that can be accessed on other platforms, you should understand how RTF works. This example also allows us to show the mechanics of creating a helper class that does not directly correspond to any objects on the screen.

Attributed strings are discussed in greater detail in Chapter 14.

PaperController.m

7. Insert the following directive after the other #import statement near the top of PaperController.m:

```
#import "RTF.h"
```

8. Insert the new **appendRTFData:** method declaration shown here into the existing NSTextView(MathPaper) category interface:

```
@interface NSTextView(MathPaper)
- (void)appendString:(NSString *)str;
- (void)appendRTFData:(NSData *)str;
@end
```

9. Insert the new **appendRTFData:** method implementation shown here into the NSTextView(MathPaper) category implementation:

```
- (void)appendRTFData:(NSData *)data
{
    int len = [ [self string] length];
    [self replaceCharactersInRange:NSMakeRange(len,0) withRTF:data];
}
```

10. Replace the **gotData:** method implementation in PaperController.m with the new implementation shown here:

```
#define USE_RTF

- (void)gotData:(NSNotification *)not
{
    NSData      *data;
    NSString    *str;
#ifdef USE_RTF
    RTF         *rtf = [[[RTF alloc] init] autorelease];
#endif

    data = [ [not userInfo]
                objectForKey:NSFileHandleNotificationDataItem];
    str = [ [NSString alloc] initWithData:data
                                 encoding:NSASCIIStringEncoding];

    [str autorelease];      /* Automatically release when done */

    // Add the data to the end of the text object
#ifdef USE_RTF
    [rtf setBold:YES];
    [rtf setJustify:NSRightTextAlignment];
    [rtf setSize:20];
    [rtf appendString:str];
    [rtf setBold:NO];
    [rtf setJustify:NSLeftTextAlignment];
    [rtf setSize:12];
    [rtf appendString:@"-------------------\n"];
    [theText appendRTFData:[rtf data]];
#else
    [theText appendString:str];
    [theText appendString:@"-------------------\n"];
#endif

    // Now scroll to the bottom
    [theText scrollRangeToVisible:
            NSMakeRange([[theText textStorage] length], 0)];

    // Register to get the notification again
    [fromEvaluator readInBackgroundAndNotify];

    // Finally, allow the user to make any changes to the text
    [theText setEditable:YES];
}
```

Notice that we used the USE_RTF conditional compilation technique so that RTF can be turned off when desired without doing a lot of editing. This is a useful technique when you are developing code. Second, notice that we **alloc**, **init**, and **autorelease** the RTF string all in one place. This assures that the string will be properly freed when we are done using it; we don't have to bother with a separate **release** message.

11. Save all pertinent files, and build and run your MathPaper project. The RTF object should behave as shown in the screen shot on the left in the earlier Figure 12-1.

12. Quit MathPaper.

Summary

In this chapter, we learned a significant amount about Rich Text Format, which helped us format the mathematical output in our MathPaper windows. We also learned more about the NSText and NSTextView classes. In particular, we learned how to exert precise control over the contents of an NSTextView object by using RTF to encode font, size, and justification information into a stream before copying the information into the NSTextView object.

In the next chapter, we'll see how to use methods built into the NSText class to save the contents of a MathPaper window into a file. We'll also learn how to implement the opening and printing of MathPaper documents (files). Finally, we'll learn how to catch the message that Window Manager generates when a user double-clicks a file icon in the Finder and how to open that file in our MathPaper application.

Exercises

1. The font size of the input text is small for an application such as Math-Paper. What changes need to be made in MathPaper to increase the font size of all mathematical expressions that are entered by the user?

2. Calculate sin(pi) using this chapter's version of MathPaper. Does anything unusual happen? If so, why, and what can be done about it?

3. Extend the RTF class in this chapter so that it implements a larger subset of the Rich Text Format specification. To find the RTF specification, search http://msdn.microsoft.com. Use your extended class to support additional fonts and other formatting features in MathPaper windows.

4. Investigate the use of the Format and Font menus in Interface Builder to support additional formatting in MathPaper. Can they be used? If so, how? Implement your ideas.

5. Reimplement the RTF class so that it uses an NSMutableAttributed-String rather than an NSMutableData object. Instead of building your own RTF, rely on the machinery inside the NSMutableAttributedString class.

6. Investigate the possibility of rewriting MathPaper so that it still supports RTF but doesn't require a helper class at all. If possible, do it! First you must carefully read Cocoa's documentation on NSText, NSTextView, and related AppKit classes. Why do you think we decided to implement MathPaper with a helper class?

CHAPTER 13

Saving, Loading, and Printing

In the previous chapter we saw how the contents of a text object can be translated into a Rich Text stream of characters. In this chapter, we'll see how to take that stream and save it into a file; we'll also see how to load one of those files and place its contents in a new window. Finally, we'll learn about printing. All of these tasks will be made dramatically easier by using the Cocoa Application Kit framework.

Data Management with NSDocument

At this point, our MathPaper application does a great job with math, fonts, and handling multiple windows. However, it's missing a lot of basic functionality, such as:

- Saving the contents of a window into a file

- Loading a saved file, so that you can continue calculating where you left off

- Marking an edited window with the "unsaved" close button with a dot inside (⦿) so that you know it has been edited (the "saved" close button has an X inside: ⊗)

- Alerting a user who tries to close an edited window without first saving the edited file

- Printing the contents of a window

- Graying out menu items that are not appropriate in a given context (e.g., the Save menu item when there are no open documents)

Writing the code for document saving and loading can be quite an ordeal in some computing platforms. However, it's easy in Cocoa because most of the required code is already part of the multiple-document framework.

Memory to Disk and Back

When you save a document to a file on your computer's hard drive, you are making a representation of a part of the computer's memory and archiving that representation in a way that can be restored later. In some cases, the easiest representation is a byte-for-byte copy of the computer's memory. Applications that use this technique are simply storing a memory snapshot on disk.

Other applications take a more intelligent approach to archiving information. For example, a vector-graphics drawing program stores the endpoints of a line rather than the positions of all of the individual pixels that make up the line. Also, an object-oriented drawing program might archive a document to disk by telling its document object to write a stream of bytes to the disk containing the values in all of the instance variables. This command would then be recursively applied to all of the objects that the document contains. In this manner, all of the text, images, lines, and other information that can be referenced from the document would be written out to disk.

There are other ways that applications can save documents to disk as well. Microsoft Word, for instance, has a feature called *fast saves*. If you open a large document with Word, make a few changes, and then try to save it, Word can simply append the change journal to the end of the first document, rather than making a whole new copy. Fast saves can be a real timesaver, but they have the disadvantage that the unmodified text remains in the document—which can produce embarrassing situations at times! Early versions of Word were also somewhat buggy, and occasionally fast saves caused document files to become corrupted.

Rethinking MathDocument and PaperController

Let's review where we are with our MathPaper program. Our MathDocument class is a subclass of NSDocument, and our PaperController class is a subclass of NSWindowController. There is also a single NSDocumentController object in our program that's mostly invisible to the programmer, even though it has overall control of the multiple-document architecture and does a lot for both the interface and the program. For example, this NSDocumentController object automatically creates a new MathDocument object when MathPaper launches and initializes another new MathDocument object every time a user chooses File → New from MathPaper's menu. NSDocumentController also maintains a list of NSDocument (i.e., MathDocument) objects and all of their NSWindowControllers. In addition, this object manages the on-screen document windows and much of the main menu.

MathDocument's **makeWindowControllers** method is automatically invoked at MathPaper launch time and when File → New is chosen. Our override of **makeWindowControllers** in the previous chapter creates a new PaperController object, unarchives PaperWindow.nib with the new PaperController object as its owner, and adds the new object to the list of window controllers.

Note that NSDocumentController implements the **saveAllDocuments:**, **newDocument:**, and **openDocument:** action methods associated with the File menu commands. These methods are all connected to the First Responder icon, as you can see in Interface Builder.

Our MathDocument class doesn't do much yet. At this point, it responds to **makeWindowControllers** and **windowNibName** messages but otherwise sits dormant. All of the controls, the state information, and the Evaluator hookup for each window are kept in the associated copy of PaperController. What is the state information? For each MathPaper window, the following information is relevant:

- The current location and size of that MathPaper window (called the window *frame*)
- The window's *history*—that is, the calculations that have been displayed

To this end, we need to redesign the way that data is kept in the application. For each MathPaper window, the MathDocument object will be responsible for keeping the "official" copy of the data, and the PaperController object will be responsible for keeping the "working copy"—that is, the copy the user is modifying.

Our changes to the MathPaper class will consist of adding two instance variables and five accessor methods. The two instance variables, frame and history, will keep track of the MathDocument's window frame and its math-expression history. The accessor methods allow us to set and inspect these variables. Later, we'll also modify the PaperController class so that it takes its data from the MathDocument class.

We'll also add a new initializer to the MathDocument class that will initialize the history variable to a default value. In this case, we'll choose a default that improves the usability of the MathPaper application by adding a line of instruction on how to use the application.

MathDocument.h

1. Back in Project Builder, insert the lines shown here in bold into the Math-Document.h class interface file:

```
#import <Cocoa/Cocoa.h>

@interface MathDocument : NSDocument
{
    NSRect              frame;
    NSMutableData       *history;
}
```

```
-(NSData *)history;
-(void)setHistory:(NSData *)theHistory;
-(NSRect)frame;
-(void)setFrame:(NSRect)aFrame;
-(BOOL)hasFrame;
@end
```

With the exception of **hasFrame**, the names of these five methods indicate what they do. The **hasFrame** method tells the invoking object whether the frame instance variable has been set. If it hasn't, it still reads the "factory default" value—that is, all zeros.

2. Insert the #import directive and add the methods shown here in bold to the MathDocument.m class implementation file:

MathDocument.m

```
#import "MathDocument.h"
#import "PaperController.h"
#import "RTF.h"

@implementation MathDocument

...

-(NSData *)history
{
    return history;
}

-(void)setHistory:(NSData *)theHistory
{
    [history setData:theHistory];
}

-(NSRect)frame
{
    return frame;
}

-(void)setFrame:(NSRect)aFrame
{
    frame = aFrame;
}

-(BOOL)hasFrame
{
    return (frame.size.height!=0 && frame.size.width!=0);
}
...
```

As you can see, these methods are all pretty straightforward. The **history** and **frame** methods return their respective instance variables, while the **setHistory:** and **setFrame:** methods set them. The **hasFrame** method returns TRUE if the frame has been set (that is, if the size of the frame is nonzero) and FALSE if it has not been set.

We also need to create a designated initializer and deallocator for the Math-Document class. The initializer will create the initial NSMutableData object for the MathPaper history instance variable and fill history with its initial content. The deallocator will release the storage that has been allocated when it's no longer needed.

MathDocument.m

3. Add the **init** and **dealloc** methods shown here in bold to the Math-Document.m class implementation file:

```
// Designated initializer; create the empty document
- (init)
{
    RTF *rtf = [ [ [RTF alloc] init] autorelease];

    [super init];
    [rtf setBold:TRUE];
    [rtf setSize:10.0];
    [rtf appendString:@"Enter a math expression and hit return:"];
    [rtf setSize:12.0];
    [rtf appendString:@"\n"];
    history = [ [NSMutableData alloc] initWithData:[rtf data] ];
    return self;
}

-(void)dealloc
{
    [history release];
    [super dealloc];
}
```

Finally, we want to modify the PaperController's **windowDidLoad** method so that it reads the value for the window's frame and history after the PaperWindow.nib file is loaded. With the code that we've written, history will always be equal to the default value and frame will never be set. That's okay for now; we'll set the frame value in the next part of this chapter.

PaperController.m

4. Insert the lines shown here in bold into the **windowDidLoad** method in the PaperController.m file:

```
#import PaperController.h;
#import RTF.h;
#import MathDocument.h;

...
- (void)windowDidLoad
{
    NSString *path;
    MathDocument *doc;

    [super windowDidLoad];
    [ [self window] makeFirstResponder:theText];

    // Initialize with document
    doc = [self document];
```

```
[theText replaceCharactersInRange:NSMakeRange(0,0)
                            withRTF:[doc history] ];

if ([doc hasFrame]) {
    [ [self window] setFrame:[doc frame] display:YES];
}

path  = [ [NSBundle mainBundle]
            pathForResource:@"Evaluator"
            ofType:@""];

toPipe    = [NSPipe pipe];    // NSTask below will retain
fromPipe  = [NSPipe pipe];    // NSTask below will retain

toEvaluator   = [toPipe fileHandleForWriting];
fromEvaluator = [fromPipe fileHandleForReading];

evaluator = [[NSTask alloc] init];
[evaluator setLaunchPath:path];

[evaluator setStandardOutput:fromPipe];
[evaluator setStandardInput:toPipe];
[evaluator launch];

[[NSNotificationCenter defaultCenter]
    addObserver:self
    selector:@selector(gotData:)
    name:NSFileHandleReadCompletionNotification
    object:fromEvaluator];

[fromEvaluator readInBackgroundAndNotify];
}
```

5. Build and run the MathPaper application. Type Command-N a few times to create a few windows. Each window should contain the brief instructions that we'll now create in MathPaper's designated initializer, init. (See Figure 13-1.)

Many simple document-based applications don't bother with separate subclasses of both the NSDocument and NSWindowController classes. Instead, they simply put all of the document-management and window-control functionality inside the NSDocument subclass. This approach works fine until you want to display two different kinds of document windows—for example, plain text and RTF text windows in TextEdit, or two windows on a single document.

Because most Cocoa programmers will eventually need to subclass both the NSWindowController and NSDocument classes, we decided to simply start that way in our demonstration program. We hope it hasn't been too confusing!

In the next section, we'll build upon this framework by having Cocoa save the contents and the position of the window into a file.

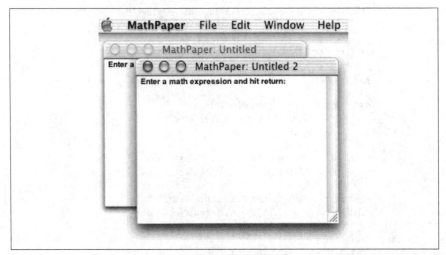

Figure 13-1. MathPaper with prompt output from the designated initializer method

Saving to a File

Before we can save the contents of a MathPaper window into a file, we first need to know what kind of file our application will create. Specifically, we need to know the file's HFS creator code, its HFS type code, and its file extension.

Creator codes are used so that when you double-click on a filename in the Finder, Cocoa knows to open the correct application. Creator codes are also used to locate applications on the computer's hard disk. You may remember that, in the section "Customizing the Document-Based Project Information in PB" in Chapter 10, we were assigned by Apple a creator code for the Math-Paper application. That creator code was MATP.

Because a single application can create many different kinds of files, and because multiple applications are sometimes able to read the same file, document files stored on HFS filesystems also have a *type code*. Like creator codes, file type codes are 4-byte strings or 32-bit quantities. In many cases, the file type is the same as the file's extension in the world of Windows and Unix: GIF and JPEG are used for image files, for example.

In addition to creator codes, Mac OS X uses *file extensions* to match up applications and their document files. A file extension is the set of letters that come after the *last* period (dot) in a file's name. Unlike the Mac OS 9 Finder, the Mac OS X Finder makes it somewhat difficult for the user to accidentally change a file extension. It does this by generally hiding file extensions and by warning the user before an extension is changed. Mac OS relies on file extensions more and more as time goes on, which generally improves interoperability with other platforms that do not have creator and type codes.

Many of the commonly used extensions and their meanings are listed in Table 13-1. These are some of the standard extensions used by Mac OS X.

Table 13-1. Common Mac OS X file extensions

File extension	File type
`.a`	Unix library file
`.app`	Directory containing an application
`.c`	C-language source file
`.eps`	Encapsulated PostScript file
`.gif`	Graphics Interchange Format file
`.h`	C (or Objective-C) header file
`.jpeg` or `.jpg`	Joint Photographic Expert's Group format file
`.l` or `.lex`	`lex` source file
`.lproj`	Directory containing language-specific nibs
`.m`	Objective-C language source file
`.mbox`	Directory containing a `Mail.app` mailbox
`.midi`	File containing binary MIDI data
`.mp3`	MPEG2 Level 3 audio file
`.nib`	IB file
`.o`	Unix object code file
`.pdf`	Portable Document Format file
`.pbproj`	Project file for use with PB
`.rtf`	Rich Text Format file
`.rtfd`	Rich Text Format directory containing `.rtf` and image files such as `.tiff` and `.eps`
`.s`	File containing assembler source
`.tar`	Tape Archive format file (see the Unix manpage for `tar`)
`.tiff` or `.tif`	Tagged Image File Format file
`.txt`	Plain text file
`.uu`	Uuencoded file
`.y`	`yacc` source file
`.Z`	File that has been compressed

For our application, we'll use the string "MATP" as the MathPaper file type and the extension `.matp` for MathPaper document files. Now we'll set up icons.

Icons for MathPaper

1. Create a high-resolution icon for MathPaper document files and save it in your MathPaper folder with the name `papericon.tiff`.

+0*./=sin(%)
MathPaper

The icon should be saved in the following four resolutions: 16×16, 32×32, 48×48, and 128×128 pixels. If you want to make only one icon, make the 128×128 icon and let the system scale the others. We came up with the icon shown at the edge of the page. (A quick way to create an icon is to use the Grab application to grab a small screen-shot selection and save it in the TIFF format. Grab is located in the /Applications/Utilities folder.)

IconComposer

2. In IconComposer, create a `PaperIcon.icns` file from your icon files. Refer to the section "Creating Application Icon Files with IconComposer" in Chapter 6 for details on using the IconComposer program.

3. Open `MathPaper.pbproj` in PB.

Project Builder

4. Choose PB's Project → Add Files menu command and add the `PaperIcon.icns` file to the Resources group in the Groups & Files pane (or simply drag the file from the Finder and drop it in the Resources group in PB). Make sure that you add `PaperIcon.icns` to the MathPaper target.

5. Select the Targets vertical tab, then click on the MathPaper target.

6. Click on the newly visible Application Settings tab, scroll down to the Document Types section, and select the MathPaper document type.

7. Enter `PaperIcon.icns` in the Icon file field and click the Change (not Add) button. The pertinent part of PB's main window can be seen in Figure 13-2.

At this point, PB knows that MathPaper can handle only one kind of document—a MathPaper document that has the extension .matp and the HFS type code "MATP". MathPaper is an Editor for this file type, meaning that it can both read and write these files.

Synchronizing PaperController with MathDocument

Saving the contents of a window means writing all of the states associated with the window into a file, so that we can reconstruct the window's current state as closely as possible when it's reloaded. In the case of a MathPaper window, not many states need to be saved. Because the Evaluator back end doesn't retain state between launches, the only information that we need to save in a MathPaper document file is:

- The current location of the window (the frame)
- The window's history

This is precisely the information that we decided to store in the MathDocument instance variables—how convenient! To implement file saving, all we need to do is to write the code to migrate this information from each window's PaperController object to its matching MathDocument object, then arrange for the pertinent instance variables to be saved in a file on disk.

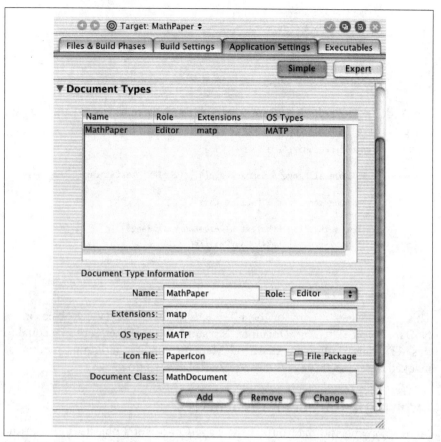

Figure 13-2. Adding the PaperIcon.icns icon file to MathPaper's Application settings

In Step 4 in the previous section, we modified the **windowDidLoad** method in PaperController.h so that the MathPaper window's initial frame and the contents of the NSTextView would be taken from the MathDocument object. To save a MathPaper document to a file, we need to perform the reverse operation—we need to copy the contents of the NSTextView object and the window's frame back into the MathDocument instance variables. That's what the new PaperController **synchronizeData** method shown below will do.

8. Insert the new **synchronizeData** method declaration shown here in bold into the PaperController.h file:

```
#import <Cocoa/Cocoa.h>

@interface PaperController : NSWindowController
{
    NSTask      *evaluator;
    NSPipe      *toPipe;
    NSPipe      *fromPipe;
```

PaperController.h

```
        NSFileHandle *toEvaluator;
        NSFileHandle *fromEvaluator;
        IBOutlet NSTextView  *theText;
}

- (void)synchronizeData;
@end
```

PaperController.m

9. Add the **synchronizeData** method implementation to the Paper-Controller.m file:

```
- (void)synchronizeData
{
    NSRange allRange = NSMakeRange(0,[ [theText textStorage] length]);

    MathDocument *doc = [self document];

    [doc setHistory:[theText RTFFromRange:allRange] ];
    [doc setFrame:[ [self window] frame] ];
}

...
@end
```

This method gets a copy of the RTF data in the NSTextView object in an NSData object. The MathDocument's history object is then set to be equal to this RTF data. Following that, the MathDocument's **setFrame:** method is invoked to set the frame of the PaperController's window.

Archiving MathPaper Documents

Merely copying the data out of the PaperController's objects and into the MathDocument is not sufficient; to save this data on the hard disk, we need to create a method that will turn this information into a byte stream.

To create that byte stream, we will use Cocoa's NSCoder, NSArchiver, and NSUnarchiver classes. These classes are responsible for archiving and restoring data. With these classes, you can archive an object to a byte stream that is stored in an NSData object with a single method invocation, as follows:

```
NSData *theData = [NSArchiver archiveDataWithRootObject:anObject];
```

After this message is sent, the NSArchiver class creates an NSCoder instance that is responsible for doing the actual encoding. The NSCoder instance then invokes a version of the **encodeWithCoder:** method that we create, passing a pointer to itself as the argument.

Thus, to operate with the NSCoder system, our MathDocument class needs to implement the **encodeWithCoder:** method. This method is quite simple; it usually consists of a message to the coder object argument for each instance variable that needs to be archived. For example, if you had a class with a single instance variable called `frame`, your **encodeWithCoder:** method would look like this:

```
-(void)encodeWithCoder:(NSCoder *)coder
{
    [coder encodeRect:frame];
}
```

The real power of the NSCoder system comes when you are archiving complicated objects that contain references to many other objects. Each object that is archived automatically archives all of its subobjects, resulting in an entire tree or graph of objects being archived in the NSData object. The system transparently handles objects that are referenced in more than one location, as well as circular references.

If you casually read the NSCoder documentation or the `NSCoder.h` include file, you may feel that the NSCoder system is powerful but somewhat difficult to use. That's because the NSCoder class just defines the base methods that are used for writing out raw data, byte arrays, and objects. There are many higher-level NSCoder methods that are defined as category methods in other include files, such as `NSGeometry.h`. Table 13-2 contains a list of many of the NSCoder methods that you may use in creating your applications.

Table 13-2. Common methods in the NSCoder class

Method	Purpose
- (void)**encodeObject:**(id)*object*	Encodes an object
- (void)**encodePropertyList:**(id)*aPropertyList*	Encodes a property list
- (void)**encodePoint:**(NSPoint)*aPoint*	Encodes an NSPoint structure
- (void)**encodeSize:**(NSSize)*aSize*	Encodes an NSSize structure
- (void)**encodeRect:**(NSRect)*aRect*	Encodes an NSRect structure
- (void)**encodeDataObject:**(NSData *)*data*	Encodes an NSData object
- (void)**encodeValuesOfObjCTypes:**@encode(int)*i*	Encodes an integer
- (void)**encodeValuesOfObjCTypes:**@encode(float)*f*	Encodes a floating-point value
- (void)**encodeArrayOfObjcCTypes:**@encode(*type*) **count:**(unsigned)*aCount* **at:**(void *)*addr*	Encodes an array of type *type*

To use the NSCoder class, we will create an **encodeWithCoder:** method for MathDocument:

10. Add the **encodeWithCoder:** method shown here in bold to the Math-Document.m file:

```
#import "MathDocument.h"
#import "PaperController.h"
#import "RTF.h"
```

MathDocument.m

```
@implementation MathDocument
...
- (void)encodeWithCoder:(NSCoder *)coder
{
    [coder encodeRect:frame];
    [coder encodeObject:history];
}
...
@end
```

Many implementations of the **encodeWithCoder:** method will invoke their superclass's **encodeWithCoder:** method (e.g., [**super encodeWithCoder: coder**]) so that the instance variables of the superclass are automatically encoded. This is not the correct approach with subclasses of the NSDocument class, however, because we do not actually want the instance variables of the NSDocument class stored in the byte stream. (Another reason not to send the [**super encodeWithCoder:coder**] message is that the NSDocument class does not implement the **encodeWithCoder:** method, so calling the super method would result in an error.)

Writing the Save Methods

We have created one method for copying the state of each MathPaper window into the MathDocument object and another method for copying these instance variables into an NSData object. All that remains for us to do to implement file saving is to display the appropriate Save panel when the user chooses File → Save (or types Command-S). The Save panel will prompt for a filename, get the filename, get the NSData for the instance variables, and put all of this information into a file. Fortunately, we need to write only five lines of code to implement this functionality; Cocoa gives almost all of it to us for free.

First Responder

To understand how all this happens, we'll first focus on the First Responder icon that we first discussed back in Chapter 3. We've already discussed the First Responder in the context of the File menu items. Now we're going to find out what it means.

The First Responder icon in the Nib File window is a placeholder for the application's current first responder; that is, the object that will be the first to try to respond to keyboard events and menu commands such as Cut, Copy, and Paste. Any message sent to the First Responder icon is sent in order to each of the following objects, until an object is found that can receive the message and respond with a value other than nil:

- The key window
- The key window's delegate
- The key window's NSWindowController (if you are using the document application framework)

- The key window's NSDocument
- The application's main window
- The application's main window's delegate
- The main window's NSWindowController
- The main window's NSDocument
- The application's NSApplication object
- The application's NSApplication object's delegate
- The application's NSDocumentController

If you open MathPaper's `MainMenu.nib` file in IB and choose the File → Save menu item, you will see that it sends the **saveDocument:** action message to the First Responder icon, as shown in Figure 13-3. (Note that we saw a similar premade connection from File → New in Chapter 10.)

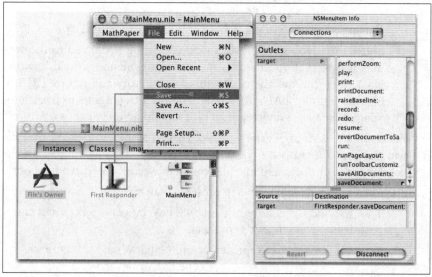

Figure 13-3. MathPaper's File → Save connection to the First Responder in IB

Thus, when a user chooses the File → Save menu command in a running MathPaper program, the **saveDocument:** message will be sent to the Math-Document object that controls the key (active) window. Cocoa implements the **saveDocument:** method in the NSDocument class. The behavior of this method depends on whether or not a filename has been assigned to the document. If a filename has not been assigned, the NSDocument class runs a modal Save panel to get a document and type. (A modal Save panel requires user action and must be dismissed before anything else can be done in the application.) After the user enters an appropriate name, etc., the document is saved and its "edited" status is cleared.

After the NSDocument class gets the filename, it needs to create an NSData object to contain the archived instance variables of your class. This NSData then needs to be written into a file on disk. The NSDocument architecture gives you not one, but three different ways for providing this information in your subclass, as well as for reading back the files from disk after they are created:

- If you simply want to be able to save a document to disk and load it back in, all you need to do in your NSDocument subclass is to override the following two methods:

  (NSData *)**dataRepresentationOfType:**(NSString *)*type;*

  > This method returns an NSData object that contains a sequence of bytes that corresponds to the document currently in memory. Some documents can be stored as multiple types, so you should check the NSString argument and provide the requested type.

  (BOOL)**loadDataRepresentation:**(NSData *)*data*
  > > **ofType:**(NSString *)*type;*

  > This method is passed an NSData object that contains the sequence of bytes that you should load, and an NSString that contains the document type that you need to read in. Your method should load the NSData object into the NSDocument's memory and return TRUE if it's successful or FALSE if it fails. The NSString argument is useful if your application knows how to load more than one kind of file.

- For some kinds of applications, it is easier to store a document in a *file wrapper* that consists of a folder and multiple files. If you want to store the contents of your document in a file wrapper, override these two methods:

  (NSFileWrapper *)**fileWrapperRepresentationOfType:**(NSString *)*type;*

  > This method should return an NSFileWrapper object that corresponds to the document's contents.

  (BOOL)**loadFileWrapperRepresentation:**(NSFileWrapper *)*wrapper*
  > > **ofType:**(NSString *)*type;*

  > This method loads the current document from the NSFileWrapper wrapper.

- If you need still more control over the saving and loading of your documents, you can override these four methods:

  (BOOL)**writeToFile:**(NSString *)*fileName* **ofType:**(NSString *)*type;*
  (BOOL)**writeToURL:**(NSURL *)*url* **ofType:**(NSString *)*type;*
  (BOOL)**readFromFile:**(NSString *)*fileName* **ofType:**(NSString *)*type;*
  (BOOL)**readFromURL:**(NSURL *)*url* **ofType:**(NSString *)*type;*

The NSDocument class contains additional methods that you can use to control whether or not backup files are preserved, if you need to access the previous version of a file when you are saving a new version (for example, if the entire document cannot fit in memory) or if your "revert" action needs to have some sort of specific behavior. As with all classes discussed in this book, you can consult the Cocoa documentation for a further explanation of the methods mentioned here, as well as additional methods that we have not described.

To help implement file saving in MathPaper, we will override NSDocument's **dataRepresentationOfType:** method in our MathDocument subclass. Our implementation will get a list of all the PaperController objects associated with the current MathDocument document (object), send each of those objects a **synchronizeData** message, and then return the NSData object that results when an NSArchiver is asked to archive the MathDocument object.

11. Insert the new code shown here in bold into the **dataRepresentation-OfType:** method in the MathDocument.m file:

```
- (NSData *)dataRepresentationOfType:(NSString *)aType
{
    if ([aType isEqualToString:@"MathPaper"]) {

        // Ask our windows to synchronize their data
        [ [self windowControllers]
            makeObjectsPerformSelector:@selector(synchronizeData)];

        // Encode the data
        return [NSArchiver archivedDataWithRootObject:self];
    }
    return nil;    // Cannot encode
}
```

The "list of all the PaperControllers" approach may seem like overkill, because we know that our application has only one PaperController per MathDocument window. Indeed, the second statement could have been written like this:

```
...
    // Ask our one window to synchronize its data
    [[ [self windowControllers] objectAtIndex:0]] synchronizeData];
...
```

But because the NSDocument architecture returns an NSArray * reference when we send it the **windowControllers** message, it's actually easier to write the generalized code that sends the **synchronizeData** message to every object in the NSArray (even though we know that only a single element is there). With this code, if a second NSWindowController instance is ever added to the MathPaper application—for example, if we should want to have two windows for every MathDocument—we'll be prepared. See the "Exercises" section at the end of the chapter for more on this topic.

Testing the Save Features

After you've made the changes, it's time to test them.

12. Build and run MathPaper. Save all pertinent files before building.

13. Create four MathPaper windows and drag them to the four corners of your screen.

14. Type some equations in each of the four windows.

15. Choose the MathPaper → Save (or Save As) menu command for each window. Because you haven't given this window a filename yet, both functions do the same thing—bring up the Save panel. Note that the application icon automatically appears in the Save panel.

16. We'll save each window with a name such as "upper-left", "lower-left", "upper-right", and "lower-right", as shown in Figure 13-4. If necessary, click Home in the Save panel to open your Home directory. Then type a filename and click OK (or hit Return) to save the file in your Home directory. The document icon will appear above your chosen filename in your File Viewer, as shown in Figure 13-5.

17. Quit MathPaper.

Note that each time you save a file, the title of the window bar changes. If you look closely, you'll also see that each window has the MathPaper document icon in its title bar, as shown in Figure 13-4.

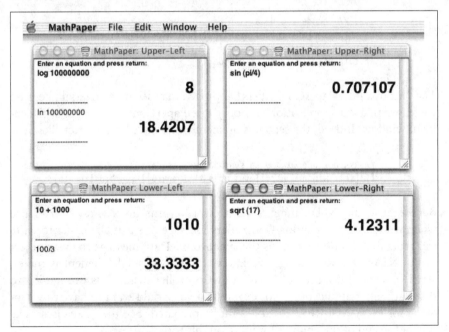

Figure 13-4. Saving several MathPaper windows

The document icon that you've created should also show up in the Finder, as it does in Figure 13-5. If the document icon does not show up, log out of your computer and log back in—the Mac OS X Finder doesn't always recognize new icons when they are manufactured by applications under development. If that doesn't work, try putting a copy of the MathPaper.app application icon in your Dock.

The NSDocument architecture automatically adds the file extension .matp to the documents that we create. You can use the Finder's Show Info panel (Command-I) to control whether the extension is shown or displayed on a file-by-file basis.

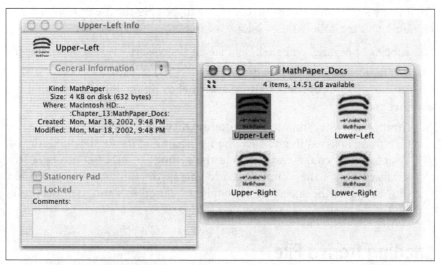

Figure 13-5. The MathPaper document icons should show up in the Finder

Advanced Save Panel Options

There may be circumstances in which the Save panel that is produced by the NSDocument architecture is not sufficient for what you wish to do. For example, you may wish to have a radio button or a checkbox on the Save panel. Cocoa makes it easy to customize both Save panels and Open panels with your own accessory views. We won't need such customization here, but this is a good place to provide an overview of how it's done.

When the NSDocument class (or your subclass) attempts to invoke **saveDocument:** and no filename is specified, or when the user asks to do a Save As or a Save To operation, the following methods in your NSDocument subclass are called, in this order:

i. (void)**runModalSavePanelForSaveOperation:**
(NSSaveOperationType)*saveOperation*
delegate:(id)*delegate*
didSaveSelector:(SEL)*didSaveSelector*
contextInfo:(void *)*contextInfo*

ii. (BOOL)**prepareSavePanel:**(NSSavePanel *)*savePanel*

iii. (void)**saveToFile:**(NSString *)*fileName*
      saveOperation:(NSSaveOperationType)*saveOperation*
         delegate:(id)*delegate*
    didSaveSelector:(SEL)*didSaveSelector*
      contextInfo:(void *)*contextInfo*

iv. (NSString *)**fileTypeFromLastRunSavePanel**

So, if you want to have a custom control that specifies the file type for a file to be saved, you can follow this sequence of steps:

i. Subclass **prepareSavePanel:** so that an "accessory view" containing the control is inserted into the Save panel.

ii. Subclass **fileTypeFromLastRunSavePanel** to return the file type that the user chose.

iii. Arrange for your **dataRepresentationOfType:** method to examine the type that is passed in and save the file according to the specified format. Your method could also examine the settings of other controls on the auxiliary view if they can be used to change the format of the saved file. (For example, the accessory view might be used in a program that saves JPEG files to specify a compression setting.)

Loading from a File

Loading means that there is already a file on the computer's disk that we want to read and use in an application. Writing the code to load a file is usually considerably easier than writing the code to save it, because the hard work of figuring out which instance variables to save and getting them on the disk has (presumably) already been done.

A user can load a file into the MathPaper application by doing any of the following:

- Choosing MathPaper's File → Open menu command and specifying a file in the Open panel
- Choosing a file from MathPaper's File → Open Recent submenu
- Double-clicking a MathPaper document file icon in the Finder
- Dragging a MathPaper document on top of the MathPaper.app application icon and dropping it

The NSDocument framework handles all of these file-opening techniques for us automatically! All we need to do is to implement a single method called **loadDataRepresentation:ofType:**.

1. Insert the following **loadDataRepresentation:ofType** method into the implementation of the MathController class in the file `MathController.m`:

MathController.m

```
- (BOOL)loadDataRepresentation:(NSData *)newHistory
                        ofType:(NSString *)aType
{
    if ([aType isEqualToString:@"MathPaper"]) {
        MathDocument *temp;

        temp = [NSUnarchiver unarchiveObjectWithData:newHistory];
        if (temp) {
            [self setFrame:[temp frame] ];
            [self setHistory:[temp history] ];
            return YES;
        }
    }
    return NO;
}
```

When any of the actions described at the beginning of this section take place, the NSDocument architecture will open the requested file, copy the file's data into the NSData object, and then pass this object and the document file type to our method. Our method makes sure that the NSData object is of the correct type. If it is, we ask the NSUnarchiver class to unarchive the NSData object into a temporary MathDocument object called `temp`. If the load is successful, the instance variables `frame` and `history` are set from the unarchived object. (We need to do this two-stage process because we decided to use the MathDocument class itself as the repository for the information in the document, rather than using a separate class created for that purpose.)

Unarchiving is the reverse of archiving: the NSUnarchiver class reads bytes from the NSData object and creates integers, floating-point values, and objects. Just as the NSArchiver class called the method **encodeWithCoder:** to perform the actual archiving, the NSUnarchiver class calls the method **initWithCoder:** to perform the actual unarchiving. Thus, in order to support unarchiving, we need to implement **initWithCoder:** as well.

2. Insert the **initWithCoder:** method shown here before the @end directive in `MathController.m`:

MathController.m

```
- initWithCoder:(NSCoder *)coder
{
    frame   = [coder decodeRect];
    history = [[coder decodeObject] retain];
    return self;
}
```

At this point, note the following important things. First, the MathPaper instance variables are decoded in the same order in which they were encoded. This is very important! If you're trying to decode the variables in a different order, the decoding operation will generate an error. (In fact, an exception will be raised. You will not get corrupt data, as you might on other systems.)

Second, note that the history object is sent a **retain** message. Objects that are decoded are sent an **autorelease** message so that they will be freed when they are no longer needed; it is the responsibility of the class implementation to retain objects that are required for long-term use.

What happens if you save a MathPaper window in the upper-right corner when your screen resolution is set to something like 1280×1024, and then you attempt to read it back in at a different resolution, such as 1024×768? On some other operating systems, such as Microsoft Windows, you might discover that the window is "off the screen" and unusable. However, Cocoa looks at the size of the window whenever you call its **setFrame:display:** method, and tries to keep windows on the computer's screen.

3. Compile and run your program. Try to open the files that you saved in the last section. The files should appear with the contents that they had when you saved them, and they should appear in the same places on the computer screen.

4. Quit MathPaper.

Marking a Document Window as Edited

An application should properly handle the closing of a document window by setting the docEdited flag, an instance variable declared in the NSWindow class. The docEdited flag determines whether an on-screen window's close button (in the upper-left corner of the window) is a solid red disk (docEdited=NO) or has a dot (◉) in its center (docEdited=YES). The two possibilities are shown in Figure 13-6.

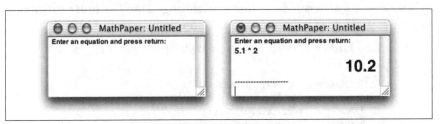

Figure 13-6. MathPaper windows without (left) and with (right) dot in close button

In addition to providing feedback to the user in the close button, the docEdited flag is used by Cocoa programs to determine whether a document window can safely be closed without any loss of data. Obviously, the docEdited flag should be set when the text inside the MathPaper page has been edited and unset when it has been saved or newly opened.

The Cocoa multiple-document architecture automates much of the maintenance of the docEdited flag with a second flag, called the *change count*. The framework knows to reset a document's change count when it is saved. All you need to do is to set the change count when the document is first "dirtied."[*]

1. Insert the statement shown here in bold into the **textDidChange:** method in PaperController.m:

PaperController.m

```
- (void)textDidChange:(NSNotification *)notification
{
    NSString *str = [ [ [self window] currentEvent] characters];

    [[self document] updateChangeCount:NSChangeDone];

    if ([str isEqualToString:@"\r"]) {
        // Get the last line of text and send it to Evaluator
        NSString *str = [theText string];
        int i;
        for (i=[str length]-2;i>=0;i--) {
            if (i==0 || [ str characterAtIndex:i-1] == '\n') {
                NSRange llRange = NSMakeRange(i,[str length]-i);
                NSString *lastLine = [str substringWithRange:llRange];
                [toEvaluator writeData:
                [lastLine dataUsingEncoding:NSASCIIStringEncoding
                    allowLossyConversion:YES] ];

                // Do not allow any more changes to the text
                [theText setEditable:NO];
                return;
            }
        }
    }
}
```

Recall that the **textDidChange:** method is called every time a character is typed in a MathPaper window. Thus, immediately after the first character is typed, the **textDidChange:** method sets the change count flag to NSChange-Done, which tells the multiple-document architecture that a change has been made to the document. When this happens, the architecture places the dot in the window's close button.

You might think that we need to reset the change count flag when the file is saved, but it turns out that this is not necessary; the multiple-document architecture handles this for us automatically.

---

[*] Alternatively, you can manually set the NSWindow's docEdited flag when the document is dirtied and unset this flag when it is saved. If you do this, you will need to implement a method called - **(BOOL)isDocumentEdited** inside the MathDocument class. There are two important advantages to using the change count technique. The first, obviously, is that there is less code. The second is that the change count interfaces cleanly with the NSUndo class, which automates the process of handling undos and redos.

Well, that's it for the "save" code! Let's test it out:

2. Build and run the MathPaper application. Move your mouse into the MathPaper window. Notice that the red close button does not have a dot in it. (However, if you mouse over the button itself, you'll see an X inside: 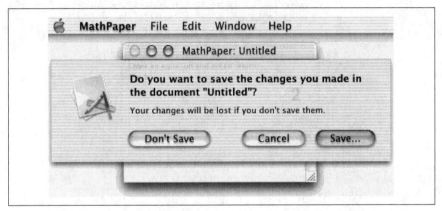.)

3. Type an equation in the MathPaper window. Notice that the dot appears automatically as soon as the first character is typed.

4. Choose File → Save and save the MathPaper document. Notice that the dot disappears.

5. Now type another equation in the MathPaper window, and the dot will reappear.

6. Click the red close button with a dot in it. The MathPaper application should ask you, via a Save sheet, if you want to save the window's contents before you close it, as shown in Figure 13-7.

Figure 13-7. A Save sheet appears when a user tries to close a window with a dot in its close button

7. Click Cancel in the Save sheet.

8. Try to quit MathPaper. You should be alerted that the window is still not saved and get the same Save sheet shown in Figure 13-7.

9. Click the Don't Save button to exit MathPaper.

Adding Printing Capability

We've made our way through a lot in this chapter, and now it's time for a quick dessert. We haven't done anything with printing so far. One of Cocoa's most powerful programming features is that printing is extremely easy. Mac OS X's Quartz, which is used to display things on the screen, is also used to send images to the printer. If your program can display itself on the screen, it can print. It's that simple.

As we'll see in Chapter 15, when an NSView object receives a **drawRect:** message, the view responds by drawing itself in the current graphics context. Normally, the current graphics context is the screen, and the **drawRect:** message results in the view's drawing itself on the computer's display. But if the current graphics context is the printer, the **drawRect:** method causes the view to generate instructions that cause itself to be printed. Under normal circumstances, you never send the **drawRect:** message directly to a view. This message is sent for you by the AppKit when the view needs to display itself. You can force a view to display itself by sending it a **display** message.

Printing is very similar. To have a view print itself, you just send the view a **print:** message. This causes the AppKit to display a Print panel (dialog), ask the user which printer he wishes to use, and then create a printer context. The view is then sent a sequence of **drawRect:** messages, one for each page. The result of the drawing operations is captured and then sent to the printer. Thus, the only thing that you need do to make an NSView object print its contents is send it the **print:** message!

You can override other methods in the NSView class to get more control over printing. For example, you can override the **printJobTitle** method to change the name of your print job. The **beginDocument** method is invoked when your document starts printing, and **endDocument** is invoked when the printing is finished. Each page's printing begins with the **beginPageInRect:** method's being invoked.

One of the truisms of object-oriented programming, and especially programming with Cocoa, is that the easiest line of code that you can possibly write, the line of code that is the easiest to debug, and the line of code that is easiest to keep in sync with future versions of the operating system, is the line of code that you *don't* write. By default, the File → Print menu command in the multiple-document framework sends the **print:** action message to the first responder (you can check this premade connection by looking at MainMenu.nib in IB).

Recall that when a message is sent to the first responder object, the message is sent to the following objects in the following order, until a recipient for the message is found:

- The key window
- The key window's delegate
- The application's main window
- The application's main window's delegate
- The application's Application object
- The application's Application object's delegate

When MathPaper is running, the first object that the AppKit queries with the **print:** method is the NSTextView in the key MathPaper window. The NSText-View, a subclass of NSView, knows how to respond to the **print:** message and it prints itself. You don't need to add printing to your MathPaper application—it's already there!*

1. Run MathPaper from PB or the Finder (no new build is necessary).

2. Type an equation or two into the MathPaper window.

3. Choose MathPaper's File → Print menu command to get the Print panel, as shown in Figure 13-8.

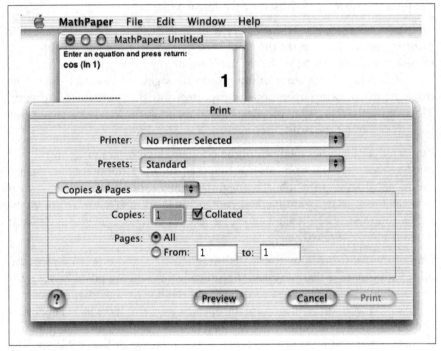

Figure 13-8. Print panel in MathPaper

4. Select a printer and click Print. The contents of the MathPaper window will appear on the printed page.

5. Alternatively, click the Preview button in the Print panel. MathPaper will then create a PDF file and launch the Preview application to display it.

6. Quit MathPaper.

It's that simple—no additional programming is required for printing!

---

* For more detailed control over document printing in a document-based application, use the **print-Document:** method instead of the **print:** method.

Summary

In this chapter, we learned how to save and load the contents of a window using Cocoa's multiple-document architecture. Saving took some effort because we needed to figure out how to archive the contents of a MathPaper document. After that, loading was relatively easy. We also learned how to mark a window as edited and how to erase that mark after the window's contents are saved. Finally, as frosting on the cake, we learned that printing was already set up for us as part of the multiple-document architecture.

In the next chapter, we'll have some fun with a little animation. It's the last of five chapters that build MathPaper. Then, in Chapter 15, we'll go into more depth about custom views.

Exercises

1. Save a MathPaper file containing several calculations and then view the contents of the file in a Terminal window with the catcommand (or by using an editor). Look up and identify any RTF commands that we didn't discuss in Chapter 12.

2. Reimplement the methods **dataRepresentationOfType:** and **loadData-Representation:ofType:** so that the NSData object contains a serialized NSDictionary object that itself contains the window's history and frame. The advantage of using an NSDictionary object for archiving is that it can give you both forward and backward compatibility with your saved documents—provided that later versions create the fields that the older versions expect to find.

3. Reimplement the methods **dataRepresentationOfType:** and **loadData-Representation:ofType:** so that the NSData object contains an XML representation of the window's history and frame. What are the advantages of using XML?

4. Add a calculator-like keypad to MathPaper so that users can click buttons to create mathematical expressions in MathPaper's key window. Implement this so that only one of these calculator-like keypads is needed for all of MathPaper—the new window should be a floating panel (utility window) that automatically inserts characters into the key window.

5. For each MathPaper document window, add an auxiliary window that displays the contents of the history instance variable as it's being filled with mathematical expressions and results. You will need to upgrade the MathDocument class and create a separate NSWindowController object for each new auxiliary window.

CHAPTER 14

Drawing with Quartz

Although we've mentioned Quartz several times, we've never used it to do much in the way of customized drawing. The reason for this is largely a result of the power of the Cocoa Application Kit—most of the objects that we've used up to this point already know how to generate Quartz to display themselves on the screen, so we haven't had to generate it ourselves.

Quartz is itself a complete graphics drawing system. It is a subject far too vast to cover fully in this chapter, so instead of even trying to give you a complete description of Quartz, this chapter is designed simply to give you a sense of how Quartz drawing is done in the Cocoa environment. At the end of the chapter, we'll provide some references for further information.

Animation in an About Panel

The ultimate goal of this chapter is to create an animation in an About panel (box) for our MathPaper application. The MathPaper About panel will have four kinds of drawing in it, each of which will require different Quartz primitives. We will draw an icon, a Bezier curve, some straight lines, and some text, as shown in Figure 14-1. We will also demonstrate animation: the Bezier curve will spin and the icon will pulsate. This chapter is dedicated to learning enough about Quartz and Cocoa to develop this About panel. It'll be fun!

The Quartz Window Server

The Quartz Window Server is the part of the Mac OS X operating system that manages the location of windows on the computer's screen and organizes the flow of events from the mouse and the keyboard. While the Window Server is mostly transparent to you as a programmer, you will occasionally see behavior in Mac OS X that is very different from what you might experience in Mac OS 9 or in Windows, and it's important to understand why. For example, you

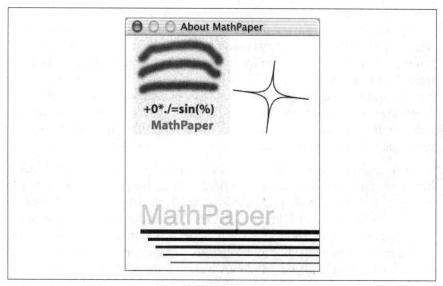

Figure 14-1. MathPaper's About panel: the icon pulsates and the star spins

can still move the windows of a Mac OS X application that is trapped inside an infinite loop (i.e., "hung"), because the moving of the windows is done by the Window Server itself, not by the application. Another result of the Window Server is that if you wish to draw on the screen, you must draw on a window—you cannot draw on the screen's background itself.[*]

Quartz uses a mechanism called *graphics context* to present each Quartz client program with its own independent copy of the Quartz environment. NSViews can also have their own graphics contexts. A graphics context can be thought of as a "virtual printer." Each has its own independent set of resources for drawing. You may have noticed on some Macs running Mac OS 9 that when you switch from one application to another, the colors of the application windows change. That sort of change never happens on Mac OS X, because the colors of each window are completely independent of one another.

Buffered, Retained, and Nonretained Windows

The underlying communication channel between an application and Quartz is buffered and bidirectional. *Buffered* means that the Quartz commands are drawn to an off-screen window that is periodically flushed to the computer's display, so that the user sees only the final result. *Bidirectional* means that you can ask questions of the Quartz environment and get back sensible answers.

---

[*] In practice, this isn't much of a restriction, because you can always create a transparent, borderless window without a title bar that covers the entire screen, and draw on that.

Normally, buffered drawing is precisely what you want, because it makes your program run with fewer distractions to the user. Instead of having every one of your program's drawing commands made visible directly on the screen, the program draws into the buffer. When the drawing is finished, the buffer is flushed to the screen. The user sees only the final state, rather than how the window was created. Buffering has a second advantage as well: when a window is covered over and then exposed, the window's contents are redrawn directly from the off-screen buffer, so the application does not need to reissue the drawing commands. This results in smooth, fast redisplay.

In some cases, however, you may want to partially or fully disable window buffering. You may have already noticed that in Interface Builder you can change the drawing type of a window from the default Buffered type to Retained or Nonretained. Windows that are *Retained* are drawn directly to the screen but are copied to an off-screen buffer when they are moved off the screen or obscured. Drawing to a Retained window can be somewhat faster than drawing to a Buffered window when you are working with very large images with lots of colors, because the image needs to be copied only once. *Nonretained* windows are just that: nonretained. You see all of the drawing as it takes place, and the window contents are lost when the window is covered up or moved off the screen. Nonretained windows can be useful if you are trying to optimize the speed of your drawing routines and want to see precisely what they are doing—that is, when you are developing and debugging your application—but it is unlikely that you will want to use Nonretained windows.

If you optimize your drawing commands properly, you may find that drawing in a Retained window can be marginally faster than drawing in a Buffered window. To create a Retained window, simply select the window's icon in IB's Nib File window, type Command-1 to bring up the Window Info panel, and change the Backing radio-button selection from Buffered to Retained.

 The Window Info panel is associated with an instance of the NSWindow class, whereas the NSWindow Info panel is associated with the NSWindow class itself. They are different!

You may find that there are times that you need to flush the current graphics context in order to force a screen update. You can use the following Objective-C statement to do this:

```
[ [NSGraphicsContext currentContext] flush];
```

There is a lot more to the NSView and NSGraphicsContext classes than we can possibly cover here. We recommend that you spend some time looking over the documentation for these two classes before going on to the next section. While you're at it, you might also spend some time with the documentation for NSView, NSGraphicsContext, and Quartz.

Drawing in an NSView with Quartz

There are two techniques you can use to draw in an NSView:

- Place Quartz function calls in the NSView's **drawRect:** method. When the window is displayed or redisplayed, this **drawRect:** method will automatically be invoked, and your specified drawing will take place.

- Bracket your Quartz calls within a call to the NSView's **lockFocus** and **unlockFocus** methods (e.g., **[myView lockFocus]**, followed by your Quartz calls, followed by **[myView unlockFocus]**). The **lockFocus** method tells the Quartz system that all subsequent drawing should take place in the view that you specify.

You should use the **drawRect:** method for any code that you write from scratch. With this technique, you partition your program into two parts: the first part changes instance variables of your NSView subclass, and the second part draws in the NSView's rectangle based on the current values of these state variables. When your view needs to be redrawn, it is sent the message **setNeedsDisplay:YES**. The AppKit then automatically invokes **lockFocus** and **unlockFocus** and calls **drawRect:** as needed. This is the most efficient way to draw with Cocoa and also the easiest to implement: all you need to concentrate on is *how* to draw the object; Cocoa handles the *when*.

The **lockFocus/unlockFocus** approach is often used by programmers who are coming to the Cocoa environment from other application frameworks and who are comfortable with the idea of drawing directly to the window in response to some sort of event. This technique is also useful when porting code from other operating systems.

We will use the **drawRect:** method for animating our About panel. This will allow us to divide the animation logic into two separate parts—one section that controls the movement of the animated figures and another that does the actual drawing. Dividing up the code in this manner makes it easier to debug.

Implementing the About Panel in MathPaper

In this section, we'll start implementing the animated About panel that we discussed earlier in the MathPaper application. The first thing we'll do is to add a new module for the About panel's nib file and arrange for the nib to be loaded automatically the first time the user chooses the MathPaper → About MathPaper menu command. (Recall that it's more efficient to use a separate nib module for an About panel, as we did in our four-function Calculator in Chapter 6. Then the nib needs to be loaded into memory only if it's used, and About panels aren't used very often.)

Project Builder

Interface Builder

1. Open `MathPaper.pbproj` in Project Builder.

2. Double-click on `MainMenu.nib` in the Groups & Files pane of PB's main window to open this nib file in IB.

3. Choose IB's File → New menu command, select Cocoa → Empty in the Starting Point panel, and then click the New button.

4. Choose IB's File → Save menu command and save the new nib with the name `AboutPanel.nib` in your `~/MathPaper/English.lproj` folder (not the `~/MathPaper` folder). When prompted, add this file to the MathPaper project, as shown in Figure 14-2.

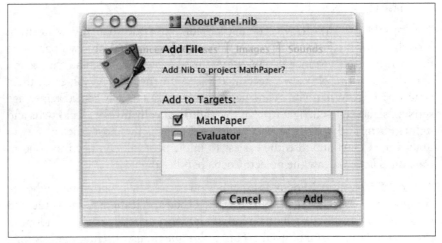

Figure 14-2. Adding AboutPanel.nib to the MathPaper project

Note that the File's Owner of the `MainMenu.nib` file is an instance of the NSApplication class (to see this in IB, click `MainMenu.nib`'s File's Owner icon and type Command-1). Also note that by default, the MathPaper → About MathPaper menu command sends the **orderFrontStandardAboutPanel:** action message to the File's Owner—that is, the NSApplication object. (To see this in IB, choose the MathPaper → About MathPaper menu item, type Command-2, and then single-click the **orderFrontStandardAboutPanel:** method with the dimple.)

NSApplication's **orderFrontStandardAboutPanel:** method actually invokes the **orderFrontStandardAboutPanelWithOptions:** method. This causes the standard About panel to appear and display the following: credits taken from the file called `Credits.rtf`; the ApplicationName and ApplicationIcon taken from the application's main bundle; and the version, copyright, and other information taken from the application property list.

This is all useful behavior for a default About panel. To customize it, however, we'll need to create our own subclass of the NSApplication class, change the application configuration so that MathPaper is built using our subclass, and override the **orderFrontStandardAboutPanel:** method.

First we'll create the NSApplication subclass called MathApplication. Then we'll add an outlet called `aboutPanel` that will eventually be set to point to our customized About panel:

File's Owner

5. Click the File's Owner icon in the `MainMenu.nib` window in IB, and then click the Classes tab in the same window. The NSApplication class should be selected. (If it is not selected, use the Search field to find it and then select it.)

6. Choose IB's Classes → Subclass NSApplication menu command, and you'll see the new subclass, called MyApplication, in the `MainMenu.nib` window.

7. Change the subclass's name from "MyApplication" to "MathApplication".

8. Type Command-1 to bring up the MathApplication Class Info dialog and add an outlet called `aboutPanel` to the class, as shown in Figure 14-3.

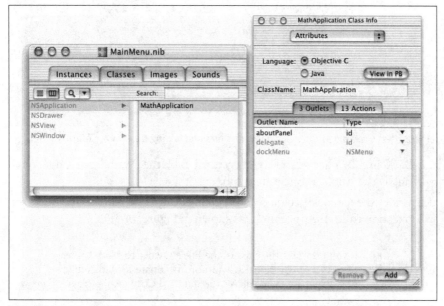

Figure 14-3. MathApplication subclass of NSApplication with new aboutPanel outlet

9. Choose IB's Classes → Create Files for MathApplication menu command and browse to your ~/MathPaper folder in the resulting Save panel.

10. Make sure that all three checkboxes are selected so that IB will save the `MathApplication.h` and `MathApplication.m` files in the ~/MathPaper folder and add them to the MathPaper target (see Figure 14-4). Click the Choose button.

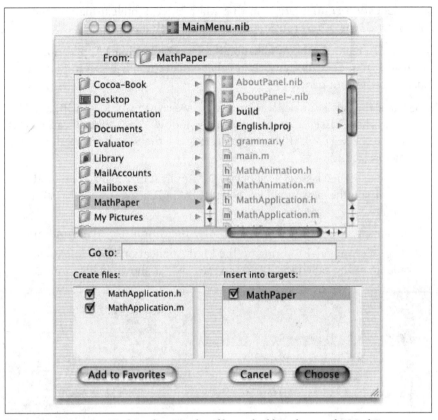

Figure 14-4. Creating MathApplication class files and adding them to the MathPaper target

Project Builder

11. Back in PB, click the Targets vertical tab, the MathPaper target, and finally the Application Settings tab.

12. Under the Cocoa-Specific section, change the Principal class from NSApplication to MathApplication, as shown in Figure 14-5.

If you don't set the class of the File's Owner to MathApplication, the Application Kit will not instantiate a MathApplication object, and you will see the standard Cocoa About panel.

Now let's make sure that both the `MainMenu.nib` and `AboutPanel.nib` files know about the new MathApplication class.

File's Owner

13. Back in IB, click the File's Owner icon under the Instances tab in the `MathPaper.nib` window.

14. Type Command-5 and change the File's Owner's class from NSApplication to MathApplication (two classes above NSApplication).

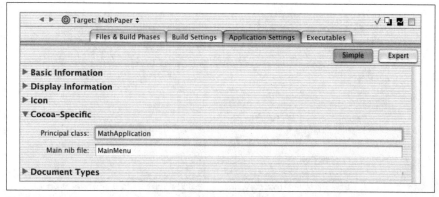

Figure 14-5. Changing MathPaper's principal class to MathApplication

15. Type Command-S to save the `MathPaper.nib` file.

Because our MathApplication subclass was created in `MainMenu.nib`, it isn't yet "known" to `AboutPanel.nib`. We'll change that in the next two steps:

16. Click anywhere in the `AboutPanel.nib` window to select the nib.

17. Go out to the Finder and select the `MathApplication.h` file icon in your ~/MathPaper folder.

18. Drag the `MathApplication.h` file icon from the Finder and drop it in the `AboutPanel.nib` window. (This is an alternative to choosing Classes → Read MathApplication.h.) The MathApplication class should now show up as a subclass of NSApplication in the `AboutPanel.nib` window.

MathApplication.h

19. Click the Instances tab and then select the File's Owner icon in the `AboutPanel.nib` window.

20. As you did in `MainMenu.nib`, change the class of the File's Owner icon to MathApplication.

File's Owner

Now we need to create the empty About panel itself:

21. Choose IB's Tools → Palettes → Show Palettes menu command to make sure that the Palettes window is visible.

22. Click the Cocoa-Windows button (shown at the edge of the page) in the Palettes window toolbar to select the Cocoa-Windows palette (which can be seen in Figure 14-6).

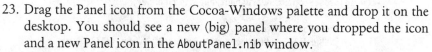

23. Drag the Panel icon from the Cocoa-Windows palette and drop it on the desktop. You should see a new (big) panel where you dropped the icon and a new Panel icon in the `AboutPanel.nib` window.

24. Move this new panel to the center of the screen (where About panels should open) and resize it so that it's about the same size as the panel with the title "About MathPaper" in Figure 14-6.

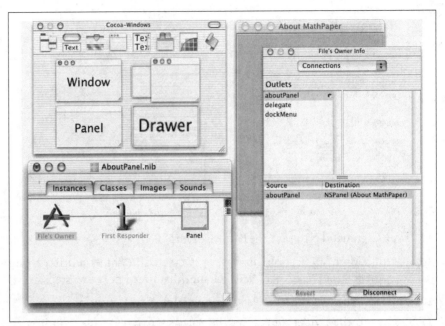

Figure 14-6. Connecting the File's Owner to the About MathPaper panel

25. With the new panel selected, type Command-1 to display the Window Info inspector.

26. Change the title of the window from "Panel" to "About MathPaper".

27. Now Control-drag a connection from the File's Owner icon to the Panel icon in the AboutPanel.nib window (or drag directly to the About Math-Paper panel itself).

28. Double-click the aboutPanel outlet to complete the connection, as shown in Figure 14-6.

29. Back in PB, double-click the MathApplication.m file under the Classes group and add the **orderFrontStandardAboutPanel:** method (shown here in bold) that we discussed earlier:

```
#import "MathApplication.h"

@implementation MathApplication

- (void)orderFrontStandardAboutPanel:(id)sender
{
    if (aboutPanel == nil) {
        [NSBundle loadNibNamed:@"AboutPanel" owner:self];
    }
    [aboutPanel makeKeyAndOrderFront:self];
}

@end
```

MathApplication.m

30. Build and run MathPaper. Save all files when prompted.

31. With MathPaper running, choose MathPaper → About MathPaper and make sure that the new About panel appears in the middle of the screen (where you left it in IB).

32. Quit MathPaper.

It is very important that your MathPaper application display an empty About panel before you go further, because our animation will get complicated. If your application does not display an About panel, go back and check your work.

Creating the MathAnimation View

MathPaper's animation subsystem will consist of four parts:

- An initialization method that sets up the whole thing
- A timer that "ticks" every 30th of a second and causes the animation to advance to the next frame
- A method that knows how to advance the state variables used to keep track of the animation
- A method that knows how to draw the current state of the MathPaper animation based on the values of the state variables

All of this logic will be encapsulated within a new subclass of the NSView class, which we'll call MathAnimation:

33. Back in IB, select the NSView class under the Classes tab in the About-Panel.nib window.

Interface Builder

34. Choose IB's Classes → Subclass NSView menu command to create a new subclass called "MyView".

35. Change the name of "MyView" to "MathAnimation".

36. Type Command-1 and add the new action method called **tick:** to the MathAnimation class, as shown in Figure 14-7.

37. Choose IB's Classes → Create Files for MathAnimation menu command to create the two MathAnimation class files. Insert them to the MathPaper target, and click Choose.

38. Still in IB, click the Cocoa-Containers button (shown at the edge of the page) in the Palettes window toolbar to select the Cocoa-Containers palette (shown in Figure 14-8).

39. Drag the CustomView icon from the Cocoa-Containers palette and drop it inside the About MathPaper panel.

40. Resize the CustomView so that it fills the About MathPaper panel.

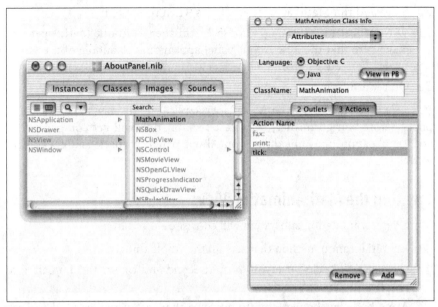

Figure 14-7. Adding the tick: action method to the MathAnimation class

41. Type Command-1 and change the class of the CustomView from NSView to MathAnimation, as shown in Figure 14-8.

42. Type Command-S to save the AboutPanel.nib file.

The MathAnimation view in the About panel will draw the four distinct elements shown in Figure 14-1:

- The application's name, MathPaper
- The five lines underneath the application's name
- The pulsating icon
- The spinning star

Drawing each of these elements requires use of a different part of the Quartz API. To do all this, we'll first need to learn more about Quartz. (Quartz, as you probably know, is also the name of a very hard mineral—fortunately, using Mac OS X's Quartz isn't hard at all!)

Quartz Graphics Data Types

As we discussed earlier, the Application Kit defines a number of data types and structures that are useful for drawing with Quartz. These data types are defined in the file NSGeometry.h, and we'll describe some of them in this section.

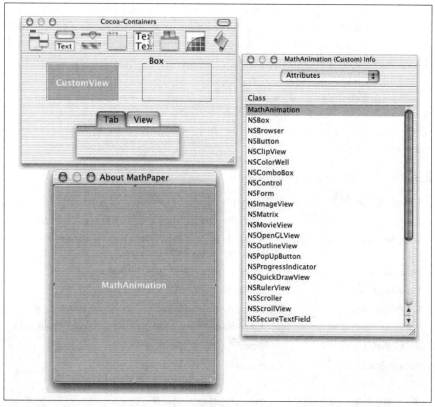

Figure 14-8. Changing the CustomView class to MathAnimation

Any point on the computer's screen is defined by an NSPoint structure:

```
typedef struct _NSPoint {
    float x;
    float y;
} NSPoint;
```

An extent in space is defined by an NSSize structure:

```
typedef struct _NSSize {
    float width;            // should never be negative
    float height;           // should never be negative
} NSSize;
```

Conveniently, a rectangle, NSRect, is defined by an extent from a point:

```
typedef struct _NSRect {
    NSPoint origin;
    NSSize size;
} NSRect;
```

Cocoa defines a number of inline functions for creating and managing these structures. The code for an inline function is integrated directly into the code for its callers, so there is no function call overhead associated with using them. These functions allow you to create an unnamed structure that is used as an argument in a function call or method invocation and then destroyed. The functions are:

```
NSPoint NSMakePoint(float x, float y)
NSSize  NSMakeSize(float w, float h)
NSRect  NSMakeRect(float x, float y, float w, float h)
```

There are also a number of convenience functions in Cocoa, which are summarized in Table 14-1.

Table 14-1. Convenience graphics functions

Graphics function	Purpose
float **NSMaxX**(*aRect*)	Returns the maximum X coordinate (the right side) of the rectangle
float **NSMaxY**(*aRect*)	Returns the maximum Y coordinate (usually the top, unless the coordinate system is flipped) of the rectangle
float **NSMidX**(*aRect*)	Returns the horizontal median of the rectangle
float **NSMidY**(*aRect*)	Returns the vertical median of the rectangle
float **NSMinX**(*aRect*)	Returns the minimum X coordinate (the left side) of the rectangle
float **NSMinY**(*aRect*)	Returns the minimum Y coordinate (usually the bottom) of the rectangle
float **NSWidth**(*aRect*)	Returns the width of the rectangle
float **NSHeight**(*aRect*)	Returns the height of the rectangle
BOOL **NSEqualPoints**(*point1*,*point2*)	Returns YES if *point1==point2*
BOOL **NSEqualSizes**(*size1*,*size2*)	Returns YES if *size1==size2*
BOOL **NSEqualRects**(*rect1*,*rect2*)	Returns YES if *rect1==rect2*
BOOL **NSIsEmptyRect**(*aRect*)	Returns YES if *aRect* has a zero size
NSRect **NSUnionRect**(*rect1*,*rect2*)	Returns the union of two rectangles
NSRect **NSIntersectionRect**(*rect1*,*rect2*)	Returns the intersection of two rectangles
BOOL **NSPointInRect**(*aPoint*,*aRect*)	Returns YES if *aPoint* is inside *aRect*
BOOL **NSContainsRect**(*aRect*,*bRect*)	Returns YES if *bRect* is inside *aRect*
BOOL **NSIntersectsRect**(*aRect*,*bRect*)	Returns YES if the two rectangles intersect
NSString *****NSStringFromPoint**(*aPoint*)	Returns a standard string coding of a point
NSString *****NSStringFromSize**(*aSize*)	Returns a standard string coding of a size
NSString *****NSStringFromRect**(*aRect*)	Returns a standard string coding of a rectangle
NSPoint **NSPointFromString**(*aString*)	Maps the string back to a point
NSSize **NSSizeFromString**(*aString*)	Maps the string back to a size
NSRect **NSRectFromString**(*aString*)	Maps the string back to a rectangle

There are other functions as well; you should review the file NSGeometry.h or the "Functions" section of the Foundation framework documentation to learn about them.

Setting Colors, Drawing Rectangles, and Drawing Lines

The NSColor class is used both to specify a particular color and to set it to be the current color in the current drawing context.

The NSColor class predefines 15 colors as class (or factory) methods. They are shown in Table 14-2 (the + means they are class methods).

Table 14-2. Predefined color methods in the NSColor class

+ blackColor	+ blueColor	+ brownColor
+ clearColor	+ cyanColor	+ darkGrayColor
+ grayColor	+ greenColor	+ lightGrayColor
+ magentaColor	+ orangeColor	+ purpleColor
+ redColor	+ whiteColor	+ yellowColor

You can also create a color by specifying its components using a variety of color models, including RGB, CYMK, HSB, and Pantone colors. These NSColor class methods are listed in Table 14-3.

Table 14-3. Factory methods for creating colors

+ colorWithCalibratedHue:saturation:brightness:alpha:

+ colorWithCalibratedRed:green:blue:alpha:

+ colorWithCalibratedWhite:alpha:

+ colorWithCatalogName:colorName:

+ colorWithDeviceCyan:magenta:yellow:black:alpha:

+ colorWithDeviceHue:saturation:brightness:alpha:

+ colorWithDeviceRed:green:blue:alpha:

+ colorWithDeviceWhite:alpha:

After you have created an NSColor object, you can make it the current drawing color by sending it the **set** method. Remember that before you call this method, a view must be established as the current drawing context with the **lockFocus** method (and have its drawing method called with **drawRect:**).

After you set a color, you can draw in that color. In the NSGraphics.h file, you'll find an extensive list of functions for drawing a variety of rectangles, bitmaps, bezeled rectangles, and so on. More complicated objects can be drawn using the NSBezierPath class. One way to think of this class is as a variable-length storage object that allows you to create a path with a particular combination of lines and curves. This object can have a specific line width, fill, end caps, etc. When you're done, you send the instance the **stroke** method to perform all of the drawing.

For example, we could use the following two statements to draw a white rectangle in the currently selected drawing view:

```
[ [NSColor whiteColor] set];
[NSBezierPath fillRect:rect];
```

We could draw four horizontal black lines, each two points thick, using the following sequence:

```
[ [NSColor blackColor] set];
[NSBezierPath setDefaultLineWidth:2.0];
[NSBezierPath strokeLineFromPoint:NSMakePoint(20,20)
                          toPoint:NSMakePoint(300,20)];
[NSBezierPath strokeLineFromPoint:NSMakePoint(20,30)
                          toPoint:NSMakePoint(300,30)];
[NSBezierPath strokeLineFromPoint:NSMakePoint(20,40)
                          toPoint:NSMakePoint(300,40)];
[NSBezierPath strokeLineFromPoint:NSMakePoint(20,50)
                          toPoint:NSMakePoint(300,50)];
```

To create a simple four-pointed star, we could use four Bezier curves that have their endpoints at the corners of the star and their control points in the star's center (see the documentation for more on Bezier curves), as shown in this code:

```
NSBezierPath *path = [NSBezierPath bezierPath];
NSPoint center = NSMakePoint(50,50);

[ [NSColor blackColor] set];
[path setLineWidth:1.0];
[path moveToPoint:NSMakePoint(50,0)];
[path curveToPoint:NSMakePoint(100,50)
    controlPoint1:center controlPoint2:center];
[path curveToPoint:NSMakePoint(50,100)
    controlPoint1:center controlPoint2:center];
[path curveToPoint:NSMakePoint(0,50)
    controlPoint1:center controlPoint2:center];
[path curveToPoint:NSMakePoint(50,0)
    controlPoint1:center controlPoint2:center];
[path stroke];
```

Drawing Text with Quartz

To draw text with Quartz, you need the following:

- A view in which to draw
- The actual text that you want to draw

- The font, font size, and other attribute information for the text
- A location in the selected view where you want the text to be drawn

You can draw text in Cocoa with either the NSString class or the NSAttributedString class. The classes themselves don't do the actual drawings; instead, the AppKit adds a category to each called NSStringDrawing. Details of this category can be found in the include file `NSStringDrawing.h`.

The view in which you want to draw is selected with the **lockFocus** method. The text is specified by the contents of the NSString or NSAttributedString class with which you are drawing.

The AppKit allows you to specify a wide variety of attributes when you draw text. These attributes can be stored in an NSDictionary. If you are drawing text with the NSString class, the NSDictionary must be provided to the NSString object when the drawing begins. If you are drawing with an NSAttributedString object, the attributes can be applied to a range of characters within the NSAttributedString class before you actually draw. Table 14-4 lists the available attributes. These attributes are defined in the file `NSAttributedString.h`, and they are all `NSString *` values.

Table 14-4. Drawing attributes for the NSAttributedString and NSString classes

Attribute identifier	Value class	Default value
NSFontAttributeName	NSFont	12-point Helvetica
NSForegroundColorAttributeName	NSColor	Black
NSBackgroundColorAttributeName	NSColor	None (no background drawn)
NSUnderlineStyleAttributeName	NSNumber, as an int	None (no underline)
NSSuperscriptAttributeName	NSNumber, as an int	0
NSBaselineOffsetAttributeName	NSNumber, as a float	0.0
NSKernAttributeName	NSNumber, as a float	0.0
NSLigatureAttributeName	NSNumber, as an int	1 (standard ligatures)
NSParagraphStyleAttributeName	NSParagraphStyle	Value returned by NSParagraphStyle's **defaultParagraphStyle** method
NSAttachmentAttributeName	NSTextAttachment	None (no attachment)

For example, let's say that we want to draw some text in green, 36-point Helvetica. First we need to create the font. We can do this using the **fontWithName:size:** class method, as follows:

```
NSFont *font = [NSFont fontWithName:@"Helvetica" size:36.0];
```

Next we need to create an NSMutableDictionary of key/value pairs that contains this font as the value for the key NSFontAttributeName and the green NSColor object as the value for the NSForegroundColorAttributeName key.

The NSMutableDictionary should look like this:

```
NSMutableDictionary *attrs = [NSMutableDictionary dictionary];
[attrs setObject:font forKey:NSFontAttributeName];
[attrs setObject:[NSColor greenColor]forKey:NSForegroundColorAttributeName];
```

With the NSMutableDictionary set up, we can now create an NSAttributed-String that contains the text that we want to draw, modified by the new attributes:

```
str = [ [NSMutableAttributedString alloc]
        initWithString:@"MathPaper" attributes:attrs];
```

To draw with this string, we need to lock focus on a particular view and use the NSAttributeString's **drawAtPoint:** method:

```
[aView lockFocus];
[str drawAtPoint:NSMakePoint(20,50)];
[aView unlockFocus];
```

Even better would be implementing a **drawRect:** method to draw the text:

```
- (void)drawRect:(NSRect)rect
{
    [str drawAtPoint:NSMakePoint(20,50)];
}
```

As an alternative to drawing with an NSAttributedString class, we can simply use an NSString object. We can use any NSString object, even one created with the @"" operator:

```
- (void)drawRect:(NSRect)rect
{
    [@"Text" drawAtPoint:NSMakePoint(20,20) withAttributes:attrs];
}
```

If we know that the text should fit within a particular size box, we can use the **drawInRect:withAttributes:** method:

```
- (void)drawRect:(NSRect)rect
{
    [@"Text" drawAInRect:NSMakeRect(20,20,100,100)
            withAttributes:attrs];
}
```

The **drawInRect:withAttributes:** method is also useful for displaying text that is wrapped to a particular width.

Drawing Images with Quartz

It's just as easy to draw pictures with Quartz as it is to draw text. In fact, in some ways it's even easier. Practically anything that you'll ever need to do with an image in Cocoa can be done with the NSImage class for manipulating images.

Using the NSImage class, you can do all of the following:

- Read an image from a file.
- Scale an image to a particular size.
- Convert an image from one representation to another.
- Draw an image in a view, or combine the contents of the image with the contents already present in the view.

NSImage accomplishes this magic by using objects of another class, called NSImageRep, to perform the actual work of storing the image. A single NSImage instance can have several NSImageRep representations of an image. For example, it might have both a bitmap representation for quick redisplay on the screen and a PDF representation for detailed display on a printer. (At this point, we recommend that you read the Cocoa documentation for the NSImage class.)

The NSImage class transfers images to the screen through a process called *compositing*. Compositing is a way of combining two images, a *source image* and a *destination image* (the image already in place on the screen). The combining is done with a special function called the *compositing operator*, which combines the two images on a pixel-by-pixel basis and displays the result.

When you composite, you can specify the following:

- The source image for the compositing.
- The destination image.
- The compositing operation.
- The fraction of the compositing operation that should be used for calculating the final result. A fraction of 1.0 means that the source pixels should be set entirely depending on the results of the compositing. A fraction of 0.5 means that half of the pixel's final value should come from the result of the compositing operation, and half of the pixel's final value should be the same as the original value.

Cocoa supports 14 different compositing operations. These operations are defined in the file NSGraphics.h. The two most common compositing operations are NSCompositeCopy and NSCompositeSourceOver. NSCompositeCopy copies the rectangle bounded by the source image into the destination image; everything in the destination image is lost. NSCompositeSourceOver is similar, but the source image is placed on top of the destination image, so that you may be able to see parts of the destination image through any pixels in the source image that are transparent or partially transparent. Because of the way Aqua handles transparency, you should generally use NSCompositeSourceOver and *not* NSCompositeCopy. If you have a few transparent pixels in your source image, NSCompositeCopy will copy these transparent pixels to the destination, making it transparent as well. This is not usually what you want.

The most common compositing operations are listed in Table 14-5. In each case, the source is defined as the image stored inside the NSImage object, while the destination is the region in which the NSImage is being composited. The destination can be any locked focus, including an NSView, another NSImage, or even a Quartz graphics state.

Table 14-5. Common compositing operations

Compositing operation	Meaning
NSCompositeSourceOver	"Source over destination" composites with attention to transparency in NSImage. This is the operation that you should normally use to "copy" an image into a window.
NSCompositeCopy	Copies the image to the NSView (destination). You generally should not use this operation, as it can cause your windows to be "promoted" to windows that contain alpha (transparency) if the source image has alpha.
NSCompositeClear	Clears the area where the image is to be copied. This isn't used much.
NSCompositeXOR	Performs an exclusive-OR between the NSImage and the NSView destination.
NSCompositePlusDarker	Performs mathematical addition between the source and the NSView. Whites get brighter and blacks get darker.
NSCompositeHighlight	Highlights the source image.

The key method for compositing is **compositeToPoint:operation**. Because this method is a Quartz drawing operation, it should be used only inside a **drawRect:** method or between invocations of the **lockFocus** and **unlockFocus** methods sent to the NSView object in which the compositing is to occur.

For example, to display an NSImage in a view is to lock focus on the view and then to composite the image to a point. To do this, you might use code that looks like this:

```
- drawRect:(NSRect)aRect
{
    image = [NSImage imageNamed:@"PaperIcon"];
    [image compositeToPoint:NSMakePoint(100,100)
                operation:NSCompositeSourceOver];
}
```

Timers

Modern applications are filled with animation. Press a mouse in the middle of a word-processor window and drag the mouse cursor up, off the window: the window scrolls until you release it. Press the mouse on the window's down arrow: the window scrolls in the other direction. Clocks have animated hands. Even web browsers have animated icons that tell you they are fetching the next page.

An animation basically consists of three things:

- An event that is repeated, perhaps in different locations
- A frequency with which the event is repeated
- A condition that causes the repetition to stop

Let's look back at our dragging example and see how it complies with these requirements. When you drag the mouse beyond the top of a word-processor window or click the down arrow, the word processor needs to move down in the document, redraw the window, wait to see if you have released the mouse, and then repeat the process. This is exactly the procedure that programs like Microsoft Word for Windows follow, and as a result, they have an annoying problem: as computers have gotten faster, these programs have scrolled faster. That was fine when PC users were moving from a 100-MHz to a 200-MHz Pentium processor. But now that PC users have 1.4-GHz Pentium processors, Word scrolls so fast that it's difficult to control.

Cocoa takes a different approach to scrolling. When you drag the mouse off the window or press the mouse on the down arrow, the Application Kit creates a *timer* to manage the scrolling. The timer triggers a sequence of instructions that moves the contents of the window down and redraws the screen. The timer is registered with the program's main event loop, so that it is run on a periodic basis—typically 10 times a second. This provides for smooth, continuous scrolling that doesn't get faster when you switch to a faster computer. (We wish that Microsoft had taken this approach with Word!)

Adding and Removing Timers

Timers are implemented with Cocoa's NSTimer class, which is part of Cocoa's Foundation. The most common way to create a timer is to use the NSTimer class method. The declaration of this method is:

```
@interface NSTimer : NSObject
...
+ (NSTimer *)scheduledTimerWithTimeInterval:(NSTimeInterval)ti
                                     target:(id)aTarget
                                   selector:(SEL)aSelector
                                   userInfo:(id)userInfo
                                    repeats:(BOOL)yesOrNo;
```

When you create a timer, you specify four arguments:

- The fire time for the timer—that is, how long from now it should be fired. This argument is expressed in floating-point seconds.
- The target of the timer—that is, the object that will receive the message when the timer fires.
- The selector to call in the target.

- Data to be provided to the handler each time it is called.
- A Boolean flag indicating whether the timer should repeat.

Two things are guaranteed about timers: they will not fire early and they can fire only when the event loop has control. Beyond that, you're on your own. If you ask that your handler be called every 5 seconds, it may actually be called every 5.3 seconds as a result of all of the other things going on in your Mac. Thus, your handler might be called at 5 seconds, then at 10.3 seconds, then at 15.7 seconds, then at 21 seconds. Your program must be tolerant of this issue.

When the timer is no longer needed, you should get rid of it by invoking its **invalidate** method:

```
[aTimer invalidate];
```

Timed entries are ideal for animation, because they let your program animate some motion in a manner that is independent of the computer's speed. Even better, the program can still accept events from the user while the animation is taking place.

Putting It All Together

In the remainder of this chapter, we'll implement the MathAnimation view, as well as a special surprise.

1. Insert the statements shown here in bold into the `MathAnimation.h` file:

```
#import <Cocoa/Cocoa.h>

@interface MathAnimation : NSView
{
    float theta;        // Current rotation for the star
    float fraction;     // Current intensity for the pulsing icon
    float ddelta;       // Density delta for icon

    NSMutableAttributedString *str;   // "MathPaper" string
    NSImage *image;
    NSTimer *timer;                   // Our timer
}
- (IBAction)tick:(id)sender;

@end
```

The purpose of these six instance variables is easier to understand with the About panel from Figure 14-1 in mind, so you might want to go back and take a quick look at it. The first three variables, `theta`, `fraction`, and `ddelta`, will be used to keep track of the animation's rotation, intensity, and density, respectively. They will be updated by NSTimer methods as they are invoked. The NSMutableAttributedString variable `str` will be used to hold the attributed "MathPaper" text. We'll create this string when the MathAnimation view is first initialized, and then draw it on the view each time that we are asked to draw the view. The same is true for the image held in the NSImage instance variable, image. Finally, the NSTimer variable timer will be used to keep track of the timer. This timer is created when the window is exposed. We need to keep the instance variable so we can invalidate the timer when the window is closed.

2. Edit the file MathAnimation.m and add the #define statements and the **awakeFromNib** method shown here:

MathAnimation.m

```
@implementation MathAnimation

#define FPS 30.0     // Frames per second

- (void)awakeFromNib
{
    // Set up the attributed text
    NSFont *font = [NSFont fontWithName:@"Helvetica" size:36.0];
    NSMutableDictionary *attrs = [NSMutableDictionary dictionary];

    [attrs setObject:font forKey:NSFontAttributeName];
    [attrs setObject:[NSColor greenColor]
            forKey:NSForegroundColorAttributeName];

    str = [ [NSMutableAttributedString alloc]
            initWithString:@"MathPaper"
                attributes:attrs];

    ddelta = (1.0 / FPS) / 5.0;
    theta = 0.0;

    image = [[NSImage imageNamed:@"PaperIcon"] retain];

    [ [NSNotificationCenter defaultCenter]
      addObserver:self selector:@selector(start:)
      name:NSWindowDidBecomeKeyNotification object:[self window]];

    [ [NSNotificationCenter defaultCenter]
       addObserver:self selector:@selector(stop:)
       name:NSWindowWillCloseNotification object:[self window] ];
}
```

The **awakeFromNib** method is automatically invoked when the MathAnimation view is first unpacked from AboutPanel.nib. The first half of the method sets up the attributed text that will draw "MathPaper" in the window. The text is drawn in 36-point green Helvetica, which is positively ugly! The variable ddelta is the increment that will be added to the variable fraction each time the timer clicks. We initialize theta to the initial rotation angle for the star. The NSImage object image is set to be the same image that we use for the document icon. Finally, we add two "observers" for the default notification center. The first observer will be self—that is, the MathAnimation view—

and will receive the **start:** message when the window in which it resides becomes the key window. The second observer will cause the **stop:** message to be sent to the MathAnimation view when the window is closed. *Notifications* are similar to delegate messages, except that any number of objects can receive the same notification. This completes the initialization logic.

Next, we implement the **start:** and **stop:** methods that were referenced earlier:

3. Insert the **start:** and **stop:** methods in `MathAnimation.m`:

MathAnimation.m

```objc
- (void)start:(void *)userInfo
{
    if (!timer) {
        timer = [NSTimer scheduledTimerWithTimeInterval:1.0/FPS
                         target:self
                         selector:@selector(tick:)
                         userInfo:0
                          repeats:YES];
    }
}


- (void)stop:(void *)userInfo
{
    if (timer) {
        [timer invalidate];
        timer = nil;  // No need to release; we did not retain the
                      // NSTimer object because scheduled timers are
                      // automatically retained by the AppKit
    }
}
```

The **start:** method starts the NSTimer if it does not already exist. The **stop:** method stops the timer and then resets the `timer` instance variable to 0. This is necessary so that the timer will be recreated if the window is exposed again.

4. Insert the following updated **drawRect:** method near the end of `MathAnimation.m`:

MathAnimation.m

```objc
- (void)drawRect:(NSRect)rect
{
    float x,y,t2;
    NSBezierPath *oval;

    // Paint the background white
    [ [NSColor whiteColor] set];
    NSRectFill([self bounds]);

    // Draw the name "MathPaper"; str was set in awakeFromNib
    [str drawAtPoint:NSMakePoint(20,50)];

    // Draw those cool straight black lines
    [ [NSColor blackColor] set];
    for (x=0; x<50; x+=10) {
        [NSBezierPath setDefaultLineWidth:(50-x)/10.0];
```

```
        [NSBezierPath strokeLineFromPoint:NSMakePoint(20+x,50-x)
                             toPoint:NSMakePoint(300.0,50-x)];
    }

    // Put the PaperIcon in the upper-left corner of the panel
    [image compositeToPoint:
            NSMakePoint(10.0, [self bounds].size.height-128.0)
                operation:NSCompositeSourceOver fraction:fraction];

    // Make a path for the star
    x = [self bounds].size.width * .75;
    y = [self bounds].size.height * .75;
    oval = [NSBezierPath bezierPath];

    [oval moveToPoint:
            NSMakePoint(x + cos(theta)*50, y + sin(theta) * 50)];
    for (t2=0; t2<=2*M_PI+.1; t2+=M_PI*.5) {
        [oval curveToPoint:NSMakePoint(x + cos(theta+t2)*50,
                                        y + sin(theta+t2)*50)
            controlPoint1:NSMakePoint(x,y)
            controlPoint2:NSMakePoint(x,y)];
    }
    [ [NSColor blackColor] set];
    [oval stroke];
}
```

This method may seem complicated, but it is actually quite straightforward.
This is what it does:

- Paints the entire view (background) white
- Draws the word "MathPaper"
- Draws those five black lines
- Composites the PaperIcon in the upper-left corner
- Creates an NSBezierPath for the star, sets the drawing color to black, and
  strokes (actually draws) the star

M_PI is the ANSI C–defined constant for pi, which is the ratio
of a circumference of a circle to its radius.

There is only one method left to create—the **tick:** method that supports our
animation:

5. Insert the statements shown here in bold into the implementation of the
   tick: method in MathAnimation.m:

MathAnimation.m

```
- (IBAction)tick:(id)sender
{
    theta   += (2.0 * M_PI / FPS) / 2.0; // Spin every 2 seconds
    fraction += ddelta;                  // Pulse every 5 seconds
```

```
      if (fraction<0 || fraction>1) { // Do we need to reverse pulse?
         ddelta   = -ddelta;
         fraction += ddelta;
      }
      [self setNeedsDisplay:YES];
   }
```

All this method does is increment the theta and fraction variables and then display the updated view. If fraction is out of range, that means that it has gone too far, and it's time to reverse direction. After the instance variables are updated, [**self display**] causes focus to be locked on the MathAnimation view and **drawRect:** to be called.

6. Build and run MathPaper.

7. Choose MathPaper → About MathPaper and admire your animation.

8. Quit MathPaper.

Pretty cool, eh? But you haven't seen anything yet!

Adding an Easter Egg

What good would an About panel be without an Easter egg?[*] This Easter egg will show up when the MathPaper → About MathPaper menu command is chosen with either the Shift or Option (Alt) modifier key held down. To implement this, we'll need to modify our MathApplication class so that it can detect this menu/key combination and pass the information along to our MathAnimation class. Then we'll need to modify the MathAnimation class to detect the fact that it should display an Easter Egg, and then to actually display it.

We will store an easterEgg flag in the MathApplication class to indicate whether a modifier key was held down when the user chose MathPaper → About MathPaper.

MathApplication.h

9. Insert the two lines shown here in bold into the MathApplication.h file:

```
#import <Cocoa/Cocoa.h>

@interface MathApplication : NSApplication
{
    IBOutlet id aboutPanel;
    BOOL easterEgg;
}

-(BOOL)doEasterEgg;

@end
```

---

[*] An Easter egg is an undocumented frill inserted by playful programmers into shipping programs, often without the knowledge of their managers. In this context, it's a surprise that users find in About panels by selecting key combinations or by other arcane methods. It has nothing to do with an egg!

It's actually fairly easy to find out if the Option key is down—just query the current event! We'll do that in the following modification to the MathApplication implementation:

10. Insert the lines shown here in bold into the `MathApplication.m` file:

MathApplication.m

```
@implementation MathApplication

- (void)orderFrontStandardAboutPanel:(id)sender
{
    if (aboutPanel == nil) {
        [NSBundle loadNibNamed:@"AboutPanel" owner:self];
    }

    easterEgg =
        ([ [self currentEvent] modifierFlags]
         & (NSShiftKeyMask | NSAlternateKeyMask)) != 0;

    [aboutPanel makeKeyAndOrderFront:self];
}

-(BOOL)doEasterEgg
{
    return easterEgg;
}

@end
```

To finish this off, we need to modify the MathAnimation class to check the value of the easterEgg flag and act accordingly:

11. Insert the following #import directive near the top of the `MathAnimation.m` file:

```
#import "MathApplication.h"
```

12. Replace the first statement in the **tick:** method in the `MathAnimation.m` file with the statements shown here in bold:

MathAnimation.m

```
- (IBAction)tick:(id)sender
{
    if ([ ((MathApplication *)NSApp) doEasterEgg] ) {
        theta -= (4.0 * M_PI / FPS) / 2.0; // Spin reverse faster
    }
    else {
        theta += (2.0 * M_PI / FPS) / 2.0; // Spin every 2 seconds
    }

    fraction += ddelta; // Pulse every 5 seconds
    if (fraction<0 || fraction>1) {
        ddelta = -ddelta;
        fraction += ddelta;
    }
    [self display];
}
```

13. Build and run MathPaper.

14. Hold down the Option key and choose MathPaper → About MathPaper, then admire your Easter Egg!

15. Quit MathPaper.

Summary

In this chapter, we learned about Quartz 2D and the way that the Cocoa Application Kit communicates with the Quartz Window Server. We also learned a little bit about drawing directly with Quartz inside an NSView object, and then explored Quartz timed entries.

This chapter marks the end of our MathPaper odyssey, although we'll use parts of it in our next major application, GraphPaper, which starts in Chapter 16. Before we get to GraphPaper, however, we'll learn much more about the **drawRect:** method—the proper way to make your NSView show its stuff.

Exercises

1. When the About MathPaper panel first opens, there is an annoying flash where the pulsating icon is located. What is it? Fix it.

2. Change the star in the About MathPaper panel to a fancier design that animates well.

3. Instead of subclassing the NSApplication object, you could have implemented the About panel by creating an Application Delegate class and having the AboutMathPaper menu command send a message directly to an instance of the delegate class. What would be the advantages and the disadvantages to this approach? Try implementing it.

4. The About panel has a memory leak: the NSImage for the PaperIcon is retained but it is never released. The image should be released in a **dealloc** method. Implement this method. Will the method ever be invoked? If not, what's the point of writing it?

References

1. Mac OS X home page for Cocoa drawing and imaging:

```
http://developer.apple.com/techpubs/macosx/Cocoa/TasksAndConcepts/
ProgrammingTopics/Misc/DrawingPage.html
```

2. Home page for Apple's Quartz system (mainly for Carbon programmers):

```
http://developer.apple.com/quartz/
```

At this site, you will find:

"Quartz Primer"

An introduction to drawing with Quartz. This document explains how Quartz is different from Mac OS 9's QuickDraw and explains issues such as color management, transparency, and the Quartz graphics primitives. It is designed for Carbon programmers.

"Drawing with Quartz 2D"

This document provides more information about drawing with Quartz. It is also aimed at Carbon programmers.

"Quartz 2D Reference"

This document includes the entire Quartz 2D API that is accessible from Carbon.

CHAPTER 15

Drawing in a Rectangle: More Fun with Cocoa Views

In the previous chapter, we saw how to draw in an NSView using Quartz drawing commands. The purpose of this chapter is to learn more about NSView's **drawRect:** method and Cocoa views in general. Recall that to us a *view* is any object that is a member of the NSView class or any of its subclasses (just as a *responder* is any object that is a member of the NSResponder class or any of its subclasses).

The Advantages of NSView's drawRect: Method

As we saw in Chapter 14, the main advantage of the **drawRect:** method is that it localizes all of the drawing commands necessary to draw your NSView in a single method. In practice, this allows you to separate the code in your application that controls layout from the code that controls drawing. This leads to an application that is cleaner, easier to maintain, and, in many cases, more efficient.

The **drawRect:** method can be invoked under a variety of circumstances:

- The NSView draws "itself" the first time that it is displayed in its window.
- If the NSView's window is not buffered, the NSView redraws itself every time the window is exposed.
- If the NSView is displayed in an NSScrollView, it redraws part of itself whenever the user makes a new part of it visible by dragging the scrollbar.
- If the user wants to print the NSView, the NSView's **drawRect:** method is invoked to perform the appropriate Quartz calls for the given device.
- If the user wants to save the contents of the NSView as a PDF file, the NSView can generate the PDF file too.

Putting the drawing of an NSView in **drawRect:** makes redisplay happen in the most efficient manner possible and lets your view print and create PDF files without requiring any additional code.

NSView's **drawRect:** method is designed to be overridden by the programmer. The **drawRect:** method in NSView itself does nothing; when you subclass the NSView class, you *must* override the do-nothing **drawRect:** method to handle the drawing for your custom NSView.

BlackView: An NSView That Paints Itself Black

In this chapter, we'll play with a number of simple, trivial NSView subclasses to learn more about how **drawRect:** and Interface Builder work. The first view is BlackView, an NSView whose **drawRect:** method fills the NSView with black.

1. Launch Project Builder and choose PB's File → New Project menu command.

Project Builder

2. Choose Application → Cocoa Application in the New Project Assistant and give your new project the name "ViewDemo".

3. Double-click the MainMenu.nib file in the Resources group in the Groups & Files pane to launch IB and display the MainMenu.nib window.

Interface Builder

4. Select the NSView class under the Classes tab of IB's Nib File window and subclass NSView by choosing the Classes → Subclass NSView menu command.

5. Change the name of the new subclass from "MyView" to "BlackView".

6. Choose Classes → Create Files for BlackView and insert the class files into the ViewDemo project.

7. Back in PB, insert the **drawRect:** method shown here in bold into BlackView.m:

```
#import "BlackView.h"
@implementation BlackView

- (void)drawRect:(NSRect)aRect
{
    [ [NSColor blackColor] set];
    [NSBezierPath fillRect:aRect];
}
@end
```

BlackView.m

8. Back in IB, resize the empty window titled "Window" so it's about three inches wide and one inch tall. The exact size isn't important here.

9. Drag a CustomView icon from IB's Cocoa-Containers palette and drop it in the empty window.

10. Type Command-1 and then change the class of the custom NSView to BlackView in the NSView (Custom) Info window. See Figure 15-1.

11. Resize the BlackView instance so it's about the size shown in the window in Figure 15-1.

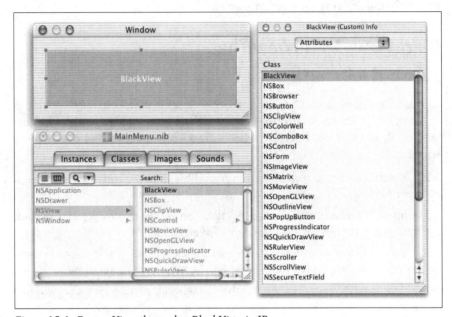

Figure 15-1. CustomView changed to BlackView in IB

12. Back in IB, choose File → Test Interface to test the ViewDemo interface. The window titled "Window" is empty—it contains no BlackView.

Now let's take a short diversion to find out a little bit about IB using the system console application Console, which resides in the /Applications/Utilities folder. The Console application displays technical messages from Mac OS X, including errors and logged output from NSLog( ) calls in applications (the same ones that show up in PB's Run pane when an application is run from within PB).

Console

13. Launch the Console application with the icon shown at the edge of the page. In the Console window, you'll see a message like the following one, which you can also see in Figure 15-2:

```
2002-03-27 21:34:17.628 Interface Builder[451] Unknown class 'BlackView'
in nib file, using 'NSView' instead.
```

14. Quit Test Interface mode by typing Command-Q.

This message appears because IB doesn't know about BlackView's implementation—it isn't compiled into the version of IB that you're using. Note that

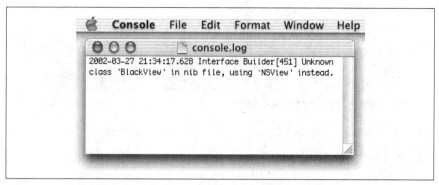

Figure 15-2. Console application with logged message about BlackView in IB

you can create your own custom palettes (e.g., a palette including a compiled BlackView similar to CustomView) in IB if you wish; consult the IB documentation to learn how to do this.

To see BlackView work, we first need to build the application in PB.

15. Back in PB, build and run ViewDemo with BlackView, saving all files when prompted.

ViewDemo

16. This time you'll see the BlackView instance in all its glory, as shown in the window in Figure 15-3.

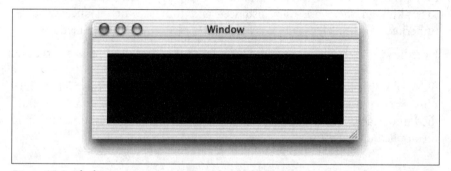

Figure 15-3. BlackView appears on-screen after the BlackView class has been compiled in PB

17. Quit ViewDemo.

That's all there is to it! BlackView's **drawRect:** method is invoked automatically when the window is first drawn on the screen; there's no need to explicitly invoke the **drawRect:** method yourself. (In fact, you're never supposed to invoke **drawRect:** directly.) Likewise, if we tried to print this window, BlackView's **drawRect:** method would automatically be invoked to generate the commands necessary to send the image to the printer.

To stress this point, let's modify the window by adding a few more BlackViews, as shown in the window on the left in Figure 15-4. You can do this with the help of IB's Edit → Copy to and Edit → Paste menu commands.

Figure 15-4. Window with four BlackViews in IB (left); running ViewDemo program (right)

Interface Builder

18. Back in IB, resize the BlackView so that it's only about one-fourth of its original size.

19. With the BlackView selected, choose IB's Edit → Copy to and then Edit → Paste menu commands.

20. Choose Edit → Paste twice more so you have a total of four BlackViews, then move and resize them in the window (see the window on the left in Figure 15-4).

ViewDemo

21. Back in PB, build and run ViewDemo again. Quit after admiring your creation.

When we run ViewDemo this time, we get a window that looks like the one on the right in Figure 15-4. Cocoa automatically calls the **drawRect:** method for each of the four BlackView instances when the window is displayed. Note that although there are four instances and four sets of instance variables (inherited from NSView), there is only one copy of **drawRect:** in memory.

Note how quickly ViewDemo was built in PB this time. The reason is that no code had to be compiled. The only changes made were in the `MainMenu.nib` file—PB only had to swap out the old nib for this new one to create the new `ViewDemo.app` application bundle. This works because nib files are not bundled into Mac OS executables—they are stored as separate resources (files) in the application bundle

A Closer Look at the NSView Class

NSView is one of Cocoa's most complicated classes. If you understand how it works, you can control the display of information on the computer's screen and have it updated quickly and efficiently.

NSView Coordinate Systems

Each Cocoa NSView has its own coordinate system that can be rotated, scaled, or otherwise transformed from the coordinate system of its superview.

Each NSView also has the following two methods that describe its position in its window:

- (NSRect)**frame**

   Returns the NSView's frame in the coordinate system of its superview

- (NSRect)**bounds**

   Returns the NSView's frame (i.e., bounds) in its own coordinate system

When you change an NSView's coordinate system, its bounds instance variable is automatically updated to reflect the change, while its frame instance variable remains the same. The NSView class provides the following methods for inspecting and changing an NSView's coordinate system:

- (float)**boundsRotation**

   Returns a floating-point number for the angle, in degrees, between an NSView's coordinate system and the coordinate system of its superview.

- (float)**frameRotation**

   Returns the angle of the NSView's frame relative to its superview's coordinate system. A value of 0 means that the NSView has not been rotated (but its coordinate system may have been).

- (BOOL)**isRotatedFromBase**

   Returns TRUE if an NSView or any of its ancestors have been rotated from the window coordinate system.

- (BOOL)**isRotatedOrScaledFromBase**

   Returns TRUE if an NSView or any of its ancestors have been rotated or scaled from the window coordinate system.

- (void)**rotateByAngle:**(NSCoord)*angle*

   Rotates an NSView's coordinate system around the NSView's origin (0,0). This method rotates the contents of the view but not the view itself.

- (void)**scaleUnitSquareToSize:**(NSSize)*newUnitSize*

   Scales an NSView's coordinate system. For example, a *newUnitSize* of (2,2) doubles the size of units along the respective axis.

- (void)**translateOriginToPoint:**(NSPoint)*aPoint*

   Translates an NSView's coordinate system so that its origin has the coordinates (*aPoint.x*, *aPoint.y*).

- (void)**rotateByAngle:**(float)*angle*

   Rotates an NSView's coordinate system so that *angle* is the angle between the NSView's coordinate system and its frame.

You can convert a point or rectangle from one NSView's coordinate system to or from another NSView's coordinate system with one of these methods:

```
- (NSPoint)convertPoint:(NSPoint)aPoint fromView:(NSView *)aView
- (NSPoint)convertPoint:(NSPoint)aPoint toView:(NSView *)aView
- (NSSize)convertSize:(NSSize)aSize fromView:(NSView *)aView
- (NSSize)convertSize:(NSSize)aSize toView:(NSView *)aView
- (NSRect)convertRect:(NSRect)aRect fromView:(NSView *)aView
- (NSRect)convertRect:(NSRect)aRect toView:(NSView *)aView
```

If you supply nil as an argument to any of the methods that take *aView* as an argument, the methods will convert to or from window coordinates.

There are many, many more methods—consult the NSView documentation for further information.

Moving and Resizing Views

You can move the position of an NSView relative to its superview's coordinate system. This usually has the effect of changing where the NSView draws itself inside the window.

The following methods control the placement and movement of an NSView:

- (void)**setFrameOrigin:**(NSPoint)*newOrigin*

   Moves the origin of the NSView's frame to a precise position in its superview's coordinate system

- (void)**setFrameRotation:**(float)*angle*

   Rotates an NSView's frame to an absolute position

- (void)**setFrame:**(NSRect)*frameRect*

   Repositions and resizes an NSView within its superview's coordinate system

- (void)**setFrameSize:**(NSSize)*newSize*

   Resizes an NSView by an absolute amount in its superview's coordinate system

Flipping

Views can be *flipped*, which means that the ordinal value of the y coordinate increases as it moves down the screen. Flipped coordinate systems are used for building subclasses of NSView such as the NSText object, which naturally move down from the upper-right corner. For these views, it's easy to calculate the y coordinate by multiplying a line number by a constant.

The following NSView method deals with flipped views:

- (BOOL)**isFlipped**

   NSView returns NO. NSView subclasses that need a flipped Y axis should override this method and return YES, in which case the Cocoa view mechanism will adjust accordingly.

Most application frameworks available for Microsoft Windows, X Windows, and Mac OS 9 operate only with flipped coordinate systems. If you are coming from these platforms, you may think it's easier to simply flip the coordinate systems of the views that you create, rather than flipping your thinking. Resist this temptation! Many functions and NSView methods do not work the way that you would expect them to if the NSView's coordinates are flipped. Flipped NSViews also seem to exercise some bugs within the AppKit. If you can avoid using flipped NSViews, we recommend that you do so.

The NSView Hierarchy

All views are arranged in a hierarchy. Each NSView has exactly one superview and can have zero to many subviews:

- (NSView *)**ancestorSharedWithView:**(NSView *)*aView*

    Searches up the hierarchy for an NSView that is in common with the receiving NSView and *aView*.

- (id)**viewWithTag:**(int)*aTag*

    Finds the nearest descendant NSView of the receiver that has *aTag* as its tag.

- (BOOL)**isDescendantOf:**(NSView *)*aView*

    Returns whether or not the receiver is a descendant of *aView*.

- (void)**setPostsFrameChangedNotification:**(BOOL)*flag*

    If *flag* is YES, this method causes the view to post a **FrameChangedNotification** when its frame changes. This is used with the NSScrollView to automatically update the size of the scrollbars. This notification is on by default; you should turn it off only for very special, temporary circumstances.

- (void)**replaceSubview:**(NSView *)*oldView* **with:**(NSView *)*newView*

    If *oldView* is a subview of the receiver, it is removed from the NSView hierarchy and replaced with *newView*.

- (NSArray *)**subviews**

    Returns an NSArray containing the NSView's subviews. Do not modify this list directly.

- (NSView *)**superview**

    Returns the NSView's superview.

Opaque and Nonrectangular Views

Cocoa represents views by rectangular regions on the screen, but nothing forces the drawing that an NSView does to be rectangular. A drawing can be an odd shape, and it can even have holes through which you can see what's behind it.

Each NSView specifies whether or not it completely fills its frame when it is drawn (so that you can't see anything behind the NSView). If your NSView has holes in it or does not completely set every pixel within its frame, **isOpaque** should return NO. It is important to set this return value properly to reflect what your NSView does; this minimizes the amount of redrawing that needs to be done when your views are redisplayed.

These methods help you manage opaqueness:

- (BOOL)**isOpaque**
  NSView returns NO by default. If your NSView subclass completely fills its bounds when it is drawn, you should should override this method and return YES.

- (NSView *)**opaqueAncestor**
  Returns the NSView's nearest ancestor NSView that is opaque. If the NSView is opaque, it will return `self`.

When the mouse is clicked in your NSView, the NSWindow object uses the **hitTest:** method to determine whether or not the NSView was clicked. You can override this method if parts of your NSView should not be mouse-sensitive—for example, if your NSView displays itself as a triangle.

- (NSView *)**hitTest:**(NSPoint)*aPoint*
  Returns the lowest subview in the view hierarchy of NSViews that contains *aPoint*. The NSWindow class uses this method to determine in which NSView a mouseclick occurs. You can subclass this method to make some parts of your NSView "invisible" to the mouse.

Controlling Display and Redisplay

Two methods are used in display:

- (void)**display**
  Causes the NSView to redisplay itself and its subviews by locking focus on itself and calling **displayRect:**. You should almost never call this method yourself; call **setNeedsDisplay:** instead.

- (void)**displayRect:**(NSRect)*rect*
  Redisplays the portion of the NSView and its subviews specified by the argument *rect*.

Most Cocoa views need to redisplay themselves when something about their internal state changes. For example, an NSTextField object needs to redisplay itself when the contents of the NSTextField change. If you write your own custom NSView, you may override these methods to improve drawing performance under certain circumstances.

The following methods are used for managing the redisplay of views:

- (void)**displayIfNeeded**

Displays the receiving NSView and any of its subviews that need to be redisplayed.

- (BOOL)**needsDisplay**

Returns YES if the receiving view needs to be redisplayed.

- (void)**setNeedsDisplay:**(BOOL)*flag*

Tells the NSView that it needs to be redisplayed when *flag* = YES. Views that need to be redisplayed are automatically sent a display message each time the NSApplication class finishes handling an event. Thus, multiple actions that might cause a view to require displays may result in a single display call's being dispatched, which increases efficiency.

- (void)**setNeedsDisplayInRect:**(NSRect)*invalidRect*

Tells an NSView that a region of itself and its subviews is no longer valid and needs to be redisplayed. This is used by the NSScrollView class. You can use it to improve drawing performance if you know that only part of a view needs to be redrawn.

Mac OS X Version 10.1 does not implement optimal redraw algorithms in the Application Kit. As a result, if you develop an application under Version 10.1, you will find that your NSView subclasses end up being displayed and redisplayed far more often than necessary. Nevertheless, you should still use the **needsDisplay/setNeedsDisplay:/setNeedsDisplayInRect:** architecture outlined above. When Apple addresses the bugs in the AppKit, your programs will run faster without additional modification.

Resizing

When a window is resized, the NSWindow class automatically sends a **resizeSubviews:** method to the NSWindow's content view. The **resizeSubviews:** method is then passed down through the view hierarchy, resizing or not resizing the subviews as necessary.

Normally, you control resizing with IB's Autosizing Info dialog. But there are times that you might want to catch resize events and do something special. Here are the methods used by Cocoa's resizing machinery:

- (void)**resizeSubviewsWithOldSize:**(NSSize)*oldFrameSize*

Informs the NSView's subviews that the NSView's size has been changed from *oldFrameSize*.

- (void)**setAutoresizesSubviews:**(BOOL)*flag*

Makes an NSView automatically resize its subviews when it is resized.

- (void)**setAutoresizingMask:**(unsigned int)*mask*

    Controls how an NSView resizes when its superview is resized.

- (void)**viewWillStartLiveResize**
- (void)**viewDidEndLiveResize**
- (BOOL)**inLiveResize**

    Control "live resizing," in which the window's contents visibly change as the window is resized. By informing the view when live resizing is taking place, you can have the view do a "quick-and-dirty" draw operation during live resizing, and then do an "expensive-but-clean" draw operation when the live resize is finished.

BarView: An NSView with a Scaled Coordinate System

In this section we'll subclass NSView to create a class called BarView to demonstrate a scaled coordinate system. A BarView object will display a simple bar graph that draws a graph between the range 0 to 100, depending on the value of a slider. It will scale its coordinate system and control redrawing with the appropriate display methods. We'll use the same ViewDemo project we created for BlackView so that we won't have to go through the project-creation process again.

Interface Builder

1. Back in IB, remove all BlackView instances from your ViewDemo window (select them one by one and type Control-X).

2. Select the NSView class under the Classes tab of IB's Nib File window and subclass NSView by choosing IB's Classes → Subclass NSView menu command.

3. Change the name of the new subclass from "MyView" to "BarView".

4. Drag a CustomView icon from IB's Cocoa-Containers palette and drop it in the empty window.

5. Type Command-1, then change the class of the CustomView to BarView in the NSView (Custom) Info panel.

6. Resize the BarView instance, as shown in Figure 15-5.

7. Drag a vertical slider (shown at the edge of the page) from IB's Cocoa-Other palette and drop it next to the BarView, as shown in Figure 15-5.

8. With the slider selected, type Command-1 and note that the slider has a default range (Minimum/Maximum) from 0.0 to 100.0 and a Current setting of 50.0.

9. Change the Current value of the slider to 0.0 in the NSSlider Info panel.

10. Make sure that the Marker Values Only checkbox is *not* checked so that you can pick any (float) value between 0 and 100.

11. Make sure that the Continuous checkbox is checked so that the slider updates when you move it, rather than when you let go.

Your window and slider attributes should now look like those in Figure 15-5.

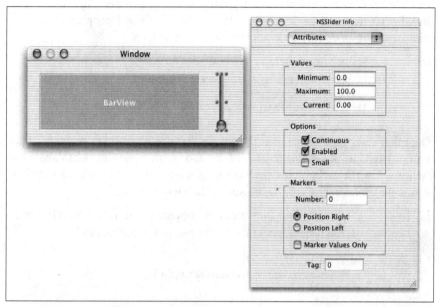

Figure 15-5. BarView, slider, and slider attributes in IB

12. Select BarView under the Classes tab in the `MainMenu.nib` window and type Command-1 to see the BarView Attributes.

13. Add the **takePercentage:** action method to the BarView class in the BarView Class inspector. (By the way, you cannot select the rectangular BarView instance in the window to add outlets or action methods because that represents an instance, not the BarView class).

14. Control-drag from the slider to the BarView instance and connect with the **takePercentage:** action method.

15. Select BarView under the Classes tab in the `MainMenu.nib` window again.

16. Choose Classes → Create Files for BarView and insert the class files into the ViewDemo project.

17. Back in PB, insert the lines shown here in bold into `BarView.h`:

```
#import <Cocoa/Cocoa.h>

@interface BarView : NSView
{
    float percentage;
}
- (id)initWithFrame:(NSRect)r;
- (BOOL)isOpaque;
```

BarView.h

```
- (void)drawRect:(NSRect)aRect;
- (void)setPercentage:(float)newPercentage;
- (IBAction)takePercentage:(id)sender;
@end
```

It's not necessary to place declarations of overridden methods (e.g.,
drawRect:) in the class interface (.h) file, but it's good programming style
because doing so documents that they were overridden.

BarView.m

18. Insert the line shown here in bold into BarView.m:

```
- (IBAction)takePercentage:(id)sender
{
    [self setPercentage:[sender floatValue] ];
}
```

The **takePercentage:** method is the action that the slider takes when it's been
manipulated. It first gets the value of the slider using **[sender floatValue]** and
then invokes the **setPercentage:** method (shown in the following example) to
set the percentage (size) of the on-screen BarView instance.

19. Insert the following four new method implementations into BarView.m:

```
- (id)initWithFrame:(NSRect)r      // Designated initializer
{
    [super initWithFrame:r];
    [self setBoundsSize:NSMakeSize(100.0,1.0)];
    return self;
}

- (BOOL)isOpaque
{
    return YES;
}

- (void)drawRect:(NSRect)aRect
{
    [ [NSColor blackColor] set];
    NSRectFill( NSMakeRect(0,0,percentage,1) );

    NSDrawWindowBackground(
            NSMakeRect(percentage,0,100-percentage,1) );
}

- (void)setPercentage:(float)val
{
    percentage = val;
    [self setNeedsDisplay:YES];
}
```

The **initWithFrame:** method in BarView.m invokes the inherited **setBounds-
Size:** method to scale BarView's drawing coordinates so that width scales 0 to
100 (to match the slider control) and height scales 0 to 1.0. This makes it very
easy for the **drawRect:** method to draw the bar graph. The **isOpaque** method

---

tells the BarView superview(s) that this method is opaque. The **drawRect:** method draws a black rectangle from the left of the NSView to the line specified by the variable percentage, then paints the rest of the NSView with the window background.

The **setPercentage:** method sets the percentage instance variable and tells the NSView's superclass that redisplay is needed.

Even though it's not used, the **setPercentage:** method is included in the class interface so that you can set the value in the BarView directly from an Objective-C statement in your program, without having to use an NSControl object such as a slider. When designing classes, you should include accessor methods for all of the instance variables that a user of your class might want to access or modify, even if the particular application you are working on does not require those accessor methods. This improves code reusability.

20. Build and run ViewDemo with BarView. Save all pertinent files when prompted.

ViewDemo

21. Drag the slider knob up and the BarView will get wider, as shown in Figure 15-6.

Figure 15-6. Slider controls the width of the BarView

22. Quit ViewDemo.

PolygonView: A Non-Opaque NSView

In this section we'll subclass NSView once again and create a class called PolygonView with some "holes" in it. It will draw a polygon with a specified number of sides (the range will be from 3 to 20 sides). We will use the View-Demo project for a third time.

1. Back in IB with ViewDemo's MainMenu.nib, subclass NSView again by choosing IB's Classes → Subclass NSView menu command.

Interface Builder

2. Change the name of the new subclass from "MyView" to "PolygonView".

3. Select the BarView instance in the window titled "Window", type Command-1, and change the class of the BarView to PolygonView in the NSView (Custom) Info window.

4. IB will alert you that "This operation will break existing connections" because the PolygonView does not respond to the **takePercentageValue:** message. Click OK.

5. Select the slider, type Command-1, and change the slider's Minimum to 3, Maximum to 20, and Current to 3. Use the Tab key to jump from text field to text field.

6. In the Markers box, change the number of marks to 18 and click the Marker Values Only checkbox.

7. Select the PolygonView class in the MainMenu.nib window, type Command-1, and then add the **takeNumSidesFrom:** action to the Polygon-View class in the PolygonView Class Info panel.

8. Connect the slider to the PolygonView instance so that it sends the **take-NumSidesFrom:** action message.

9. Select the PolygonView class in the MainMenu.nib window and choose Classes → Create Files for PolygonView. Insert the class files into the ViewDemo project.

PolygonView.h

10. Back in PB, insert the two lines shown here in bold into PolygonView.h:

```
#import <Cocoa/Cocoa.h>

@interface PolygonView : NSView
{
    int sides;
}
- (IBAction)takeNumSidesFrom:(id)sender;
- (void)setNumSides:(int)val;
@end
```

PolygonView.m

11. Insert the lines shown here in bold into PolygonView.m:

```
#import "PolygonView.h"

@implementation PolygonView

- (IBAction)takeNumSidesFrom:sender
{
    [self setNumSides:[sender intValue] ];
}

- (id)initWithFrame:(NSRect)rect
{
    [super initWithFrame:rect];
    [self setBounds:NSMakeRect(-1,-1,2,2)];
    [self setNumSides:3];
    return self;
}

- (BOOL)isOpaque
```

```
    {
        return NO;
    }
```

The **initFrame:** method sets the coordinates for the drawing system to range from (–1,–1) to (1,1). It then sets the number of sides for the polygon to be 3 and returns the initialized object. The **isOpaque** method tells the superview that the PolygonView is not opaque.

12. Insert the following two methods into PolygonView.m:

PolygonView.m

```
- (void)setNumSides:(int)val
{
    if (val>2 && sides!=val) {
        sides = val;
        [self setNeedsDisplay:YES];
    }
}

-(void)drawRect:(NSRect)rect
{
    NSBezierPath *shape = [NSBezierPath bezierPath];
    float theta;

    [shape moveToPoint:NSMakePoint(sin(0.0),cos(0.0))];

    // M_PI is a predefined value of PI.
    // M_PI*2.0 is number of radians in a circle.
    // The for( ) statement below sweeps through each
    // pie-section of the polygon for each side.

    for (theta=0.0;
         theta <= 2*M_PI;
         theta += (M_PI*2.0)/sides) {

        [shape lineToPoint:NSMakePoint(sin(theta),cos(theta)) ];
    }

    [ [NSColor blackColor] set];
    [shape fill];
}
```

The **takeNumSidesFrom:** and **setNumSides:** methods work together to react to slider manipulations and set the number of sides of the polygon to be displayed. The **drawRect:** method creates an NSBezierPath whose outline matches the sides of a polygon, then sets the current color to be black and fills the shape.

Notice that this view doesn't paint the background. That is because the PolygonView is not opaque. It has holes around the edges of the polygon where you can see the views that are behind it. When the window displays this view it will notice that the view is not opaque, and the window will first draw the view that is behind our PolygonView so that the window looks correct.

ViewDemo

13. Back in PB, build and run ViewDemo with PolygonView, saving all pertinent files when prompted.

14. A triangle should appear first (as shown in the window on the left in Figure 15-7), because we set Current to 3 in IB. Drag the slider knob up and note that the number of sides of the displayed polygon should change, as shown in the window on the right in Figure 15-7.

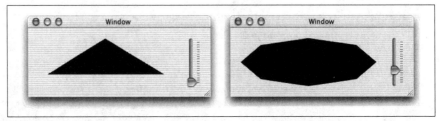

Figure 15-7. PolygonView instance with three (left) and eight (right) sides

15. Quit ViewDemo.

Changing the PolygonView's Size

Let's add a second control (another slider) to PolygonView that lets the user change the size of the polygon. Well do this by changing the size of the PolygonView instance itself. This time we'll insert code into the PolygonView class files first, then we'll work in IB.

PolygonView.h

16. Insert the two new method declarations shown here into PolygonView.h:

```
- (void)setSize:(float)size;
- (IBAction)takeFloatSize:(id)sender;
```

PolygonView.m

17. Insert the two new method implementations shown here into PolygonView.m:

```
- (void)setSize:(float)size
{
    [self setFrameSize:NSMakeSize(size,size)];
    [self setBounds:NSMakeRect(-1,-1,2,2)];
    [self setNeedsDisplay:YES];
}

- (void)takeFloatSize:(id)sender
{
    [self setSize:[sender floatValue] ];
}
```

The **setSize:** method is sublime. It takes the floating-point parameter size and resizes the PolygonView to be this size. Remember that this size is expressed in the coordinate system of the containing NSView, rather than the Polygon-View itself (which is scaled from −1 to 1 in each dimension, for easy drawing).

That's fine, but once the PolygonView is resized, it is no longer scaled from –1 to 1 in each dimension, so we have to set bounds again. Finally, we need to alert the view mechanism that this view needs to be resized.

Note that the **takeFloatSize:** method is an action method, so it can be invoked from a slider.

18. Save the `PolygonView.h` and `PolygonView.m` class files.

19. Drag the `PolygonView.h` file icon from PB's Groups & Files pane and drop it in the `MainMenu.nib` window in IB. (You can also do this step by choosing Classes → Create Files for PolygonView, but dragging and dropping is more fun).

PolygonView.h

Before dropping the file icon in the previous step, you should have seen a plus sign (+) appear next to the cursor, indicating that the class information was about to be added to PolygonView. The reason we did this was to inform IB about the new **takeFloatSize:** action method so we can use it in a new connection in IB.

20. Back in IB, make the window a little taller and then drag a horizontal slider from the Cocoa-Other palette and drop it in the window below PolygonView, as shown in the top-left window in Figure 15-8.

Interface Builder

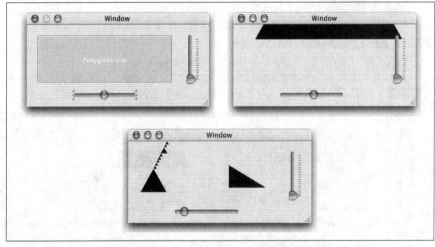

Figure 15-8. PolygonView class with horizontal slider for size in IB (top left); PolygonView instance draws outside frame (top right) and doesn't properly erase old PolygonViews (bottom)

21. Select the horizontal slider, type Command-1, and set the slider's Minimum to 0, Maximum to 600, and Current to 100.

22. Connect the horizontal slider to the PolygonView instance so that it sends the **takeFloatSize:** message.

ViewDemo

23. Back in PB, build and run ViewDemo again. Save all files when prompted.

24. Drag the horizontal slider knob to the right and you'll notice some peculiar behavior, as shown in the top-right window in Figure 15-8. Then drag the horizontal slider to the left and note even more peculiar behavior, shown in the window at the bottom of Figure 15-8.

The polygon gets larger and trespasses into territory where it shouldn't! As it gets smaller, it doesn't erase the old triangles, because they are now outside the view. This whole thing looks terrible and is not the correct way to handle such a situation. We'll discuss a remedy right away.

25. Quit ViewDemo.

Placing an NSView Inside an NSScrollView

Cocoa's solution to the PolygonView drawing problem is to place it inside another NSView called an NSScrollView. We first experimented with NSScroll-Views back in Chapter 10, with our MathPaper application. At that time, we used an NSTextView inside the NSScrollView. In this section we'll learn how to put *any* NSView into an NSScrollView and how to set up a window so that it can be resized properly.

Interface Builder

26. Back in IB, select the PolygonView instance and make it a little smaller by dragging its lower-right handle up and to the left.

27. Choose IB's Layout → Make subviews of → Scroll View menu command. Your PolygonView instance will be surrounded by two scroller areas, as shown in the window on the left in Figure 15-9. (You may need to reposition the NSScrollView so that it still fits properly in the window.)

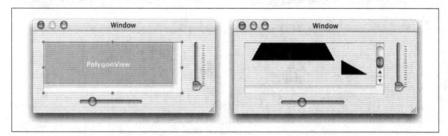

Figure 15-9. PolygonView contained in a ScrollView in IB (left) and running (right)

ViewDemo

28. Back in PB, build and run ViewDemo again with PolygonView, saving all pertinent files when prompted.

29. Drag the knob on the horizontal scroller to the right and then to the left.

This time, as you make the PolygonView bigger, the NSScrollView will automatically scale the scroll knobs to accommodate the change in size, as shown in the window on the right in Figure 15-9. Notice that the scroll knobs and

---

buttons automatically appear and disappear as needed; they are handled automatically for you by the Cocoa NSScrollView and NSScroller objects. When you make the PolygonView smaller, some of the background where the view existed is erased, but it's still not perfect (see the "Exercises" section for more). Best of all, the PolygonView object doesn't know that it is being drawn inside an NSScrollView; we didn't have to modify any of the code!

The NSScrollView automatically sets the Quartz clipping rectangle so that any attempts to draw outside the ScrollView are not permitted. This further simplifies the task of writing our own custom views.

30. Quit ViewDemo.

Responding to Events in an NSView

In addition to drawing, the NSView class can also process events (because it's a subclass of the NSResponder abstract superclass). To receive mouse-down or mouse-up events, all your custom NSView needs to do is override one of the following event-handling methods (there are others) that are declared in the NSResponder class:

```
- (void)mouseDown:(NSEvent *)theEvent
- (void)rightMouseDown:(NSEvent *)theEvent
- (void)mouseUp:(NSEvent *)theEvent
- (void)rightMouseUp:(NSEvent *)theEvent
- (void)mouseDragged:(NSEvent *)theEvent
- (void)rightMouseDragged:(NSEvent *)theEvent
```

To receive mouse-entered or mouse-exited events, your custom NSView needs to override one of the following event methods and set up a tracking rectangle—something we will describe later, in Chapter 18.

```
- (void)mouseEntered:(NSEvent *)theEvent
- (void)mouseExited:(NSEvent *)theEvent
```

Additionally, if your custom NSView is made the first responder of its containing window, it will receive the following keyboard and mouse events:

```
- (void)keyDown:(NSEvent *)theEvent
- (void)keyUp:(NSEvent *)theEvent
- (void)mouseMoved:(NSEvent *)theEvent
```

mouseMoved: events must be turned on explicitly. We will discuss this topic in Chapter 18.

In the remainder of this section, we'll show you how to receive and interpret mouse-related events and how to detect whether or not a point is within a polygon.

Getting a Mouse-Down Event

Overriding an event method can be as simple as adding a single method to your PolygonView class definition. Determining whether a mouseclick is inside or outside a polygon, a process called *hit detection*, is a bit more complicated. Fortunately, the NSBezierPath object that we use to draw the polygon will also take care of hit detection. We just need to keep the object intact, rather than letting it be autoreleased.

The following modifications will change the PolygonView class so that it has a list of colors for drawing the polygon. Each time you click the polygon, it will be redisplayed in a different color. If you click outside the polygon, an alert panel will be displayed instead.

PolygonView.h

1. Back in PB, insert the three lines shown here in bold into `PolygonView.h`:

```
#import <Cocoa/Cocoa.h>

@interface PolygonView : NSView
{
    int sides;
    NSBezierPath   *shape;
    NSMutableArray *colors;
    int colorNum;
}
- (IBAction)takeNumSidesFrom:(id)sender;
- (void)setNumSides:(int)val;

- (void)setSize:(float)size;
- (IBAction)takeFloatSize:(id)sender;
@end
```

The shape instance variable will replace the local variable with the same name in the **drawRect:** method in our previous PolygonView example, so that we can perform hit detection. The colors array will be used to keep track of the list of colors, while colorNum will track the current color. The latter two instance variables need to be set up.

PolygonView.m

2. Insert the six lines shown here in bold into the **initWithFrame:** method in PolygonView.m:

```
- initWithFrame:(NSRect)rect
{
    [super initWithFrame:rect];
    [self setBounds:NSMakeRect(-1,-1,2,2)];
    [self setNumSides:3];

    colors = [[NSMutableArray alloc] init];

    [colors addObject:[NSColor blackColor]];
    [colors addObject:[NSColor blueColor]];
    [colors addObject:[NSColor redColor]];
```

```
    [colors addObject:[NSColor greenColor]];
    [colors addObject:[NSColor whiteColor]];

    return self;
}
```

3. Replace the **drawRect:** method in PolygonView.m with the new version that follows:

PolygonView.m

```
-(void)drawRect:(NSRect)rect
{
    float theta;

    if (shape) {  // New
        [shape release];
        shape = nil;
    }

    shape = [ [NSBezierPath bezierPath] retain];  // New

    [shape moveToPoint:NSMakePoint(sin(0.0),cos(0.0))];

    // M_PI is a predefined value of PI.
    // M_PI*2.0 is number of radians in a circle.
    // The for( ) statement below sweeps through each
    // pie-section of the polygon for each side.

    for (theta=0.0;
        theta <= 2*M_PI;
        theta += (M_PI*2.0)/sides) {

        [shape lineToPoint:NSMakePoint(sin(theta),cos(theta)) ];
    }
    [ [colors objectAtIndex:colorNum] set];  // New
    [shape fill];
}
```

These code changes accomplish two things. By retaining the shape variable (as an instance variable rather than as a local variable), we assure that it will not be freed and will be available to perform hit detection. The second change causes the polygon to be drawn in the currently selected color, rather than always in black.

Finally, we need to implement the **mouseDown:** event:

4. Insert the following **mouseDown:** method into PolygonView.m:

PolygonView.m

```
- (void)mouseDown:(NSEvent *)theEvent
{
    NSPoint loc = [self convertPoint:
                    [theEvent locationInWindow] fromView:nil];

    if ([shape containsPoint:loc]) {
        colorNum = (colorNum+1) % [colors count];
```

```
                [self setNeedsDisplay:YES];
        }
        else {
            NSRunAlertPanel([self description],
                            @"You missed the shape!",nil,nil,nil);
        }
    }
```

This **mouseDown:** method is passed a pointer to the theEvent object and sends the object the **locationInWindow** message to find out the point (loc) where the **mouseDown:** event took place. The returned NSPoint is then converted from NSWindow coordinates to the NSView coordinates using the **convertPoint:fromView:** method.

We next invoke the NSBezierPath method called **containsPoint:**, which returns YES if the passed point (loc) is inside the path and NO of it is not. If the point is within the path, we increment colorNum to the next color (mod [**colors count**]), where [**colors count**] returns the number of colors in the colors array. If the event is not inside the path, we use the NSRunAlertPanel( ) function to display an alert panel.

The NSRunAlertPanel( ) function takes five mandatory arguments: the title for the alert panel, the text, and the text of up to three buttons. If the second argument is a format string, you can provide additional arguments after the fifth argument. In this example, the title of the alert panel is the Objective-C description string for the PolygonView itself, provided using the NSObject-inherited **description** method.

ViewDemo

5. Build and run ViewDemo with PolygonView. Save all pertinent files when prompted.

6. Click the mouse inside the polygon, and it will change color. Click the mouse outside the polygon (but in the PolygonView), and you will see an alert panel, as shown in Figure 15-10.

7. Quit ViewDemo.

Autosizing Multiple Views in a Window

Most windows that contain scrollers should be resizable. In Chapter 10, we showed how to set up an NSScrollView so that it would resize when its containing window was resized. Recall that we set the Autosizing attributes for the NSScrollView in IB's Size Info dialog. That was easy to do for our Math-Paper application because there was only one view—the NSScrollView—that covered the window's content area. With the ViewDemo window, however, handling window resizing requires a little more thought because there are multiple view objects. Let's first see what the current situation is.

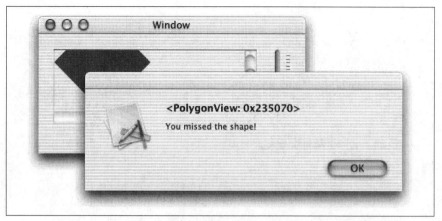

Figure 15-10. Clicking outside the polygon causes an NSAlertPanel to be displayed

1. Back in IB with PolygonView, choose the File → Test Interface menu command.

2. Resize the window up and to the left. Note that the view objects in the window don't change size and thus become obscured when the window is small, as shown in the window on the left in Figure 15-11.

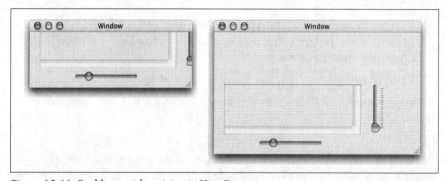

Figure 15-11. Problems with resizing in ViewDemo

3. Now resize the window down and to the right, and note that the objects still don't change size or position relative to the lower-left corner. The result is ugly, as shown in the window on the right in Figure 15-11.

4. Quit Test Interface mode by typing Command-Q.

5. Select the NSScrollView/PolygonView instance and type Command-3 to bring up IB's Size Info dialog with the Autosizing feature.

6. Click the lines in the *inner* Autosizing square so that the four springs appear, as shown on the bottom right in Figure 15-12.

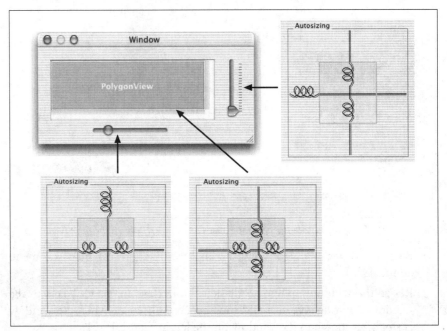

Figure 15-12. Setting up the autosizing for the widgets in the PolygonView demo

7. Choose IB's File → Test Interface menu command again and note that the NSScrollView resizes properly but eventually covers the vertical slider—obviously not what we want.

8. Quit Test Interface mode by typing Command-Q.

Note how wonderful IB is for testing interfaces! We'll use Test Interface mode again shortly.

Clearly, the NSScrollView should stretch in two dimensions when the window is stretched—we have that working now. The vertical slider, on the other hand, should stick to the righthand side of the window and grow only when the window is resized vertically. The horizontal slider should stick to the bottom of the window and grow only when the window is stretched horizontally. If we were using other frameworks, implementing these various resizing operations would be a real pain. But with Cocoa, it's easy: simply set Autosizing attributes in IB's Size Info dialog. This is basic visual programming in Cocoa.

In the Autosizing square, the horizontal springs are for horizontal resizes while the vertical springs are for vertical ones. The inside square is for stretching, while the outside square is for anchoring. A spring in the inside box indicates that the selected object should stretch when it is resized, while a line indicates that it should stay a fixed size. A line on the outside box indicates that the distance between the object and the side of the window should remain fixed if possible; a spring indicates that it should be resizable.

9. Still in IB, select the horizontal slider and click the lines in the associated Autosizing square so that the springs appear, as shown on the bottom left in Figure 15-12.

10. Now select the vertical slider and click the lines in the associated Autosizing square so that the springs appear, as shown on the top right in Figure 15-12. Choose IB's File → Test Interface menu command one more time and resize the window. Note that the views all resize properly (e.g., the sliders grow), as shown in Figure 15-13.

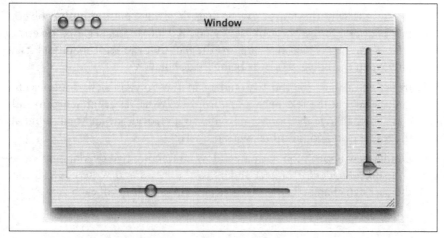

Figure 15-13. Autosizing works when testing the interface in IB

11. Quit Test Interface mode by typing Command-Q.

The one remaining problem with resizing has to do not with stretching, but with shrinking. If you make the window too small, you'll end up with junk. To prevent this from happening, you can set a minimum size for the window in the Window's Size inspector (see the upcoming "Exercises" section).

Summary

In this chapter, we learned a lot more about the NSView class (in particular, the **drawRect:** method) and a lot about resizing. NSView is such an important class that we devoted an entire chapter to it. In the next chapter, we'll start building our final major application, GraphPaper, which has a window that graphs equations. We'll use a lot of what we learned in this chapter to build GraphPaper.

Exercises

1. Change the color of the BlackView instance to the one with RGB values (0.5, 0.0, 0.5). Start by launching PB and searching for blackColor in the Find pane. After that, use a function other than NSRectFill( ) to display something in the view.

2. Revise the BarView instance so that the bar goes up and down instead of right and left. Change the vertical slider attributes so that the bar can only have an integral height in the range 0 to 10.

3. Take care of the PolygonView example problem that occurs when the window is resized very small by setting a minimum size for the window.

4. Figure out why the PolygonView doesn't always erase the old polygon that is drawn in the NSScrollView when it is made smaller. Fix the error. (Hint: The bug is closely related to the fact that the error manifests itself only when the PolygonView is being made smaller.)

5. Insert text labels for the two sliders in the PolygonView example and make sure that the text behaves appropriately (no resize, attached to sliders). Then change the horizontal slider to a vertical one and make sure all the resizing and connections work properly.

6. Build a new application with a window containing two overlapping views and several sliders. Connect sliders to the views and write code so that the user can change the RGB values and alpha channel of each view.

GraphPaper:
A Multithreaded,
Mouse-Tracking Application

Part IV, Chapters 16 through 21, focuses on building our last major application, called GraphPaper. Given a range and step, GraphPaper will graph a mathematical function in color and use mouseovers to identify graph points. We also embed in GraphPaper many of the standard features of commercial Mac OS X applications, such as services, copy and paste, and the use of the Mac OS X preferences database.

- Chapter 16, *GraphPaper: A Multithreaded Application with a Display List*
- Chapter 17, *Color*
- Chapter 18, *Tracking the Mouse*
- Chapter 19, *Zooming and Saving Graphics Files*
- Chapter 20, *Pasteboards, Services, Modal Sessions, and Drag-and-Drop*
- Chapter 21, *Preferences and Defaults*

GraphPaper: A Multithreaded Application with a Display List

In this chapter, we'll use the Evaluator back end that we built in Chapter 10 as the basis for an application that graphs single-valued functions. By the end of the chapter, the menu bar and main window of the application will look like those shown in Figure 16-1.

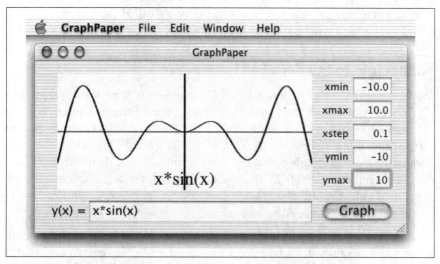

Figure 16-1. The GraphPaper application

In the process of developing this program, we'll learn more about the **drawRect:** method, see how to construct a complicated image out of many individual pieces, and learn a little bit about threads.

GraphPaper's Design

Conceptually, our program to graph a function will contain four main parts, as described in the list that follows.

Interface
Lets the user specify the function and graph parameters, and start and stop the graphing process

Pair generator
Takes the graph parameters set by the user and generates pairs of (x,y) points to be plotted

Graph builder
Takes the pairs from the pair generator and builds the graph's data structure

Graph displayer
Takes the data structure and displays it on the screen

The Interface

We'll build GraphPaper's interface with Interface Builder (of course!). The interface will consist of a Cocoa NSForm object containing several text fields ("xmin", "ymax", etc., as shown in Figure 16-1), a button (labeled "Graph") to start the graphing process, and a custom NSView called the GraphView. The GraphView object will be the overall controller of the GraphPaper application.

Connecting to the Back End

When GraphPaper starts up, a GraphView object will be instantiated. The GraphView object will then start up a single copy of the Evaluator program (as MathPaper did in Chapter 11). When the user clicks the Graph button in GraphPaper's main window, the GraphView object will first check to make sure that all of the graph parameters make sense. It will then start up a second task (called a *thread*) that will send pairs of numeric algebraic expressions to Evaluator for processing. Each of these numeric algebraic pairs corresponds to an (x,y) pair.

Because Evaluator doesn't know how to process variables, GraphView will substitute the value of the variable x for the letter "x" for every point that it graphs before it sends it to Evaluator. That's what we mean when we say "numeric" algebraic pairs. For example, suppose the user wants to graph the following equation:

```
y(x) = 2*x + 1
```

over the range of 0 to 10 with a step of 1. GraphView's subsidiary thread will send the following sequence of 11 pairs to Evaluator:

```
0, 2*0+1
1, 2*1+1
2, 2*2+1
...
10, 2*10+1
```

Evaluator, in turn, will evaluate each of these expressions and send them back in a format like this:

```
0, 1
1, 3
2, 5
...
10, 21
```

The GraphView object will also "watch" for the results from Evaluator and incorporate them into a data structure called a *display list*. The display list that GraphView will use is a Cocoa NSMutableArray object, which will contain an array (list) of objects. Each object in this list will know how to respond to two methods: **bounds** and **stroke**. We will have to implement these methods for each class whose members we want to put into the display list.

When an object in the display list receives the **bounds** message, the object returns a pointer to an NSRect structure that describes the object's size and position. When an object in the display list receives a **stroke** message, it generates the appropriate Quartz calls to draw itself.

Initially, we'll have only one kind of object that can be put into the display list, a Segment object. Each Segment object will be used to represent a line segment of the final plot, from one (x,y) pair to another. In addition to responding to the **bounds** and **stroke** messages, the Segment class that we'll create will have a special **initFrom:to:** method for initialization.

Why Use a Display List?

The advantage of using a display list of objects, rather than simply an array of (x,y) structures, is the following: we can easily add new kinds of objects to be drawn in the on-screen GraphView by simply creating new classes and inserting instances of those classes into the display list. For example, we might want to add a title to the graph's background. With the flexibility of the display list, all we have to do is to create a Title class that responds to the same **bounds** and **stroke** messages. After we create the new class, it's easy to integrate its instances into the existing display list.

The GraphView class will manage the display list. When a new object is added to the display list, the GraphView class will indicate that the region occupied by that object needs to be redrawn. Additional methods that we'll add to the GraphView class will take care of scaling the GraphView's coordinate system when the view is resized.

The GraphView object also does the actual drawing of the graph, using the **drawRect:** method. The **drawRect:** method will look at the rectangle where it has been requested to perform drawing and will send a message to the objects in the display list that intersect that region.

Working with Multiple Threads

GraphPaper is a tricky application because it has to do three things at the same time:

   i. Respond to user events.

   ii. "Listen" for data from Evaluator and graph it when it arrives.

   iii. Send data to Evaluator.

Handling (i) and (ii) at the same time is no problem: we saw how to do that in the MathPaper application in Chapter 11. The NSApplication object's event loop, which watches for user events, will also watch for data on a file descriptor* using the NSTask, NSPipe, and NSFileHandle classes. The problem is (iii)—sending data to the Evaluator process. Doing this concurrently with (i) and (ii) presents a problem in Cocoa that has to do with the way that operating systems handle pipes.

Unix Pipes and Evaluator

When two programs are connected with a Unix *pipe*, the operating system allocates a buffer to address the possibility that the program at the "write end" of the pipe might send data before the program at the "read end" of the pipe is ready to accept it. Of course, each pipe buffer is only so big, and thus if the program at the read end of the pipe doesn't read the data fast enough, the pipe buffer gets filled. If the pipe buffer is filled and the program that is writing tries to keep sending data down the pipe, that program will be blocked until the pipe buffer has some empty space.

It is much faster to send data to Evaluator than it is for Evaluator to process the data and send it back, so it's reasonable to assume that any process sending data to Evaluator through a pipe will eventually be blocked. In addition, Evaluator will send results data through another pipe back to the same process from which the data came. That second pipe can fill up just as easily as the pipe that sends data to Evaluator. This can result in a *deadlock condition*, with both pipes filled and both processes blocked, each waiting for the other to empty the pipe from which it is reading. In our example, the main Graph-Paper process would be blocked because Evaluator couldn't accept any more data, and Evaluator would be blocked because the GraphPaper application wasn't emptying its pipe either. The user would see one of those never-ending spinning disks indicating that the GraphPaper application had hung—a very undesirable result.

---

* File descriptors are also called *file handles*. They are the small integers that are returned by the Unix open( ) system function and are used by the read( ), write( ), and close( ) functions.

One way to solve this problem would be to have GraphPaper and Evaluator work in a lock-step fashion: GraphPaper could send a single line to Evaluator, then wait for that line to be returned. Many programmers take this approach, but you shouldn't. Forcing two programs to run in lock-step invariably makes them both run very slowly, because the operating system needs to constantly switch between the two of them.

A far better approach is to let the GraphPaper process fill up the pipe and then go on to other tasks, such as accepting user input and emptying the pipe of data from the Evaluator process. While GraphPaper may be blocked because the pipe buffer directing data to Evaluator is full, the operating system will allow the Evaluator process to run. It will run as fast as it can, processing data from its input and writing the data to its output. The operating system will allow the Evaluator process to run in blocks, perhaps because its output buffer is filled, or until it has used up the maximum amount of CPU time that a process may use before the operating system forces a context switch. The Graph-Paper process will then start up and start reading data returned from Evaluator.

This is the approach we will follow. Because there is no easy way for a process to see if writing to a pipe will block, our solution is to use a third execution thread—one that has only the job of sending data to Evaluator. In GraphPaper, we will call this process the *stuffer*. When Evaluator gets busy and the pipe buffer gets filled, the stuffer thread blocks. Because all the stuffer thread does is send data to Evaluator, it doesn't matter if it gets blocked temporarily, because no blocked process will be waiting for the stuffer.

Threads

Although we could send the data to Evaluator with a completely different process using another NSTask object, a far more elegant (and efficient) way to do it is with a lightweight process called a *thread*. Simply put, a thread is another process that shares the same program and data space with the program that created it. A thread can access the same global variables as its creator, but it runs on its own schedule and can lock its own resources. Threads also have their own stacks, local variables, and, in Cocoa, their own autorelease pools. If you have a computer with two processors, multiple threads can run at the same time, each on its own CPU. Threads and multithread programming are an important part of Cocoa.

The power of threads does not come without a price—it's harder to write a multithreaded application than to write a single-threaded one, because two processes executing in the same address space can cause adverse interactions. Programmers must be careful to anticipate and avoid such interactions—for example, some kinds of global variables must be locked every time they are used, to prevent accidental modification by another thread.

To see how such an interaction could happen, consider the following simple example. Suppose a function in a multithreaded program wanted to increment a global variable called count. In a single-threaded program, you would use an expression like this:

```
extern int count;
count = count + 1;
```

This simple increment operation might cause problems in a multithreaded application. Suppose that one thread read the value of count from memory, but before it could increment count and write the value back to memory, that thread was suspended and a second thread started up. Suppose that the second thread also read the value of count from memory (the same location) and incremented it. The second thread would have read the old, unincremented value of count from memory and incremented that value. Regardless of the order in which the threads write their values back to memory, the resulting value of count will be increased by only 1 (instead of by 2) when both threads are finished. A bug!

Locking with NSLock

The way around this problem is to use a *mutually exclusive (mutex) lock*. All programming environments that provide for multiple threads support some kind of locking system. In Cocoa, locks are implemented with the NSLock, NSConditionLock, and NSRecursiveLock Foundation classes.

Using these locking classes is quite simple. To implement an interthread variable called count, for example, we could create and initialize an NSLock object as follows:

```
int count = 0;
NSLock *countLock = [ [NSLock alloc] init];
```

Then we could increment the count variable in a thread as follows:

```
extern int count;
extern NSLock countLock;

[countLock lock];
count++;
[countLock unlock;]
```

If a second thread attempts to lock the countLock while the first thread has it locked, the second thread halts execution until the countLock is unlocked. This prevents two threads from simultaneously trying to access and modify the value of the variable count.

It's obviously more work to write an application that uses multiple threads, and these applications are also dramatically harder to debug. Applications that are multithreaded also have somewhat more overhead than nonmulti-threaded applications, because of the need to lock and unlock. For these reasons, the original NeXTSTEP Foundation and Application Kit were not multithreaded.

In recent years, Apple has worked to make Cocoa multithreaded. Today the Objective-C runtime and the Foundation and Application Kits are largely multithreaded. But the multithreaded implementation is not perfect. This means that if you write a multithreaded application, *you should send messages to AppKit objects only from your application's main thread.* Before you write your own multithreaded application, you should also review the Apple documentation entitled "Overview of Programming Topic: Multithreading." This document includes several sections, including:

"Threads"
>   Describes what threads are and how they are used

"Thread Safety"
>   Describes problems that can arise when using multiple threads

"Locks"
>   Describes the Cocoa locking system

Don't let this discussion scare you off from writing multithreaded applications. These applications can be a lot of fun to write and debug. You will find your job considerably easier, however, if you restrict your use of Cocoa's Application Kit objects to a single thread—the application's main thread. Although the Application Kit is not fully multithreaded, that doesn't mean that you shouldn't use multiple threads—just don't use them to access the defaults system or update the screen. It's not a good idea to make users of your application wait for CPU-intensive processes to finish when they could be doing other useful things with your application. For this reason, programmers usually use threads for performing time-intensive tasks to be done in the background, so they won't interfere with your main program's handling of events.

Launching Threads with NSThread

Every Mac OS X application has at least one thread, called the *main thread.* The main thread is responsible for processing events and performs the primary communication with the Window Server. If you want to create a second thread, you use the NSThread class. This class is surprisingly simple; its most important methods are described in Table 16-1.

Table 16-1. Important methods in the NSThread class

Method	Purpose
+ (void)**detachNewThreadSelector:** (SEL)*aSelector* **toTarget:**(id)*aTarget* **withObject:**(id)*anArgument*	Creates a new thread. The thread starts up by sending the selector *aSelector* with the argument *anArgument* to the target *aTarget*. When the method returns, the thread dies.
+ (void)**exit**	Terminates the current thread.

Table 16-1. Important methods in the NSThread class (continued)

Method	Purpose
+ (BOOL)**isMultiThreaded**	Returns true if the application is multithreaded—that is, if the application has executed the **detachNewThreadSelector:toTarget:withObject** method.
+ (void)**sleepUntilDate:** (NSDate *)*aDate*	Pauses the current thread until *aDate*.

Threads can communicate through TCP/IP connections, through NSPipes, by using shared memory, and by using Cocoa's distributed object system. However, they cannot communicate via normal Objective-C messages. Although threads share the same address space, they are truly independent processes—each is separately scheduled and separately controllable. As such, there is no easy way for one thread to terminate another thread, although you can have one thread send another thread a message that causes the second thread to terminate itself when it reads and processes the message.

Building the GraphPaper Application

Now that we've thought about GraphPaper a bit, let's get on with the work of building the application.

Changes to the Evaluator Back End

We need to make one change to Evaluator so that it can recognize more than a single expression on a line—that's important, because GraphPaper will be sending (x,y) pairs such as (3,2*3+1) to Evaluator. (If we sent only y values, we might get confused.)

The easy way to do this is to make Evaluator recognize two expressions separated by a comma and terminated with a newline. Because we built Evaluator with lex and yacc, this change is easy to make and is confined to a single file, `grammar.y`.

Project Builder

1. Launch Project Builder, choose File → New Project, and double-click "Cocoa Application".

2. Type "GraphPaper" in the Project Name field, hit the Tab key so that the project is saved in the folder ~/GraphPaper, and then click Finish.

3. Create a second target called Evaluator in the GraphPaper project by choosing PB's Project → New Target menu command, double-clicking Tool at the bottom of the list in the resulting sheet, typing "Evaluator", and clicking Finish in the second sheet in the project window.

4. Click the Files vertical tab in PB's main window and disclose the Resources group.

5. Activate the Finder, open your ~/MathPaper folder, single-click grammar.y, and then Command-click rules.l to select these two files. We'll add them to the GraphPaper project in the next step.

6. Drag the two-file selection from the Finder and drop it on the Resources group in PB's Groups & Files pane. In the resulting sheet, click the checkbox next to "Copy items into destination group's folder", make sure the Evaluator target is checked, and finally click Add.

7. In PB's editor, insert the six lines shown here in bold into grammar.y:

grammar.y

```
stat  : expr '\n'
      {
        printf("%10g\n", $1);
        printingError = 0;
        fflush(stdout);
      }
      | expr ',' expr '\n'
      {
        printf("%g,%g\n", $1, $3);
        printingError = 0;
        fflush(stdout);
      }
      ;
```

These changes enable us to send to Evaluator two expressions on the same line, separated by a comma. Evaluator will evaluate each expression and print the results, separated by a comma, on a single line.

8. Select Evaluator in the pop-up menu at the top center of PB's main window, then click the build and run button to build the Evaluator target. Save grammar.y before building.

9. Test the new running Evaluator process in PB's Run pane by typing the expressions shown here in bold. The nonbold lines are output from Evaluator.

```
0,2*0+1
0,1
1,2*1+1
1,3
2,2*2+1
2,5
```

In this example, we typed the seven-character string "0,2*0+1" and Evaluator responded with "0,1". Note that the upgraded Evaluator can now handle the numeric algebraic pairs that we plan to send it later.

10. Quit Evaluator by clicking the Stop button in PB's toolbar.

11. Still in PB, add the Evaluator file to the GraphPaper target. To do this, select the GraphPaper target in PB's pop-up menu, choose Project → Add Files, and add Evaluator (in the build folder) to the GraphPaper target.

Building GraphPaper's Interface

In this section, we will put in place the underlying framework for the Graph-Paper application:

1. Using a graphics program, create a 128×128 bit application icon for GraphPaper. Our amateurish attempt is shown at the edge of the page. You might also create the 48×48, 32×32, and 16×16 icon sizes to use in GraphPaper's .icns file.

IconComposer

2. Launch IconComposer, create a GraphPaper.icns icons file using the icon(s) that you created in the previous step, and save this file in the ~/GraphPaper project folder.

GraphPaper.icns

3. Drag the GraphPaper.icns icon from the Finder and drop it in the Resources section of PB's Groups & Files pane. Add the GraphPaper.icns file to your GraphPaper target.

4. Click PB's Targets vertical tab and select the GraphPaper target. Click the Application Settings tab and establish the application settings, as specified in Table 16-2.

Table 16-2. Application settings for GraphPaper

Setting name	Value
Executable	GraphPaper
Identifier	GraphPaper
Type	AAPL
Signature	GRFP
Version	1.0
Display Name	GraphPaper graphical calculator
Get-Info String	GraphPaper
Short version	GraphPaper
Icon file	GraphPaper
Principal class	NSApplication
Main nib file	MainMenu

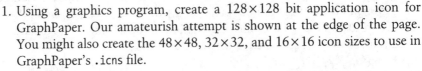

InfoPlist.strings

5. Single-click the InfoPlist.strings filename (under Resources) in PB's Groups & Files pane. Edit the copyright messages in PB as appropriate.

6. Double-click the MainMenu.nib filename (under Resources) in PB's Groups & Files pane. IB will automatically launch and display the default MainMenu.nib interface created by PB.

Interface Builder

7. Modify the GraphPaper menus, changing "NewApplication" to "Graph-Paper" in four places in the application menu. Also, rename "MyApp" in the Help menu.

Earlier, we mentioned that a class called GraphView will be used to display function graphs. As you might expect, GraphView will be a subclass of Cocoa's NSView class. GraphView will need outlets to point to most of the on-screen objects, as well as action methods to start and stop the graphing.

8. Select NSView in the `MainMenu.nib` window and choose Classes → Subclass NSView to create a new subclass. Rename the new subclass "GraphView".

9. Type Command-1 to open the GraphView Class Info dialog. Add the following outlets and action methods to GraphView:

Outlets	Action Methods
graphButton	graph:
xminCell	stopGraph:
xmaxCell	
xstepCell	
yminCell	
ymaxCell	
formulaField	

10. Choose Classes → Create Files for GraphView to create the files for the GraphView class and insert them into the GraphPaper target.

Next we'll set up GraphPaper's main window, as shown in Figure 16-2.

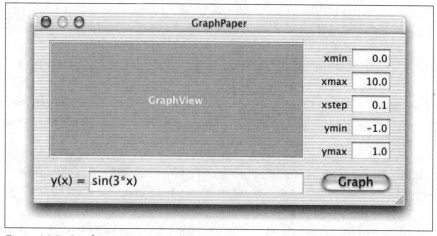

Figure 16-2. GraphPaper's main window in IB

11. Still in IB, change the main window's title from "Window" to "GraphPaper" in the Window Info dialog.

12. Resize the window so that it is about two inches tall and four inches wide.

13. Drag a CustomView icon from IB's Cocoa-Views palette and drop it in the GraphPaper window. Enlarge it and position it as shown in Figure 16-2.

14. Change the class of the CustomView to GraphView in the Info dialog.

15. Drag an NSForm object (shown at the edge of the page) from IB's Cocoa-Views palette and drop it in the right side of the GraphPaper window.

16. Option-drag the bottom-center handle of the NSForm object to create three more NSFormCells, for a total of five NSFormCells.

17. Change the labels on the NSFormCells to "xmin", "xmax", "xstep", "ymin", and "ymax", as shown in Figure 16-2. (Use the Tab key to move quickly from one NSFormCell to the next.)

18. Enter the numbers "0.0", "10.0", "0.1", "–1.0", and "1.0" in the five text areas of the NSForm, as shown in Figure 16-2. We'll use these initial graphing parameters to show the user a good-looking graph at launch time.

19. Select the entire NSForm matrix and change the text to be right-aligned in the Text Alignment box in the NSForm Info dialog.

20. Drag a SystemFont Text icon from IB's Cocoa-Views palette and drop it in the lower-left corner of the GraphPaper window. Change the text to "y(x)=", as shown in Figure 16-2, and make it larger (16 point) using IB's Font dialog (Command-T). This SystemFont Text icon represents an NSTextField object with attributes such as uneditable, etc.

21. Drag an NSTextField icon (shown at the edge of the page) from IB's Cocoa-Views palette and drop it at the right of the "y(x)=" in the Graph-Paper window.

22. Make the text in the NSTextField larger (16 point) using IB's Font dialog. Make the NSTextField wider as well.

23. Enter a function that has an interesting graph in the white NSTextField. We'll use sin(3*x), which will produce an interesting graph at launch time.

24. Drag an NSButton object from IB's Cocoa-Views palette and drop it in the GraphPaper window below the NSForm, as shown in Figure 16-2. Change the title on the NSButton object to "Graph" and make the text size 16 point. Use the blue guidelines to align the on-screen objects.

25. Connect the seven GraphView outlets to the appropriate on-screen objects. For example, Control-drag from the GraphView on-screen instance to the Graph button and double-click the graphButton outlet. Similarly, connect the xmaxCell outlet to the NSFormCell labeled "xmax", the xminCell outlet to the NSFormCell labeled "xmin", and so on. The formulaField outlet should be connected to the NSTextField object containing the formula (see the GraphView Connections Info dialog at the left of Figure 16-3). Note that all of the outlet connections are listed at the bottom of the Info dialog.

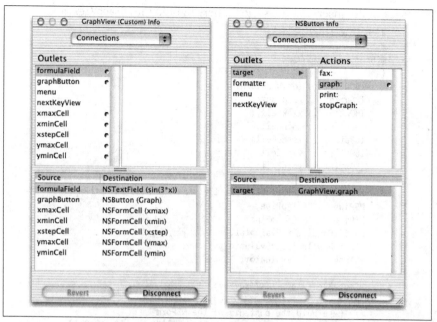

Figure 16-3. GraphView's outlet connections (left) and Graph button action connection (right)

Later in this chapter, we'll use the graphButton outlet to temporarily change the title on the button from "Graph" to "Stop" while GraphPaper is drawing a graph.

26. Connect the Graph button to the on-screen GraphView instance. Make it send the **graph:** action message to GraphView. See the corresponding NSButton Info dialog in Figure 16-3.

We won't use the **stopGraph:** action as part of the connections we set up in IB, but we will connect the Graph button to **stopGraph:** programmatically. One tiny advantage of adding **stopGraph:** to the GraphView class in IB is that IB's Create Files command will create the skeleton code for the method, which saves a bit of typing. Another advantage is that **stopGraph:** will be visible while you're working in IB.

27. Save the MainMenu.nib file.

The GraphView Class Interface File

GraphView will be the most complicated class that we build in this book, so we'll go over it in pieces. When learning any new class, the best place to start is with the interface file. In this case, that file is GraphView.h.

GraphView.h

28. Back in PB, insert the lines shown here in bold into GraphView.h:

```
#import <Cocoa/Cocoa.h>

@interface GraphView : NSView
{
    IBOutlet id formulaField;
    IBOutlet id graphButton;
    IBOutlet id xmaxCell;
    IBOutlet id xminCell;
    IBOutlet id xstepCell;
    IBOutlet id ymaxCell;
    IBOutlet id yminCell;

    // These five variables are the same as those in MathPaper
    NSPipe       *toPipe;
    NSPipe       *fromPipe;
    NSFileHandle *toEvaluator;
    NSFileHandle *fromEvaluator;
    NSTask       *evaluator;

    NSMutableString    *fromBuf;

    // These hold the contents of the NSForm
    // double      xmin;   These three will be public variables
    // double      xmax;   See the @public directive below
    // double      xstep;
    double       ymin;
    double       ymax;

    // Display list
    NSMutableArray *displayList;
    BOOL          first;      // Getting the first point?
    NSPoint       lastPt;     // Last point received

    // Communication with stuffer thread
    BOOL     stop_sending;
    BOOL     sending;
    BOOL     receiving;

@public     // For use by stuffer thread

    BOOL     graphing;
    char     *formula;
    int      toFd;
    double   xmin, xmax, xstep;
}

- (IBAction)graph:(id)sender;
- (IBAction)stopGraph:(id)sender;
- (void)doStop:(int)which;
- (void)getFormAndScaleView;
- (void)addGraphElement:(id)element;
- (void)clear;
- (void)sendData;
```

```
@end
```

```
#define STOP_SENDER    1
#define STOP_RECEIVER  2
```

```
#define GRAPH_TAG  1
#define AXES_TAG   2
#define LABEL_TAG  3
```

The first seven `id` statements declare the outlets we set up and connected in IB. The remaining instance variables are a little more complicated. Here is a brief description of what they do:

toPipe, fromPipe, toEvaluator, fromEvaluator, evaluator

These variables all have the same functions as the corresponding variables in the MathPaper application. The MathPaper variables were initially defined in Chapter 11.

fromBuf

It's possible to get a variable amount of information back from Evaluator (including a partial line), so it's necessary to buffer Evaluator's content. We'll use `fromBuf`, an NSString instance variable, as the buffer.

The next group of instance variables holds a copy of the graphing parameters that are read from the NSForm. We use instance variables to store the graphing parameters so that they can be referenced by both the main thread and the stuffer thread.

xmin, xmax

These two variables determine the horizontal scale of the graph that is drawn.

xstep

This variable determines the step increment in the horizontal (x) direction, used for drawing the graph.

ymin, ymax

These two variables determine the vertical scale of the graph that is drawn.

The next group of variables is used for holding and maintaining the display list:

displayList

This is the actual display list itself, implemented with an NSMutableArray.

first

This boolean variable is set before the first pair is received from Evaluator. It enables the GraphView object to distinguish between the first pair of coordinates returned and the others.

lastPt

The (x,y) coordinate pair of the last point read from Evaluator. This variable is valid only if `first=NO`. It is used to construct the line segment from the last point received to the current point.

The last group of instance variables is used for communication between the main thread and the stuffer thread. Because of the design of the GraphView class, it won't be necessary to use an NSLock.

stop_sending
> When set to YES, this boolean variable forces the stuffer thread to exit.

sending
> This boolean variable is set to YES just before the stuffer thread starts up. When the stuffer thread is finished, it will send the termination code (999) to Evaluator and resets this variable to NO.

receiving
> This boolean variable is set to YES just before the stuffer thread starts up. When the main thread receives the termination code (999) from Evaluator, it resets this variable to NO.

The @public declarations mean that the four instance variables (graphing, formula, etc.) will be visible everywhere, including to the stuffer thread. We'll discuss the new methods declared in GraphView.h as we progress through this chapter. Finally, the #define statements set up the tags that we will use for various parts of the GraphView class.

The GraphView Class Implementation File

Now let's look at the GraphView class implementation code in GraphView.m. The first part of the file requires another #import directive:

GraphView.m

29. Insert the #import directive for the Segment.h file near the beginning of GraphView.m:

```
#import "GraphView.h"
#import "Segment.h"

@implementation GraphView
```

The new Segment class will be used to create line segments to draw pieces of the graph. We'll create the Segment class later in this chapter.

The initWithFrame: Method

The first method we'll discuss in our GraphView class definition is **initWith-Frame:**, the view's designated initializer. This method will set up the connection to Evaluator and will initialize the displayList and fromBuf instance variables.

GraphView.m

30. Insert the following **initWithFrame:** method into GraphView.m:

```
- initWithFrame:(NSRect)frame
{
    NSString *path;
```

```
    [super initWithFrame:frame];

    displayList = [ [NSMutableArray alloc] init];
    fromBuf = [ [NSMutableString alloc] init];

    // What follows is largely from MathPaper
    path = [ [NSBundle mainBundle]
                pathForResource:@"Evaluator" ofType:@""];

    if (!path) {
        NSLog(@"%@: Cannot find Evaluator", [self description]);
    }
    else {
        toPipe   = [NSPipe pipe];
        fromPipe = [NSPipe pipe];

        toEvaluator   = [toPipe fileHandleForWriting];
        fromEvaluator = [fromPipe fileHandleForReading];

        evaluator = [ [NSTask alloc] init] retain;
        [evaluator setLaunchPath:path];

        [evaluator setStandardOutput:fromPipe];
        [evaluator setStandardInput:toPipe];
        [evaluator launch];

        [ [NSNotificationCenter defaultCenter]
            addObserver:self
                selector:@selector(gotData:)
                    name:NSFileHandleReadCompletionNotification
                  object:fromEvaluator ];

        [fromEvaluator readInBackgroundAndNotify];
    }

    // The notification below causes the getFormAndScaleView
    // method to be invoked whenever this view is resized
    [ [NSNotificationCenter defaultCenter]
                    addObserver:self
                    selector:@selector(getFormAndScaleView)
                        name:NSViewFrameDidChangeNotification
                      object:self];
    return self;
}
```

The **initWithFrame:** method starts by creating the displayList and fromBuf
objects. Then it creates Evaluator, using code that is largely borrowed from
MathPaper (see Chapter 11). Finally, it makes GraphView a receiver of notifications of the NSViewFrameDidChangeNotification type. This notification
ensures that the GraphView will be sent a **getFormAndScaleView** message if
its on-screen view area changes size. By doing this, we avoid having to make
GraphView a delegate of the NSWindow in which it resides.

Implementing the Display List

Recall that the data stuffer thread sends to Evaluator a series of expressions that looks like this (for y=2*x+1):

```
0, 2*0+1
1, 2*1+1
2, 2*2+1
```

And Evaluator sends back a series of numbers that looks like this:

```
0, 1
1, 3
2, 5
```

The GraphView object uses those pairs of numbers to construct a graph. For this to happen, we must create a *display list*—a list of objects that will be used to describe the drawing of a graph.

Our display list will be implemented with a series of objects that adopt a new *formal protocol* that we'll call GraphViewElement. We say that an Objective-C class *adopts* a protocol if it implements all the methods in that protocol. A formal protocol is a group of methods declared between the @protocol and @end directives. A formal protocol is adopted in code by listing its name between angle brackets in a class declaration, as we'll see later.

The methods in our GraphViewElement protocol are described in Table 16-3.

Table 16-3. GraphViewElement protocol methods

Method	Purpose
- (int)**tag**	Returns the object's tag (used later)
- (void)**setTag:**(int)*aTag*	Sets the object's tag
- (void)**stroke**	Draws the object
- (NSRect)**bounds**	Returns the element's bounding box
- (void)**setColor:**(NSColor *)*aColor*	Sets the element's color
- (NSColor *)**color**	Returns the object's color

The GraphView class will maintain a list of objects that respond to this protocol in the displayList mutable array. The following GraphView methods will be used to implement this display list functionality:

- (void)**clear**
    Empties the display list

- (void)**addGraphElement:**(id)*element*
    Adds an element to the display list

- (void)**drawRect:**(NSRect)*aRect*
    Draws the portion of the GraphView (and the GraphView display list) that appears within *aRect*

31. Insert the GraphViewElement protocol into the `GraphView.h` file, after the @end directive that ends the GraphView interface:

GraphView.h

```
@protocol GraphViewElement
- (int)tag;
- (void)setTag:(int)aTag;
- (void)stroke;
- (NSRect)bounds;
- (void)setColor:(NSColor *)aColor;
- (NSColor *)color;
@end
```

Placing this protocol definition in the file `GraphView.h` informs the Graph-View class about the declarations for each of these methods.

32. Insert the following **clear** method into the `GraphView.m` file, after the @implementation directive but before the @end directive:

GraphView.m

```
// Display list maintenance
- (void)clear
{
    [displayList removeAllObjects];
    [self setNeedsDisplay:YES];
}
```

This **clear** method removes all of the objects from the displayList and then sends a message to itself indicating that the entire GraphView needs to be redisplayed.

33. Insert the following **addGraphElement:** method into `GraphView.m`:

GraphView.m

```
- (void)addGraphElement:(id)element
{
    [displayList addObject:element];
    [self setNeedsDisplayInRect:[element bounds]];
}
```

This method adds the element object argument to the display list, then invokes NSView's **setNeedsDisplayInRect:** method to tell the Graph-View's superclass that the region within the bounding box of the added element needs to be redrawn.

Scaling the GraphView and the drawRect: Method

As with PolygonView in the previous chapter, GraphView will use Quartz and the NSView architecture to provide all of the scaling that we need to draw our mathematical functions.

The only thing that our program needs to do is provide information for the required scaling. This will be done by the method **getFormAndScaleView**, which will read the current parameters from the on-screen window's form, set up the GraphView's instance variables, and then scale the GraphView's **bounds** to the appropriate size.

GraphView.m

34. Insert the following **getFormAndScaleView** method into GraphView.m:

```
- (void)getFormAndScaleView
{
    xmin = [xminCell doubleValue];
    xmax = [xmaxCell doubleValue];
    xstep = [xstepCell doubleValue];
    ymin = [yminCell doubleValue];
    ymax = [ymaxCell doubleValue];
    [self setBounds:(NSMakeRect(xmin, ymin, xmax-xmin, ymax-ymin) ) ];
    [self setNeedsDisplay:YES];
}
```

You might think that the **drawRect:** method, which we show in the next step, would be the workhorse of the GraphView class. After all, this method does all of the work of actually drawing the graph, right? But in fact, this method is very simple in GraphView. First it initializes the background color to white, then it determines an appropriate line width for drawing the graph and sets the current line width accordingly. (The default line width is 1 point, but because we will be rescaling the coordinate system of this NSView to match that of our graph, we need to calculate the "true" size of 1 point in our scaled coordinate system.) Finally, the **drawRect:** method iterates through all of the objects in the display list, determines whether or not they intersect the area that is being redrawn, and draws them if they do.

GraphView.m

35. Insert the following **isOpaque** and **drawRect:** methods into GraphView.m:

```
-(BOOL)isOpaque { return YES; }    // Because GraphView is opaque

-(void)drawRect:(NSRect )rect
{
    id obj=nil;
    NSEnumerator *en;
    NSSize sz;

    [ [NSColor whiteColor] set];
    NSRectFill(rect);

    sz = [self convertSize:NSMakeSize(1,1) fromView:nil];
    [NSBezierPath setDefaultLineWidth:MAX(sz.width,sz.height)];

    en = [displayList objectEnumerator];
    while (obj = [en nextObject]) {
        if (NSIntersectsRect(rect,[obj bounds]) ) {
            [obj stroke];
        }
    }
}
```

Note that for the first time we are using the **drawRect:** argument rect for more than simply drawing a rectangle: we use it to determine the intersection of GraphView and the object (line segment) to be drawn. The **drawRect:**

method that we constructed for the PolygonView class in the previous chapter drew the entire polygon every time the method was invoked. That was okay because drawing the polygon involved very few drawing operations, but when drawing complex images, it's wasteful to redraw the entire image—especially if you need to redraw only a tiny sliver of the image.

We'll use **drawRect:**'s rect argument to help us determine which part of the screen to redraw. rect is passed as an argument to the Cocoa function NSIntersectsRect( ), which provides a handy way to determine if rect and the new area to be drawn intersect.

NSIntersectsRect( ) is one of the many Cocoa utility rectangle functions. Similar functions will tell you if one rectangle contains another rectangle or a specified point, or if two rectangles are the same. The function NSUnionRect( ) will compute the smallest rectangle large enough to contain two other rectangles, while the function NSIntersectionRect( ) will compute the region of overlap.

That's it for the **drawRect:** method. This simple method is not only optimized to redraw the absolute minimum amount of the graph that's ever required; it will also handle printing, faxing, and generating PDF files.

The Data Stuffer Methods

The part of GraphView that sets up and uses the data stuffer thread consists of the following four methods:

- (void)**graph:**(id)*sender*
    Sets up global variables and starts the data stuffer thread.

- (void)**stopGraph:**(id)*sender*
    Lets a user interrupt the graph currently being drawn.

- (void)**sendData**
    The data stuffer method that will be executed in a separate thread by the NSThread class.

- (void)**doStop:**(int)*which*
    The common logic for stopping the graph and resetting the GUI. This method is invoked regardless of whether the graph stops normally or by user intervention.

36. Insert the lines shown here in bold into the **graph:** action method in GraphView.m:

GraphView.m

```
- (IBAction)graph:(id)sender
{
    // Set instance variables from the form
    [self getFormAndScaleView];
```

```
// Check the parameters of the graph
if (xmax < xmin || ymax < ymin) {
    NSRunAlertPanel( nil, @"Invalid min/max combination",
                     @"OK", nil, nil);
    return;
}

if ( xstep <= 0 ) {
    NSRunAlertPanel(0, @"The step size must be positive",
                    @"OK", nil, nil);
    return;
}

[self clear];

first = YES;
stop_sending = NO;
sending = YES;
receiving = YES;

[graphButton setTitle:@"Stop"];
[graphButton setAction:@selector(stopGraph:)];

[NSThread detachNewThreadSelector:@selector(sendData)
                         toTarget:self
                       withObject:nil];
}
```

The **graph:** action method first validates the values entered by the user for the graphing parameters xmin, xmax, ymin, ymax, and xstep. If these values are not acceptable, an alert panel is displayed and the method returns.

If the values are acceptable, the display list is cleared and the state variables are initialized. The statement first=YES sets the first instance variable so that the method that builds the graph will know that a new graph is being created. The statement stop_sending=NO resets the instance variable that is used to control the stuffer thread. The sending=YES and receiving=YES statements set toggles that will be used in the **doStop:** and **gotData:** methods described a bit later.

The **setTitle:** message changes the title of the on-screen button from "Graph" to "Stop". The related statement that follows changes the action method associated with the button from **graph:** to **stopGraph:**. If the user clicks the button when its title is "Stop", the **stopGraph:** message is sent to the GraphView. This is the way to rewire (change the connection in) an application while it is running. You can't do that in IB.

The last line in the **graph:** action method sends a message to the NSThread class to detach the stuffer thread. Although we haven't seen it yet, the thread starts up with the **sendData** message being sent to the same GraphView object that was previously running. The trick here, of course, is that the **sendData** method executes simultaneously with the rest of the GraphView object.

37. Insert the following **sendData** method into `GraphView.m`:

```objc
- (void)sendData
{
    NSAutoreleasePool *threadPool = [ [NSAutoreleasePool alloc] init];
    NSString *formula;
    double x;
    int i;

    formula = [formulaField stringValue];

    for (x=xmin; stop_sending==NO && x<=xmax; x+=xstep) {

        NSMutableString *fsend =
          [NSMutableString stringWithString:@"x,"];
        NSString *xString = [NSString stringWithFormat:@"%g",x];

        [fsend appendString:formula];
        [fsend appendString:@"\n"];

        // Now go through the formula and change every 'x' to a '%g'

        for (i=[fsend length]-1; i>=0; i--) {
            if ([fsend characterAtIndex:i] == 'x') {
                [fsend replaceCharactersInRange:NSMakeRange(i,1)
                                     withString:xString];
            }
        }

        // Send this to the other side
        [toEvaluator writeData:
                [fsend dataUsingEncoding:NSASCIIStringEncoding
                    allowLossyConversion:YES] ];
    }

    // Now send through the termination code
    [toEvaluator writeData:[@"999\n"
        dataUsingEncoding:NSASCIIStringEncoding
      allowLossyConversion:YES] ];

    [self doStop:STOP_SENDER];

    // Release the pool before the thread exits
    [threadPool release];
}
```

GraphView.m

The **sendData** method implements the entire stuffer thread, so it is understandably complicated (we hope that you'll find it understandable as well!). The first thing this thread does is set up its own NSAutoreleasePool. Each thread must have its own autorelease pool: it would do no good to have one thread's releasing another thread's data!

After the autorelease pool is set up, the **sendData** method makes a copy of the formula that is presently in the GraphView's formulaField. It then sets up a loop that will step the variable x from xmin to xmax by xstep (recall that these instance variables were set up by the message [**self getFormAndScaleView**] in the **graph:** method. Each time through the loop, the method creates a new NSMutableString that contains the formula that is to be solved. The x variables are then replaced with the current value of x. This algebraic formula is then sent to Evaluator.

When the loop finishes, the data stuffer sends the number 999 to Evaluator. This number is used as a flag to indicate that no more data is coming through the pipe. The procedure that constructs the graph will look for a 999 on a line by itself and will use that flag as its way of knowing that the graph is finished. The specific digits 999 really don't matter: what's important is that Evaluator is sent a line of data with one expression and no comma.

When the whole process is finished, the **doStop:** method is invoked with the argument STOP_SENDER to indicate that the stuffer has finished. Finally, the autorelease pool is released, which causes all of the temporary strings that were created to be freed.

Stopping a Running Graph

The **stopGraph:** method stops a running graph. It is invoked when the user clicks the Stop button ("Stop" replaces "Graph" as the button's title only when a graph is being drawn).

GraphView.m

38. Insert the line shown here in bold into the **stopGraph:** method in GraphView.m:

```
- (IBAction)stopGraph:(id)sender
{
    stop_sending = YES;
}
```

As part of its main loop, the data stuffer monitors the status of the stop_sending Boolean variable. When this variable is set to YES, the data stuffer immediately stops what it is doing and sends the termination code 999 to Evaluator.

The **doStop:** method is invoked twice, once when the stuffer stops sending, and again when Evaluator receives the stuffer's termination code, which is the last line that the stuffer sends prior to terminating.

GraphView.m

39. Insert the following **doStop:** method into GraphView.m:

```
- (void)doStop:(int)which
{
    switch (which) {
        case STOP_SENDER:
            sending = NO;
            break;
```

```
    case STOP_RECEIVER:
        receiving = NO;
        break;
}

if (sending==NO && receiving==NO) {  // Reinitialize
    [graphButton setTitle:@"Graph"];
    [graphButton setAction:@selector(graph:)];
    [graphButton setEnabled:YES];
}

if (sending==NO && receiving==YES) { // Wait for results data
    [graphButton setEnabled:FALSE];
    [graphButton setTitle:@"Waiting..."];
}

if (sending==YES && receiving==NO) { // A problem
    NSLog(@"Synchronization error");
}
}
```

This **doStop:** method controls the on-screen Graph button. When the user first clicks the Graph button, its label changes from "Graph" to "Stop". Pressing the button when it is labeled "Stop" causes the stop_sending flag to be set, as discussed earlier. But after the stuffer flag has finished sending its data, neither "Graph" nor "Stop" is really an appropriate setting for this button. Instead, there is a third mode: the button displays "Waiting…" and is disabled. At this point, the application is simply waiting for Evaluator to process all of the information that it has been sent and to return the calculated results.

The Graph Displayer

Now it's time to implement the method that receives data from Evaluator and constructs line segments that make up the graph.

40. Insert the following **gotData:** method into GraphView.m:

GraphView.m

```
- (void)gotData:(NSNotification *)not
{
    NSData      *data;
    NSString    *str;
    NSPoint     pt;
    int         num;
    NSString    *line=0;

    data = [ [not userInfo]
            objectForKey:NSFileHandleNotificationDataItem];
    str  = [ [NSString alloc] initWithData:data
                        encoding:NSASCIIStringEncoding];

    // Add the data to the end of the text buffer
    [fromBuf appendString:str];
```

```
                        // Register to get the notification again
                        [fromEvaluator readInBackgroundAndNotify];

                        // Now, process all complete lines we have
                        do {
                            NSRange r1;

                            r1 = [fromBuf rangeOfString:@"\n"];
                            if (r1.length<1) break;

                            line = [fromBuf substringToIndex:r1.location];
                            [fromBuf
                                    replaceCharactersInRange:NSMakeRange(0,r1.location+1)
                                                  withString:@""];

                            num = sscanf( [line cString], "%f, %f", &pt.x, &pt.y);
                            if (num!=2) {
                                [self doStop:STOP_RECEIVER];
                                return;
                            }

                            if (!first && !stop_sending) {
                                Segment *seg = [ [ [Segment alloc]
                                                      initFrom:lastPt to:pt ] autorelease];
                                [seg setTag:GRAPH_TAG];
                                [self addGraphElement:seg];
                            }

                            first = NO;              // No longer first
                            lastPt = pt;             // Remember this point

                        } while (line);
                        // End of data
                    }
```

This method is invoked whenever new data is available. Its main complication is that it needs to break the block of data it receives into individual lines. Each of these lines is then used to create a Segment object, and these objects are then added to the display list with the **addGraphElement:** method.

The reason for the line-by-line buffering is that Evaluator might send more than one line of data to the GraphView object before it is scheduled to read the data (because the data is being generated by a different execution thread). It might also send an incomplete line, due to blocking on the pipe. The GraphView object therefore needs to buffer the data that it receives and then read it out one line at a time.

Note that the **addBufToGraph:** method ignores the data it receives if the stop_sending instance variable is set to YES. This means that after the user clicks the Stop button all of the rest of the data in the pipeline is ignored, giving the application a nice snappy response time.

The **gotData:** method uses the `sscanf( )` function to turn the line of text from Evaluator back into numbers. If `num!=2`, then there were not two numbers separated by a comma to read; in this case, the method invokes the **stopGraph:** method and the graph stops.

If this data pair is the first data pair, the execution drops down to the last four lines. These lines set the instance variables `lastx` and `lasty` to be the coordinates of the current point, then unsets the first variable and returns.

On all data pairs other than the first, the middle section of this method gets executed. This conditional code first creates a Segment object (described in the next section) with endpoints at (`lastPt.x`, `lastPt.y`) and (`pt.x`, `pt.y`) and adds this segment to the display list.

This method also sets the tag of the segment to `GRAPH_TAG`. We'll use tags later to distinguish between different objects stored inside the display list.

The Segment Class

Although a GraphView object constructs graphs, it relies upon a Segment object to actually draw the lines that make up the graph. The GraphView object invokes two Segment instance methods:

bounds
> Returns a rectangle bounding the Segment's line

stroke
> Causes the Segment object to draw itself in the current view

By using a separate class that interacts with the GraphView class according to a well-defined protocol, we open up the possibility of adding new objects to the graph with very little work. To make the Segment class even more general, it supports a `tag` internal variable (which we'll use later, when we add more types of objects).

41. Choose PB's File → New File command, select Cocoa → Objective-C class, and click Next.

42. Name the file `Segment.m`. Leave the checkbox checked so that `Segment.h` is also created in the `~/GraphPaper` folder, GraphPaper project, and GraphPaper target. Click Finish.

43. Edit the `Segment.h` file so that it looks like the following:

```
#import <Cocoa/Cocoa.h>
#import "GraphView.h"

@interface Segment:NSObject <GraphViewElement>
{
    NSPoint     start;
    NSPoint     end;
```

Segment.h

```
            NSColor    *color;
            int         tag;
      }

      - initFrom:(NSPoint)start to:(NSPoint)end;
      - (NSPoint) segmentCenter;

      @end
```

The @interface directive with the angle brackets (<>) tells the Objective-C
compiler that Segment is a subclass of NSObject that follows the Graph-
ViewElement protocol, and thus that it must implement the six methods
declared previously in that protocol.

Segment.m

44. Edit the Segment.m file so that it looks like the following:

```
      #import "Segment.h"

      @implementation Segment

      - initFrom:(NSPoint)theStart to:(NSPoint)theEnd
      {
          [super init];              // Init the NSObject superclass

          start = theStart;
          end   = theEnd;
          color = [ [NSColor blackColor] retain];
          return self;
      }

      - (void)dealloc
      {
          [color release];  // Release what you retain
          [super dealloc];  // and dealloc the superclass
      }

      // Accessor methods
      - (int)tag       { return tag; }
      - (void)setTag:(int)aTag
      {
          tag = aTag;
      }

      - (void)setColor:(NSColor *)aColor
      {
          [color release];
          color = [aColor retain];
      }

      - (NSColor *)color
      {
          return color;
```

```
    // Methods that derive information for the caller
    - (NSRect)bounds
    {
        return NSMakeRect( MIN(start.x,end.x),
                           MIN(start.y,end.y),
                           fabs(start.x-end.x) + FLT_MIN,
                           fabs(start.y-end.y) + FLT_MIN );
    }

    - (NSPoint)segmentCenter
    {
        return NSMakePoint((start.x+end.x)/2.0, (start.y+end.y)/2.0);
    }

    - (void)stroke
    {
        [color set];
        [NSBezierPath strokeLineFromPoint:start toPoint:end];
    }

@end
```

The Segment class implementation is fairly straightforward. Notice that there is no bounds instance variable; instead, we calculate each segment's bounding box on demand from other instance variables and return what was calculated. This is known as *data hiding*—an object's internal representation of data does not have to be the same representation that is used by its accessor methods.

We use FLT_MIN in the **bounds** method so that lines that are vertical or horizontal will still have a width or height that is non-zero. FLT_MIN is the smallest floating-point number that the IEEE floating-point package can represent. By adding FLT_MIN to the calculated width and height, we guarantee that these values will not be zero. If they are computed to be a number that is larger than FLT_MIN—for example, the number 5—adding FLT_MIN will have no significant effect, as it's a very tiny value.

Testing GraphPaper

Now that we've built the interface, made the connections, and implemented all the classes, we're finally ready to make and test GraphPaper.

45. Build and run GraphPaper. Save all files first.

46. With GraphPaper running, click the Graph button. You'll see the graph of y=sin(3*x) over the x range [0,10], as shown in Figure 16-4. Because xstep=0.1, 100 line segments (steps) made up the graph of sin(3*x).

47. Change the value of xstep to 0.001 and click the Graph button again. This time, the graph of sin(3*x) will be displayed slowly, and the Graph button title will change to "Stop" and then a dimmed "Waiting...". Try clicking the Stop button.

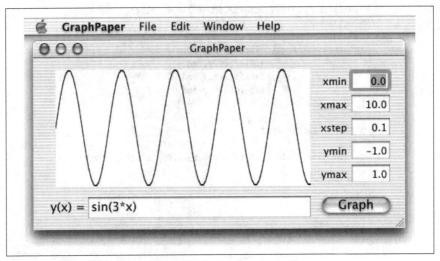

Figure 16-4. Graphing sin(3*x) with GraphPaper

48. Try graphing another function, such as x*cos(4*x), with a different step and ranges.

49. Try entering a negative value for xstep and click the Graph button. An alert should show up. Try entering min values greater than the max values, and you should get another alert.

50. Quit GraphPaper.

In Chapter 18, we'll clean up the GraphPaper application a bit and make it respond properly to resizing, and we'll arrange for the (x,y) coordinates of each point to be displayed as the mouse is moved over the graph. We'll finish off this chapter by showing how to add two different objects to GraphPaper's display list.

Extending the Display List

GraphView's display list and **drawRect:** method can easily be extended to draw objects other than graphs in the on-screen GraphView. In this section, we'll add axes and labels to the graph.

Adding Axes

Adding X and Y axes to GraphView is quite simple, because we already have the Segment class to draw the line. All we need to do to draw the axes is to create a new method that draws the axes and then arrange for it to be invoked by GraphView's **graph:** method.

1. Insert the following **addAxesFrom:to:** method declaration into GraphView.h:

   ```
   - (void)addAxesFrom:(NSPoint)pt1 to:(NSPoint)pt2;
   ```

2. Insert the following **addAxesFrom:to:** method implementation into GraphView.m:

   ```
   - (void)addAxesFrom:(NSPoint)pt1 to:(NSPoint)pt2
   {
       Segment *seg = [ [ [Segment alloc] initFrom:pt1 to:pt2] autorelease];
       [seg setTag:AXES_TAG];
       [self addGraphElement:seg];
   }
   ```

3. Insert the lines shown here in bold into the **graph:** method in GraphView.m:

   ```
   - (IBAction)graph:(id)sender
   {
       ...
       [self clear];

       // Display the axes
       [self addAxesFrom:NSMakePoint(xmin,0.0) to:NSMakePoint(xmax,0.0)];
       [self addAxesFrom:NSMakePoint(0.0,ymin) to:NSMakePoint(0.0,ymax)];
       ...
   ```

4. Build and run GraphPaper. Save all files first.

5. To see both the axes in GraphPaper, enter the values shown in Figure 16-5.

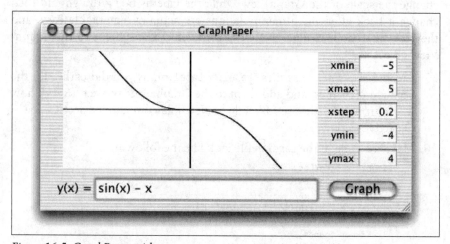

Figure 16-5. GraphPaper with axes

6. Try other functions and graphing parameters, and then Quit GraphPaper.

When the first data point comes through, the new statements in the **graph:** method create two Segment objects that correspond to the X and Y axes. The tags for each of these objects are set to 1. The axis lines are added to the display list, and then the graph is displayed. The window in Figure 16-5 shows what the graph looks like with axes. We set the tag to AXES_TAG so that we can distinguish these segments from the segments used to draw the graph itself. This distinction will be important in Chapter 18, when we want to make the graph segments (but not the axes) sensitive to mouseovers.

Adding Labeling

In addition to axes, we can add a function label fairly easily by creating a Label class that responds to the same **bounds** and **stroke** methods as the Segment class. Because Objective-C uses dynamic binding—where messages are resolved when they are sent, rather than when the program is compiled—we won't need to make any changes to GraphView's **drawRect:** method. Label objects will be stored in the display list, along with the Segment objects. Label objects must have their own initialization methods, however, because line segments and text labels need to be set up in different ways.

As we'll see, drawing text also represents an interesting problem: the Quartz fonts assume that they are drawing on a grid with a square scale—that is, they assume that the scale on the X axis is the same as the scale on the Y axis. It's possible to override this assumption by providing a two-dimensional transformation matrix when creating the font. However, it's easier to change the scale of the GraphView while the label is being drawn and then change it back after. Such manipulations are actually remarkably easy, and they can be done in a manner that is completely transparent to the GraphView object itself.

7. Create new Label class files (Label.h, Label.m), as you did earlier for the Segment class files, and add them to the GraphPaper project. (Recall how we did it before: choose PB's File → New File command, select Cocoa → Objective-C class, etc.).

8. Make the code in the Label.h file look like the following code:

```
#import <Cocoa/Cocoa.h>
#import "GraphView.h"

@interface Label:NSObject <GraphViewElement>
{
    NSRect bounds;
    NSMutableAttributedString *text;
    NSColor             *color;
    int                 tag;
    NSFont              *font;
    NSMutableDictionary *dict;
}

- initRect:(NSRect)bounds text:(NSString *)aText size:(float)aSize;
@end
```

Label.h

Notice that this interface is very similar to the interface used by Segment. In particular, it adopts the GraphViewElement protocol. The main difference is that the two objects use different initialization methods, as of course they must. The Label class implementation is a bit more complicated than the Segment class implementation. It starts out with the **initRect:text:size:** method, which we show in the next step.

9. Make the code in the Label.m file look like the following (incomplete) code:

Label.m

```
#import "Label.h"

@implementation Label
- initRect:(NSRect)aBounds text:(NSString *)aText size:(float)aSize
{
    [super init];
    bounds = aBounds;

    font = [NSFont fontWithName:@"Times-Roman" size:aSize];
    dict = [ [NSMutableDictionary alloc] init];
    [dict setObject:font forKey:NSFontAttributeName];

    text = [ [NSMutableAttributedString alloc]
                initWithString:aText attributes:dict];
    [self  setColor:[NSColor blackColor] ];
    return self;
}
```

This **initRect:text:size:** method sets the bounds of the Label object. It then creates an NSMutableAttributedString that will draw centered text in Times Roman in the requested point size.

Because the Label class uses the **alloc** method to create the NSMutableDictionary and the NSMutableAttributedString, these objects must be released when the Label object itself is freed. This is done by the **dealloc** method.

10. Insert the following **dealloc** method into Label.m:

Label.m

```
- (void)dealloc
{
    [dict release]
    [text release];
    [super dealloc];
}
```

The following **setColor:**, **bounds**, **tag**, and **setTag:** accessor methods provide access to these values of the Label class from outside. Notice that the Label class's implementation of **setColor:** is completely different from the Segment class's. In particular, Label's **setColor:** method adds the color to the attribute dictionary and then reapplies the attribute to the attributed string. Then, because of a bug in the AppKit (present in Cocoa 10.1), this implementation reapplies the NSCenterTextAlignment to the string.

This is an example of a case where the structure of the AppKit makes it easy to work around some bugs or limitations in the existing Cocoa release.

Label.m

11. Insert the following five methods into Label.m:

```
- (NSRect)bounds          { return bounds;}
- (int)tag                { return tag;}
- (void)setTag:(int)aTag  { tag=aTag;}

- (void)setColor:(NSColor *)aColor
{
    [dict setObject:aColor forKey:NSForegroundColorAttributeName];
    [text setAttributes:dict range:NSMakeRange(0,[text length])];

    // Now reapply the alignment because of a Cocoa bug
    [text setAlignment:NSCenterTextAlignment
                range:NSMakeRange(0,[text length])];
}

- (NSColor *)color {return color;}
```

Finally, the Label class implements a **stroke** method to generate the Quartz commands necessary to display the label.

Label.m

12. Insert the following **stroke** method and @end directive into Label.m:

```
// This works, but it requires a subview
- (void)stroke
{
    NSView *fv = [NSView focusView];
    NSView *tempView;

    tempView = [ [NSView alloc] initWithFrame:bounds];

    [fv addSubview:tempView];

    // Scale the tempView to screen coordinates
    [tempView setBounds:
            [tempView convertRect:[self bounds] toView:nil] ];

    [tempView lockFocus];
    [color set];
    [text drawInRect:[tempView bounds] ];
    [tempView unlockFocus];
    [tempView removeFromSuperviewWithoutNeedingDisplay];
}

@end
```

This method is pretty wacky, and we had hoped to replace it with a better one before this book was published. The problem here is that the GraphView usually has a nonsquare transformation, but Quartz provides few mechanisms for drawing fonts with nonsquare transformations. To get around this limitation, this method first creates a new NSView in the area in the GraphView where the label is to be drawn. This view is then scaled so that its coordinate system matches that of the NSWindow it contains. We then lock focus on this view, draw the label, unlock the focus, and remove the view from the superview using a method that prevents the superview from being redisplayed. This works and is reasonably fast, but it would be better to use the NSAffineTransformation and NSGraphicsContext classes. So far, though, we haven't been able to get them to work. If you figure out how, please send us email, and we'll post the solution on the O'Reilly web site.

Using the Label Class

To use this new class, we'll need to make several changes to GraphView.m. First we need to import the new Label class into the GraphView class, and then we need to make another modification to the **graph:** method.

13. Insert the #import statement shown here in bold into GraphView.m:

```
#import "GraphView.h"
#import "Segment.h"
#import "Label.h"

@implementation GraphView
```

GraphView.m

14. Insert the new statements shown here in bold into the **graph:** method in GraphView.m:

```
...
// Add the axes
[self addAxesFrom:NSMakePoint(xmin,0.0) to:NSMakePoint(xmax,0.0)];
[self addAxesFrom:NSMakePoint(0.0,ymin) to:NSMakePoint(0.0,ymax)];

// Add a label
{
    Label *label = [ [Label alloc]
    initRect:NSMakeRect(xmin, ymin, xmax-xmin, (ymax-ymin)*.2)
        text:[formulaField stringValue]
        size:24.0];

    [label autorelease];
    [label setTag:LABEL_TAG];
    [self addGraphElement:label];
}
...
```

GraphView.m

Notice that we inserted a new block of code so that we can have a local variable called label that is limited in scope to these statements.

15. Build and run GraphPaper. Save all files first.

16. Enter a function and ranges, as shown in Figure 16-1 at the beginning of this chapter, and then click the Graph button to see the function label.

17. Play around with GraphPaper and then quit.

Summary

Wow, we've really done a lot in this chapter! In the first half of the chapter, we got a taste of multithreaded programming in Mach by creating an application with two execution threads—one that sends data to a back end program and another that reads the resulting values. In the second half, we learned how to draw a picture by building a display list of objects, each of which knows how to draw itself.

In the next chapter, we'll see how GraphView's modular design makes it easy to add new functionality to the class. In particular, we'll see how to add color by subclassing the GraphView class and overriding some of its methods.

Exercises

1. What happens if the **autorelease** message is not sent to the Segment and Label objects? Will the program still work if the message is taken out?

2. Make the GraphView draw the graph when a formula is typed and the user hits Return (instead of clicking the Graph button).

3. Instead of being implemented as a formal protocol, GraphViewElement could have been implemented as an abstract parent class of both Segment and Label. (We didn't implement the classes with a common parent class because we wanted to show how to create and implement a protocol.) If we had used a common parent class, we could have factored the common code out of the Segment and Label classes and put it into the parent class.

   Reimplement the Segment and Label classes with a common parent class. Explain the advantages and disadvantages of this approach versus the formal protocol approach. Is one of the approaches better than the other? Why or why not? Can you imagine a situation in which you would want to use both a common parent class and a protocol in the same application?

4. When the width of the bounds does not equal the height, the line drawing is not square—that is, horizontal lines will not have the same thickness as vertical lines. Explain why this is so, and reimplement GraphView and Segment so that drawing is always square. (Hint: Try this using the same coordinate-transformation technique that the Label class uses.)

5. Our GraphView class needs a **dealloc** method that properly releases all of the allocated and retained objects, as well as providing other general-purpose cleanup. Write it. Will your **dealloc** method ever be called in the GraphPaper application? If not, why write it?

References

Multithreading:

```
http://developer.apple.com/techpubs/macosx/Cocoa/TasksAndConcepts/
ProgrammingTopics/Multithreading/index.html
```

CHAPTER 17

Color

Although we have used color in most of our examples, we have used it in only a cursory fashion—just black and white. That might have been fine back in the 1980s and early 1990s, when lots of people still had monochrome displays, but these days almost every computer has a full-color display. As you might expect, Cocoa's Quartz drawing environment makes drawing in color beautiful and easy.

Colors and Color Objects

Cocoa colors have two components: color and alpha. *Color* is the way that the color looks when it is displayed on an empty background. *Alpha* is a measure of the color's *transparency*—it tells Quartz how to blend a color with the colors already present in the background when the color is displayed. Alpha is measured on a scale from 0.0 to 1.0. An alpha of 0.0 is completely transparent; an alpha of 1.0 is opaque (nothing shows through it).

Cocoa enables you to specify the color using several different models, called *color spaces*. As with most computer systems, one option is to specify values for the amount of red, green, and blue (RGB). RGB is an *additive color model*—the colors are added together like colored lights (mix them all in equal amounts and you get white). Alternatively, you can specify a color by specifying a hue, saturation, and brightness (HSB). You can also specify the amount of cyan, yellow, magenta, and black (CMYK) "inks" to mix at any point. CMYK is called a *subtractive color model* because the colors are subtracted from white; mix them all and you get a muddy brown. CMYK colors are device-dependent.

Cocoa also allows the user to specify colors by name. Apple supplies a predefined set of names, but other organizations can make color lists available as well. For instance, Pantone's ColorWeb Pro makes Pantone colors available for Mac OS X. On black-and-white devices, such as laser printers, colors are automatically mapped to corresponding shades of gray by the Quartz system.

Colors from a Programmer's Point of View

Internally, Cocoa represents color with the NSColor class. This class provides a large number of class methods for creating NSColor objects. Mac OS X Version 10.1 provides the following named colors as NSColor objects:

+ blackColor	+ darkGrayColor	+ orangeColor
+ blueColor	+ grayColor	+ purpleColor
+ brownColor	+ greenColor	+ redColor
+ clearColor	+ lightGrayColor	+ whiteColor
+ cyanColor	+ magentaColor	+ yellowColor

Cocoa also provides the following class methods for creating colors using one of several color models:

```
+ (NSColor *)colorWithCalibratedHue:(float)hue
                        saturation:(float)saturation
                        brightness:(float)brightness
                             alpha:(float)alpha;

+ (NSColor *)colorWithCalibratedRed:(float)red
                             green:(float)green
                              blue:(float)blue
                             alpha:(float)alpha;

+ (NSColor *)colorWithCalibratedWhite:(float)white
                               alpha:(float)alpha;

+ (NSColor *)colorWithCatalogName:(NSString *)listName
                        colorName:(NSString *)colorName;

+ (NSColor *)colorWithDeviceCyan:(float)cyan
                         magenta:(float)magenta
                          yellow:(float)yellow
                           black:(float)black
                           alpha:(float)alpha;

+ (NSColor *)colorWithDeviceHue:(float)hue
                     saturation:(float)saturation
                     brightness:(float)brightness
                          alpha:(float)alpha;

+ (NSColor *)colorWithDeviceRed:(float)red
                          green:(float)green
                           blue:(float)blue
                          alpha:(float)alpha;

+ (NSColor *)colorWithDeviceWhite:(float)white
                            alpha:(float)alpha;
```

Colors can be copied to and from the pasteboard (or clipboard). You can use the instance methods to learn the components of each color. See the NSColor documentation for details.

Colors from a User's Point of View

Mac OS X gives users a variety of options for choosing colors through a standard interface called the *Colors panel* (or dialog), an instance object of the NSColorPanel class. (We'll use the term "panel" in this chapter in deference to the name of the class.) The Colors panel enables the user to specify a color (or shade of gray) using any of the color models mentioned earlier. The panel also lets the user set the amount of alpha (transparency) used by each color. Figure 17-1 contains the Color Wheel, Color Palettes, and Image Palettes views of the Colors panel.

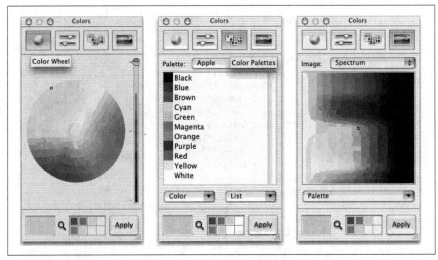

Figure 17-1. Saturated green shown in three different panes in the Colors panel

The buttons in the toolbar of the Colors panel change the model that the panel uses to display colors. If you select a color and then change the color model, you can see how the same color is represented in the different color models. For example, in the Colors panel on the left in Figure 17-2, we chose fully saturated green in RGB mode. Then we clicked two buttons below the toolbar to see the corresponding representations of saturated green in the CMYK and HSB modes, as shown in the middle and right screen shots in Figure 17-2. Unfortunately, it's hard to display a good "green" in a monochrome book—you'll have to play with the Colors panel on a Mac OS X system to get a good feel for it.

The space along the bottom of the Colors panel is a holding area for eight colors. You can drag a color "chip" from the color well in the lower-left corner of the panel into the holding area. You can also drag colors directly into applications. Pressing the button with the magnifying glass icon near the bottom of the Colors panel allows you to steal a color from anywhere else on the screen. Try it—it's fun!

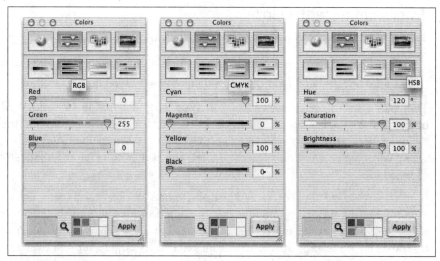

Figure 17-2. Saturated green shown in three different color models

The Colors panel works closely with another Cocoa class, called the NSColor-Well. The NSColorWell icon from Interface Builder's Cocoa-Views palette is shown at the edge of the page. If you press the mouse in an NSColorWell instance and drag it away, you'll take a little dab of color, called a *color chip*, with you (see Figure 17-3). Every NSColorWell has a color; you can change its color by dragging a color chip from a different NSColorWell and dropping it inside.

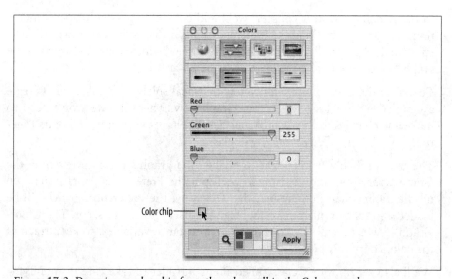

Figure 17-3. Dragging a color chip from the color well in the Colors panel

Programming with Color

To add color to our GraphPaper application, we need to do two things:

- Give the user a way to specify a color.
- Modify our drawing methods so that color is displayed in the window.

The easiest way to let a user specify a color is by placing an NSColorWell object in your application. If a user clicks the *border* of an NSColorWell, the Colors panel is displayed. The Colors panel is "linked" to the NSColorWell— when you change the color on the panel, the well's color is automatically changed too.

Both the NSColorPanel object and the NSColorWell object support Cocoa's target/action paradigm. Normally, they send action messages to their targets when their colors are changed. But if you send the NSColorWell the **setContinuous:TRUE** message, it will send a message to its target over and over as a slider is moved. This lets the user watch the drawing change color as she moves the Colors panel sliders. The receiver of the action message from the NSColorWell can find out which color was selected by sending the NSColorWell a **color** message, which returns the well's NSColor structure. Sending the **set** instance method to an NSColor object causes that color to become the current drawing color for any NSView.

Adding Color to GraphPaper

In the remainder of this chapter, we'll add color to our GraphPaper application. To do this, we'll add a Preferences panel (users refer to it as a Preferences dialog) that will let the user choose three distinct colors for drawing the graph, the equation, and the axes.

To isolate the parts of the GraphView that deal solely with color, we'll create a GraphView subclass called ColorGraphView. This way, we won't need to make any changes to the GraphView class itself, yet we can use all of its functionality. This is called *reusability* of classes.

The user probably won't want to change the graph's colors every time the GraphPaper application is run, so we'll put the Preferences panel in its own nib file rather than in MainMenu.nib. That way, the Preferences panel will be loaded and take up memory only when the user chooses to see it. The ColorGraphView class will have three NSColor instance variables, to keep track of the colors currently being used.

We'll also set up a new class called PrefController to take care of modifying these instance variables when the Preferences panel is displayed. If the Preferences panel isn't loaded, the ColorGraphView class will use reasonable defaults for the color instance variables. In Chapter 21, we'll see how to set the values for these colors from the Mac OS X defaults database, application-defaults information stored in every user's ~/Library/Preferences folder. (The application's defaults database was introduced in Chapter 2).

Creating a Preferences Panel

A Preferences panel is a panel that an application provides to let users change preferences and configuration options. It gives the user an easy way to read the contents of the defaults database for his particular application and to make modifications. Every configuration or installation option that your program supports should be settable via the Preferences panel.

Preferences panels can be simple or complex; usually, there is little correlation between the complexity of a program's Preferences panel and the complexity of the program itself. However, you should try to keep the number of options in your application's Preferences panel under control. When in doubt, let ease of use be your guide.

In the upcoming sections, we'll make a simple Preferences panel for setting the colors of the graph, the axes, and the function in GraphPaper. This panel won't be fully functional, though, because it will be missing the OK and Revert buttons for saving the Preferences information into the defaults database. We'll add those in Chapter 21.

First we'll create a Controller class for our application, which will act as a central coordinator of the activity of the GraphView object and the Preferences panel. Contrast this with the PrefController class, which will control only the preferences in GraphPaper.

The Controller Class

As with most Cocoa applications, the purpose of GraphPaper's Controller class will be to load nibs and provide a central means for finding the ids of important objects. It won't be a very complicated class, but it will be very important.

We'll set up the Controller object so that it is the NSApp delegate. The delegate outlet will make it possible for any object in our application to get the id of the GraphView instance (pointed to by graphView) by evaluating the following message:

```
[ [NSApp delegate] graphView]
```

Putting accessor methods in classes when you design them is good programming practice. We're just planning ahead.

To have the Preferences panel in its own nib, we will also need to arrange for the Controller class to load the nib on demand. We'll use code similar to that we used in previous chapters to load the About box nib on demand.

Project Builder

1. Open your GraphPaper project in Project Builder and the `MainMenu.nib` file in IB.

2. Subclass the NSObject class in IB (Classes → Subclass NSObject) and rename the new class "Controller".

3. Add an outlet called `graphView` to the Controller class in the Controller Info dialog.

4. Add another outlet, called `prefController`, to the Controller class.

5. Add an action method called **showPrefs:** to the Controller class.

6. Create the files for the Controller class (Classes → Create Files for Controller) and insert the new class files to the GraphPaper project.

7. Instantiate the Controller class (Classes → Instantiate Controller). A new icon labeled "Controller" will show up in the Instances pane of the `MainMenu.nib` window.

8. Make the Controller the File's Owner's delegate by Control-dragging from the File's Owner icon to the Controller icon and double-clicking delegate in the File's Owner Info dialog.

9. Connect the Controller's `graphView` outlet to the on-screen GraphView instance in GraphPaper's main window.

Controller.h

10. Insert the `@class` directive and **graphView** method declaration shown here in bold into `Controller.h`:

```
#import <Cocoa/Cocoa.h>

@class GraphView;
@interface Controller : NSObject
{
    IBOutlet id graphView;
    IBOutlet id prefController;
}
- (IBAction)showPrefs:(id)sender;
- (GraphView *)graphView;
@end
```

The `@class` directive allows the Controller class to declare that it returns an object of the GraphView type without including the whole GraphView class definition.

Controller.m

11. Insert the lines shown here in bold into `Controller.m`:

```
#import "Controller.h"
#import "GraphView.h"

@implementation Controller
```

```
- (GraphView *)graphView
{
    return graphView;
}

- (IBAction)showPrefs:(id)sender
{
    if (!prefController) {
        [NSBundle loadNibNamed:@"Preferences.nib" owner:self];
    }
    [ [prefController window] makeKeyAndOrderFront:sender];
}

@end
```

Controller may appear to be a gratuitous class—why not just make the GraphView instance the delegate of the NSApp object? The answer will become clear as we add more features to the GraphPaper application: having a separate Controller object will make it easier to add new functionality.

The prefController outlet will be initialized to point to a PrefController object (which will control the Preferences panel) that we'll create in the next section. The **showPrefs:** action will be invoked in response to a user's choosing GraphPaper → Preferences and will pass the request along to the PrefController object through the prefController outlet.

The first time the **showPrefs:** action method is invoked, it will load Preferences.nib. Every time the **showPrefs:** action method is invoked, it asks the prefController for the id of its window and then exposes the window with the **makeKeyAndOrderFront:** message.

12. Back in IB, Control-drag from the MainMenu.nib application menu item GraphPaper → Preferences to the Controller instance (see Figure 17-4).

Interface Builder

13. Connect the GraphPaper → Preferences menu cell to the Controller instance so that it sends the **showPrefs:** action message, as shown in Figure 17-4.

14. Save MainMenu.nib and minimize the MainMenu.nib window by clicking its yellow minimize button (working with two on-screen nibs in IB can be confusing).

Creating the Preferences Nib, Panel, and PrefController

The Preferences panel will be loaded by a PrefController object in response to the user's choosing the GraphPaper → Preferences menu command. In this section we'll set up the nib and create the PrefController class. These next few steps all refer to the file Preferences.nib, not to MainMenu.nib.

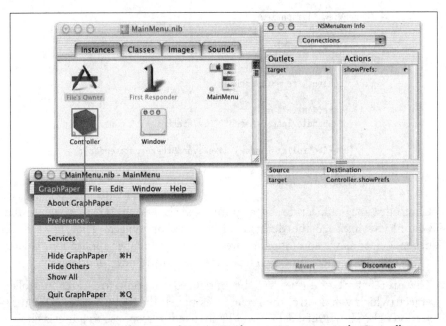

Figure 17-4. Connection from GraphPaper's Preferences Menu item to the Controller

15. Choose IB's File → New command and then choose Cocoa → Empty from the resulting Starting Point panel.

16. Save the new nib module in the `Preferences.nib` file in GraphPaper's `English.lproj` folder and add it to the GraphPaper target.

Controller.h

17. Read (parse) the definition of the Controller class (Classes → Read Files) by reading the declarations in `Controller.h`. The Controller class should appear as a subclass of the NSObject class, and thus `Preferences.nib` should now know about the Controller class.

18. Change the class of `Preferences.nib`'s File's Owner to the Controller class. To do this, select the File's Owner icon under the Instances tab in the `Preferences.nib` window, type Command-1, and then change the class of the File's Owner from NSObject to Controller.

19. Subclass the NSObject class again (Classes → Subclass NSObject) and rename the new class "PrefController".

20. Add these four outlets and two actions to the PrefController class:

Outlets	Action Methods
graphColorWell	okay:
axesColorWell	revert:
labelColorWell	
window	

Don't worry about the **revert:** and **okay:** actions now; we won't use them until Chapter 21.

21. Create the files for the PrefController class (Classes → Create Files for PrefController) and insert the new class files to the GraphPaper project.

22. Instantiate the Controller class (Classes → Instantiate PrefController). A new icon labeled "PrefController" will show up in the Instances pane of the `Preferences.nib` window.

23. Connect the `prefController` outlet in the File's Owner (Controller) object to the PrefController instance in the `Preferences.nib` window.

24. Set up a Preferences panel in `Preferences.nib` that looks like the one in Figure 17-5. To do this, drag a Panel icon from IB's Cocoa-Windows palette and drop it on the desktop. Rename it "Preferences". Then drag three NSColorWells from the Cocoa-Other palette and three Message Text icons from the Cocoa-Views palette and drop them all in the new panel. Use IB's blue guidelines and the Layout → Alignment menu command to align these objects. Then choose Layout → Group In → Box to get the boundary (Box) and rename it "Colors", as shown in Figure 17-5.

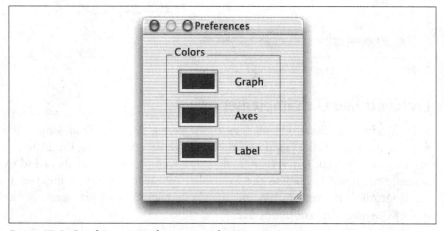

Figure 17-5. GraphPaper's Preferences panel in IB

25. Set the tag of the NSColorWell labeled "Graph" to "1" (make sure you set the tag on the NSColorWell and not the text label).

26. Set the tag of the NSColorWell labeled "Axes" to "2".

27. Set the tag of the NSColorWell labeled "Label" to "3".

28. Connect each color-well outlet in PrefController to the appropriate NSColorWell object in the Preferences panel. Be sure that you are connecting to the NSColorWell object and not to the labels! See Figure 17-6 for the `labelColorWell` outlet connection.

29. Connect PrefController's `window` outlet to the Preferences panel's title bar.

30. Save `Preferences.nib`.

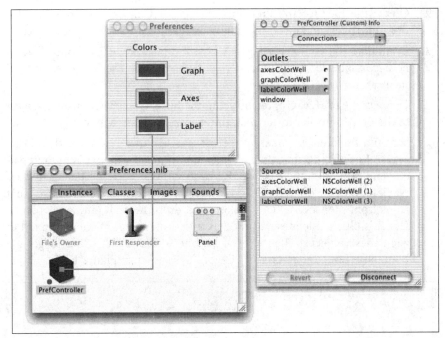

Figure 17-6. Connecting PrefController outlets to color wells

PrefController Class Implementation

A PrefController object will manage the Preferences panel. Following is the implementation of the **awakeFromNib** method and the method that it invokes (**setUpWell:**) to set up each color well. In addition, the **window** accessor method is added so the Controller can send a **window** message to PrefController to get the id of the Preferences panel to send it the **makeKeyAndOrderFront:** message.

Project Builder

PrefController.h

31. Back in PB, insert the three method declarations shown here in bold into PrefController.h:

```
#import <Cocoa/Cocoa.h>

@interface PrefController : NSObject
{
    IBOutlet id axesColorWell;
    IBOutlet id graphColorWell;
    IBOutlet id labelColorWell;
    IBOutlet id window;
}
- (IBAction)okay:(id)sender;
- (IBAction)revert:(id)sender;

- (NSWindow *)window;
```

```
- (void)setUpWell:(NSColorWell *)well;
- (NSColorWell *)colorWellForTag:(int)aTag;

@end
```

32. Insert these two #import directives into PrefController.m:

```
#import "Controller.h"
#import "ColorGraphView.h"
```

PrefController.m

33. Insert the following two method implementations into PrefController.m:

```
- (NSWindow *)window
{
    return window;
}

- (void)setUpWell:(NSColorWell *)well
{
    id colorGraphView = [ [NSApp delegate] graphView] ;

    [well setTarget:colorGraphView];
    [well setAction:@selector(setObjectsToColor:) ];
    [well setColor:[colorGraphView colorForTag:[well tag]] ];
}
```

The **setUpWell:** method arranges for the NSColorWell to send the **setObjects-ToColor:** action message (described later) directly to the ColorGraphView target object. It gets the ColorGraphView id (graphView) by sending the **graphView** accessor message to the Controller (NSApp's delegate). This allows us to overcome Cocoa's apparent inability to send messages between nibs. In fact, it's easy to send messages between objects that are in different nibs—you just can't wire it up graphically using IB.

After the NSColorWell's action and target are set, the **setUpWell:** method goes to the colorGraphView, asks for the color that is associated with the particular tag, and then sets the NSColorWell to be this color. We'll implement the **colorForTag:** method later in this chapter.

34. Insert the following **awakeFromNib** method implementation into PrefController.m:

PrefController.m

```
- (void)awakeFromNib
{
    [ [NSColorPanel sharedColorPanel] setContinuous:YES];

    [self setUpWell:axesColorWell ];
    [self setUpWell:labelColorWell ];
    [self setUpWell:graphColorWell ];
}
```

The Application Kit uses a single NSColorPanel object for each running application. The method [**NSColorPanel sharedInstance:YES**] returns the id of that shared instance; if the Colors panel hasn't been created yet, it gets created.

PrefController's **awakeFromNib** method first creates a shared Colors panel, then sets the continuous flag for the Colors panel. It is necessary to set the continuous flags in both the color well and the Colors panel if you want a color well to automatically send a message to its target as the color on the Colors panel is changed. The **awakeFromNib** method also invokes the **setUp-Well:** method for each of the three color wells.

Finally, we will add a method that will allow other objects to obtain the id of an NSColorWell on the Preferences panel by specifying the tag. Because all of the color wells are subviews of the window's content view, this is easy.

PrefController.m

35. Insert the following method implementation for the **colorWellForTag:** method into PrefController.m:

```
-(NSColorWell *)colorWellForTag:(int)aTag
{
    return [ [window contentView] viewWithTag:aTag];
}
```

ColorGraphView

In this section we'll create the ColorGraphView class, which knows how to draw a graph in color and how to change the colors of the objects in the display list. The ColorGraphView class will have two jobs: managing the drawing of the graph in color, and changing the colors of objects in the display list when requested.

Interface Builder

36. Back in IB, open (or maximize) the MainMenu.nib file if it is not already open. (Make sure that you are no longer working in Preferences.nib by minimizing it.)

37. Subclass the GraphView class (which itself is a subclass of NSView) in the MainMenu.nib file. Rename the new class "ColorGraphView".

38. Change the class of the on-screen GraphView instance in GraphPaper's main window to ColorGraphView in the Info dialog (Command-1).

    Changing the class of GraphView to ColorGraphView shouldn't break any of the connections we made with GraphView. However, if you inadvertently changed the class to one that didn't implement the **graph:** action (such as NSView), IB may have broken the Graph button's connection. If this or any other connection was broken, reconnect it.

39. Add a new action called **setObjectsToColor:** to ColorGraphView.

    Note that because GraphView is ColorGraphView's superclass, its outlets and actions show up as dimmed, uneditable text in the Info dialog.

40. Create the files for the ColorGraphView class and insert the new class files to the GraphPaper project.

41. Insert the lines shown here in bold into `ColorGraphView.h`:

```
#import <Cocoa/Cocoa.h>
#import "GraphView.h"

@interface ColorGraphView : GraphView
{
    NSColor *axesColor;
    NSColor *graphColor;
    NSColor *labelColor;
}
- (NSColor *)colorForTag:(int)aTag;
- (void)setObjectsToColor:(NSColor *)theColor forTag:(int)aTag;
- (void)addGraphElement:(id)element;
- (IBAction)setObjectsToColor:(id)sender;

@end
```

ColorGraphView.h

The `axesColor`, `graphColor`, and `labelColor` instance variables will store the current colors for the axes, graph, and label, respectively. The color wells in the Preferences panel will send the **setObjectsToColor:** message to tell the ColorGraphView when the user wants to change the color of the axes, graph, or label (the **setObjectsToColor** method was referenced in **setUpWell:** and will be implemented later). This method, in turn, will invoke the **setObjects-ToColor:forTag:** method, which will cause ColorGraphView to change the colors of all of the objects in the display list that have a matching tag. The **colorForTag:** method returns the color of the particular NSColor that matches the provided tag.

The ColorGraphView Class Implementation

The ColorGraphView implementation isn't very complicated, because most of the work of actually drawing the graph is done in the GraphView class. The only thing the ColorGraphView class has to manage is the color of the newly drawn objects on the graph, as well as changing the colors of existing objects when the user changes a color in one of the color wells in the Colors panel.

42. Insert the following `#import` directives into `ColorGraphView.m`:

```
#import "Segment.h"
#import "Label.h"
```

ColorGraphView.m

The key definitions that we need for color are contained in Cocoa's `NSColorWell.h` and `NSColorPanel.h` files. It's a good idea to look briefly at these files, as well as at `NSColor.h`, to learn the basic structures, constants, and methods Cocoa provides for handling color. All of these files can be viewed using PB's Find pane.

The first two methods in the following ColorGraphView class implementation provide for the basic mapping between tags and the three color-containing instance variables in ColorGraphView. The **colorForTag:** method takes a tag and returns the matching color instance variable. The **setObjectsToColor: forTag:** method sets the appropriate instance variable to be the passed-in color. It then goes through the entire display list, finds all of the elements with matching tags, and sets their colors as well.

43. Insert the following two method implementations into ColorGraphView.m:

ColorGraphView.m

```
- (NSColor *)colorForTag:(int)aTag
{
    switch (aTag) {
      case AXES_TAG:    return axesColor;
      case GRAPH_TAG:   return graphColor;
      case LABEL_TAG:   return labelColor;
    }
    return nil;         // no color?
}


- (void)setObjectsToColor:(NSColor *)theColor forTag:(int)aTag
{
    NSEnumerator *en;
    id obj=nil;

    // First set the correct instance variable
    switch (aTag) {
      case AXES_TAG:
        [axesColor release];
        axesColor = [theColor retain];
        break;

      case GRAPH_TAG:
        [graphColor release];
        graphColor = [theColor retain];
        break;

      case LABEL_TAG:
        [labelColor release];
        labelColor = [theColor retain];
        break;
    }

    // Now set the elements in the display list
    en = [displayList objectEnumerator];
    while (obj = [en nextObject]) {
        if ([obj tag]==aTag) {
            [obj setColor:theColor];
            [self setNeedsDisplayInRect:[obj bounds] ];
        }
    }
}
```

When new objects are added to the display list, their colors must be set in accordance with their tags. We can set the colors quite simply by overriding

GraphView's **addGraphElement:** method. Notice that our implementation of this method uses the **colorForTag:** method to find out what the color for the passed-in element should be.

44. Insert the following **addGraphElement:** method implementation into ColorGraphView.m:

ColorGraphView.m

```
- (void)addGraphElement:(id)element
{
    // Set the color to match the request
    [element setColor:[self colorForTag:[element tag]] ];

    // Add the element to the display list
    [super addGraphElement:element];
}
```

As this example shows, part of a good class design is being able to easily change or enhance functionality by subclassing.[*]

These three methods are all that are necessary to display newly drawn graphs in the colors requested by the user. But if you want to respond to color-change requests from the user, we will need one more method.

Setting the Colors

When the user changes a color using an NSColorWell object, the NSColorWell sends the **setObjectsToColor:** action to the ColorGraphView object (the target and action were set up in PrefController's **setUpWell:** method). The **setObjectsToColor:** method in ColorGraphView needs to change the value of the appropriate color instance variable as well as the elements in the display list. We'll use the NSColorWell's tag instance variable to figure out which NSColorWell sent the message. (Recall that we set each color well to have a different tag.)

45. Insert the following **setObjectsToColor:** method implementation into ColorGraphView.m:

ColorGraphView.m

```
- (IBAction)setObjectsToColor:(id)sender
{
    [self setObjectsToColor:[sender color] forTag:[sender tag] ];
}
```

---

[*] An earlier version of the GraphView class that is not shown in this book didn't have a separate method for adding graph elements to the display list. Instead, there was duplicate code throughout the GraphView class for manipulating the display list. Not only was this version of the program longer, but it also proved to be impossible to add color to that version of GraphView without making changes to the GraphView class itself (i.e., subclassing didn't work). The new version of GraphView—the one we showed in the previous chapter—overcame those problems through better design.

Setting the Initial Color

There's a problem with the code that we've written so far: if the user tries to make a graph without first invoking the Preferences panel, nothing will be drawn, because all of the NSColor instance variables for setting the graph, axes, and label colors will be zero. The logical way to set the initial values for these instance variables is by overriding the GraphView's **initWithFrame:** method. For now, we'll just hardcode in values. In Chapter 21, we'll see how to set these values from the defaults database system.

ColorGraphView.m

46. Override GraphView's **initWithFrame:** method implementation by inserting the following method into ColorGraphView.m:

```
- initWithFrame:(NSRect)frame
{
    [super initWithFrame:frame];
    axesColor = [ [NSColor lightGrayColor] retain];
    graphColor = [ [NSColor blackColor] retain];
    labelColor = [ [NSColor darkGrayColor] retain];
    return self;
}
```

The GraphView, Segment, and Label Classes

We were very careful in the last chapter to build in flexibility when we designed the GraphView, Segment, and Label classes. Because these classes have proper abstractions, instance variables, and protocols, not a single line of code in them needs to be changed.

Testing GraphPaper's Color

47. Build and run GraphPaper. Save all files first.

48. Click the Graph button to make a graph with axes and a function label appear.

49. Choose GraphPaper → Preferences to make the Preferences panel appear.

50. Click the border of the Graph color well to expose the Colors panel, which will be linked to the color well you clicked.

51. Try changing the color in the Colors panel. The color of the graph will change immediately (and continuously, if you drag the Colors panel sliders).

52. Now try changing the colors of the axes and function label. In Figure 17-7, we have changed the colors of all three items displayed for the function x*cos(x).

53. Quit GraphPaper.

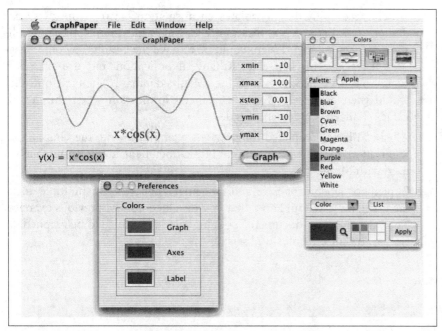

Figure 17-7. GraphPaper running with colors chosen via the Preferences panel

Summary

In this chapter, we learned that drawing in color with Quartz is nearly as easy as drawing in black and white. Then we saw how easy it is to improve the functionality of a well-designed class through subclassing. Finally, we showed another way to use the tag facility with the display list to change the color attributes for a set of objects.

In the next chapter, we'll learn more about NSViews—specifically, we'll see how to put any view in a scroller and how to add a pop-up magnification control. We'll also show how to subclass the ColorGraphView class to handle mouse tracking.

Exercises

1. Some of the functions that we implement in the PrefController class are provided as part of the NSWindowController class. Reimplement the PrefController class as a subclass of NSWindowController, removing any code possible.

2. In our implementation of the GraphPaper application, the PrefController communicates directly with the GraphView object when the preferences

are changed. This design violates encapsulation between the two class designs and limits the application to having a maximum of one Graph-View object. A better design would be to have the GraphView object register to receive an NSDefaultsChangedNotification and use this as a signal to reread the values from the defaults database. The PrefController would then post an NSDefaultsChangedNotification when the default values changed. Implement this design.

3. After you have completed the previous exercise, rewrite the GraphPaper application so that it uses the multiple-document architecture that we used with MathPaper.

4. Implement Document Save and Document Load for the multiple-document version of GraphPaper that you developed in the previous exercise. Your GraphPaper "document" should include formulae to be graphed, as well as the current color-well settings.

CHAPTER 18

Tracking the Mouse

We're in the home stretch! In this and the following three chapters, we're going to fill in many of the standard Mac OS X features that you need to know in order to write commercial-level Cocoa applications.

Tracking the Mouse

Today's users are so demanding! A few years ago you could write an application that would just sit there and wait for you to click a mouse button or press a key, but these days users expect your application to be always prepared to respond. When a user moves the mouse over something in an application's window, if there is some way that your application can possibly convey information, the user expects it to happen.

What kind of information are we talking about? For example, if a user mouses over (i.e., lets the cursor hover over) the toolbar icons in the Mail application or the Colors panel, he will expect to get feedback about what clicking those icons will do. This is an example of Cocoa tool tips—something that is so simple to set with Interface Builder that we haven't even bothered showing you how to do it. Can we arrange for even more sophisticated mouseover behavior within GraphPaper? Of course we can, and in this chapter we'll show you how!

Tracking Rectangles

Until now, we've thought of Cocoa events as being in two categories: mouse events and keyboard events (although there are periodic and other types of events as well). Another way of classifying events is according to the type of programmatic gyrations that you have to go through in order to receive them.

The simplest events to program are those that require no setup; you merely subclass NSView and implement the corresponding event methods to receive the events. Some of the methods that handle these simple events are:

- **mouseDown:**(NSEvent *)*theEvent*
- **mouseUp:**(NSEvent *)*theEvent*
- **mouseDragged:**(NSEvent *)*theEvent*
- **rightMouseDown:**(NSEvent *)*theEvent*
- **rightMouseUp:**(NSEvent *)*theEvent*
- **rightMouseDragged:**(NSEvent *)*theEvent*

A second group of mouse events involves the responder chain. Usually, your NSView subclass receives these events by making itself a first responder. This can happen automatically if the user clicks the mouse in your NSView and your NSView responds YES to the **acceptsFirstResponder:** message. The responder-chain events include keyboard events as well as events that have to deal with simple mouse motion. Some of the methods that handle these first responder events are:

- **keyDown:**(NSEvent *)*theEvent*
- **keyUp:**(NSEvent *)*theEvent*
- **flagsChanged:**(NSEvent *)*theEvent*

The last group of events has to do with *tracking rectangles*, rectangular regions within windows that track the mouse cursor. You can arrange to have messages sent to an object whenever a tracking rectangle is *entered* or *exited* (no click) by the mouse. Some of the methods that handle these tracking events are:

- **mouseMoved:**(NSEvent *)*theEvent*
- **mouseEntered:**(NSEvent *)*theEvent*
- **mouseExited:**(NSEvent *)*theEvent*

To set up a tracking rectangle, send the **addTrackingRect:owner:userData: assumeInside:** message to an NSWindow object:

- (NSTrackingRectTag)**addTrackingRect:**(NSRect)*aRect*
                           owner:(id)*anObject*
                        userData:(void *)*userData*
                    assumeInside:(BOOL)*insideFlag*

These arguments are described in Table 18-1.

Table 18-1. Method arguments of NSTrackingRectTag

Argument	Meaning
addTrackingRect:	A pointer to the tracking rectangle in the NSWindow's coordinate system. The tracking rectangle does not change if the NSWindow is resized.
owner:	The object that will be sent **mouseEntered:** and **mouseExited:** messages when the mouse moves in or out of the tracking rectangle. Normally the owner will be the NSView itself, but it can be any object that responds to **mouseEntered:** and **mouseExited:** messages.

Table 18-1. Method arguments of NSTrackingRectTag (continued)

Argument	Meaning
userData:	Data that is provided in the NSEvent object with the **mouseEntered:** or **mouseExited:** events.
assumeInside:	Set this flag to indicate whether you think the mouse cursor is initially inside or outside the tracking rectangle. If this flag is NO, the **mouseEntered:** event will be sent the first time the cursor moves into the tracking rectangle. If this flag is YES, the first tracking event sent will be a **mouseExited:** event, when the cursor leaves the tracking rectangle.

Tracking rectangles are actually handled by windows, not by views. Unfortunately, you normally want to manage and use tracking rectangles from within views. Cocoa meets you halfway in this pursuit—for example, tracking rectangles are created by sending messages to NSViews. Nevertheless, the fact that tracking rectangles are managed by windows results in some weirdness:

- If you change your NSView's frame, you need to remove the old tracking rectangle and create a new one.

- An NSView receives **mouseMoved:** events only when it is the NSWindow's first responder.

- There is no default tracking rectangle. If you don't set a tracking rectangle, you won't get **mouseEntered:** and **mouseExited:** events.

If your only reason for using a tracking rectangle is to give your NSView subclass a custom cursor, don't use a tracking rectangle; use NSView's **addCursorRect:cursor:** method instead.

Accepting Mouse-Moved Events

Each window maintains an internal flag called acceptsMouseMovedEvents that determines whether the Window Server will send it mouse-moved events. The reason for this, once again, is efficiency—most applications simply don't need to know every time the mouse moves. The default, therefore, is not to send these events. If you set the acceptsMouseMovedEvents flag, you'll get the events regardless of whether your application is the active application. That's useful, but it can slow down your entire computer, so be judicious in your use of mouse-moved events.

To receive mouse-moved events from an NSWindow object called aWindow, send aWindow the following message:

```
[aWindow setAcceptsMouseMovedEvents:YES]
```

When you don't need these events anymore, send the following message:

```
[aWindow setAcceptsMouseMovedEvents:NO]
```

Adding Mouse Tracking to GraphPaper

Now we know enough to add mouse tracking to GraphPaper. The modifications will involve the following four parts:

- Modifying the **initWithFrame:** method to set up the tracking rectangle around the on-screen ColorGraphView instance
- Adding a **mouseEntered:** method that will tell the NSWindow to start sending mouse-moved events
- Adding a **mouseMoved:** method to process mouse-moved events
- Adding a **mouseExited:** method that will reset the window's event-handling status

Rather than adding this new functionality to the GraphView or ColorGraphView classes, we'll subclass ColorGraphView to make a TrackingGraphView class. Tracking functionality is separate from graphing functionality, and it makes sense to separate them in the code.

Let's get on with it!

Changes to the GraphPaper Interface

Interface Builder

1. Back in IB, make sure that `MainMenu.nib` is open and is the selected window (again, we recommend that you minimize the other nibs that are open in IB).

2. Subclass the ColorGraphView class and rename the new subclass "TrackingGraphView".

3. Add outlets called xCell and yCell to the TrackingGraphView class.

4. Change the class of the ColorGraphView instance in the GraphPaper window to TrackingGraphView in the Class Info dialog.

5. Verify that the Graph button is still connected to the TrackingGraphView instance. Make sure it sends the **graph:** action.

6. Add two NSTextField objects inside the GraphPaper window and label them "x:" and "y:", as shown in Figure 18-1. It may be necessary to resize the GraphPaper window to accommodate the two text fields.

7. Make the two new NSTextFields uneditable but selectable in the Attributes Info dialog. Set their borders to be solid lines, as shown in Figure 18-1.

8. Using the Size inspector, set the "springs" for both NSTextFields in the same way you did for the Graph button: the topmost and leftmost lines should be springs, so that the text fields do not resize but instead move with the lower-right corner.

9. Connect the TrackingGraphView's xCell outlet to the NSTextField labeled "x:" and the yCell outlet to the one labeled "y:".

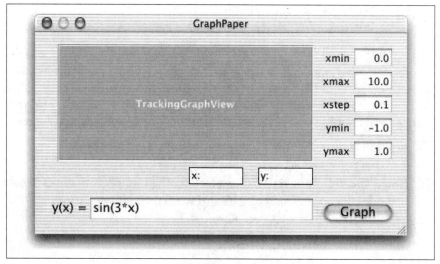

Figure 18-1. New x: and y: text fields to identify points on a graph in GraphPaper

10. Create the TrackingGraphView class files and insert them into your project.

Changes to the TrackingGraphView Class Files

In addition to the two outlets we set up in IB, the TrackingGraphView class needs two more instance variables. The trackingRect instance variable will remember the NSTrackingRectTag that is returned when the tracking rectangle is created. (We don't use the variable in this class, but it is conceivable that a subclass might use it.) We will also create a second NSMutableArray, called annotations, that we'll use to keep track of the additional annotations (i.e., two lines that make up a big crosshair) that we will display on the TrackingGraphView.

11. Insert the lines shown here in bold into TrackingGraphView.h:

TrackingGraphView.h

```
#import <Cocoa/Cocoa.h>
#import "ColorGraphView.h"

@interface TrackingGraphView : ColorGraphView
{
    IBOutlet id xCell;
    IBOutlet id yCell;
    NSTrackingRectTag trackingRect;
    NSMutableArray *annotations;
}

- (id)initWithFrame:(NSRect)frame;
- (void)mouseEntered:(NSEvent *)theEvent;
- (void)mouseExited:(NSEvent *)theEvent;
- (void)mouseMoved:(NSEvent *)theEvent;
```

```
- (void)addAnnotation:(id)anObject;
- (void)removeAnnotations;

@end
```

We'll set up seven methods in the TrackingGraphView class to make it draw a big crosshair over the entire view when the mouse cursor moves over the graph (the mouse cursor itself will remain a pointer). The first method, **initWith-Frame:**, will establish a tracking rectangle around the TrackingGraphView.

12. Insert the following #import directive into TrackingGraphView.m:

```
#import "Segment.h"
```

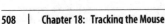
TrackingGraphView.m

13. Insert the following **initWithFrame:** method implementation (which overrides the one in ColorGraphView) into TrackingGraphView.m:

```
- (id)initWithFrame:(NSRect)frame
{
    [super initWithFrame:frame];

    annotations = [ [NSMutableArray alloc] init];

    trackingRect = [self addTrackingRect:[self visibleRect]
                                   owner:self
                                userData:nil
                            assumeInside:NO];
    return self;
}
```

The **initWithFrame:** method is the NSView designated initializer. This method calls the designated initializer in the superclass, then adds an NSMutableArray to keep track of the annotations. Finally, a tracking rectangle is created for the portion of the TrackingGraphView that is currently visible on the screen.

If the user resizes GraphPaper's main window, the tracking rectangle will no longer be correct. The override of the **getFormAndScaleView** method shown in the next step resizes the tracking rectangle whenever the TrackingGraph-View is resized.

14. Insert the following **getFormAndScaleView** method implementation into TrackingGraphView.m:

```
- (void)getFormAndScaleView
{
    [self removeTrackingRect:trackingRect]; // Remove the old
    [super getFormAndScaleView];
    trackingRect = [self addTrackingRect:[self visibleRect]
                                   owner:self
                                userData:nil
                            assumeInside:NO];
}
```

The next pair of methods responds to events generated by the cursor's entering and exiting the tracking rectangle.

15. Insert the following **mouseEntered:** and **mouseExited:** method implementations into TrackingGraphView.m:

```
- (void)mouseEntered:(NSEvent *)theEvent
{
    [ [self window] setAcceptsMouseMovedEvents:YES];
    [ [self window] makeFirstResponder:self];
}

- (void)mouseExited:(NSEvent *)theEvent
{
    [self removeAnnotations];
    [ [self window] setAcceptsMouseMovedEvents:NO];
}
```

The **mouseEntered:** method makes the TrackingGraphView the NSWindow's first responder and changes the NSWindow's event mask so that it gets all mouse-moved events. The **mouseExited:** method restores the original event mask. (We'll discuss the **removeAnnotations** method shortly.)

The next two methods maintain the annotation list. The crosshair that TrackingGraphView draws will be added to two display lists: the first is the normal display list maintained by the GraphView; the second is the list of *annotations*. This second list allows us to remove the annotations from the primary display list without recomputing the entire graph.

16. Insert the following **addAnnotation:** and **removeAnnotations** methods into TrackingGraphView.m:

TrackingGraphView.m

```
- (void)addAnnotation:(id)obj
{
    [annotations addObject:obj];
    [self addGraphElement:obj];
}

- (void)removeAnnotations
{
    NSEnumerator *en = [annotations objectEnumerator];
    id obj;

    while (obj = [en nextObject]) {
        [self setNeedsDisplayInRect:[obj bounds] ];
    }

    [displayList removeObjectsInArray:annotations];
    [annotations removeAllObjects];
}
```

17. Insert the following **mouseMoved:** method into TrackingGraphView.m:

```
- (void)mouseMoved:(NSEvent *)theEvent
{
    NSPoint pt;
    NSEnumerator *en;
    id obj;
```

```
                    pt = [self convertPoint:[theEvent locationInWindow]
                            fromView:nil];

                    en = [displayList objectEnumerator];
                    while (obj = [en nextObject]) {

                        if ([obj tag]==GRAPH_TAG &&
                            pt.x >= [obj bounds].origin.x &&
                            pt.x <= [obj bounds].origin.x +
                                    [obj bounds].size.width) {

                    // Are we within 30 pixels of the line in screen coordinates?
                            NSPoint ptMouse = [theEvent locationInWindow];
                            NSPoint ptLine = [self convertPoint:[obj segmentCenter]
                                                    toView:nil];

                            double dist = sqrt(pow(ptMouse.x - ptLine.x,2) +
                                                pow(ptMouse.y - ptLine.y,2));

                            if (dist<30.0) {
                                // Add two segments to annotations
                                NSRect vb = [self bounds];
                                NSRect ob = [obj bounds];
                                id seg;

                                [self removeAnnotations];   // Remove the old

                                // Horizontal line intersecting cursor hot spot
                                seg = [ [Segment alloc]
                                        initFrom:NSMakePoint(vb.origin.x,ob.origin.y)
                                            to:NSMakePoint(vb.origin.x+vb.size.width,
                                                            ob.origin.y)];
                                [seg autorelease];
                                [self addAnnotation:seg];
                                [seg setColor:[NSColor greenColor] ];

                                // Vertical line intersecting cursor hot spot
                                seg = [ [Segment alloc]
                                        initFrom:NSMakePoint(ob.origin.x,vb.origin.y)
                                            to:NSMakePoint(ob.origin.x,
                                                            vb.origin.y+vb.size.height)];
                                [seg autorelease];
                                [self addAnnotation:seg];
                                [seg setColor:[NSColor greenColor]];

                                // Update positions in the x and y text fields
                                [xCell setStringValue:
                                        [NSString stringWithFormat:@"x: %g",
                                            [obj segmentCenter].x] ];
                                [yCell setStringValue:
                                        [NSString stringWithFormat:@"y: %g",
                                            [obj segmentCenter].y] ];

                                [self setNeedsDisplay:YES];
```

```
            return;
        }
    }
}

// No segment should be highlighted
[self removeAnnotations];
[self display];
[xCell setStringValue:@"x:"];
[yCell setStringValue:@"y:"];
}
```

Despite the length of this **mouseMoved:** method, it isn't very complicated. First it converts the new mouse location from NSWindow to NSView coordinates. Then it iterates through the display list, searching for a segment that has the GRAPH_TAG tag and also contains the point corresponding to the mouse position. If it finds such a segment, and if the mouse is within 30 pixels of the segment's center, it removes the old annotation (crosshair) lines and adds two new ones— a horizontal line and a vertical one. The x: and y: text fields are then filled in, and the entire view is redisplayed. (Ideally, you should be able to do a redisplay of only the region that has been updated, but that code didn't work for us, possibly due to a Cocoa 10.1 bug.) If the mouse position doesn't correspond to any Segment, the annotations are removed and the x: and y: values are erased.

18. Build and run GraphPaper. Save all files first.

19. Click the Graph button and move the cursor over the graph.

The window in Figure 18-2 shows what the x: and y: cells and highlighted Segment look like when GraphPaper runs. Note that the arrow cursor is at the center of the big crosshair.

20. Quit GraphPaper.

Summary

In this chapter, we continued our investigation of the NSView class by looking at the way the class handles resize events. In the next chapter we'll learn more about Cocoa NSScrollViews and add a zoom feature to the GraphPaper application. We'll also make provisions for saving a graph as a PDF or TIFF file.

Exercises

1. Explain the purpose of the assumeInside: flag in the **addTrackingRect: owner:userData:assumeInside:** method.

2. Why do you think it is necessary to manually add a tracking rectangle to an NSView in order to have that NSView track the mouse? Why is it necessary to make the tracking view the first responder?

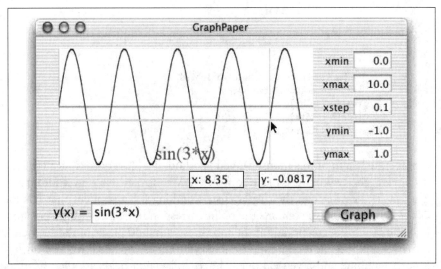

Figure 18-2. GraphPaper window with crosshair at cursor hot spot and with x and y values on graph

3. Instead of being added to a separate display list, the annotations could have been integrated with the primary display list. Try to implement the program in this manner. What are the advantages and disadvantages of this approach?

4. Modify the GraphPaper application so that the displayed formula changes color when you move the mouse over it.

5. Further modify the GraphPaper application so that you can click the formula and drag it to other locations in the GraphView window.

6. Investigate the NSFormatter class. Instead of specifying the string values "x:" and "y:" in the **mouseMoved:** event, create your own NSFormatter that prepends these labels to the floating-point value before it is displayed. Which approach is better—using an NSFormatter or creating the formatted display in the **mouseMoved:** event?

References

1. NSView and NSWindow class descriptions:

   http://developer.apple.com/techpubs/macosx/Cocoa/Reference/
   ApplicationKit/ObjC_classic/AppKitTOC.html

2. Handling tracking-rectangle and cursor-update events in views:

   http://developer.apple.com/techpubs/macosx/Cocoa/TasksAndConcepts/
   ProgrammingTopics/CursorMgmt/index.html

CHAPTER 19

Zooming and Saving Graphics Files

This chapter shows how to do a few interesting things with NSViews. In the first part, we'll show how to put a zoom pop-up menu in an NSScrollView. In the second part, we'll show how to generate Encapsulated PostScript (EPS), PDF, or TIFF files from an NSView; how to save a graph into an EPS, PDF, or TIFF file; and how to add controls to a Save panel (dialog).

Adding a Zoom Button to GraphPaper

In the previous chapter, we arranged for the GraphView object to rescale its coordinate system when its containing window was resized. Although the scaled coordinate system is appropriate for our graphing application and is a good way to show how to catch resizing events, stretching an application's window isn't the right way for a user to get a magnified view of the window's contents. Consider the Aqua interface standard: a window is supposed to be just that—a window into a page of a virtual document. The document itself shouldn't get bigger or smaller when the window is resized; rather, a bigger or smaller window should let the user see more or less of a document.

Mac OS X applications should enable the user to see more detail using a zoom button—not the green zoom button in a window's title bar, but a little pop-up menu button, typically located at the bottom of an NSScrollView, that allows you to change the magnification of the NSScrollView. Microsoft Word and Stone Design's Create applications both have such a button (see Figure 19-1).

The window on the left in Figure 19-1 is set to a zoom factor of 100%. Pressing the zoom button reveals a pop-up menu of different magnification settings, which in turn lets you change the size of the text that is displayed. In the right window, we changed the setting to 200%.

It's easy to add a zoom button to any NSScrollView, but you have to know a little bit about how the NSScrollView works first.

Figure 19-1. Zoom pop-up menu button in Stone Design's Create

The NSScrollView Class Revisited

Each NSScrollView object has another object "inside" it, called its *docView*, which is the actual NSView being displayed. In addition to the docView, each NSScrollView has the following three NSView objects to help it perform its scrolling tasks:

- An NSScroller to control horizontal scrolling
- An NSScroller to control vertical scrolling
- An NSClipView that displays the part of the docView that is visible

We can change the magnification of the NSView displayed in the NSScroll-View simply by sending a **scale:** message to the NSClipView. The NSClip-View will scale the NSView that it contains when it is drawn. Zooming happens without the knowledge or cooperation of the docView.

Whenever an NSScrollView changes size (for example, when it is resized), and whenever the NSView that it contains changes size, the NSScrollView sends the **tile** message to itself to alert its subviews to change their sizes. By subclassing the NSScrollView class and overriding the **tile** method, we can place additional objects (such as rulers and zoom buttons) over or next to the scrollers that the NSScrollView displays.

In this section, we will subclass the NSScrollView class to make a new class called ZoomScrollView. This class will have outlets for its docView—the TrackingGraphView that we created in the previous chapter—as well as for the zoom pop-up menu. We'll control the ZoomScrollView instance from the Controller object that we created in Chapter 17.

Changes to MainMenu.nib

Project Builder

1. Open your GraphPaper project in Project Builder and the MainMenu.nib file in Interface Builder.

2. Resize the TrackingGraphView in the GraphPaper window so that it's smaller, and put it somewhere in the window that is out of the way.

   Don't worry about the size or position of the TrackingGraphView—it will automatically be resized and placed in the proper position when GraphPaper runs.

3. Subclass the NSScrollView class and rename the new subclass "Zoom-ScrollView".

4. Add the subView and zoomButton outlets and the **changeZoom:** action method to the new ZoomScrollView class.

5. Drag a CustomView icon from IB's Cocoa-Containers palette and drop it in the GraphPaper window. Change its class to ZoomScrollView.

6. Resize the on-screen ZoomScrollView instance to be as large as the previous TrackingGraphView instance. Note that the TrackingGraphView instance shows through the ZoomScrollView a bit.

7. Choose IB's Layout → Send To Back menu command to put the Zoom-ScrollView instance "behind" the TrackingGraphView instance, as shown in Figure 19-2.

   The only reason to send the ZoomScrollView to the back is so we can easily see both NSViews at the same time; it won't make a difference in the way GraphPaper runs.

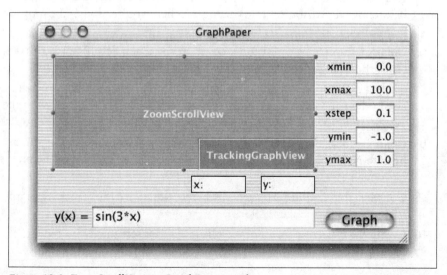

Figure 19-2. ZoomScrollView in GraphPaper window

8. Drag a pop-up menu button (shown at the edge of the page) from IB's Cocoa-Other palette and place it below the ZoomScrollView, to the left of the x: field (see Figure 19-3). Do not place it on the ZoomScrollView.

9. Double-click the pop-up menu button.

When you double-click the pop-up menu button in IB, you'll see the three menu cells that the associated pop-up menu initially contains, as shown at the edge of the page. The on-screen pop-up menu is controlled by an instance of the NSPopUpButton class. The NSPopUpButton class, a subclass of the NSButton class, creates an NSMenu object to handle its menu-like functionality.

You can add a new item to an open pop-up menu in IB by dragging the Item menu cell from the Cocoa-Menus palette and dropping it in the pop-up menu. You can't add submenus to a pop-up menu, however, because that would violate the Aqua interface guidelines.

You can give an individual target and action to each item within the pop-up menu. Alternatively, you can simply give an action to the button on top, which is called the *cover* (a type of NSPopUpButton). After a selection is made, the NSPopUpButton automatically changes the title of the button by sending it the **setTitle:** message.

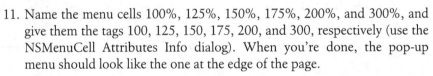

10. One by one, drag three more menu items from the Cocoa-Menus palette and drop them in the pop-up menu. Make the width of the pop-up menu smaller.

11. Name the menu cells 100%, 125%, 150%, 175%, 200%, and 300%, and give them the tags 100, 125, 150, 175, 200, and 300, respectively (use the NSMenuCell Attributes Info dialog). When you're done, the pop-up menu should look like the one at the edge of the page.

12. Connect the NSPopUpButton's cover to the ZoomScrollView so that it sends the **changeZoom:** action message (see Figure 19-3).

13. Click the 100% item and close the pop-up menu by clicking somewhere else in the window. This ensures that the initial condition will be with the pop-up menu at 100%.

14. Connect the ZoomScrollView's zoomButton outlet to the pop-up menu button. Note that this connection is in the opposite direction of the previous one.

15. Connect the ZoomScrollView's subView outlet to the TrackingGraphView, as shown in Figure 19-4.

16. Create the class files for ZoomScrollView and insert them into the GraphPaper project.

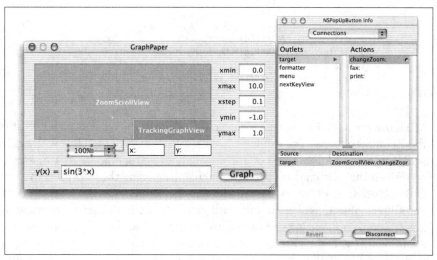

Figure 19-3. changeZoom: action connection from PopUpButton to ZoomScrollView in IB

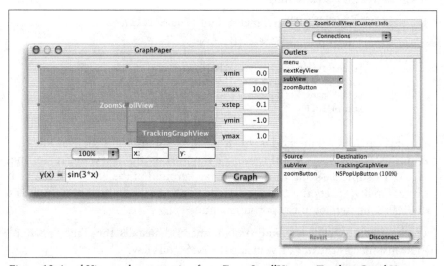

Figure 19-4. subView outlet connection from ZoomScrollView to TrackingGraphView

Changes to ZoomScrollView

17. Insert the lines shown here in bold into ZoomScrollView.h:

ZoomScrollView.h

```
#import <Cocoa/Cocoa.h>

@interface ZoomScrollView : NSScrollView
{
    IBOutlet id subView;
    IBOutlet id zoomButton;
```

```
    double scaleFactor;
}
- (IBAction)changeZoom:(id)sender;
- (id)initWithFrame:(NSRect)theFrame;
- (void)awakeFromNib;
- (void)setScaleFactor:(float)aFloat;
- (void)tile;
@end
```

We'll use the scaleFactor instance variable to store the current scale factor of the ZoomScrollView. For example, a user's zoom choice of 100% will yield a scaleFactor of 1.0, a choice of 150% will yield a scaleFactor of 1.5, and so on. When the user changes the zoom percentage using the pop-up menu, the NSPopUpButton object will send the **changeZoom:** message to the Zoom-ScrollView object, which in turn will send the **setScaleFactor:** message to itself. ZoomScrollView's **setScaleFactor:** method will then compare the new zoom factor with the current one and calculate the proper arguments to the **scale:** message. If the new magnification is the same as the old, the Zoom-ScrollView won't do anything.

ZoomScrollView.m

18. Insert the **initWithFrame:** method into ZoomScrollView.m:

```
- (id)initWithFrame:(NSRect)theFrame
{
    [super initWithFrame:theFrame];
    [self setBackgroundColor:[NSColor whiteColor]];
    scaleFactor = 1.0;
    return self;
}
```

The **initWithFrame:** method is the designated initializer for the NSView class. ZoomScrollView's **initWithFrame:** method sends the **initWithFrame:** message to its superclass and then sets the background of the NSScrollView to be white. Finally, it sets the current scale factor to be 1.0, which corresponds to the 100% menu item in the pop-up menu.

TrackingGraphView's **awakeFromNib** method installs the TrackingGraph-View instance as the docView inside the NSScrollView.

ZoomScrollView.m

19. Insert the following **awakeFromNib** method into ZoomScrollView.m:

```
-(void) awakeFromNib
{
    [self setHasHorizontalScroller:YES];
    [self setHasVerticalScroller:YES];
    [self setBorderType:NSLineBorder];

    // Set up the zoom button
    [[zoomButton cell] setBordered:NO];
    [[zoomButton cell] setBezeled:YES];
    [[zoomButton cell] setFont:[NSFont labelFontOfSize:10.0]];
    [self addSubview:zoomButton];
```

```
    // The next two lines install the subView (TrackingGraphView)
    // and set its size to be the same as the NSScrollView
    [self setDocumentView:subView];
    [subView setFrame:[[self contentView] frame]];
}
```

This method tells the ZoomScrollView that both scrollers are required and that its border should be of type NSLineBorder (as opposed to NSNoBorder, NSBezelBorder, or NSGrooveBorder, all of which are defined in NSView.h). Finally, it sizes the TrackingGraphView (the subView) to be the size of the NSScrollView's contentView, which is the NSClipView.

The next method is the one that actually changes the magnification of the NSClipView object. NSClipViews are used by the NSScrollView class to do the actual displaying of the NSView.

20. Insert the following **setScaleFactor:** method into ZoomScrollView.m:

```
- (void)setScaleFactor:(float)aFactor
{
    NSAssert(aFactor!=0,@"Illegal scale factor. Set the tag!");

    if (scaleFactor != aFactor) {
        float delta = aFactor/scaleFactor;
        scaleFactor = aFactor;
        [[self contentView]
          scaleUnitSquareToSize:NSMakeSize(delta,delta)];
    }
}
```

The **scaleUnitSquareToSize:** method rescales the NSClipView (the content-View), with the arguments being the delta (change) necessary to make the NSClipView have the magnification that the user wants. This method uses the NSAssert() macro, which is similar to the ANSI C assert() macro, except that it allows you to specify a printf-style string that is printed if the assertion is false. If aFactor==0, the NSAssert() macro will raise the exception NSInternalInconsistencyException.

The next method is the action that is invoked when the user clicks the pop-up menu button.

21. Insert the line shown here in bold into the **changeZoom:** method in ZoomScrollView.m:

```
- (IBAction)changeZoom:(id)sender
{
    [self setScaleFactor:[[sender selectedCell] tag] / 100.0];
}
```

ZoomScrollView.m

Finally, there is our **tile** method, an override of NSScrollView's **tile** method. It is invoked automatically when the ZoomScrollView's size changes.

22. Insert the following **tile** method into `ZoomScrollView.m`:

```
- (void)tile
{
    NSRect scrollerRect, buttonRect;

    [super tile];

    // Place the pop-up button next to the scroller
    scrollerRect = [[self horizontalScroller] frame];
    NSDivideRect(scrollerRect, &buttonRect, &scrollerRect, 50.0,
                 NSMaxXEdge);
    [[self horizontalScroller] setFrame: scrollerRect];
    [zoomButton setFrame: NSInsetRect(buttonRect, 1.0, 1.0)];
}
```

This **tile** method gets the frame of the horizontal scroller, snips off 50 pixels, and gives that space to the zoom button. The 50-pixel limit was determined by trial and error. Note how handy the Application Kit functions (e.g., `NSDivideRect()` and `NSInsetRect()`) are for manipulating rectangles!

Testing the Zoom Button

23. Build and run GraphPaper, saving all files first.

24. You should get a magnification button in the lower-right corner of the ZoomScrollView, as shown in the window at the top of Figure 19-5. Enter a function and click the Graph button.

25. Press the pop-up menu button, drag to 175%, and release the mouse button. The zoom button's title should change, as shown in the window at the bottom of Figure 19-5.

26. Resize the GraphPaper window—oops, we haven't taken care of Autosizing yet! We'll show you how to do that in the next section.

27. Resize the GraphPaper window anyway and drag the scroll knobs. The ZoomScrollView should stretch, making more of the graph visible, rather than changing its scale, as it did previously.

28. Quit GraphPaper.

Autosizing in GraphPaper

The zoom pop-up menu will make it more likely that a user will want to resize (probably enlarge) the GraphPaper window, but we didn't take care of that possibility yet. We'll do that now.

29. Back in IB, select ZoomScrollView and type Command-3. Make Zoom-ScrollView's Autosizing box look like the one on the left in Figure 19-6.

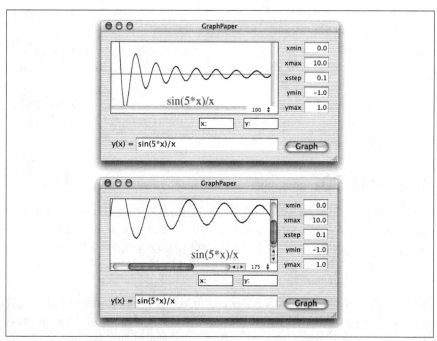

Figure 19-5. Zooming GraphPaper's graph from 100% (top) to 175% (bottom)

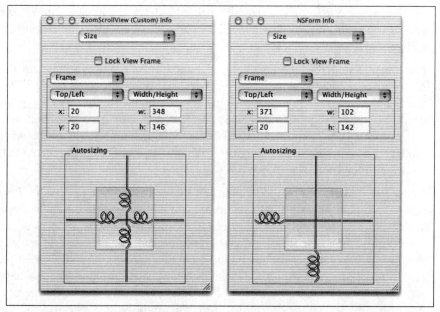

Figure 19-6. Autosizing for ZoomScrollView and NSForm instances in GraphPaper window

30. Then select the NSForm (xmin, xmax, etc.) and make its Autosizing box look like the one on the right in Figure 19-6.

31. Build and run GraphPaper, saving the nib file. Note how quickly the building process took this time—PB only had to stuff a new nib file in the .app directory, not much work.

32. Graph a function and resize GraphPaper. It works better but is still not perfect. See the "Exercises" section at the end of this chapter for more.

33. Quit GraphPaper.

Saving to PDF

Although making a graph (or any other picture) is a nice start, it's important to be able to save the graph in a format that can work with other Mac OS X applications. For example, you might want to put the graph in a word processor document that you are making with Microsoft Word, or paste the image into a Create drawing.

One of the most common file formats in the graphics industry today is the *Encapsulated PostScript* (EPS) standard. EPS contains a series of device-independent commands that can be used to draw any image on any graphics device.

EPS is a great way to move graphics between applications. EPS retains all of the information that was originally used to draw the image: fonts, line strokes, bitmaps—it's all in there. EPS images can be scaled and displayed, and they're beautiful and easy to work with.

But over the years, Adobe PostScript has not been a runaway success in the marketplace. Although PostScript was extremely popular on the NeXTSTEP, Unix, and Macintosh operating systems, it never really caught on in the Windows world. Throughout the 1990s, there were also a growing number of security concerns with PostScript, because it is more than an imaging model—it's a programming language. Finally, as PostScript was extended, some of its device-independence was lost.

In the 1990s, Adobe developed a new graphics imaging format called the Portable Document Format (PDF). In many ways, PDF is a successor to PostScript. Like PostScript, it is device-independent and has provisions for embedding fonts, compressing images, and more. But PDF also has built-in security: documents can be encrypted to control access. Unlike PostScript, PDF is not a programming language, which means that PDF documents have less chance of containing viruses or hostile code. And unlike PostScript, Adobe has made a strong commitment to PDF on the Windows platform.

The Mac OS X operating system extends PDF, allowing it to be used as a general graphics file format for images and line drawings. In this way, PDF documents can be embedded directly in other documents, similar to the way that EPS documents are embedded in documents. But unlike PostScript, there is no "encapsulated" form of PDF—it's just regular PDF.

As this book goes to press, PDF is still a relatively immature technology for embedding graphics images. We can make GraphPaper produce a PDF of the GraphView graph, but we need to "trick" it because of some issues with the 10.1 AppKit. We can embed the resulting PDF image into a variety of applications, but, as we'll see, it scales properly in only one or two of them. A PDF of a GraphPaper graph is great for printing entire pages, but it's still immature as a format for moving images between applications.

Producing PDFs from NSView

Cocoa's NSView class makes it possible to generate an EPS or PDF file with a single message. Just send a **dataWithEPSInsideRect:** message, and the NSView will return an NSData object that contains the EPS file. Similarly, **dataWithPDFInsideRect:** will return an NSData object that contains a PDF file. The NSView object will invoke the appropriate **drawRect:** method, but instead of sending the drawing code to the Window Server, it will capture the output and send it to the stream that you designate.

Unfortunately, in Mac OS X Version 10.1, these methods do not work properly for views that are not scaled in screen coordinates. Although these bugs may be fixed in a future release, in order to make this demonstration program work with Version 10.1, we were forced to find a workaround. Specifically, to generate a PDF file, we had to remove the GraphView from the ZoomScrollView, place it in an off-screen window, and ask the off-screen window to generate the PDF file for us. Once the PDF file was created, we put the GraphView back into the ZoomScrollView. This worked, but it's not ideal.

In the rest of this section, we'll add a Save command to GraphPaper's menu and then modify the Controller object to capture the PDF and write it to a file.

Changes to MainMenu.nib

1. Back in IB, edit GraphPaper's File menu. Remove (with the Delete key) the New, Open, Open Recent, Close, Save As, and Revert menu items, leaving only the Save, Page Setup, and Print items.

Interface Builder

2. Rename the Save menu item "Save Graph".

3. Connect the Save Graph menu cell so that it sends the **saveDocumentTo:** action message to the First Responder object in the Instances pane of the MainMenu.nib window (see Figure 19-7).

4. Save MainMenu.nib.

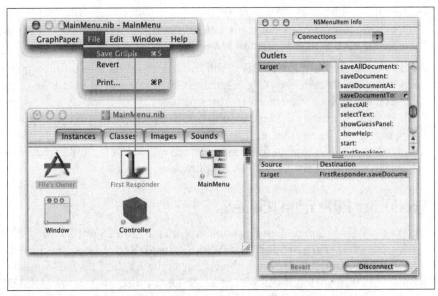

Figure 19-7. Connection from the Save Graph menu item to the First Responder

Changes to the Controller Class

We need to add three methods to the Controller class to make the Save Graph menu command work:

PDFForView:
    The first method, **PDFForView:**, will generate an NSData object that contains the PDF representation for the view.

saveDocumentTo:
    The second method, **saveDocumentTo:**, will be invoked in response to a user's choosing the Save Graph menu command. It will display a sheet that will prompt the user for the filename under which the PDF file should be saved.

savePanelDidEnd:returnCode:contextInfo:
    Finally, we will implement a **savePanelDidEnd:returnCode:contextInfo:** method that is called by the Save panel to actually save the PDF in a file.

Using this last method to generate the PDF output will make it easier to adapt the **saveDocumentTo:** method later to save the file as either PDF or TIFF.

Controller.h

5. Insert these three method declarations into `Controller.h`:

```
- (NSData *)PDFForView:(NSView *)aView;
- (IBAction)saveDocumentTo:(id)sender;
- (void)savePanelDidEnd:(NSSavePanel *)sheet
        returnCode:(int)returnCode contextInfo:(void *)contextInfo;
```

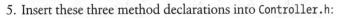

6. Insert the **PDFForView:** action method into Controller.m:

```
// This implementation works around an AppKit bug in Cocoa 10.1
// by placing the view in a different window and asking that
// window to create the PDF for the view.

- (NSData *)PDFForView:(NSView *)aView
{
    NSRect frame        = [aView frame];
    NSView *oldSuperview = [aView superview];
    NSWindow *tempWindow;
    NSData *pdf;

    tempWindow = [[NSWindow alloc]
                    initWithContentRect:frame
                            styleMask:NSBorderlessWindowMask
                              backing:NSBackingStoreRetained
                                defer:NO];

    [[tempWindow contentView] addSubview:aView];
    pdf = [tempWindow dataWithPDFInsideRect:[tempWindow frame]];
    [oldSuperview addSubview:aView];
    [tempWindow release];
    return pdf;
}
```

Controller.m

This method creates a temporary off-screen window that has the same size as the frame of the view that is passed as an argument (aView). The argument view, which will be TrackingGraphView, is ripped out of its current location and is made a subview of the temporary window's content view. Then NSWindow's **dataWithPDFInsideRect:** method is used to create an NSData object that contains the PDF representation of this window. Finally, the passed-in view is returned to its original superview.

Both the NSView and NSWindow classes support the **dataWithPDFInsideRect:** method. Ideally, we should be able to invoke this method in the passed-in view without putting the view in its own NSWindow. But when we tried that, we ended up with a tiny PDF image that couldn't be displayed by any of the standard tools. This method is less elegant, but it works.

7. Insert the following **saveDocumentTo:** method into Controller.m:

```
- (IBAction)saveDocumentTo:(id)sender
{
    NSSavePanel *pan = [NSSavePanel savePanel];

    [pan setRequiredFileType:@"pdf"];
    [pan setTitle:@"Save Graph"];

    [pan beginSheetForDirectory:nil
                          file:nil
                 modalForWindow:[graphView window]
                 modalDelegate:self
```

```
        didEndSelector:@selector(savePanelDidEnd:returnCode:contextInfo:)
            contextInfo:nil];
}
```

This **saveDocumentTo:** method implements the Save Graph action (recall the connection from the menu item we made earlier). The method creates an NSSavePanel, sets the required file type for this panel to be "pdf", and then starts a modal sheet (with one of the longest method names in Cocoa!). When the user dismisses the sheet, the **savePanelDidEnd:returnCode:contextInfo:** message is sent to the modalDelegate, which is self—the Controller object.

8. Insert the following **savePanelDidEnd:returnCode:contextInfo:** method into Controller.m:

```
- (void)savePanelDidEnd:(NSSavePanel *)sheet
        returnCode:(int)returnCode
       contextInfo:(void *)contextInfo
{
    NSData *graphPDF;

    if (returnCode==0) return;     // User did not click OK
                                   // Take no action
    graphPDF = [self PDFForView:graphView];

    if ([graphPDF writeToFile:[sheet filename] atomically:NO]==NO) {
        NSRunAlertPanel(nil,@"Cannot save file '%@': %s",nil,nil,nil,
                        [sheet filename],strerror(errno));
    }
}
```

This method is the delegate method for the Save panel. It first checks the return code to see if the user exited the sheet by hitting the OK or Cancel buttons. If the user did not click OK, the method returns. Otherwise, the method creates a PDF for the graphView and writes it to a file using the **writeToFile:atomically:** method from the NSData class. If the **writeToFile:atomically:** method fails, the appropriate error message is displayed by an NSRunAlertPanel( ) function.

Testing the Save Graph Menu Command

9. Build and run GraphPaper. Save all files first.

10. Click the Graph button and then choose the Save Graph menu command. You should see a standard Mac OS X document-modal sheet, as shown in Figure 19-8.

sin-plot.pdf

11. Enter a filename such sin-plot and click Save. A new icon like the one shown at the edge of the page will show up in the Documents folder in the Finder.

12. Quit GraphPaper.

13. Now double-click the saved sin-plot.pdf file in the Finder. The graph should open in the Preview application, as shown in Figure 19-9.

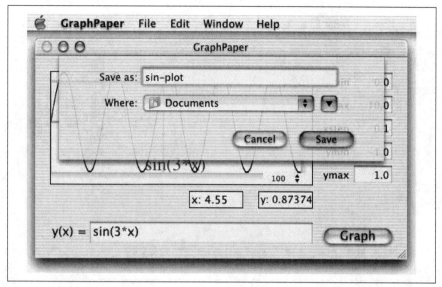

Figure 19-8. Saving a PDF file in GraphPaper

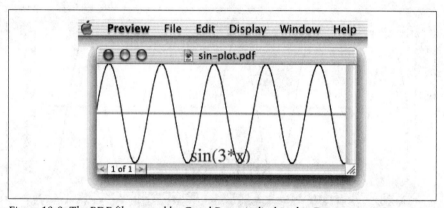

Figure 19-9. The PDF file created by GraphPaper is displayed in Preview

You can incorporate this PDF file directly into many Mac OS X applications. In theory, PDF files should automatically scale to different display sizes. Unfortunately, some applications do not currently support PDF properly. Instead of asking the Quartz system to redisplay the PDF image at the appropriate resolution, these programs appear to simply create a TIFF image of the PDF and then scale the PDF as necessary.

For an example of a program that handles PDF files properly, consider Stone Design's Create. If you drag the PDF file into a Create window, the image will appear as it did in Preview, as shown in Figure 19-10. If you increase the resolution to 200% (or other), you'll see that the image is rendered again in higher detail, as it is in Figure 19-11.

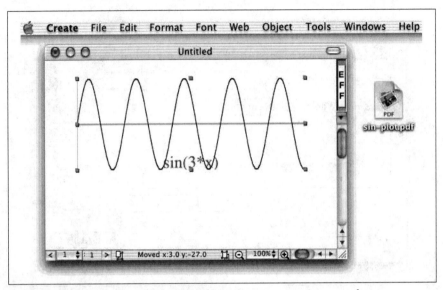

Figure 19-10. Our sin-plot.pdf file dragged into Stone Design's Create application

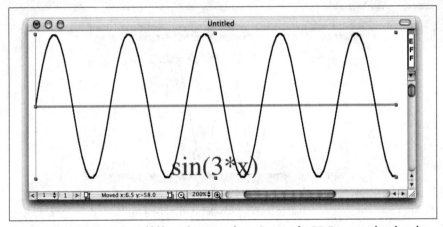

Figure 19-11. Our sin-plot.pdf file scales properly in Create; the PDF is rerendered at the higher resolution

On the other hand, Microsoft Word and PowerPoint for the Mac do not properly display PDF images. Figure 19-12 shows the same PDF file dragged into a Word presentation. The image is then scaled up by a factor of 200%. Unlike Create, Word simply scales up the image, rather than rerendering the PDF, and these ugly "jaggies" appear.

This is not merely of academic interest. If you are preparing images for publication, you need to use EPS and PDF types so that the images are properly rendered at the resolution of your output device. Figure 19-13 shows an EPS

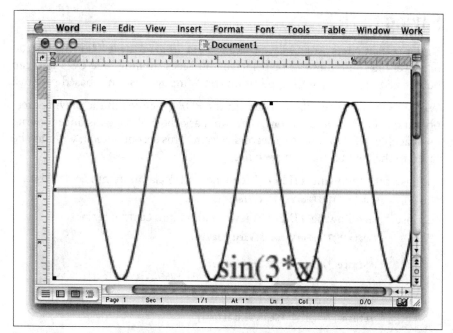

Figure 19-12. The PDF file in Word does not scale properly

file created from GraphPaper (by converting every "pdf" to an "eps" in the Controller class) that was then directly included in this book. If you compare this image of the GraphView with the others in this book, you'll see that the letters sin(3*x) have no jaggies and that the line itself looks smoother. That's because the PostScript file has been imaged at the 1200 dpi (dots per inch) resolution of our phototypesetter. The other images of the GraphView were captured off the screen at 92 dpi (approximately) and had their pixels replicated to get to the 1200 dpi of the phototypesetter.

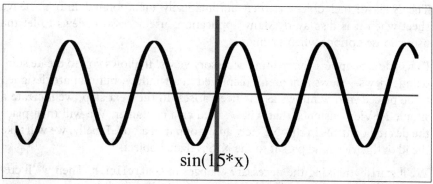

Figure 19-13. An EPS image created with GraphPaper and rendered directly in this book

Saving to TIFF

Under certain circumstances, you might want to generate a TIFF file instead of a PDF file. TIFF files can be displayed on Macs running Mac OS 9 and can be transferred to numerous applications on Windows- or Unix-based systems.

We'll use the NSImage class to convert the PDF generated in the previous section into a TIFF representation. Then we'll ask the NSImage instance to write its image, in TIFF format, to a second stream. This second stream will then be saved to the file that the user specifies.

Controller.h

Controller.m

1. Insert the following **TIFFForView:** method declaration into Controller.h:

   ```
   - (NSData *)TIFFForView:(NSView *)aView;
   ```

2. Insert the following **TIFFForView:** method into Controller.m:

   ```
   - (NSData *)TIFFForView:(NSView *)aView
   {
       NSImage *image = [[NSImage alloc]
                            initWithData:[self PDFForView:aView]];

       [image autorelease];
       return [image TIFFRepresentation];
   }
   ```

Now that we have our **TIFFForView:** method to save in TIFF format, how should we invoke it? One way would be to create a second menu item—for example, "Save Graph as TIFF". But a better (and more common) interface technique is to provide the user with file-format choices in the Save sheet. The way to do this is with an accessory view.

Creating an Accessory NSView

An *accessory view* is an NSView that you provide to the NSSavePanel object. The NSSavePanel object is then automatically incorporated into the Save sheet when it is displayed. Many applications use accessory views to let the user choose options when saving.

IB has direct support for creating accessory views. It allows you to create standalone views—views that aren't displayed in a window, but that are designed to be placed into windows as the need arises. In the next step, we'll create a simple NSView instance that will be used as a container. We will then place the desired controls in this NSView and group it in a box. Finally, we will take the id of this view and pass it to the NSSavePanel object.

We'll start by making the necessary changes to Controller.h. Then we'll create the accessory view and make connections in IB. Finally, we'll implement the necessary method in Controller.m to allow us to specify the file type.

3. Insert the `formatBox` and `formatMatrix` outlets and the `savePanel` instance variable into `Controller.h`:

Controller.h

```
@interface Controller : NSObject
{
    IBOutlet id graphView;
    IBOutlet id prefController;

    IBOutlet  id  formatBox;
    IBOutlet  id  formatMatrix;
    NSSavePanel  *savePanel;
}
```

4. Insert the following **setFormat:** action method declaration into `Controller.h`:

```
- (IBAction)setFormat:(id)sender;
```

5. Save `Controller.h`.

6. Activate IB and make sure that `MainMenu.nib` is the active window.

7. Read (parse) the updated Controller class definition into `MainMenu.nib`.

   An easy way to do this is to drag the `Controller.h` icon from PB's Groups & Files pane into the `MainMenu.nib` window in IB. Check the Info dialog to make sure that the newly added action method and outlets are in the Controller class of `MainMenu.nib`.

Next, we'll create the accessory NSView.

8. Drag a CustomView icon from IB's Cocoa-Containers palette and drop it into the `MainMenu.nib` window, as shown in Figure 19-14.

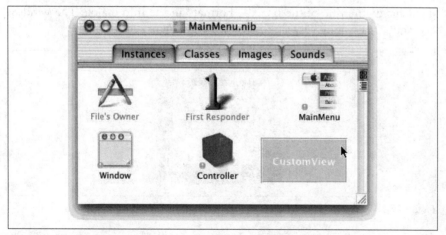

Figure 19-14. Dragging a CustomView from the Cocoa-Containers palette into the MainMenu.nib window

View

A new NSView will be added to the file MainMenu.nib and a small window titled "View" will appear, as shown in Figure 19-15. This odd-looking window represents the accessory view. The icon titled "View" in the Nib File window (shown at the edge of the page) represents the accessory view window.

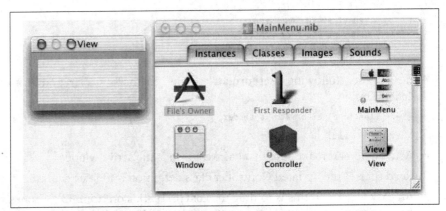

Figure 19-15. Accessory view window (left) and its icon representation (right)

9. Drag a radio-button matrix from IB's Cocoa-Views palette and drop it in the accessory view. Allow two radio-button choices, PDF and TIFF, with PDF the default. Change the font of the radio-button labels if you like.

10. Select the radio-button matrix and choose IB's Layout → Make subviews of → Box menu command to group it in a box.

11. Change the title of the box to "Format" in the Info dialog. The window should now look very similar to the one in Figure 19-16.

Figure 19-16. The completed accessory view in IB

12. Connect the Controller's formatBox outlet to the box titled "Format".

13. Connect the Controller's formatMatrix outlet to the radio-button matrix, as shown in Figure 19-17. Refer to the text near the bottom of the Info dialog, and verify that each outlet was connected to the correct object.

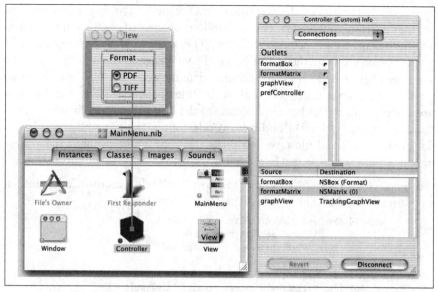

Figure 19-17. Connection (formatMatrix) from Controller to radio-button matrix

14. Connect the radio-button matrix to the Controller instance icon so that it sends the **setFormat:** action. Again, be sure to connect the NSMatrix and not the containing box (check the title of the Info dialog). Note that this connection is in the opposite direction of the one in the previous step.

Changes to the Controller Class

In addition to the **PDFForView:** and **TIFFForView:** methods we discussed earlier, we'll need to implement a **setFormat:** action method that is invoked when the user changes the file-format type in the Save panel. Cocoa provides only a single instance of the NSSavePanel object, so we can use the [**Save-Panel new**] statement to get the panel's id. We'll do that later, in the **save-DocumentTo** method. The SavePanel object lets us change its required file types inside its modal loop, so when the user changes the format, the required file type is automatically changed.

15. Insert the following **setFormat:** method into Controller.m:

```
- (IBAction)setFormat:(id)sender
{
    savePanel = [NSSavePanel savePanel];
    [savePanel setRequiredFileType:
        [ [[sender selectedCell] title] lowercaseString] ];
}
```

Controller.m

It's a complicated statement, but by now you should be able to figure it out on your own. Notice that we directly read the title of the selected cell in the matrix, so you can add new file types simply by adding their extensions to the control.

Now we need to modify the **saveDocumentTo:** method to rip the box (and the subviews that it contains) out of the window we created earlier and put it into the Save panel as an accessory NSView. This is done with the NSSavePanel's **setAccessoryView:** method. The NSSavePanel object automatically resizes the on-screen Save panel (sheet) to accommodate the accessory NSView. We need to modify the **save:** method to look at the title of the selected cell and choose the appropriate method to send output to the stream. And finally, we need to modify the **savePanelDidEnd:returnCode:contextInfo:** method so that it looks at the selected file type and picks the appropriate format. All of these modifications are presented in the following steps.

Controller.m

16. Replace the previous version of the **savePanelDidEnd:returnCode:context-Info:** method in Controller.m with the following one:

```
- (void)savePanelDidEnd:(NSSavePanel *)sheet
            returnCode:(int)returnCode
            contextInfo:(void  *)contextInfo
{
    NSData *image=0;
    NSString *filetype = [sheet requiredFileType];

    if (returnCode==0) return;    // User did not click OK

    if ([filetype isEqualToString:@"pdf"]) {
        image = [self PDFForView:graphView];
    }

    if ([filetype isEqualToString:@"tiff"]) {
        image = [self TIFFForView:graphView];
    }

    if (image==0) {
        NSRunAlertPanel(nil,@"Unknown file type '%@'",
                        nil,nil,nil,filetype);
        return;
    }

    if ([image writeToFile:[sheet filename] atomically:NO]==NO) {
        NSRunAlertPanel(nil,@"Cannot save file '%@': %s",nil,nil,nil,
                        [sheet filename],strerror(errno));
    }
}
```

17. Replace the previous version of the **saveDocumentTo:** method in Controller.m with the following one:

```
- (IBAction)saveDocumentTo:(id)sender
{
    NSString    *type = [ [ [formatMatrix selectedCell] title]
                                lowercaseString];

    // Get a Save panel
    savePanel = [NSSavePanel savePanel];
```

```
        [savePanel setTitle:@"Save Graph Image"];

        // Set the initial file type
        [savePanel setRequiredFileType:type];

        // Put the format box in the Save Panel
        [savePanel setAccessoryView:formatBox];

        [formatBox retain];                 // Keep a copy!

        // And run
        [savePanel beginSheetForDirectory:nil
                                     file:nil
                          modalForWindow:[graphView window]
                           modalDelegate:self
                  didEndSelector:@selector(savePanelDidEnd:returnCode:contextInfo:)
                             contextInfo:nil];
    }
```

Note that this method retains the formatBox instance variable. This is necessary because the savePanel automatically releases its accessory view. If the Controller class does not retain the formatBox, it will be freed, and an error will be generated the next time the Save panel (sheet) is displayed.

Testing the PDF and TIFF Save Feature

18. Build and run GraphPaper, saving all files first.

19. Click the Graph button, then choose the Save Graph menu command. You should see a Save panel with the accessory NSView containing the radio-button matrix, as shown in Figure 19-18.

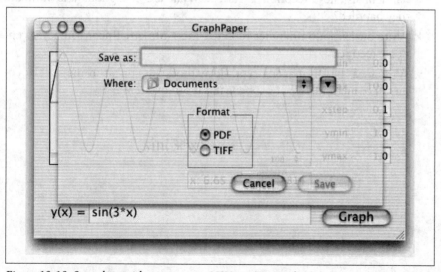

Figure 19-18. Save sheet with an accessory NSView (Format box)

20. Try saving the same graph as PDF and as TIFF. Then double-click the PDF and TIFF file icons in your Finder to see them in Preview. You might also try to import the files into a word processor or other application.

21. Quit GraphPaper.

Summary

You may notice that things are starting to happen really quickly—that's because we've reached critical mass with Cocoa. Everything we've learned is starting to jell and build on everything else that we've learned. The result is that with each step we now take, we can do more things with less effort.

From here on, you could probably figure out everything else about Cocoa simply by reading the documentation, because you've now mastered the basic concepts. The last two chapters of this book will walk you through a few special Cocoa systems that you'll find very useful: the cut-and-paste system and the Mac OS X defaults database system.

Exercises

1. In addition to PDF, the NSView and NSWindow classes can also generate EPS files. Extend the GraphPaper application so that it can also save files as EPS.

2. Can you improve GraphPaper's handling of resizing? If so, how?

3. Try setting the tag of one of the pop-up cells to "0" so that the NSInternalInconsistencyException is raised. What are exceptions and how are they handled?

4. Write an exception handler to catch the NSInternalInconsistencyException exception.

5. Why does the [**formatBox retain**]; method call appear in the **saveDocumentTo:** method? What happens if it is removed? Why?

CHAPTER 20

Pasteboards, Services, Modal Sessions, and Drag-and-Drop

In the previous chapter, we showed how images produced by the Graph-Paper application can be incorporated into other programs by saving the images in PDF or TIFF files. In this chapter, we'll show more ways that Cocoa provides for making applications work together: the cut, copy, and paste system; the Services system; and the drag-and-drop system. To make the Services system work, we'll also need to introduce the concept of *modal sessions*—that is, event loops other than the primary event loop. You'll enjoy this chapter, because Services and drag-and-drop are really nifty features.

Cut, Copy, and Paste with the Pasteboard

The Cocoa NSPasteboard object provides a simple and direct way for users to transfer data between applications using familiar copy, cut, and paste commands. In fact, every application we've created already implements copy, cut, and paste inside the text fields: this behavior is built into the NSTextView class.

Cocoa extends the traditional notions of cut, copy, and paste by providing multiple pasteboards (clipboards), each of which can hold several different data representations simultaneously. It also provides *lazy evaluation*, a system whereby information is not put onto the pasteboard unless it is needed by a receiving application.

Types of Pasteboards

Cocoa provides the following five basic pasteboards:

General pasteboard (NSGeneralPboard)
> Used to cut, copy, and paste data between applications. This pasteboard supports the ordinary Cut, Copy, and Paste menu commands. (It was

formerly called the NSSelectionPboard, because it's the pasteboard used for selections.)

Ruler pasteboard (NSRulerPboard)
Holds information about margins and tab stops. This pasteboard supports Copy Ruler and Paste Ruler commands such as those often found in word processor applications.

Font pasteboard (NSFontPboard)
Holds information about character font size, format, and style. This pasteboard supports Copy Font and Paste Font menu commands.

Find pasteboard (NSFindPboard)
Holds information about the current state of each application's Find panel. Although most applications don't use the Find pasteboard, it is designed so that you can execute a Find command in one application and then execute a Find-Next command in another application without having to retype the search string.

Drag pasteboard (NSDragPboard)
Holds information when objects (such as color chips) are dragged from one window (or application) to another.

You can also create your own pasteboards and use them between different applications that you write. Of course, other people's applications are not likely to know of their existence.

Users and Pasteboards

Pasteboards are generally transparent to the user. That is, users don't realize that there are five distinct pasteboards—they simply benefit from the fact that, for example, cutting text from one application and pasting it into another doesn't change the last ruler that they copied or pasted. Likewise, a user might search for the word "Cocoa" in one application, not find it, switch to another application and type Command-F again, and then be pleased to discover that the "default" search string is still "Cocoa" (because the string was put onto the NSFindPboard by the first application and then read from there by the second one). Users are also generally unaware that Cocoa pasteboards can hold data in multiple representations at the same time—they simply like the results when they paste from one application into another.

Consider this: if you create a complex image with Stone's Create program, copy it to the pasteboard, switch to TextEdit, and then choose the Paste command, TextEdit may paste the image into the window in PDF, TIFF, and possibly a number of other formats. If you quit Create and then start it up again and paste the image from the pasteboard into the new Create document, you will actually paste in a fully editable Create document, rather than just an image. This is because Create puts several different kinds of representations of the copied illustration onto the pasteboard, including the PDF and TIFF formats, which other programs can use, and Create's internal file format.

There's also nothing like the pasteboard for showing bugs and implementation errors in Cocoa applications. For example, if you copy an image from Create and paste it into OmniGraffle, you'll discover that OmniGraffle pastes in the TIFF representation, even though the PDF representation is also on the pasteboard. Paste in a tiny star and then stretch it to make it big, and you'll see lots of pixelation and jaggies. Likewise, if you make an illustration in OmniGraffle and paste it into Create, you'll see that it gets pasted in as a TIFF, not as a PDF. It turns out that both of these are the same bug, a bug in the NSImage implementation that is part of the Mac OS X Version 10.1 operating system. NSImage in Version 10.1 always returns a TIFF image, even if only a PDF file is located on the pasteboard.

Unfortunately, when you find one of these bugs, all you can do is report it to the program's author and go on: the pasteboard system doesn't give you a way to fix bugs in other people's programs (Andrew Stone at Stone Design fixed that bug in Create just a few hours after it was reported, by coding around the bug in the NSImage class).

Providing Data to the Pasteboard

Cocoa keeps data on the pasteboard using a separate program called pbs, or the pasteboard server. (Use the ProcessViewer utility application or enter the Unix command ps aux in a shell window to see the running pbs server.) You can communicate with the pasteboard server only indirectly, by sending messages to the NSPasteboard object.

There are seven commonly used NSPasteboard methods. The following two class methods return the id of an NSPasteboard object:

+ (NSPasteboard *)**generalPasteboard**
    Returns the id of the general pasteboard

+ (NSPasteboard *)**pasteboardWithName:**(NSString *)*name*
    Returns the id of a pasteboard with a given name.

The following two instance methods put data onto a pasteboard. They are usually invoked by the **cut:** or **copy:** methods that handle the Cut or Copy menu commands (or by your overrides of these methods).

- (int)**declareTypes:**(NSArray *)*newTypes* **owner:**(id)*newOwner*
    Tells the pasteboard which types you can provide

- (BOOL)**setData:**(NSData *)*data* **forType:**(NSString *)*dataType*
    Writes the data for a particular type to the pasteboard

The following instance methods take data from the pasteboard. These are usually invoked by a **paste:** method that handles the Paste menu command.

- (NSArray *)**types**

    Returns an array listing the kinds of types available for pasting

- (NSString *)**availableTypeFromArray:**(NSArray *)*types*

    Scans the array of types and returns the first type on the pasteboard that matches one of the types in the array

- (NSData *)**dataForType:**(NSString *)*dataType*

    Reads data of the specified type from the pasteboard server; returns nil if the type is not available

Cocoa defines 15 basic pasteboard data types, as shown in Table 20-1.

Table 20-1. Cocoa pasteboard types

Type	Contents
NSColorPboardType	NSColor data
NSFileContentsPboardType	A representation of a file's contents
NSFilenamesPboardType	An NSString designating one or more filenames
NSFontPboardType	Font and character information
NSHTMLPboardType	HTML (which NSTextView can read from, but not write to)
NSPDFPboardType	PDF data
NSPICTPboardType	QuickDraw Picture data
NSPostScriptPboardType	Encapsulated PostScript (EPS) code
NSRulerPboardType	Paragraph formatting information
NSRTFPboardType	Rich Text Format (RTF)
NSRTFDPboardType	RTFD-formatted file contents
NSStringPboardType	NSString data
NSTabularTextPboardType	An NSString containing tab-separated fields of text
NSTIFFPboardType	Tagged Image File Format (TIFF)
NSURLPboardType	NSURL data

Data on the pasteboard is stored as an array of bytes, in a way similar to the way that you might store it in a file, but you'll always get the contents of the pasteboard in an NSData or an NSString object.

Programs can put data on the pasteboard in two ways:

Immediately

    For example, when the user types Command-C, the program puts all of the selected data on the pasteboard.

Lazily

> When the user presses Command-C, the program simply tells the pasteboard what kinds of data it could provide if asked. Then, when the user does a paste in another application, the program that originally copied the data onto the pasteboard is asked to provide the requested data.

Most Cocoa programs write one format onto the pasteboard when the user performs a cut or copy operation and use lazy evaluation to provide the other kinds of representations that the application knows about. The representation written first should be the most "rich" representation of the data possible—a representation that can be used to reconstruct all the others. If the application performing the paste operation wants data in a different format, the first application reads the richest description from the pasteboard, converts the data to the requested format, and writes it back.

Using the Pasteboard in GraphPaper

To demonstrate how to use the pasteboard, we'll first modify the GraphPaper application so that a user can copy a graph to the pasteboard by choosing the Edit → Copy menu command.

When you create a new project in Project Builder and then open the new `MainMenu.nib` file in Interface Builder, you are automatically provided with an Edit submenu like the one shown in Figure 20-1. The top seven menu items listed (all but the Find and Spelling submenus) come preconnected to the First Responder icon (a proxy icon in IB that represents the current First Responder object, which changes in response to user events). The methods invoked by the First Responder object in response to these menu commands are **undo:**, **redo:**, **cut:**, **copy:**, **paste:**, **clear:**, and **selectAll:**, respectively. Thus, to implement Cut and Copy menu commands for the graph, all we need to do is add **cut:** and **copy:** methods to GraphPaper's Controller class and make Controller the NSApp (NSApplication object) delegate. (Note that we already made Controller the NSApp delegate, in Chapter 17.) The **cut:** and **copy:** messages will automatically be forwarded to NSApp's delegate, unless another responder in the responder chain intercepts them first.

GraphPaper's implementation of cut, copy, and paste will be able to provide data in two formats: PDF and TIFF. Because PDF is the richer of these two formats, GraphPaper will put PDF on the pasteboard first and then convert it to TIFF if requested by lazy evaluation.

Now we're ready to discuss the implementations of Controller's **copyToPasteboard:** and **copy:** methods. The supporting **copyToPasteboard:** method is the one that does most of the work.

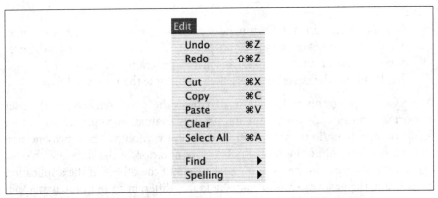

Figure 20-1. Default Edit menu provided for a new Cocoa application in IB

Controller.h

1. Insert the following four method declarations into `Controller.h`:

```
- (void)copyToPasteboard:(NSPasteboard *)pboard;
- (IBAction)copy:(id)sender;
- (void)pasteboard:(NSPasteboard *)sender
        provideDataForType:(NSString *)type;
- (IBAction)cut:(id)sender;
```

Controller.m

2. Insert the following **copyToPasteboard:** and **copy:** methods into `Controller.m`:

```
- (void)copyToPasteboard:(NSPasteboard *)pboard
{
    // Declare that we can handle PDF and TIFF
    [pboard declareTypes:[NSArray arrayWithObjects:
        NSPDFPboardType,NSTIFFPboardType,nil] owner:self];

    // Now put a PDF on the pasteboard
    [pboard setData:[self PDFForView:graphView] forType:NSPDFPboardType];
}

- (IBAction)copy:(id)sender
{
    [self copyToPasteboard: [NSPasteboard generalPasteboard] ];
}
```

The **copyToPasteboard:** method begins by constructing a disposable array of two elements, NSPDFPboardType and NSTIFFPboardType. The order of these two elements is important: it specifies the preferred order in which the types should be used (PDF is better than TIFF). It then sends the **declareTypes:owner:** message to the pasteboard object (which is passed from the **copy:** method) to do three things:

i. Erase any existing data on the pasteboard.

ii. Tell the pasteboard that your object can provide data of type PDF or TIFF.

iii. Specify an object (via the **owner:** argument) that the pasteboard can message to provide any types necessary for lazy evaluation. Whenever there is a request for lazy data from the NSPasteboard, the pasteboard will send the **pasteboard:provideDataForType:** message to the object specified by the **owner:** argument.

The **setData:forType:** message in the **copyToPasteboard:** method gets an NSData object with the PDF representation and puts it on the pasteboard.

The **copy:** method simply calls **copyToPasteboard:** with a general NSPasteboard. We use this methodology so that we can use the **copyToPasteboard:** method later in this chapter to copy the PDF and TIFF representations to pasteboards other than the general pasteboard.

Providing Data Through Lazy Evaluation

Suppose that a user has copied a GraphPaper graph to the pasteboard and wants to paste it into another application, such as TextEdit (which we'll refer to as the receiving application). When the user chooses the Paste command to paste the graph, the receiving application obtains access to the selection pasteboard with the **[NSPasteboard generalPasteboard]** message and then sends the **types** message to find out what types are available. The **types** message will return the following array of two types that the GraphPaper put on the pasteboard with the **declareTypes:owner:** method:

```
{NSPDFPboardType, NSTIFFPboardType}
```

Even if the receiving program knows what kind of data it wants, the program must first send the NSPasteboard the **types** message to set it up for returning the requested data. Once the **types** message is sent, the receiving program can ask for either type and be reasonably well assured of getting it.

If the receiving application wants the NSPDFPboardType, it will simply take the data off the pasteboard when it invokes the **dataForType:** method. However, if it wants the NSTIFFPboardType, it will wait while the NSPasteboard object sends the **pasteboard:provideDataForType:** message to GraphPaper's Controller object and receives a reply. This lazy evaluation is completely transparent to the program that is receiving the pasted data.

The **pasteboard:provideDataForType:** method that performs the conversion from PDF to TIFF is a little tricky. We can't just use the Controller instance method **TIFFForView:** (as in the previous chapter), because it is possible that the graph that was copied to the pasteboard is no longer the one displayed in the GraphPaper window. Instead, this method needs to take the PDF image from the pasteboard and convert it to a TIFF image. It does this conversion by using an NSImage object.

Controller.m

3. Insert the following **pasteboard:provideDataForType:** method into Controller.m:

```
- (void)pasteboard:(NSPasteboard *)sender
        provideDataForType:(NSString *)type
{
    if ([type isEqualToString:NSTIFFPboardType]) {
        NSImage *image = [[NSImage alloc]
                        initWithData:[sender dataForType:NSPDFPboardType]];

        [sender setData:[image TIFFRepresentation]
                forType:NSTIFFPboardType];
        [image release];
    }
}
```

This method both reads information off the pasteboard and puts new data on the pasteboard. The data is read off the pasteboard with the method **dataFor-Type:**. Data from the pasteboard arrives in the form of an NSData object. Although this NSData object looks like the others, the kernel may implement the copy by mapping the data from the address space of one application to another without actually copying the data. This is why Cocoa doesn't "choke" when you cut and paste tens of megabytes of information at once.

If the user quits GraphPaper after some of its data has been copied to the pasteboard, its NSApplication object will automatically force the pasteboard owner to turn all of the lazy data into real data (or at least ask the user if the copied data will be needed by another application). This lets the user paste data into another application even if the source (application) of the data copied to the pasteboard is no longer running.

Implementing the Cut Command

Cutting data is similar to copying it, except the data in the application is deleted after the copy operation is performed. For GraphPaper, it doesn't make a lot of sense to cut out a graph from the ZoomScrollView, but implementing it still makes sense from a user-interface point of view (it's good practice to give the user the expected feedback from a well-known and widely used command). Therefore, if the user tries to cut a graph, GraphPaper will copy the graph onto the pasteboard and then erase the ZoomScrollView.

Controller.m

4. Insert the following directive at the top of Controller.m:

```
#import "ZoomScrollView.h"
```

5. Insert the following **cut:** method implementation into Controller.m:

```
- (IBAction)cut:(id)sender
{
    [self copy:sender];
    [graphView clear];
}
```

Testing GraphPaper's Copy and Cut Commands

6. Build and run GraphPaper, saving all files first.

7. Graph an equation and click the cursor on the graph (otherwise, one of the text fields might be the first responder).

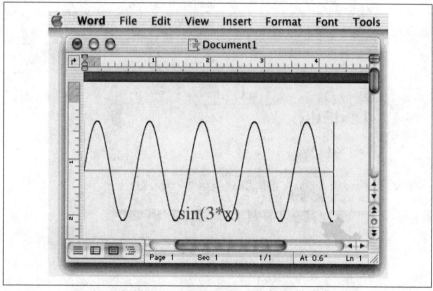

8. Choose GraphPaper's Edit → Copy menu command to copy the graph to the pasteboard. GraphPaper's NSApplication object will send the **copy:** message to its delegate Controller object.

9. Open a document in Word, Create, or any other application that supports graphics (TextEdit does so in Rich Text mode) and choose the Edit → Paste menu command.

If the modifications to GraphPaper are correct and the program you're using can handle the appropriate pasteboard types, the graph will appear in your word-processor document. (An example of pasting into Word is shown in Figure 20-2.) If you don't have any such applications, download a trial version from the Web.

Figure 20-2. A GraphPaper graph pasted into Word

10. Now graph a different equation and click in the ZoomScrollView area.

11. Choose GraphPaper's Edit → Cut menu command this time. The graph should disappear.

12. Again choose the Edit → Paste menu command in the word processor, and the second graph should appear.

13. Quit GraphPaper.

Services

In addition to cut, copy, and paste, Cocoa provides a nearly transparent system for applications to work together called *Services*. Services work with Cocoa's concept of "selection" to provide a system for automatically sending information from one application to accomplish a specific function in another.

Services can send information, retrieve it, or do bidirectional processing. For example, say you're looking at an article in a TextEdit file. To clip a paragraph from the article and place it in a "Sticky" on the desktop, you can simply select the paragraph and choose Services → Make Sticky, as shown in Figure 20-3.

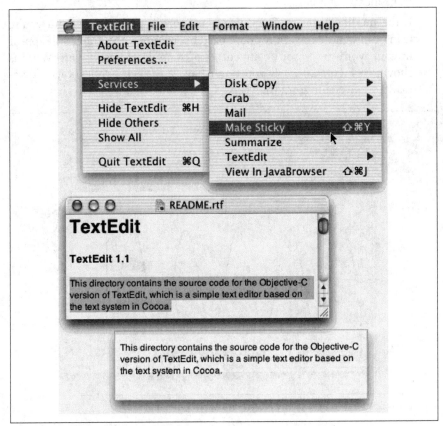

Figure 20-3. The Services menu provides interapplication messaging without prior agreement between applications

How Services Work

Unlike most menus, the Services menu is *not* controlled by the application in which it appears. Instead, the content of the Services menu is controlled by the operating system.

When a user logs in, the Cocoa environment scans all of the folders listed in Table 20-2 for applications that advertise that they can handle the Services protocol. This advertisement consists of a list of the messages that the program can handle, what kinds of data types it can accept, and what kinds of data types it can return.

Table 20-2. Folders scanned for applications offering services during user login

/Applications[a]	~/Applications[b]
/Library/Services	~/Library/Services
/System/Services	/Network/Applications
/Network/Library/Services	

[a] And all subdirectories.
[b] The character "~" indicates the user's home directory.

 If the services for a newly installed application do not appear in your Services menu, try logging out of your computer and logging back in. If that doesn't work, wait 15 minutes, shut down your computer, start it up again, and log in again. At some point, the services should appear.

For example, the Stickies advertisement is as follows:

```
NSExecutable: Stickies
NSKeyEquivalent: Y
NSMenuItem: Make Sticky
NSMessage: makeStickyFromTextServices
NSPortName: Stickies
NSSendTypes: NSStringPboardType, NSRTFPboardType
```

It's also possible for an application to have an NSReturnTypes field, but Stickies doesn't.

The advertisements that an application makes are stored in the Info.plist file contained inside the application's .app wrapper (folder). When a user runs an application, the application sends the following message to NSApp to register which types it can send and receive:

```
(void)registerServicesMenuSendTypes:(NSArray *)sendTypes
                andReturnTypes:(NSArray *)returnTypes
```

sendTypes and *returnTypes* are both NSArrays of NSString objects that are similar to those used by NSPasteboard's **declareTypes:owner:** method. After the program starts running, the following method:

```
(id)validRequestorForSendType:(NSString *)typeSent
                returnType:(NSString *)typeReturned
```

is sent down the responder chain for every combination of send and return types that the application can handle. If a responder can handle a particular combination, it should return something other than NULL (such as `self`). For example, the NSTextView class implements this method, returning `self` for the combinations shown in Table 20-3 and NULL for all others.

Table 20-3. NSTextView send and return types

Send type	Return type	Comments
NULL	NSStringPboardType	Inserts new text
NULL	NSRTFPboardType	Inserts new Rich Text
NSStringPboardType	NULL	Sends text, no return
NSRTFPboardType	NULL	Sends Rich Text, no return
NSStringPboardType	NSStringPboardType	Sends text, gets a response, and replaces the sent text with the received text
NSStringPboardType	NSStringPboardType	
NSStringPboardType	NSRTFPboardType	
NSRTFPboardType	NSStringPboardType	
NSRTFPboardType	NSRTFPboardType	

The **validRequestorForSendType:returnType:** method is invoked often, so it should be as efficient as possible. Normally, it simply looks for combinations of send and return types and returns a value.

When the user selects an item from the Services menu in your application, your object will be sent the **writeSelectionToPasteboard:types:** message declared as follows:

```
@interface NSObject(NSServicesRequests)
- (BOOL)writeSelectionToPasteboard:(NSPasteboard *)pboard
                            types:(NSArray *)types;
@end
```

This method is defined by the Application Kit as a category of the NSObject class, so it can be sent to any object in your application. Normally, though, it will be sent only to objects that can handle selection. When this method in an object in your application gets invoked, it should write whatever is selected to the pasteboard pboard. The method should return YES if the data can be provided and NO if it cannot.

If the service returns data, your object should also implement the **readSelectionFromPasteboard:** method:

```
@interface NSObject(NSServicesRequests)
- (BOOL)readSelectionFromPasteboard:(NSPasteboard *)pboard;
@end
```

If you are creating an object that does not handle selection, you do not need to implement or even worry about these methods. (The NSTextView object is an example of an object that handles selection.) For the remainder of this chapter, we will concentrate solely on the other half of the process—offering services to other applications.

 Carbon applications can also interoperate with the Services system, but these require additional work on the part of the programmer—services aren't as easy to implement under Carbon as they are under Cocoa.

Creating Your Own Service

Services advertisements, such as the one we listed earlier for the Stickies application, are stored in the application's Info.plist file, an XML-encoded file stored inside the .app wrapper. When Mac OS X registers a new application, it opens up the Info.plist file and looks for the application's application icon, its document icons, and its Services advertisement (if it exists). This information is cached to improve performance.

Table 20-4 lists all of the fields allowed in the Services advertisement.

Table 20-4. Services advertisement fields

Field	Meaning
Message	Name of the message to be sent.
NSExecutable	Name of the application's executable.
NSKeyEquivalent	Key equivalent, if any, that the Services menu item should have.
NSMenuItem	Name that should appear in the Services menu. If you want to have a submenu, use the forward slash (/). For example, to have "equation" be a submenu of "graph", you would use the string "graph/equation".
NSMessage	Actual message that is sent to your application to cause the service to be executed. Messages are implemented with the Cocoa distributed object system.
NSPortName	Name of the Mach port where the message should be sent. Normally, this will be the name of your application's "Identifier," defined in the Application Settings tab in PB.
NSReturnTypes	Pasteboard types that the method can return.
NSSendTypes	Pasteboard types that the method can send.
NSTimeout	Numerical string that is the time, in milliseconds, that the sending application should wait before timing out. The default is 30,000 (30 seconds).
NSUserData	Optional string that contains any value of your choice. This can be used to distinguish several different services from each other, as an alternative to giving the services different messages.

When your application starts up, you should register an object that will receive the incoming services messages. The easiest way to register an object is using the NSApplication **setServicesProvider:** message. (You can also use the NSRegisterServicesProvider( ) function.) The Services system uses a private pasteboard to exchange data between the sending and receiving applications.

To respond to a services message, you must implement a method in the Services delegate object that has the following form:

```
- (void)<serviceName>:(NSPasteboard *)pasteboard
          userData:(NSString *)userData
             error:(NSString **)msg
```

The `msg` argument is for returning an error condition. If your method needs to return an error, set *msg to an NSString describing the error. The string will be displayed on the system console.

Modifications Required for GraphPaper to Implement Services

To show how services work, we're going to modify the GraphPaper application so that it is accessible through the Services menus of other applications. The graph service will take a formula selected by the user, graph it using the current graph parameters, and return the completed graph. To perform this operation, the method that implements the service will need to read a formula from the pasteboard, draw the graph, and then put the graph back on the pasteboard.

GraphPaper requires a few minor modifications and one significant one to work as a service. The minor modifications will take care of advertising the service, receiving the service message, making the graph, and returning the result. This is all fairly straightforward and will be based on the same pasteboard code that we have developed up to this point.

The significant modification will allow the service provided to initiate a graph and determine when the graph is completed. When GraphPaper is running as a service, it will not use the standard Cocoa event loop. Instead, it will run its own modal session.

A *modal session* is like the standard application event loop that we have used until now, except the application object ignores events from all windows other than the window designated in the **runModalSession:** message. This is how Cocoa implements Alert alerts.

The GraphView object will signal that the graph is finished by sending the **stop:** message to NSApp. This method is normally used to stop the main event loop. When you are running a modal session, it stops the modal session, which then returns control to the location where the modal session was started. In our example, it will return control to our Controller object and signal for the completed graph to be sent to the application that requested the service.

Don't worry if this seems complicated—it will be quite simple to implement.

Creating the Services Advertisement

Services advertisements are stored in the Info.plist file that is one of the application resources. The Info.plist file is in XML format and should not be edited directly. Instead, you should use PB to edit it.

Unfortunately, with Mac OS X Version 10.1 it is necessary to (painstakingly) use PB's "Expert" XML editing mode to manually create the XML structure necessary for the Services advertisement (PropertyListEditor is about the same hassle). It is possible that Apple will have added an easier-to-use mode for creating Services advertisements by the time you read this book—if so, you might want to experiment with it. Nevertheless, even if such a "Services wizard" is created, the following steps should still work.

1. Activate PB, if it's not already running. Click the Targets vertical tab and the GraphPaper target in the Targets pane.

Project Builder

2. Click the Application Settings tab and the Expert button at the right.

3. Next, click the New Sibling button. A new sibling named "New item" should appear in the property list, with the class String.

4. Change the name of the sibling to "NSServices", as shown near the bottom of the window in Figure 20-4.

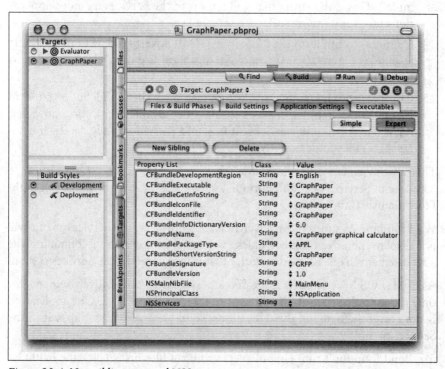

Figure 20-4. New sibling renamed NSServices

5. Change the class of the sibling to Array by pressing the stepper (up-down arrow) next to String and selecting Array from the resulting pop-up menu.

6. Click the disclosure triangle (which appears for Arrays) to the left of NSServices so that it points downward.

7. Make sure that the word "NSServices" is selected. Note that the New Sibling button is now labeled "New Child".

8. Click the New Child button, and a new row of information will appear under NSServices.

    You have created the first entry in the NSServices array. Its name, "0", cannot be changed, because the name of this child is its index in the NSServices array.

9. Change the class of this new entry to Dictionary using the stepper.

10. Now click the disclosure triangle to the left of the 0 under NSServices so that it points downward, and click the New Child button again.

11. Rename the new item "NSMenuItem" and change its class to Dictionary.

12. Click the disclosure triangle to the left of the NSMenuItem so that it points downward, and click the New Child button once again.

13. Give it the name "default", the class String, and the value "Graph Formula". This is the string that will appear in the Services menu of applications that support GraphPaper's service.

14. Continue to build up the NSServices XML advertisement until it exactly resembles Figure 20-5. If you make mistakes, use the Delete button next to the New Child button.

15. Change "Development" to "Deployment" in the Build Styles pane in Figure 20-5. GraphPaper has become a deployable application now that it has pasteboard and service features, and we will actually deploy it in an /Applications folder shortly.

This advertisement tells Mac OS X that your service should have a single menu item, Services → Graph Formula, which responds to the message **graphFormula:userData:error:**.

We have now completed the advertisement. However, the Services menu will not display the advertisement unless we place an application containing the advertisement in one of the directories that is monitored by the Services system.

As of Mac OS X Version 10.1, the Services system scans for advertisements for only those applications in the directories listed in Table 20-2. Our application is not currently in any of these locations, so its services will not appear in the Services menu!

16. Build (but don't run) GraphPaper, saving all files first. (Click the hammer-only button in PB's toolbar.)

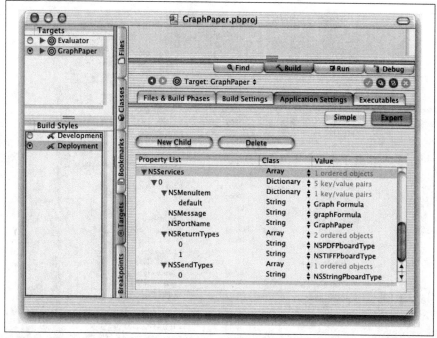

Figure 20-5. The completed NSServices property list

Before we check to see if the new service works, we'll verify that the Info.
plist file in your newly built GraphPaper application contains the XML property list for your Services advertisement. The easiest way to do that is to use
the PropertyListEditor application in the /Developer/Applications folder.

17. Back in the Finder, choose Go → Go to Folder and enter the folder
    name ~/GraphPaper/build/GraphPaper.app/Contents. You should see the
    Info.plist file bundled into the GraphPaper.app application.

18. Double-click the Info.plist file in the Contents directory to open it in the
    PropertyListEditor developer application.

PropertyListEditor

19. Click the disclosure triangles within the NSServices Property List item in
    PropertyListEditor until you get the window shown in Figure 20-6. We
    have verified that the Info.plist file was properly created by PB.

20. Quit PropertyListEditor.

You can also view the Info.plist file's contents in a Terminal shell window
using the Unix cat command, as follows:

    cat ~/GraphPaper/build/GraphPaper.app/Contents/Info.plist

but the output is less palatable.

Next, we'll duplicate our application and put the copy in a directory that gets
scanned for services.

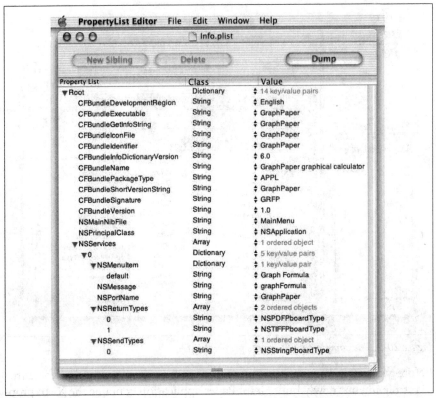

Property List	Class	Value
▼ Root	Dictionary	⬍ 14 key/value pairs
CFBundleDevelopmentRegion	String	⬍ English
CFBundleExecutable	String	⬍ GraphPaper
CFBundleGetInfoString	String	⬍ GraphPaper
CFBundleIconFile	String	⬍ GraphPaper
CFBundleIdentifier	String	⬍ GraphPaper
CFBundleInfoDictionaryVersion	String	⬍ 6.0
CFBundleName	String	⬍ GraphPaper graphical calculator
CFBundlePackageType	String	⬍ APPL
CFBundleShortVersionString	String	⬍ GraphPaper
CFBundleSignature	String	⬍ GRFP
CFBundleVersion	String	⬍ 1.0
NSMainNibFile	String	⬍ MainMenu
NSPrincipalClass	String	⬍ NSApplication
▼ NSServices	Array	⬍ 1 ordered object
▼ 0	Dictionary	⬍ 5 key/value pairs
▼ NSMenuItem	Dictionary	⬍ 1 key/value pair
default	String	⬍ Graph Formula
NSMessage	String	⬍ graphFormula
NSPortName	String	⬍ GraphPaper
▼ NSReturnTypes	Array	⬍ 2 ordered objects
0	String	⬍ NSPDFPboardType
1	String	⬍ NSTIFFPboardType
▼ NSSendTypes	Array	⬍ 1 ordered object
0	String	⬍ NSStringPboardType

Figure 20-6. GraphPaper's Info.plist file as viewed in PropertyListEditor

21. In the Finder, locate and open the directory called ~/GraphPaper/build.

    A copy of the GraphPaper application should be in the build directory. It will appear as the file GraphPaper, but it's actually a directory called GraphPaper.app (recall that the Finder doesn't display the extension). This is the copy of the application that is built every time you build your program within PB. It is also the copy of the program that gets run within the debugger.

22. Select GraphPaper in the ~/GraphPaper/build directory in the Finder and then choose the File → Duplicate menu command.

    You should see a new file icon called "GraphPaper copy" in the same directory. This copy will eventually be moved into a folder that is scanned for services.

GraphPaper copy

23. Drag the GraphPaper copy icon out of your build directory and drop it on the desktop.

24. Change the name of the icon from "GraphPaper copy" to "GraphPaper" (single-click the name, double-click Copy, press Delete twice, and then hit Return).

25. Drag the GraphPaper desktop icon into the /Applications folder. If you don't have the permissions to do that, create a folder called Applications in your Home folder and drag the GraphPaper alias into it.

26. Log out of your computer. This is needed to make the Graph Formula service available.

27. Log back into your computer.

When you log back into your computer, the Services system will begin scanning the monitored directories for any new applications. When the Services system finds GraphPaper alias, it will discover the Info.plist file and read the Services advertisement. (If this doesn't work, try restarting and even shutting down your computer. If you've configured the Info.plist correctly, the service should show up eventually.)

On some versions of Mac OS X, the Services system will not follow the alias. If you are unable to get the GraphPaper Services menu to appear using the steps here, try putting the entire application (GraphPaper.app) into the /Applications directory.

Modification of GraphView

In the following steps, we will modify the GraphView class so that it can be effectively commanded by the Controller class to run as a service.

28. Insert the following instance variable into GraphView.h:

```
BOOL runningAsService;
```

GraphView.h

29. Insert the following two method declarations into GraphView.h:

```
- (void)setFormula:(NSString *)aString;
- (void)setRunningAsService:(BOOL)flag;
```

We'll use the runningAsService instance variable to tell GraphView that it should stop the modal loop when the graph is finished being drawn.

30. Insert the three lines shown here in bold into the **doStop:** method in GraphView.m:

GraphView.m

```
- (void)doStop:(int)which
{
    switch (which){
        case STOP_SENDER:
            sending = NO;
            break;
        case STOP_RECEIVER:
            receiving = NO;
            break;
    }
}
```

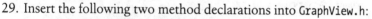

```
if (sending==NO && receiving==NO) {
    [graphButton setTitle:@"Graph"];
    [graphButton setAction:@selector(graph:)];
    [graphButton setEnabled:YES];

    // For service support
    if (runningAsService) {
        [NSApp stop:nil];
    }
}

if (sending==NO && receiving!=NO) {
    [graphButton setEnabled:FALSE];
    [graphButton setTitle:@"Waiting..."];
}

if (sending!=NO && receiving==NO) {
    NSLog(@"Synchronization error");
}
}
```

This addition causes the **stop:** message to be sent to GraphPaper's Application object when the graph is stopped or finished.

31. Insert these two accessor methods into GraphView.m:

```
- (void)setFormula:(NSString *)aString
{
    [formulaField setStringValue:aString];
}

- (void)setRunningAsService:(BOOL)aFlag
{
    runningAsService = aFlag;
}
```

That's it for the changes to GraphView.

Changes to Controller

Finally, we need to modify the Controller class to register as a service so that it can receive the advertisement, and to actually handle the services request when that request arrives.

Services registration should be the last thing that your application does before it starts to accept events, because your application may receive a services request right after it registers. Thus, we cannot register for receiving services requests in an **awakeFromNib** or an **initWithFrame:** method (which may be followed by additional initializations). Instead, we will register our service in the application delegate method **applicationDidFinishLaunching:**.

32. Insert the following two method declarations into Controller.h (not GraphView.h):

Controller.h

```
// Services
- (void)applicationDidFinishLaunching:(NSNotification *)aNot;
- (void)graphFormula:(NSPasteboard *)pboard
            userData:(NSString *)userData
               error:(NSString **)error;
```

33. Insert the **applicationDidFinishLaunching:** delegate method into the file Controller.m:

Controller.m

```
- (void)applicationDidFinishLaunching:(NSNotification *)aNot
{
    NSLog(@"Registering as a Services Provider");
    [NSApp setServicesProvider:self];
}
```

This method sets the Controller object as the services provider. You must do this in order to receive services messages. The call to NSLog( ) is for our benefit—it tells us that the application has properly initialized. When you are running the application from within PB, you'll see this notice in the PB window (Run pane). Otherwise, the notice will be visible within the Console application.

34. Insert the **graphFormula:userData:error:** method into Controller.m:

```
- (void)graphFormula:(NSPasteboard *)pboard
            userData:(NSString *)userData
               error:(NSString **)error
{
    BOOL wasHidden = [NSApp isHidden];

    [pboard types];                        // Get the types
    [graphView setRunningAsService:YES];
    [graphView setFormula:[pboard stringForType:NSStringPboardType]];
    [graphView graph:nil];                 // Do the graph

    // The NSEvent will cause periodic events to flow so that
    // the window will pick up events form the NSTask.
    // This may be a bug in the AppKit.
    [NSEvent startPeriodicEventsAfterDelay:0 withPeriod:0.1];
    [NSApp runModalForWindow:[graphView window]];
    [NSEvent stopPeriodicEvents];

    [graphView setRunningAsService:NO];
    [self copyToPasteboard:pboard ];

    if (wasHidden) {
        [NSApp hide:self];
    }
}
```

Although this **graphFormula:userData:error:** method may seem complex, it's fairly self-explanatory. The method first sends the **types** message to the pasteboard, because if you don't do that, you can't read data from the object. Next it asks the pasteboard for its string data and puts this into the formula field, using the newly written **setFormula:** method. It then sends the **graph:** message to the GraphView object to start the graphing process.

Recall that the **graph:** message actually starts up the stuffer thread that sends (x,y) pairs to the Evaluator program. The results are read by the GraphView object because it has registered its **gotData:** method as an observer for the NSFileHandleReadCompletionNotification notification. All of this happens behind the scenes, as part of the application's main event loop. When an application is being run as a service, however, you don't want to be running the application's main event loop, because you don't want to be taking input from the user.

The way around this apparent conundrum is to create your own event loop, which Cocoa calls a *modal session*. This is what is done by the following command:

```
[NSApp runModalForWindow:[graphView window]];
```

This modal session runs until the GraphView object sends the **stop:** message to the NSApp object (which is done in the **doStop:** method).

So what's with the call to NSEvent to create a periodic event? It turns out that when a modal session is created for a window, the NSApplication class will wake up only for events that are destined for that window and for timer events—not for events generated by a watched file handle. We use the NSEvent class to create a stream of periodic events. These periodic events cause the NSApplication class to wake up, at which point it checks the NSFileHandle object to see if there is any pending data. After the modal session, we need to terminate the stream of timed events—hence the bracketing of the **runModalForWindow:** message with the two messages to NSEvent:

```
[NSEvent startPeriodicEventsAfterDelay:0 withPeriod:0.1];
[NSApp runModalForWindow:[graphView window]];
[NSEvent stopPeriodicEvents];
```

By the way, you might try running this example with the two calls to NSEvent commented out, just to see how your application runs within a modal session. If you do this, you'll see the graph appear whenever you generate an event in the GraphView window—for example, by clicking on the window or by choosing a menu.

When the modal session is finished, this method resets the runningAsService flag and copies the graph to the pasteboard that was provided by the Services manager. The **copyToPasteboard:** method puts the PDF representation of the graph on the pasteboard; if the requesting application wants the TIFF representation, this data will be provided through lazy evaluation. Finally, if the GraphPaper application was originally hidden, it hides itself again. This is good manners.

Testing GraphPaper's Service

Well, it's time to give everything a whirl.

35. Build (but don't run) GraphPaper, saving all files first.

36. Start up TextEdit and make sure your active window supports Rich Text Format (check the TextEdit's Format menu, third item).

37. Type the formula sin(3*x) into a TextEdit window. Select the text and choose TextEdit's Services → Graph Formula menu command, as shown in Figure 20-7.

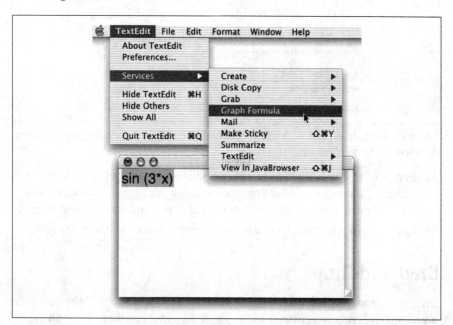

Figure 20-7. Requesting the GraphPaper service from the TextEdit application

If GraphPaper is not already running, Mac OS X will start it up. GraphPaper will then generate the graph, and the graph will replace the selected formula in the word processor, as shown in Figure 20-8.

If you get an "Error providing services Graph Formula" in PB's Run pane, you probably made a spelling error in either the Info.plist file or the Controller.m file.

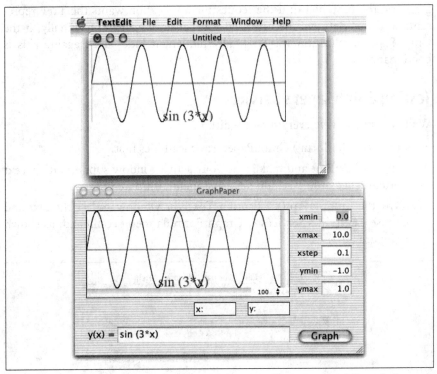

Figure 20-8. Result in TextEdit (top) after receiving GraphPaper-generated graph (bottom) via a Services menu request

38. Play around with services in other applications—for example, type and select a function in a Mail compose window and then choose Services → Graph Formula to create a lovely graph that you can send to your friends.

39. Quit GraphPaper (which launches or activates when you choose its service).

Drag-and-Drop

Drag-and-drop is another way for applications to interoperate: the user simply drags information from one application into another. Drag-and-drop requires more work on the part of the user than the Services system, because the data must be manually dragged across application boundaries. Drag-and-drop is also less powerful than Services because it does not offer the bidirectional interaction of services that receive information, act on it, and return a result. Nevertheless, drag-and-drop is easier than Services for many people to understand, largely because drag-and-drop is more familiar: it is present both in Windows and in previous versions of the Macintosh operating system.

Although we've already done a lot in this chapter, with just a little more work we can implement drag-and-drop functionality as well. So let's do it!

Being a Drag-and-Drop Source

We can make GraphPaper a drag-and-drop source by making a few small changes to the GraphView class. Unfortunately, one aspect of this process will be a little awkward because of our decision earlier in this chapter and the previous one to have the PDF- and TIFF-generation functionality centralized in the Controller class. (Fixing this design flaw is left to the user as an exercise.)

1. Add the following three new method declarations to the `GraphView.h` interface file:

   ```
   -(BOOL)acceptsFirstMouse:(NSEvent *)theEvent;
   -(NSDragOperation)draggingSourceOperationMaskForLocal:(BOOL)flag;
   -(void)mouseDragged:(NSEvent *)theEvent;
   ```

GraphView.h

2. Insert the `#import` directive shown here in bold at the beginning of `GraphView.m`:

   ```
   #import "GraphView.h"
   #import "Segment.h"
   #import "Label.h"
   #import "Controller.h"
   ```

GraphView.m

3. Add the **acceptsFirstMouse:** method to `GraphView.m`:

   ```
   - (BOOL)acceptsFirstMouse:(NSEvent *)theEvent
   {
       return YES;
   }
   ```

The Macintosh operating system is a click-to-focus window environment. This means that you click on a window to focus the keyboard on that window. But this can lead to confusing behavior. Sometimes you want a view to react immediately to an activating click, such as when you are clicking on a button of an application that is not active. Other times you do not want the application to react to this activating click. Whether or not an NSView reacts to an activating click is controlled by the **acceptsFirstMouse:** method. If this method returns YES, the NSWindow object will both activate and pass the event along to the NSView in which an activating click occurs. This is the behavior that we want for dragging operations, because, for example, the GraphPaper application will probably not be the active application when you are attempting to drag an image out of it.

You must override two methods to implement drag-and-drop in your view. The first method, **draggingSourceOperationMaskForLocal:**, tells Cocoa which drag-and-drop operations you support. The `flag` argument allows you to specify whether you support these operations only for other applications, or also within your own application.

The second method, **mouseDragged:**, is used to initiate a drag-and-drop operation. Your NSView subclass is sent this message when the mouse is dragged.

GraphView.m

4. Add the following **draggingSourceOperationMaskForLocal:** method to GraphView.m:

```
- (NSDragOperation)draggingSourceOperationMaskForLocal:(BOOL)flag
{
    if (flag==YES) return NSDragOperationNone;
    return NSDragOperationCopy;
}
```

This method returns an NSDragOperation type that indicates what kind of operation is supported. If flag is YES, we are being asked about drag operations within the same application. Otherwise, we are being asked about drag operations into other applications. This method tells the drag-and-drop system that we do not support dragging into the same application; we only support the copy operation into other applications.

Finally, we need to implement the method that does the actual dragging. Instead of hooking onto the **mouseDown:** event, we'll actually hook onto the **mouseDragged:** event, so that merely clicking in the GraphView will not initiate the dragging operation. (We tried the application both ways and decided that this way was better.)

5. Add the **mouseDragged:** method to GraphView.m:

```
- (void)mouseDragged:(NSEvent *)theEvent
{
    NSImage *pdfImage = [[NSWorkspace sharedWorkspace]
                            iconForFileType:@"pdf"];
    NSPasteboard *pboard;

    pboard = [NSPasteboard pasteboardWithName:NSDragPboard];
    [[NSApp delegate] copyToPasteboard:pboard];

    [self dragImage:pdfImage
                 at:[self convertPoint:[theEvent locationInWindow]
                        fromView:nil]
             offset:NSMakeSize(0,0)
              event:theEvent
         pasteboard:pboard
             source:self
          slideBack:YES];
}
```

This method first gets an image of a PDF file's icon. We don't really know what that image looks like, but the operating system knows, so we ask it and store the results in the pdfImage variable. We then ask the NSPasteboard class for the NSDragPboard and ask the Controller class to copy to this pasteboard. (This is the inelegant part, by the way. Ideally, the **copyToPasteboard** code should have been put in the GraphView class, rather than in the Controller class.)

Finally, we use the NSView **dragImage:at:offset:event:pasteboard:source: slideBack:** method to initiate the dragging operation. This method takes the arguments listed in Table 20-5.

Table 20-5. Method arguments of dragImage:at:offset:event:pasteboard:source:slideBack:

Argument	Meaning
at:	Location where the dragging should start.
offset:	Offset into the image for the dragging. We make this (0,0), but it could be a point within the image itself.
event:	Event that initiated the dragging operation.
pasteboard:	Pasteboard to use for the dragging operation.
source:	Source of the dragging operation; it is usually `self`, but it doesn't have to be.
slideBack:	If this argument is true, a released drag icon will appear to slide back to its source.

6. Build and run GraphPaper, saving all files first.

7. Start the TextEdit application and make sure the active window is in Rich Text mode.

8. Click the Graph button to graph a function.

9. Press your mouse on the graph and drag. A PDF icon should appear, as shown in Figure 20-9.

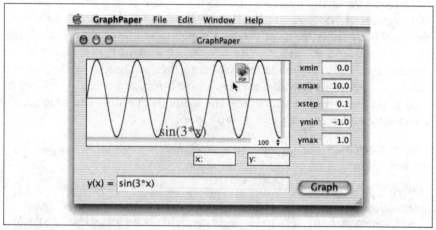

Figure 20-9. Dragging a PDF icon from GraphPaper

10. Drop the PDF icon into the TextEdit application. The graph should appear!

11. Quit GraphPaper.

Pretty neat, isn't it? Cocoa programming is actually lots of fun once you get the hang of it.

Being a Drag-and-Drop Receiver

As long as we are implementing drag-and-drop, we should implement the ability to receive drag-and-drop events as well. Of course, just what an application such as GraphPaper should do when it receives a drag-and-drop event might be subject to some debate. After all, what would it mean to drop something into a GraphView?

A drag-and-drop event contains both the data being dragged in and a type associated with that data. This information is on the pasteboard that is provided to the drag-and-drop receiver. (You should always interrogate the incoming drag-and-drop event for its pasteboard, rather than simply getting the global NSDragPboard.) We're not sure what it means to drag an image into the GraphPaper application. However, there are two obvious drag-and-drop types to which the GraphPaper application could respond:

- If the user drags in a color and drops it on an item in the GraphView, we should set the item to be that color.
- If the user drags in a piece of text and drops it on the GraphView, we should set the formula to be that text and initiate a graph.

We'll implement both of these.

Drag-and-drop receiving applications must implement one or more of the NSDraggingDestination category methods. These methods are implemented as categories of NSObject, rather than as informational protocols or categories of NSResponder. Because they are implemented as categories of NSObject, you can send the messages to any object without first checking to see whether that object responds to them. And they are probably categories of NSObject, rather than NSResponder, so both responders and cells can be used as drag-and-drop destinations. The methods that drag-and-drop receivers need to implement are listed in Table 20-6.

Table 20-6. NSObject (NSDraggingDestination) methods implemented by drag-and-drop receivers

Method	Purpose
- (NSDragOperation)**draggingEntered:** (id <NSDraggingInfo>)*sender*	Sent to a potential drag-and-drop receiver. NSObject returns NSDragOperationNone, which indicates that the object cannot receive drag-and-drop events.
- (NSDragOperation)**draggingUpdated:** (id <NSDraggingInfo>)*sender*	Sent periodically while a drag-and-drop object is held over a potential receiver. The receiver can use this to implement some sort of animation.
- (void)**draggingExited:** (id <NSDraggingInfo>)*sender*	Sent to the potential drag-and-drop receiver if no drag-and-drop took place.
- (BOOL)**prepareForDragOperation:** (id <NSDraggingInfo>)*sender*	Sent to the potential receiver when the drag-and-drop image is released. The receiver should return YES if it can receive the drag-and-drop object and NO if it cannot.
- (BOOL)**performDragOperation:** (id <NSDraggingInfo>)*sender*	Sent after the drag-and-drop object has been released. This is where the receiver should do the actual work of receiving the drag-and-drop object. Returns YES if the action was successful.

Table 20-6. NSObject (NSDraggingDestination) methods implemented by drag-and-drop receivers (continued)

Method	Purpose
- (void)**concludeDragOperation:**(id <NSDraggingInfo>)*sender*	Sent when the drag-and-drop operation is finished.
- (void)**draggingEnded:**(id <NSDraggingInfo>)*sender*	According to Apple's documentation, this is sent when the drag-and-drop operation concludes in some other destination. In fact, though, it isn't sent, because the document also indicates that this method hasn't been implemented.

Each of these methods has a single argument, an object that responds to the NSDraggingInfo protocol. The accessor methods for the NSDraggingInfo protocol are listed in Table 20-7.

Table 20-7. NSDraggingInfo protocol accessor methods

Method	Purpose
- (NSWindow *)**draggingDestinationWindow**	Returns the destination window of the drag operation.
- (NSDragOperation)**draggingSourceOperationMask**	Returns the dragging source operation mask, which indicates what sort of dragging operation the source supports.
- (NSPoint)**draggingLocation**	Returns the cursor's current location in the dragging operation, in the destination window's coordinate system.
- (NSPoint)**draggedImageLocation**	Returns the location of the dragged image.
- (NSImage *)**draggedImage**	Returns the actual image being dragged.
- (NSPasteboard *)**draggingPasteboard**	Returns the pasteboard that contains the data that is being dragged in.
- (id)**draggingSource**	Returns the source of the dragging operation.
- (int)**draggingSequenceNumber**	Returns the integer that uniquely identifies the dragging session.
- (void)**slideDraggedImageTo:**(NSPoint)*screenPoint*	Slides the image to *screenPoint*. Use this method to snap the image down to a particular location. Read the documentation for details.

We're going to implement the methods to receive a drag operation by modifying the ColorGraphView class.

12. Add the following method declarations to the ColorGraphView.h interface definition:

ColorGraphView.h

```
// Dragging support
- (int)tagAtPoint:(NSPoint)pt;
- (unsigned int)draggingEntered:(id <NSDraggingInfo>)sender;
- (unsigned int)draggingUpdated:(id <NSDraggingInfo>)sender;
- (BOOL)performDragOperation:(id <NSDraggingInfo>)sender;
@end
```

ColorGraphView.m

13. Modify the **initWithFrame:** method in ColorGraphView.m by inserting the lines shown here in bold:

```
- initWithFrame:(NSRect)frame
{
    [super initWithFrame:frame];
    axesColor = [[NSColor darkGrayColor] retain];
    graphColor = [[NSColor blackColor] retain];
    labelColor = [[NSColor blackColor] retain];

    [self registerForDraggedTypes:
        [NSArray arrayWithObjects:NSStringPboardType,
            NSColorPboardType,nil]];
    return self;
}
```

The **tagAtPoint:** method allows the methods that implement drag receiving to determine what object is underneath the cursor's hot spot.

14. Add the following **tagAtPoint:** method to the ColorGraphView.m class implementation file:

```
- (int)tagAtPoint:(NSPoint)pt
{
    NSEnumerator *en;
    id obj;

    en = [displayList objectEnumerator];
    while (obj = [en nextObject]) {
        if (NSPointInRect(pt,[obj bounds])) {
            return [obj tag];
        }
    }
    return 0;
}
```

The **draggingEntered:** method simply informs the dragging system that we accept dragging only for copy operations.

ColorGraphView.m

15. Add the **draggingEntered:** method to ColorGraphView.m:

```
- (unsigned int)draggingEntered:(id <NSDraggingInfo>)sender
{
    return NSDragOperationCopy;
}
```

16. Add the **draggingUpdated:** method to ColorGraphView.m:

```
- (unsigned int)draggingUpdated:(id <NSDraggingInfo>)sender
{
    NSPasteboard *pboard = [sender draggingPasteboard];

    // If it is a string, we can take it here
    if ([pboard stringForType:NSStringPboardType]) {
        return NSDragOperationCopy;
    }
```

```
// If is a color, we support dropping only
// on objects in the display list
if ([pboard dataForType:NSColorPboardType]) {

    // Get the dragging location in the view's coordinates
    NSPoint pt = [self convertPoint:[sender draggingLocation]
                          fromView:nil];

    // See if there is an intersection.
    // If so, say we support a copy.
     if ([self tagAtPoint:pt]) {
         return NSDragOperationCopy;
     }
    }
   return NSDragOperationNone;
}
```

This method is more complicated than the **draggingEntered:** method. If we are receiving a text drag, we tell the dragging system that we can accept it anywhere. But if we are receiving a color drag, we can receive it only at points where we actually have something drawn (that is, on a piece of the graph, on the labels, or on the axes).

The next method that will actually implement the drag operation.

17. Add the **performDragOperation:** to the ColorGraphView.m class implementation file:

ColorGraphView.m

```
- (BOOL)performDragOperation:(id <NSDraggingInfo>)sender
{
    NSPasteboard *pboard = [sender draggingPasteboard];
    NSString *str =0 ;
    NSColor  *color=0;

    // If there is text, do the graph
    [pboard types];
    str = [pboard stringForType:NSStringPboardType];
    if (str) {
        [self setFormula:str];
        [self graph:nil];
        return YES;
    }

    // If there is color, find the tag that the user is dragging
    // onto and set the objects with that tag to be that color
    color = [NSColor colorFromPasteboard:pboard];
    if (color) {
        NSPoint pt = [self convertPoint:[sender draggingLocation]
                              fromView:nil];
        int tag = [self tagAtPoint:pt];

        if (tag!=-1) {
            [self setObjectsToColor:color forTag:tag];
```

```
                return YES;
            }
        }
        return NO;
    }
```

This method first sees if there is a string on the dragging pasteboard. If there is, the method sets the formula to be the value and performs a graph operation. If a color is passed in, the method determines the tag over which the color chip was dropped, then sets all of the objects with that tag to be that color.

18. Build and run GraphPaper, saving all files first. Don't graph a function yet.

19. Open up the TextEdit application. Type sin(x) (or any function that Evaluator can handle) into an empty window and select the text by typing Command-A.

20. Now drag the selected text (i.e., the text expression sin(x)) and let it hover over the GraphPaper graphing area, as shown in Figure 20-10.

Note that a plus sign (+) accompanies the arrow cursor, indicating that the view will accept a copy of the dropped item (the plus sign is not shown in Figure 20-10).

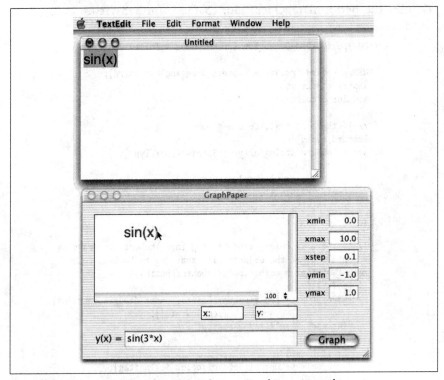

Figure 20-10. Drag-and-drop from TextEdit into GraphPaper's graphing area

21. Now drop the dragged text into GraphPaper's graphing area, and voila—GraphPaper graphs the dropped function sin(x)! See Figure 20-11.

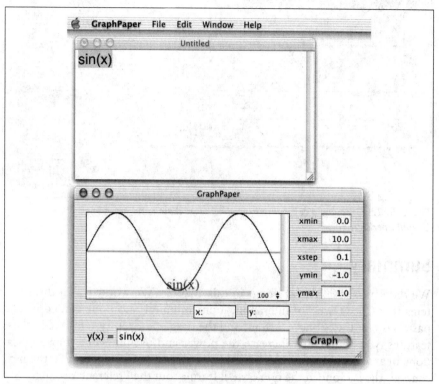

Figure 20-11. The resulting graph of the dropped function (bottom)

Next we'll test the color drag-and-drop feature.

22. Back in the TextEdit application, choose Format → Font → Colors (or type Command-Shift-C) to display the Colors panel.

23. Choose a color and drag a color chip to the actual graph (not just the graphing area) in GraphPaper, as shown in Figure 20-12.

   Note that the arrow cursor changes to the arrow cursor with the plus sign only when the mouse is over an object in the window that can receive a color. (Again, the plus sign doesn't appear in the screen shot.)

24. Drop the color chip on top of the graph and see it change color.

25. Now drag-and-drop another color chip on the function name (label) and see it change color as well! (We didn't write code for the axes to accept drag-and-drop color chips.)

26. Quit GraphPaper and rejoice!

This completes our implementation of pasteboard-related services.

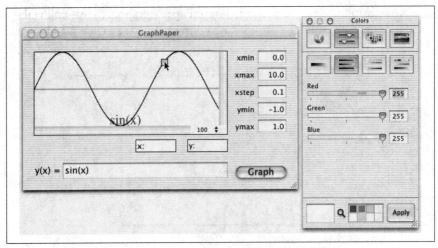

Figure 20-12. Dragging a color chip from the Colors dialog and dropping it on GraphPaper's graph

Summary

We did several really neat things in this chapter. We worked with three systems that Cocoa uses for interapplication communication: the cut, copy, and paste system; the Services system; and the drag-and-drop system. Using these features, you can greatly increase the power and usefulness of your applications by making their features available to other Cocoa programs. In the next chapter, the last one in the book, we'll learn about the Preferences system.

Exercises

1. Move the PDF- and TIFF-generation functionality from the Controller to the GraphView class. What are the advantages of having it in each class? Which is better? Does this make the implementation of drag-and-drop easier or more complex?

2. It's relatively easy to drag a color chip onto the graph or the function text, but it is very difficult to drag a chip onto the axes. Why? How would you fix this problem?

3. Instead of implementing all of the drag-receiving functionality in the ColorGraphView class, we should have implemented receiving of dragged-in color objects in the ColorGraphView class and of dragged-in text objects in the GraphView class. We didn't do this for the sake of brevity—it actually takes less typing to implement drag-receiving in one

place. Try to implement each kind of functionality in the appropriate class. What are the advantages of implementing the two kinds of drag functionality in two different classes instead of one class?

4. Implement a text drag-and-drop receiver (i.e., the NSTextField labeled "y(x)="), so that when a formula is dragged in, it automatically gets graphed.

5. If we use the Cocoa drag-and-drop system, it is not possible for the source of a drag-and-drop event to determine a drag-and-drop destination. This is possible, however, using Apple's underlying Core framework system. Investigate this Core Foundation framework and modify the GraphView application so that it displays information about the drag-and-drop recipient.

6. When you drag out the icon representing the PDF file of the graph, the icon is not centered underneath the mouse pointer. Fix the **performDragOperation** method so it is.

CHAPTER 21

Preferences and Defaults

If you've used an operating environment other than Mac OS X (such as Windows or Unix), you've probably had to worry about environment variables and configuration files. Such nuisances are pointedly missing from most Mac OS X applications, because Mac OS X uses a database to store all such configuration and user-preferences information. This database is called the *defaults database*.

The Mac OS X defaults database stores the preferences set in the Preferences dialogs of *all* applications. As a Cocoa programmer, you can use the defaults database system to store whatever information you want.

The Mac OS X defaults database is similar to the registry in Microsoft Windows, but with one critical difference—Mac OS X applications use this database only for storing preferences, not for storing critical information that is necessary for the proper operation of an application. Unlike Windows, where registry keys must be created when an application is installed, Mac OS X applications create their defaults entries when they run—and they automatically recreate the settings if they are accidentally or intentionally removed. Furthermore, the settings in the defaults system never contain full application pathnames—applications find where they are installed by examining their MainBundles (the directory from which the application is run). Thus, you can move an application and it will still work properly.

In this chapter, we'll modify the GraphPaper program to work with the defaults database system. We'll use the database to store the colors used to draw the graph, axes, and labels. In the second half of this chapter, we'll use the defaults system to store the initial values for the graph parameters. Finally, we'll create a multi-view Info dialog to switch between these two preferences options.

Preferences and the Defaults Database System

Mac OS X stores preferences information for each application in a file located in the user's ~/Library/Preferences/ folder. The preferences files are actually XML-encoded property lists with the .plist extension. To prevent namespace collisions, each file is named using the reversed fully-qualified hostname of the company that created the application (e.g., "com.apple"), followed by the application name (e.g., "clock"). Apple calls these names *domains*. Defaults domains are similar in appearance and spirit to class names in the Java programming language. For example, the Clock application stores its preferences information in a file called com.apple.clock.plist.

Because the ~/Library/Preferences folder is stored under the user's Home folder, each user has her own preferences information. If you NFS-mount a user's Home directory in a networked environment, that user will have access to her preferences information regardless of which computer she uses for login.

Accessing the Defaults Database with PropertyListEditor

If you double-click ~/Library/Preferences/com.apple.clock.plist in the Finder, the PropertyListEditor application will open and display a window similar to that in Figure 21-1 (click the disclosure triangle next to Root, if necessary).

PropertyListEditor

You can edit a .plist file in PropertyListEditor using the steppers and New Sibling and New Child buttons (recall that we did this earlier in PB). Try changing the InDock property of the Clock from Yes to No (or vice versa) using the stepper at the far right of the window, and then save the com.apple.clock.plist file. If the Clock is already running, it won't change its Dock status immediately. However, if you quit the Clock application and then restart it, it should change its Dock status. Changing preferences of a running application in PropertyListEditor is dangerous, because the running application may also change the preferences, which can lead to inconsistent results. It's like two people editing the same exact file on a server and saving it at different times.

When we clicked the Dump button in the upper-right corner of the Property-ListEditor window, we got the window containing the ASCII dump of the com.apple.clock.plist file, as shown in Figure 21-2.

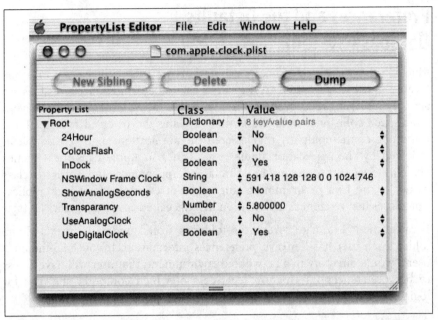

Figure 21-1. Property list for Apple's Clock application displayed in PropertyListEditor

When we listed the exact same com.apple.clock.plist file in a Terminal shell, we got the same listing as in the PropertyListEditor dump:

```
% cd ~/Library/Preferences/
% cat com.apple.clock.plist
<?xml version="1.0" encoding="UTF-8"?>
<!DOCTYPE plist SYSTEM "file://localhost/System/Library/DTDs/
  PropertyList.dtd">
<plist version="0.9">
<dict>
        <key>24Hour</key>
        <false/>
        <key>ColonsFlash</key>
        <false/>
        <key>InDock</key>
        <true/>
        <key>NSWindow Frame Clock</key>
        <string>591 418 128 128 0 0 1024 746 </string>
        <key>ShowAnalogSeconds</key>
        <false/>
        <key>Transparancy</key>
        <real>5.800000e+00</real>
        <key>UseAnalogClock</key>
        <false/>
        <key>UseDigitalClock</key>
        <true/>
</dict>
</plist>
%
```

```
000                    com.apple.clock.plist

    New Sibling            Delete                    Dump

Property List               Class                  Value
▶ Root                      Dictionary             ↕ 8 key/value pairs


<?xml version="1.0" encoding="UTF-8"?>
<!DOCTYPE plist SYSTEM "file://localhost/System/Library/DTDs/PropertyList.dtd">
<plist version="0.9">
<dict>
    <key>24Hour</key>
    <false/>
    <key>ColonsFlash</key>
    <false/>
    <key>InDock</key>
    <true/>
    <key>NSWindow Frame Clock</key>
    <string>591 418 128 128 0 0 1024 746 </string>
    <key>ShowAnalogSeconds</key>
    <false/>
    <key>Transparancy</key>
    <real>5.800000000000000e+00</real>
    <key>UseAnalogClock</key>
    <false/>
    <key>UseDigitalClock</key>
    <true/>
</dict>
</plist>
```

Figure 21-2. ASCII dump of com.apple.clock.plist file

Only printable ASCII text should be stored in the database, but Apple's XML encoding system should take care of this for you automatically.

Accessing the Defaults Database in a Terminal

In addition to PropertyListEditor, Mac OS X provides a Unix command-line program called defaults for reading and modifying the contents of the defaults database.

Terminal

The defaults command makes it possible to use and modify the defaults database without having to start up a Mac OS X program and read the XML property list. That's handy if you're writing a shell script or just trying to learn your way around the defaults system. The defaults command can also read the contents of the defaults databases on other computers, provided you have sufficient permissions to do so.

The primary functions of the defaults command are summarized in Table 21-1.

Table 21-1. Defaults system commands

Command	Purpose
defaults [-host *host*] read *domain key*	Reads the defaults value of the key in the specified domain. If *key* is omitted, all of the keys are read. If *domain* is omitted, all of the domains are read. This can be incredibly verbose!
defaults [-host *host*] read *domain key*	Reads the type of the key in the specified domain. If *key* is omitted, all of the keys are read. If *domain* is omitted, all of the domains are read.
defaults [-host *host*] write *domain plist*	Adds the property list *plist* to the preferences values for the domain.
defaults [-host *host*] write *domain name value*	Adds the (*name,value*) pair to the set of preferences for the domain.
defaults [-host *host*] rename *domain old new*	Renames the key *old* to have the name *new* in the domain.
defaults [-host *host*] delete *domain key*	Deletes the specified key in the domain. If *key* is omitted, all of the keys are removed. If *domain* is omitted, all of the user's domains are removed.
defaults [-host *host*] domains	Lists all of the domains on the command line.
defaults [-host *host*] domains find *word*	Lists all of the domains that contain a key or value that contains *word*.

We can use the `defaults read` command in a Terminal window to see *all* of the variables and defaults for the Clock application:

```
% cd ~/Library/Preferences/
% defaults read com.apple.MenuBarClock
{
    AppendAMPM = 1;
    ClockDigital = 1;
    ClockEnabled = 1;
    DisplaySeconds = 1;
    FlashSeparators = 0;
    PreferencesVersion = 1;
    ShowDay = 1;
}
%
```

If we wanted to make the clock's AM/PM indicator disappear, we could execute this command:

```
% defaults write com.apple.MenuBarClock AppendAMPM 0
%
```

That wasn't terribly informative. What's worse, if you execute this command and then look at your clock, you'll see that the AM/PM indicator is still there. Did the command take?

```
% defaults read com.apple.MenuBarClock
{
    AppendAMPM = 0;
    ClockDigital = 1;
```

```
    ClockEnabled = 1;
    DisplaySeconds = 1;
    FlashSeparators = 0;
    PreferencesVersion = 1;
    ShowDay = 1;
}
```

It looks as if the command worked, but its effects haven't shown up yet. Try clicking the menu bar clock and then choose View → as Icon. Click the menu bar clock once again and choose View → as Text. Now the AM/PM indicator should disappear. The behavior of preferences in other applications may differ—it depends on how often the program checks the defaults database stored in its .plist file.

Defaults Domains

The Mac OS X defaults system is designed to accommodate multiple defaults domains. Each domain is a collection of names and values. Internally, Cocoa implements defaults domains as NSDictionary objects that store zero or more other objects. The key to the NSDictionary is the name of each defaults value; it is determined by an NSString object. The value can be any object that can be stored in a property list—that is, an NSData, NSString, NSNumber, NSDate, or NSArray object, or another NSDictionary object.

Every application that you run can have its own defaults domain. The name of this domain is the same as the application's application identifier, which is set in Project Builder.

Persistent versus volatile defaults

Defaults domains can be persistent or volatile. A *persistent domain* is a domain that is stored after an application exits and is made available again the next time that application runs. The contents of a *volatile domain* are simply lost when the application finishes executing—but that doesn't matter, because they are recreated the next time the application runs.

Persistent defaults domains are typically stored as files in the user's ~/Library/ Preferences folder, but they could in theory be stored in other locations, such as in a SQL database or an LDAP server. In fact, the mechanics of how persistent defaults are stored and then loaded back into memory are intentionally hidden from the programmer.

Standard defaults domains

Mac OS X provides each application with five standard defaults domains, described in Table 21-2.

Table 21-2. Defaults domains available to every application

Domain	Purpose	Type
NSArgumentDomain	Stores the command-line arguments provided when the program is run.	Volatile
Application[a]	Provides persistent storage of the user's preferences and other values.	Persistent
NSGlobalDomain	Used by user-interface objects that require a consistent behavior between user applications.	Persistent
Languages[b]	Used for language-specific default values. For example, NSGregorian-CalendarDate, NSDate, NSTimeZone, NSString, and NSScanner use this defaults domain to remember language-specific defaults (such as the names of the days of the week).	Volatile
NSRegistrationDomain	Stores application-specific defaults of applications before they are changed by the user.	Volatile

[a] The name of this domain is the same as the name of the application identifier.
[b] The names of these domains correspond to the name of the language.

The NSUserDefaults Class

The NSUserDefaults class is the standard interface that you will use to communicate with the defaults system. Your application will create a single instance of this class; you can get the id of this instance using the class method **+standardUserDefaults**. For example:

```
NSUserDefaults *defaults = [NSUserDefaults standardUserDefaults];
```

The NSUserDefaults object implements a search system by which successive domains are searched when you ask to look up an object by key. The domains are searched in the order given in Table 21-2:

1. The NSUserDefaults object first checks the NSArgumentDomain, which is built from the command line that was used to launch the application, if one exists. This lets you temporarily change the value of a preference for a single run of an application.

2. If no command-line value was given, it next checks the application domain, as specified by the application's bundle identifier.

3. If no owner/name combination is found in the defaults database, the NSUserDefaults object next checks for a default in the NSGlobalDomain.

4. If no NSGlobalDomain default is found, the NSUserDefaults object checks the domains for each of the user's preferred languages.

5. If no default has been found up to this point, the NSUserDefaults object returns the value that was specified in the registration table that was registered in the NSRegistrationDomain.

This search order of the application's compiled-in defaults will be honored unless they are superseded by defaults specific to the user's language, defaults that have been stored, or command-line arguments.

If we want the GraphPaper application to start up with an xstep of 5, we could launch it with the following command line in the Terminal:

```
% build/GraphPaper.app/Contents/MacOS/GraphPaper -xstep 5
```

When your application starts up, it needs to read the user's default values and set the state of its associated objects. Recall that in Chapter 17 we simply hardcoded values to use for defaults in ColorGraphView.m and in Interface Builder. We'll change that in the next section.

The most obvious use of the defaults system is to remember user preferences between successive invocations of an application, but the defaults system is actually used throughout the Mac OS X environment. For example, Cocoa's NSRulerView class references the NSGlobalDomain to remember if the user's preferred unit of measurement is picas, points, inches, or centimeters. The internationalization of Cocoa is provided through the AppleLanguages key that is stored in the NSGlobalDomain defaults domain, which allows users to specify which languages they want to use, and in which order.

Adding Defaults to GraphPaper

In this section, we'll modify the GraphPaper application to work with the defaults database. We will do this by making changes to both the Controller and the ColorGraphView classes.

Cocoa applications use a single instance of the Foundation class NSUser-Defaults for managing the defaults database. Apple's documentation notes that the NSUserDefaults class is *not* thread-safe, so you should use it only from your application's main thread.

To use the NSUserDefaults class, you must first decide what default values your application will need to store. Each of these values should be given a name that will be its key in the defaults database. For each value, you must also decide upon a representation—that is, how the representation will be stored. Table 21-3 shows the defaults that we will use for GraphPaper.

Table 21-3. Defaults for the GraphPaper application

Default name	#define	Our default
AxesColor	GP_AxesColor	[NSColor red]
LabelColor	GP_LabelColor	[NSColor blue]
GraphColor	GP_GraphColor	[NSColor black]
xstep	GP_xstep	0.1
xmin	GP_xmin	−10.0
xmax	GP_xmax	10.0
ymin	GP_ymin	−5.0

Table 21-3. Defaults for the GraphPaper application (continued)

Default name	#define	Our default
ymax	GP_ymax	5.0
formula	GP_Formula	cos(x)
GraphPaper window frame	Not needed	NSMakeRect(0,0,500,500)

Once you have decided on the default values that your application will be using, you need to write the code that will install these into the default registration table. This table will provide the *default* default values for your application—that is, the values that the application will use before any are set by the user.

Apple recommends that you register the defaults that each of your classes will use in a method you create called **+initialize**. The **+initialize** method is a special class method that is invoked when your class is first used (recall that the plus (+) means class method, whereas a minus (-) means instance method). The Objective-C runtime system ensures that the **initialize** message* is sent once and only once to each class in your program. The **initialize** message is always sent to a class's superclass before it is sent to the class itself.

The GraphPaper application will use the defaults system in three locations:

 i. The GraphView class will use the defaults system to determine the initial values of the xmin, xmax, xstep, ymin, ymax, and formula values, overriding the information stored in the NSForm instance in MainMenu.nib.

 ii. The ColorGraphView class will use the defaults system to determine the initial values of the AxesColor, LabelColor, and GraphColor colors, overriding the values that were hardcoded into the ColorGraphView class.

 iii. The NSWindow class will use the defaults system to determine the initial location of the GraphPaper window.

For consistency and to prevent typographical errors, we will create a separate file called defaults.h that will contain #define values for each of the default keys.

defaults.h

 1. Create the defaults.h file (in PB or elsewhere) and save it in your ~/Graph-Paper folder.

```
// defaults.h
// Define the default values used in GraphPaper

#define GP_AxesColor    @"AxesColor"
#define GP_LabelColor   @"LabelColor"
```

---

* Remember, the message sent does not have a plus sign. Because the receiver of the message is a class, the Objective-C runtime looks for a class method called **initialize** rather than an instance method.

```
#define GP_GraphColor    @"GraphColor"
#define GP_xstep         @"xstep"
#define GP_xmin          @"xmin"
#define GP_xmax          @"xmax"
#define GP_ymin          @"ymin"
#define GP_ymax          @"ymax"
#define GP_Formula       @"Formula"
```

2. Add defaults.h to your GraphPaper project in the group Other Sources.

Registering the Default Values

We will need to add two methods to each of the GraphView and ColorGraph-View classes: an **initialize** method that will register the appropriate defaults, and an **awakeFromNib** method that will set the appropriate controls based on the values in the defaults system.

3. Insert the following declarations into GraphView.h:

   ```
   + (void)initialize;
   - (void)awakeFromNib;
   ```

GraphView.h

4. Insert the #import directive and the #define macro shown here in bold into GraphView.m:

   ```
   #import "GraphView.h"
   #import "Segment.h"
   #import "Label.h"
   #import "Controller.h"
   #import "defaults.h"

   #define FLOAT(x) [NSNumber numberWithFloat:x]

   @implementation GraphView
   ```

GraphView.m

5. Insert the implementation for the **initialize** class method into GraphView.m:

   ```
   +(void)initialize
   {
       NSUserDefaults *defaults = [NSUserDefaults standardUserDefaults];
       NSMutableDictionary *appDefs = [NSMutableDictionary dictionary];

       [appDefs setObject:@"0.1"    forKey:GP_xstep];
       [appDefs setObject:@"-10.0"  forKey:GP_xmin];
       [appDefs setObject:@"10.0"   forKey:GP_xmax];
       [appDefs setObject:@"-5.0"   forKey:GP_ymin];
       [appDefs setObject:@"5.0"    forKey:GP_ymax];
       [appDefs setObject:@"cos(x)" forKey:GP_Formula];

       [defaults registerDefaults:appDefs];
   }
   ```

For ease of typing and reading, this **initialize** method uses string values, rather than creating an NSNumber with the appropriate float value.

Next we'll make the necessary changes to the ColorGraphView class.

ColorGraphView.h

6. Insert the method and function declarations shown here in bold into ColorGraphView.h:

```
+ (void) initialize;
- (void) awakeFromNib;
@end

NSData *DataForColor(NSColor *aColor);
NSColor *ColorForData(NSData *data);
```

ColorGraphView.m

7. Insert the #include directive shown here in bold into ColorGraphView.m:

```
#import "ColorGraphView.h"
#import "Segment.h"
#import "Label.h"
#import "defaults.h"
```

8. Insert the following two transformation functions and the class method declaration for **initialize** into ColorGraphView.m:

```
NSData *DataForColor(NSColor *aColor)
{
    return [NSArchiver archivedDataWithRootObject:aColor];
}

NSColor *ColorForData(NSData *data)
{
    return [NSUnarchiver unarchiveObjectWithData:data];
}

@implementation ColorGraphView

+(void)initialize
{
    NSUserDefaults *defaults = [NSUserDefaults standardUserDefaults];
    NSMutableDictionary *appDefs = [NSMutableDictionary dictionary];

    [appDefs setObject:DataForColor([NSColor redColor])
            forKey:GP_AxesColor];

    [appDefs setObject:DataForColor([NSColor blueColor])
            forKey:GP_LabelColor];

    [appDefs setObject:DataForColor([NSColor blackColor])
            forKey:GP_GraphColor];

    [defaults registerDefaults:appDefs];
}
```

In addition to providing the **initialize** method, we must equip the Color-GraphView implementation with two functions—one for converting an NSColor object into an NSData object, and one for converting back. We need to do this because the defaults system cannot store NSColor objects by themselves. The defaults system can store NSData objects, however, so we can store colors in the defaults system by first converting them to NSData objects.

(Indeed, because any object can be archived in an NSData structure, it is possible to store any object in the defaults system.)

Notice that the **initialize** method does not need to call the **initialize** method in the superclass; the Objective-C runtime system handles this for us automatically.

Reading Values from the Defaults Database

When GraphPaper starts up, it will read the defaults database to discover the user's preferences for graph, axes, and label colors. (We'll add the initial graph parameters to this list in a later section.) To read the database, we use the **standardUserDefaults** method.

9. Insert the following **awakeFromNib** instance method into GraphView.m:

```
- (void)awakeFromNib
{
    NSUserDefaults *defs = [NSUserDefaults standardUserDefaults];

    [xminCell  setObjectValue:[defs objectForKey:GP_xmin]];
    [xmaxCell  setObjectValue:[defs objectForKey:GP_xmax]];
    [xstepCell setObjectValue:[defs objectForKey:GP_xstep]];
    [yminCell  setObjectValue:[defs objectForKey:GP_ymin]];
    [ymaxCell  setObjectValue:[defs objectForKey:GP_ymax]];

    [formulaField setObjectValue:[defs objectForKey:GP_Formula]];
}
```

GraphView.m

This method queries the defaults system for the value that corresponds to each key. The first time that this version of GraphPaper is run, these values will correspond to the values that are registered in the **initialize** class method. However, if any of the values are changed and saved in the defaults system, those values will override the values that are registered.

10. Insert the following **awakeFromNib** method into the ColorGraphView.m implementation file:

```
- (void)awakeFromNib
{
    NSUserDefaults *defs = [NSUserDefaults standardUserDefaults];

    [super awakeFromNib];

    [self setObjectsToColor:ColorForData([defs dataForKey:GP_AxesColor])
                forTag:AXES_TAG];

    [self setObjectsToColor:ColorForData([defs dataForKey:GP_GraphColor])
                forTag:GRAPH_TAG];

    [self setObjectsToColor:ColorForData([defs dataForKey:GP_LabelColor])
                forTag:LABEL_TAG];
}
```

ColorGraphView.m

This method queries the defaults system for the NSColor object for each color, then uses the ColorGraphView **setObjectsToColor:forTag:** method to set the color. We use the **setObjectsToColor:forTag:** method because it performs the proper sequence of release and retain steps to ensure that we do not leak memory.

Finally, we'll take advantage of some machinery that is built into the NSWindow class that automatically remembers where the GraphPaper window is dragged by the user and restores the window to that location when the program runs again.

Controller.h

11. Insert the following class method into `Controller.h`:

```
- (void)awakeFromNib;
```

Controller.m

12. Insert the following **awakeFromNib** method into the `Controller.m` implementation file:

```
- (void)awakeFromNib
{
    [[graphView window]  setFrameUsingName:@"Main Window"];
    [[graphView window]  setFrameAutosaveName:@"Main Window"];
}
```

Now let's test the work we've done so far:

13. Build and run GraphPaper, saving all files first. Click the Graph button. You should see the window shown in Figure 21-3.

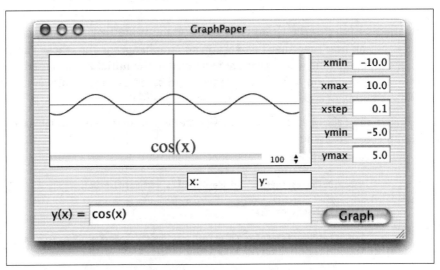

Figure 21-3. GraphPaper window with defaults

Notice that the values for xmin, xmax, step, ymin, ymax, and formula are the values that were registered in the **initialize** method, rather than the values that are stored in the nib.

14. Move the GraphPaper window to a different location and then quit GraphPaper.

15. Restart GraphPaper. Notice that the GraphPaper window now appears where you previously left it, rather than in the original location (where the window was positioned in IB).

16. Now move the GraphPaper window so that it's partially off-screen.

17. Quit GraphPaper and restart it again. Note that the window is completely visible!

18. Quit GraphPaper.

Restoring a window to the location where it was positioned the last time that the application ran is a very friendly feature, but it needs to be implemented correctly. For example, suppose your screen's resolution is set to 1600×1280, and you leave an application's window in a corner of the screen and then quit the application. If you then lower your screen's resolution to 1024×768 and run the application again, you might not be able to find the application's window because it is off-screen. Fortunately, the Cocoa implementation of **setFrameUsingName:** (which we used in Controller's **awakeFromNib** method) and related methods will *never* restore a window in a position where it cannot be seen. These methods interrogate the screen to find out its current resolution and, if the stored frame of the window will not completely appear on the screen, the frame is modified so that it will fit before the window is restored.

Finally, let's see what the property list for the GraphPaper application looks like at this point:

19. Restart GraphPaper again, choose GraphPaper → Preferences, and then open the Colors panel and make changes to the colors. Quit GraphPaper.

20. Now double-click the `~/Library/Preferences/GraphPaper.plist` file in the Finder to view the GraphPaper defaults in PropertyListEditor, as shown in Figure 21-4.

PropertyListEditor

The defaults in your `GraphPaper.plist` file will probably differ from those in Figure 21-4. You may even have different properties listed—it depends on what you did while GraphPaper was running.

As you can see, other parts of the application kit have been using the defaults system without our knowledge! In particular, the NSColorPanel uses the defaults system to remember its position on the screen as well as its current mode. Note that the main GraphPaper window's position is stored as well.

Notice also that there is no entry in the defaults system for xmin, xmax, xstep, ymin, ymax, or formula. That's because the default values for these items are never changed in our current code. To do that, we'll need to implement the **okay:** method associated with the GraphPaper Preferences panel.

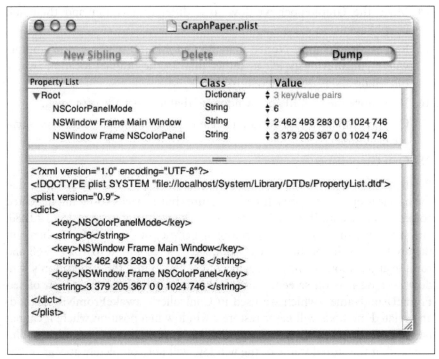

Figure 21-4. GraphPaper.plist file in PropertyListEditor

Cocoa, Carbon, and the Core Framework

Cocoa's preferences system is implemented on top of the Carbon and Core Foundation framework APIs. The interface made available through the Cocoa API allows you to access preferences only for your own application. However, by using the Core Foundation directly, it is possible to inspect and manipulate the defaults for other applications. To do this, you will need to use the Core framework string type, CFStringRef, which is the class from which the NSString object is derived. (You can cast a CFStringRef into an NSString, and vice versa.) You will then use the CFPreferencesAppSynchronize( ), CFPreferencesSetAppValue( ), and CFPreferencesCopyAppValue( ) functions. Good luck!

Making the Preferences Panel Work with Defaults

Now that we've arranged for the GraphView and ColorGraphView classes to set their initial values from the defaults database, we will modify Graph-Paper's Preferences panel to let the user see those values and change them.

We'll use the same Preferences panel that we created back in Chapter 17, except that we'll add two new controls—OK and Revert buttons.

The OK button will write the current Preferences panel values into the defaults database. This button will send the **okay:** action message to the Preferences panel controller object (PrefController).

The Revert button will redisplay the information in the Preferences panel by reading it out of the database. This button will send the **revert:** action message to PrefController. (Recall that we added the **okay:** and **revert:** action methods in IB and unparsed them into PrefController class files back in Chapter 17).

We'll also modify the PrefController class so that the code for setting up the initial value of each color well is moved from the **awakeFromNib** method to the **revert:** method. This way, we won't have to duplicate the same code in two different methods.

Modifying the Preferences Panel

1. Open GraphPaper's auxiliary nib file, `Preferences.nib`, in IB (double-click it in PB).

Interface Builder

2. Make the Preferences panel big enough to add Revert and OK buttons, as shown in Figure 21-5.

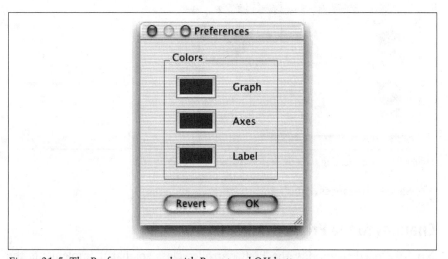

Figure 21-5. The Preferences panel with Revert and OK buttons

3. Add the Revert and OK buttons (using the Cocoa-Views palette), as shown in Figure 21-5. Make them line up nicely with the box using the blue guidelines.

4. Make the OK button the default button. To do this, select the button, type Command-1 to display the NSPanel Attributes Info dialog, click the

pop-up menu labeled "<no key>", and drag to Return (to make the Return key a key equivalent for the OK button).

The OK button should turn blue (or whatever "Appearance" color you've selected in System Preferences).

5. Connect the Revert button to the PrefController instance icon so that it sends the **revert:** message.

6. Connect the OK button to the PrefController instance icon so that it sends the **okay:** message, as shown in Figure 21-6.

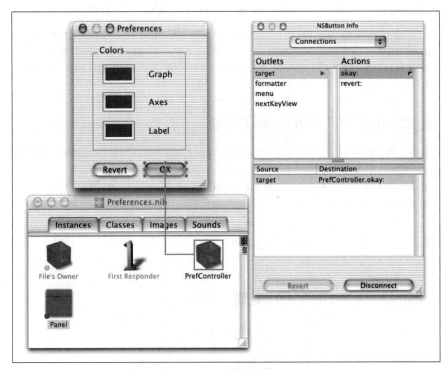

Figure 21-6. Connecting the OK button to PrefController in IB

7. Save Preferences.nib.

Changes to the PrefController Class

Now we need to modify the PrefController class so that it implements the **revert:** and **okay:** methods.

8. Back in PB, add the following #import directive to the beginning of the PrefController.m class file:

```
#import "defaults.h"
```

9. *Move* the three lines that set color wells from the **awakeFromNib** method in the PrefController.m file to the **revert:** method. The **revert:** method should look like this:

```
- (IBAction)revert:(id)sender
{
    [self setUpWell:axesColorWell ];
    [self setUpWell:labelColorWell ];
    [self setUpWell:graphColorWell ];
}
```

The **revert:** method calls the **setUpWell:** method for each of the color wells. Recall that the **setUpWell:** method asks the ColorGraphView class for these values. Because we previously modified the ColorGraphView to get these values from the defaults database, no further modification is required in the PrefController class.

We will also arrange for the Preferences window to show up where it was last left by the user in **awakeFromNib**.

10. Add the lines shown here in bold to **awakeFromNib**:

```
- (void)awakeFromNib
{
    [ [NSColorPanel sharedColorPanel] setContinuous:YES];

    [window setFrameUsingName:@"Preferences"];
    [window setFrameAutosaveName:@"Preferences"];
    [self revert:nil];
}
```

11. Insert the lines shown here in bold into the **okay:** method in PrefController.m (the method stub should already be there, as it was for **revert:**):

PrefController.m

```
- (IBAction)okay:(id)sender
{
    NSUserDefaults *defs = [NSUserDefaults standardUserDefaults];

    [defs setObject:DataForColor([axesColorWell color])
            forKey:GP_AxesColor];

    [defs setObject:DataForColor([labelColorWell color])
            forKey:GP_LabelColor];

    [defs setObject:DataForColor([graphColorWell color])
            forKey:GP_GraphColor];

    [window orderOut:nil];
}
```

The **okay:** method gets the current value for each of the color wells, converts each value to an NSData object using our DataForColor( ) function, and stores these objects in the defaults database. Finally, it orders out (i.e., dismisses) the Preferences window, because most users expect the Preferences window to disappear when they press the OK button.

Testing the Updated Preferences Panel

12. Graph a function and choose the GraphPaper → Preferences menu command to bring up the Preferences panel.

13. Change some colors and click the Revert button; notice how the original colors return to the Preferences panel.

14. Change some colors and click OK.

15. Quit GraphPaper.

16. Run GraphPaper again and graph a function. Note that the values that you set in the Preferences panel during the last run of the GraphPaper are still in effect. Quit GraphPaper.

PropertyListEditor

17. Double-click the ~/Library/Preferences/GraphPaper.plist file in the Finder to view the GraphPaper defaults in PropertyListEditor, as shown in Figure 21-7. The long hexadecimal strings are the NSData representations of the NSColor objects.

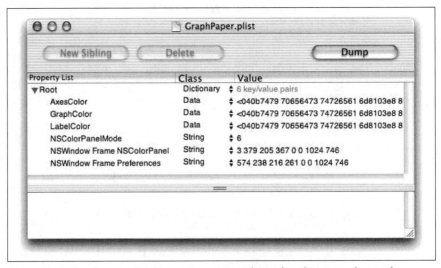

Figure 21-7. GraphPaper.plist file in PropertyListEditor after changing colors in the Preferences panel

There is one last problem that needs to be resolved to complete this phase. Earlier in this chapter, we said that the default values should be stored in a file that has the fully-qualified domain name of the application's publisher. But

GraphPaper's default values are being stored in a file called GraphPaper.plist, not something like com.nitroba.GraphPaper.plist. This needs to be fixed!

It turns out that the NSUserDefaults class decides which name to use based on the application identifier that is set in PB. In previous chapters, we set this application identifier to the name of the application. Now it's time to change this.

18. Activate PB.

19. Click on the Targets vertical tab and select the GraphPaper target.

20. Click the Application Settings tab.

Project Builder

21. Change the name in the Identifier field from "GraphPaper" to "com. nitroba.GraphPaper" (the .plist extension will be added automatically).

22. Build and run GraphPaper, saving all files first.

23. Make a change to the Preferences panel, then quit the program.

24. Verify that the preferences are now saved in the file com.nitroba. GraphPaper.plist in your ~/Library/Preferences folder, and not in GraphPaper.plist.

Setting Up a Multi-View Panel

In this section, we're going to change the Preferences panel into a multi-view panel, so that we can use it to change either the initial colors or the initial graph parameters (e.g., xmin, ymax). Figure 21-8 shows the pop-up menu and two NSViews that will show up in our new Preferences panel. The particular view that shows up depends on which tab (Colors or Initial) the user selects. In the final section of this chapter (and the book!), we'll modify GraphView to read its initial graph conditions out of the defaults database.

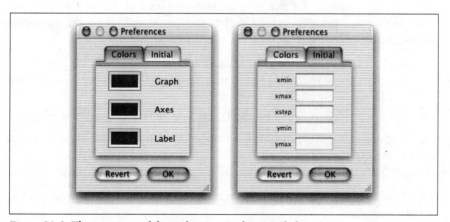

Figure 21-8. The two views of the multi-view Preferences dialog

Tab Views

It's quite easy to set up a tab view with Cocoa: just drag out the tab view and drop your GUI elements into place. Before we do this, however, we need to set up instance variables to hold the additional controls.

PrefController.h

1. Insert the five outlet instance variables shown here in bold into `PrefController.h`:

```
#import <Cocoa/Cocoa.h>

@interface PrefController : NSObject
{
    // Colors tab
    IBOutlet id axesColorWell;
    IBOutlet id graphColorWell;
    IBOutlet id labelColorWell;

    // Initial tab
    IBOutlet id xminCell;
    IBOutlet id xmaxCell;
    IBOutlet id xstepCell;
    IBOutlet id yminCell;
    IBOutlet id ymaxCell;

    IBOutlet id window;
}
...
@end
```

2. Save `PrefController.h`.

3. Open `Preferences.nib` in IB.

4. Drag the `PrefController.h` icon from PB and drop it in the `Preferences.nib` window in IB.

PrefController.h

The last step brought the five new outlet variables into IB. In the next few steps, we'll put a tab view on the Preferences panel and set up the appropriate controls.

5. Select a color well in the Preferences panel in IB and then Shift-select the other two color wells and the labels. Then type Command-X to cut the six selected items (we'll paste them back later).

6. Select the Colors box and hit the Delete key (we won't need it anymore).

7. Drag a Tab/View icon from IB's Cocoa-Containers palette and drop it in the Preferences panel.

8. Size the Tab/View to fit in the Preferences panel (see Figure 21-8).

9. Double-click inside the Tab/View to tell IB that you want to work within the container.

10. Type Command-V to paste in the three color wells and their labels.

11. Reconnect the PrefController's `axesColorWell`, `graphColorWell`, and `labelColorWell` outlets to their respective color wells (Control-drag from PrefController to each well).

12. Double-click on the tab labeled "Tab" in the Tab/View and change the label to read "Colors".

13. Click the tab labeled "View" in the Tab/View. Note that your controls disappear! (Don't worry—they're still there—you can make them reappear by clicking the Colors tab.)

14. Change the word "View" to "Initial".

15. Drag out a Field1/Field2 NSForm from the Cocoa-Views palette and drop it in the Initial tab (pane).

16. Expand the NSForm to five cells. You may want (or need) to shrink the font size or change the intercell spacing. (You can change the intercell spacing by holding down the Command key while resizing the matrix.)

17. Connect the appropriate PrefController outlets (`xmaxCell`, `xminCell`, `xstepCell`, `yminCell`, and `ymaxCell`) to the appropriate cells in the form (Control-drag from PrefController to the fields).

18. Save the `Preferences.nib` file.

Loading and Saving the Default Values

Finally, we need to modify the **revert:** and **okay:** methods for the PrefController class so that the `xmin`, `xmax`, `xstep`, `ymin`, and `ymax` values are read from the defaults database when the Preferences window is displayed and saved back into the defaults database when the OK button is pressed. (Recall that we have already modified the GraphView class so that it initializes these values from the defaults database.)

19. Insert the lines shown here in bold into the **revert:** method in the `PrefController.m` class file:

PrefController.m

```
- (IBAction)revert:(id)sender
{
    NSUserDefaults *defs = [NSUserDefaults standardUserDefaults];

    [self setUpWell:axesColorWell ];
    [self setUpWell:labelColorWell ];
    [self setUpWell:graphColorWell ];

    [xminCell  setObjectValue:[defs objectForKey:GP_xmin]];
    [xmaxCell  setObjectValue:[defs objectForKey:GP_xmax]];
    [xstepCell setObjectValue:[defs objectForKey:GP_xstep]];
    [yminCell  setObjectValue:[defs objectForKey:GP_ymin]];
    [ymaxCell  setObjectValue:[defs objectForKey:GP_ymax]];
}
```

20. Insert the five lines shown here in bold into the **okay:** method in PrefController.m:

```
- (IBAction)okay:(id)sender
{
    NSUserDefaults *defs = [NSUserDefaults standardUserDefaults];

    [defs setObject:DataForColor([axesColorWell color])
            forKey:GP_AxesColor];

    [defs setObject:DataForColor([labelColorWell color])
            forKey:GP_LabelColor];

    [defs setObject:DataForColor([graphColorWell color])
            forKey:GP_GraphColor];

    [defs setObject:[xminCell objectValue] forKey:GP_xmin];
    [defs setObject:[xmaxCell objectValue] forKey:GP_xmax];
    [defs setObject:[xstepCell objectValue] forKey:GP_xstep];
    [defs setObject:[yminCell objectValue] forKey:GP_ymin];
    [defs setObject:[ymaxCell objectValue] forKey:GP_ymax];

    [window orderOut:nil];
}
```

21. Build and run GraphPaper, saving all files first.

22. Choose GraphPaper → Preferences.

23. Select the Initial tab in the Preferences panel, and you should see the initial defaults, as shown in Figure 21-9.

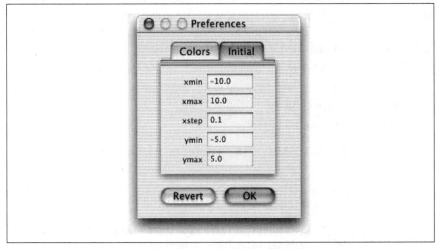

Figure 21-9. GraphPaper's Preferences panel with initial defaults

24. Enter values for all of the initial parameters and click OK (or hit Return). The OK and Revert buttons work as before.

---

25. Quit GraphPaper.

26. Now run GraphPaper again, and the initial values should show up in both the GraphPaper window and the Preferences panel.

27. Quit GraphPaper.

28. Double-click the `~/Library/Preferences/com.nitroba.GraphPaper.plist` file in the Finder to view the GraphPaper defaults in PropertyListEditor, as shown in Figure 21-10.

PropertyListEditor

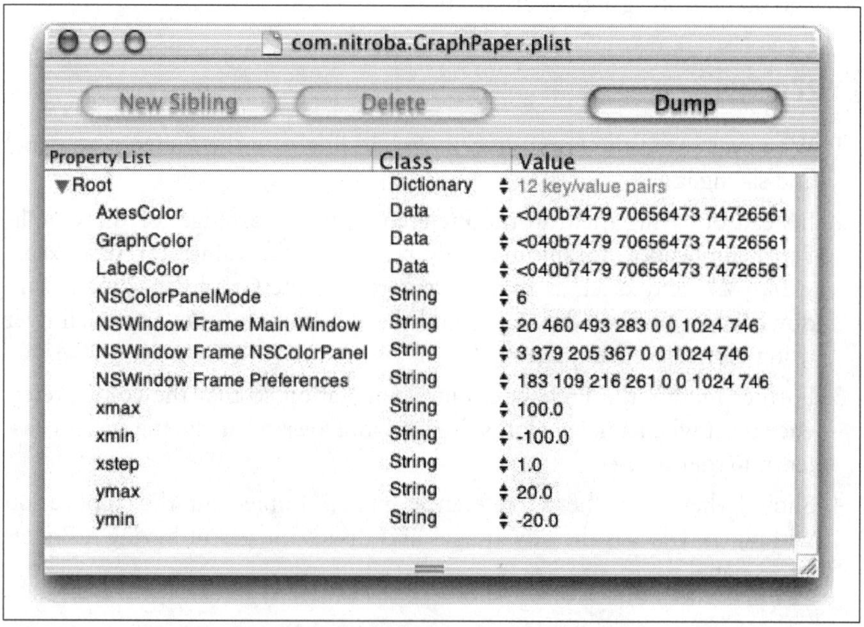

Property List	Class	Value
▼ Root	Dictionary	12 key/value pairs
AxesColor	Data	<040b7479 70656473 74726561
GraphColor	Data	<040b7479 70656473 74726561
LabelColor	Data	<040b7479 70656473 74726561
NSColorPanelMode	String	6
NSWindow Frame Main Window	String	20 460 493 283 0 0 1024 746
NSWindow Frame NSColorPanel	String	3 379 205 367 0 0 1024 746
NSWindow Frame Preferences	String	183 109 216 261 0 0 1024 746
xmax	String	100.0
xmin	String	-100.0
xstep	String	1.0
ymax	String	20.0
ymin	String	-20.0

Figure 21-10. com.nitroba.GraphPaper.plist file after setting initial values in the Preferences panel

29. Quit GraphPaper.

Congratulate yourself for making it through this book! We salute you! We thank you! We honor you!

Summary

Well, we've finally come to the end of the book. In this chapter, we learned some more about how to write a professional quality Cocoa application program and, in particular, how to use the Mac OS X defaults database.

Although there's lots more to learn about Cocoa, from here on you should be able to get most of what you need from the online documentation (or from our next book!). If you've been with us until now, you've learned the basics of

Cocoa's three main classes (NSApplication, NSView, and NSWindow), how they interact, and how to modify their functions as necessary to get done just about anything that you want to get done.

Cocoa establishes a framework into which all of the Application Kit objects neatly fit, like carved wooden pieces into a Chinese puzzle. The longer you program Cocoa, the more you'll learn about using the pieces that Apple provides; you'll also learn more and more about adding your own pieces.

Now go out and write a killer application!

Exercises

1. We never saved the Formula cell. Try adding it to the Preferences panel and saving it.

2. Instead of saving them in the Preferences panel, arrange for the Graph-Paper application to automatically remember the values for xmin, xmax, ymin, ymax, and xstep as they are entered on the GraphPaper main window. What are the advantages and disadvantages of this approach over using the Preferences panel?

3. Further modify the Preferences implementation so that the color preference is set when a new color is dragged in. Does this make the system easier or harder to use?

4. Should there even be a Preferences panel? Implement the application without it. Discuss the advantages and disadvantages of having a Preferences panel.

Cocoa Resources

Although you now know enough to write a Cocoa application, the truth of the matter is that we have only scratched the surface of what there is to learn. There are dozens of classes that we haven't explained. There are frameworks that we've only hinted at. There's a lot of functionality that we didn't include because, frankly, it still has bugs. And finally, there's the fact that Cocoa is still a work-in-progress, with Apple sure to make more changes.

So, now that we've reached the end of this little course in learning Cocoa, what we hope to leave you with is instructions for finding out more. Fortunately, there are many, many Cocoa references online. We've tried to assemble a list of some here. You'll find still more on the Web. The references included here were accurate as of the time this book went to press, but some may have changed by the time you read the book.

For additional information about the material presented in this book, we recommend that you first check this book's own web site, located at:

```
http://www.oreilly.com/catalog/buildcocoa/
```

At this site, you'll find the book's sample code available for download, errata, and other book-related information, such as plans for future editions.

Apple Resources

Over the years Apple has made a significant effort to make the Macintosh a friendly platform for developers and users alike. With Mac OS X, Apple has redoubled its efforts. A staggering amount of technical information for the Mac OS X platform is available online. Much of this information you can access without registering or paying a penny.

Online Documentation

The most important reference available for developing Cocoa applications is Apple's own documentation. This documentation describes every Cocoa class, method, and function is great detail. Apple has also created higher-level "concepts" documentation that discusses many higher-level issues in Cocoa programming, from memory allocation and drawing to advanced interprocess communications issues.

When you install the developer tools from the Mac OS X Developer Tools CD-ROM, you are given an option to install the developer documentation on your computer. The documentation installs as both a series of HTML files and a PDF file of the entire manual. The HTML files can be viewed from within Project Builder itself by choosing Cocoa Help from the Project Builder Help menu. If you wish, you can print the PDF files to create your own bound copy of the documentation.

As an alternative to reading the Apple documentation on your computer, we recommend reading it from Apple's web site. The documentation on the web site is the most up-to-date, and it frequently has more detailed explanations and discussions than you will find on the Developer CD-ROM. An added advantage of the online documentation is that it is easily searchable.

You will find Apple's online documentation at:

```
http://developer.apple.com/techpubs/
```

Apple also makes much of its developer documentation available in hardcopy form. On the technical publications web site, you will find information about how to order hardcopy documentation.

In writing this book, we found the following Apple technical publications to be extremely useful:

Mac OS X Developer Documentation
```
http://developer.apple.com/techpubs/macosx/macosx.html
```
This is the primary entry point for documentation about developing software for the Mac OS X environment. This documentation area is divided into the following categories: Essentials; Carbon; Cocoa; Developer Tools; Core Technologies; Additional Technologies; Networking; Release Notes; Legacy; and Darwin.

Cocoa Developer Documentation
```
http://developer.apple.com/techpubs/macosx/Cocoa/CocoaTopics.html
```
This is the primary entry point for documentation about developing software using Cocoa. This documentation area is divided into the following categories: Site Information; Getting Started; Java Framework Reference; Objective-C Framework Reference; Legacy; Program Design; Data Management; File, Resource, and Process Management; Events and Other

Input; Drawing and Imaging; Text Handling; User Interface Elements; Interapplication Communication; and Multimedia.

Introduction to the Aqua Human Interface Guidelines

http://developer.apple.com/techpubs/macosx/Essentials/AquaHIGuidelines/
index.html

This book describes how to design your application for the Aqua user interface. The information in this book will allow you to make your application operate in a manner that is consistent with other Aqua applications, which ultimately makes it easier for people to use your application without additional training. If you are going to be developing applications that will be used by a large group of people, we recommend that you read this book.

Foundation Objective-C API Reference

http://developer.apple.com/techpubs/macosx/Cocoa/Reference/Foundation/
ObjC_classic/FoundationTOC.html

Application Kit Objective-C API Reference

http://developer.apple.com/techpubs/macosx/Cocoa/Reference/ApplicationKit/
ObjC_classic/AppKitTOC.html

These pages list all of the Objective-C classes and informal protocols that make up the Cocoa Foundation and Application Kit, respectively. In writing this book, we found that the fastest way to look up the documentation for a particular class was to go to these pages and then select the class name. If you are a serious Cocoa programmer, we strongly recommend that you bookmark these pages.

Apple Developer Connection

The Apple Developer Connection (ADC) is Apple's primary tool for communicating with Macintosh developers. Registered developers receive regular bulletins by email, access to Apple's developer resources, and more.

Basic membership for the ADC is free. This free membership allows you to download the latest development tools, file bug reports, gain access to certain early software releases, and receive weekly technical updates via email.

If you'd rather have this type of information mailed to you, you can pay to become an ADC Mailing customer. You will then receive the latest in development tools, system software, development kits, and reference materials via a CD-ROM series delivered to you monthly via postal mail.

A low-cost ADC Student Program is aimed at university students around the world. ADC Student developers receive special introductory tools, access to a student community of Mac programmers, and other educational opportunities, including the chance to win scholarships to the Worldwide Developers Conference.

For more money, you can sign up for the Select and Premier levels of service. These programs offer a multitude of high-end products and services, including discounts on Apple hardware and third-party products and services and access to Apple's technical support engineers.

You will find information about the Apple Developer Connection at:

```
http://developer.apple.com
```

Information about signing up for these programs can be found at:

```
http://developer.apple.com/membership/
```

Sample Code

We believe that the best way to learn to program a new environment is through a combination of writing your own source code and reading well-written code that others have developed. That's why we have presented a combination of source code and exercises in this volume.

If you're looking for more programming examples, you need look no further than your own hard drive: the Cocoa Developer Tools come with source code for a large number of sample programs. You'll find these programs in the /Developer/Examples/AppKit and /Developer/Examples/Carbon directories. Of particular interest are the following:

/Developer/Examples/AppKit/CircleView
> CircleView is a simple application that demonstrates NSView subclassing and text display.

/Developer/Examples/AppKit/CompositeLab
> There are 13 distinct compositing operations. This application allows you to use each of those operations with a source and destination of your choice. This is a great lab for showing you how the compositing system works and how to incorporate image-manipulation functionality into your application.

/Developer/Examples/AppKit/DragNDropOutlineView
> This demonstration shows you how to construct an outline view and enable drag-and-drop. The application also allows you to experiment with the many different options to consider when you enable drag-and-drop in an outline view.

/Developer/Examples/AppKit/Rulers
> A ruler is a view that tracks along with the content view of a scroll view. You are probably familiar with rulers from the word-processor application, but here you can actually create your own rulers and use them for a variety of purposes.

```
/Developer/Examples/AppKit/SimpleImageFilter
```
The Cocoa image filter system allows you to give existing Cocoa applications the ability to read nonstandard graphics file formats. Although we did not discuss image filters in this book, they are similar in practice to services. This code shows you how to implement them.

```
/Developer/Examples/AppKit/SimpleToolbar
```
Many Cocoa applications have toolbars. This source code shows you how to add toolbars to your own applications. Try Control-clicking on the toolbar to customize it.

```
/Developer/Examples/AppKit/Sketch
```
Sketch is a full-blown drawing application that implements a ton of functionality. If you want to respond to events, draw text, print, implement services, or do practically anything with graphics, you should check out Sketch.

```
/Developer/Examples/AppKit/TextEdit
```
This is the source code for the TextEdit application. It's a good place for information-building applications that use the multiple-document architecture.

Worldwide Developers Conference

The Apple Worldwide Developers Conference (WWDC) is an annual meeting of Macintosh developers, hosted by Apple Computer. The conference features tutorials, classes, introductions to the latest Apple technologies, and a show floor with the latest and greatest tools for Macintosh developers. You should be there! Check out:

```
http://developer.apple.com/wwdc/
```

Registering Creator Codes

The future of creator codes is presently in doubt. Nevertheless, when you start developing a commercial application of your own, you should register a unique creator code with Apple at this web site:

```
http://developer.apple.com/dev/cftype/
```

Bug Reporting

If you find a bug in Cocoa or any other part of the Macintosh environment, you are encouraged to report it at:

```
http://bugreporter.apple.com
```

Apple also welcomes any feedback that you might have regarding Cocoa. You can send your comments to cocoa@apple.com.

Third-Party Resources

This section summarizes the best of the many third-party resources that you'll find helpful in learning more about Cocoa.

Mailing Lists

Online mailing lists are a great way to stay up-to-date on developer issues:

`cocoa-dev`

> Apple's `cocoa-dev` is a mailing list focused exclusively on Cocoa development issues. The mailing list is a forum for both technical and nontechnical questions. Although most of the participants are outside of Apple, many people on Apple's Cocoa development team read the mailing list and answer questions. For information on how to subscribe to this mailing list, go to:
>
> > `http://lists.apple.com/mailman/listinfo/cocoa-development`

`MacDev-1`

> This list is cosponsored by *MacTech Magazine*, Developer Depot (a retailer of programming tools), and Apple. `MacDev-1` is a source of news, information, updates, and special offers for the Mac programmer community. The goals of the `MacDev-1` list are to make developers more aware of available programming resources and to provide vendors of Mac development tools with an efficient channel through which to spread the word about product releases. This list is moderated by the *MacTech Magazine* staff. For information on how to participate in `MacDev-1`, go to:
>
> > `http://www.mactech.com/macdev-1/`

Web Sites

You'll find the following web sites helpful:

Mac DevCenter

> Affiliated with O'Reilly & Associates, Inc., the O'Reilly Network is home to the Mac DevCenter, a hub site that offers news, FAQs, original articles, and other technical information for Mac OS X developers. Various online and offline resources aimed especially at Cocoa developers are available at:
>
> > `http://www.oreillynet.com/mac/`

MacTech

> The web site run by *MacTech Magazine* (described under "Printed Resources") contains extensive resources for Mac developers, including downloadable source code that Cocoa developers should find helpful and

a web version of "MacTech Online," a monthly column from the magazine that provides online technologies and resources. It also contains links to web pages, shareware archives, newsgroups, mailing lists, and castanet channels aimed at Macintosh programmers. Go to the home page at:

```
http://www.mactech.com
```

SourceForge

SourceForge.net is the world's largest open source development web site, with the largest repository of open source code and applications available on the Internet. SourceForge.net provides free services to open source developers, including project hosting, version control, bug and issue tracking, project management, backups and archives, and communication and collaboration resources.

There are many open source projects based on the Cocoa framework. You can explore them by searching for the word "Cocoa" in the search field on SourceForge's home page:

```
http://www.sourceforge.net
```

Printed Resources

We recommend that you take a look at the following books and magazines:

Cocoa Programming for Mac OS X, by Aaron Hillegass (Addison Wesley)
Naturally, if you are buying just one book on Cocoa programming, you should buy the book you are holding in your hands. But if you are looking for another point of view, you might want to check out Aaron Hillegass's book. Aaron was a developer trainer at NeXT and has worked on developing some fairly sophisticated Cocoa applications. Even better, just as we cover many topics not mentioned in Aaron's book, Aaron covers many topics not mentioned in this book, making the two books quite complementary.

Learning Cocoa, by James Duncan Davidson and Apple Computer (O'Reilly)
The first edition of this book was written by Apple Computer; a second edition was in the works as this book went to press. It provides an introduction to the Cocoa environment, taking you through the process of creating single-window applications and building up to more complex, multiple-window, document-based applications. While *Learning Cocoa* assumes some knowledge of C programming, the book teaches you the basic concepts of object-oriented programming with Objective-C while introducing you to Cocoa.

Learning Carbon, by Apple Computer (O'Reilly)
Even if you plan to build your applications using Cocoa, you can still benefit from time to time by dipping into the Macintosh Core framework

and Carbon layers. This book provides you with all of the information you need to access these system resources.

Learning Unix for Mac OS X, by Dave Taylor and Jerry Peek (O'Reilly)
This concise introduction summarizes what users need to know to get started with Unix functions on Mac OS X. The book explains how to use the Terminal application, become familiar with the command-line interface, explore many Unix applications, and—most importantly—take advantage of the power of Unix on the Mac platform.

Mac OS X for Unix Developers, by Brian Jepson and Ernest E. Rothman (O'Reilly)
Although Mac OS X is based on Unix, it is different from most standard Unix implementations. This book will help advanced Unix users acclimate themselves to this familiar, yet foreign, Unix environment; it provides information useful to Unix programmers, such as the details of linking, compiling, and packaging their applications.

Mac OS X Pocket Reference, by Chuck Toporek (O'Reilly)
This handy book introduces Mac, Windows, and Unix users to the fundamental concepts of Mac OS X. It starts with a "Mac OS X Survival Guide," which shows Mac users what has changed from Mac OS 9 and helps Windows and Unix converts get acclimated to their new OS. The book concludes with a "Task and Setting" index, which answers questions users might have when configuring their systems.

Mac OS X: The Missing Manual, by David Pogue (Pogue Press/O'Reilly)
This book illuminates both the big-ticket features and the fine points of Mac OS X Version 10.1: its Unix-like folder structure, powerful networking and Internet features, and even the command-line interface of its Unix underbelly. It also covers each of the control panels and bonus programs that come with Mac OS X, including iTunes, Mail, Sherlock, and Apache, the built-in web server.

MacTech Magazine
MacTech is a monthly print journal that presents programming articles and news about Macintosh technology and development. For subscription information, go to:

```
http://www.mactech.com
```

The *MacTech* web site was described earlier in this appendix, under "Web Sites."

Index

Symbols

/* and */, as comment delimiter, 129
<> (angle brackets), 464
\ (backslash), 351, 354
: (colon, in Objective-C messages), 99
{ } (curly braces), 351
// (double forward slash), as comment
            delimiter, 129
| (pipe), 74
+ (plus sign), in method names, 124
[ ] (square brackets), 98

A

About box, 191
    application icon, adding to, 211
    customizing, 196
aboutPanel outlet, 193
AboutPanel.nib file, 197–205
    icon activation, 211
abstract superclass, 135, 252
acceptsFirstMouse: method, 253, 561
acceptsFirstResponder message, 257
acceptsMouseMovedEvents flag, 505
accessor methods, 116
    rules for use, 127
accessory views, 530
action buttons, 25
action methods
    Controller class, adding to, 193
    declaration, 183
actions, 98–102, 156
active application, 4, 47, 52
active window, 4

ADC (Apple Developer Connection), 599
addAnnotation: method, 509
addAxesFrom:to: method, 477
addBufToGraph: method, 472
adder.m file, 126
addGraphElement: method, 464, 465, 472, 499
additive color models, 484
addTrackingRect:owner:userData:assumeInside:
            method, 254
addWindowController: method, 329
administrator (or root) processes, viewing, 284
Adobe PostScript, 522
AIFF files, opening, 56
alerts, 15
+alloc class method, 124
alloc method, 117
    rules for use, 127
alpha (transparency), 484
ancestorSharedWithView: method, 425
angle brackets (<>), 464
angle changes, fonts in RTF, 352
animation, 408
.app file extension, 146
app wrapper, 146
appendRTFData: method, 360
appendString: method, 341
app.icns file, 206
AppIcon.icns file, 207
AppKit, 4
    delegates, classes that support, 227
    document-based architecture, 302
    important classes, 129
Apple Developer Connection (ADC), 599
Apple Foundation library, xviii

We'd like to hear your suggestions for improving our indexes. Send email to *index@oreilly.com*.

integrated development environment (IDE), Project Builder, 61
interactive systems, development of, 70
Interface Builder (see IB)
@interface directive, 118
introspection, 114
isDescendantOf: method, 425
isFlipped method, 424
isOpaque method, 426, 430, 433
isRotatedFromBase method, 423
isRotatedOrScaledFromBase method, 423

J

Java, compared to Objective-C, xviii

K

key window, 12, 18
keyboard equivalents, 22, 43
  Application menu, 44
  Edit menu, 45
  File menu, 45
  Find submenu, 46
  Font submenu, 47
  Window menu, 48
keyboard event handling, 255
keyDown: message, 255, 271
keyPad outlet, 233
keyTable instance variable, 268
keyWindow id pointer, 253

L

Label class, 478, 500
  dealloc method, 479
  using, 481
lazy allocation, 273
lazy evaluation, 537, 543
length method, 124
lex, 297
lexical analysis, 296
lex.yy.c file, 297
loadDataRepresentation:ofType: method, 378, 382
loadFileWrapperRepresentation:wrapper ofType: method, 378
loading from a file (MathPaper), 382–384
loadNibNamed:owner: method, 195
lockFocus method, 393
locking classes, 452
locks, 452
ltob( ) function, 220

M

.m file extension, 104
Mac OS X, xiv, 3, 277
  applications, About box, 191
  common file extensions, 371
  defaults database, 572
  defaults domains, 577
  desktop configuration, 33
  developer tools, 61–69
  development environment, 4
  Dock, 22–24
  Finder (see Finder)
  GUI, 3
    (see also Aqua)
  hidden directories, 78
  imaging model, 4
  keyboard commands, 8
  Mac OS 9 applications and, xix, 7
  main thread, 453
  online documentation, 598
  preferences, 573
  Terminal (see Terminal application)
  Version 10.1 AppKit display bugs, 427
  Window Server, 282–284
Mach operating system, 279–282
  messages, 280
  process numbers, 282
mach_init Unix process, 288
Macintosh Toolbox, 7
mailing lists, 602
main( ) function, 130, 185, 261
main event loop, 262
main thread, 453
main window, 12, 18
MainBundle directory, 572
main.m file, 185, 261
MainMenu.nib file, 145
  customizing, 188–192
  delegate specification, 228
  for MathPaper, 303
  memory resources and, 192
  modifying, 196
Makefile, 298–302
  tab characters and spaces in, 298
makeFirst Responder: message, 258
makeKeyAndOrderFront: message, 136
makeWindowControllers method, 329, 366
man ps command, 288
managing files, 49–58
MathAnimation view, creating, 399–401, 410–414

N

needsDisplay method, 427
NetInfo (network administrative information)
    system, 281
newDocument: method, 366
NeXT Interface Builder, 145
nextEventMatchingMask:untilDate:inMode:
    dequeue: method, 263
nextResponder instance variable, 252
NeXTSTEP operating system, xvii, 97, 279
nib, 88
Nib File window, 88–92
    Classes tab, 90
    First Responder, 90
    Images tab, 91
    Instances tab, 89
    Sounds tab, 91
nib files, 145
    managing multiple, 192
nonretained windows, 392
notification system, 224, 334, 341, 412
"NS" prefix, 97
NSActionCell class, 259
NSApp object, 107, 131
    main event loop, 262
NSApp delegate, 489
[NSApp terminate:self] message, 99
NSApplication class, 129
    Controller instance, delegate
        specification, 228
    event handling, 251
    MathApplication subclass, 395
NSApplicationIcon system icon, 91
NSApplicationMain( ) function, 185
NSApplicationNotifications category, 231
NSArray class, 233
NSAssert( ) macro, 519
NSAttributedString class, 360
NSAutoreleasePool class, 127
NSBezierPath class, 137
NSBundle class, 195
NSCell objects, 149
NSCell subclasses, 149
NSClipView class, 335
NSCoder class, 374
    common methods, 375
NSColor class, 403, 485
NSColorPanel.h file, 497
NSColorWell class, 487
NSColorWell.h file, 497

NSControl objects, 149
NSControl subclasses, 149
NSDictionary class, 266
NSDocument class
    data management with, 364–369
    MathDocument subclass, 293, 307–309
    save methods, 377
NSDocumentController class, 365
    File menu action methods, 366
NSDraggingDestination methods, 564
NSDraggingInfo protocol methods, 565
NSEvent class, 249
NSFileHandle class, 322
NSFileHandleReadCompletionNotification
    message, 334
NSFont class, 348
NSFontAttributeName key, 405
NSGeometry.h file, 400
NSHumanReadableCopyright string, 191
NSImage class, 213, 407
NSLayoutManager class, 335
NSLock class, 452
NSMakeRange( ) function, 348
NSMatrix class, 149
    sizing and dragging, 150
NSMutableArray class, 233, 449
NSMutableAttributedString class, 360
NSMutableDictionary class, 266
    for drawing fonts, 405
    setObject:forKey: method, 270
NSMutableString class, 125
NSObject class, 124, 225
    RTF class, creating, 356–359
NSPasteboard class, 537–545
NSPipe class, 322
NSPoint structure, 401
NSPopUpButton class, 216, 516
    cover, 516
NSRange class, 348
NSRectFill( ) function, 137
NSRegisterServicesProvider( ) function, 549
NSResponder class
    chain and action messages, 258
    event methods, 250–253
NSScrollView class, 514
    embedded classes, 335
    ZoomScrollView subclass, 514
NSSimpleHorizontalTypesetter class, 335
NSSize structure, 401
NSString class, 125
    using autorelease pool, 128

Q

Quartz, xix
drawing inside a view object, 136
drawing text, 404–406
graphics context, 391
graphics data types, 400
imaging model, 4
NSMutableDictionary for drawing fonts, 405
NSView drawing methods, 393
PDF files, support of, xix
Window Server, 390–393

R

radio buttons, 25, 215
radix, 215
RAM (random-access memory), 280
readSelectionFromPasteboard: method, 548
receiver, 113
release message, 121
rules for use, 127
release method, 122, 127
removeAnnotations method, 509
replaceSubview:with: method, 425
resignFirstResponder message, 258
resizeSubviewsWithOldSize: method, 427
resizing windows, 237–243
responder, 90
responder chain, 252
action messages and, 258
respondsToSelector: message, 225
retain message, 121
reference count incrementation, 122
retained windows, 392
returnTypes, 547
revert: method, 589, 593
RGB color model, 484
Rich Text Format (see RTF)
root system user, 280
viewing root processes, 284
rotateByAngle: method, 423
RTF class, 356–359
dependencies on other classes, 359
implementation, 357
instance methods, 356
MathPaper, integration into, 359–362
RTF (Rich Text Format), 347, 350–355
angle, 352
classes, creating, 356–359
control words and symbols, 353–355

fonts, 353
groups, 351
states, 351
weight, 352
{\rtf0 and {\rtf1, 354
rubberbanding, 9
rules.l file, 300
MathPaper, adding to, 322, 325
run message, 262
runModalSession: message, 550
runningAsService instance variable, 555
runtime binding, 97

S

Save Graph command, 523
save methods, 376–379
save options, supporting, 530–535
saveAllDocuments: method, 366
saveDocument: message, 377
saveDocumentTo: method, 524, 525, 534
savePanel instance variable, 531
savePanelDidEnd:returnCode:contextInfo:
method, 524, 526
saving data, 365
saving files, 370–382
customizing features, 381–382
Save As or Save To, 381
without filename, 381
scale: message, 514
scaled coordinate system, 428–431
scaleFactor instance variable, 518
scaleUnitSquareToSize: method, 423, 519
screen resolution and saved windows, 384
scroll arrows, 27
scrollers, 27
scrolling, 409
scrolling lists, 27
Segment class, 473
self, 163, 204
[self bounds] message, 137
semiautomatic memory management, Cocoa
environment, 64
sendAction:to: method, 258, 260
sendData method, 467
[[sender selectedCell] tag] message, 177
senders, 156
sendTypes, 547
services, 546–560
aliases, Mac OS X version dependency, 555
Controller class, registration as, 556

services (*continued*)
   creating, 549–560
     GraphPaper implementation, 550
     GraphView class, conversion to, 555
     Info.plist file, 549, 551
       XML property list verification, 553
     InfoPlist.strings file, 191
     operating system, control by, 546
     Services advertisements, 549
       creating, 551–555
       fields, 549
       XML editing, 551
Services submenu and commands, 48
setAutoresizesSubviews: method, 427
setAutoresizingMask: method, 428
setBoundsSize: method, 430
setColor: method, 479
setData:Type: method, 539
setDelegate: method, 228
setEnd: method, 119
   memory leaks and, 123
setFormat: method, 531, 533
setFrame: method, 424
setFrame:display: method, 384
setFrame:display:animate: method, 242
setFrameOrigin: method, 424
setFrameRotation: method, 424
setFrameSize: method, 424
setHasHorizontalScroller: message, 335
setHasVerticalScroller: message, 335
setNeedsDisplay message, 242
setNeedsDisplay: method, 427
setNeedsDisplayInRect: method, 427
setNumSides: method, 433
setObject:forKey: method, 270
setObjectsToColor: method, 496
setObjectsToColor:forTag: method, 497,
     498, 584
setPercentage: method, 430
setPostsFrameChangedNotification: method, 425
setRadius: method, 115
setRadix: method, 219–225
   hexadecimal operations, modifying for, 240
   multi-base applications, modifying for, 232,
     234–237
setScaleFactor: method, 518, 519
setServicesProvider: message, 549
setSize: method, 434
setStart: method, 119, 121
   memory leaks and, 123

setTag: method, 479
setup( ) function, 132
setUpWell: method, 495, 589
setX:andY: method, 116
shape instance variable, 438
Shell menu, 72
shells (Unix), 72
Should messages, 225
   examples, 226
showAboutPanel: method, 193–197
showPrefs: method, 491
Size Info dialog, 238
sizeToCells message, 242
sliders, 27
source code examples, resources, 600
source image, 407
spaces vs. tab characters, Unix, 298
square brackets ([ ]), 98
sscanf( ) function, 473
stack-trace, 84
standard state, 34
+standardUserDefaults method, 578, 583
start method, 119
states, 351
static input fields, 27
static typing, 117
Stickies advertisement, 547
stop: message, 262
stopGraph: method, 459, 467, 470
string tables, 191
stringWithFormat: method, 128
stroke method, 449, 480
strong typing, 243
stuffer, 451
subclassing vs. delegation, 227
submenu, 44
submenu indicator, 22
subtractive color models, 484
subView outlet, 515
subviews, 130
subviews method, 425
[super encodeWithCoder:coder] message, 376
superuser, 280
superview, 252
superview method, 425
swapping, 280
synchronizeData method, 373
System Preferences, 39–42
system users, 280

Simson Garfinkel is a developer with 24 years of programming experience, the author or coauthor of 12 books, an entrepreneur, and a journalist. He is the founder and Chief Technology Officer of Sandstorm Enterprises, a Boston-based firm that develops state-of-the-art computer security tools. He is also a columnist for *Technology Review Magazine* and has published more than 500 articles in more than 50 magazines and journals.

Garfinkel bought his first Macintosh computer in the fall of 1984. He went on to develop software for the Macintosh, DOS, Windows, Unix, and NeXT-STEP platforms. Garfinkel was a Senior Editor at *NeXTWORLD Magazine* and was the coauthor (with Michael K. Mahoney) of the first programming book that covered the NeXT operating system, *NeXTSTEP Programming, Step One: Object-Oriented Applications* (Springer-Verlag).

Back in 1988, Garfinkel interviewed for a job at NeXT Computer, Inc. and, during the interview, advised NeXT to avoid the planned magneto-optical drive and instead ship the radical new CD-ROM technology on every new NeXT computer. As a result of his insubordination, he was not hired; however, he was brought in as a consultant two years later to create the CD-ROM filesystem for NeXTSTEP Version 3.0.

Garfinkel earned a Master's degree in Journalism at Columbia University in 1988 and holds three undergraduate degrees from MIT.

Michael K. Mahoney is Dean of the College of Engineering at California State University, Long Beach, where he is also a Professor of Computer Engineering and Computer Science. Formerly, he was the Associate Vice President for Academic Information Technology and Chair of the Department of Computer Engineering and Computer Science.

Dr. Mahoney started programming at NeXT Computer, Inc. in January 1989 and coauthored (with Simson Garfinkel) *NeXTSTEP Programming, Step One: Object-Oriented Applications* (Springer-Verlag). He has given presentations on object-oriented programming and NeXTSTEP's Interface Builder at ACM meetings in Seattle, Los Angeles, Monterey, and New Orleans. Before becoming dean, he regularly taught university courses in computer graphics, user interface design, object-oriented programming, discrete mathematics, and web development. He has supervised eight Master's theses.

Mahoney earned his Ph.D. in mathematics at the University of California, Santa Barbara, in 1979. He has published papers in computer graphics, computer science education, and mathematics. He has won campuswide teaching awards at both UCSB and CSULB. His web site is http://www.csulb.edu/~mahoney/.

Colophon

Our look is the result of reader comments, our own experimentation, and feedback from distribution channels. Distinctive covers complement our distinctive approach to technical topics, breathing personality and life into potentially dry subjects.

The animal on the cover of *Building Cocoa Applications* is a Mastiff (also known as an English or Old English Mastiff). The Mastiff is a large-breed working dog with a long history—Mastiffs have been used as guard and fighting dogs in England for more than 2,000 years, and dogs of this type are found in European and Asian records dating back to 3000 BC. Shakespeare referred to Mastiffs as "the dogs of war," and Henry VIII is known to have given King Charles V of Spain several hundred Mastiffs to use as fighting dogs on the battlefield. Trained fighting mastiffs were also used by the ancient Celts, by Kubla Khan, and by Hannibal when he crossed the Alps. Even as recently as the two World Wars, Mastiffs were used to pull munitions carts on the fronts.

Mastiff owners are often first attracted to the breed by its large size—Mastiffs are the heaviest dog breed, weighing in at an average of 180–220 pounds. Despite their history as fighting dogs, modern breeders have bred the Mastiff for gentleness and have created an excellent companion, large enough to deter intruders yet gentle enough to be dependable around children. Mastiffs are loyal, patient, affectionate, and protective, and they tend to bond strongly to their owners and become depressed during long periods of separation.

Rachel Wheeler was the production editor and copyeditor for *Building Cocoa Applications*. Leanne Soylemez was the proofreader. Linley Dolby provided quality control, and Mary Brady, David Chu, Phil Dangler, Julie Flanagan, and Sue Willing provided production assistance. John Bickelhaupt wrote the index.

Emma Colby designed the cover of this book, based on a series design by Edie Freedman. The cover image is from the *Dover Treasury of Animal Illustrations*, edited by Carol Belanger Grafton. Emma Colby produced the cover layout with QuarkXPress 4.1 using Adobe's ITC Garamond font.

David Futato designed the interior layout. This book was converted into FrameMaker 5.5.6 with a format conversion tool created by Erik Ray, Jason McIntosh, Neil Walls, and Mike Sierra that uses Perl and XML technologies. The text font is Linotype Birka; the heading font is Adobe Myriad Condensed; and the code font is LucasFont's TheSans Mono Condensed. The illustrations that appear in the book were produced by Robert Romano and Jessamyn Read using Macromedia FreeHand 9 and Adobe Photoshop 6. The tip and warning icons were drawn by Christopher Bing. This colophon was written by Rachel Wheeler.